T0336868

Practical Foundations for Programming Languages

This text develops a comprehensive theory of programming languages based on type systems and structural operational semantics. Language concepts are precisely defined by their static and dynamic semantics, presenting the essential tools both intuitively and rigorously while relying on only elementary mathematics. These tools are used to analyze and prove properties of languages and provide the framework for combining and comparing language features. The broad range of concepts includes fundamental data types such as sums and products, polymorphic and abstract types, dynamic typing, dynamic dispatch, subtyping and refinement types, symbols and dynamic classification, parallelism and cost semantics, and concurrency and distribution. The methods are directly applicable to language implementation, to the development of logics for reasoning about programs, and to the formal verification language properties such as type safety.

This thoroughly revised second edition includes exercises at the end of nearly every chapter and a new chapter on type refinements.

Robert Harper is a professor in the Computer Science Department at Carnegie Mellon University. His main research interest is in the application of type theory to the design and implementation of programming languages and to the mechanization of their metatheory. Harper is a recipient of the Allen Newell Medal for Research Excellence and the Herbert A. Simon Award for Teaching Excellence, and is an Association for Computing Machinery Fellow.

Practical Foundations for Programming Languages

Second Edition

Robert Harper

Carnegie Mellon University

CAMBRIDGE
UNIVERSITY PRESS

CAMBRIDGE
UNIVERSITY PRESS

University Printing House, Cambridge CB2 8BS, United Kingdom

One Liberty Plaza, 20th Floor, New York, NY 10006, USA

477 Williamstown Road, Port Melbourne, VIC 3207, Australia

4843/24, 2nd Floor, Ansari Road, Daryaganj, Delhi - 110002, India

79 Anson Road, #06-04/06, Singapore 079906

Cambridge University Press is part of the University of Cambridge.

It furthers the University's mission by disseminating knowledge in the pursuit of education, learning and research at the highest international levels of excellence.

www.cambridge.org
Information on this title: www.cambridge.org/9781107150300

First published 2016

A catalogue record for this publication is available from the British Library

Library of Congress Cataloging in Publication data
Names: Harper, Robert, 1957–
Title: Practical foundations for programming languages / Robert Harper, Carnegie Mellon University.
Description: Second edition. | New York NY : Cambridge University Press, 2016. | Includes bibliographical references and index.
Identifiers: LCCN 2015045380 | ISBN 9781107150300 (alk. paper)
Subjects: LCSH: Programming languages (Electronic computers)
Classification: LCC QA76.7 .H377 2016 | DDC 005.13–dc23
LC record available at http://lccn.loc.gov/2015045380

ISBN 978-1-107-15030-0 Hardback

Contents

Part III   Total Functions

Part IV   Finite Data Types

Part V   Types and Propositions

Part VI   Infinite Data Types

Part VII   Variable Types

Part VIII   Partiality and Recursive Types

Part IX   Dynamic Types

Part X   Subtyping

Part XI   Dynamic Dispatch

Part XII   Control Flow

Part XIII   Symbolic Data

Part XIV   Mutable State

Part XV   Parallelism

Part XVI   Concurrency and Distribution

Part XVII   Modularity

Part XVIII   Equational Reasoning

Part XIX   Appendices

Preface to the Second Edition

Writing the second edition to a textbook incurs the same risk as building the second version of a software system. It is difficult to make substantive improvements, while avoiding the temptation to overburden and undermine the foundation on which one is building. With the hope of avoiding the second system effect, I have sought to make corrections, revisions, expansions, and deletions that improve the coherence of the development, remove some topics that distract from the main themes, add new topics that were omitted from the first edition, and include exercises for almost every chapter.

The revision removes a number of typographical errors, corrects a few material errors (especially the formulation of the parallel abstract machine and of concurrency in Algol), and improves the writing throughout. Some chapters have been deleted (general pattern matching and polarization, restricted forms of polymorphism), some have been completely rewritten (the chapter on higher kinds), some have been substantially revised (general and parametric inductive definitions, concurrent and distributed Algol), several have been reorganized (to better distinguish partial from total type theories), and a new chapter has been added (on type refinements). Titular attributions on several chapters have been removed, not to diminish credit, but to avoid confusion between the present and the original formulations of several topics. A new system of (pronounceable!) language names has been introduced throughout. The exercises generally seek to expand on the ideas in the main text, and their solutions often involve significant technical ideas that merit study. Routine exercises of the kind one might include in a homework assignment are deliberately few.

My purpose in writing this book is to establish a comprehensive framework for formulating and analyzing a broad range of ideas in programming languages. If language design and programming methodology are to advance from a trade-craft to a rigorous discipline, it is essential that we first get the definitions right. Then, and only then, can there be meaningful analysis and consolidation of ideas. My hope is that I have helped to build such a foundation.

I am grateful to Stephen Brookes, Evan Cavallo, Karl Crary, Jon Sterling, James R. Wilcox and Todd Wilson for their help in critiquing drafts of this edition and for their suggestions for modification and revision. I thank my department head, Frank Pfenning, for his support of my work on the completion of this edition. Thanks also to my editors, Ada Brunstein and Lauren Cowles, for their guidance and assistance. And thanks to Andrew Shulaev for corrections to the draft.

Neither the author nor the publisher make any warranty, express or implied, that the definitions, theorems, and proofs contained in this volume are free of error, or are consistent with any particular standard of merchantability, or that they will meet requirements for any particular application. They should not be relied on for solving a problem whose incorrect solution could result in injury to a person or loss of property. If you do use this material in such a manner, it is at your own risk. The author and publisher disclaim all liability for direct or consequential damage resulting from its use.

Pittsburgh
July 2015

Preface to the First Edition

Types are the central organizing principle of the theory of programming languages. Language features are manifestations of type structure. The syntax of a language is governed by the constructs that define its types, and its semantics is determined by the interactions among those constructs. The soundness of a language design—the absence of ill-defined programs—follows naturally.

The purpose of this book is to explain this remark. A variety of programming language features are analyzed in the unifying framework of type theory. A language feature is defined by its *statics*, the rules governing the use of the feature in a program, and its *dynamics*, the rules defining how programs using this feature are to be executed. The concept of *safety* emerges as the coherence of the statics and the dynamics of a language.

In this way, we establish a foundation for the study of programming languages. But why these particular methods? The main justification is provided by the book itself. The methods we use are both *precise* and *intuitive*, providing a uniform framework for explaining programming language concepts. Importantly, these methods *scale* to a wide range of programming language concepts, supporting rigorous analysis of their properties. Although it would require another book in itself to justify this assertion, these methods are also *practical* in that they are *directly applicable* to implementation and *uniquely effective* as a basis for mechanized reasoning. No other framework offers as much.

Being a consolidation and distillation of decades of research, this book does not provide an exhaustive account of the history of the ideas that inform it. Suffice it to say that much of the development is not original but rather is largely a reformulation of what has gone before. The notes at the end of each chapter signpost the major developments but are not intended as a complete guide to the literature. For further information and alternative perspectives, the reader is referred to such excellent sources as Constable (1986, 1998), Girard (1989), Martin-Löf (1984), Mitchell (1996), Pierce (2002, 2004), and Reynolds (1998).

The book is divided into parts that are, in the main, independent of one another. Parts I and II, however, provide the foundation for the rest of the book and must therefore be considered prior to all other parts. On first reading, it may be best to skim Part I, and begin in earnest with Part II, returning to Part I for clarification of the logical framework in which the rest of the book is cast.

Numerous people have read and commented on earlier editions of this book and have suggested corrections and improvements to it. I am particularly grateful to Umut Acar, Jesper Louis Andersen, Carlo Angiuli, Andrew Appel, Stephanie Balzer, Eric Bergstrom, Guy E. Blelloch, Iliano Cervesato, Lin Chase, Karl Crary, Rowan Davies, Derek Dreyer, Dan Licata, Zhong Shao, Rob Simmons, and Todd Wilson for their extensive efforts in reading and criticizing the book. I also thank the following people for their suggestions: Joseph Abrahamson, Arbob Ahmad, Zena Ariola, Eric Bergstrome, William Byrd, Alejandro Cabrera, Luis Caires, Luca Cardelli, Manuel Chakravarty, Richard C. Cobbe, James Cooper, Yi Dai, Daniel Dantas, Anupam Datta, Jake Donham, Bill Duff, Matthias Felleisen, Kathleen Fisher, Dan Friedman, Peter Gammie, Maia Ginsburg, Byron Hawkins, Kevin Hely, Kuen-Bang Hou (Favonia), Justin Hsu, Wojciech Jedynak, Cao Jing, Salil Joshi, Gabriele Keller, Scott Kilpatrick, Danielle Kramer, Dan Kreysa, Akiva Leffert, Ruy Ley-Wild, Karen Liu, Dave MacQueen, Chris Martens, Greg Morrisett, Stefan Muller, Tom Murphy, Aleksandar Nanevski, Georg Neis, David Neville, Adrian Trejo Nuñez, Cyrus Omar, Doug Perkins, Frank Pfenning, Jean Pichon, Benjamin Pierce, Andrew M. Pitts, Gordon Plotkin, David Renshaw, John Reynolds, Andreas Rossberg, Carter Schonwald, Dale Schumacher, Dana Scott, Shayak Sen, Pawel Sobocinski, Kristina Sojakova, Daniel Spoonhower, Paulo Tanimoto, Joe Tassarotti, Peter Thiemann, Bernardo Toninho, Michael Tschantz, Kami Vaniea, Carsten Varming, David Walker, Dan Wang, Jack Wileden, Sergei Winitzki, Roger Wolff, Omer Zach, Luke Zarko, and Yu Zhang. I am very grateful to the students of 15-312 and 15-814 at Carnegie Mellon who have provided the impetus for the preparation of this book and who have endured the many revisions to it over the last ten years.

I thank the Max Planck Institute for Software Systems for its hospitality and support. I also thank Espresso a Mano in Pittsburgh, CB2 Cafe in Cambridge, and Thonet Cafe in Saarbrücken for providing a steady supply of coffee and a conducive atmosphere for writing.

This material is, in part, based on work supported by the National Science Foundation under Grant Nos. 0702381 and 0716469. Any opinions, findings, and conclusions or recommendations expressed in this material are those of the author(s) and do not necessarily reflect the views of the National Science Foundation.

Robert Harper
Pittsburgh
March 2012

PART I

Judgments and Rules

1 Abstract Syntax

Programming languages express computations in a form comprehensible to both people and machines. The syntax of a language specifies how various sorts of phrases (expressions, commands, declarations, and so forth) may be combined to form programs. But what are these phrases? What is a program made of?

The informal concept of syntax involves several distinct concepts. The *surface*, or *concrete*, *syntax* is concerned with how phrases are entered and displayed on a computer. The surface syntax is usually thought of as given by strings of characters from some alphabet (say, ASCII or Unicode). The *structural*, or *abstract*, *syntax* is concerned with the structure of phrases, specifically how they are composed from other phrases. At this level, a phrase is a tree, called an *abstract syntax tree*, whose nodes are operators that combine several phrases to form another phrase. The *binding* structure of syntax is concerned with the introduction and use of identifiers: how they are declared, and how declared identifiers can be used. At this level, phrases are *abstract binding trees*, which enrich abstract syntax trees with the concepts of binding and scope.

We will not concern ourselves in this book with concrete syntax but will instead consider pieces of syntax to be finite trees augmented with a means of expressing the binding and scope of identifiers within a syntax tree. To prepare the ground for the rest of the book, we define in this chapter what is a "piece of syntax" in two stages. First, we define abstract syntax trees, or ast's, which capture the hierarchical structure of a piece of syntax, while avoiding commitment to their concrete representation as a string. Second, we augment abstract syntax trees with the means of specifying the binding (declaration) and scope (range of significance) of an identifier. Such enriched forms of abstract syntax are called abstract binding trees, or abt's for short.

Several functions and relations on abt's are defined that give precise meaning to the informal ideas of binding and scope of identifiers. The concepts are infamously difficult to define properly and are the mother lode of bugs for language implementors. Consequently, precise definitions are essential, but they are also fairly technical and take some getting used to. It is probably best to skim this chapter on first reading to get the main ideas, and return to it for clarification as necessary.

1.1 Abstract Syntax Trees

An *abstract syntax tree*, or *ast* for short, is an ordered tree whose leaves are *variables*, and whose interior nodes are *operators* whose *arguments* are its children. Ast's are classified into a variety of *sorts* corresponding to different forms of syntax. A *variable* stands for an unspecified, or generic, piece of syntax of a specified sort. Ast's can be combined by an *operator*, which has an *arity* specifying the sort of the operator and the number and sorts of its arguments. An operator of sort s and arity $s_1, \ldots, s_n$ combines $n \geq 0$ ast's of sort $s_1, \ldots, s_n$, respectively, into a compound ast of sort s.

The concept of a variable is central and therefore deserves special emphasis. A variable is an *unknown* object drawn from some domain. The unknown can become known by *substitution* of a particular object for all occurrences of a variable in a formula, thereby specializing a general formula to a particular instance. For example, in school algebra variables range over real numbers, and we may form polynomials, such as $x^2 + 2x + 1$, that can be specialized by substitution of, say, 7 for x to obtain $7^2 + (2 \times 7) + 1$, which can be simplified according to the laws of arithmetic to obtain 64, which is $(7 + 1)^2$.

Abstract syntax trees are classified by *sorts* that divide ast's into syntactic categories. For example, familiar programming languages often have a syntactic distinction between expressions and commands; these are two sorts of abstract syntax trees. Variables in abstract syntax trees range over sorts in the sense that only ast's of the specified sort of the variable can be plugged in for that variable. Thus, it would make no sense to replace an expression variable by a command, nor a command variable by an expression, the two being different sorts of things. But the core idea carries over from school mathematics, namely that *a variable is an unknown, or a place-holder, whose meaning is given by substitution.*

As an example, consider a language of arithmetic expressions built from numbers, addition, and multiplication. The abstract syntax of such a language consists of a single sort Exp generated by these operators:

1. An operator num[n] of sort Exp for each $n \in \mathbb{N}$.
2. Two operators, plus and times, of sort Exp, each with two arguments of sort Exp.

The expression $2 + (3 \times x)$, which involves a variable, x, would be represented by the ast

$$\text{plus}(\text{num}[2]; \text{times}(\text{num}[3]; x))$$

of sort Exp, under the assumption that x is also of this sort. Because, say, num[4], is an ast of sort Exp, we may plug it in for x in the above ast to obtain the ast

$$\text{plus}(\text{num}[2]; \text{times}(\text{num}[3]; \text{num}[4])),$$

which is written informally as $2 + (3 \times 4)$. We may, of course, plug in more complex ast's of sort Exp for x to obtain other ast's as result.

The tree structure of ast's provides a very useful principle of reasoning, called *structural induction*. Suppose that we wish to prove that some property $\mathcal{P}(a)$ holds for all ast's a of a given sort. To show this, it is enough to consider all the ways in which a can be generated and show that the property holds in each case under the assumption that it holds for its constituent ast's (if any). So, in the case of the sort Exp just described, we must show

1. The property holds for any variable x of sort Exp: prove that $\mathcal{P}(x)$.
2. The property holds for any number, num[n]: for every $n \in \mathbb{N}$, prove that $\mathcal{P}(\text{num}[n])$.

3. Assuming that the property holds for a_1 and a_2, prove that it holds for $\text{plus}(a_1; a_2)$ and $\text{times}(a_1; a_2)$: if $\mathcal{P}(a_1)$ and $\mathcal{P}(a_2)$, then $\mathcal{P}(\text{plus}(a_1; a_2))$ and $\mathcal{P}(\text{times}(a_1; a_2))$.

Because these cases exhaust all possibilities for the formation of a, we are assured that $\mathcal{P}(a)$ holds for any ast a of sort Exp.

It is common to apply the principle of structural induction in a form that takes account of the interpretation of variables as place-holders for ast's of the appropriate sort. Informally, it is often useful to prove a property of an ast involving variables in a form that is conditional on the property holding for the variables. Doing so anticipates that the variables will be replaced with ast's that ought to have the property assumed for them, so that the result of the replacement will have the property as well. This amounts to applying the principle of structural induction to properties $\mathcal{P}(a)$ of the form "if a involves variables $x_1, \ldots, x_k$, and $\mathcal{Q}$ holds of each x_i, then $\mathcal{Q}$ holds of a," so that a proof of $\mathcal{P}(a)$ for all ast's a by structural induction is just a proof that $\mathcal{Q}(a)$ holds for all ast's a under the assumption that $\mathcal{Q}$ holds for its variables. When there are no variables, there are no assumptions, and the proof of $\mathcal{P}$ is a proof that $\mathcal{Q}$ holds for all *closed* ast's. On the other hand, if x is a variable in a, and we replace it by an ast b for which $\mathcal{Q}$ holds, then $\mathcal{Q}$ will hold for the result of replacing x by b in a.

For the sake of precision, we now give precise definitions of these concepts. Let $\mathcal{S}$ be a finite set of sorts. For a given set $\mathcal{S}$ of sorts, an *arity* has the form $(s_1, \ldots, s_n)s$, which specifies the sort $s \in \mathcal{S}$ of an operator taking $n \geq 0$ arguments, each of sort $s_i \in \mathcal{S}$. Let $\mathcal{O} = \{ \mathcal{O}_\alpha \}$ be an arity-indexed family of disjoint sets of *operators* $\mathcal{O}_\alpha$ of arity α. If o is an operator of arity $(s_1, \ldots, s_n)s$, we say that o has sort s and has n arguments of sorts $s_1, \ldots, s_n$.

Fix a set $\mathcal{S}$ of sorts and an arity-indexed family $\mathcal{O}$ of sets of operators of each arity. Let $\mathcal{X} = \{ \mathcal{X}_s \}_{s \in \mathcal{S}}$ be a sort-indexed family of disjoint finite sets $\mathcal{X}_s$ of *variables* x of sort s. When $\mathcal{X}$ is clear from context, we say that a variable x is of sort s if $x \in \mathcal{X}_s$, and we say that x is *fresh for* $\mathcal{X}$, or just *fresh* when $\mathcal{X}$ is understood, if $x \notin \mathcal{X}_s$ for any sort s. If x is fresh for $\mathcal{X}$ and s is a sort, then $\mathcal{X}, x$ is the family of sets of variables obtained by adding x to $\mathcal{X}_s$. The notation is ambiguous in that the sort s is not explicitly stated but determined from context.

The family $\mathcal{A}[\mathcal{X}] = \{ \mathcal{A}[\mathcal{X}]_s \}_{s \in \mathcal{S}}$ of *abstract syntax trees*, or *ast's*, of sort s is the smallest family satisfying the following conditions:

1. A variable of sort s is an ast of sort s: if $x \in \mathcal{X}_s$, then $x \in \mathcal{A}[\mathcal{X}]_s$.
2. Operators combine ast's: if o is an operator of arity $(s_1, \ldots, s_n)s$, and if $a_1 \in \mathcal{A}[\mathcal{X}]_{s_1}$, $\ldots, a_n \in \mathcal{A}[\mathcal{X}]_{s_n}$, then $o(a_1; \ldots; a_n) \in \mathcal{A}[\mathcal{X}]_s$.

It follows from this definition that the principle of *structural induction* can be used to prove that some property $\mathcal{P}$ holds of every ast. To show $\mathcal{P}(a)$ holds for every $a \in \mathcal{A}[\mathcal{X}]$, it is enough to show:

1. If $x \in \mathcal{X}_s$, then $\mathcal{P}_s(x)$.
2. If o has arity $(s_1, \ldots, s_n)s$ and $\mathcal{P}_{s_1}(a_1)$ and $\ldots$ and $\mathcal{P}_{s_n}(a_n)$, then $\mathcal{P}_s(o(a_1; \ldots; a_n))$.

For example, it is easy to prove by structural induction that $\mathcal{A}[\mathcal{X}] \subseteq \mathcal{A}[\mathcal{Y}]$ whenever $\mathcal{X} \subseteq \mathcal{Y}$.

Variables are given meaning by *substitution*. If $a \in \mathcal{A}[\mathcal{X}, x]_{s'}$, and $b \in \mathcal{A}[\mathcal{X}]_s$, then $[b/x]a \in \mathcal{A}[\mathcal{X}]_{s'}$ is the result of substituting b for every occurrence of x in a. The ast a is called the *target*, and x is called the *subject*, of the substitution. Substitution is defined by the following equations:

1. $[b/x]x = b$ and $[b/x]y = y$ if $x \neq y$.
2. $[b/x]o(a_1; \ldots; a_n) = o([b/x]a_1; \ldots; [b/x]a_n)$.

For example, we may check that

$$[\mathtt{num}[2]/x]\mathtt{plus}(x; \mathtt{num}[3]) = \mathtt{plus}(\mathtt{num}[2]; \mathtt{num}[3]).$$

We may prove by structural induction that substitution on ast's is well-defined.

Theorem 1.1. *If $a \in \mathcal{A}[\mathcal{X}, x]$, then for every $b \in \mathcal{A}[\mathcal{X}]$ there exists a unique $c \in \mathcal{A}[\mathcal{X}]$ such that $[b/x]a = c$*

Proof By structural induction on a. If $a = x$, then $c = b$ by definition; otherwise, if $a = y \neq x$, then $c = y$, also by definition. Otherwise, $a = o(a_1, \ldots, a_n)$, and we have by induction unique $c_1, \ldots, c_n$ such that $[b/x]a_1 = c_1$ and $\ldots$ $[b/x]a_n = c_n$, and so c is $c = o(c_1; \ldots; c_n)$, by definition of substitution. □

1.2 Abstract Binding Trees

Abstract binding trees, or *abt's*, enrich ast's with the means to introduce new variables and symbols, called a *binding*, with a specified range of significance, called its *scope*. The scope of a binding is an abt within which the bound identifier can be used, either as a place-holder (in the case of a variable declaration) or as the index of some operator (in the case of a symbol declaration). Thus, the set of active identifiers can be larger within a subtree of an abt than it is within the surrounding tree. Moreover, different subtrees may introduce identifiers with disjoint scopes. The crucial principle is that any use of an identifier should be understood as a reference, or abstract pointer, to its binding. One consequence is that the choice of identifiers is immaterial, so long as we can always associate a unique binding with each use of an identifier.

As a motivating example, consider the expression $\mathtt{let}\,x\,\mathtt{be}\,a_1\,\mathtt{in}\,a_2$, which introduces a variable x for use within the expression a_2 to stand for the expression a_1. The variable x is bound by the $\mathtt{let}$ expression for use within a_2; any use of x within a_1 refers to a different variable that happens to have the same name. For example, in the expression $\mathtt{let}\,x\,\mathtt{be}\,7\,\mathtt{in}\,x + x$ occurrences of x in the addition refer to the variable introduced by the $\mathtt{let}$. On the other hand, in the expression $\mathtt{let}\,x\,\mathtt{be}\,x * x\,\mathtt{in}\,x + x$, occurrences of x within the multiplication refer to a different variable than those occurring within the addition. The latter occurrences refer to the binding introduced by the let, whereas the former refer to some outer binding not displayed here.

The names of bound variables are immaterial insofar as they determine the same binding. So, for example, let x be $x * x$ in $x + x$ could just as well have been written let y be $x * x$ in $y + y$, without changing its meaning. In the former case, the variable x is bound within the addition, and in the latter, it is the variable y, but the "pointer structure" remains the same. On the other hand, the expression let x be $y * y$ in $x + x$ has a different meaning to these two expressions, because now the variable y within the multiplication refers to a different surrounding variable. Renaming of bound variables is constrained to the extent that it must not alter the reference structure of the expression. For example, the expression

$$\text{let } x \text{ be } 2 \text{ in let } y \text{ be } 3 \text{ in } x + x$$

has a different meaning than the expression

$$\text{let } y \text{ be } 2 \text{ in let } y \text{ be } 3 \text{ in } y + y,$$

because the y in the expression $y + y$ in the second case refers to the inner declaration, not the outer one as before.

The concept of an ast can be enriched to account for binding and scope of a variable. These enriched ast's are called *abstract binding trees*, or *abt's* for short. Abt's generalize ast's by allowing an operator to bind any finite number (possibly zero) of variables in each argument. An argument to an operator is called an *abstractor* and has the form $x_1, \ldots, x_k.a$. The sequence of variables $x_1, \ldots, x_k$ are bound within the abt a. (When k is zero, we elide the distinction between $.a$ and a itself.) Written in the form of an abt, the expression let x be a_1 in a_2 has the form $\text{let}(a_1; x.a_2)$, which more clearly specifies that the variable x is bound within a_2, and not within a_1. We often write $\vec{x}$ to stand for a finite sequence $x_1, \ldots, x_n$ of distinct variables and write $\vec{x}.a$ to mean $x_1, \ldots, x_n.a$.

To account for binding, operators are assigned *generalized arities* of the form $(\upsilon_1, \ldots, \upsilon_n)s$, which specifies operators of sort s with n arguments of *valence* $\upsilon_1, \ldots, \upsilon_n$. In general a valence υ has the form $s_1, \ldots, s_k.s$, which specifies the sort of an argument as well as the number and sorts of the variables bound within it. We say that a sequence $\vec{x}$ of variables is of sort $\vec{s}$ to mean that the two sequences have the same length k and that the variable x_i is of sort s_i for each $1 \leq i \leq k$.

Thus, to specify that the operator let has arity (Exp, Exp.Exp)Exp indicates that it is of sort Exp whose first argument is of sort Exp and binds no variables and whose second argument is also of sort Exp and within which is bound one variable of sort Exp. The informal expression let x be $2 + 2$ in $x \times x$ may then be written as the abt

$$\text{let}(\text{plus}(\text{num}[2]; \text{num}[2]); x.\text{times}(x; x))$$

in which the operator let has two arguments, the first of which is an expression, and the second of which is an abstractor that binds one expression variable.

Fix a set $\mathcal{S}$ of sorts and a family $\mathcal{O}$ of disjoint sets of operators indexed by their generalized arities. For a given family of disjoint sets of variables $\mathcal{X}$, the family of *abstract binding trees*, or *abt's* $\mathcal{B}[\mathcal{X}]$, is defined similarly to $\mathcal{A}[\mathcal{X}]$, except that $\mathcal{X}$ is not fixed throughout the definition but rather changes as we enter the scopes of abstractors.

This simple idea is surprisingly hard to make precise. A first attempt at the definition is as the least family of sets closed under the following conditions:

1. If $x \in \mathcal{X}_s$, then $x \in \mathcal{B}[\mathcal{X}]_s$.
2. For each operator o of arity $(\vec{s}_1.s_1, \ldots, \vec{s}_n.s_n)s$, if $a_1 \in \mathcal{B}[\mathcal{X}, \vec{x}_1]_{s_1}$, $\ldots$, and $a_n \in \mathcal{B}[\mathcal{X}, \vec{x}_n]_{s_n}$, then $o(\vec{x}_1.a_1; \ldots; \vec{x}_n.a_n) \in \mathcal{B}[\mathcal{X}]_s$.

The bound variables are adjoined to the set of active variables within each argument, with the sort of each variable determined by the valence of the operator.

This definition is *almost* correct but fails to properly account for renaming of bound variables. An abt of the form $\mathtt{let}(a_1; x.\mathtt{let}(a_2; x.a_3))$ is ill-formed according to this definition, because the first binding adds x to $\mathcal{X}$, which implies that the second cannot also add x to $\mathcal{X}, x$, because it is not fresh for $\mathcal{X}, x$. The solution is to ensure that each of the arguments is well-formed regardless of the choice of bound variable names, which is achieved using *fresh renamings*, which are bijections between sequences of variables. Specifically, a fresh renaming (relative to $\mathcal{X}$) of a finite sequence of variables $\vec{x}$ is a bijection $\rho : \vec{x} \leftrightarrow \vec{x}'$ between $\vec{x}$ and $\vec{x}'$, where $\vec{x}'$ is fresh for $\mathcal{X}$. We write $\widehat{\rho}(a)$ for the result of replacing each occurrence of x_i in a by $\rho(x_i)$, its fresh counterpart.

This is achieved by altering the second clause of the definition of abt's using fresh renamings as follows:

> For each operator o of arity $(\vec{s}_1.s_1, \ldots, \vec{s}_n.s_n)s$, if for each $1 \leq i \leq n$ and each fresh renaming $\rho_i : \vec{x}_i \leftrightarrow \vec{x}'_i$, we have $\widehat{\rho}_i(a_i) \in \mathcal{B}[\mathcal{X}, \vec{x}'_i]$, then $o(\vec{x}_1.a_1; \ldots; \vec{x}_n.a_n) \in \mathcal{B}[\mathcal{X}]_s$.

The renaming $\widehat{\rho}_i(a_i)$ of each a_i ensures that collisions cannot occur and that the abt is valid for almost all renamings of any bound variables that occur within it.

The principle of structural induction extends to abt's and is called *structural induction modulo fresh renaming*. It states that to show that $\mathcal{P}[\mathcal{X}](a)$ holds for every $a \in \mathcal{B}[\mathcal{X}]$, it is enough to show the following:

1. if $x \in \mathcal{X}_s$, then $\mathcal{P}[\mathcal{X}]_s(x)$.
2. For every o of arity $(\vec{s}_1.s_1, \ldots, \vec{s}_n.s_n)s$, if for each $1 \leq i \leq n$, $\mathcal{P}[\mathcal{X}, \vec{x}'_i]_{s_i}(\widehat{\rho}_i(a_i))$ holds for every $\rho_i : \vec{x}_i \leftrightarrow \vec{x}'_i$ with $\vec{x}'_i \notin \mathcal{X}$, then $\mathcal{P}[\mathcal{X}]_s(o(\vec{x}_1.a_1; \ldots; \vec{x}_n.a_n))$.

The second condition ensures that the inductive hypothesis holds for *all* fresh choices of bound variable names, and not just the ones actually given in the abt.

As an example let us define the judgment $x \in a$, where $a \in \mathcal{B}[\mathcal{X}, x]$, to mean that x *occurs free* in a. Informally, this means that x is bound somewhere outside of a, rather than within a itself. If x is bound within a, then those occurrences of x are different from those occurring outside the binding. The following definition ensures that this is the case:

1. $x \in x$.
2. $x \in o(\vec{x}_1.a_1; \ldots; \vec{x}_n.a_n)$ if there exists $1 \leq i \leq n$ such that for every fresh renaming $\rho : \vec{x}_i \leftrightarrow \vec{z}_i$ we have $x \in \widehat{\rho}(a_i)$.

The first condition states that x is free in x but not free in y for any variable y other than x. The second condition states that if x is free in some argument, independently of the choice of bound variable names in that argument, then it is free in the overall abt.

The relation $a =_\alpha b$ of *α-equivalence* (so-called for historical reasons) means that a and b are identical up to the choice of bound variable names. The α-equivalence relation is the strongest congruence containing the following two conditions:

1. $x =_\alpha x$.
2. $o(\vec{x}_1.a_1; \ldots; \vec{x}_n.a_n) =_\alpha o(\vec{x}'_1.a'_1; \ldots; \vec{x}'_n.a'_n)$ if for every $1 \leq i \leq n$, $\widehat{\rho}_i(a_i) =_\alpha \widehat{\rho}'_i(a'_i)$ for all fresh renamings $\rho_i : \vec{x}_i \leftrightarrow \vec{z}_i$ and $\rho'_i : \vec{x}'_i \leftrightarrow \vec{z}_i$.

The idea is that we rename $\vec{x}_i$ and $\vec{x}'_i$ consistently, avoiding confusion, and check that a_i and a'_i are α-equivalent. If $a =_\alpha b$, then a and b are *α-variants* of each other.

Some care is required in the definition of *substitution* of an abt b of sort s for free occurrences of a variable x of sort s in some abt a of some sort, written $[b/x]a$. Substitution is partially defined by the following conditions:

1. $[b/x]x = b$, and $[b/x]y = y$ if $x \neq y$.
2. $[b/x]o(\vec{x}_1.a_1; \ldots; \vec{x}_n.a_n) = o(\vec{x}_1.a'_1; \ldots; \vec{x}_n.a'_n)$, where, for each $1 \leq i \leq n$, we require that $\vec{x}_i \notin b$, and we set $a'_i = [b/x]a_i$ if $x \notin \vec{x}_i$, and $a'_i = a_i$ otherwise.

The definition of $[b/x]a$ is quite delicate and merits careful consideration.

One trouble spot for substitution is to notice that if x is bound by an abstractor within a, then x does not occur free within the abstractor and hence is unchanged by substitution. For example, $[b/x]\text{let}(a_1; x.a_2) = \text{let}([b/x]a_1; x.a_2)$, there being no free occurrences of x in $x.a_2$. Another trouble spot is the *capture* of a free variable of b during substitution. For example, if $y \in b$ and $x \neq y$, then $[b/x]\text{let}(a_1; y.a_2)$ is undefined, rather than being $\text{let}([b/x]a_1; y.[b/x]a_2)$, as one might at first suspect. For example, provided that $x \neq y, [y/x]\text{let}(\text{num}[0]; y.\text{plus}(x; y))$ is undefined, not $\text{let}(\text{num}[0]; y.\text{plus}(y; y))$, which confuses two different variables named y.

Although capture avoidance is an essential characteristic of substitution, it is, in a sense, merely a technical nuisance. If the names of bound variables have no significance, then capture can always be avoided by first renaming the bound variables in a to avoid any free variables in b. In the foregoing example, if we rename the bound variable y to y' to obtain $a' \triangleq \text{let}(\text{num}[0]; y'.\text{plus}(x; y'))$, then $[b/x]a'$ *is* defined and is equal to $\text{let}(\text{num}[0]; y'.\text{plus}(b; y'))$. The price for avoiding capture in this way is that substitution is only determined up to α-equivalence, and so we may no longer think of substitution as a function but only as a proper relation.

To restore the functional character of substitution, it is sufficient to adopt the *identification convention*, which is stated as follows:

Abstract binding trees are always identified up to α-equivalence.

That is, α-equivalent abt's are regarded as identical. Substitution can be extended to α-equivalence classes of abt's to avoid capture by choosing representatives of the equivalence classes of b and a in such a way that substitution is defined, then forming the equivalence class of the result. Any two choices of representatives for which substitution is defined gives α-equivalent results, so that substitution becomes a well-defined total function. *We will adopt the identification convention for abt's throughout this book.*

It will often be necessary to consider languages whose abstract syntax cannot be specified by a fixed set of operators but rather requires that the available operators be sensitive to the context in which they occur. For our purposes, it will suffice to consider a set of *symbolic parameters*, or *symbols*, that index families of operators so that as the set of symbols varies, so does the set of operators. An *indexed operator* o is a family of operators indexed by symbols u, so that $o[u]$ is an operator when u is an available symbol. If $\mathcal{U}$ is a finite set of symbols, then $\mathcal{B}[\mathcal{U}; \mathcal{X}]$ is the sort-indexed family of abt's that are generated by operators and variables as before, admitting all indexed operator instances by symbols $u \in \mathcal{U}$. Whereas a variable is a place-holder that stands for an unknown abt of its sort, a symbol *does not stand for anything*, and is not, itself, an abt. The only significance of symbol is whether it is the same as or differs from another symbol; the operator instances $o[u]$ and $o[u']$ are the same exactly when u is u' and are the same symbol.

The set of symbols is extended by introducing a *new*, or *fresh*, symbol within a scope using the abstractor $u.a$, which binds the symbol u within the abt a. An abstracted symbol is "new" in the same sense as for an abstracted variable: the name of the bound symbol can be varied at will provided that no conflicts arise. This renaming property ensures that an abstracted symbol is distinct from all others in scope. The only difference between symbols and variables is that the only operation on symbols is renaming; there is no notion of substitution for a symbol.

Finally, a word about notation: to help improve the readability we often "group" and "stage" the arguments to an operator, using round brackets and braces to show grouping, and generally regarding stages to progress from right to left. All arguments in a group are considered to occur at the same stage, though their order is significant, and successive groups are considered to occur in sequential stages. Staging and grouping is often a helpful mnemonic device, but has no fundamental significance. For example, the abt $o\{a_1; a_2\}(a_3; x.a_4)$ is the same as the abt $o(a_1; a_2; a_3; x.a_4)$, as would be any other order-preserving grouping or staging of its arguments.

1.3 Notes

The concept of abstract syntax has its origins in the pioneering work of Church, Turing, and Gödel, who first considered writing programs that act on representations of programs.

Originally, programs were represented by natural numbers, using encodings, now called *Gödel-numberings*, based on the prime factorization theorem. Any standard text on mathematical logic, such as Kleene (1952), has a thorough account of such representations. The Lisp language (McCarthy, 1965; Allen, 1978) introduced a much more practical and direct representation of syntax as *symbolic expressions*. These ideas were developed further in the language ML (Gordon et al., 1979), which featured a type system capable of expressing abstract syntax trees. The AUTOMATH project (Nederpelt et al., 1994) introduced the idea of using Church's λ notation (Church, 1941) to account for the binding and scope of variables. These ideas were developed further in LF (Harper et al., 1993).

The concept of abstract binding trees presented here was inspired by the system of notation developed in the NuPRL Project, which is described in Constable (1986) and from Martin-Löf's system of arities, which is described in Nordstrom et al. (1990). Their enrichment with symbol binders is influenced by Pitts and Stark (1993).

Exercises

1.1. Prove by structural induction on abstract syntax trees that if $\mathcal{X} \subseteq \mathcal{Y}$, then $\mathcal{A}[\mathcal{X}] \subseteq \mathcal{A}[\mathcal{Y}]$.

1.2. Prove by structural induction modulo renaming on abstract binding trees that if $\mathcal{X} \subseteq \mathcal{Y}$, then $\mathcal{B}[\mathcal{X}] \subseteq \mathcal{B}[\mathcal{Y}]$.

1.3. Show that if $a =_\alpha a'$ and $b =_\alpha b'$ and both $[b/x]a$ and $[b'/x]a'$ are defined, then $[b/x]a =_\alpha [b'/x]a'$.

1.4. Bound variables can be seen as the formal analogs of pronouns in natural languages. The binding occurrence of a variable at an abstractor fixes a "fresh" pronoun for use within its body that refers unambiguously to that variable (in contrast to English, in which the referent of a pronoun can often be ambiguous). This observation suggests an alternative representation of abt's, called *abstract binding graphs*, or *abg's* for short, as directed graphs constructed as follows:

(a) Free variables are atomic nodes with no outgoing edges.

(b) Operators with n arguments are n-ary nodes, with one outgoing edge directed at each of their children.

(c) Abstractors are nodes with one edge directed to the scope of the abstracted variable.

(d) Bound variables are back edges directed at the abstractor that introduced it.

Notice that ast's, thought of as abt's with no abstractors, are *acyclic* directed graphs (more precisely, variadic trees), whereas general abt's can be *cyclic*. Draw a few examples of abg's corresponding to the example abt's given in this chapter. Give a precise definition of the sort-indexed family $\mathcal{G}[\mathcal{X}]$ of abstract binding graphs. What representation would you use for bound variables (back edges)?

2 Inductive Definitions

Inductive definitions are an indispensable tool in the study of programming languages. In this chapter we will develop the basic framework of inductive definitions and give some examples of their use. An inductive definition consists of a set of *rules* for deriving *judgments*, or *assertions*, of a variety of forms. Judgments are statements about one or more abstract binding trees of some sort. The rules specify necessary and sufficient conditions for the validity of a judgment, and hence fully determine its meaning.

2.1 Judgments

We start with the notion of a *judgment*, or *assertion*, about an abstract binding tree. We shall make use of many forms of judgment, including examples such as these:

n nat	n is a natural number
$n_1 + n_2 = n$	n is the sum of n_1 and n_2
τ type	τ is a type
$e : \tau$	expression e has type τ
$e \Downarrow v$	expression e has value v

A judgment states that one or more abstract binding trees have a property or stand in some relation to one another. The property or relation itself is called a *judgment form*, and the judgment that an object or objects have that property or stand in that relation is said to be an *instance* of that judgment form. A judgment form is also called a *predicate*, and the objects constituting an instance are its *subjects*. We write a J or J a, for the judgment asserting that J holds of the abt a. Correspondingly, we sometimes notate the judgment form J by $-$ J, or J $-$, using a dash to indicate the absence of an argument to J. When it is not important to stress the subject of the judgment, we write J to stand for an unspecified judgment, that is, an instance of some judgment form. For particular judgment forms, we freely use prefix, infix, or mix-fix notation, as illustrated by the above examples, in order to enhance readability.

2.2 Inference Rules

An *inductive definition* of a judgment form consists of a collection of *rules* of the form

$$\frac{J_1 \quad \cdots \quad J_k}{J} \tag{2.1}$$

in which J and $J_1, \ldots, J_k$ are all judgments of the form being defined. The judgments above the horizontal line are called the *premises* of the rule, and the judgment below the line is called its *conclusion*. If a rule has no premises (that is, when k is zero), the rule is called an *axiom*; otherwise, it is called a *proper rule*.

An inference rule can be read as stating that the premises are *sufficient* for the conclusion: to show J, it is enough to show $J_1, \ldots, J_k$. When k is zero, a rule states that its conclusion holds unconditionally. Bear in mind that there may be, in general, many rules with the same conclusion, each specifying sufficient conditions for the conclusion. Consequently, if the conclusion of a rule holds, then it is not necessary that the premises hold, for it might have been derived by another rule.

For example, the following rules form an inductive definition of the judgment form $-$ nat:

$$\frac{}{\texttt{zero nat}} \tag{2.2a}$$

$$\frac{a \text{ nat}}{\texttt{succ}(a) \text{ nat}} \tag{2.2b}$$

These rules specify that a nat holds whenever either a is $\texttt{zero}$, or a is $\texttt{succ}(b)$ where b nat for some b. Taking these rules to be exhaustive, it follows that a nat iff a is a natural number.

Similarly, the following rules constitute an inductive definition of the judgment form $-$ tree:

$$\frac{}{\texttt{empty tree}} \tag{2.3a}$$

$$\frac{a_1 \text{ tree} \quad a_2 \text{ tree}}{\texttt{node}(a_1;a_2) \text{ tree}} \tag{2.3b}$$

These rules specify that a tree holds if either a is $\texttt{empty}$, or a is $\texttt{node}(a_1;a_2)$, where a_1 tree and a_2 tree. Taking these to be exhaustive, these rules state that a is a binary tree, which is to say it is either empty, or a node consisting of two children, each of which is also a binary tree.

The judgment form a is b expresses the equality of two abt's a and b such that a nat and b nat is inductively defined by the following rules:

$$\frac{}{\texttt{zero is zero}} \tag{2.4a}$$

$$\frac{a \text{ is } b}{\texttt{succ}(a) \text{ is } \texttt{succ}(b)} \tag{2.4b}$$

In each of the preceding examples, we have made use of a notational convention for specifying an infinite family of rules by a finite number of patterns, or *rule schemes*. For example, rule (2.2b) is a rule scheme that determines one rule, called an *instance* of the rule scheme, for each choice of object a in the rule. We will rely on context to determine whether a rule is stated for a *specific* object a or is instead intended as a rule scheme specifying a rule for *each choice* of objects in the rule.

A collection of rules is considered to define the *strongest* judgment form that is *closed under*, or *respects*, those rules. To be closed under the rules simply means that the rules are *sufficient* to show the validity of a judgment: J holds *if* there is a way to obtain it using the given rules. To be the *strongest* judgment form closed under the rules means that the rules are also *necessary*: J holds *only if* there is a way to obtain it by applying the rules. The sufficiency of the rules means that we may show that J holds by *deriving* it by composing rules. Their necessity means that we may reason about it using *rule induction*.

2.3 Derivations

To show that an inductively defined judgment holds, it is enough to exhibit a *derivation* of it. A derivation of a judgment is a finite composition of rules, starting with axioms and ending with that judgment. It can be thought of as a tree in which each node is a rule whose children are derivations of its premises. We sometimes say that a derivation of J is evidence for the validity of an inductively defined judgment J.

We usually depict derivations as trees with the conclusion at the bottom, and with the children of a node corresponding to a rule appearing above it as evidence for the premises of that rule. Thus, if

$$\frac{J_1 \quad \ldots \quad J_k}{J}$$

is an inference rule and $\nabla_1, \ldots, \nabla_k$ are derivations of its premises, then

$$\frac{\nabla_1 \quad \cdots \quad \nabla_k}{J}$$

is a derivation of its conclusion. In particular, if $k = 0$, then the node has no children.

For example, this is a derivation of $\texttt{succ(succ(succ(zero)))}$ nat:

$$\frac{\dfrac{\dfrac{\dfrac{}{\texttt{zero nat}}}{\texttt{succ(zero) nat}}}{\texttt{succ(succ(zero)) nat}}}{\texttt{succ(succ(succ(zero))) nat}} . \tag{2.5}$$

Similarly, here is a derivation of $\texttt{node(node(empty;empty);empty)}$ tree:

$$\frac{\dfrac{\dfrac{}{\texttt{empty tree}} \quad \dfrac{}{\texttt{empty tree}}}{\texttt{node(empty;empty) tree}} \quad \dfrac{}{\texttt{empty tree}}}{\texttt{node(node(empty;empty);empty) tree}} . \tag{2.6}$$

To show that an inductively defined judgment is derivable, we need only find a derivation for it. There are two main methods for finding derivations, called *forward chaining*, or *bottom-up construction*, and *backward chaining*, or *top-down construction*. Forward chaining starts with the axioms and works forward towards the desired conclusion, whereas backward chaining starts with the desired conclusion and works backwards towards the axioms.

More precisely, forward chaining search maintains a set of derivable judgments and continually extends this set by adding to it the conclusion of any rule all of whose premises are in that set. Initially, the set is empty; the process terminates when the desired judgment occurs in the set. Assuming that all rules are considered at every stage, forward chaining will eventually find a derivation of any derivable judgment, but it is impossible (in general) to decide algorithmically when to stop extending the set and conclude that the desired judgment is not derivable. We may go on and on adding more judgments to the derivable set without ever achieving the intended goal. It is a matter of understanding the global properties of the rules to determine that a given judgment is not derivable.

Forward chaining is undirected in the sense that it does not take account of the end goal when deciding how to proceed at each step. In contrast, backward chaining is goal-directed. Backward chaining search maintains a queue of current goals, judgments whose derivations are to be sought. Initially, this set consists solely of the judgment we wish to derive. At each stage, we remove a judgment from the queue and consider all rules whose conclusion is that judgment. For each such rule, we add the premises of that rule to the back of the queue, and continue. If there is more than one such rule, this process must be repeated, with the same starting queue, for each candidate rule. The process terminates whenever the queue is empty, all goals having been achieved; any pending consideration of candidate rules along the way can be discarded. As with forward chaining, backward chaining will eventually find a derivation of any derivable judgment, but there is, in general, no algorithmic method for determining in general whether the current goal is derivable. If it is not, we may futilely add more and more judgments to the goal set, never reaching a point at which all goals have been satisfied.

2.4 Rule Induction

Because an inductive definition specifies the *strongest* judgment form closed under a collection of rules, we may reason about them by *rule induction*. The principle of rule induction states that to show that a property $a \; \mathcal{P}$ holds whenever $a \; \mathsf{J}$ is derivable, it is enough to show that $\mathcal{P}$ is *closed under*, or *respects*, the rules defining the judgment form J. More precisely, the property $\mathcal{P}$ respects the rule

$$\frac{a_1 \; \mathsf{J} \quad \ldots \quad a_k \; \mathsf{J}}{a \; \mathsf{J}}$$

if $\mathcal{P}(a)$ holds whenever $\mathcal{P}(a_1), \ldots, \mathcal{P}(a_k)$ do. The assumptions $\mathcal{P}(a_1), \ldots, \mathcal{P}(a_k)$ are called the *inductive hypotheses*, and $\mathcal{P}(a)$ is called the *inductive conclusion* of the inference.

The principle of rule induction is simply the expression of the definition of an inductively defined judgment form as the *strongest* judgment form closed under the rules comprising the definition. Thus, the judgment form defined by a set of rules is both (a) closed under those rules, and (b) sufficient for any other property also closed under those rules. The former means that a derivation is evidence for the validity of a judgment; the latter means that we may reason about an inductively defined judgment form by rule induction.

When specialized to rules (2.2), the principle of rule induction states that to show $\mathcal{P}(a)$ whenever a nat, it is enough to show:

1. $\mathcal{P}(\texttt{zero})$.
2. for every a, if $\mathcal{P}(a)$, then $\mathcal{P}(\texttt{succ}(a))$.

The sufficiency of these conditions is the familiar principle of *mathematical induction*.

Similarly, rule induction for rules (2.3) states that to show $\mathcal{P}(a)$ whenever a tree, it is enough to show

1. $\mathcal{P}(\texttt{empty})$.
2. for every a_1 and a_2, if $\mathcal{P}(a_1)$, and if $\mathcal{P}(a_2)$, then $\mathcal{P}(\texttt{node}(a_1;a_2))$.

The sufficiency of these conditions is called the principle of *tree induction*.

We may also show by rule induction that the predecessor of a natural number is also a natural number. Although this may seem self-evident, the point of the example is to show how to derive this from first principles.

Lemma 2.1. *If* $\texttt{succ}(a)$ nat, *then* a nat.

Proof It suffices to show that the property $\mathcal{P}(a)$ stating that a nat and that $a = \texttt{succ}(b)$ implies b nat is closed under rules (2.2).

> **Rule (2.2a)** Clearly $\texttt{zero}$ nat, and the second condition holds vacuously, because $\texttt{zero}$ is not of the form $\texttt{succ}(-)$.
> **Rule (2.2b)** Inductively, we know that a nat and that if a is of the form $\texttt{succ}(b)$, then b nat. We are to show that $\texttt{succ}(a)$ nat, which is immediate, and that if $\texttt{succ}(a)$ is of the form $\texttt{succ}(b)$, then b nat, and we have b nat by the inductive hypothesis. □

Using rule induction, we may show that equality, as defined by rules (2.4) is reflexive.

Lemma 2.2. *If* a nat, *then* a is a.

Proof By rule induction on rules (2.2):

> **Rule (2.2a)** Applying rule (2.4a) we obtain $\texttt{zero}$ is $\texttt{zero}$.
> **Rule (2.2b)** Assume that a is a. It follows that $\texttt{succ}(a)$ is $\texttt{succ}(a)$ by an application of rule (2.4b). □

Similarly, we may show that the successor operation is injective.

Lemma 2.3. *If* $\text{succ}(a_1)$ *is* $\text{succ}(a_2)$, *then* a_1 *is* a_2.

Proof   Similar to the proof of Lemma 2.1.   □

2.5 Iterated and Simultaneous Inductive Definitions

Inductive definitions are often *iterated*, meaning that one inductive definition builds on top of another. In an iterated inductive definition, the premises of a rule

$$\frac{J_1 \quad \ldots \quad J_k}{J}$$

may be instances of either a previously defined judgment form, or the judgment form being defined. For example, the following rules define the judgment form — list, which states that a is a list of natural numbers:

$$\frac{}{\text{nil list}} \tag{2.7a}$$

$$\frac{a \text{ nat} \quad b \text{ list}}{\text{cons}(a;b) \text{ list}} \tag{2.7b}$$

The first premise of rule (2.7b) is an instance of the judgment form a nat, which was defined previously, whereas the premise b list is an instance of the judgment form being defined by these rules.

Frequently two or more judgments are defined at once by a *simultaneous inductive definition*. A simultaneous inductive definition consists of a set of rules for deriving instances of several different judgment forms, any of which may appear as the premise of any rule. Because the rules defining each judgment form may involve any of the others, none of the judgment forms can be taken to be defined prior to the others. Instead, we must understand that all of the judgment forms are being defined at once by the entire collection of rules. The judgment forms defined by these rules are, as before, the strongest judgment forms that are closed under the rules. Therefore, the principle of proof by rule induction continues to apply, albeit in a form that requires us to prove a property of each of the defined judgment forms simultaneously.

For example, consider the following rules, which constitute a simultaneous inductive definition of the judgments a even, stating that a is an even natural number, and a odd, stating that a is an odd natural number:

$$\frac{}{\text{zero even}} \tag{2.8a}$$

$$\frac{b \text{ odd}}{\text{succ}(b) \text{ even}} \tag{2.8b}$$

$$\frac{a \text{ even}}{\text{succ}(a) \text{ odd}} \tag{2.8c}$$

The principle of rule induction for these rules states that to show simultaneously that $\mathcal{P}(a)$ whenever a even and $\mathcal{Q}(b)$ whenever b odd, it is enough to show the following:

1. $\mathcal{P}(\mathtt{zero})$;
2. if $\mathcal{Q}(b)$, then $\mathcal{P}(\mathtt{succ}(b))$;
3. if $\mathcal{P}(a)$, then $\mathcal{Q}(\mathtt{succ}(a))$.

As an example, we may use simultaneous rule induction to prove that (1) if a even, then either a is $\mathtt{zero}$ or a is $\mathtt{succ}(b)$ with b odd, and (2) if a odd, then a is $\mathtt{succ}(b)$ with b even. We define $\mathcal{P}(a)$ to hold iff a is $\mathtt{zero}$ or a is $\mathtt{succ}(b)$ for some b with b odd, and define $\mathcal{Q}(b)$ to hold iff b is $\mathtt{succ}(a)$ for some a with a even. The desired result follows by rule induction, because we can prove the following facts:

1. $\mathcal{P}(\mathtt{zero})$, which holds because $\mathtt{zero}$ is $\mathtt{zero}$.
2. If $\mathcal{Q}(b)$, then $\mathtt{succ}(b)$ is $\mathtt{succ}(b')$ for some b' with $\mathcal{Q}(b')$. Take b' to be b and apply the inductive assumption.
3. If $\mathcal{P}(a)$, then $\mathtt{succ}(a)$ is $\mathtt{succ}(a')$ for some a' with $\mathcal{P}(a')$. Take a' to be a and apply the inductive assumption.

2.6 Defining Functions by Rules

A common use of inductive definitions is to define a function by giving an inductive definition of its *graph* relating inputs to outputs, and then showing that the relation uniquely determines the outputs for given inputs. For example, we may define the addition function on natural numbers as the relation $\mathtt{sum}(a;b;c)$, with the intended meaning that c is the sum of a and b, as follows:

$$\frac{b\ \mathtt{nat}}{\mathtt{sum}(\mathtt{zero};b;b)} \tag{2.9a}$$

$$\frac{\mathtt{sum}(a;b;c)}{\mathtt{sum}(\mathtt{succ}(a);b;\mathtt{succ}(c))} \tag{2.9b}$$

The rules define a ternary (three-place) relation $\mathtt{sum}(a;b;c)$ among natural numbers a, b, and c. We may show that c is determined by a and b in this relation.

Theorem 2.4. *For every a* nat *and b* nat, *there exists a unique c* nat *such that* $\mathtt{sum}(a;b;c)$.

Proof   The proof decomposes into two parts:

1. (Existence) If a nat and b nat, then there exists c nat such that $\mathtt{sum}(a;b;c)$.
2. (Uniqueness) If $\mathtt{sum}(a;b;c)$, and $\mathtt{sum}(a;b;c')$, then c is c'.

For existence, let $\mathcal{P}(a)$ be the proposition *if* b nat *then there exists* c nat *such that* $\mathrm{sum}(a;b;c)$. We prove that if a nat then $\mathcal{P}(a)$ by rule induction on rules (2.2). We have two cases to consider:

Rule (2.2a) We are to show $\mathcal{P}(\mathtt{zero})$. Assuming b nat and taking c to be b, we obtain $\mathrm{sum}(\mathtt{zero};b;c)$ by rule (2.9a).

Rule (2.2b) Assuming $\mathcal{P}(a)$, we are to show $\mathcal{P}(\mathtt{succ}(a))$. That is, we assume that if b nat then there exists c such that $\mathrm{sum}(a;b;c)$ and are to show that if b' nat, then there exists c' such that $\mathrm{sum}(\mathtt{succ}(a);b';c')$. To this end, suppose that b' nat. Then by induction there exists c such that $\mathrm{sum}(a;b';c)$. Taking c' to be $\mathtt{succ}(c)$, and applying rule (2.9b), we obtain $\mathrm{sum}(\mathtt{succ}(a);b';c')$, as required.

For uniqueness, we prove that *if* $\mathrm{sum}(a;b;c_1)$, *then if* $\mathrm{sum}(a;b;c_2)$, *then* c_1 is c_2 by rule induction based on rules (2.9).

Rule (2.9a) We have a is $\mathtt{zero}$ and c_1 is b. By an inner induction on the same rules, we may show that if $\mathrm{sum}(\mathtt{zero};b;c_2)$, then c_2 is b. By Lemma 2.2, we obtain b is b.

Rule (2.9b) We have that a is $\mathtt{succ}(a')$ and c_1 is $\mathtt{succ}(c_1')$, where $\mathrm{sum}(a';b;c_1')$. By an inner induction on the same rules, we may show that if $\mathrm{sum}(a;b;c_2)$, then c_2 is $\mathtt{succ}(c_2')$ where $\mathrm{sum}(a';b;c_2')$. By the outer inductive hypothesis, c_1' is c_2' and so c_1 is c_2.   □

2.7 Notes

Aczel (1977) provides a thorough account of the theory of inductive definitions on which the present account is based. A significant difference is that we consider inductive definitions of judgments over abt's as defined in Chapter 1, rather than with natural numbers. The emphasis on judgments is inspired by Martin-Löf's logic of judgments (Martin-Löf, 1983, 1987).

Exercises

2.1. Give an inductive definition of the judgment $\max(m;n;p)$, where m nat, n nat, and p nat, with the meaning that p is the larger of m and n. Prove that every m and n are related to a unique p by this judgment.

2.2. Consider the following rules, which define the judgment $\mathrm{hgt}(t;n)$ stating that the binary tree t has *height* n.

$$\frac{}{\mathrm{hgt}(\mathtt{empty};\mathtt{zero})} \tag{2.10a}$$

$$\frac{\mathrm{hgt}(t_1;n_1) \quad \mathrm{hgt}(t_2;n_2) \quad \max(n_1;n_2;n)}{\mathrm{hgt}(\mathtt{node}(t_1;t_2);\mathtt{succ}(n))} \tag{2.10b}$$

Prove that the judgment hgt defines a function from trees to natural numbers.

2.3. Given an inductive definition of *ordered variadic trees* whose nodes have a finite, but variable, number of children with a specified left-to-right ordering among them. Your solution should consist of a simultaneous definition of two judgments, t tree, stating that t is a variadic tree, and f forest, stating that f is a "forest" (finite sequence) of variadic trees.

2.4. Give an inductive definition of the height of a variadic tree of the kind defined in Exercise **2.3**. Your definition should make use of an auxiliary judgment defining the height of a forest of variadic trees and will be defined simultaneously with the height of a variadic tree. Show that the two judgments so defined each define a function.

2.5. Give an inductive definition of the *binary natural numbers*, which are either zero, twice a binary number, or one more than twice a binary number. The size of such a representation is logarithmic, rather than linear, in the natural number it represents.

2.6. Give an inductive definition of addition of binary natural numbers as defined in Exercise **2.5**. *Hint*: Proceed by analyzing both arguments to the addition, and make use of an auxiliary function to compute the successor of a binary number. *Hint*: Alternatively, define both the sum and the sum-plus-one of two binary numbers mutually recursively.

3 Hypothetical and General Judgments

A *hypothetical judgment* expresses an entailment between one or more hypotheses and a conclusion. We will consider two notions of entailment, called *derivability* and *admissibility*. Both express a form of entailment, but they differ in that derivability is stable under extension with new rules, admissibility is not. A *general judgment* expresses the universality, or genericity, of a judgment. There are two forms of general judgment, the *generic* and the *parametric*. The generic judgment expresses generality with respect to all substitution instances for variables in a judgment. The parametric judgment expresses generality with respect to renamings of symbols.

3.1 Hypothetical Judgments

The hypothetical judgment codifies the rules for expressing the validity of a conclusion conditional on the validity of one or more hypotheses. There are two forms of hypothetical judgment that differ according to the sense in which the conclusion is conditional on the hypotheses. One is stable under extension with more rules, and the other is not.

3.1.1 Derivability

For a given set $\mathcal{R}$ of rules, we define the *derivability* judgment, written $J_1, \ldots, J_k \vdash_\mathcal{R} K$, where each J_i and K are basic judgments, to mean that we may derive K from the *expansion* $\mathcal{R} \cup \{ J_1, \ldots, J_k \}$ of the rules $\mathcal{R}$ with the axioms

$$\frac{}{J_1} \quad \cdots \quad \frac{}{J_k}.$$

We treat the *hypotheses*, or *antecedents*, of the judgment, $J_1, \ldots, J_k$ as "temporary axioms," and derive the *conclusion*, or *consequent*, by composing rules in $\mathcal{R}$. Thus, evidence for a hypothetical judgment consists of a derivation of the conclusion from the hypotheses using the rules in $\mathcal{R}$.

We use capital Greek letters, usually Γ or Δ, to stand for a finite set of basic judgments, and write $\mathcal{R} \cup \Gamma$ for the expansion of $\mathcal{R}$ with an axiom corresponding to each judgment in Γ. The judgment $\Gamma \vdash_\mathcal{R} K$ means that K is derivable from rules $\mathcal{R} \cup \Gamma$, and the judgment $\vdash_\mathcal{R} \Gamma$ means that $\vdash_\mathcal{R} J$ for each J in Γ. An equivalent way of defining $J_1, \ldots, J_n \vdash_\mathcal{R} J$ is to say that the rule

$$\frac{J_1 \quad \ldots \quad J_n}{J} \tag{3.1}$$

is *derivable* from $\mathcal{R}$, which means that there is a derivation of J composed of the rules in $\mathcal{R}$ augmented by treating $J_1, \ldots, J_n$ as axioms.

For example, consider the derivability judgment

$$a \text{ nat} \vdash_{(2.2)} \text{succ}(\text{succ}(a)) \text{ nat} \tag{3.2}$$

relative to rules (2.2). This judgment is valid for *any* choice of object a, as shown by the derivation

$$\frac{\dfrac{a \text{ nat}}{\text{succ}(a) \text{ nat}}}{\text{succ}(\text{succ}(a)) \text{ nat}} \tag{3.3}$$

which composes rules (2.2), starting with a nat as an axiom, and ending with $\text{succ}(\text{succ}(a))$ nat. Equivalently, the validity of (3.2) may also be expressed by stating that the rule

$$\frac{a \text{ nat}}{\text{succ}(\text{succ}(a)) \text{ nat}} \tag{3.4}$$

is derivable from rules (2.2).

It follows directly from the definition of derivability that it is stable under extension with new rules.

Theorem 3.1 (Stability). *If $\Gamma \vdash_{\mathcal{R}} J$, then $\Gamma \vdash_{\mathcal{R} \cup \mathcal{R}'} J$.*

Proof Any derivation of J from $\mathcal{R} \cup \Gamma$ is also a derivation from $(\mathcal{R} \cup \mathcal{R}') \cup \Gamma$, because any rule in $\mathcal{R}$ is also a rule in $\mathcal{R} \cup \mathcal{R}'$. $\qquad\qquad\square$

Derivability enjoys a number of *structural properties* that follow from its definition, independently of the rules $\mathcal{R}$ in question.

Reflexivity Every judgment is a consequence of itself: $\Gamma, J \vdash_{\mathcal{R}} J$. Each hypothesis justifies itself as conclusion.

Weakening If $\Gamma \vdash_{\mathcal{R}} J$, then $\Gamma, K \vdash_{\mathcal{R}} J$. Entailment is not influenced by un-exercised options.

Transitivity If $\Gamma, K \vdash_{\mathcal{R}} J$ and $\Gamma \vdash_{\mathcal{R}} K$, then $\Gamma \vdash_{\mathcal{R}} J$. If we replace an axiom by a derivation of it, the result is a derivation of its consequent without that hypothesis.

Reflexivity follows directly from the meaning of derivability. Weakening follows directly from the definition of derivability. Transitivity is proved by rule induction on the first premise.

3.1.2 Admissibility

Admissibility, written $\Gamma \models_\mathcal{R} J$, is a weaker form of hypothetical judgment stating that $\vdash_\mathcal{R} \Gamma$ implies $\vdash_\mathcal{R} J$. That is, the conclusion J is derivable from rules $\mathcal{R}$ when the assumptions Γ are all derivable from rules $\mathcal{R}$. In particular if any of the hypotheses are *not* derivable relative to $\mathcal{R}$, then the judgment is *vacuously* true. An equivalent way to define the judgment $J_1, \ldots, J_n \models_\mathcal{R} J$ is to state that the rule

$$\frac{J_1 \quad \ldots \quad J_n}{J} \tag{3.5}$$

is *admissible* relative to the rules in $\mathcal{R}$. Given any derivations of $J_1, \ldots, J_n$ using the rules in $\mathcal{R}$, we may build a derivation of J using the rules in $\mathcal{R}$.

For example, the admissibility judgment

$$\texttt{succ}(a) \text{ even} \models_{(2.8)} a \text{ odd} \tag{3.6}$$

is valid, because any derivation of $\texttt{succ}(a)$ even from rules (2.2) must contain a subderivation of a odd from the same rules, which justifies the conclusion. This fact can be proved by induction on rules (2.8). That judgment (3.6) is valid may also be expressed by saying that the rule

$$\frac{\texttt{succ}(a) \text{ even}}{a \text{ odd}} \tag{3.7}$$

is *admissible* relative to rules (2.8).

In contrast to derivability the admissibility judgment is *not* stable under extension to the rules. For example, if we enrich rules (2.8) with the axiom

$$\frac{}{\texttt{succ(zero)} \text{ even}} \,, \tag{3.8}$$

then rule (3.6) is *inadmissible*, because there is no composition of rules deriving $\texttt{zero}$ odd. Admissibility is as sensitive to which rules are *absent* from an inductive definition as it is to which rules are *present* in it.

The structural properties of derivability ensure that derivability is stronger than admissibility.

Theorem 3.2. *If* $\Gamma \vdash_\mathcal{R} J$, *then* $\Gamma \models_\mathcal{R} J$.

Proof Repeated application of the transitivity of derivability shows that if $\Gamma \vdash_\mathcal{R} J$ and $\vdash_\mathcal{R} \Gamma$, then $\vdash_\mathcal{R} J$.   □

To see that the converse fails, note that

$$\texttt{succ(zero)} \text{ even} \nvDash_{(2.8)} \texttt{zero} \text{ odd},$$

because there is no derivation of the right-hand side when the left-hand side is added as an axiom to rules (2.8). Yet the corresponding admissibility judgment

$$\texttt{succ(zero)} \text{ even} \models_{(2.8)} \texttt{zero} \text{ odd}$$

is valid, because the hypothesis is false: there is no derivation of $\texttt{succ(zero)}$ even from rules (2.8). Even so, the derivability

$$\texttt{succ(zero) even} \vdash_{(2.8)} \texttt{succ(succ(zero)) odd}$$

is valid, because we may derive the right-hand side from the left-hand side by composing rules (2.8).

Evidence for admissibility can be thought of as a mathematical function transforming derivations $\nabla_1, \ldots, \nabla_n$ of the hypotheses into a derivation ∇ of the consequent. Therefore, the admissibility judgment enjoys the same structural properties as derivability and hence is a form of hypothetical judgment:

Reflexivity If J is derivable from the original rules, then J is derivable from the original rules: $J \models_{\mathcal{R}} J$.

Weakening If J is derivable from the original rules assuming that each of the judgments in Γ are derivable from these rules, then J must also be derivable assuming that Γ and K are derivable from the original rules: if $\Gamma \models_{\mathcal{R}} J$, then $\Gamma, K \models_{\mathcal{R}} J$.

Transitivity If $\Gamma, K \models_{\mathcal{R}} J$ and $\Gamma \models_{\mathcal{R}} K$, then $\Gamma \models_{\mathcal{R}} J$. If the judgments in Γ are derivable, so is K, by assumption, and hence so are the judgments in Γ, K, and hence so is J.

Theorem 3.3. *The admissibility judgment* $\Gamma \models_{\mathcal{R}} J$ *enjoys the structural properties of entailment.*

Proof Follows immediately from the definition of admissibility as stating that if the hypotheses are derivable relative to $\mathcal{R}$, then so is the conclusion. $\qquad\qquad\square$

If a rule r is admissible with respect to a rule set $\mathcal{R}$, then $\vdash_{\mathcal{R},r} J$ is equivalent to $\vdash_{\mathcal{R}} J$. For if $\vdash_{\mathcal{R}} J$, then obviously $\vdash_{\mathcal{R},r} J$, by simply disregarding r. Conversely, if $\vdash_{\mathcal{R},r} J$, then we may replace any use of r by its expansion in terms of the rules in $\mathcal{R}$. It follows by rule induction on $\mathcal{R}, r$ that every derivation from the expanded set of rules $\mathcal{R}, r$ can be transformed into a derivation from $\mathcal{R}$ alone. Consequently, if we wish to prove a property of the judgments derivable from $\mathcal{R}, r$, when r is admissible with respect to $\mathcal{R}$, it suffices show that the property is closed under rules $\mathcal{R}$ alone, because its admissibility states that the consequences of rule r are implicit in those of rules $\mathcal{R}$.

3.2 Hypothetical Inductive Definitions

It is useful to enrich the concept of an inductive definition to allow rules with derivability judgments as premises and conclusions. Doing so lets us introduce *local hypotheses* that apply only in the derivation of a particular premise, and also allows us to constrain inferences based on the *global hypotheses* in effect at the point where the rule is applied.

A *hypothetical inductive definition* consists of a set of *hypothetical rules* of the following form:

$$\frac{\Gamma\,\Gamma_1 \vdash J_1 \quad \ldots \quad \Gamma\,\Gamma_n \vdash J_n}{\Gamma \vdash J}\,. \tag{3.9}$$

The hypotheses Γ are the *global hypotheses* of the rule, and the hypotheses Γ_i are the *local hypotheses* of the ith premise of the rule. Informally, this rule states that J is a derivable consequence of Γ when each J_i is a derivable consequence of Γ, augmented with the hypotheses Γ_i. Thus, one way to show that J is derivable from Γ is to show, in turn, that each J_i is derivable from $\Gamma\,\Gamma_i$. The derivation of each premise involves a "context switch" in which we extend the global hypotheses with the local hypotheses of that premise, establishing a new set of global hypotheses for use within that derivation.

We require that all rules in a hypothetical inductive definition be *uniform* in the sense that they are applicable in *all* global contexts. Uniformity ensures that a rule can be presented in *implicit*, or *local form*,

$$\frac{\Gamma_1 \vdash J_1 \quad \ldots \quad \Gamma_n \vdash J_n}{J}\,, \tag{3.10}$$

in which the global context has been suppressed with the understanding that the rule applies for any choice of global hypotheses.

A hypothetical inductive definition is to be regarded as an ordinary inductive definition of a *formal derivability judgment* $\Gamma \vdash J$ consisting of a finite set of basic judgments Γ and a basic judgment J. A set of hypothetical rules $\mathcal{R}$ defines the strongest formal derivability judgment that is *structural* and *closed* under uniform rules $\mathcal{R}$. Structurality means that the formal derivability judgment must be closed under the following rules:

$$\frac{}{\Gamma, J \vdash J} \tag{3.11a}$$

$$\frac{\Gamma \vdash J}{\Gamma, K \vdash J} \tag{3.11b}$$

$$\frac{\Gamma \vdash K \quad \Gamma, K \vdash J}{\Gamma \vdash J} \tag{3.11c}$$

These rules ensure that formal derivability behaves like a hypothetical judgment. We write $\Gamma \vdash_{\mathcal{R}} J$ to mean that $\Gamma \vdash J$ is derivable from rules $\mathcal{R}$.

The principle of *hypothetical rule induction* is just the principle of rule induction applied to the formal hypothetical judgment. So to show that $\mathcal{P}(\Gamma \vdash J)$ when $\Gamma \vdash_{\mathcal{R}} J$, it is enough to show that $\mathcal{P}$ is closed under the rules of $\mathcal{R}$ and under the structural rules.[1] Thus, for each rule of the form (3.9), whether structural or in $\mathcal{R}$, we must show that

if $\mathcal{P}(\Gamma\,\Gamma_1 \vdash J_1)$ and $\ldots$ and $\mathcal{P}(\Gamma\,\Gamma_n \vdash J_n)$, then $\mathcal{P}(\Gamma \vdash J)$.

But this is just a restatement of the principle of rule induction given in Chapter 2, specialized to the formal derivability judgment $\Gamma \vdash J$.

In practice, we usually dispense with the structural rules by the method described in Section 3.1.2. By proving that the structural rules are admissible, any proof by rule induction may restrict attention to the rules in $\mathcal{R}$ alone. If all rules of a hypothetical inductive definition are uniform, the structural rules (3.11b) and (3.11c) are clearly admissible. Usually, rule (3.11a) must be postulated explicitly as a rule, rather than shown to be admissible on the basis of the other rules.

3.3 General Judgments

General judgments codify the rules for handling variables in a judgment. As in mathematics in general, a variable is treated as an *unknown*, ranging over a specified set of objects. A *generic* judgment states that a judgment holds for any choice of objects replacing designated variables in the judgment. Another form of general judgment codifies the handling of symbolic parameters. A *parametric* judgment expresses generality over any choice of fresh renamings of designated symbols of a judgment. To keep track of the active variables and symbols in a derivation, we write $\Gamma \vdash_{\mathcal{R}}^{\mathcal{U};\mathcal{X}} J$ to say that J is derivable from Γ according to rules $\mathcal{R}$, with objects consisting of abt's over symbols $\mathcal{U}$ and variables $\mathcal{X}$.

The concept of uniformity of a rule must be extended to require that rules be *closed under renaming and substitution* for variables and *closed under renaming* for parameters. More precisely, if $\mathcal{R}$ is a set of rules containing a free variable x of sort s, then it must also contain all possible substitution instances of abt's a of sort s for x, including those that contain other free variables. Similarly, if $\mathcal{R}$ contains rules with a parameter u, then it must contain all instances of that rule obtained by renaming u of a sort to any u' of the same sort. Uniformity rules out stating a rule for a variable, without also stating it for all instances of that variable. It also rules out stating a rule for a parameter without stating it for all possible renamings of that parameter.

Generic derivability judgment is defined by

$$\mathcal{Y} \mid \Gamma \vdash_{\mathcal{R}}^{\mathcal{X}} J \quad \text{iff} \quad \Gamma \vdash_{\mathcal{R}}^{\mathcal{X}\mathcal{Y}} J,$$

where $\mathcal{Y} \cap \mathcal{X} = \varnothing$. Evidence for generic derivability consists of a *generic derivation* ∇ involving the variables $\mathcal{X}\,\mathcal{Y}$. So long as the rules are uniform, the choice of $\mathcal{Y}$ does not matter, in a sense to be explained shortly.

For example, the generic derivation ∇,

$$\frac{\dfrac{\overline{x \text{ nat}}}{\text{succ}(x) \text{ nat}}}{\text{succ}(\text{succ}(x)) \text{ nat}},$$

is evidence for the judgment

$$x \mid x \text{ nat} \vdash_{(2.2)}^{x} \text{succ}(\text{succ}(x)) \text{ nat}$$

provided $x \notin \mathcal{X}$. Any other choice of x would work just as well, as long as all rules are uniform.

The generic derivability judgment enjoys the following *structural properties* governing the behavior of variables, provided that $\mathcal{R}$ is uniform.

Proliferation If $\mathcal{Y} \mid \Gamma \vdash^{\mathcal{X}}_{\mathcal{R}} J$, then $\mathcal{Y}, y \mid \Gamma \vdash^{\mathcal{X}}_{\mathcal{R}} J$.

Renaming If $\mathcal{Y}, y \mid \Gamma \vdash^{\mathcal{X}}_{\mathcal{R}} J$, then $\mathcal{Y}, y' \mid [y \leftrightarrow y']\Gamma \vdash^{\mathcal{X}}_{\mathcal{R}} [y \leftrightarrow y']J$ for any $y' \notin \mathcal{X} \mathcal{Y}$.

Substitution If $\mathcal{Y}, y \mid \Gamma \vdash^{\mathcal{X}}_{\mathcal{R}} J$ and $a \in \mathcal{B}[\mathcal{X} \mathcal{Y}]$, then $\mathcal{Y} \mid [a/y]\Gamma \vdash^{\mathcal{X}}_{\mathcal{R}} [a/y]J$.

Proliferation is guaranteed by the interpretation of rule schemes as ranging over all expansions of the universe. Renaming is built into the meaning of the generic judgment. It is left implicit in the principle of substitution that the substituting abt is of the same sort as the substituted variable.

Parametric derivability is defined analogously to generic derivability, albeit by generalizing over symbols, rather than variables. Parametric derivability is defined by

$$\mathcal{V} \parallel \mathcal{Y} \mid \Gamma \vdash^{\mathcal{U};\mathcal{X}}_{\mathcal{R}} J \quad \text{iff} \quad \mathcal{Y} \mid \Gamma \vdash^{\mathcal{U}\mathcal{V};\mathcal{X}}_{\mathcal{R}} J,$$

where $\mathcal{V} \cap \mathcal{U} = \emptyset$. Evidence for parametric derivability consists of a derivation ∇ involving the symbols $\mathcal{V}$. Uniformity of $\mathcal{R}$ ensures that any choice of parameter names is as good as any other; derivability is stable under renaming.

3.4 Generic Inductive Definitions

A *generic inductive definition* admits generic hypothetical judgments in the premises of rules, with the effect of augmenting the variables, as well as the rules, within those premises. A *generic rule* has the form

$$\frac{\mathcal{Y} \mathcal{Y}_1 \mid \Gamma \Gamma_1 \vdash J_1 \quad \dots \quad \mathcal{Y} \mathcal{Y}_n \mid \Gamma \Gamma_n \vdash J_n}{\mathcal{Y} \mid \Gamma \vdash J}. \tag{3.12}$$

The variables $\mathcal{Y}$ are the *global variables* of the inference, and, for each $1 \leq i \leq n$, the variables $\mathcal{Y}_i$ are the *local variables* of the ith premise. In most cases, a rule is stated for *all* choices of global variables and global hypotheses. Such rules can be given in *implicit form*,

$$\frac{\mathcal{Y}_1 \mid \Gamma_1 \vdash J_1 \quad \dots \quad \mathcal{Y}_n \mid \Gamma_n \vdash J_n}{J}. \tag{3.13}$$

A generic inductive definition is just an ordinary inductive definition of a family of *formal generic judgments* of the form $\mathcal{Y} \mid \Gamma \vdash J$. Formal generic judgments are identified up to renaming of variables, so that the latter judgment is treated as identical to the judgment $\mathcal{Y}' \mid \widehat{\rho}(\Gamma) \vdash \widehat{\rho}(J)$ for any renaming $\rho : \mathcal{Y} \leftrightarrow \mathcal{Y}'$. If $\mathcal{R}$ is a collection of generic rules, we write $\mathcal{Y} \mid \Gamma \vdash_{\mathcal{R}} J$ to mean that the formal generic judgment $\mathcal{Y} \mid \Gamma \vdash J$ is derivable from rules $\mathcal{R}$.

When specialized to a set of generic rules, the principle of rule induction states that to show $\mathcal{P}(\mathcal{Y} \mid \Gamma \vdash J)$ when $\mathcal{Y} \mid \Gamma \vdash_{\mathcal{R}} J$, it is enough to show that $\mathcal{P}$ is closed under the rules

$\mathcal{R}$. Specifically, for each rule in $\mathcal{R}$ of the form (3.12), we must show that

$$\text{if } \mathcal{P}(\mathcal{Y}\, \mathcal{Y}_1 \mid \Gamma\, \Gamma_1 \vdash J_1) \ \dots \ \mathcal{P}(\mathcal{Y}\, \mathcal{Y}_n \mid \Gamma\, \Gamma_n \vdash J_n) \text{ then } \mathcal{P}(\mathcal{Y} \mid \Gamma \vdash J).$$

By the identification convention (stated in Chapter 1), the property $\mathcal{P}$ must respect renamings of the variables in a formal generic judgment.

To ensure that the formal generic judgment behaves like a generic judgment, we must always ensure that the following *structural rules* are admissible:

$$\frac{}{\mathcal{Y} \mid \Gamma, J \vdash J} \tag{3.14a}$$

$$\frac{\mathcal{Y} \mid \Gamma \vdash J}{\mathcal{Y} \mid \Gamma, J' \vdash J} \tag{3.14b}$$

$$\frac{\mathcal{Y} \mid \Gamma \vdash J}{\mathcal{Y}, x \mid \Gamma \vdash J} \tag{3.14c}$$

$$\frac{\mathcal{Y}, x' \mid [x \leftrightarrow x']\Gamma \vdash [x \leftrightarrow x']J}{\mathcal{Y}, x \mid \Gamma \vdash J} \tag{3.14d}$$

$$\frac{\mathcal{Y} \mid \Gamma \vdash J \quad \mathcal{Y} \mid \Gamma, J \vdash J'}{\mathcal{Y} \mid \Gamma \vdash J'} \tag{3.14e}$$

$$\frac{\mathcal{Y}, x \mid \Gamma \vdash J \quad a \in \mathcal{B}[\mathcal{Y}]}{\mathcal{Y} \mid [a/x]\Gamma \vdash [a/x]J} \tag{3.14f}$$

The admissibility of rule (3.14a) is, in practice, ensured by explicitly including it. The admissibility of rules (3.14b) and (3.14c) is assured if each of the generic rules is uniform, because we may assimilate the added variable x to the global variables, and the added hypothesis J, to the global hypotheses. The admissibility of rule (3.14d) is ensured by the identification convention for the formal generic judgment. Rule (3.14f) must be verified explicitly for each inductive definition.

The concept of a generic inductive definition extends to parametric judgments as well. Briefly, rules are defined on formal parametric judgments of the form $\mathcal{V} \parallel \mathcal{Y} \mid \Gamma \vdash J$, with symbols $\mathcal{V}$, as well as variables, $\mathcal{Y}$. Such formal judgments are identified up to renaming of its variables and its symbols to ensure that the meaning is independent of the choice of variable and symbol names.

3.5 Notes

The concepts of entailment and generality are fundamental to logic and programming languages. The formulation given here builds on Martin-Löf (1983, 1987) and Avron (1991). Hypothetical and general reasoning are consolidated into a single concept in the AU-TOMATH languages (Nederpelt et al., 1994) and in the LF Logical Framework (Harper et al., 1993). These systems allow arbitrarily nested combinations of hypothetical and general judgments, whereas the present account considers only general hypothetical judgments over basic judgment forms. On the other hand, we consider here symbols, as well as variables, which are not present in these previous accounts. Parametric judgments are required for specifying languages that admit the dynamic creation of "new" objects (see Chapter 34).

Exercises

3.1. *Combinators* are inductively defined by the rule set $\mathcal{C}$ given as follows:

$$\frac{}{\text{s comb}} \tag{3.15a}$$

$$\frac{}{\text{k comb}} \tag{3.15b}$$

$$\frac{a_1 \text{ comb} \quad a_2 \text{ comb}}{\text{ap}(a_1;a_2) \text{ comb}} \tag{3.15c}$$

Give an inductive definition of the *length* of a combinator defined as the number of occurrences of S and K within it.

3.2. The general judgment

$$x_1, \ldots, x_n \mid x_1 \text{ comb}, \ldots, x_n \text{ comb} \vdash_{\mathcal{C}} A \text{ comb}$$

states that A is a combinator that may involve the variables $x_1, \ldots, x_n$. Prove that if $x \mid x$ comb $\vdash_{\mathcal{C}} a_2$ comb and a_1 comb, then $[a_1/x]a_2$ comb by induction on the derivation of the first hypothesis of the implication.

3.3. *Conversion*, or *equivalence*, of combinators is expressed by the judgment $A \equiv B$ defined by the rule set $\mathcal{E}$ extending $\mathcal{C}$ as follows:[2]

$$\frac{a \text{ comb}}{a \equiv a} \tag{3.16a}$$

$$\frac{a_2 \equiv a_1}{a_1 \equiv a_2} \tag{3.16b}$$

$$\frac{a_1 \equiv a_2 \quad a_2 \equiv a_3}{a_1 \equiv a_3} \tag{3.16c}$$

$$\frac{a_1 \equiv a_1' \quad a_2 \equiv a_2'}{a_1 \, a_2 \equiv a_1' \, a_2'} \tag{3.16d}$$

$$\frac{a_1 \text{ comb} \quad a_2 \text{ comb}}{\text{k} \, a_1 \, a_2 \equiv a_1} \tag{3.16e}$$

$$\frac{a_1 \text{ comb} \quad a_2 \text{ comb} \quad a_3 \text{ comb}}{\text{s} \, a_1 \, a_2 \, a_3 \equiv (a_1 \, a_3)(a_2 \, a_3)} \tag{3.16f}$$

The no-doubt mysterious motivation for the last two equations will become clearer in a moment. For now, show that

$$x \mid x \text{ comb} \vdash_{\mathcal{C} \cup \mathcal{E}} \text{s} \, \text{k} \, \text{k} \, x \equiv x.$$

3.4. Show that if $x \mid x$ comb $\vdash_C a$ comb, then there is a combinator a', written $[x]\, a$ and called *bracket abstraction*, such that

$$x \mid x \text{ comb} \vdash_{C \cup \mathcal{E}} a'\, x \equiv a.$$

Consequently, by Exercise **3.2**, if a'' comb, then

$$([x]\, a)\, a'' \equiv [a''/x]a.$$

Hint: Inductively define the judgment

$$x \mid x \text{ comb} \vdash \text{abs}_x\, a \text{ is } a',$$

where $x \mid x$ comb $\vdash a$ comb. Then argue that it defines a' as a binary function of x and a. The motivation for the conversion axioms governing k and s should become clear while developing the proof of the desired equivalence.

3.5. Prove that bracket abstraction, as defined in Exercise **3.4**, is *non-compositional* by exhibiting a and b such that a comb and

$$x\, y \mid x \text{ comb } y \text{ comb} \vdash_C b \text{ comb}$$

such that $[a/y]([x]\, b) \neq [x]\,([a/y]b)$. *Hint*: Consider the case that b is y.

Suggest a modification to the definition of bracket abstraction that is *compositional* by showing under the same conditions given above that

$$[a/y]([x]\, b) = [x]\,([a/y]b).$$

3.6. Consider the set $\mathcal{B}[\mathcal{X}]$ of abt's generated by the operators ap, with arity (Exp, Exp)Exp, and λ, with arity (Exp.Exp)Exp, and possibly involving variables in $\mathcal{X}$, all of which are of sort Exp. Give an inductive definition of the judgment b closed, which specifies that b has no free occurrences of the variables in $\mathcal{X}$. *Hint*: it is essential to give an inductive definition of the hypothetical, general judgment

$$x_1, \ldots, x_n \mid x_1 \text{ closed}, \ldots, x_n \text{ closed} \vdash b \text{ closed}$$

in order to account for the binding of a variable by the λ operator. The hypothesis that a variable is closed seems self-contradictory in that a variable obviously occurs free in itself. Explain why this is not the case by examining carefully the meaning of the hypothetical and general judgments.

Notes

1 Writing $\mathcal{P}(\Gamma \vdash J)$ is a mild abuse of notation in which the turnstile is used to separate the two arguments to $\mathcal{P}$ for the sake of readability.
2 The combinator $\text{ap}(a_1; a_2)$ is written $a_1\, a_2$ for short, left-associatively when used in succession.

PART II

Statics and Dynamics

4 Statics

Most programming languages exhibit a *phase distinction* between the *static* and *dynamic* phases of processing. The static phase consists of parsing and type checking to ensure that the program is well-formed; the dynamic phase consists of execution of well-formed programs. A language is said to be *safe* exactly when well-formed programs are well-behaved when executed.

The static phase is specified by a *statics* comprising a set of rules for deriving *typing judgments* stating that an expression is well-formed of a certain type. Types mediate the interaction between the constituent parts of a program by "predicting" some aspects of the execution behavior of the parts so that we may ensure they fit together properly at run-time. Type safety tells us that these predictions are correct; if not, the statics is considered to be improperly defined, and the language is deemed *unsafe* for execution.

In this chapter, we present the statics of a simple expression language, **E**, as an illustration of the method that we will employ throughout this book.

4.1 Syntax

When defining a language we shall be primarily concerned with its abstract syntax, specified by a collection of operators and their arities. The abstract syntax provides a systematic, unambiguous account of the hierarchical and binding structure of the language and is considered the official presentation of the language. However, for the sake of clarity, it is also useful to specify minimal concrete syntax conventions, without going through the trouble to set up a fully precise grammar for it.

We will accomplish both of these purposes with a *syntax chart*, whose meaning is best illustrated by example. The following chart summarizes the abstract and concrete syntax of **E**.

Typ	τ	::=	num	num	numbers
			str	str	strings
Exp	e	::=	x	x	variable
			$\text{num}[n]$	n	numeral
			$\text{str}[s]$	$"s"$	literal
			$\text{plus}(e_1; e_2)$	$e_1 + e_2$	addition
			$\text{times}(e_1; e_2)$	$e_1 * e_2$	multiplication
			$\text{cat}(e_1; e_2)$	$e_1 \char94 e_2$	concatenation
			$\text{len}(e)$	$|e|$	length
			$\text{let}(e_1; x.e_2)$	$\text{let } x \text{ be } e_1 \text{ in } e_2$	definition

This chart defines two sorts, Typ, ranged over by τ, and Exp, ranged over by e. The chart defines a set of operators and their arities. For example, it specifies that the operator let has arity (Exp, Exp.Exp)Exp, which specifies that it has two arguments of sort Exp, and binds a variable of sort Exp in the second argument.

4.2 Type System

The role of a type system is to impose constraints on the formations of phrases that are sensitive to the context in which they occur. For example, whether the expression $\text{plus}(x; \text{num}[n])$ is sensible depends on whether the variable x is restricted to have type num in the surrounding context of the expression. This example is, in fact, illustrative of the general case, in that the *only* information required about the context of an expression is the type of the variables within whose scope the expression lies. Consequently, the statics of **E** consists of an inductive definition of generic hypothetical judgments of the form

$$\vec{x} \mid \Gamma \vdash e : \tau,$$

where $\vec{x}$ is a finite set of variables, and Γ is a *typing context* consisting of hypotheses of the form $x : \tau$, one for each $x \in \vec{x}$. We rely on typographical conventions to determine the set of variables, using the letters x and y to stand for them. We write $x \notin dom(\Gamma)$ to say that there is no assumption in Γ of the form $x : \tau$ for any type τ, in which case we say that the variable x is *fresh* for Γ.

The rules defining the statics of **E** are as follows:

$$\frac{}{\Gamma, x : \tau \vdash x : \tau} \tag{4.1a}$$

$$\frac{}{\Gamma \vdash \text{str}[s] : \text{str}} \tag{4.1b}$$

$$\frac{}{\Gamma \vdash \text{num}[n] : \text{num}} \tag{4.1c}$$

$$\frac{\Gamma \vdash e_1 : \text{num} \quad \Gamma \vdash e_2 : \text{num}}{\Gamma \vdash \text{plus}(e_1; e_2) : \text{num}} \tag{4.1d}$$

$$\frac{\Gamma \vdash e_1 : \text{num} \quad \Gamma \vdash e_2 : \text{num}}{\Gamma \vdash \text{times}(e_1; e_2) : \text{num}} \tag{4.1e}$$

$$\frac{\Gamma \vdash e_1 : \text{str} \quad \Gamma \vdash e_2 : \text{str}}{\Gamma \vdash \text{cat}(e_1; e_2) : \text{str}} \tag{4.1f}$$

$$\frac{\Gamma \vdash e : \text{str}}{\Gamma \vdash \text{len}(e) : \text{num}} \tag{4.1g}$$

$$\frac{\Gamma \vdash e_1 : \tau_1 \quad \Gamma, x : \tau_1 \vdash e_2 : \tau_2}{\Gamma \vdash \text{let}(e_1; x.e_2) : \tau_2} \tag{4.1h}$$

In rule (4.1h), we tacitly assume that the variable x is not already declared in Γ. This condition may always be met by choosing a suitable representative of the α-equivalence class of the let expression.

It is easy to check that every expression has at most one type by *induction on typing*, which is rule induction applied to rules (4.1).

Lemma 4.1 (Unicity of Typing). *For every typing context Γ and expression e, there exists at most one τ such that $\Gamma \vdash e : \tau$.*

Proof By rule induction on rules (4.1), making use of the fact that variables have at most one type in any typing context.   □

The typing rules are *syntax-directed* in the sense that there is exactly one rule for each form of expression. Consequently, it is easy to give necessary conditions for typing an expression that invert the sufficient conditions expressed by the corresponding typing rule.

Lemma 4.2 (Inversion for Typing). *Suppose that $\Gamma \vdash e : \tau$. If $e = \mathtt{plus}(e_1; e_2)$, then $\tau = \mathtt{num}$, $\Gamma \vdash e_1 : \mathtt{num}$, and $\Gamma \vdash e_2 : \mathtt{num}$, and similarly for the other constructs of the language.*

Proof These may all be proved by induction on the derivation of the typing judgment $\Gamma \vdash e : \tau$.   □

In richer languages such inversion principles are more difficult to state and to prove.

4.3 Structural Properties

The statics enjoys the structural properties of the generic hypothetical judgment.

Lemma 4.3 (Weakening). *If $\Gamma \vdash e' : \tau'$, then $\Gamma, x : \tau \vdash e' : \tau'$ for any $x \notin dom(\Gamma)$ and any type τ.*

Proof By induction on the derivation of $\Gamma \vdash e' : \tau'$. We will give one case here, for rule (4.1h). We have that $e' = \mathtt{let}(e_1; z.e_2)$, where by the conventions on variables we may assume z is chosen such that $z \notin dom(\Gamma)$ and $z \neq x$. By induction, we have

1. $\Gamma, x : \tau \vdash e_1 : \tau_1$,
2. $\Gamma, x : \tau, z : \tau_1 \vdash e_2 : \tau'$,

from which the result follows by rule (4.1h).   □

Lemma 4.4 (Substitution). *If $\Gamma, x : \tau \vdash e' : \tau'$ and $\Gamma \vdash e : \tau$, then $\Gamma \vdash [e/x]e' : \tau'$.*

Proof By induction on the derivation of $\Gamma, x : \tau \vdash e' : \tau'$. We again consider only rule (4.1h). As in the preceding case, $e' = \mathtt{let}(e_1; z.e_2)$, where z is chosen so that $z \neq x$ and $z \notin dom(\Gamma)$. We have by induction and Lemma 4.3 that

1. $\Gamma \vdash [e/x]e_1 : \tau_1$,
2. $\Gamma, z : \tau_1 \vdash [e/x]e_2 : \tau'$.

By the choice of z, we have

$$[e/x]\mathtt{let}(e_1; z.e_2) = \mathtt{let}([e/x]e_1; z.[e/x]e_2).$$

It follows by rule (4.1h) that $\Gamma \vdash [e/x]\mathtt{let}(e_1; z.e_2) : \tau'$, as desired. □

From a programming point of view, Lemma 4.3 allows us to use an expression in any context that binds its free variables: if e is well-typed in a context Γ, then we may "import" it into any context that includes the assumptions Γ. In other words, introducing new variables beyond those required by an expression e does not invalidate e itself; it remains well-formed, with the same type.[1] More importantly, Lemma 4.4 expresses the important concepts of *modularity* and *linking*. We may think of the expressions e and e' as two *components* of a larger system in which e' is a *client* of the *implementation e*. The client declares a variable specifying the type of the implementation and is type checked knowing only this information. The implementation must be of the specified type to satisfy the assumptions of the client. If so, then we may link them to form the composite system $[e/x]e'$. This implementation may itself be the client of another component, represented by a variable y that is replaced by that component during linking. When all such variables have been implemented, the result is a *closed expression* that is ready for execution (evaluation).

The converse of Lemma 4.4 is called *decomposition*. It states that any (large) expression can be decomposed into a client and implementor by introducing a variable to mediate their interaction.

Lemma 4.5 (Decomposition). *If* $\Gamma \vdash [e/x]e' : \tau'$, *then for every type* τ *such that* $\Gamma \vdash e : \tau$, *we have* $\Gamma, x : \tau \vdash e' : \tau'$.

Proof The typing of $[e/x]e'$ depends only on the type of e wherever it occurs, if at all. □

Lemma 4.5 tells us that any sub-expression can be isolated as a separate module of a larger system. This property is especially useful when the variable x occurs more than once in e', because then one copy of e suffices for all occurrences of x in e'.

The statics of **E** given by rules (4.1) exemplifies a recurrent pattern. The constructs of a language are classified into one of two forms, the *introduction* and the *elimination*. The introduction forms for a type determine the *values*, or *canonical forms*, of that type. The elimination forms determine how to manipulate the values of a type to form a computation of another (possibly the same) type. In the language **E**, the introduction forms for the type num are the numerals, and those for the type str are the literals. The elimination forms for the type num are addition and multiplication, and those for the type str are concatenation and length.

The importance of this classification will become clear once we have defined the dynamics of the language in Chapter 5. Then we will see that the elimination forms are *inverse* to the introduction forms in that they "take apart" what the introduction forms have "put together." The coherence of the statics and dynamics of a language expresses the concept of *type safety*, the subject of Chapter 6.

4.4 Notes

The concept of the static semantics of a programming language was historically slow to develop, perhaps because the earliest languages had relatively few features and only very weak type systems. The concept of a static semantics in the sense considered here was introduced in the definition of the Standard ML programming language (Milner et al., 1997), building on earlier work by Church and others on the typed λ-calculus (Barendregt, 1992). The concept of introduction and elimination, and the associated inversion principle, was introduced by Gentzen in his pioneering work on natural deduction (Gentzen, 1969). These principles were applied to the structure of programming languages by Martin-Löf (1984, 1980).

Exercises

4.1. It is sometimes useful to give the typing judgment $\Gamma \vdash e : \tau$ an "operational" reading that specifies more precisely the flow of information required to derive a typing judgment (or determine that it is not derivable). The *analytic* mode corresponds to the context, expression, and type being given, with the goal to determine whether the typing judgment is derivable. The *synthetic* mode corresponds to the context and expression being given, with the goal to find the unique type τ, if any, possessed by the expression in that context. These two readings can be made explicit as judgments of the form $e \downarrow \tau$, corresponding to the analytic mode, and $e \uparrow \tau$, corresponding to the synthetic mode.

Give a simultaneous inductive definition of these two judgments according to the following guidelines:

(a) Variables are introduced in synthetic form.

(b) If we can synthesize a unique type for an expression, then we can analyze it with respect to a given type by checking type equality.

(c) Definitions need care, because the type of the defined expression is not given, even when the type of the result is given.

There is room for variation; the point of the exercise is to explore the possibilities.

4.2. One way to limit the range of possibilities in the solution to Exercise **4.1** is to restrict and extend the syntax of the language so that every expression is either synthetic or analytic according to the following suggestions:

(a) Variables are analytic.

(b) Introduction forms are analytic, elimination forms are synthetic.

(c) An analytic expression can be made synthetic by introducing a *type cast* of the form cast$\{\tau\}(e)$ specifying that e must check against the specified type τ, which is synthesized for the whole expression.

(d) The defining expression of a definition must be synthetic, but the scope of the definition can be either synthetic or analytic.

Reformulate your solution to Exercise **4.1** to take account of these guidelines.

Note

1 This point may seem so obvious that it is not worthy of mention, but, surprisingly, there are useful type systems that lack this property. Because they do not validate the structural principle of weakening, they are called *substructural* type systems.

5 Dynamics

The *dynamics* of a language describes how programs are executed. The most important way to define the dynamics of a language is by the method of *structural dynamics*, which defines a *transition system* that inductively specifies the step-by-step process of executing a program. Another method for presenting dynamics, called *contextual dynamics*, is a variation of structural dynamics in which the transition rules are specified in a slightly different way. An *equational dynamics* presents the dynamics of a language by a collection of rules defining when one program is *definitionally equivalent* to another.

5.1 Transition Systems

A *transition system* is specified by the following four forms of judgment:

1. s state, asserting that s is a *state* of the transition system.
2. s final, where s state, asserting that s is a *final* state.
3. s initial, where s state, asserting that s is an *initial* state.
4. $s \longmapsto s'$, where s state and s' state, asserting that state s may transition to state s'.

In practice, we always arrange things so that no transition is possible from a final state: if s final, then there is no s' state such that $s \longmapsto s'$. A state from which no transition is possible is *stuck*. Whereas all final states are, by convention, stuck, there may be stuck states in a transition system that are not final. A transition system is *deterministic* iff for every state s there exists at most one state s' such that $s \longmapsto s'$; otherwise, it is *non-deterministic*.

A *transition sequence* is a sequence of states $s_0, \ldots, s_n$ such that s_0 initial, and $s_i \longmapsto s_{i+1}$ for every $0 \leq i < n$. A transition sequence is *maximal* iff there is no s such that $s_n \longmapsto s$, and it is *complete* iff it is maximal and s_n final. Thus, every complete transition sequence is maximal, but maximal sequences are not necessarily complete. The judgment $s \downarrow$ means that there is a complete transition sequence starting from s, which is to say that there exists s' final such that $s \longmapsto^* s'$.

The *iteration* of transition judgment $s \longmapsto^* s'$ is inductively defined by the following rules:

$$\frac{}{s \longmapsto^* s} \tag{5.1a}$$

$$\frac{s \longmapsto s' \quad s' \longmapsto^* s''}{s \longmapsto^* s''} \tag{5.1b}$$

When applied to the definition of iterated transition, the principle of rule induction states that to show that $P(s, s')$ holds when $s \longmapsto^* s'$, it is enough to show these two properties of P:

1. $P(s, s)$.
2. if $s \longmapsto s'$ and $P(s', s'')$, then $P(s, s'')$.

The first requirement is to show that P is reflexive. The second is to show that P is *closed under head expansion*, or *closed under inverse evaluation*. Using this principle, it is easy to prove that $\longmapsto^*$ is reflexive and transitive.

The *n-times iterated* transition judgment $s \longmapsto^n s'$, where $n \geq 0$, is inductively defined by the following rules:

$$\frac{}{s \longmapsto^0 s} \tag{5.2a}$$

$$\frac{s \longmapsto s' \quad s' \longmapsto^n s''}{s \longmapsto^{n+1} s''} \tag{5.2b}$$

Theorem 5.1. *For all states s and s', $s \longmapsto^* s'$ iff $s \longmapsto^k s'$ for some $k \geq 0$.*

Proof From left to right, by induction on the definition of multi-step transition. From right to left, by mathematical induction on $k \geq 0$. □

5.2 Structural Dynamics

A *structural dynamics* for the language **E** is given by a transition system whose states are closed expressions. All states are initial. The final states are the *(closed) values*, which represent the completed computations. The judgment e val, which states that e is a value, is inductively defined by the following rules:

$$\frac{}{\text{num}[n] \text{ val}} \tag{5.3a}$$

$$\frac{}{\text{str}[s] \text{ val}} \tag{5.3b}$$

The transition judgment $e \longmapsto e'$ between states is inductively defined by the following rules:

$$\frac{n_1 + n_2 = n}{\text{plus}(\text{num}[n_1]; \text{num}[n_2]) \longmapsto \text{num}[n]} \tag{5.4a}$$

$$\frac{e_1 \longmapsto e_1'}{\text{plus}(e_1; e_2) \longmapsto \text{plus}(e_1'; e_2)} \tag{5.4b}$$

$$\frac{e_1 \text{ val} \quad e_2 \longmapsto e_2'}{\text{plus}(e_1; e_2) \longmapsto \text{plus}(e_1; e_2')} \tag{5.4c}$$

$$\frac{s_1 \, \hat{} \, s_2 = s \; \mathsf{str}}{\mathsf{cat}(\mathsf{str}[s_1]; \mathsf{str}[s_2]) \longmapsto \mathsf{str}[s]} \tag{5.4d}$$

$$\frac{e_1 \longmapsto e_1'}{\mathsf{cat}(e_1; e_2) \longmapsto \mathsf{cat}(e_1'; e_2)} \tag{5.4e}$$

$$\frac{e_1 \; \mathsf{val} \quad e_2 \longmapsto e_2'}{\mathsf{cat}(e_1; e_2) \longmapsto \mathsf{cat}(e_1; e_2')} \tag{5.4f}$$

$$\left[\frac{e_1 \longmapsto e_1'}{\mathsf{let}(e_1; x.e_2) \longmapsto \mathsf{let}(e_1'; x.e_2)} \right] \tag{5.4g}$$

$$\frac{[e_1 \; \mathsf{val}]}{\mathsf{let}(e_1; x.e_2) \longmapsto [e_1/x]e_2} \tag{5.4h}$$

We have omitted rules for multiplication and computing the length of a string, which follow a similar pattern. Rules (5.4a), (5.4d), and (5.4h) are *instruction transitions*, because they correspond to the primitive steps of evaluation. The remaining rules are *search transitions* that determine the order of execution of instructions.

The bracketed rule (5.4g) and bracketed premise on rule (5.4h) are included for a *by-value* interpretation of let and omitted for a *by-name* interpretation. The by-value interpretation evaluates an expression before binding it to the defined variable, whereas the by-name interpretation binds it in unevaluated form. The by-value interpretation saves work if the defined variable is used more than once but wastes work if it is not used at all. Conversely, the by-name interpretation saves work if the defined variable is not used and wastes work if it is used more than once.

A derivation sequence in a structural dynamics has a two-dimensional structure, with the number of steps in the sequence being its "width" and the derivation tree for each step being its "height." For example, consider the following evaluation sequence:

$$\mathsf{let}(\mathsf{plus}(\mathsf{num}[1]; \mathsf{num}[2]); x.\mathsf{plus}(\mathsf{plus}(x; \mathsf{num}[3]); \mathsf{num}[4]))$$
$$\longmapsto \quad \mathsf{let}(\mathsf{num}[3]; x.\mathsf{plus}(\mathsf{plus}(x; \mathsf{num}[3]); \mathsf{num}[4]))$$
$$\longmapsto \quad \mathsf{plus}(\mathsf{plus}(\mathsf{num}[3]; \mathsf{num}[3]); \mathsf{num}[4])$$
$$\longmapsto \quad \mathsf{plus}(\mathsf{num}[6]; \mathsf{num}[4])$$
$$\longmapsto \quad \mathsf{num}[10]$$

Each step in this sequence of transitions is justified by a derivation according to rules (5.4). For example, the third transition in the preceding example is justified by the following derivation:

$$\frac{\dfrac{}{\mathsf{plus}(\mathsf{num}[3]; \mathsf{num}[3]) \longmapsto \mathsf{num}[6]} \; (5.4a)}{\mathsf{plus}(\mathsf{plus}(\mathsf{num}[3]; \mathsf{num}[3]); \mathsf{num}[4]) \longmapsto \mathsf{plus}(\mathsf{num}[6]; \mathsf{num}[4])} \; (5.4b)$$

The other steps are similarly justified by composing rules.

The principle of rule induction for the structural dynamics of **E** states that to show $\mathcal{P}(e \longmapsto e')$ when $e \longmapsto e'$, it is enough to show that $\mathcal{P}$ is closed under rules (5.4). For example, we may show by rule induction that the structural dynamics of **E** is *determinate*, which means that an expression may transition to at most one other expression. The proof requires a simple lemma relating transition to values.

Lemma 5.2 (Finality of Values). *For no expression e do we have both e* val, *and e* $\longmapsto$ *e′ for some e′.*

Proof   By rule induction on rules (5.3) and (5.4).   □

Lemma 5.3 (Determinacy). *If e* $\longmapsto$ *e′ and e* $\longmapsto$ *e″, then e′ and e″ are α-equivalent.*

Proof   By rule induction on the premises $e \longmapsto e'$ and $e \longmapsto e''$, carried out either simultaneously or in either order. The primitive operators, such as addition, are assumed to have a unique value when applied to values.   □

Rules (5.4) exemplify the *inversion principle* of language design, which states that the elimination forms are *inverse* to the introduction forms of a language. The search rules determine the *principal arguments* of each elimination form, and the instruction rules specify how to evaluate an elimination form when all of its principal arguments are in introduction form. For example, rules (5.4) specify that both arguments of addition are principal and specify how to evaluate an addition once its principal arguments are evaluated to numerals. The inversion principle is central to ensuring that a programming language is properly defined, the exact statement of which is given in Chapter 6.

5.3 Contextual Dynamics

A variant of structural dynamics, called *contextual dynamics*, is sometimes useful. There is no fundamental difference between contextual and structural dynamics, but rather one of style. The main idea is to isolate instruction steps as a special form of judgment, called *instruction transition*, and to formalize the process of locating the next instruction using a device called an *evaluation context*. The judgment e val defining whether an expression is a value, remains unchanged.

The instruction transition judgment $e_1 \to e_2$ for **E** is defined by the following rules, together with similar rules for multiplication of numbers and the length of a string.

$$\frac{m + n \text{ is } p \text{ nat}}{\mathtt{plus}(\mathtt{num}[m]; \mathtt{num}[n]) \to \mathtt{num}[p]} \tag{5.5a}$$

$$\frac{s \,\hat{}\, t = u \text{ str}}{\mathtt{cat}(\mathtt{str}[s]; \mathtt{str}[t]) \to \mathtt{str}[u]} \tag{5.5b}$$

$$\frac{}{\mathtt{let}(e_1; x.e_2) \to [e_1/x]e_2} \tag{5.5c}$$

The judgment $\mathcal{E}$ ectxt determines the location of the next instruction to execute in a larger expression. The position of the next instruction step is specified by a "hole," written $\circ$, into which the next instruction is placed, as we shall detail shortly. (The rules for multiplication and length are omitted for concision, as they are handled similarly.)

$$\overline{\circ \text{ ectxt}} \tag{5.6a}$$

$$\frac{\mathcal{E}_1 \text{ ectxt}}{\text{plus}(\mathcal{E}_1; e_2) \text{ ectxt}} \tag{5.6b}$$

$$\frac{e_1 \text{ val} \quad \mathcal{E}_2 \text{ ectxt}}{\text{plus}(e_1; \mathcal{E}_2) \text{ ectxt}} \tag{5.6c}$$

The first rule for evaluation contexts specifies that the next instruction may occur "here," at the occurrence of the hole. The remaining rules correspond one-for-one to the search rules of the structural dynamics. For example, rule (5.6c) states that in an expression $\text{plus}(e_1; e_2)$, if the first argument, e_1, is a value, then the next instruction step, if any, lies at or within the second argument, e_2.

An evaluation context is a template that is instantiated by replacing the hole with an instruction to be executed. The judgment $e' = \mathcal{E}\{e\}$ states that the expression e' is the result of filling the hole in the evaluation context $\mathcal{E}$ with the expression e. It is inductively defined by the following rules:

$$\overline{e = \circ\{e\}} \tag{5.7a}$$

$$\frac{e_1 = \mathcal{E}_1\{e\}}{\text{plus}(e_1; e_2) = \text{plus}(\mathcal{E}_1; e_2)\{e\}} \tag{5.7b}$$

$$\frac{e_1 \text{ val} \quad e_2 = \mathcal{E}_2\{e\}}{\text{plus}(e_1; e_2) = \text{plus}(e_1; \mathcal{E}_2)\{e\}} \tag{5.7c}$$

There is one rule for each form of evaluation context. Filling the hole with e results in e; otherwise, we proceed inductively over the structure of the evaluation context.

Finally, the contextual dynamics for **E** is defined by a single rule:

$$\frac{e = \mathcal{E}\{e_0\} \quad e_0 \rightarrow e_0' \quad e' = \mathcal{E}\{e_0'\}}{e \longmapsto e'} \tag{5.8}$$

Thus, a transition from e to e' consists of (1) decomposing e into an evaluation context and an instruction, (2) execution of that instruction, and (3) replacing the instruction by the result of its execution in the same spot within e to obtain e'.

The structural and contextual dynamics define the same transition relation. For the sake of the proof, let us write $e \longmapsto_s e'$ for the transition relation defined by the structural dynamics (rules (5.4)), and $e \longmapsto_c e'$ for the transition relation defined by the contextual dynamics (rules (5.8)).

Theorem 5.4. $e \longmapsto_s e'$ *if, and only if,* $e \longmapsto_c e'$.

Proof From left to right, proceed by rule induction on rules (5.4). It is enough in each case to exhibit an evaluation context $\mathcal{E}$ such that $e = \mathcal{E}\{e_0\}$, $e' = \mathcal{E}\{e_0'\}$, and $e_0 \to e_0'$. For example, for rule (5.4a), take $\mathcal{E} = \circ$, and note that $e \to e'$. For rule (5.4b), we have by induction that there exists an evaluation context $\mathcal{E}_1$ such that $e_1 = \mathcal{E}_1\{e_0\}$, $e_1' = \mathcal{E}_1\{e_0'\}$, and $e_0 \to e_0'$. Take $\mathcal{E} = \text{plus}(\mathcal{E}_1; e_2)$, and note that $e = \text{plus}(\mathcal{E}_1; e_2)\{e_0\}$ and $e' = \text{plus}(\mathcal{E}_1; e_2)\{e_0'\}$ with $e_0 \to e_0'$.

From right to left, note that if $e \longmapsto_{\mathsf{c}} e'$, then there exists an evaluation context $\mathcal{E}$ such that $e = \mathcal{E}\{e_0\}$, $e' = \mathcal{E}\{e_0'\}$, and $e_0 \to e_0'$. We prove by induction on rules (5.7) that $e \longmapsto_{\mathsf{s}} e'$. For example, for rule (5.7a), e_0 is e, e_0' is e', and $e \to e'$. Hence, $e \longmapsto_{\mathsf{s}} e'$. For rule (5.7b), we have that $\mathcal{E} = \text{plus}(\mathcal{E}_1; e_2)$, $e_1 = \mathcal{E}_1\{e_0\}$, $e_1' = \mathcal{E}_1\{e_0'\}$, and $e_1 \longmapsto_{\mathsf{s}} e_1'$. Therefore, e is $\text{plus}(e_1; e_2)$, e' is $\text{plus}(e_1'; e_2)$, and therefore by rule (5.4b), $e \longmapsto_{\mathsf{s}} e'$. $\square$

Because the two transition judgments coincide, contextual dynamics can be considered an alternative presentation of a structural dynamics. It has two advantages over structural dynamics, one relatively superficial, one rather less so. The superficial advantage stems from writing rule (5.8) in the simpler form

$$\frac{e_0 \to e_0'}{\mathcal{E}\{e_0\} \longmapsto \mathcal{E}\{e_0'\}} \ . \tag{5.9}$$

This formulation is superficially simpler in that it does not make explicit how an expression is decomposed into an evaluation context and a reducible expression. The deeper advantage of contextual dynamics is that all transitions are between complete programs. One need never consider a transition between expressions of any type other than the observable type, which simplifies certain arguments, such as the proof of Lemma 47.16.

5.4 Equational Dynamics

Another formulation of the dynamics of a language regards computation as a form of equational deduction, much in the style of elementary algebra. For example, in algebra, we may show that the polynomials $x^2 + 2x + 1$ and $(x + 1)^2$ are equivalent by a simple process of calculation and re-organization using the familiar laws of addition and multiplication. The same laws are enough to determine the value of any polynomial, given the values of its variables. So, for example, we may plug in 2 for x in the polynomial $x^2 + 2x + 1$ and calculate that $2^2 + 2 \times 2 + 1 = 9$, which is indeed $(2 + 1)^2$. We thus obtain a model of computation in which the value of a polynomial for a given value of its variable is determined by substitution and simplification.

Very similar ideas give rise to the concept of *definitional*, or *computational*, *equivalence* of expressions in **E**, which we write as $\mathcal{X} \mid \Gamma \vdash e \equiv e' : \tau$, where Γ consists of one assumption of the form $x : \tau$ for each $x \in \mathcal{X}$. We only consider definitional equality of well-typed expressions, so that when considering the judgment $\Gamma \vdash e \equiv e' : \tau$, we tacitly assume that $\Gamma \vdash e : \tau$ and $\Gamma \vdash e' : \tau$. Here, as usual, we omit explicit mention of the variables $\mathcal{X}$ when they can be determined from the forms of the assumptions Γ.

Definitional equality of expressions in **E** under the by-name interpretation of let is inductively defined by the following rules:

$$\frac{}{\Gamma \vdash e \equiv e : \tau} \tag{5.10a}$$

$$\frac{\Gamma \vdash e' \equiv e : \tau}{\Gamma \vdash e \equiv e' : \tau} \tag{5.10b}$$

$$\frac{\Gamma \vdash e \equiv e' : \tau \quad \Gamma \vdash e' \equiv e'' : \tau}{\Gamma \vdash e \equiv e'' : \tau} \tag{5.10c}$$

$$\frac{\Gamma \vdash e_1 \equiv e_1' : \mathtt{num} \quad \Gamma \vdash e_2 \equiv e_2' : \mathtt{num}}{\Gamma \vdash \mathtt{plus}(e_1; e_2) \equiv \mathtt{plus}(e_1'; e_2') : \mathtt{num}} \tag{5.10d}$$

$$\frac{\Gamma \vdash e_1 \equiv e_1' : \mathtt{str} \quad \Gamma \vdash e_2 \equiv e_2' : \mathtt{str}}{\Gamma \vdash \mathtt{cat}(e_1; e_2) \equiv \mathtt{cat}(e_1'; e_2') : \mathtt{str}} \tag{5.10e}$$

$$\frac{\Gamma \vdash e_1 \equiv e_1' : \tau_1 \quad \Gamma, x : \tau_1 \vdash e_2 \equiv e_2' : \tau_2}{\Gamma \vdash \mathtt{let}(e_1; x.e_2) \equiv \mathtt{let}(e_1'; x.e_2') : \tau_2} \tag{5.10f}$$

$$\frac{n_1 + n_2 \text{ is } n \text{ nat}}{\Gamma \vdash \mathtt{plus}(\mathtt{num}[n_1]; \mathtt{num}[n_2]) \equiv \mathtt{num}[n] : \mathtt{num}} \tag{5.10g}$$

$$\frac{s_1 \,\hat{}\, s_2 = s \text{ str}}{\Gamma \vdash \mathtt{cat}(\mathtt{str}[s_1]; \mathtt{str}[s_2]) \equiv \mathtt{str}[s] : \mathtt{str}} \tag{5.10h}$$

$$\frac{}{\Gamma \vdash \mathtt{let}(e_1; x.e_2) \equiv [e_1/x]e_2 : \tau} \tag{5.10i}$$

Rules (5.10a) through (5.10c) state that definitional equality is an *equivalence relation*. Rules (5.10d) through (5.10f) state that it is a *congruence relation*, which means that it is compatible with all expression-forming constructs in the language. Rules (5.10g) through (5.10i) specify the meanings of the primitive constructs of **E**. We say that rules (5.10) define the *strongest congruence* closed under rules (5.10g), (5.10h), and (5.10i).

Rules (5.10) suffice to calculate the value of an expression by a deduction similar to that used in high school algebra. For example, we may derive the equation

$$\mathtt{let}\, x \,\mathtt{be}\, 1 + 2 \,\mathtt{in}\, x + 3 + 4 \equiv 10 : \mathtt{num}$$

by applying rules (5.10). Here, as in general, there may be many different ways to derive the same equation, but we need find only one derivation in order to carry out an evaluation.

Definitional equality is rather weak in that many equivalences that we might intuitively think are true are not derivable from rules (5.10). A prototypical example is the putative equivalence

$$x_1 : \mathtt{num}, x_2 : \mathtt{num} \vdash x_1 + x_2 \equiv x_2 + x_1 : \mathtt{num}, \tag{5.11}$$

which, intuitively, expresses the commutativity of addition. Although we shall not prove this here, this equivalence is *not* derivable from rules (5.10). And yet we *may* derive all of its closed instances,

$$n_1 + n_2 \equiv n_2 + n_1 : \texttt{num}, \tag{5.12}$$

where n_1 nat and n_2 nat are particular numbers.

The "gap" between a general law, such as Equation (5.11), and all of its instances, given by Equation (5.12), may be filled by enriching the notion of equivalence to include a principle of proof by mathematical induction. Such a notion of equivalence is sometimes called *semantic equivalence*, because it expresses relationships that hold by virtue of the dynamics of the expressions involved. (Semantic equivalence is developed rigorously for a related language in Chapter 46.)

Theorem 5.5. *For the expression language* **E**, *the relation* $e \equiv e' : \tau$ *holds iff there exists* e_0 *val such that* $e \longmapsto^* e_0$ *and* $e' \longmapsto^* e_0$.

Proof The proof from right to left is direct, because every transition step is a valid equation. The converse follows from the following, more general, proposition, which is proved by induction on rules (5.10): if $x_1 : \tau_1, \ldots, x_n : \tau_n \vdash e \equiv e' : \tau$, then when $e_1 : \tau_1, e_1' : \tau_1, \ldots, e_n : \tau_n, e_n' : \tau_n$, if for each $1 \leq i \leq n$ the expressions e_i and e_i' evaluate to a common value v_i, then there exists e_0 val such that

$$[e_1, \ldots, e_n / x_1, \ldots, x_n]e \longmapsto^* e_0$$

and

$$[e_1', \ldots, e_n' / x_1, \ldots, x_n]e' \longmapsto^* e_0. \qquad \square$$

5.5 Notes

The use of transition systems to specify the behavior of programs goes back to the early work of Church and Turing on computability. Turing's approach emphasized the concept of an abstract machine consisting of a finite program together with unbounded memory. Computation proceeds by changing the memory in accordance with the instructions in the program. Much early work on the operational semantics of programming languages, such as the SECD machine (Landin, 1965), emphasized machine models. Church's approach emphasized the language for expressing computations and defined execution in terms of the programs themselves, rather than in terms of auxiliary concepts such as memories or tapes. Plotkin's elegant formulation of structural operational semantics (Plotkin, 1981), which we use heavily throughout this book, was inspired by Church's and Landin's ideas (Plotkin, 2004). Contextual semantics, which was introduced by Felleisen and Hieb (1992), may be seen as an alternative formulation of structural semantics in which "search rules" are replaced by "context matching." Computation viewed as equational deduction goes back to the early work of Herbrand, Gödel, and Church.

Exercises

5.1. Prove that if $s \longmapsto^* s'$ and $s' \longmapsto^* s''$, then $s \longmapsto^* s''$.

5.2. Complete the proof of Theorem 5.1 along the lines suggested there.

5.3. Complete the proof of Theorem 5.5 along the lines suggested there.

6   Type Safety

Most programming languages are *safe* (or, *type safe*, or *strongly typed*). Informally, this means that certain kinds of mismatches cannot arise during execution. For example, type safety for **E** states that it will never arise that a number is added to a string, or that two numbers are concatenated, neither of which is meaningful.

In general, type safety expresses the coherence between the statics and the dynamics. The statics may be seen as predicting that the value of an expression will have a certain form so that the dynamics of that expression is well-defined. Consequently, evaluation cannot "get stuck" in a state for which no transition is possible, corresponding in implementation terms to the absence of "illegal instruction" errors at execution time. Safety is proved by showing that each step of transition preserves typability and by showing that typable states are well-defined. Consequently, evaluation can never "go off into the weeds" and, hence, can never encounter an illegal instruction.

Type safety for the language **E** is stated precisely as follows:

Theorem 6.1 (Type Safety).

1. *If $e : \tau$ and $e \longmapsto e'$, then $e' : \tau$.*
2. *If $e : \tau$, then either e val, or there exists e' such that $e \longmapsto e'$.*

The first part, called *preservation*, says that the steps of evaluation preserve typing; the second, called *progress*, ensures that well-typed expressions are either values or can be further evaluated. Safety is the conjunction of preservation and progress.

We say that an expression e is *stuck* iff it is not a value, yet there is no e' such that $e \longmapsto e'$. It follows from the safety theorem that a stuck state is necessarily ill-typed. Or, putting it the other way around, that well-typed states do not get stuck.

6.1 Preservation

The preservation theorem for **E** defined in Chapters 4 and 5 is proved by rule induction on the transition system (rules (5.4)).

Theorem 6.2 (Preservation). *If $e : \tau$ and $e \longmapsto e'$, then $e' : \tau$.*

Proof We will give the proof in two cases, leaving the rest to the reader. Consider rule (5.4b),

$$\frac{e_1 \longmapsto e_1'}{\text{plus}(e_1; e_2) \longmapsto \text{plus}(e_1'; e_2)}.$$

Assume that $\text{plus}(e_1; e_2) : \tau$. By inversion for typing, we have that $\tau = \text{num}$, $e_1 : \text{num}$, and $e_2 : \text{num}$. By induction, we have that $e_1' : \text{num}$, and hence $\text{plus}(e_1'; e_2) : \text{num}$. The case for concatenation is handled similarly.

Now consider rule (5.4h),

$$\frac{}{\text{let}(e_1; x.e_2) \longmapsto [e_1/x]e_2}.$$

Assume that $\text{let}(e_1; x.e_2) : \tau_2$. By the inversion Lemma 4.2, $e_1 : \tau_1$ for some τ_1 such that $x : \tau_1 \vdash e_2 : \tau_2$. By the substitution Lemma 4.4 $[e_1/x]e_2 : \tau_2$, as desired.

It is easy to check that the primitive operations are all type-preserving; for example, if a nat and b nat and $a + b$ is c nat, then c nat. $\qquad\square$

The proof of preservation is naturally structured as an induction on the transition judgment, because the argument hinges on examining all possible transitions from a given expression. In some cases, we may manage to carry out a proof by structural induction on e, or by an induction on typing, but experience shows that this often leads to awkward arguments, or, sometimes, cannot be made to work at all.

6.2 Progress

The progress theorem captures the idea that well-typed programs cannot "get stuck." The proof depends crucially on the following lemma, which characterizes the values of each type.

Lemma 6.3 (Canonical Forms). *If e val and e : τ, then*

1. *If $\tau = \text{num}$, then $e = \text{num}[n]$ for some number n.*
2. *If $\tau = \text{str}$, then $e = \text{str}[s]$ for some string s.*

Proof By induction on rules (4.1) and (5.3). $\qquad\square$

Progress is proved by rule induction on rules (4.1) defining the statics of the language.

Theorem 6.4 (Progress). *If e : τ, then either e val, or there exists e' such that $e \longmapsto e'$.*

Proof The proof proceeds by induction on the typing derivation. We will consider only one case, for rule (4.1d),

$$\frac{e_1 : \mathtt{num} \quad e_2 : \mathtt{num}}{\mathtt{plus}(e_1; e_2) : \mathtt{num}},$$

where the context is empty because we are considering only closed terms.

By induction, we have that either e_1 val, or there exists e_1' such that $e_1 \longmapsto e_1'$. In the latter case, it follows that $\mathtt{plus}(e_1; e_2) \longmapsto \mathtt{plus}(e_1'; e_2)$, as required. In the former, we also have by induction that either e_2 val, or there exists e_2' such that $e_2 \longmapsto e_2'$. In the latter case, we have that $\mathtt{plus}(e_1; e_2) \longmapsto \mathtt{plus}(e_1; e_2')$, as required. In the former, we have, by the Canonical Forms Lemma 6.3, $e_1 = \mathtt{num}[n_1]$ and $e_2 = \mathtt{num}[n_2]$, and hence

$$\mathtt{plus}(\mathtt{num}[n_1]; \mathtt{num}[n_2]) \longmapsto \mathtt{num}[n_1 + n_2]. \qquad \square$$

Because the typing rules for expressions are syntax-directed, the progress theorem could equally well be proved by induction on the structure of e, appealing to the inversion theorem at each step to characterize the types of the parts of e. But this approach breaks down when the typing rules are not syntax-directed, that is, when there is more than one rule for a given expression form. Such rules present no difficulties, so long as the proof proceeds by induction on the typing rules and not on the structure of the expression.

Summing up, the combination of preservation and progress together constitute the proof of safety. The progress theorem ensures that well-typed expressions do not "get stuck" in an ill-defined state, and the preservation theorem ensures that if a step is taken, the result remains well-typed (with the same type). Thus, the two parts work together to ensure that the statics and dynamics are coherent and that no ill-defined states can ever be encountered while evaluating a well-typed expression.

6.3 Run-Time Errors

Suppose that we wish to extend **E** with, say, a quotient operation that is undefined for a zero divisor. The natural typing rule for quotients is given by the following rule:

$$\frac{e_1 : \mathtt{num} \quad e_2 : \mathtt{num}}{\mathtt{div}(e_1; e_2) : \mathtt{num}}.$$

But the expression $\mathtt{div}(\mathtt{num}[3]; \mathtt{num}[0])$ is well-typed, yet stuck! We have two options to correct this situation:

1. Enhance the type system, so that no well-typed program may divide by zero.
2. Add dynamic checks, so that division by zero signals an error as the outcome of evaluation.

Either option is, in principle, practical, but the most common approach is the second. The first requires that the type checker prove that an expression be non-zero before permitting it to be used in the denominator of a quotient. It is difficult to do this without ruling out too many programs as ill-formed. We cannot predict statically whether an expression will be non-zero when evaluated, so the second approach is most often used in practice.

The overall idea is to distinguish *checked* from *unchecked* errors. An unchecked error is one that is ruled out by the type system. No run-time checking is performed to ensure that such an error does not occur, because the type system rules out the possibility of it arising. For example, the dynamics need not check, when performing an addition, that its two arguments are, in fact, numbers, as opposed to strings, because the type system ensures that this is the case. On the other hand, the dynamics for quotient *must* check for a zero divisor, because the type system does not rule out the possibility.

One approach to modeling checked errors is to give an inductive definition of the judgment e err stating that the expression e incurs a checked run-time error, such as division by zero. Here are some representative rules that would be present in a full inductive definition of this judgment:

$$\frac{e_1 \text{ val}}{\text{div}(e_1; \text{num}[0]) \text{ err}} \tag{6.1a}$$

$$\frac{e_1 \text{ err}}{\text{div}(e_1; e_2) \text{ err}} \tag{6.1b}$$

$$\frac{e_1 \text{ val} \quad e_2 \text{ err}}{\text{div}(e_1; e_2) \text{ err}} \tag{6.1c}$$

Rule (6.1a) signals an error condition for division by zero. The other rules propagate this error upwards: if an evaluated sub-expression is a checked error, then so is the overall expression.

Once the error judgment is available, we may also consider an expression, error, which forcibly induces an error, with the following static and dynamic semantics:

$$\frac{}{\Gamma \vdash \text{error} : \tau} \tag{6.2a}$$

$$\frac{}{\text{error err}} \tag{6.2b}$$

The preservation theorem is not affected by checked errors. However, the statement (and proof) of progress is modified to account for checked errors.

Theorem 6.5 (Progress With Error). *If $e : \tau$, then either e err, or e val, or there exists e' such that $e \longmapsto e'$.*

Proof The proof is by induction on typing, and proceeds similarly to the proof given earlier, except that there are now three cases to consider at each point in the proof. ☐

6.4 Notes

The concept of type safety was first formulated by Milner (1978), who invented the slogan "well-typed programs do not go wrong." Whereas Milner relied on an explicit notion of "going wrong" to express the concept of a type error, Wright and Felleisen (1994) observed that we can instead show that ill-defined states cannot arise in a well-typed program, giving rise to the slogan "well-typed programs do not get stuck." However, their formulation relied on an analysis showing that no stuck state is well-typed. The progress theorem, which relies on the characterization of canonical forms in the style of Martin-Löf (1980), eliminates this analysis.

Exercises

6.1. Complete the proof of Theorem 6.2 in full detail.

6.2. Complete the proof of Theorem 6.4 in full detail.

6.3. Give several cases of the proof of Theorem 6.5 to illustrate how checked errors are handled in type safety proofs.

7   Evaluation Dynamics

In Chapter 5, we defined evaluation of expressions in **E** using a structural dynamics. Structural dynamics is very useful for proving safety, but for some purposes, such as writing a user manual, another formulation, called *evaluation dynamics*, is preferable. An evaluation dynamics is a relation between a phrase and its value that is defined without detailing the step-by-step process of evaluation. A *cost dynamics* enriches an evaluation dynamics with a *cost measure* specifying the resource usage of evaluation. A prime example is time, measured as the number of transition steps required to evaluate an expression according to its structural dynamics.

7.1   Evaluation Dynamics

An *evaluation dynamics* consists of an inductive definition of the evaluation judgment $e \Downarrow v$ stating that the closed expression e evaluates to the value v. The evaluation dynamics of **E** is defined by the following rules:

$$\frac{}{\text{num}[n] \Downarrow \text{num}[n]} \tag{7.1a}$$

$$\frac{}{\text{str}[s] \Downarrow \text{str}[s]} \tag{7.1b}$$

$$\frac{e_1 \Downarrow \text{num}[n_1] \quad e_2 \Downarrow \text{num}[n_2] \quad n_1 + n_2 \text{ is } n \text{ nat}}{\text{plus}(e_1; e_2) \Downarrow \text{num}[n]} \tag{7.1c}$$

$$\frac{e_1 \Downarrow \text{str}[s_1] \quad e_2 \Downarrow \text{str}[s_2] \quad s_1 \char`\^ s_2 = s \text{ str}}{\text{cat}(e_1; e_2) \Downarrow \text{str}[s]} \tag{7.1d}$$

$$\frac{e \Downarrow \text{str}[s] \quad |s| = n \text{ nat}}{\text{len}(e) \Downarrow \text{num}[n]} \tag{7.1e}$$

$$\frac{[e_1/x]e_2 \Downarrow v_2}{\text{let}(e_1; x.e_2) \Downarrow v_2} \tag{7.1f}$$

The value of a `let` expression is determined by substitution of the binding into the body. The rules are not syntax-directed, because the premise of rule (7.1f) is not a sub-expression of the expression in the conclusion of that rule.

Rule (7.1f) specifies a by-name interpretation of definitions. For a by-value interpretation, the following rule should be used instead:

$$\frac{e_1 \Downarrow v_1 \quad [v_1/x]e_2 \Downarrow v_2}{\mathtt{let}(e_1; x.e_2) \Downarrow v_2} \tag{7.2}$$

Because the evaluation judgment is inductively defined, we prove properties of it by rule induction. Specifically, to show that the property $\mathcal{P}(e \Downarrow v)$ holds, it is enough to show that $\mathcal{P}$ is closed under rules (7.1):

1. Show that $\mathcal{P}(\mathtt{num}[n] \Downarrow \mathtt{num}[n])$.
2. Show that $\mathcal{P}(\mathtt{str}[s] \Downarrow \mathtt{str}[s])$.
3. Show that $\mathcal{P}(\mathtt{plus}(e_1; e_2) \Downarrow \mathtt{num}[n])$, if $\mathcal{P}(e_1 \Downarrow \mathtt{num}[n_1])$, $\mathcal{P}(e_2 \Downarrow \mathtt{num}[n_2])$, and $n_1 + n_2$ is n nat.
4. Show that $\mathcal{P}(\mathtt{cat}(e_1; e_2) \Downarrow \mathtt{str}[s])$, if $\mathcal{P}(e_1 \Downarrow \mathtt{str}[s_1])$, $\mathcal{P}(e_2 \Downarrow \mathtt{str}[s_2])$, and $s_1 \,\hat{}\, s_2 = s$ str.
5. Show that $\mathcal{P}(\mathtt{let}(e_1; x.e_2) \Downarrow v_2)$, if $\mathcal{P}([e_1/x]e_2 \Downarrow v_2)$.

This induction principle is *not* the same as structural induction on e itself, because the evaluation rules are not syntax-directed.

Lemma 7.1. *If $e \Downarrow v$, then v val.*

Proof By induction on rules (7.1). All cases except rule (7.1f) are immediate. For the latter case, the result follows directly by an appeal to the inductive hypothesis for the premise of the evaluation rule.   □

7.2 Relating Structural and Evaluation Dynamics

We have given two different forms of dynamics for **E**. It is natural to ask whether they are equivalent, but to do so first requires that we consider carefully what we mean by equivalence. The structural dynamics describes a step-by-step process of execution, whereas the evaluation dynamics suppresses the intermediate states, focusing attention on the initial and final states alone. This remark suggests that the right correspondence is between *complete* execution sequences in the structural dynamics and the evaluation judgment in the evaluation dynamics.

Theorem 7.2. *For all closed expressions e and values v, $e \longmapsto^* v$ iff $e \Downarrow v$.*

How might we prove such a theorem? We will consider each direction separately. We consider the easier case first.

Lemma 7.3. *If $e \Downarrow v$, then $e \longmapsto^* v$.*

Proof By induction on the definition of the evaluation judgment. For example, suppose that $\text{plus}(e_1; e_2) \Downarrow \text{num}[n]$ by the rule for evaluating additions. By induction, we know that $e_1 \longmapsto^* \text{num}[n_1]$ and $e_2 \longmapsto^* \text{num}[n_2]$. We reason as follows:

$$
\begin{aligned}
\text{plus}(e_1; e_2) \quad &\longmapsto^* \quad \text{plus}(\text{num}[n_1]; e_2) \\
&\longmapsto^* \quad \text{plus}(\text{num}[n_1]; \text{num}[n_2]) \\
&\longmapsto \quad \text{num}[n_1 + n_2]
\end{aligned}
$$

Therefore, $\text{plus}(e_1; e_2) \longmapsto^* \text{num}[n_1 + n_2]$, as required. The other cases are handled similarly.   □

For the converse, recall from Chapter 5 the definitions of multi-step evaluation and complete evaluation. Because $v \Downarrow v$ when v val, it suffices to show that evaluation is closed under converse evaluation:[1]

Lemma 7.4. *If* $e \longmapsto e'$ *and* $e' \Downarrow v$, *then* $e \Downarrow v$.

Proof By induction on the definition of the transition judgment. For example, suppose that $\text{plus}(e_1; e_2) \longmapsto \text{plus}(e_1'; e_2)$, where $e_1 \longmapsto e_1'$. Suppose further that $\text{plus}(e_1'; e_2) \Downarrow v$, so that $e_1' \Downarrow \text{num}[n_1]$, and $e_2 \Downarrow \text{num}[n_2]$, and $n_1 + n_2$ is n nat, and v is $\text{num}[n]$. By induction $e_1 \Downarrow \text{num}[n_1]$, and hence $\text{plus}(e_1; e_2) \Downarrow \text{num}[n]$, as required.   □

7.3 Type Safety, Revisited

Type safety is defined in Chapter 6 as preservation and progress (Theorem 6.1). These concepts are meaningful when applied to a dynamics given by a transition system, as we shall do throughout this book. But what if we had instead given the dynamics as an evaluation relation? How is type safety proved in that case?

The answer, unfortunately, is that we cannot. Although there is an analog of the preservation property for an evaluation dynamics, there is no clear analog of the progress property. Preservation may be stated as saying that if $e \Downarrow v$ and $e : \tau$, then $v : \tau$. It can be readily proved by induction on the evaluation rules. But what is the analog of progress? We might be tempted to phrase progress as saying that if $e : \tau$, then $e \Downarrow v$ for some v. Although this property is true for **E**, it demands much more than just progress—it requires that every expression evaluate to a value! If **E** were extended to admit operations that may result in an error (as discussed in Section 6.3), or to admit non-terminating expressions, then this property would fail, even though progress would remain valid.

One possible attitude towards this situation is to conclude that type safety cannot be properly discussed in the context of an evaluation dynamics, but only by reference to a structural dynamics. Another point of view is to instrument the dynamics with explicit checks for dynamic type errors, and to show that any expression with a dynamic type fault must be statically ill-typed. Re-stated in the contrapositive, this means that a statically well-typed program cannot incur a dynamic type error. A difficulty with this point of view is that we must explicitly account for a form of error solely to prove that it cannot arise! Nevertheless, a semblance of type safety can be established using evaluation dynamics.

We define a judgment e err stating that the expression e *goes wrong* when executed. The exact definition of "going wrong" is given by a set of rules, but the intention is that it should cover all situations that correspond to type errors. The following rules are representative of the general case:

$$\frac{}{\texttt{plus}(\texttt{str}[s]; e_2) \text{ err}} \tag{7.3a}$$

$$\frac{e_1 \text{ val}}{\texttt{plus}(e_1; \texttt{str}[s]) \text{ err}} \tag{7.3b}$$

These rules explicitly check for the misapplication of addition to a string; similar rules govern each of the primitive constructs of the language.

Theorem 7.5. *If e err, then there is no τ such that $e : \tau$.*

Proof By rule induction on rules (7.3). For example, for rule (7.3a), we note that $\texttt{str}[s]$: str, and hence $\texttt{plus}(\texttt{str}[s]; e_2)$ is ill-typed.   □

Corollary 7.6. *If $e : \tau$, then $\neg(e$ err$)$.*

Apart from the inconvenience of having to define the judgment e err only to show that it is irrelevant for well-typed programs, this approach suffers a very significant methodological weakness. If we should omit one or more rules defining the judgment e err, the proof of Theorem 7.5 remains valid; there is nothing to ensure that we have included sufficiently many checks for run-time type errors. We can prove that the ones we define cannot arise in a well-typed program, but we cannot prove that we have covered all possible cases. By contrast the structural dynamics does not specify any behavior for ill-typed expressions. Consequently, any ill-typed expression will "get stuck" without our explicit intervention, and the progress theorem rules out all such cases. Moreover, the transition system corresponds more closely to implementation—a compiler need not make any provisions for checking for run-time type errors. Instead, it relies on the statics to ensure that these cannot arise, and assigns no meaning to any ill-typed program. Therefore, execution is more efficient, and the language definition is simpler.

7.4 Cost Dynamics

A structural dynamics provides a natural notion of *time complexity* for programs, namely the number of steps required to reach a final state. An evaluation dynamics, however, does not provide such a direct notion of time. Because the individual steps required to complete an evaluation are suppressed, we cannot directly read off the number of steps required to evaluate to a value. Instead, we must augment the evaluation relation with a cost measure, resulting in a *cost dynamics*.

Evaluation judgments have the form $e \Downarrow^k v$, with the meaning that e evaluates to v in k steps.

$$\overline{\text{num}[n] \Downarrow^0 \text{num}[n]} \tag{7.4a}$$

$$\frac{e_1 \Downarrow^{k_1} \text{num}[n_1] \quad e_2 \Downarrow^{k_2} \text{num}[n_2]}{\text{plus}(e_1; e_2) \Downarrow^{k_1+k_2+1} \text{num}[n_1 + n_2]} \tag{7.4b}$$

$$\overline{\text{str}[s] \Downarrow^0 \text{str}[s]} \tag{7.4c}$$

$$\frac{e_1 \Downarrow^{k_1} s_1 \quad e_2 \Downarrow^{k_2} s_2}{\text{cat}(e_1; e_2) \Downarrow^{k_1+k_2+1} \text{str}[s_1 \,\hat{}\, s_2]} \tag{7.4d}$$

$$\frac{[e_1/x]e_2 \Downarrow^{k_2} v_2}{\text{let}(e_1; x.e_2) \Downarrow^{k_2+1} v_2} \tag{7.4e}$$

For a by-value interpretation of let, rule (7.4e) is replaced by the following rule:

$$\frac{e_1 \Downarrow^{k_1} v_1 \quad [v_1/x]e_2 \Downarrow^{k_2} v_2}{\text{let}(e_1; x.e_2) \Downarrow^{k_1+k_2+1} v_2} \tag{7.5}$$

Theorem 7.7. *For any closed expression e and closed value v of the same type, $e \Downarrow^k v$ iff $e \longmapsto^k v$.*

Proof From left to right, proceed by rule induction on the definition of the cost dynamics. From right to left, proceed by induction on k, with an inner rule induction on the definition of the structural dynamics. ▯

7.5 Notes

The structural similarity between evaluation dynamics and typing rules was first developed in *The Definition of Standard ML* (Milner et al., 1997). The advantage of evaluation semantics is its directness; its disadvantage is that it is not well-suited to proving properties such as type safety. Robin Milner introduced the apt phrase "going wrong" as a description of a type error. Cost dynamics was introduced by Blelloch and Greiner (1996) in a study of parallel computation (see Chapter 37).

Exercises

7.1. Show that evaluation is deterministic: if $e \Downarrow v_1$ and $e \Downarrow v_2$, then $v_1 = v_2$.

7.2. Complete the proof of Lemma 7.3.

7.3. Complete the proof of Lemma 7.4. Then show that if $e \longmapsto^* e'$ with e' val, then $e \Downarrow e'$.

7.4. Augment the evaluation dynamics with checked errors, along the lines sketched in Chapter 5, using e err to say that e incurs a checked (or an unchecked) error. What remains unsatisfactory about the type safety proof? Can you think of a better alternative?

7.5. Consider generic hypothetical judgments of the form

$$x_1 \Downarrow v_1, \ldots, x_n \Downarrow v_n \vdash e \Downarrow v$$

where v_1 val, $\ldots$, v_n val, and v val. The hypotheses, written Δ, are called the *environment* of the evaluation; they provide the values of the free variables in e. The hypothetical judgment $\Delta \vdash e \Downarrow v$ is called an *environmental evaluation dynamics*.

Give a hypothetical inductive definition of the environmental evaluation dynamics *without making any use of substitution*. In particular, you should include the rule

$$\frac{}{\Delta, x \Downarrow v \vdash x \Downarrow v}$$

defining the evaluation of a free variable.

Show that $x_1 \Downarrow v_1, \ldots, x_n \Downarrow v_n \vdash e \Downarrow v$ iff $[v_1, \ldots, v_n/x_1, \ldots, x_n]e \Downarrow v$ (using the by-value form of evaluation).

Note

1 Converse evaluation is also known as *head expansion*.

PART III

Total Functions

Function Definitions and Values

In the language **E**, we may perform calculations such as the doubling of a given expression, but we cannot express doubling as a concept in itself. To capture the pattern of doubling a number, we abstract away from the particular number being doubled using a *variable* to stand for a fixed, but unspecified, number, to express the doubling of an arbitrary number. Any particular instance of doubling may then be obtained by substituting a numeric expression for that variable. In general, an expression may involve many distinct variables, necessitating that we specify which of several possible variables is varying in a particular context, giving rise to a *function* of that variable.

In this chapter, we will consider two extensions of **E** with functions. The first, and perhaps most obvious, extension is by adding *function definitions* to the language. A function is defined by binding a name to an abt with a bound variable that serves as the argument of that function. A function is *applied* by substituting a particular expression (of suitable type) for the bound variable, obtaining an expression.

The domain and range of defined functions are limited to the types nat and str, because these are the only types of expression. Such functions are called *first-order* functions, in contrast to *higher-order functions*, which permit functions as arguments and results of other functions. Because the domain and range of a function are types, this requires that we introduce *function types* whose elements are functions. Consequently, we may form functions of *higher type*, those whose domain and range may themselves be function types.

8.1 First-Order Functions

The language **ED** extends **E** with function definitions and function applications as described by the following grammar:

$$\text{Exp} \quad e \quad ::= \quad \text{apply}\{f\}(e) \qquad f(e) \qquad\qquad\qquad \text{application}$$
$$\qquad\qquad\qquad \text{fun}\{\tau_1; \tau_2\}(x_1.e_2; f.e) \quad \text{fun } f(x_1 : \tau_1) : \tau_2 = e_2 \text{ in } e \quad \text{definition}$$

The expression $\text{fun}\{\tau_1; \tau_2\}(x_1.e_2; f.e)$ binds the function name f within e to the pattern $x_1.e_2$, which has argument x_1 and definition e_2. The domain and range of the function are, respectively, the types τ_1 and τ_2. The expression $\text{apply}\{f\}(e)$ instantiates the binding of f with the argument e.

The statics of **ED** defines two forms of judgment:

1. Expression typing, $e : \tau$, stating that e has type τ;
2. Function typing, $f(\tau_1) : \tau_2$, stating that f is a function with argument type τ_1 and result type τ_2.

The judgment $f(\tau_1) : \tau_2$ is called the *function header* of f; it specifies the domain type and the range type of a function.

The statics of **ED** is defined by the following rules:

$$\frac{\Gamma, x_1 : \tau_1 \vdash e_2 : \tau_2 \quad \Gamma, f(\tau_1) : \tau_2 \vdash e : \tau}{\Gamma \vdash \mathtt{fun}\{\tau_1; \tau_2\}(x_1.e_2; f.e) : \tau} \tag{8.1a}$$

$$\frac{\Gamma \vdash f(\tau_1) : \tau_2 \quad \Gamma \vdash e : \tau_1}{\Gamma \vdash \mathtt{apply}\{f\}(e) : \tau_2} \tag{8.1b}$$

Function substitution, written $[\![x.e/f]\!]e'$, is defined by induction on the structure of e' much like ordinary substitution. However, a function name f does not stand for an expression and can only occur in an application of the form $\mathtt{apply}\{f\}(e)$. Function substitution is defined by the following rule:

$$\frac{}{[\![x.e/f]\!]\mathtt{apply}\{f\}(e') = \mathtt{let}([\![x.e/f]\!]e'; x.e)} \tag{8.2}$$

At application sites to f with argument e', function substitution yields a $\mathtt{let}$ expression that binds x to the result of expanding any further applications to f within e'.

Lemma 8.1. *If* $\Gamma, f(\tau_1) : \tau_2 \vdash e : \tau$ *and* $\Gamma, x_1 : \tau_1 \vdash e_2 : \tau_2$, *then* $\Gamma \vdash [\![x_1.e_2/f]\!]e : \tau$.

Proof   By rule induction on the first premise, similarly to the proof of Lemma 4.4.   □

The dynamics of **ED** is defined using function substitution:

$$\frac{}{\mathtt{fun}\{\tau_1; \tau_2\}(x_1.e_2; f.e) \longmapsto [\![x_1.e_2/f]\!]e} \tag{8.3}$$

Because function substitution replaces all applications of f by appropriate $\mathtt{let}$ expressions, there is no need to give a rule for application expressions (essentially, they behave like variables that are replaced during evaluation, and not like a primitive operation of the language).

The safety of **ED** may, with some effort, be derived from the safety theorem for higher-order functions, which we discuss next.

8.2 Higher-Order Functions

The similarity between variable definitions and function definitions in **ED** is striking. Is it possible to combine them? The gap that must be bridged is the segregation of functions from expressions. A function name f is bound to an abstractor $x.e$ specifying a pattern that is instantiated when f is applied. To reduce function definitions to ordinary definitions, we *reify* the abstractor into a form of expression, called a λ-*abstraction*, written $\mathtt{lam}\{\tau_1\}(x.e)$. Applications generalize to $\mathtt{ap}(e_1; e_2)$, where e_1 is an expression denoting a function, and not just a function name. λ-abstraction and application are the introduction and elimination forms for the *function type* $\mathtt{arr}(\tau_1; \tau_2)$, which classifies functions with domain τ_1 and range τ_2.

The language **EF** enriches **E** with function types, as specified by the following grammar:

$$
\begin{array}{llllll}
\mathsf{Typ} & \tau & ::= & \mathtt{arr}(\tau_1; \tau_2) & \tau_1 \to \tau_2 & \text{function} \\
\mathsf{Exp} & e & ::= & \mathtt{lam}\{\tau\}(x.e) & \lambda\,(x : \tau)\,e & \text{abstraction} \\
& & & \mathtt{ap}(e_1; e_2) & e_1(e_2) & \text{application}
\end{array}
$$

In **EF** functions are *first-class* in that they are a form of expression that can be used like any other. In particular, functions may be passed as arguments to, and returned as results from, other functions. For this reason, first-class functions are said to be *higher-order*, rather than *first-order*.

The statics of **EF** is given by extending rules (4.1) with the following rules:

$$
\frac{\Gamma, x : \tau_1 \vdash e : \tau_2}{\Gamma \vdash \mathtt{lam}\{\tau_1\}(x.e) : \mathtt{arr}(\tau_1; \tau_2)} \tag{8.4a}
$$

$$
\frac{\Gamma \vdash e_1 : \mathtt{arr}(\tau_2; \tau) \quad \Gamma \vdash e_2 : \tau_2}{\Gamma \vdash \mathtt{ap}(e_1; e_2) : \tau} \tag{8.4b}
$$

Lemma 8.2 (Inversion). *Suppose that* $\Gamma \vdash e : \tau$.

1. *If* $e = \mathtt{lam}\{\tau_1\}(x.e_2)$, *then* $\tau = \mathtt{arr}(\tau_1; \tau_2)$ *and* $\Gamma, x : \tau_1 \vdash e_2 : \tau_2$.
2. *If* $e = \mathtt{ap}(e_1; e_2)$, *then there exists* τ_2 *such that* $\Gamma \vdash e_1 : \mathtt{arr}(\tau_2; \tau)$ *and* $\Gamma \vdash e_2 : \tau_2$.

Proof The proof proceeds by rule induction on the typing rules. Observe that for each rule, exactly one case applies and that the premises of the rule provide the required result.   □

Lemma 8.3 (Substitution). *If* $\Gamma, x : \tau \vdash e' : \tau'$, *and* $\Gamma \vdash e : \tau$, *then* $\Gamma \vdash [e/x]e' : \tau'$.

Proof By rule induction on the derivation of the first judgment.   □

The dynamics of **EF** extends that of **E** with the following rules:

$$
\frac{}{\mathtt{lam}\{\tau\}(x.e)\ \mathsf{val}} \tag{8.5a}
$$

$$
\frac{e_1 \longmapsto e_1'}{\mathtt{ap}(e_1; e_2) \longmapsto \mathtt{ap}(e_1'; e_2)} \tag{8.5b}
$$

$$\left[\frac{e_1 \text{ val} \quad e_2 \longmapsto e_2'}{\text{ap}(e_1 ; e_2) \longmapsto \text{ap}(e_1 ; e_2')} \right] \tag{8.5c}$$

$$\frac{[e_2 \text{ val}]}{\text{ap}(\text{lam}\{\tau_2\}(x.e_1) ; e_2) \longmapsto [e_2/x]e_1} \tag{8.5d}$$

The bracketed rule and premise are included for a *call-by-value* interpretation of function application and excluded for a *call-by-name* interpretation.[1]

When functions are first class, there is no need for function declarations: simply replace the function declaration $\text{fun } f(x_1 : \tau_1) : \tau_2 = e_2 \text{ in } e$ by the definition $\text{let } \lambda (x : \tau_1) e_2 \text{ be } f \text{ in } e$, and replace second-class function application $f(e)$ by the first-class function application $f(e)$. Because λ-abstractions are values, it makes no difference whether the definition is evaluated by-value or by-name for this replacement to make sense. However, using ordinary definitions, we may, for example, give a name to a partially applied function, as in the following example:

$\text{let } k \text{ be } \lambda (x_1 : \text{num}) \lambda (x_2 : \text{num}) x_1$
$\text{in let } kz \text{ be } k(0) \text{ in } kz(3) + kz(5).$

Without first-class functions, we cannot even form the function k, which returns a function as result when applied to its first argument.

Theorem 8.4 (Preservation). *If $e : \tau$ and $e \longmapsto e'$, then $e' : \tau$.*

Proof The proof is by induction on rules (8.5), which define the dynamics of the language. Consider rule (8.5d),

$$\frac{}{\text{ap}(\text{lam}\{\tau_2\}(x.e_1) ; e_2) \longmapsto [e_2/x]e_1} .$$

Suppose that $\text{ap}(\text{lam}\{\tau_2\}(x.e_1) ; e_2) : \tau_1$. By Lemma 8.2, we have $e_2 : \tau_2$ and $x : \tau_2 \vdash e_1 : \tau_1$, so by Lemma 8.3, $[e_2/x]e_1 : \tau_1$.

The other rules governing application are handled similarly. $\qquad\qquad\square$

Lemma 8.5 (Canonical Forms). *If $e : \text{arr}(\tau_1 ; \tau_2)$ and e val, then $e = \lambda (x : \tau_1) e_2$ for some variable x and expression e_2 such that $x : \tau_1 \vdash e_2 : \tau_2$.*

Proof By induction on the typing rules, using the assumption e val. $\qquad\qquad\square$

Theorem 8.6 (Progress). *If $e : \tau$, then either e val, or there exists e' such that $e \longmapsto e'$.*

Proof The proof is by induction on rules (8.4). Note that because we consider only closed terms, there are no hypotheses on typing derivations.

Consider rule (8.4b) (under the by-name interpretation). By induction either e_1 val or $e_1 \longmapsto e_1'$. In the latter case, we have $\text{ap}(e_1 ; e_2) \longmapsto \text{ap}(e_1' ; e_2)$. In the former case, we have by Lemma 8.5 that $e_1 = \mathtt{lam}\{\tau_2\}(x.e)$ for some x and e. But then $\mathtt{ap}(e_1; e_2) \longmapsto [e_2/x]e$. □

8.3 Evaluation Dynamics and Definitional Equality

An inductive definition of the evaluation judgment $e \Downarrow v$ for **EF** is given by the following rules:

$$\frac{}{\mathtt{lam}\{\tau\}(x.e) \Downarrow \mathtt{lam}\{\tau\}(x.e)} \tag{8.6a}$$

$$\frac{e_1 \Downarrow \mathtt{lam}\{\tau\}(x.e) \quad [e_2/x]e \Downarrow v}{\mathtt{ap}(e_1; e_2) \Downarrow v} \tag{8.6b}$$

It is easy to check that if $e \Downarrow v$, then v val, and that if e val, then $e \Downarrow e$.

Theorem 8.7. $e \Downarrow v$ iff $e \longmapsto^* v$ and v val.

Proof In the forward direction, we proceed by rule induction on rules (8.6), following along similar lines as the proof of Theorem 7.2.

In the reverse direction, we proceed by rule induction on rules (5.1). The proof relies on an analog of Lemma 7.4, which states that evaluation is closed under converse execution, which is proved by induction on rules (8.5). □

Definitional equality for the call-by-name dynamics of **EF** is defined by extension of rules (5.10).

$$\frac{}{\Gamma \vdash \mathtt{ap}(\mathtt{lam}\{\tau\}(x.e_2); e_1) \equiv [e_1/x]e_2 : \tau_2} \tag{8.7a}$$

$$\frac{\Gamma \vdash e_1 \equiv e_1' : \tau_2 \rightarrow \tau \quad \Gamma \vdash e_2 \equiv e_2' : \tau_2}{\Gamma \vdash \mathtt{ap}(e_1; e_2) \equiv \mathtt{ap}(e_1'; e_2') : \tau} \tag{8.7b}$$

$$\frac{\Gamma, x : \tau_1 \vdash e_2 \equiv e_2' : \tau_2}{\Gamma \vdash \mathtt{lam}\{\tau_1\}(x.e_2) \equiv \mathtt{lam}\{\tau_1\}(x.e_2') : \tau_1 \rightarrow \tau_2} \tag{8.7c}$$

Definitional equality for call-by-value requires a bit more machinery. The main idea is to restrict rule (8.7a) to require that the argument be a value. In addition, values must be expanded to include variables, because in call-by-value, the argument variable of a function stands for the value of its argument. The call-by-value definitional equality judgment takes the form

$$\Gamma \vdash e_1 \equiv e_2 : \tau,$$

where Γ consists of paired hypotheses $x : \tau, x$ val stating, for each variable x in scope, its type and that it is a value. We write $\Gamma \vdash e$ val to show that e is a value under these hypotheses, so that $x : \tau, x$ val $\vdash x$ val.

8.4 Dynamic Scope

The dynamics of function application given by rules (8.5) is defined only for expressions without free variables. When a function is applied, the argument is substituted for the argument variable, ensuring that the result remains closed. Moreover, because substitution of closed expressions can never incur capture, the scopes of variables are not disturbed by the dynamics, ensuring that the principles of binding and scope described in Chapter 1 are respected. This treatment of variables is called *static scoping*, or *static binding*, to contrast it with an alternative approach that we now describe.

Another approach, called *dynamic scoping*, or *dynamic binding*, is sometimes advocated as an alternative to static binding. The crucial difference is that with dynamic scoping the principle of identification of abt's up to renaming of bound variables is *denied*. Consequently, capture-avoiding substitution is not available. Instead, evaluation is defined for open terms, with the bindings of free variables provided by an *environment* mapping variable names to (possibly open) values. The binding of a variable is determined as late as possible, at the point where the variable is evaluated, rather than where it is bound. If the environment does not provide a binding for a variable, evaluation is aborted with a run-time error.

For first-order functions, dynamic and static scoping coincide, but in the higher-order case, the two approaches diverge. For example, there is no difference between static and dynamic scope when it comes to evaluation of an expression such as $(\lambda\,(x:\texttt{num})\,x + 7)(42)$. Whether 42 is substituted for x in the body of the function before evaluation, or the body is evaluated in the presence of the binding of x to 42, the outcome is the same.

In the higher-order case, the equivalence of static and dynamic scope breaks down. For example, consider the expression

$$e \triangleq (\lambda\,(x:\texttt{num})\,\lambda\,(y:\texttt{num})\,x + y)(42).$$

With static scoping e evaluates to the closed value $v \triangleq \lambda\,(y:\texttt{num})\,42 + y$, which, if applied, would add 42 to its argument. It makes no difference how the bound variable x is chosen, the outcome will always be the same. With dynamic scoping, e evaluates to the open value $v' \triangleq \lambda\,(y:\texttt{num})\,x + y$ in which the variable x occurs free. When this expression is evaluated, the variable x is bound to 42, but this is irrelevant because the binding is not needed to evaluate the λ-abstraction. The binding of x is not retrieved until such time as v' is applied to an argument, at which point the binding for x in force at that time is retrieved, and not the one in force at the point where e is evaluated.

Therein lies the difference. For example, consider the expression

$$e' \triangleq (\lambda\,(f:\texttt{num} \rightarrow \texttt{num})\,(\lambda\,(x:\texttt{num})\,f(0))(7))(e).$$

When evaluated using dynamic scope, the value of e' is 7, whereas its value is 42 under static scope. The discrepancy can be traced to the re-binding of x to 7 before the value of e, namely v', is applied to 0, altering the outcome.

Dynamic scope violates the basic principle that variables are given meaning by capture-avoiding substitution as defined in Chapter 1. Violating this principle has at least two undesirable consequences. One is that the names of bound variables matter, in contrast to static scope which obeys the identification principle. For example, had the innermost λ-abstraction of e' bound the variable y, rather than x, then its value would have been 42, rather than 7. Thus, one component of a program may be sensitive to the names of bound variables chosen in another component, a clear violation of modular decomposition.

Another problem is that dynamic scope is not, in general, type-safe. For example, consider the expression

$$e' \triangleq (\lambda\,(f : \text{num} \to \text{num})\,(\lambda\,(x : \text{str})\, f(\text{"zero"}))(7))(e).$$

Under dynamic scoping this expression gets stuck attempting to evaluate $x + y$ with x bound to the string "*zero*," and no further progress can be made. For this reason dynamic scope is only ever advocated for so-called dynamically typed languages, which replace static consistency checks by dynamic consistency checks to ensure a weak form of progress. Compile-time errors are thereby transformed into run-time errors.

(For more on dynamic typing, see Chapter 22, and for more on dynamic scope, see Chapter 32.)

8.5 Notes

Nearly all programming languages provide some form of function definition mechanism of the kind illustrated here. The main point of the present account is to demonstrate that a more natural, and more powerful, approach is to separate the generic concept of a definition from the specific concept of a function. Function types codify the general notion in a systematic way that encompasses function definitions as a special case, and moreover, admits passing functions as arguments and returning them as results without special provision. The essential contribution of Church's λ-calculus (Church, 1941) was to take functions as primary, and to show that nothing more is needed to get a fully expressive programming language.

Exercises

8.1. Formulate an environmental evaluation dynamics (see Exercise **7.5**) for **ED**. *Hint*: Introduce a new form of judgment for evaluation of function identifiers.

8.2. Consider an environmental dynamics for **EF**, which includes higher-order functions. What difficulties arise? Can you think of a way to evade these difficulties? *Hint*: One approach is to "substitute away" all free variables in a λ-abstraction at the point at which it is evaluated. The second is to "freeze" the values of each of the free variables in a λ-abstraction, and to "thaw" them when such a function is applied. What problems arise in each case?

Note

1 Although the term "call-by-value" is accurately descriptive, the origin of the term "call-by-name" remains shrouded in mystery.

9 System T of Higher-Order Recursion

System **T**, well-known as *Gödel's T*, is the combination of function types with the type of natural numbers. In contrast to **E**, which equips the naturals with some arbitrarily chosen arithmetic operations, the language **T** provides a general mechanism, called *primitive recursion*, from which these primitives may be defined. Primitive recursion captures the essential inductive character of the natural numbers, and hence may be seen as an intrinsic termination proof for each program in the language. Consequently, we may only define *total* functions in the language, those that always return a value for each argument. In essence, every program in **T** "comes equipped" with a proof of its termination. Although this may seem like a shield against infinite loops, it is also a weapon that can be used to show that some programs cannot be written in **T**. To do so would demand a master termination proof for every possible program in the language, something that we shall prove does not exist.

9.1 Statics

The syntax of **T** is given by the following grammar:

Typ	τ	::=	nat	nat	naturals
			$\text{arr}(\tau_1; \tau_2)$	$\tau_1 \to \tau_2$	function
Exp	e	::=	x	x	variable
			z	z	zero
			$\text{s}(e)$	$\text{s}(e)$	successor
			$\text{rec}\{e_0; x.y.e_1\}(e)$	$\text{rec } e \{\text{z} \hookrightarrow e_0 \mid \text{s}(x) \text{ with } y \hookrightarrow e_1\}$	
					recursion
			$\text{lam}\{\tau\}(x.e)$	$\lambda(x:\tau)e$	abstraction
			$\text{ap}(e_1; e_2)$	$e_1(e_2)$	application

We write $\bar{n}$ for the expression $\text{s}(\ldots \text{s}(\text{z}))$, in which the successor is applied $n \geq 0$ times to zero. The expression $\text{rec}\{e_0; x.y.e_1\}(e)$ is called the *recursor*. It represents the e-fold iteration of the transformation $x.y.e_1$ starting from e_0. The bound variable x represents the predecessor and the bound variable y represents the result of the x-fold iteration. The "with" clause in the concrete syntax for the recursor binds the variable y to the result of the recursive call, as will become clear shortly.

Sometimes the *iterator*, $\text{iter}\{e_0; y.e_1\}(e)$, is considered as an alternative to the recursor. It has essentially the same meaning as the recursor, except that only the result of the recursive call is bound to y in e_1, and no binding is made for the predecessor. Clearly, the iterator is a special case of the recursor, because we can always ignore the predecessor binding. Conversely, the recursor is definable from the iterator, provided that we have product types (Chapter 10) at our disposal. To define the recursor from the iterator, we simultaneously compute the predecessor while iterating the specified computation.

The statics of **T** is given by the following typing rules:

$$\frac{}{\Gamma, x : \tau \vdash x : \tau} \tag{9.1a}$$

$$\frac{}{\Gamma \vdash \mathtt{z} : \mathtt{nat}} \tag{9.1b}$$

$$\frac{\Gamma \vdash e : \mathtt{nat}}{\Gamma \vdash \mathtt{s}(e) : \mathtt{nat}} \tag{9.1c}$$

$$\frac{\Gamma \vdash e : \mathtt{nat} \quad \Gamma \vdash e_0 : \tau \quad \Gamma, x : \mathtt{nat}, y : \tau \vdash e_1 : \tau}{\Gamma \vdash \mathtt{rec}\{e_0; x.y.e_1\}(e) : \tau} \tag{9.1d}$$

$$\frac{\Gamma, x : \tau_1 \vdash e : \tau_2}{\Gamma \vdash \mathtt{lam}\{\tau_1\}(x.e) : \mathtt{arr}(\tau_1; \tau_2)} \tag{9.1e}$$

$$\frac{\Gamma \vdash e_1 : \mathtt{arr}(\tau_2; \tau) \quad \Gamma \vdash e_2 : \tau_2}{\Gamma \vdash \mathtt{ap}(e_1; e_2) : \tau} \tag{9.1f}$$

As usual, admissibility of the structural rule of substitution is crucially important.

Lemma 9.1. *If* $\Gamma \vdash e : \tau$ *and* $\Gamma, x : \tau \vdash e' : \tau'$, *then* $\Gamma \vdash [e/x]e' : \tau'$.

9.2 Dynamics

The closed values of **T** are defined by the following rules:

$$\frac{}{\mathtt{z} \: \mathsf{val}} \tag{9.2a}$$

$$\frac{[e \: \mathsf{val}]}{\mathtt{s}(e) \: \mathsf{val}} \tag{9.2b}$$

$$\frac{}{\mathtt{lam}\{\tau\}(x.e) \: \mathsf{val}} \tag{9.2c}$$

The premise of rule (9.2b) is included for an *eager* interpretation of successor, and excluded for a *lazy* interpretation.

The transition rules for the dynamics of **T** are as follows:

$$\left[\frac{e \longmapsto e'}{\mathtt{s}(e) \longmapsto \mathtt{s}(e')} \right] \tag{9.3a}$$

$$\frac{e_1 \longmapsto e_1'}{\mathrm{ap}(e_1; e_2) \longmapsto \mathrm{ap}(e_1'; e_2)} \tag{9.3b}$$

$$\left[\frac{e_1 \text{ val} \quad e_2 \longmapsto e_2'}{\mathrm{ap}(e_1; e_2) \longmapsto \mathrm{ap}(e_1; e_2')}\right] \tag{9.3c}$$

$$\frac{[e_2 \text{ val}]}{\mathrm{ap}(\mathrm{lam}\{\tau\}(x.e); e_2) \longmapsto [e_2/x]e} \tag{9.3d}$$

$$\frac{e \longmapsto e'}{\mathrm{rec}\{e_0; x.y.e_1\}(e) \longmapsto \mathrm{rec}\{e_0; x.y.e_1\}(e')} \tag{9.3e}$$

$$\frac{}{\mathrm{rec}\{e_0; x.y.e_1\}(\mathrm{z}) \longmapsto e_0} \tag{9.3f}$$

$$\frac{s(e) \text{ val}}{\mathrm{rec}\{e_0; x.y.e_1\}(s(e)) \longmapsto [e, \mathrm{rec}\{e_0; x.y.e_1\}(e)/x, y]e_1} \tag{9.3g}$$

The bracketed rules and premises are included for an eager successor and call-by-value application, and omitted for a lazy successor and call-by-name application. Rules (9.3f) and (9.3g) specify the behavior of the recursor on z and $s(e)$. In the former case, the recursor reduces to e_0, and in the latter case, the variable x is bound to the predecessor e and y is bound to the (unevaluated) recursion on e. If the value of y is not required in the rest of the computation, the recursive call is not evaluated.

Lemma 9.2 (Canonical Forms). *If $e : \tau$ and e val, then*

1. If $\tau = \mathrm{nat}$, then $e = s(e')$ for some e'.
2. If $\tau = \tau_1 \to \tau_2$, then $e = \lambda(x : \tau_1) e_2$ for some e_2.

Theorem 9.3 (Safety). *1. If $e : \tau$ and $e \longmapsto e'$, then $e' : \tau$.*
2. If $e : \tau$, then either e val or $e \longmapsto e'$ for some e'.

9.3 Definability

A mathematical function $f : \mathbb{N} \to \mathbb{N}$ on the natural numbers is *definable* in **T** iff there exists an expression e_f of type $\mathrm{nat} \to \mathrm{nat}$ such that for every $n \in \mathbb{N}$,

$$e_f(\overline{n}) \equiv \overline{f(n)} : \mathrm{nat}. \tag{9.4}$$

That is, the numeric function $f : \mathbb{N} \to \mathbb{N}$ is definable iff there is an expression e_f of type $\mathrm{nat} \to \mathrm{nat}$ such that, when applied to the numeral representing the argument $n \in \mathbb{N}$, the application is definitionally equal to the numeral corresponding to $f(n) \in \mathbb{N}$.

Definitional equality for **T**, written $\Gamma \vdash e \equiv e' : \tau$, is the strongest congruence containing these axioms:

$$\frac{\Gamma, x : \tau_1 \vdash e_2 : \tau_2 \quad \Gamma \vdash e_1 : \tau_1}{\Gamma \vdash \mathtt{ap}(\mathtt{lam}\{\tau_1\}(x.e_2); e_1) \equiv [e_1/x]e_2 : \tau_2} \tag{9.5a}$$

$$\frac{\Gamma \vdash e_0 : \tau \quad \Gamma, x : \tau \vdash e_1 : \tau}{\Gamma \vdash \mathtt{rec}\{e_0; x.y.e_1\}(\mathtt{z}) \equiv e_0 : \tau} \tag{9.5b}$$

$$\frac{\Gamma \vdash e_0 : \tau \quad \Gamma, x : \tau \vdash e_1 : \tau}{\Gamma \vdash \mathtt{rec}\{e_0; x.y.e_1\}(\mathtt{s}(e)) \equiv [e, \mathtt{rec}\{e_0; x.y.e_1\}(e)/x, y]e_1 : \tau} \tag{9.5c}$$

For example, the doubling function, $d(n) = 2 \times n$, is definable in **T** by the expression $e_d : \mathtt{nat} \to \mathtt{nat}$ given by

$$\lambda\,(x : \mathtt{nat})\,\mathtt{rec}\,x\,\{\mathtt{z} \hookrightarrow \mathtt{z} \mid \mathtt{s}(u)\,\mathtt{with}\,v \hookrightarrow \mathtt{s}(\mathtt{s}(v))\}.$$

To check that this defines the doubling function, we proceed by induction on $n \in \mathbb{N}$. For the basis, it is easy to check that

$$e_d(\overline{0}) \equiv \overline{0} : \mathtt{nat}.$$

For the induction, assume that

$$e_d(\overline{n}) \equiv \overline{d(n)} : \mathtt{nat}.$$

Then calculate using the rules of definitional equality:

$$\begin{aligned}
e_d(\overline{n+1}) &\equiv \mathtt{s}(\mathtt{s}(e_d(\overline{n}))) \\
&\equiv \mathtt{s}(\mathtt{s}(\overline{2 \times n})) \\
&= \overline{2 \times (n+1)} \\
&= \overline{d(n+1)}.
\end{aligned}$$

As another example, consider the following function, called *Ackermann's function*, defined by the following equations:

$$\begin{aligned}
A(0, n) &= n + 1 \\
A(m + 1, 0) &= A(m, 1) \\
A(m + 1, n + 1) &= A(m, A(m + 1, n)).
\end{aligned}$$

The Ackermann function grows very quickly. For example, $A(4, 2) \approx 2^{65,536}$, which is often cited as being larger than the number of atoms in the universe! Yet we can show that the Ackermann function is total by a lexicographic induction on the pair of arguments (m, n). On each recursive call, either m decreases, or else m remains the same, and n decreases, so inductively the recursive calls are well-defined, and hence so is $A(m, n)$.

A *first-order primitive recursive function* is a function of type $\mathtt{nat} \to \mathtt{nat}$ that is defined using the recursor, but without using any higher-order functions. Ackermann's function is defined so that it is not first-order primitive recursive but is higher-order primitive recursive. The key to showing that it is definable in **T** is to note that $A(m + 1, n)$ iterates n times the function $A(m, -)$, starting with $A(m, 1)$. As an auxiliary, let us define the higher-order function

$$\texttt{it} : (\texttt{nat} \rightarrow \texttt{nat}) \rightarrow \texttt{nat} \rightarrow \texttt{nat} \rightarrow \texttt{nat}$$

to be the λ-abstraction

$$\lambda\,(f : \texttt{nat} \rightarrow \texttt{nat})\,\lambda\,(n : \texttt{nat})\,\texttt{rec}\,n\,\{\texttt{z} \hookrightarrow \texttt{id} \mid \texttt{s}(\_)\,\texttt{with}\,g \hookrightarrow f \circ g\},$$

where $\texttt{id} = \lambda\,(x : \texttt{nat})\,x$ is the identity, and $f \circ g = \lambda\,(x : \texttt{nat})\,f(g(x))$ is the composition of f and g. It is easy to check that

$$\texttt{it}(f)(\overline{n})(\overline{m}) \equiv f^{(n)}(\overline{m}) : \texttt{nat},$$

where the latter expression is the n-fold composition of f starting with $\overline{m}$. We may then define the Ackermann function

$$e_a : \texttt{nat} \rightarrow \texttt{nat} \rightarrow \texttt{nat}$$

to be the expression

$$\lambda\,(m : \texttt{nat})\,\texttt{rec}\,m\,\{\texttt{z} \hookrightarrow \texttt{s} \mid \texttt{s}(\_)\,\texttt{with}\,f \hookrightarrow \lambda\,(n : \texttt{nat})\,\texttt{it}(f)(n)(f(\overline{1}))\}.$$

It is instructive to check that the following equivalences are valid:

$$e_a(\overline{0})(\overline{n}) \equiv \texttt{s}(\overline{n}) \tag{9.6}$$

$$e_a(\overline{m+1})(\overline{0}) \equiv e_a(\overline{m})(\overline{1}) \tag{9.7}$$

$$e_a(\overline{m+1})(\overline{n+1}) \equiv e_a(\overline{m})(e_a(\texttt{s}(\overline{m}))(\overline{n})). \tag{9.8}$$

That is, the Ackermann function is definable in **T**.

9.4 Undefinability

It is impossible to define an infinite loop in **T**.

Theorem 9.4. *If $e : \tau$, then there exists v val such that $e \equiv v : \tau$.*

Proof   See Corollary 46.15.   □

Consequently, values of function type in **T** behave like mathematical functions: if $e : \tau_1 \rightarrow \tau_2$ and $e_1 : \tau_1$, then $e(e_1)$ evaluates to a value of type τ_2. Moreover, if $e : \texttt{nat}$, then there exists a natural number n such that $e \equiv \overline{n} : \texttt{nat}$.

Using this, we can show, using a technique called *diagonalization*, that there are functions on the natural numbers that are not definable in **T**. We make use of a technique, called *Gödel-numbering*, that assigns a unique natural number to each closed expression of **T**. By assigning a unique number to each expression, we may manipulate expressions as data values in **T** so that **T** is able to compute with its own programs.[1]

The essence of Gödel-numbering is captured by the following simple construction on abstract syntax trees. (The generalization to abstract binding trees is slightly more difficult, the main complication being to ensure that all α-equivalent expressions are assigned the same Gödel number.) Recall that a general ast a has the form $o(a_1, \ldots, a_k)$, where o is an operator of arity k. Enumerate the operators so that every operator has an index $i \in \mathbb{N}$, and let m be the index of o in this enumeration. Define the *Gödel number* $\ulcorner a \urcorner$ of a to be the number

$$2^m \, 3^{n_1} \, 5^{n_2} \ldots p_k^{n_k},$$

where p_k is the kth prime number (so that $p_0 = 2$, $p_1 = 3$, and so on), and $n_1, \ldots, n_k$ are the Gödel numbers of $a_1, \ldots, a_k$, respectively. This procedure assigns a natural number to each ast. Conversely, given a natural number, n, we may apply the prime factorization theorem to "parse" n as a unique abstract syntax tree. (If the factorization is not of the right form, which can only be because the arity of the operator does not match the number of factors, then n does not code any ast.)

Now, using this representation, we may define a (mathematical) function $f_{univ} : \mathbb{N} \to \mathbb{N} \to \mathbb{N}$ such that, for any $e :$ nat $\to$ nat, $f_{univ}(\ulcorner e \urcorner)(m) = n$ iff $e(\overline{m}) \equiv \overline{n} :$ nat.[2] The determinacy of the dynamics, together with Theorem 9.4, ensure that f_{univ} is a well-defined function. It is called the *universal function* for **T** because it specifies the behavior of any expression e of type nat $\to$ nat. Using the universal function, let us define an auxiliary mathematical function, called the *diagonal function* $\delta : \mathbb{N} \to \mathbb{N}$, by the equation $\delta(m) = f_{univ}(m)(m)$. The δ function is chosen so that $\delta(\ulcorner e \urcorner) = n$ iff $e(\ulcorner e \urcorner) \equiv \overline{n} :$ nat. (The motivation for its definition will become clear in a moment.)

The function f_{univ} is not definable in **T**. Suppose that it were definable by the expression e_{univ}, then the diagonal function δ would be definable by the expression

$$e_\delta = \lambda \, (m : \text{nat}) \, e_{univ}(m)(m).$$

But in that case we would have the equations

$$e_\delta(\overline{\ulcorner e \urcorner}) \equiv e_{univ}(\overline{\ulcorner e \urcorner})(\overline{\ulcorner e \urcorner})$$
$$\equiv e(\overline{\ulcorner e \urcorner}).$$

Now let e_Δ be the function expression

$$\lambda \, (x : \text{nat}) \, \text{s}(e_\delta(x)),$$

so that we may deduce

$$e_\Delta(\overline{\ulcorner e_\Delta \urcorner}) \equiv \text{s}(e_\delta(\overline{\ulcorner e_\Delta \urcorner}))$$
$$\equiv \text{s}(e_\Delta(\overline{\ulcorner e_\Delta \urcorner})).$$

But the termination theorem implies that there exists n such that $e_\Delta(\overline{\ulcorner e_\Delta \urcorner}) \equiv \overline{n}$, and hence we have $\overline{n} \equiv \text{s}(\overline{n})$, which is impossible.

We say that a language $\mathcal{L}$ is *universal* if it is possible to write an interpreter for $\mathcal{L}$ in $\mathcal{L}$ itself. It is intuitively clear that f_{univ} is computable in the sense that we can define it in *some* sufficiently powerful programming language. But the preceding argument shows that **T** is not up to the task; it is not a universal programming language. Examination of the foregoing proof reveals an inescapable trade-off: by insisting that all expressions terminate, we necessarily lose universality—there are computable functions that are not definable in the language.

9.5 Notes

System **T** was introduced by Gödel (1958) in his study of the consistency of arithmetic (Gödel, 1980). Gödel showed how to "compile" proofs in arithmetic into well-typed terms of system **T**, and to reduce the consistency problem for arithmetic to the termination of programs in **T**. It was perhaps the first programming language whose design was directly influenced by the verification (of termination) of its programs.

Exercises

9.1. Prove Lemma 9.2.

9.2. Prove Theorem 9.3.

9.3. Attempt to prove that if e : nat is closed, then there exists n such that $e \longmapsto^* \overline{n}$ under the eager dynamics. Where does the proof break down?

9.4. Attempt to prove termination for all well-typed closed terms: if $e : \tau$, then there exists e' val such that $e \longmapsto^* e'$. You are free to appeal to Lemma 9.2 and Theorem 9.3 as necessary. Where does the attempt break down? Can you think of a stronger inductive hypothesis that might evade the difficulty?

9.5. Define a closed term e of type τ in **T** to be *hereditarily terminating at type τ* by induction on the structure of τ as follows:

(a) If $\tau = $ nat, then e is hereditarily terminating at type τ iff e is terminating (that is, iff $e \longmapsto^* \overline{n}$ for some n.)

(b) If $\tau = \tau_1 \rightarrow \tau_2$, then e is hereditarily terminating iff when e_1 is hereditarily terminating at type τ_1, then $e(e_1)$ is hereditarily terminating at type τ_2.

Attempt to prove hereditary termination for well-typed terms: if $e : \tau$, then e is hereditarily terminating at type τ. The stronger inductive hypothesis bypasses the difficulty that arose in Exercise **9.4** but introduces another obstacle. What is the complication? Can you think of an even stronger inductive hypothesis that would suffice for the proof?

9.6. Show that if e is hereditarily terminating at type τ, $e' : \tau$, and $e' \longmapsto e$, then e is also hereditarily terminating at type τ. (The need for this result will become clear in the solution to Exercise **9.5**.)

9.7. Define an open, well-typed term

$$x_1 : \tau_1, \ldots, x_n : \tau_n \vdash e : \tau$$

to be *open hereditarily terminating* iff every substitution instance

$$[e_1, \ldots, e_n/x_1, \ldots, x_n]e$$

is closed hereditarily terminating at type τ when each e_i is closed hereditarily terminating at type τ_i for each $1 \le i \le n$. Derive Exercise **9.3** from this result.

Notes

1 The same technique lies at the heart of the proof of Gödel's celebrated incompleteness theorem. The undefinability of certain functions on the natural numbers within **T** may be seen as a form of incompleteness like that considered by Gödel.

2 The value of $f_{univ}(k)(m)$ may be chosen arbitrarily to be zero when k is not the code of any expression e.

PART IV

Finite Data Types

10 Product Types

The *binary product* of two types consists of *ordered pairs* of values, one from each type in the order specified. The associated elimination forms are *projections*, which select the first and second component of a pair. The *nullary product*, or *unit*, type consists solely of the unique "null tuple" of no values and has no associated elimination form. The product type admits both a *lazy* and an *eager* dynamics. According to the lazy dynamics, a pair is a value without regard to whether its components are values; they are not evaluated until (if ever) they are accessed and used in another computation. According to the eager dynamics, a pair is a value only if its components are values; they are evaluated when the pair is created.

More generally, we may consider the *finite product*, $\langle \tau_i \rangle_{i \in I}$, indexed by a finite set of *indices I*. The elements of the finite product type are *I-indexed tuples* whose ith component is an element of the type τ_i, for each $i \in I$. The components are accessed by *I-indexed projection* operations, generalizing the binary case. Special cases of the finite product include *n-tuples*, indexed by sets of the form $I = \{0, \dots, n - 1\}$, and *labeled tuples*, or *records*, indexed by finite sets of symbols. Similarly to binary products, finite products admit both an eager and a lazy interpretation.

10.1 Nullary and Binary Products

The abstract syntax of products is given by the following grammar:

Typ	τ	::=	unit	unit	nullary product
			$\mathrm{prod}(\tau_1; \tau_2)$	$\tau_1 \times \tau_2$	binary product
Exp	e	::=	triv	$\langle \rangle$	null tuple
			$\mathrm{pair}(e_1; e_2)$	$\langle e_1, e_2 \rangle$	ordered pair
			$\mathrm{pr}[\mathrm{l}](e)$	$e \cdot \mathrm{l}$	left projection
			$\mathrm{pr}[\mathrm{r}](e)$	$e \cdot \mathrm{r}$	right projection

There is no elimination form for the unit type, there being nothing to extract from the null tuple.

The statics of product types is given by the following rules.

$$\frac{}{\Gamma \vdash \langle \rangle : \mathtt{unit}} \tag{10.1a}$$

$$\frac{\Gamma \vdash e_1 : \tau_1 \quad \Gamma \vdash e_2 : \tau_2}{\Gamma \vdash \langle e_1, e_2 \rangle : \tau_1 \times \tau_2} \tag{10.1b}$$

$$\frac{\Gamma \vdash e : \tau_1 \times \tau_2}{\Gamma \vdash e \cdot 1 : \tau_1} \tag{10.1c}$$

$$\frac{\Gamma \vdash e : \tau_1 \times \tau_2}{\Gamma \vdash e \cdot \mathbf{r} : \tau_2} \tag{10.1d}$$

The dynamics of product types is defined by the following rules:

$$\frac{}{\langle \rangle \text{ val}} \tag{10.2a}$$

$$\frac{[e_1 \text{ val}] \quad [e_2 \text{ val}]}{\langle e_1, e_2 \rangle \text{ val}} \tag{10.2b}$$

$$\left[\frac{e_1 \longmapsto e_1'}{\langle e_1, e_2 \rangle \longmapsto \langle e_1', e_2 \rangle} \right] \tag{10.2c}$$

$$\left[\frac{e_1 \text{ val} \quad e_2 \longmapsto e_2'}{\langle e_1, e_2 \rangle \longmapsto \langle e_1, e_2' \rangle} \right] \tag{10.2d}$$

$$\frac{e \longmapsto e'}{e \cdot 1 \longmapsto e' \cdot 1} \tag{10.2e}$$

$$\frac{e \longmapsto e'}{e \cdot \mathbf{r} \longmapsto e' \cdot \mathbf{r}} \tag{10.2f}$$

$$\frac{[e_1 \text{ val}] \quad [e_2 \text{ val}]}{\langle e_1, e_2 \rangle \cdot 1 \longmapsto e_1} \tag{10.2g}$$

$$\frac{[e_1 \text{ val}] \quad [e_2 \text{ val}]}{\langle e_1, e_2 \rangle \cdot \mathbf{r} \longmapsto e_2} \tag{10.2h}$$

The bracketed rules and premises are omitted for a lazy dynamics and included for an eager dynamics of pairing.

The safety theorem applies to both the eager and the lazy dynamics, with the proof proceeding along similar lines in each case.

Theorem 10.1 (Safety). *1. If $e : \tau$ and $e \longmapsto e'$, then $e' : \tau$.*
2. If $e : \tau$ then either e val or there exists e' such that $e \longmapsto e'$.

Proof Preservation is proved by induction on transition defined by rules (10.2). Progress is proved by induction on typing defined by rules (10.1). □

10.2 Finite Products

The syntax of finite product types is given by the following grammar:

$$
\begin{array}{llll}
\text{Typ} & \tau & ::= & \text{prod}(\{i \hookrightarrow \tau_i\}_{i \in I}) \quad \langle \tau_i \rangle_{i \in I} \quad \text{product} \\
\text{Exp} & e & ::= & \text{tpl}(\{i \hookrightarrow e_i\}_{i \in I}) \quad \langle e_i \rangle_{i \in I} \quad \text{tuple} \\
& & & \text{pr}[i](e) \qquad\qquad\quad e \cdot i \qquad\;\; \text{projection}
\end{array}
$$

The variable I stands for a finite *index set* over which products are formed. The type $\text{prod}(\{i \hookrightarrow \tau_i\}_{i \in I})$, or $\prod_{i \in I} \tau_i$ for short, is the type of I-*tuples* of expressions e_i of type τ_i, one for each $i \in I$. An I-tuple has the form $\text{tpl}(\{i \hookrightarrow e_i\}_{i \in I})$, or $\langle e_i \rangle_{i \in I}$ for short, and for each $i \in I$ the ith projection from an I-tuple e is written $\text{pr}[i](e)$, or $e \cdot i$ for short.

When $I = \{i_1, \ldots, i_n\}$, the I-tuple type may be written in the form

$$
\langle i_1 \hookrightarrow \tau_1, \ldots, i_n \hookrightarrow \tau_n \rangle
$$

where we make explicit the association of a type to each index $i \in I$. Similarly, we may write

$$
\langle i_1 \hookrightarrow e_1, \ldots, i_n \hookrightarrow e_n \rangle
$$

for the I-tuple whose ith component is e_i.

Finite products generalize empty and binary products by choosing I to be empty or the two-element set $\{1, r\}$, respectively. In practice, I is often chosen to be a finite set of symbols that serve as labels for the components of the tuple to enhance readability.

The statics of finite products is given by the following rules:

$$
\frac{\Gamma \vdash e_1 : \tau_1 \quad \ldots \quad \Gamma \vdash e_n : \tau_n}{\Gamma \vdash \langle i_1 \hookrightarrow e_1, \ldots, i_n \hookrightarrow e_n \rangle : \langle i_1 \hookrightarrow \tau_1, \ldots, i_n \hookrightarrow \tau_n \rangle} \tag{10.3a}
$$

$$
\frac{\Gamma \vdash e : \langle i_1 \hookrightarrow \tau_1, \ldots, i_n \hookrightarrow \tau_n \rangle \quad (1 \leq k \leq n)}{\Gamma \vdash e \cdot i_k : \tau_k} \tag{10.3b}
$$

In rule (10.3b), the index $i_k \in I$ is a *particular* element of the index set I, whereas in rule (10.3a), the indices $i_1, \ldots, i_n$ range over the entire index set I.

The dynamics of finite products is given by the following rules:

$$
\frac{[e_1 \text{ val} \quad \ldots \quad e_n \text{ val}]}{\langle i_1 \hookrightarrow e_1, \ldots, i_n \hookrightarrow e_n \rangle \text{ val}} \tag{10.4a}
$$

$$
\left[\frac{\left\{ \begin{array}{c} e_1 \text{ val} \quad \ldots \quad e_{j-1} \text{ val} \quad e_1' = e_1 \quad \ldots \quad e_{j-1}' = e_{j-1} \\ e_j \longmapsto e_j' \quad e_{j+1}' = e_{j+1} \quad \ldots \quad e_n' = e_n \end{array} \right\}}{\langle i_1 \hookrightarrow e_1, \ldots, i_n \hookrightarrow e_n \rangle \longmapsto \langle i_1 \hookrightarrow e_1', \ldots, i_n \hookrightarrow e_n' \rangle} \right] \tag{10.4b}
$$

$$
\frac{e \longmapsto e'}{e \cdot i \longmapsto e' \cdot i} \tag{10.4c}
$$

$$
\frac{[\langle i_1 \hookrightarrow e_1, \ldots, i_n \hookrightarrow e_n \rangle \text{ val}]}{\langle i_1 \hookrightarrow e_1, \ldots, i_n \hookrightarrow e_n \rangle \cdot i_k \longmapsto e_k} \tag{10.4d}
$$

As formulated, rule (10.4b) specifies that the components of a tuple are evaluated in *some* sequential order, without specifying the order in which the components are considered. It is not hard, but a bit technically complicated, to impose an evaluation order by imposing a total ordering on the index set and evaluating components according to this ordering.

Theorem 10.2 (Safety). *If $e : \tau$, then either e val or there exists e' such that $e' : \tau$ and $e \longmapsto e'$.*

Proof The safety theorem is decomposed into progress and preservation lemmas, which are proved as in Section 10.1.   □

10.3 Primitive Mutual Recursion

Using products we may simplify the primitive recursion construct of **T** so that only the recursive result on the predecessor, and not the predecessor itself, is passed to the successor branch. Writing this as $\mathtt{iter}\{e_0; x.e_1\}(e)$, we may define $\mathtt{rec}\{e_0; x.y.e_1\}(e)$ to be $e' \cdot \mathbf{r}$, where e' is the expression

$$\mathtt{iter}\{\langle \mathbf{z}, e_0 \rangle; x'.\langle \mathbf{s}(x' \cdot \mathbf{1}), [x' \cdot \mathbf{r}/x]e_1 \rangle\}(e).$$

The idea is to compute inductively both the number n and the result of the recursive call on n, from which we can compute both $n + 1$ and the result of another recursion using e_1. The base case is computed directly as the pair of zero and e_0. It is easy to check that the statics and dynamics of the recursor are preserved by this definition.

We may also use product types to implement *mutual primitive recursion*, in which we define two functions simultaneously by primitive recursion. For example, consider the following recursion equations defining two mathematical functions on the natural numbers:

$$e(0) = 1$$
$$o(0) = 0$$
$$e(n + 1) = o(n)$$
$$o(n + 1) = e(n)$$

Intuitively, $e(n)$ is non-zero if and only if n is even, and $o(n)$ is non-zero if and only if n is odd.

To define these functions in **T** enriched with products, we first define an auxiliary function e_{eo} of type

$$\mathtt{nat} \to (\mathtt{nat} \times \mathtt{nat})$$

that computes both results simultaneously by swapping back and forth on recursive calls:

$$\lambda\,(n : \mathtt{nat} \times \mathtt{nat})\,\mathtt{iter}\,n\,\{\mathbf{z} \hookrightarrow \langle 1, 0 \rangle \mid \mathbf{s}(b) \hookrightarrow \langle b \cdot \mathbf{r}, b \cdot \mathbf{l} \rangle\}.$$

We may then define e_{ev} and e_{od} as follows:

$$e_{\mathrm{ev}} \triangleq \lambda\,(n : \mathrm{nat})\,e_{\mathrm{eo}}(n) \cdot \mathtt{l}$$
$$e_{\mathrm{od}} \triangleq \lambda\,(n : \mathrm{nat})\,e_{\mathrm{eo}}(n) \cdot \mathtt{r}.$$

10.4 Notes

Product types are the most basic form of structured data. All languages have some form of product type but often in a form that is combined with other, separable, concepts. Common manifestations of products include (1) functions with "multiple arguments" or "multiple results"; (2) "objects" represented as tuples of mutually recursive functions; (3) "structures," which are tuples with mutable components. There are many papers on finite product types, which include record types as a special case. Pierce (2002) provides a thorough account of record types and their subtyping properties (for which, see Chapter 24). Allen et al. (2006) analyze many of the key ideas in the framework of dependent type theory.

Exercises

10.1. A *database schema* may be thought of as a finite product type $\prod_{i \in I} \tau$, in which the *columns*, or *attributes*, are labeled by the indices I whose values are restricted to *atomic* types, such as nat and str. A value of a schema type is called a *tuple*, or *instance*, of that schema. A *database* may be thought of as a finite sequence of such tuples, called the *rows* of the database. Give a representation of a database using function, product, and natural numbers types, and define the *project* operation that sends a database with columns I to a database with columns $I' \subseteq I$ by restricting each row to the specified columns.

10.2. Rather than choose between a lazy and an eager dynamics for products, we can instead distinguish two forms of product type, called the *positive* and the *negative*. The statics of the negative product is given by rules (10.1), and the dynamics is lazy. The statics of the positive product, written $\tau_1 \otimes \tau_2$, is given by the following rules:

$$\frac{\Gamma \vdash e_1 : \tau_1 \quad \Gamma \vdash e_2 : \tau_2}{\Gamma \vdash \mathtt{fuse}(e_1; e_2) : \tau_1 \otimes \tau_2} \tag{10.5a}$$

$$\frac{\Gamma \vdash e_0 : \tau_1 \otimes \tau_2 \quad \Gamma\, x_1 : \tau_1\, x_2 : \tau_2 \vdash e : \tau}{\Gamma \vdash \mathtt{split}(e_0; x_1, x_2.e) : \tau} \tag{10.5b}$$

The dynamics of $\mathtt{fuse}$, the introduction form for the positive pair, is eager, essentially because the elimination form, $\mathtt{split}$, extracts both components simultaneously.

Show that the negative product is definable in terms of the positive product using the unit and function types to express the lazy semantics of negative pairing. Show that the positive product is definable in terms of the negative product, provided that we have at our disposal a `let` expression with a by-value dynamics so that we may enforce eager evaluation of positive pairs.

10.3. Specializing Exercise **10.2** to nullary products, we obtain a positive and a negative unit type. The negative unit type is given by rules (10.1), with no elimination forms and one introduction form. Give the statics and dynamics for a positive unit type, and show that the positive and negative unit types are inter-definable without any further assumptions.

11 Sum Types

Most data structures involve alternatives such as the distinction between a leaf and an interior node in a tree, or a choice in the outermost form of a piece of abstract syntax. Importantly, the choice determines the structure of the value. For example, nodes have children, but leaves do not, and so forth. These concepts are expressed by *sum types*, specifically the *binary sum*, which offers a choice of two things, and the *nullary sum*, which offers a choice of no things. *Finite sums* generalize nullary and binary sums to allow an arbitrary number of cases indexed by a finite index set. As with products, sums come in both eager and lazy variants, differing in how values of sum type are defined.

11.1 Nullary and Binary Sums

The abstract syntax of sums is given by the following grammar:

Typ	τ	::=	void	void	nullary sum
			$\mathtt{sum}(\tau_1; \tau_2)$	$\tau_1 + \tau_2$	binary sum
Exp	e	::=	$\mathtt{abort}\{\tau\}(e)$	$\mathtt{abort}(e)$	abort
			$\mathtt{in[l]}\{\tau_1; \tau_2\}(e)$	$\mathtt{l} \cdot e$	left injection
			$\mathtt{in[r]}\{\tau_1; \tau_2\}(e)$	$\mathtt{r} \cdot e$	right injection
			$\mathtt{case}(e; x_1.e_1; x_2.e_2)$	$\mathtt{case}\, e\, \{\mathtt{l} \cdot x_1 \hookrightarrow e_1 \mid \mathtt{r} \cdot x_2 \hookrightarrow e_2\}$	case analysis

The nullary sum represents a choice of zero alternatives, and hence admits no introduction form. The elimination form, $\mathtt{abort}(e)$, aborts the computation in the event that e evaluates to a value, which it cannot do. The elements of the binary sum type are labeled to show whether they are drawn from the left or the right summand, either $\mathtt{l} \cdot e$ or $\mathtt{r} \cdot e$. A value of the sum type is eliminated by case analysis.

The statics of sum types is given by the following rules.

$$\frac{\Gamma \vdash e : \mathtt{void}}{\Gamma \vdash \mathtt{abort}(e) : \tau} \tag{11.1a}$$

$$\frac{\Gamma \vdash e : \tau_1}{\Gamma \vdash \mathtt{l} \cdot e : \tau_1 + \tau_2} \tag{11.1b}$$

$$\frac{\Gamma \vdash e : \tau_2}{\Gamma \vdash \mathtt{r} \cdot e : \tau_1 + \tau_2} \tag{11.1c}$$

$$\frac{\Gamma \vdash e : \tau_1 + \tau_2 \quad \Gamma, x_1 : \tau_1 \vdash e_1 : \tau \quad \Gamma, x_2 : \tau_2 \vdash e_2 : \tau}{\Gamma \vdash \mathtt{case}\, e\, \{\mathtt{l} \cdot x_1 \hookrightarrow e_1 \mid \mathtt{r} \cdot x_2 \hookrightarrow e_2\} : \tau} \tag{11.1d}$$

For the sake of readability, in rules (11.1b) and (11.1c) we have written $1 \cdot e$ and $r \cdot e$ in place of the abstract syntax $\texttt{in}[\texttt{l}]\{\tau_1; \tau_2\}(e)$ and $\texttt{in}[\texttt{r}]\{\tau_1; \tau_2\}(e)$, which includes the types τ_1 and τ_2 explicitly. In rule (11.1d), both branches of the case analysis must have the same type. Because a type expresses a static "prediction" on the form of the value of an expression, and because an expression of sum type could evaluate to either form at run-time, we must insist that both branches yield the same type.

The dynamics of sums is given by the following rules:

$$\frac{e \longmapsto e'}{\texttt{abort}(e) \longmapsto \texttt{abort}(e')} \tag{11.2a}$$

$$\frac{[e \; \text{val}]}{1 \cdot e \; \text{val}} \tag{11.2b}$$

$$\frac{[e \; \text{val}]}{r \cdot e \; \text{val}} \tag{11.2c}$$

$$\left[\frac{e \longmapsto e'}{1 \cdot e \longmapsto 1 \cdot e'} \right] \tag{11.2d}$$

$$\left[\frac{e \longmapsto e'}{r \cdot e \longmapsto r \cdot e'} \right] \tag{11.2e}$$

$$\frac{e \longmapsto e'}{\texttt{case} \; e \; \{1 \cdot x_1 \hookrightarrow e_1 \mid r \cdot x_2 \hookrightarrow e_2\} \longmapsto \texttt{case} \; e' \; \{1 \cdot x_1 \hookrightarrow e_1 \mid r \cdot x_2 \hookrightarrow e_2\}} \tag{11.2f}$$

$$\frac{[e \; \text{val}]}{\texttt{case} \; 1 \cdot e \; \{1 \cdot x_1 \hookrightarrow e_1 \mid r \cdot x_2 \hookrightarrow e_2\} \longmapsto [e/x_1]e_1} \tag{11.2g}$$

$$\frac{[e \; \text{val}]}{\texttt{case} \; r \cdot e \; \{1 \cdot x_1 \hookrightarrow e_1 \mid r \cdot x_2 \hookrightarrow e_2\} \longmapsto [e/x_2]e_2} \tag{11.2h}$$

The bracketed premises and rules are included for an eager dynamics and excluded for a lazy dynamics.

The coherence of the statics and dynamics is stated and proved as usual.

Theorem 11.1 (Safety). *1. If $e : \tau$ and $e \longmapsto e'$, then $e' : \tau$.*
2. If $e : \tau$, then either e val or $e \longmapsto e'$ for some e'.

Proof The proof proceeds by induction on rules (11.2) for preservation, and by induction on rules (11.1) for progress. $\square$

11.2 Finite Sums

Just as we may generalize nullary and binary products to finite products, so may we also generalize nullary and binary sums to finite sums. The syntax for finite sums is given by the following grammar:

Typ	τ	::=	$\mathrm{sum}(\{i \hookrightarrow \tau_i\}_{i \in I})$	$[\tau_i]_{i \in I}$	sum
Exp	e	::=	$\mathrm{in}[i]\{\vec{\tau}\}(e)$	$i \cdot e$	injection
			$\mathrm{case}(e; \{i \hookrightarrow x_i.e_i\}_{i \in I})$	$\mathrm{case}\, e\, \{i \cdot x_i \hookrightarrow e_i\}_{i \in I}$	case analysis

The variable I stands for a finite index set over which sums are formed. The notation $\vec{\tau}$ stands for a finite function $\{i \hookrightarrow \tau_i\}_{i \in I}$ for some index set I. The type $\mathrm{sum}(\{i \hookrightarrow \tau_i\}_{i \in I})$, or $\sum_{i \in I} \tau_i$ for short, is the type of I-classified values of the form $\mathrm{in}[i]\{I\}(e_i)$, or $i \cdot e_i$ for short, where $i \in I$ and e_i is an expression of type τ_i. An I-classified value is analyzed by an I-way case analysis of the form $\mathrm{case}(e; \{i \hookrightarrow x_i.e_i\}_{i \in I})$.

When $I = \{i_1, \ldots, i_n\}$, the type of I-classified values may be written

$$[i_1 \hookrightarrow \tau_1, \ldots, i_n \hookrightarrow \tau_n]$$

specifying the type associated with each class $I_i \in I$. Correspondingly, the I-way case analysis has the form

$$\mathrm{case}\, e\, \{i_1 \cdot x_1 \hookrightarrow e_1 \mid \ldots \mid i_n \cdot x_n \hookrightarrow e_n\}.$$

Finite sums generalize empty and binary sums by choosing I to be empty or the two-element set $\{\mathrm{l}, \mathrm{r}\}$, respectively. In practice I is often chosen to be a finite set of symbols that serve as names for the classes so as to enhance readability.

The statics of finite sums is defined by the following rules:

$$\frac{\Gamma \vdash e : \tau_k \quad (1 \leq k \leq n)}{\Gamma \vdash i_k \cdot e : [i_1 \hookrightarrow \tau_1, \ldots, i_n \hookrightarrow \tau_n]} \tag{11.3a}$$

$$\frac{\Gamma \vdash e : [i_1 \hookrightarrow \tau_1, \ldots, i_n \hookrightarrow \tau_n] \quad \Gamma, x_1 : \tau_1 \vdash e_1 : \tau \quad \ldots \quad \Gamma, x_n : \tau_n \vdash e_n : \tau}{\Gamma \vdash \mathrm{case}\, e\, \{i_1 \cdot x_1 \hookrightarrow e_1 \mid \ldots \mid i_n \cdot x_n \hookrightarrow e_n\} : \tau} \tag{11.3b}$$

These rules generalize the statics for nullary and binary sums given in Section 11.1.

The dynamics of finite sums is defined by the following rules:

$$\frac{[e\ \mathsf{val}]}{i \cdot e\ \mathsf{val}} \tag{11.4a}$$

$$\left[\frac{e \longmapsto e'}{i \cdot e \longmapsto i \cdot e'}\right] \tag{11.4b}$$

$$\frac{e \longmapsto e'}{\mathrm{case}\, e\, \{i \cdot x_i \hookrightarrow e_i\}_{i \in I} \longmapsto \mathrm{case}\, e'\, \{i \cdot x_i \hookrightarrow e_i\}_{i \in I}} \tag{11.4c}$$

$$\frac{i \cdot e\ \mathsf{val}}{\mathrm{case}\, i \cdot e\, \{i \cdot x_i \hookrightarrow e_i\}_{i \in I} \longmapsto [e/x_i]e_i} \tag{11.4d}$$

These again generalize the dynamics of binary sums given in Section 11.1.

Theorem 11.2 (Safety). *If $e : \tau$, then either $e\ \mathsf{val}$ or there exists $e' : \tau$ such that $e \longmapsto e'$.*

Proof   The proof is like that for the binary case, as described in Section 11.1.   □

11.3 Applications of Sum Types

Sum types have many uses, several of which we outline here. More interesting examples
arise once we also have induction and recursive types, which are introduced in Parts VI and
Part VIII.

11.3.1 Void and Unit

It is instructive to compare the types unit and void, which are often confused with one
another. The type unit has exactly one element, $\langle\rangle$, whereas the type void has no elements
at all. Consequently, if e : unit, then if e evaluates to a value, that value is $\langle\rangle$—in other
words, e has *no interesting value*. On the other hand, if e : void, then e *must not yield a
value*; if it were to have a value, it would have to be a value of type void, of which there
are none. Thus, what is called the void type in many languages is really the type unit
because it indicates that an expression has no interesting value, not that it has no value
at all!

11.3.2 Booleans

Perhaps the simplest example of a sum type is the familiar type of Booleans, whose syntax
is given by the following grammar:

Typ	τ	$::=$	bool	bool	booleans
Exp	e	$::=$	true	true	truth
			false	false	falsity
			if$(e; e_1; e_2)$	if e then e_1 else e_2	conditional

The expression if$(e; e_1; e_2)$ branches on the value of e : bool.

The statics of Booleans is given by the following typing rules:

$$\frac{}{\Gamma \vdash \text{true} : \text{bool}} \tag{11.5a}$$

$$\frac{}{\Gamma \vdash \text{false} : \text{bool}} \tag{11.5b}$$

$$\frac{\Gamma \vdash e : \text{bool} \quad \Gamma \vdash e_1 : \tau \quad \Gamma \vdash e_2 : \tau}{\Gamma \vdash \text{if } e \text{ then } e_1 \text{ else } e_2 : \tau} \tag{11.5c}$$

The dynamics is given by the following value and transition rules:

$$\frac{}{\text{true val}} \tag{11.6a}$$

$$\frac{}{\text{false val}} \tag{11.6b}$$

$$\frac{}{\text{if true then } e_1 \text{ else } e_2 \longmapsto e_1} \tag{11.6c}$$

$$\frac{}{\text{if false then } e_1 \text{ else } e_2 \longmapsto e_2} \tag{11.6d}$$

$$\frac{e \longmapsto e'}{\text{if } e \text{ then } e_1 \text{ else } e_2 \longmapsto \text{if } e' \text{ then } e_1 \text{ else } e_2} \tag{11.6e}$$

The type bool is definable in terms of binary sums and nullary products:

$$\text{bool} = \text{unit} + \text{unit} \tag{11.7a}$$

$$\text{true} = 1 \cdot \langle \rangle \tag{11.7b}$$

$$\text{false} = r \cdot \langle \rangle \tag{11.7c}$$

$$\text{if } e \text{ then } e_1 \text{ else } e_2 = \text{case } e \,\{1 \cdot x_1 \hookrightarrow e_1 \mid r \cdot x_2 \hookrightarrow e_2\} \tag{11.7d}$$

In Equation (11.7d), the variables x_1 and x_2 are chosen arbitrarily such that $x_1 \notin e_1$ and $x_2 \notin e_2$. It is a simple matter to check that the readily-defined statics and dynamics of the type bool are engendered by these definitions.

11.3.3 Enumerations

More generally, sum types can be used to define *finite enumeration* types, those whose values are one of an explicitly given finite set, and whose elimination form is a case analysis on the elements of that set. For example, the type suit, whose elements are ♣, ◇, ♡, and ♠, has as elimination form the case analysis

$$\text{case } e \,\{ \clubsuit \hookrightarrow e_0 \mid \diamondsuit \hookrightarrow e_1 \mid \heartsuit \hookrightarrow e_2 \mid \spadesuit \hookrightarrow e_3 \},$$

which distinguishes among the four suits. Such finite enumerations are easily representable as sums. For example, we may define suit $= [\text{unit}]_{\in I}$, where $I = \{\clubsuit, \diamondsuit, \heartsuit, \spadesuit\}$ and the type family is constant over this set. The case analysis form for a labeled sum is almost literally the desired case analysis for the given enumeration, the only difference being the binding for the uninteresting value associated with each summand, which we may ignore.

Other examples of enumeration types abound. For example, most languages have a type char of characters, which is a large enumeration type containing all possible Unicode (or other such standard classification) characters. Each character is assigned a *code* (such as UTF-8) used for interchange among programs. The type char is equipped with operations such as $\text{chcode}(n)$ that yield the char associated to the code n, and $\text{codech}(c)$ that yield the code of character c. Using the linear ordering on codes we may define a total ordering of characters, called the *collating sequence* determined by that code.

11.3.4 Options

Another use of sums is to define the *option* types, which have the following syntax:

Typ	τ	::=	$\mathtt{opt}(\tau)$	$\tau\ \mathtt{opt}$	option
Exp	e	::=	$\mathtt{null}$	$\mathtt{null}$	nothing
			$\mathtt{just}(e)$	$\mathtt{just}(e)$	something
			$\mathtt{ifnull}\{\tau\}\{e_1; x.e_2\}(e)$	$\mathtt{which}\, e\, \{\mathtt{null} \hookrightarrow e_1 \mid \mathtt{just}(x) \hookrightarrow e_2\}$	
				null test	

The type $\mathtt{opt}(\tau)$ represents the type of "optional" values of type τ. The introduction forms are $\mathtt{null}$, corresponding to "no value," and $\mathtt{just}(e)$, corresponding to a specified value of type τ. The elimination form discriminates between the two possibilities.

The option type is definable from sums and nullary products according to the following equations:[1]

$$\tau\ \mathtt{opt} = \mathtt{unit} + \tau \tag{11.8a}$$

$$\mathtt{null} = \mathtt{l} \cdot \langle\rangle \tag{11.8b}$$

$$\mathtt{just}(e) = \mathtt{r} \cdot e \tag{11.8c}$$

$$\mathtt{which}\, e\, \{\mathtt{null} \hookrightarrow e_1 \mid \mathtt{just}(x_2) \hookrightarrow e_2\} = \mathtt{case}\, e\, \{\mathtt{l} \cdot \_ \hookrightarrow e_1 \mid \mathtt{r} \cdot x_2 \hookrightarrow e_2\} \tag{11.8d}$$

We leave it to the reader to check the statics and dynamics implied by these definitions.

The option type is the key to understanding a common misconception, the *null pointer fallacy*. This fallacy arises from two related errors. The first error is to deem values of certain types to be mysterious entities called *pointers*. This terminology arises from suppositions about how these values might be represented at run-time, rather than on their semantic role in the language. The second error compounds the first. A particular value of a pointer type is distinguished as *the null pointer*, which, unlike the other elements of that type, does not stand for a value of that type at all, but rather rejects all attempts to use it.

To help avoid such failures, such languages usually include a function, say $\mathtt{null}$: $\tau \to \mathtt{bool}$, that yields $\mathtt{true}$ if its argument is null, and $\mathtt{false}$ otherwise. Such a test allows the programmer to take steps to avoid using null as a value of the type it purports to inhabit. Consequently, programs are riddled with conditionals of the form

$$\mathtt{if}\,\mathtt{null}(e)\,\mathtt{then}\ldots error \ldots \mathtt{else}\ldots proceed \ldots. \tag{11.9}$$

Despite this, "null pointer" exceptions at run-time are rampant, in part because it is quite easy to overlook the need for such a test, and in part because detection of a null pointer leaves little recourse other than abortion of the program.

The underlying problem is the failure to distinguish the type τ from the type $\tau\ \mathtt{opt}$. Rather than think of the elements of type τ as pointers, and thereby have to worry about the null pointer, we instead distinguish between a *genuine* value of type τ and an *optional* value of type τ. An optional value of type τ may or may not be present, but, if it is, the underlying value is truly a value of type τ (and cannot be null). The elimination form for the option type,

$$\mathtt{which}\, e\, \{\mathtt{null} \hookrightarrow e_{error} \mid \mathtt{just}(x) \hookrightarrow e_{ok}\}, \tag{11.10}$$

propagates the information that e is present into the non-null branch by binding a genuine value of type τ to the variable x. The case analysis effects a change of type from "optional value of type τ" to "genuine value of type τ," so that within the non-null branch no further null checks, explicit or implicit, are necessary. Note that such a change of type is not achieved by the simple Boolean-valued test exemplified by expression (11.9); the advantage of option types is precisely that they do so.

11.4 Notes

Heterogeneous data structures are ubiquitous. Sums codify heterogeneity, yet few languages support them in the form given here. The best approximation in commercial languages is the concept of a class in object-oriented programming. A class is an injection into a sum type, and dispatch is case analysis on the class of the data object. (See Chapter 26 for more on this correspondence.) The absence of sums is the origin of C.A.R. Hoare's self-described "billion dollar mistake," the null pointer (Hoare, 2009). Bad language designs put the burden of managing "null" values entirely at run-time, instead of making the possibility or the impossibility of "null" apparent at compile time.

Exercises

11.1. Complete the definition of a finite enumeration type sketched in Section 11.3.3. Derive enumeration types from finite sum types.

11.2. The essence of Hoare's mistake is the misidentification of the type τ opt with the type bool $\times \tau$. Values of the latter type are pairs consisting of a boolean "flag" and a value of type τ. The idea is that the flag indicates whether the associated value is "present." When the flag is true, the second component is present, and, when the flag is false, the second component is absent.

Analyze Hoare's mistake by attempting to define τ opt to be the type bool $\times \tau$ by filling in the following chart:

$$\text{null} \triangleq \; ?$$

$$\text{just}(e) \triangleq \; ?$$

$$\text{which} \, e \, \{\text{null} \hookrightarrow e_1 \mid \text{just}(x) \hookrightarrow e_2\} \triangleq \; ?$$

Argue that *even if* we adopt Hoare's convention of admitting a "null" value of every type, the chart cannot be properly filled.

11.3. Databases have a version of the "null pointer" problem that arises when not every tuple provides a value for every attribute (such as a person's middle name). More generally, many commercial databases are limited to a single atomic type for each attribute, presenting problems when the value of that attribute may have several types (for example, one may have different sorts of postal codes depending on the country). Consider how to address these problems using the methods discussed in Exercise **10.1**. Suggest how to handle null values and heterogeneous values that avoids some of the complications that arise in traditional formulations of databases.

11.4. A *combinational circuit* is an open expression of type

$$x_1 : \texttt{bool}, \ldots, x_n : \texttt{bool} \vdash e : \texttt{bool},$$

which computes a boolean value from n boolean inputs. Define a NOR and a NAND gate as boolean circuits with two inputs and one output. There is no reason to restrict to a single output. For example, define an HALF-ADDER that takes two boolean inputs, but produces two boolean outputs, the sum and the carry outputs of the HALF-ADDER. Then define a FULL-ADDER that takes three inputs, the addends and an incoming carry, and produces two outputs, the sum and the outgoing carry. Define the type NYBBLE to be the product `bool × bool × bool × bool`. Define the combinational circuit NYBBLE-ADDER that takes two nybbles as input and produces a nybble and a carry-out bit as output.

11.5. A *signal* is a time-varying sequence of booleans, representing the status of the signal at each time instant. An RS latch is a fundamental digital circuit with two input signals and two output signals. Define the type `signal` of signals to be the function type `nat → bool` of infinite sequences of booleans. Define an RS latch as a function of type

$$(\texttt{signal} \times \texttt{signal}) \rightarrow (\texttt{signal} \times \texttt{signal}).$$

Note

---

1 We often write an underscore in place of a bound variable that is not used within its scope.

PART V

Types and Propositions

Constructive Logic

Constructive logic codifies the principles of mathematical reasoning as it is actually practiced. In mathematics a proposition is judged true exactly when it has a proof, and is judged false exactly when it has a refutation. Because there are, and always will be, unsolved problems, we cannot expect in general that a proposition is either true or false, for in most cases, we have neither a proof nor a refutation of it. Constructive logic can be described as *logic as if people matter*, as distinct from classical logic, which can be described as *the logic of the mind of god*.

From a constructive viewpoint, a proposition is true when it has a proof. What is a proof is a social construct, an agreement among people as to what is a valid argument. The rules of logic codify a set of principles of reasoning that may be used in a valid proof. The valid forms of proof are determined by the outermost structure of the proposition whose truth is asserted. For example, a proof of a conjunction consists of a proof of each conjunct, and a proof of an implication transforms a proof of its antecedent to a proof of its consequent. When spelled out in full, the forms of proof are seen to correspond exactly to the forms of expression of a programming language. To each proposition is associated the type of its proofs; a proof is then an expression of the associated type. This association between programs and proofs induces a dynamics on proofs. In this way, proofs in constructive logic have *computational content*, which is to say that they are interpreted as executable programs of the associated type. Conversely, programs have *mathematical content* as proofs of the proposition associated to their type.

The unification of logic and programming is called the *propositions as types* principle. It is a central organizing principle of the theory of programming languages. Propositions are identified with types, and proofs are identified with programs. A programming technique corresponds to a method of proof; a proof technique corresponds to a method of programming. Viewing types as behavioral specifications of programs, propositions are problem statements whose proofs are solutions that implement the specification.

12.1 Constructive Semantics

Constructive logic is concerned with two judgments, namely ϕ prop, stating that ϕ expresses a proposition, and ϕ true, stating that ϕ is a true proposition. What distinguishes constructive from non-constructive logic is that a proposition is not conceived of as merely a truth value, but instead as a *problem statement* whose solution, if it has one, is given by a proof. A proposition is *true* exactly when it has a proof, in keeping with ordinary mathematical practice. In practice, there is no other criterion of truth than the existence of a proof.

Identifying truth with proof has important, and possibly surprising, consequences. The most important consequence is that we cannot say, in general, that a proposition is either true or false. If for a proposition to be true means to have a proof of it, what does it mean for a proposition to be false? It means that we have a *refutation* of it, showing that it cannot be proved. That is, a proposition is false if we can show that the assumption that it is true (has a proof) contradicts known facts. In this sense, constructive logic is a logic of *positive*, or *affirmative, information*—we must have explicit evidence in the form of a proof to affirm the truth or falsity of a proposition.

In light of this, it is clear that not every proposition is either true or false. For if ϕ expresses an unsolved problem, such as the famous P $\stackrel{?}{=}$ NP problem, then we have neither a proof nor a refutation of it (the mere absence of a proof not being a refutation). Such a problem is *undecided*, precisely because it has not been solved. Because there will always be unsolved problems (there being infinitely many propositions, but only finitely many proofs at a given point in time), we cannot say that every proposition is *decidable*, that is, either true or false.

Of course, some propositions are decidable, and hence are either true or false. For example, if ϕ expresses an inequality between natural numbers, then ϕ is decidable, because we can always work out, for given natural numbers m and n, whether $m \leq n$ or $m \nleq n$—we can either prove or refute the given inequality. This argument does not extend to the real numbers. To get an idea of why not, consider the representation of a real number by its decimal expansion. At any finite time, we will have explored only a finite initial segment of the expansion, which is not enough to decide if it is, say, less than 1. For if we have calculated the expansion to be $0.99\ldots9$, we cannot decide at any time, short of infinity, whether or not the number is 1.

The constructive attitude is simply to accept the situation as inevitable, and make our peace with that. When faced with a problem, we have no choice but to roll up our sleeves and try to prove it or refute it. There is no guarantee of success! Life is hard, but we muddle through somehow.

12.2 Constructive Logic

The judgments ϕ prop and ϕ true of constructive logic are rarely of interest by themselves, but rather in the context of a hypothetical judgment of the form

$$\phi_1 \text{ true}, \ldots, \phi_n \text{ true} \vdash \phi \text{ true}.$$

This judgment says that the proposition ϕ is true (has a proof), under the assumptions that each of $\phi_1, \ldots, \phi_n$ are also true (have proofs). Of course, when $n = 0$ this is just the same as the judgment ϕ true.

The structural properties of the hypothetical judgment, when specialized to constructive logic, define what we mean by reasoning under hypotheses:

$$\overline{\Gamma, \phi \text{ true} \vdash \phi \text{ true}} \tag{12.1a}$$

$$\frac{\Gamma \vdash \phi_1 \text{ true} \quad \Gamma, \phi_1 \text{ true} \vdash \phi_2 \text{ true}}{\Gamma \vdash \phi_2 \text{ true}} \tag{12.1b}$$

$$\frac{\Gamma \vdash \phi_2 \text{ true}}{\Gamma, \phi_1 \text{ true} \vdash \phi_2 \text{ true}} \tag{12.1c}$$

$$\frac{\Gamma, \phi_1 \text{ true}, \phi_1 \text{ true} \vdash \phi_2 \text{ true}}{\Gamma, \phi_1 \text{ true} \vdash \phi_2 \text{ true}} \tag{12.1d}$$

$$\frac{\Gamma_1, \phi_2 \text{ true}, \phi_1 \text{ true}, \Gamma_2 \vdash \phi \text{ true}}{\Gamma_1, \phi_1 \text{ true}, \phi_2 \text{ true}, \Gamma_2 \vdash \phi \text{ true}} \tag{12.1e}$$

The last two rules are implicit in that we regard Γ as a set of hypotheses, so that two "copies" are as good as one, and the order of hypotheses does not matter.

12.2.1 Provability

The syntax of propositional logic is given by the following grammar:

$$
\begin{array}{lllll}
\text{Prop} & \phi & ::= & \top & \top & \text{truth} \\
& & & \bot & \bot & \text{falsity} \\
& & & \wedge(\phi_1; \phi_2) & \phi_1 \wedge \phi_2 & \text{conjunction} \\
& & & \vee(\phi_1; \phi_2) & \phi_1 \vee \phi_2 & \text{disjunction} \\
& & & \supset(\phi_1; \phi_2) & \phi_1 \supset \phi_2 & \text{implication}
\end{array}
$$

The connectives of propositional logic are given meaning by rules that define (a) what constitutes a "direct" proof of a proposition formed from that connective, and (b) how to exploit the existence of such a proof in an "indirect" proof of another proposition. These are called the *introduction* and *elimination* rules for the connective. The principle of *conservation of proof* states that these rules are inverse to one another—the elimination rule cannot extract more information (in the form of a proof) than was put into it by the introduction rule, and the introduction rules can reconstruct a proof from the information extracted by the elimination rules.

Truth   Our first proposition is trivially true. No information goes into proving it, and so no information can be obtained from it.

$$\overline{\Gamma \vdash \top \text{ true}} \tag{12.2a}$$

(no elimination rule)

$$\tag{12.2b}$$

Conjunction   Conjunction expresses the truth of both of its conjuncts.

$$\frac{\Gamma \vdash \phi_1 \text{ true} \quad \Gamma \vdash \phi_2 \text{ true}}{\Gamma \vdash \phi_1 \wedge \phi_2 \text{ true}} \tag{12.3a}$$

$$\frac{\Gamma \vdash \phi_1 \wedge \phi_2 \text{ true}}{\Gamma \vdash \phi_1 \text{ true}} \tag{12.3b}$$

$$\frac{\Gamma \vdash \phi_1 \wedge \phi_2 \text{ true}}{\Gamma \vdash \phi_2 \text{ true}} \tag{12.3c}$$

Implication   Implication expresses the truth of a proposition under an assumption.

$$\frac{\Gamma, \phi_1 \text{ true} \vdash \phi_2 \text{ true}}{\Gamma \vdash \phi_1 \supset \phi_2 \text{ true}} \tag{12.4a}$$

$$\frac{\Gamma \vdash \phi_1 \supset \phi_2 \text{ true} \quad \Gamma \vdash \phi_1 \text{ true}}{\Gamma \vdash \phi_2 \text{ true}} \tag{12.4b}$$

Falsehood   Falsehood expresses the trivially false (refutable) proposition.

(no introduction rule)

$$\tag{12.5a}$$

$$\frac{\Gamma \vdash \bot \text{ true}}{\Gamma \vdash \phi \text{ true}} \tag{12.5b}$$

Disjunction   Disjunction expresses the truth of either (or both) of two propositions.

$$\frac{\Gamma \vdash \phi_1 \text{ true}}{\Gamma \vdash \phi_1 \vee \phi_2 \text{ true}} \tag{12.6a}$$

$$\frac{\Gamma \vdash \phi_2 \text{ true}}{\Gamma \vdash \phi_1 \vee \phi_2 \text{ true}} \tag{12.6b}$$

$$\frac{\Gamma \vdash \phi_1 \vee \phi_2 \text{ true} \quad \Gamma, \phi_1 \text{ true} \vdash \phi \text{ true} \quad \Gamma, \phi_2 \text{ true} \vdash \phi \text{ true}}{\Gamma \vdash \phi \text{ true}} \tag{12.6c}$$

Negation   The negation, $\neg\phi$, of a proposition ϕ is defined as the implication $\phi \supset \bot$. As a result, $\neg\phi$ true if ϕ true $\vdash \bot$ true, which is to say that the truth of ϕ is *refutable* in that we may derive a proof of falsehood from any purported proof of ϕ. Because constructive truth is defined to be the existence of a proof, the implied semantics of negation is rather strong. In particular, a problem ϕ is *open* exactly when we can neither affirm nor refute it. In contrast, the classical conception of truth assigns a fixed truth value to each proposition so that every proposition is either true or false.

12.2.2 Proof Terms

The key to the propositions-as-types principle is to make explicit the forms of proof. The basic judgment ϕ true, which states that ϕ has a proof, is replaced by the judgment $p : \phi$, stating that p is a proof of ϕ. (Sometimes p is called a "proof term," but we will simply call p a "proof.") The hypothetical judgment is modified correspondingly, with variables standing for the presumed, but unknown, proofs:

$$x_1 : \phi_1, \ldots, x_n : \phi_n \vdash p : \phi.$$

We again let Γ range over such hypothesis lists, subject to the restriction that no variable occurs more than once.

The syntax of proof terms is given by the following grammar:

Prf	p	::=	true-I	$\langle \rangle$	truth intro
			and-I$(p_1; p_2)$	$\langle p_1, p_2 \rangle$	conj. intro
			and-E[l](p)	$p \cdot \mathtt{l}$	conj. elim
			and-E[r](p)	$p \cdot \mathtt{r}$	conj. elim
			imp-I$(x.p)$	$\lambda\,(x)\,p$	impl. intro
			imp-E$(p_1; p_2)$	$p_1(p_2)$	impl. elim
			false-E(p)	$\mathtt{abort}(p)$	false elim
			or-I[l](p)	$\mathtt{l} \cdot p$	disj. intro
			or-I[r](p)	$\mathtt{r} \cdot p$	disj. intro
			or-E$(p; x_1.p_1; x_2.p_2)$	$\mathtt{case}\ p\ \{\mathtt{l} \cdot x_1 \hookrightarrow p_1 \mid \mathtt{r} \cdot x_2 \hookrightarrow p_2\}$	disj. elim

The concrete syntax of proof terms is chosen to stress the correspondence between propositions and types discussed in Section 12.4 below.

The rules of constructive propositional logic can be restated using proof terms as follows.

$$\frac{}{\Gamma \vdash \langle \rangle : \top} \tag{12.7a}$$

$$\frac{\Gamma \vdash p_1 : \phi_1 \quad \Gamma \vdash p_2 : \phi_2}{\Gamma \vdash \langle p_1, p_2 \rangle : \phi_1 \wedge \phi_2} \tag{12.7b}$$

$$\frac{\Gamma \vdash p_1 : \phi_1 \wedge \phi_2}{\Gamma \vdash p_1 \cdot \mathtt{l} : \phi_1} \tag{12.7c}$$

$$\frac{\Gamma \vdash p_1 : \phi_1 \wedge \phi_2}{\Gamma \vdash p_1 \cdot \mathtt{r} : \phi_2} \tag{12.7d}$$

$$\frac{\Gamma, x : \phi_1 \vdash p_2 : \phi_2}{\Gamma \vdash \lambda\,(x)\,p_2 : \phi_1 \supset \phi_2} \tag{12.7e}$$

$$\frac{\Gamma \vdash p : \phi_1 \supset \phi_2 \quad \Gamma \vdash p_1 : \phi_1}{\Gamma \vdash p(p_1) : \phi_2} \tag{12.7f}$$

$$\frac{\Gamma \vdash p : \bot}{\Gamma \vdash \mathtt{abort}(p) : \phi} \tag{12.7g}$$

$$\frac{\Gamma \vdash p_1 : \phi_1}{\Gamma \vdash \mathtt{l} \cdot p_1 : \phi_1 \vee \phi_2} \tag{12.7h}$$

$$\frac{\Gamma \vdash p_2 : \phi_2}{\Gamma \vdash \mathtt{r} \cdot p_2 : \phi_1 \vee \phi_2} \tag{12.7i}$$

$$\frac{\Gamma \vdash p : \phi_1 \vee \phi_2 \quad \Gamma, x_1 : \phi_1 \vdash p_1 : \phi \quad \Gamma, x_2 : \phi_2 \vdash p_2 : \phi}{\Gamma \vdash \mathtt{case}\, p \,\{\mathtt{l} \cdot x_1 \hookrightarrow p_1 \mid \mathtt{r} \cdot x_2 \hookrightarrow p_2\} : \phi} \tag{12.7j}$$

12.3 Proof Dynamics

Proof terms in constructive logic are given a dynamics by *Gentzen's Principle*. It states that the elimination forms are inverse to the introduction forms. One aspect of Gentzen's Principle is the principle of *conservation of proof*, which states that the information introduced into a proof of a proposition can be extracted without loss by elimination. For example, we may state that conjunction elimination is post-inverse to conjunction introduction by the definitional equations:

$$\frac{\Gamma \vdash p_1 : \phi_1 \quad \Gamma \vdash p_2 : \phi_2}{\Gamma \vdash \langle p_1, p_2 \rangle \cdot \mathtt{l} \equiv p_1 : \phi_1} \tag{12.8a}$$

$$\frac{\Gamma \vdash p_1 : \phi_1 \quad \Gamma \vdash p_2 : \phi_2}{\Gamma \vdash \langle p_1, p_2 \rangle \cdot \mathtt{r} \equiv p_2 : \phi_2} \tag{12.8b}$$

Another aspect of Gentzen's Principle is that principle of *reversibility of proof*, which states that every proof can be reconstructed from the information that can be extracted from it by elimination. In the case of conjunction this can be stated by the definitional equation

$$\frac{\Gamma \vdash p_1 : \phi_1 \quad \Gamma \vdash p_2 : \phi_2}{\Gamma \vdash \langle p \cdot \mathtt{l}, p \cdot \mathtt{r} \rangle \equiv p : \phi_1 \wedge \phi_2} \tag{12.9}$$

Similar equivalences can be stated for the other connectives. For example, the conservation and reversibility principles for implication are given by these rules:

$$\frac{\Gamma, x : \phi_1 \vdash p_2 : \phi_2 \quad \Gamma \vdash p_2 : \phi_2}{\Gamma \vdash (\lambda\,(x)\,p_2)(p_1) \equiv [p_1/x]p_2 : \phi_2} \tag{12.10a}$$

$$\frac{\Gamma \vdash p : \phi_1 \supset \phi_2}{\Gamma \vdash \lambda\,(x)\,(p(x)) \equiv p : \phi_1 \supset \phi_2} \tag{12.10b}$$

The corresponding rules for disjunction and falsehood are given as follows:

$$\frac{\Gamma \vdash p : \phi_1 \vee \phi_2 \quad \Gamma, x_1 : \phi_1 \vdash p_1 : \psi \quad \Gamma, x_2 : \phi_2 \vdash p_2 : \psi}{\Gamma \vdash \mathtt{case}\,\mathtt{l} \cdot p \,\{\mathtt{l} \cdot x_1 \hookrightarrow p_1 \mid \mathtt{r} \cdot x_2 \hookrightarrow p_2\} \equiv [p/x_1]p_1 : \psi} \tag{12.11a}$$

$$\frac{\Gamma \vdash p : \phi_1 \vee \phi_2 \quad \Gamma, x_1 : \phi_1 \vdash p_1 : \psi \quad \Gamma, x_2 : \phi_2 \vdash p_2 : \psi}{\Gamma \vdash \mathtt{case}\,\mathtt{r} \cdot p \,\{\mathtt{l} \cdot x_1 \hookrightarrow p_1 \mid \mathtt{r} \cdot x_2 \hookrightarrow p_2\} \equiv [p/x_2]p_2 : \psi} \tag{12.11b}$$

$$\frac{\Gamma \vdash p : \phi_1 \vee \phi_2 \quad \Gamma, x : \phi_1 \vee \phi_2 \vdash q : \psi}{\Gamma \vdash [p/x]q \equiv \mathtt{case}\ p\ \{\mathbf{l} \cdot x_1 \hookrightarrow [\mathbf{l} \cdot x_1/x]q \mid \mathbf{r} \cdot x_2 \hookrightarrow [\mathbf{r} \cdot x_2/x]q\} : \psi} \tag{12.11c}$$

$$\frac{\Gamma \vdash p : \bot \quad \Gamma, x : \bot \vdash q : \psi}{\Gamma \vdash [p/x]q \equiv \mathtt{abort}(p) : \psi} \tag{12.11d}$$

12.4 Propositions as Types

Reviewing the statics and dynamics of proofs in constructive logic reveals a striking similarity to the statics and dynamics of expressions of various types. For example, the introduction rule for conjunction specifies that a proof of a conjunction consists of a pair of proofs, one for each conjunct, and the elimination rule inverts this, allowing us to extract a proof of each conjunct from any proof of a conjunction. There is an obvious analogy with the static semantics of product types, whose introduction form is a pair and whose elimination forms are projections. Gentzen's Principle extends the analogy to the dynamics as well, so that the elimination forms for conjunction amount to projections that extract the appropriate components from an ordered pair.

The following chart summarizes the correspondence between propositions and types and between proofs and programs:

Prop	Type
$\top$	$\mathtt{unit}$
$\bot$	$\mathtt{void}$
$\phi_1 \wedge \phi_2$	$\tau_1 \times \tau_2$
$\phi_1 \supset \phi_2$	$\tau_1 \rightarrow \tau_2$
$\phi_1 \vee \phi_2$	$\tau_1 + \tau_2$

The correspondence between propositions and types is a cornerstone of the theory of programming languages. It exposes a deep connection between computation and deduction, and serves as a framework for the analysis of language constructs and reasoning principles by relating them to one another.

12.5 Notes

The propositions as types principle has its origins in the semantics of intuitionistic logic developed by Brouwer, according to which the truth of a proposition is witnessed by a construction providing computable evidence for it. The forms of evidence are determined by the form of the proposition, so that evidence for an implication is a computable function transforming evidence for the hypothesis into evidence for the conclusion. An explicit formulation of this semantics was introduced by Heyting, and further developed by several people, including de Bruijn, Curry, Gentzen, Girard, Howard, Kolmogorov, Martin-Löf, and Tait. The propositions-as-types correspondence is sometimes called the *Curry-Howard*

Isomorphism, but this terminology neglects the crucial contributions of the others just mentioned. Moreover, the correspondence is not, in general, an isomorphism; rather, it expresses Brouwer's Dictum that the concept of proof is best explained by the more general concept of construction (program).

Exercises

12.1. The *law of the excluded middle (LEM)* is the statement that every proposition ϕ is *decidable* in the sense that $\phi \vee \neg\phi$ true. Constructively, the law of the excluded middle states that, for every proposition ϕ, we either have a proof of ϕ or a refutation of ϕ (proof of its negation). Because this is manifestly not the case in general, one may suspect that the law of the excluded middle is not constructively valid. This is so, but not in the sense that the law is *refuted*, but rather in the sense that it is *not affirmed*. First, any proposition ϕ for which we have a proof or a refutation is already decided, and so is decidable. Second, there are broad classes of propositions for which we can, on demand, produce a proof or a refutation. For example, it is decidable whether or not two integers are equal. Third, and most important, there are, and always will be, propositions ϕ whose status is unresolved: it may turn out that ϕ is true, or it may turn out that ϕ is false. For all these reasons, constructive logic *does not refute* the decidability propositions: $\neg\neg(\phi \vee \neg\phi)$ true for any proposition ϕ. Prove it using the rules given in this chapter.

12.2. The proposition $\neg\neg\phi$ is no stronger than ϕ: prove $\phi \supset \neg\neg\phi$ true. The *law of double-negation elimination (DNE)* states that $(\neg\neg\phi) \supset \phi$ true for every proposition ϕ. It follows immediately from Exercise **12.1** that DNE entails LEM; prove the converse.

12.3. Define the relation $\phi \le \psi$ to mean that ϕ true $\vdash \psi$ true according to the rules of constructive logic given above. With respect to this relation, show the following facts:

(a) It is a *pre-order*, which is say that it is reflexive and transitive.

(b) $\phi \wedge \psi$ is the *meet*, or *greatest lower bound*, of ϕ and ψ, and $\top$ is the *top*, or *greatest*, element.

(c) Show that $\phi \vee \psi$ is the *join*, or *least upper bound*, of ϕ and ψ, and that $\bot$ is the *bottom*, or *least*, element.

(d) Show that $\phi \supset \psi$ is an *exponential*, or *pseudo-complement*, in the sense that it is the *largest* ρ such that $\phi \wedge \rho \le \psi$. (The exponential $\phi \supset \psi$ is sometimes written ψ^ϕ.)

Altogether these facts state that entailment in constructive propositional logic forms a *Heyting algebra*. Show that a general Heyting algebra (that is, an ordering with the above structure) is *distributive* in the sense that

$$\phi \wedge (\psi_1 \vee \psi_2) \equiv (\phi \wedge \psi_1) \vee (\phi \wedge \psi_2)$$
$$\phi \vee (\psi_1 \wedge \psi_2) \equiv (\phi \vee \psi_1) \wedge (\phi \vee \psi_2),$$

where $\phi \equiv \psi$ means $\phi \le \psi$ and $\psi \le \phi$.

12.4. In any Heyting algebra, we have $\phi \wedge \neg\phi \leq \perp$, which is to say that the negation is inconsistent with the negated. But $\neg\phi$ is not necessarily the *complement* of ϕ in the sense that $\phi \vee \neg\phi \leq \top$. A *Boolean algebra* is a Heyting algebra in which negation is always the complement of the negated: $\top \leq \phi \vee \neg\phi$ for every ϕ. Check that the two-element Boolean algebra for which meets, joins, and exponentials are given by the classical truth tables (defining $\phi \supset \psi$ as $(\neg\phi) \vee \psi$ is Boolean algebra. Conclude that it is consistent to adjoin LEM to constructive logic, which is to say that classical logic is a special case of constructive logic in which we assume that every proposition is decidable. Being a Heyting algebra, every Boolean algebra is clearly distributive. Show that every Boolean algebra also satisfies the *de Morgan duality laws*:

$$\neg(\phi \vee \psi) \equiv \neg\phi \wedge \neg\psi$$
$$\neg(\phi \wedge \psi) \equiv \neg\phi \vee \neg\psi.$$

The first of these is valid in any Heyting algebra; the second only in a Boolean algebra.

13   Classical Logic

In constructive logic, a proposition is true exactly when it has a proof, a derivation of it from axioms and assumptions, and is false exactly when it has a refutation, a derivation of a contradiction from the assumption that it is true. Constructive logic is a logic of positive evidence. To affirm or deny a proposition requires a proof, either of the proposition itself, or of a contradiction, under the assumption that it has a proof. We are not always able to affirm or deny a proposition. An open problem is one for which we have neither a proof nor a refutation—constructively speaking, it is neither true nor false.

In contrast, classical logic (the one we learned in school) is a logic of perfect information where every proposition is either true or false. We may say that classical logic corresponds to "god's view" of the world—there are no open problems, rather all propositions are either true or false. Put another way, to assert that every proposition is either true or false is to weaken the notion of truth to encompass all that is not false, dually to the constructively (and classically) valid interpretation of falsity as all that is not true. The symmetry between truth and falsity is appealing, but there is a price to pay for this: the meanings of the logical connectives are weaker in the classical case than in the constructive.

The law of the excluded middle provides a prime example. Constructively, this principle is not universally valid, as we have seen in Exercise **12.1**. Classically, however, it is valid, because every proposition is either false or not false, and being not false is the same as being true. Nevertheless, classical logic is consistent with constructive logic in that constructive logic does not refute classical logic. As we have seen, constructive logic proves that the law of the excluded middle is positively not refuted (its double negation is constructively true). Consequently, constructive logic is stronger (more expressive) than classical logic, because it can express more distinctions (namely, between affirmation and irrefutability), and because it is consistent with classical logic.

Proofs in constructive logic have computational content: they can be executed as programs, and their behavior is described by their type. Proofs in classical logic also have computational content, but in a weaker sense than in constructive logic. Rather than positively affirm a proposition, a proof in classical logic is a computation that cannot be refuted. Computationally, a refutation consists of a continuation, or control stack, that takes a proof of a proposition and derives a contradiction from it. So a proof of a proposition in classical logic is a computation that, when given a refutation of that proposition derives a contradiction, witnessing the impossibility of refuting it. In this sense, the law of the excluded middle has a proof, precisely because it is irrefutable.

13.1 Classical Logic

In constructive logic, a connective is defined by giving its introduction and elimination
rules. In classical logic, a connective is defined by giving its truth and falsity conditions.
Its truth rules correspond to introduction, and its falsity rules to elimination. The symmetry
between truth and falsity is expressed by the principle of indirect proof. To show that ϕ true
it is enough to show that ϕ false entails a contradiction, and, conversely, to show that ϕ false
it is enough to show that ϕ true leads to a contradiction. Although the second of these is
constructively valid, the first is fundamentally classical, expressing the principle of indirect
proof.

13.1.1 Provability and Refutability

There are three basic judgment forms in classical logic:

1. ϕ true, stating that the proposition ϕ is provable;
2. ϕ false, stating that the proposition ϕ is refutable;
3. #, stating that a contradiction has been derived.

These are extended to hypothetical judgments in which we admit both provability and
refutability assumptions:

$$\phi_1 \text{ false}, \ldots, \phi_m \text{ false } \psi_1 \text{ true}, \ldots, \psi_n \text{ true} \vdash J.$$

The hypotheses are divided into two zones, one for falsity assumptions, Δ, and one for
truth assumptions, Γ.

The rules of classical logic are organized around the symmetry between truth and falsity,
which is mediated by the contradiction judgment.

The hypothetical judgment is reflexive:

$$\frac{}{\Delta, \phi \text{ false } \Gamma \vdash \phi \text{ false}} \qquad (13.1a)$$

$$\frac{}{\Delta \ \Gamma, \phi \text{ true} \vdash \phi \text{ true}} \qquad (13.1b)$$

The remaining rules are stated so that the structural properties of weakening, contraction,
and transitivity are admissible.

A contradiction arises when a proposition is judged both true and false. A proposition is
true if its falsity is absurd, and is false if its truth is absurd.

$$\frac{\Delta \ \Gamma \vdash \phi \text{ false} \quad \Delta \ \Gamma \vdash \phi \text{ true}}{\Delta \ \Gamma \vdash \#} \qquad (13.1c)$$

$$\frac{\Delta, \phi \text{ false } \Gamma \vdash \#}{\Delta \ \Gamma \vdash \phi \text{ true}} \qquad (13.1d)$$

$$\frac{\Delta \ \Gamma, \phi \text{ true} \vdash \#}{\Delta \ \Gamma \vdash \phi \text{ false}} \qquad (13.1e)$$

Truth is trivially true and cannot be refuted.

$$\overline{\Delta\ \Gamma \vdash \top\ \text{true}} \tag{13.1f}$$

A conjunction is true if both conjuncts are true and is false if either conjunct is false.

$$\frac{\Delta\ \Gamma \vdash \phi_1\ \text{true} \quad \Delta\ \Gamma \vdash \phi_2\ \text{true}}{\Delta\ \Gamma \vdash \phi_1 \wedge \phi_2\ \text{true}} \tag{13.1g}$$

$$\frac{\Delta\ \Gamma \vdash \phi_1\ \text{false}}{\Delta\ \Gamma \vdash \phi_1 \wedge \phi_2\ \text{false}} \tag{13.1h}$$

$$\frac{\Delta\ \Gamma \vdash \phi_2\ \text{false}}{\Delta\ \Gamma \vdash \phi_1 \wedge \phi_2\ \text{false}} \tag{13.1i}$$

Falsity is trivially false and cannot be proved.

$$\overline{\Delta\ \Gamma \vdash \bot\ \text{false}} \tag{13.1j}$$

A disjunction is true if either disjunct is true and is false if both disjuncts are false.

$$\frac{\Delta\ \Gamma \vdash \phi_1\ \text{true}}{\Delta\ \Gamma \vdash \phi_1 \vee \phi_2\ \text{true}} \tag{13.1k}$$

$$\frac{\Delta\ \Gamma \vdash \phi_2\ \text{true}}{\Delta\ \Gamma \vdash \phi_1 \vee \phi_2\ \text{true}} \tag{13.1l}$$

$$\frac{\Delta\ \Gamma \vdash \phi_1\ \text{false} \quad \Delta\ \Gamma \vdash \phi_2\ \text{false}}{\Delta\ \Gamma \vdash \phi_1 \vee \phi_2\ \text{false}} \tag{13.1m}$$

Negation inverts the sense of each judgment:

$$\frac{\Delta\ \Gamma \vdash \phi\ \text{false}}{\Delta\ \Gamma \vdash \neg\phi\ \text{true}} \tag{13.1n}$$

$$\frac{\Delta\ \Gamma \vdash \phi\ \text{true}}{\Delta\ \Gamma \vdash \neg\phi\ \text{false}} \tag{13.1o}$$

An implication is true if its conclusion is true when the assumption is true and is false if its conclusion is false yet its assumption is true.

$$\frac{\Delta\ \Gamma, \phi_1\ \text{true} \vdash \phi_2\ \text{true}}{\Delta\ \Gamma \vdash \phi_1 \supset \phi_2\ \text{true}} \tag{13.1p}$$

$$\frac{\Delta\ \Gamma \vdash \phi_1\ \text{true} \quad \Delta\ \Gamma \vdash \phi_2\ \text{false}}{\Delta\ \Gamma \vdash \phi_1 \supset \phi_2\ \text{false}} \tag{13.1q}$$

13.1.2 Proofs and Refutations

To explain the dynamics of classical proofs, we first introduce an explicit syntax for proofs and refutations. We will define three hypothetical judgments for classical logic with explicit derivations:

1. $\Delta\ \Gamma \vdash p : \phi$, stating that p is a proof of ϕ;

2. $\Delta\ \Gamma \vdash k \div \phi$, stating that k is a refutation of ϕ;

3. $\Delta\ \Gamma \vdash k \# p$, stating that k and p are contradictory.

The falsity assumptions Δ are given by a context of the form

$$u_1 \div \phi_1, \ldots, u_m \div \phi_m,$$

where $m \geq 0$, in which the variables $u_1, \ldots, u_n$ stand for refutations. The truth assumptions Γ are given by a context of the form

$$x_1 : \psi_1, \ldots, x_n : \psi_n,$$

where $n \geq 0$, in which the variables $x_1, \ldots, x_n$ stand for proofs.

The syntax of proofs and refutations is given by the following grammar:

Prf	p	::=	true-T	$\langle\rangle$	truth
			and-T$(p_1; p_2)$	$\langle p_1, p_2 \rangle$	conjunction
			or-T[l](p)	$1 \cdot p$	disjunction left
			or-T[r](p)	$r \cdot p$	disjunction right
			not-T(k)	not(k)	negation
			imp-T$(x.p)$	$\lambda(x)\,p$	implication
			ccr$(u.(k \# p))$	ccr$(u.(k \# p))$	contradiction
Ref	k	::=	false-F	abort	falsehood
			and-F[l](k)	fst $; k$	conjunction left
			and-F[r](k)	snd $; k$	conjunction right
			or-F$(k_1; k_2)$	case$(k_1; k_2)$	disjunction
			not-F(p)	not(p)	negation
			imp-F$(p; k)$	ap$(p) ; k$	implication
			ccp$(x.(k \# p))$	ccp$(x.(k \# p))$	contradiction

Proofs serve as evidence for truth judgments, and refutations serve as evidence for false judgments. Contradictions are witnessed by the juxtaposition of a proof and a refutation.

A contradiction arises when a proposition is both true and false:

$$\frac{\Delta\ \Gamma \vdash k \div \phi \quad \Delta\ \Gamma \vdash p : \phi}{\Delta\ \Gamma \vdash k \# p} \tag{13.2a}$$

Truth and falsity are defined symmetrically in terms of contradiction:

$$\frac{\Delta, u \div \phi\ \Gamma \vdash k \# p}{\Delta\ \Gamma \vdash \text{ccr}(u.(k \# p)) : \phi} \tag{13.2b}$$

$$\frac{\Delta\ \Gamma, x : \phi \vdash k \# p}{\Delta\ \Gamma \vdash \text{ccp}(x.(k \# p)) \div \phi} \tag{13.2c}$$

Reflexivity corresponds to the use of a variable hypothesis:

$$\frac{}{\Delta, u \div \phi\ \Gamma \vdash u \div \phi} \tag{13.2d}$$

$$\frac{}{\Delta\ \Gamma, x : \phi \vdash x : \phi} \tag{13.2e}$$

The other structure properties are admissible.

Truth is trivially true and cannot be refuted.

$$\overline{\Delta\ \Gamma \vdash \langle\rangle : \top} \tag{13.2f}$$

A conjunction is true if both conjuncts are true and is false if either conjunct is false.

$$\frac{\Delta\ \Gamma \vdash p_1 : \phi_1 \quad \Delta\ \Gamma \vdash p_2 : \phi_2}{\Delta\ \Gamma \vdash \langle p_1, p_2 \rangle : \phi_1 \wedge \phi_2} \tag{13.2g}$$

$$\frac{\Delta\ \Gamma \vdash k_1 \div \phi_1}{\Delta\ \Gamma \vdash \mathtt{fst}\,;k_1 \div \phi_1 \wedge \phi_2} \tag{13.2h}$$

$$\frac{\Delta\ \Gamma \vdash k_2 \div \phi_2}{\Delta\ \Gamma \vdash \mathtt{snd}\,;k_2 \div \phi_1 \wedge \phi_2} \tag{13.2i}$$

Falsity is trivially false and cannot be proved.

$$\overline{\Delta\ \Gamma \vdash \mathtt{abort} \div \bot} \tag{13.2j}$$

A disjunction is true if either disjunct is true and is false if both disjuncts are false.

$$\frac{\Delta\ \Gamma \vdash p_1 : \phi_1}{\Delta\ \Gamma \vdash 1 \cdot p_1 : \phi_1 \vee \phi_2} \tag{13.2k}$$

$$\frac{\Delta\ \Gamma \vdash p_2 : \phi_2}{\Delta\ \Gamma \vdash \mathtt{r} \cdot p_2 : \phi_1 \vee \phi_2} \tag{13.2l}$$

$$\frac{\Delta\ \Gamma \vdash k_1 \div \phi_1 \quad \Delta\ \Gamma \vdash k_2 \div \phi_2}{\Delta\ \Gamma \vdash \mathtt{case}(k_1;k_2) \div \phi_1 \vee \phi_2} \tag{13.2m}$$

Negation inverts the sense of each judgment:

$$\frac{\Delta\ \Gamma \vdash k \div \phi}{\Delta\ \Gamma \vdash \mathtt{not}(k) : \neg\phi} \tag{13.2n}$$

$$\frac{\Delta\ \Gamma \vdash p : \phi}{\Delta\ \Gamma \vdash \mathtt{not}(p) \div \neg\phi} \tag{13.2o}$$

An implication is true if its conclusion is true when the assumption is true and is false if its conclusion is false, yet its assumption is true.

$$\frac{\Delta\ \Gamma, x : \phi_1 \vdash p_2 : \phi_2}{\Delta\ \Gamma \vdash \lambda\,(x)\,p_2 : \phi_1 \supset \phi_2} \tag{13.2p}$$

$$\frac{\Delta\ \Gamma \vdash p_1 : \phi_1 \quad \Delta\ \Gamma \vdash k_2 \div \phi_2}{\Delta\ \Gamma \vdash \mathtt{ap}(p_1)\,;k_2 \div \phi_1 \supset \phi_2} \tag{13.2q}$$

13.2 Deriving Elimination Forms

The price of achieving a symmetry between truth and falsity in classical logic is that we must very often rely on the principle of indirect proof: to show that a proposition is true, we often must derive a contradiction from the assumption of its falsity. For example, a proof of

$$(\phi \wedge (\psi \wedge \theta)) \supset (\theta \wedge \phi)$$

in classical logic has the form

$$\lambda(w) \, \mathtt{ccr}(u.(k \,\#\, w)),$$

where k is the refutation

$$\mathtt{fst} \,;\, \mathtt{ccp}(x.(\mathtt{snd} \,;\, \mathtt{ccp}(y.(\mathtt{snd} \,;\, \mathtt{ccp}(z.(u \,\#\, \langle z, x \rangle)) \,\#\, y)) \,\#\, w)).$$

And yet in constructive logic this proposition has a direct proof that avoids the circumlocutions of proof by contradiction:

$$\lambda(w) \, \langle w \cdot \mathtt{r} \cdot \mathtt{r}, \, w \cdot \mathtt{l} \rangle.$$

But this proof cannot be expressed (as is) in classical logic, because classical logic lacks the elimination forms of constructive logic.

However, we may package the use of indirect proof into a slightly more palatable form by deriving the elimination rules of constructive logic. For example, the rule

$$\frac{\Delta \; \Gamma \vdash \phi \wedge \psi \; \mathsf{true}}{\Delta \; \Gamma \vdash \phi \; \mathsf{true}}$$

is derivable in classical logic:

$$\frac{\dfrac{\Delta, \phi \; \mathsf{false} \; \Gamma \vdash \phi \; \mathsf{false}}{\Delta, \phi \; \mathsf{false} \; \Gamma \vdash \phi \wedge \psi \; \mathsf{false}} \quad \dfrac{\Delta \; \Gamma \vdash \phi \wedge \psi \; \mathsf{true}}{\Delta, \phi \; \mathsf{false} \; \Gamma \vdash \phi \wedge \psi \; \mathsf{true}}}{\dfrac{\Delta, \phi \; \mathsf{false} \; \Gamma \vdash \#}{\Delta \; \Gamma \vdash \phi \; \mathsf{true}}}$$

The other elimination forms are derivable similarly, in each case relying on indirect proof to construct a proof of the truth of a proposition from a derivation of a contradiction from the assumption of its falsity.

The derivations of the elimination forms of constructive logic are most easily exhibited using proof and refutation expressions, as follows:

$$\mathtt{abort}(p) = \mathtt{ccr}(u.(\mathtt{abort} \,\#\, p))$$

$$p \cdot \mathtt{l} = \mathtt{ccr}(u.(\mathtt{fst} \,;\, u \,\#\, p))$$

$$p \cdot \mathtt{r} = \mathtt{ccr}(u.(\mathtt{snd} \,;\, u \,\#\, p))$$

$$p_1(p_2) = \mathtt{ccr}(u.(\mathtt{ap}(p_2) \,;\, u \,\#\, p_1))$$

$$\mathtt{case} \; p_1 \; \{ \mathtt{l} \cdot x \hookrightarrow p_2 \mid \mathtt{r} \cdot y \hookrightarrow p \} = \mathtt{ccr}(u.(\mathtt{case}(\mathtt{ccp}(x.(u \,\#\, p_2)) \,;\, \mathtt{ccp}(y.(u \,\#\, p))) \,\#\, p_1))$$

The expected elimination rules are valid for these definitions. For example, the rule

$$\frac{\Delta\ \Gamma \vdash p_1 : \phi \supset \psi \quad \Delta\ \Gamma \vdash p_2 : \phi}{\Delta\ \Gamma \vdash p_1(p_2) : \psi} \tag{13.3}$$

is derivable using the definition of $p_1(p_2)$ given above. By suppressing proof terms, we may derive the corresponding provability rule

$$\frac{\Delta\ \Gamma \vdash \phi \supset \psi \text{ true} \quad \Delta\ \Gamma \vdash \phi \text{ true}}{\Delta\ \Gamma \vdash \psi \text{ true}}. \tag{13.4}$$

13.3 Proof Dynamics

The dynamics of classical logic arises from the simplification of the contradiction between a proof and a refutation of a proposition. To make this explicit, we will define a transition system whose states are contradictions $k \# p$ consisting of a proof p and a refutation k of the same proposition. The steps of the computation consist of simplifications of the contradictory state based on the form of p and k.

The truth and falsity rules for the connectives play off one another in a pleasing way:

$$\mathtt{fst}; k \# \langle p_1, p_2 \rangle \longmapsto k \# p_1 \tag{13.5a}$$

$$\mathtt{snd}; k \# \langle p_1, p_2 \rangle \longmapsto k \# p_2 \tag{13.5b}$$

$$\mathtt{case}(k_1; k_2) \# \mathtt{l} \cdot p_1 \longmapsto k_1 \# p_1 \tag{13.5c}$$

$$\mathtt{case}(k_1; k_2) \# \mathtt{r} \cdot p_2 \longmapsto k_2 \# p_2 \tag{13.5d}$$

$$\mathtt{not}(p) \# \mathtt{not}(k) \longmapsto k \# p \tag{13.5e}$$

$$\mathtt{ap}(p_1); k \# \lambda(x) p_2 \longmapsto k \# [p_1/x]p_2 \tag{13.5f}$$

The rules of indirect proof give rise to the following transitions:

$$\mathtt{ccp}(x.(k_1 \# p_1)) \# p_2 \longmapsto [p_2/x]k_1 \# [p_2/x]p_1 \tag{13.5g}$$

$$k_1 \# \mathtt{ccr}(u.(k_2 \# p_2)) \longmapsto [k_1/u]k_2 \# [k_1/u]p_2 \tag{13.5h}$$

The first of these defines the behavior of the refutation of ϕ that proceeds by contradicting the assumption that ϕ is true. Such a refutation is activated by presenting it with a proof of ϕ, which is then substituted for the assumption in the new state. Thus, "ccp" stands for "call with current proof." The second transition defines the behavior of the proof of ϕ that proceeds by contradicting the assumption that ϕ is false. Such a proof is activated by presenting it with a refutation of ϕ, which is then substituted for the assumption in the new state. Thus, "ccr" stands for "call with current refutation."

Rules (13.5g) to (13.5h) overlap in that there are two transitions for a state of the form

$$\mathtt{ccp}(x.(k_1 \# p_1)) \# \mathtt{ccr}(u.(k_2 \# p_2)),$$

one to the state $[p/x]k_1 \# [p/x]p_1$, where p is $\mathtt{ccr}(u.(k_2 \# p_2))$, and one to the state $[k/u]k_2 \# [k/u]p_2$, where k is $\mathtt{ccp}(x.(k_1 \# p_1))$. The dynamics of classical logic is non-deterministic. To avoid this one may impose a priority ordering among the two cases, preferring one transition over the other when there is a choice. Preferring the first corresponds to a "lazy" dynamics for proofs, because we pass the unevaluated proof p to the refutation on the left, which is thereby activated. Preferring the second corresponds to an "eager" dynamics for proofs, in which we pass the unevaluated refutation k to the proof, which is thereby activated.

All proofs in classical logic proceed by contradicting the assumption that it is false. In terms of the classical logic machine the initial and final states of a computation are as follows:

$$\frac{}{\texttt{halt}_\phi \ \# \ p \ \text{initial}} \tag{13.6a}$$

$$\frac{p \ \text{canonical}}{\texttt{halt}_\phi \ \# \ p \ \text{final}} \tag{13.6b}$$

where p is a proof of ϕ, and $\texttt{halt}_\phi$ is the assumed refutation of ϕ. The judgment p canonical states that p is a canonical proof, which holds of any proof other than an indirect proof. Execution consists of driving a general proof to a canonical proof, under the assumption that the theorem is false.

Theorem 13.1 (Preservation). *If $k \div \phi$, $p : \phi$, and $k \ \# \ p \longmapsto k' \ \# \ p'$, then there exists ϕ' such that $k' \div \phi'$ and $p' : \phi'$.*

Proof   By rule induction on the dynamics of classical logic.   □

Theorem 13.2 (Progress). *If $k \div \phi$ and $p : \phi$, then either $k \ \# \ p$ final or $k \ \# \ p \longmapsto k' \ \# \ p'$.*

Proof   By rule induction on the statics of classical logic.   □

13.4 Law of the Excluded Middle

The law of the excluded middle is derivable in classical logic:

$$\frac{\dfrac{\dfrac{\dfrac{\dfrac{\dfrac{\dfrac{\dfrac{\phi \vee \neg\phi \ \text{false}, \phi \ \text{true} \vdash \phi \ \text{true}}{\phi \vee \neg\phi \ \text{false}, \phi \ \text{true} \vdash \phi \vee \neg\phi \ \text{true}} \quad \phi \vee \neg\phi \ \text{false}, \phi \ \text{true} \vdash \phi \vee \neg\phi \ \text{false}}{\phi \vee \neg\phi \ \text{false}, \phi \ \text{true} \vdash \#}}{\phi \vee \neg\phi \ \text{false} \vdash \phi \ \text{false}}}{\phi \vee \neg\phi \ \text{false} \vdash \neg\phi \ \text{true}}}{\phi \vee \neg\phi \ \text{false} \vdash \phi \vee \neg\phi \ \text{true}} \quad \phi \vee \neg\phi \ \text{false} \vdash \phi \vee \neg\phi \ \text{false}}{\phi \vee \neg\phi \ \text{false} \vdash \#}}{\phi \vee \neg\phi \ \text{true}}$$

When written out using explicit proofs and refutations, we obtain the proof term p_0 : $\phi \vee \neg\phi$:

$$\text{ccr}(u.(u \# r \cdot \text{not}(\text{ccp}(x.(u \# 1 \cdot x)))))).$$

To understand the computational meaning of this proof, let us juxtapose it with a refutation $k \div \phi \vee \neg\phi$ and simplify it using the dynamics given in Section 13.3. The first step is the transition

$$k \# \text{ccr}(u.(u \# r \cdot \text{not}(\text{ccp}(x.(u \# 1 \cdot x)))))$$
$$\longmapsto$$
$$k \# r \cdot \text{not}(\text{ccp}(x.(k \# 1 \cdot x))),$$

wherein we have replicated k so that it occurs in two places in the result state. By virtue of its type, the refutation k must have the form $\text{case}(k_1; k_2)$, where $k_1 \div \phi$ and $k_2 \div \neg\phi$. Continuing the reduction, we obtain:

$$\text{case}(k_1; k_2) \# r \cdot \text{not}(\text{ccp}(x.(\text{case}(k_1; k_2) \# 1 \cdot x)))$$
$$\longmapsto$$
$$k_2 \# \text{not}(\text{ccp}(x.(\text{case}(k_1; k_2) \# 1 \cdot x))).$$

By virtue of its type k_2 must have the form $\text{not}(p_2)$, where $p_2 : \phi$, and hence the transition proceeds as follows:

$$\text{not}(p_2) \# \text{not}(\text{ccp}(x.(\text{case}(k_1; k_2) \# 1 \cdot x)))$$
$$\longmapsto$$
$$\text{ccp}(x.(\text{case}(k_1; k_2) \# 1 \cdot x)) \# p_2.$$

Observe that p_2 is a valid proof of ϕ. Proceeding, we obtain

$$\text{ccp}(x.(\text{case}(k_1; k_2) \# 1 \cdot x)) \# p_2$$
$$\longmapsto$$
$$\text{case}(k_1; k_2) \# 1 \cdot p_2$$
$$\longmapsto$$
$$k_1 \# p_2$$

The first of these two steps is the crux of the matter: the refutation, $k = \text{case}(k_1; k_2)$, which was replicated at the outset of the derivation, is re-used, but with a different argument. At the first use, the refutation k which is provided by the context of use of the law of the excluded middle, is presented with a proof $r \cdot p_1$ of $\phi \vee \neg\phi$. That is, the proof behaves as though the right disjunct of the law is true, which is to say that ϕ is false. If the context is such that it inspects this proof, it can only be by providing the proof p_2 of ϕ that refutes the claim that ϕ is false. Should this occur, the proof of the law of the excluded middle "backtracks" the context, providing instead the proof $1 \cdot p_2$ to k, which then passes p_2 to k_1 without further incident. The proof of the law of the excluded middle boldly asserts

$\neg\phi$ true, regardless of the form of ϕ. Then, if caught in its lie by the context providing a proof of ϕ, it "changes its mind" and asserts ϕ to the original context k after all. No further reversion is possible, because the context has itself provided a proof p_2 of ϕ.

The law of the excluded middle illustrates that classical proofs are interactions between proofs and refutations, which is to say interactions between a proof and the context in which it is used. In programming terms, this corresponds to an abstract machine with an explicit control stack, or continuation, representing the context of evaluation of an expression. That expression may access the context (stack, continuation) to backtrack so as to maintain the perfect symmetry between truth and falsity. The penalty is that a closed proof of a disjunction no longer need show which disjunct it proves, for as we have just seen, it may, on further inspection, "change its mind."

13.5 The Double-Negation Translation

One consequence of the greater expressiveness of constructive logic is that classical proofs may be translated systematically into constructive proofs of a classically equivalent proposition. Therefore, by systematically reorganizing the classical proof, we may, without changing its meaning from a classical perspective, turn it into a constructive proof of a constructively weaker proposition. Consequently, there is no loss in adhering to constructive proofs, because every classical proof is a constructive proof of a constructively weaker, but classically equivalent, proposition. Moreover, it proves that classical logic is weaker (less expressive) than constructive logic, contrary to a naïve interpretation which would say that the added reasoning principles, such as the law of the excluded middle, afforded by classical logic makes it stronger. In programming language terms adding a "feature" does not necessarily strengthen (improve the expressive power) of your language; on the contrary, it may weaken it.

We will define a translation ϕ^* of propositions that interprets classical into constructive logic according to the following correspondences:

Classical	*Constructive*	
$\Delta\ \Gamma \vdash \phi$ true	$\neg\Delta^*\ \Gamma^* \vdash \neg\neg\phi^*$ true	truth
$\Delta\ \Gamma \vdash \phi$ false	$\neg\Delta^*\ \Gamma^* \vdash \neg\phi^*$ true	falsity
$\Delta\ \Gamma \vdash \#$	$\neg\Delta^*\ \Gamma^* \vdash \bot$ true	contradiction

Classical truth is weakened to constructive irrefutability, but classical falsehood is constructive refutability, and classical contradiction is constructive falsehood. Falsity assumptions are negated after translation to express their falsehood; truth assumptions are merely translated as is. Because the double negations are classically cancelable, the translation will be easily seen to yield a classically equivalent proposition. But because $\neg\neg\phi$ is constructively weaker than ϕ, we also see that a proof in classical logic is translated to a constructive proof of a weaker statement.

There are many choices for the translation; here is one that makes the proof of the correspondence between classical and constructive logic especially simple:

$$\top^* = \top$$
$$(\phi_1 \wedge \phi_2)^* = \phi_1^* \wedge \phi_2^*$$
$$\bot^* = \bot$$
$$(\phi_1 \vee \phi_2)^* = \phi_1^* \vee \phi_2^*$$
$$(\phi_1 \supset \phi_2)^* = \phi_1^* \supset \neg\neg\phi_2^*$$
$$(\neg\phi)^* = \neg\phi^*$$

One may show by induction on the rules of classical logic that the correspondences summarized above hold, using constructively valid entailments such as

$$\neg\neg\phi \text{ true} \, \neg\neg\psi \text{ true} \vdash \neg\neg(\phi \wedge \psi) \text{ true}.$$

13.6 Notes

The computational interpretation of classical logic was first explored by Griffin (1990) and Murthy (1991). The present account is influenced by Wadler (2003), transposed by Nanevski from sequent calculus to natural deduction using multiple forms of judgment. The terminology is inspired by Lakatos (1976), an insightful and inspiring analysis of the discovery of proofs and refutations of conjectures in mathematics. Versions of the double-negation translation were originally given by Gödel and Gentzen. The computational content of the double-negation translation was first elucidated by Murthy (1991), who established the important relationship with continuation passing.

Exercises

13.1. If the continuation type expresses negation, the types shown to be inhabited in Exercise **30.2**, when interpreted under the proposition-as-types interpretation, look suspiciously like the following propositions:

(a) $\phi \vee \neg\phi$.

(b) $(\neg\neg\phi) \supset \phi$.

(c) $(\neg\phi_2 \supset \neg\phi_1) \supset (\phi_1 \supset \phi_2)$.

(d) $\neg(\phi_1 \vee \phi_2) \supset (\neg\phi_1 \wedge \neg\phi_2)$.

None of these propositions is true, in general, in constructive logic. Show that each of these propositions is true in classical logic by exhibiting a proof term for each. (The first one is done for you in Section 13.4; you need only do the other three.) Compare the proof term you get for each with the inhabitant of the corresponding type that you gave in your solution to Exercise **30.2**.

13.2. Complete the proof of the double-negation interpretation sketched in Section 13.5, providing explicit proof terms for clarity. Because $(\phi \vee \neg\phi)^* = \phi^* \vee \neg\phi^*$, the double-negation translation applied to the proof of LEM (for ϕ) given in Section 13.4 yields a proof of the double negation of LEM (for ϕ^*) in constructive logic. How does the translated proof compare to the one you derived by hand in Exercise **12.1**?

PART VI

Infinite Data Types

14 Generic Programming

14.1 Introduction

Many programs are instances of a pattern in a particular situation. Sometimes types determine the pattern by a technique called *(type) generic* programming. For example, in Chapter 9, recursion over the natural numbers is introduced in an *ad hoc* way. As we shall see, the pattern of recursion on values of an inductive type is expressed as a generic program.

To get a flavor of the concept, consider a function f of type $\rho \to \rho'$, which transforms values of type ρ into values of type ρ'. For example, f might be the doubling function on natural numbers. We wish to extend f to a transformation from type $[\rho/t]\tau$ to type $[\rho'/t]\tau$ by applying f to various spots in the input, where a value of type ρ occurs to obtain a value of type ρ', leaving the rest of the data structure alone. For example, τ might be $\text{bool} \times t$, in which case f could be extended to a function of type $\text{bool} \times \rho \to \text{bool} \times \rho'$ that sends the pairs $\langle a, b \rangle$ to the pair $\langle a, f(b) \rangle$.

The foregoing example glosses over an ambiguity arising from the many-one nature of substitution. A type can have the form $[\rho/t]\tau$ in many different ways, according to how many occurrences of t there are within τ. Given f as above, it is not clear how to extend it to a function from $[\rho/t]\tau$ to $[\rho'/t]\tau$. To resolve the ambiguity, we must be given a template that marks the occurrences of t in τ at which f is applied. Such a template is known as a *type operator*, $t.\tau$, which is an abstractor binding a type variable t within a type τ. Given such an abstractor, we may unambiguously extend f to instances of τ given by substitution for t in τ.

The power of generic programming depends on the type operators that are allowed. The simplest case is that of a *polynomial* type operator, one constructed from sum and product of types, including their nullary forms. These are extended to *positive* type operators, which also allow certain forms of function types.

14.2 Polynomial Type Operators

A *type operator* is a type equipped with a designated variable whose occurrences mark the spots in the type where a transformation is applied. A type operator is an abstractor $t.\tau$ such that $t \text{ type} \vdash \tau \text{ type}$. An example of a type operator is the abstractor

$$t.\text{unit} + (\text{bool} \times t)$$

in which occurrences of t mark the spots in which a transformation is applied. An *instance* of the type operator $t.\tau$ is obtained by substituting a type ρ for the variable t within the type τ.

The *polynomial* type operators are those constructed from the type variable t the types void and unit, and the product and sum type constructors $\tau_1 \times \tau_2$ and $\tau_1 + \tau_2$. More precisely, the judgment $t.\tau$ poly is inductively defined by the following rules:

$$\frac{}{t.t \text{ poly}} \tag{14.1a}$$

$$\frac{}{t.\text{unit poly}} \tag{14.1b}$$

$$\frac{t.\tau_1 \text{ poly} \quad t.\tau_2 \text{ poly}}{t.\tau_1 \times \tau_2 \text{ poly}} \tag{14.1c}$$

$$\frac{}{t.\text{void poly}} \tag{14.1d}$$

$$\frac{t.\tau_1 \text{ poly} \quad t.\tau_2 \text{ poly}}{t.\tau_1 + \tau_2 \text{ poly}} \tag{14.1e}$$

Exercise **14.1** asks for a proof that polynomial type operators are closed under substitution.

Polynomial type operators are templates describing the structure of a data structure with slots for values of a particular type. For example, the type operator $t.t \times (\text{nat} + t)$ specifies all types $\rho \times (\text{nat} + \rho)$ for any choice of type ρ. Thus a polynomial type operator designates points of interest in a data structure that have a common type. As we shall see shortly, this allows us to specify a program that applies a given function to all values lying at points of interest in a compound data structure to obtain a new one with the results of the applications at those points. Because substitution is not injective, one cannot recover the type operator from its instances. For example, if ρ were nat, then the instance would be $\text{nat} \times (\text{nat} + \text{nat})$; it is impossible to know which occurrences of nat are in designated spots unless we are given the pattern by the type operator.

The *generic extension* of a polynomial type operator is a form of expression with the following syntax

$$\text{Exp} \quad e \quad ::= \quad \text{map}\{t.\tau\}(x.e')(e) \quad \text{map}\{t.\tau\}(x.e')(e) \quad \text{generic extension.}$$

Its statics is given as follows:

$$\frac{t.\tau \text{ poly} \quad \Gamma, x : \rho \vdash e' : \rho' \quad \Gamma \vdash e : [\rho/t]\tau}{\Gamma \vdash \text{map}\{t.\tau\}(x.e')(e) : [\rho'/t]\tau} \tag{14.2}$$

The abstractor $x.e'$ specifies a mapping that sends $x : \rho$ to $e' : \rho'$. The generic extension of $t.\tau$ along $x.e'$ specifies a mapping from $[\rho/t]\tau$ to $[\rho'/t]\tau$. The latter mapping replaces values v of type ρ occurring at spots corresponding to occurrences of t in τ by the transformed value $[v/x]e'$ of type ρ' at the same spot. The type operator $t.\tau$ is a template in which certain spots, marked by occurrences of t, show where to apply the transformation $x.e'$ to a value of type $[\rho/t]\tau$ to obtain a value of type $[\rho'/t]\tau$.

The following dynamics makes precise the concept of the generic extension of a polynomial type operator.

$$\frac{}{\mathtt{map}\{t.t\}(x.e')(e) \longmapsto [e/x]e'} \tag{14.3a}$$

$$\frac{}{\mathtt{map}\{t.\mathtt{unit}\}(x.e')(e) \longmapsto e} \tag{14.3b}$$

$$\frac{}{\begin{array}{c}\mathtt{map}\{t.\tau_1 \times \tau_2\}(x.e')(e) \\ \longmapsto \\ \langle \mathtt{map}\{t.\tau_1\}(x.e')(e \cdot \mathtt{l}), \mathtt{map}\{t.\tau_2\}(x.e')(e \cdot \mathtt{r}) \rangle\end{array}} \tag{14.3c}$$

$$\frac{}{\mathtt{map}\{t.\mathtt{void}\}(x.e')(e) \longmapsto \mathtt{abort}(e)} \tag{14.3d}$$

$$\frac{}{\begin{array}{c}\mathtt{map}\{t.\tau_1 + \tau_2\}(x.e')(e) \\ \longmapsto \\ \mathtt{case}\, e \, \{\mathtt{l} \cdot x_1 \hookrightarrow \mathtt{l} \cdot \mathtt{map}\{t.\tau_1\}(x.e')(x_1) \mid \mathtt{r} \cdot x_2 \hookrightarrow \mathtt{r} \cdot \mathtt{map}\{t.\tau_2\}(x.e')(x_2)\}\end{array}} \tag{14.3e}$$

Rule (14.3a) applies the transformation $x.e'$ to e itself, because the operator $t.t$ specifies that the transformation is performed directly. Rule (14.3b) states that the empty tuple is transformed to itself. Rule (14.3c) states that to transform e according to the operator $t.\tau_1 \times \tau_2$, the first component of e is transformed according to $t.\tau_1$ and the second component of e is transformed according to $t.\tau_2$. Rule (14.3d) states that the transformation of a value of type $\mathtt{void}$ aborts, because there are no such values. Rule (14.3e) states that to transform e according to $t.\tau_1 + \tau_2$, case analyze e and reconstruct it after transforming the injected value according to $t.\tau_1$ or $t.\tau_2$.

Consider the type operator $t.\tau$ given by $t.\mathtt{unit} + (\mathtt{bool} \times t)$. Let $x.e$ be the abstractor $x.\mathtt{s}(x)$, which increments a natural number. Using rules (14.3) we may derive that

$$\mathtt{map}\{t.\tau\}(x.e)(\mathtt{r} \cdot \langle \mathtt{true}, n \rangle) \longmapsto^* \mathtt{r} \cdot \langle \mathtt{true}, n + 1 \rangle.$$

The natural number in the second component of the pair is incremented, because the type variable t occurs in that spot in the type operator $t.\tau$.

Theorem 14.1 (Preservation). *If* $\mathtt{map}\{t.\tau\}(x.e')(e) : \tau'$ *and* $\mathtt{map}\{t.\tau\}(x.e')(e) \longmapsto e''$, *then* $e'' : \tau'$.

Proof By inversion of rule (14.2), we have

1. t type $\vdash \tau$ type;
2. $x : \rho \vdash e' : \rho'$ for some ρ and ρ';

3. $e : [\rho/t]\tau$;

4. τ' is $[\rho'/t]\tau$.

The proof proceeds by cases on rules (14.3). For example, consider rule (14.3c). It follows from inversion that $\mathtt{map}\{t.\tau_1\}(x.e')(e \cdot \mathtt{l}) : [\rho'/t]\tau_1$, and similarly that $\mathtt{map}\{t.\tau_2\}(x.e')(e \cdot \mathtt{r}) : [\rho'/t]\tau_2$. It is easy to check that

$$\langle \mathtt{map}\{t.\tau_1\}(x.e')(e \cdot \mathtt{l}), \mathtt{map}\{t.\tau_2\}(x.e')(e \cdot \mathtt{r}) \rangle$$

has type $[\rho'/t](\tau_1 \times \tau_2)$, as required. $\square$

14.3 Positive Type Operators

The *positive* type operators extend the polynomial type operators to admit restricted forms of function type. Specifically, $t.\tau_1 \to \tau_2$ is a positive type operator, if (1) t *does not occur* in τ_1, and (2) $t.\tau_2$ is a positive type operator. In general, any occurrences of a type variable t in the domain of a function type are *negative occurrences*, whereas any occurrences of t within the range of a function type, or within a product or sum type, are *positive occurrences*.[1] A positive type operator is one for which only positive occurrences of the type variable t are allowed. Positive type operators, like polynomial type operators, are closed under substitution.

We define the judgment $t.\tau$ pos, which states that the abstractor $t.\tau$ is a positive type operator by the following rules:

$$\frac{}{t.t \text{ pos}} \tag{14.4a}$$

$$\frac{}{t.\mathtt{unit} \text{ pos}} \tag{14.4b}$$

$$\frac{t.\tau_1 \text{ pos} \quad t.\tau_2 \text{ pos}}{t.\tau_1 \times \tau_2 \text{ pos}} \tag{14.4c}$$

$$\frac{}{t.\mathtt{void} \text{ pos}} \tag{14.4d}$$

$$\frac{t.\tau_1 \text{ pos} \quad t.\tau_2 \text{ pos}}{t.\tau_1 + \tau_2 \text{ pos}} \tag{14.4e}$$

$$\frac{\tau_1 \text{ type} \quad t.\tau_2 \text{ pos}}{t.\tau_1 \to \tau_2 \text{ pos}} \tag{14.4f}$$

In rule (14.4f), the type variable t is excluded from the domain of the function type by demanding that it be well-formed without regard to t.

The generic extension of a positive type operator is defined similarly to that of a polynomial type operator, with the following dynamics on function types:

$$\frac{}{\mathtt{map}^+\{t.\tau_1 \to \tau_2\}(x.e')(e) \longmapsto \lambda\,(x_1 : \tau_1)\,\mathtt{map}^+\{t.\tau_2\}(x.e')(e(x_1))} \tag{14.5}$$

Because t is not allowed to occur within the domain type, the type of the result is $\tau_1 \to [\rho'/t]\tau_2$, assuming that e is of type $\tau_1 \to [\rho/t]\tau_2$. It is easy to verify preservation for the generic extension of a positive type operator.

It is instructive to consider what goes wrong if we try to extend the generic extension to an arbitrary type operator, without any positivity restriction. Consider the type operator $t.\tau_1 \to \tau_2$, without restriction on t, and suppose that $x : \rho \vdash e' : \rho'$. The generic extension $\mathtt{map}\{t.\tau_1 \to \tau_2\}(x.e')(e)$ should have type $[\rho'/t]\tau_1 \to [\rho'/t]\tau_2$, given that e has type $[\rho/t]\tau_1 \to [\rho/t]\tau_2$. The extension should yield a function of the form

$$\lambda\,(x_1 : [\rho'/t]\tau_1)\dots(e(\dots(x_1)))$$

in which we apply e to a transformation of x_1 and then transform the result. The trouble is that we are given, inductively, that $\mathtt{map}\{t.\tau_1\}(x.e')(-)$ transforms values of type $[\rho/t]\tau_1$ into values of type $[\rho'/t]\tau_1$, but *we need to go the other way around* to make x_1 suitable as an argument for e.

14.4 Notes

The generic extension of a type operator is an example of the concept of a *functor* in category theory (MacLane, 1998). Generic programming is essentially *functorial* programming, exploiting the functorial action of polynomial type operators (Hinze and Jeuring, 2003).

Exercises

14.1. Prove that if $t.\tau$ poly and $t'.\tau'$ poly, then $t.[\tau/t']\tau'$ poly.

14.2. Show that the generic extension of a constant type operator is essentially the identity in that it sends each closed value to itself. More precisely, show that, for each value e of type τ, the expression

$$\mathtt{map}\{\_.\tau\}(x.e')(e)$$

evaluates to e, regardless of the choice of e'. For simplicity, assume an eager dynamics for products and sums, and consider only polynomial type operators. What complications arise when extending this observation to positive type operators?

14.3. Consider Exercises **10.1** and **11.3** in which a database schema is represented by a finite product type indexed by the attributes of the schema, and a database with that schema is a finite sequence of instances of tuples of that type. Show that any database transformation that applies a function to one or more of the columns of each row of a database can be programmed in two steps using generic programming according to the following plan:

(a) Specify a type operator whose type variable shows which columns are transformed. All specified columns must be of the same type in order for the transformation to make sense.

(b) Specify the transformation on the type of column that will be applied to each tuple of the database to obtain an updated database.

(c) Form the generic extension of the type operator with the given transformation, and apply it to the given database.

For specificity, consider a schema whose attributes I include the attributes first and last, both of type str. Let $c : \text{str} \to \text{str}$ be a function that capitalizes strings according to some convention. Use generic programming to capitalize the first and last attributes of each row of a given database with the specified schema.

14.4. Whereas t occurs negatively in the type $t \to \text{bool}$, and does not occur only positively $(t \to \text{bool}) \to \text{bool}$, we may say that t does occur *non-negatively* in the latter type. This example illustrates that occurrences of t in the domain of a function are negative, and that occurrences in the domain of the domain of a function are non-negative. Every positive occurrence counts as non-negative, but not every non-negative occurrence is positive.[2] Give a simultaneous induction definition of the negative and non-negative type operators. Check that the type operator $t.(t \to \text{bool}) \to \text{bool}$ is non-negative according to your definition.

14.5. Using the definitions of negative and non-negative type operators requested in Exercise **14.4**, give the definition of the generic extension of a non-negative type operator. Specifically, define simultaneously $\text{map}^{--}\{t.\tau\}(x.e')(e)$ and $\text{map}^{-}\{t.\tau\}(x.e)(e')$ by induction on the structure of τ with the statics give by these rules:

$$\frac{t.\tau \text{ non-neg} \quad \Gamma, x : \rho \vdash e' : \rho' \quad \Gamma \vdash e : [\rho/t]\tau}{\Gamma \vdash \text{map}^{--}\{t.\tau\}(x.e')(e) : [\rho'/t]\tau} \tag{14.6a}$$

$$\frac{t.\tau \text{ neg} \quad \Gamma, x : \rho \vdash e' : \rho' \quad \Gamma \vdash e : [\rho'/t]\tau}{\Gamma \vdash \text{map}^{-}\{t.\tau\}(x.e')(e) : [\rho/t]\tau} \tag{14.6b}$$

Note well the reversal of the types of e and the overall type in these two rules. Calculate the generic extension of the type operator $t.(t \to \text{bool}) \to \text{bool}$.

Notes

1 The origin of this terminology is that a function type $\tau_1 \to \tau_2$ is analogous to the implication $\phi_1 \supset \phi_2$, which is classically equivalent to $\neg\phi_1 \vee \phi_2$, so that occurrences in the domain are under the negation.

2 Often what we have called "positive" is called "strictly positive," and what we have called "non-negative" is called "positive."

15 Inductive and Coinductive Types

The *inductive* and the *coinductive* types are two important forms of recursive type. Inductive types correspond to *least*, or *initial*, solutions of certain type equations, and coinductive types correspond to their *greatest*, or *final*, solutions. Intuitively, the elements of an inductive type are those that are given by a finite composition of its introduction forms. Consequently, if we specify the behavior of a function on each of the introduction forms of an inductive type, then its behavior is defined for all values of that type. Such a function is a *recursor*, or *catamorphism*. Dually, the elements of a coinductive type are those that behave properly in response to a finite composition of its elimination forms. Consequently, if we specify the behavior of an element on each elimination form, then we have fully specified a value of that type. Such an element is a *generator*, or *anamorphism*.

15.1 Motivating Examples

The most important example of an inductive type is the type of natural numbers as formalized in Chapter 9. The type $\mathtt{nat}$ is the *least* type containing $\mathtt{z}$ and closed under $\mathtt{s}(-)$. The minimality condition is expressed by the existence of the iterator, $\mathtt{iter}\, e\, \{\mathtt{z} \hookrightarrow e_0 \mid \mathtt{s}(x) \hookrightarrow e_1\}$, which transforms a natural number into a value of type τ, given its value for zero, and a transformation from its value on a number to its value on the successor of that number. This operation is well-defined precisely because there are no other natural numbers.

With a view towards deriving the type $\mathtt{nat}$ as a special case of an inductive type, it is useful to combine zero and successor into a single introduction form, and to correspondingly combine the basis and inductive step of the iterator. The following rules specify the statics of this reformulation:

$$\frac{\Gamma \vdash e : \mathtt{unit} + \mathtt{nat}}{\Gamma \vdash \mathtt{fold}_{\mathtt{nat}}(e) : \mathtt{nat}} \tag{15.1a}$$

$$\frac{\Gamma, x : \mathtt{unit} + \tau \vdash e_1 : \tau \quad \Gamma \vdash e_2 : \mathtt{nat}}{\Gamma \vdash \mathtt{rec}_{\mathtt{nat}}(x.e_1; e_2) : \tau} \tag{15.1b}$$

The expression $\mathtt{fold}_{\mathtt{nat}}(e)$ is the unique introduction form of the type $\mathtt{nat}$. Using this, the expression $\mathtt{z}$ is $\mathtt{fold}_{\mathtt{nat}}(\mathtt{l} \cdot \langle \rangle)$, and $\mathtt{s}(e)$ is $\mathtt{fold}_{\mathtt{nat}}(\mathtt{r} \cdot e)$. The recursor, $\mathtt{rec}_{\mathtt{nat}}(x.e_1; e_2)$, takes as argument the abstractor $x.e_1$ that combines the basis and inductive step into a single computation that, given a value of type $\mathtt{unit} + \tau$, yields a value of type τ. Intuitively, if

x is replaced by the value $1 \cdot \langle\rangle$, then e_1 computes the base case of the recursion, and if x is replaced by the value $\mathbf{r} \cdot e$, then e_1 computes the inductive step from the result e of the recursive call.

The dynamics of the combined representation of natural numbers is given by the following rules:

$$\frac{}{\texttt{fold}_{\texttt{nat}}(e) \ \texttt{val}} \tag{15.2a}$$

$$\frac{e_2 \longmapsto e_2'}{\texttt{rec}_{\texttt{nat}}(x.e_1; e_2) \longmapsto \texttt{rec}_{\texttt{nat}}(x.e_1; e_2')} \tag{15.2b}$$

$$\frac{\texttt{rec}_{\texttt{nat}}(x.e_1; \texttt{fold}_{\texttt{nat}}(e_2))}{\underset{\longmapsto}{\quad}} \tag{15.2c}$$
$$[\texttt{map}\{t.\texttt{unit} + t\}(y.\texttt{rec}_{\texttt{nat}}(x.e_1; y))(e_2)/x]e_1$$

Rule (15.2c) uses (polynomial) generic extension (see Chapter 14) to apply the recursor to the predecessor, if any, of a natural number. If we expand the definition of the generic extension in place, we obtain this rule:

$$\frac{\texttt{rec}_{\texttt{nat}}(x.e_1; \texttt{fold}_{\texttt{nat}}(e_2))}{\underset{\longmapsto}{\quad}}$$
$$[\texttt{case} \ e_2 \ \{1 \cdot \_ \hookrightarrow 1 \cdot \langle\rangle \mid \mathbf{r} \cdot y \hookrightarrow \mathbf{r} \cdot \texttt{rec}_{\texttt{nat}}(x.e_1; y)\}/x]e_1$$

Exercise **15.2** asks for a derivation of the iterator, as defined in Chapter 9, from the recursor just given.

An illustrative example of a coinductive type is the type of *streams* of natural numbers. A stream is an infinite sequence of natural numbers such that an element of the stream can be computed only after computing all preceding elements in that stream. That is, the computations of successive elements of the stream are sequentially dependent in that the computation of one element influences the computation of the next. In this sense, the introduction form for streams is dual to the elimination form for natural numbers.

A stream is given by its behavior under the elimination forms for the stream type: $\texttt{hd}(e)$ returns the next, or head, element of the stream, and $\texttt{tl}(e)$ returns the tail of the stream, the stream resulting when the head element is removed. A stream is introduced by a *generator*, the dual of a recursor, that defines the head and the tail of the stream in terms of the current state of the stream, which is represented by a value of some type. The statics of streams is given by the following rules:

$$\frac{\Gamma \vdash e : \texttt{stream}}{\Gamma \vdash \texttt{hd}(e) : \texttt{nat}} \tag{15.3a}$$

$$\frac{\Gamma \vdash e : \texttt{stream}}{\Gamma \vdash \texttt{tl}(e) : \texttt{stream}} \tag{15.3b}$$

$$\frac{\Gamma \vdash e : \tau \quad \Gamma, x : \tau \vdash e_1 : \mathtt{nat} \quad \Gamma, x : \tau \vdash e_2 : \tau}{\Gamma \vdash \mathtt{strgen}\, x \,\mathtt{is}\, e \,\mathtt{in}\, \mathtt{<hd} \hookrightarrow e_1, \mathtt{tl} \hookrightarrow e_2\mathtt{>} : \mathtt{stream}} \tag{15.3c}$$

In rule (15.3c), the current state of the stream is given by the expression e of some type τ, and the head and tail of the stream are determined by the expressions e_1 and e_2, respectively, as a function of the current state. (The notation for the generator is chosen to emphasize that every stream has both a head *and* a tail.)

The dynamics of streams is given by the following rules:

$$\frac{}{\mathtt{strgen}\, x \,\mathtt{is}\, e \,\mathtt{in}\, \mathtt{<hd} \hookrightarrow e_1, \mathtt{tl} \hookrightarrow e_2\mathtt{>}\ \mathsf{val}} \tag{15.4a}$$

$$\frac{e \longmapsto e'}{\mathtt{hd}(e) \longmapsto \mathtt{hd}(e')} \tag{15.4b}$$

$$\frac{}{\mathtt{hd}(\mathtt{strgen}\, x \,\mathtt{is}\, e \,\mathtt{in}\, \mathtt{<hd} \hookrightarrow e_1, \mathtt{tl} \hookrightarrow e_2\mathtt{>}) \longmapsto [e/x]e_1} \tag{15.4c}$$

$$\frac{e \longmapsto e'}{\mathtt{tl}(e) \longmapsto \mathtt{tl}(e')} \tag{15.4d}$$

$$\frac{}{\begin{array}{c} \mathtt{tl}(\mathtt{strgen}\, x \,\mathtt{is}\, e \,\mathtt{in}\, \mathtt{<hd} \hookrightarrow e_1, \mathtt{tl} \hookrightarrow e_2\mathtt{>}) \\ \longmapsto \\ \mathtt{strgen}\, x \,\mathtt{is}\, [e/x]e_2 \,\mathtt{in}\, \mathtt{<hd} \hookrightarrow e_1, \mathtt{tl} \hookrightarrow e_2\mathtt{>} \end{array}} \tag{15.4e}$$

Rules (15.4c) and (15.4e) express the dependency of the head and tail of the stream on its current state. Observe that the tail is obtained by applying the generator to the new state determined by e_2 from the current state.

To derive streams as a special case of a coinductive type, we combine the head and the tail into a single elimination form, and reorganize the generator correspondingly. Thus, we consider the following statics:

$$\frac{\Gamma \vdash e : \mathtt{stream}}{\Gamma \vdash \mathtt{unfold}_{\mathtt{stream}}(e) : \mathtt{nat} \times \mathtt{stream}} \tag{15.5a}$$

$$\frac{\Gamma, x : \tau \vdash e_1 : \mathtt{nat} \times \tau \quad \Gamma \vdash e_2 : \tau}{\Gamma \vdash \mathtt{gen}_{\mathtt{stream}}(x.e_1 ; e_2) : \mathtt{stream}} \tag{15.5b}$$

Rule (15.5a) states that a stream may be unfolded into a pair consisting of its head, a natural number, and its tail, another stream. The head $\mathtt{hd}(e)$ and tail $\mathtt{tl}(e)$ of a stream e are the projections $\mathtt{unfold}_{\mathtt{stream}}(e) \cdot \mathtt{l}$ and $\mathtt{unfold}_{\mathtt{stream}}(e) \cdot \mathtt{r}$, respectively. Rule (15.5b) states that a stream is generated from the state element e_2 by an expression e_1 that yields the head element and the next state as a function of the current state.

The dynamics of streams is given by the following rules:

$$\frac{}{\mathtt{gen}_{\mathtt{stream}}(x.e_1 ; e_2)\ \mathsf{val}} \tag{15.6a}$$

$$\frac{e \longmapsto e'}{\texttt{unfold}_{\texttt{stream}}(e) \longmapsto \texttt{unfold}_{\texttt{stream}}(e')} \tag{15.6b}$$

$$\frac{}{\begin{array}{c} \texttt{unfold}_{\texttt{stream}}(\texttt{gen}_{\texttt{stream}}(x.e_1; e_2)) \\ \longmapsto \\ \texttt{map}\{t.\texttt{nat} \times t\}(y.\texttt{gen}_{\texttt{stream}}(x.e_1; y))([e_2/x]e_1) \end{array}} \tag{15.6c}$$

Rule (15.6c) uses generic extension to generate a new stream whose state is the second component of $[e_2/x]e_1$. Expanding the generic extension we obtain the following reformulation of this rule:

$$\frac{}{\begin{array}{c} \texttt{unfold}_{\texttt{stream}}(\texttt{gen}_{\texttt{stream}}(x.e_1; e_2)) \\ \longmapsto \\ \langle ([e_2/x]e_1) \cdot \texttt{l}, \texttt{gen}_{\texttt{stream}}(x.e_1; ([e_2/x]e_1) \cdot \texttt{r}) \rangle \end{array}}$$

Exercise **15.3** asks for a derivation of $\texttt{strgen}\, x\, \texttt{is}\, e\, \texttt{in} <\texttt{hd} \hookrightarrow e_1, \texttt{tl} \hookrightarrow e_2>$ from the coinductive generation form.

15.2 Statics

We may now give a general account of inductive and coinductive types, which are defined in terms of positive type operators. We will consider a variant of **T**, which we will call **M**, with natural numbers replaced by functions, products, sums, and a rich class of inductive and coinductive types.

15.2.1 Types

The syntax of inductive and coinductive types involves *type variables*, which are, of course, variables ranging over types. The abstract syntax of inductive and coinductive types is given by the following grammar:

$$
\begin{array}{llllll}
\text{Typ} & \tau & ::= & t & t & \text{self-reference} \\
& & & \texttt{ind}(t.\tau) & \mu(t.\tau) & \text{inductive} \\
& & & \texttt{coi}(t.\tau) & \nu(t.\tau) & \text{coinductive}
\end{array}
$$

Type formation judgments have the form

$$t_1 \text{ type}, \dots, t_n \text{ type} \vdash \tau \text{ type},$$

where $t_1, \dots, t_n$ are type names. We let Δ range over finite sets of hypotheses of the form t type, where t is a type name. The type formation judgment is inductively defined by the following rules:

$$\frac{}{\Delta, t \text{ type} \vdash t \text{ type}} \tag{15.7a}$$

$$\frac{}{\Delta \vdash \text{unit type}} \tag{15.7b}$$

$$\frac{\Delta \vdash \tau_1 \text{ type} \quad \Delta \vdash \tau_2 \text{ type}}{\Delta \vdash \text{prod}(\tau_1; \tau_2) \text{ type}} \tag{15.7c}$$

$$\frac{}{\Delta \vdash \text{void type}} \tag{15.7d}$$

$$\frac{\Delta \vdash \tau_1 \text{ type} \quad \Delta \vdash \tau_2 \text{ type}}{\Delta \vdash \text{sum}(\tau_1; \tau_2) \text{ type}} \tag{15.7e}$$

$$\frac{\Delta \vdash \tau_1 \text{ type} \quad \Delta \vdash \tau_2 \text{ type}}{\Delta \vdash \text{arr}(\tau_1; \tau_2) \text{ type}} \tag{15.7f}$$

$$\frac{\Delta, t \text{ type} \vdash \tau \text{ type} \quad \Delta \vdash t.\tau \text{ pos}}{\Delta \vdash \text{ind}(t.\tau) \text{ type}} \tag{15.7g}$$

$$\frac{\Delta, t \text{ type} \vdash \tau \text{ type} \quad \Delta \vdash t.\tau \text{ pos}}{\Delta \vdash \text{coi}(t.\tau) \text{ type}} \tag{15.7h}$$

15.2.2 Expressions

The abstract syntax of **M** is given by the following grammar:

$$
\begin{array}{llll}
\text{Exp} & e & ::= & \text{fold}\{t.\tau\}(e) \quad\quad \text{fold}_{t.\tau}(e) \quad\quad \text{constructor} \\
& & & \text{rec}\{t.\tau\}(x.e_1; e_2) \quad \text{rec}(x.e_1; e_2) \quad \text{recursor} \\
& & & \text{unfold}\{t.\tau\}(e) \quad\quad \text{unfold}_{t.\tau}(e) \quad \text{destructor} \\
& & & \text{gen}\{t.\tau\}(x.e_1; e_2) \quad \text{gen}(x.e_1; e_2) \quad \text{generator}
\end{array}
$$

The subscripts on the concrete syntax forms are often omitted when they are clear from context.

The statics for **M** is given by the following typing rules:

$$\frac{\Gamma \vdash e : [\text{ind}(t.\tau)/t]\tau}{\Gamma \vdash \text{fold}\{t.\tau\}(e) : \text{ind}(t.\tau)} \tag{15.8a}$$

$$\frac{\Gamma, x : [\tau'/t]\tau \vdash e_1 : \tau' \quad \Gamma \vdash e_2 : \text{ind}(t.\tau)}{\Gamma \vdash \text{rec}\{t.\tau\}(x.e_1; e_2) : \tau'} \tag{15.8b}$$

$$\frac{\Gamma \vdash e : \text{coi}(t.\tau)}{\Gamma \vdash \text{unfold}\{t.\tau\}(e) : [\text{coi}(t.\tau)/t]\tau} \tag{15.8c}$$

$$\frac{\Gamma \vdash e_2 : \tau_2 \quad \Gamma, x : \tau_2 \vdash e_1 : [\tau_2/t]\tau}{\Gamma \vdash \text{gen}\{t.\tau\}(x.e_1; e_2) : \text{coi}(t.\tau)} \tag{15.8d}$$

15.3 Dynamics

The dynamics of **M** is given in terms of the positive generic extension operation described in Chapter 14. The following rules specify a lazy dynamics for **M**:

$$\frac{}{\texttt{fold}\{t.\tau\}(e) \text{ val}} \tag{15.9a}$$

$$\frac{e_2 \longmapsto e_2'}{\texttt{rec}\{t.\tau\}(x.e_1; e_2) \longmapsto \texttt{rec}\{t.\tau\}(x.e_1; e_2')} \tag{15.9b}$$

$$\frac{\texttt{rec}\{t.\tau\}(x.e_1; \texttt{fold}\{t.\tau\}(e_2))}{\longmapsto} \tag{15.9c}$$
$$[\texttt{map}^+\{t.\tau\}(y.\texttt{rec}\{t.\tau\}(x.e_1; y))(e_2)/x]e_1$$

$$\frac{}{\texttt{gen}\{t.\tau\}(x.e_1; e_2) \text{ val}} \tag{15.9d}$$

$$\frac{e \longmapsto e'}{\texttt{unfold}\{t.\tau\}(e) \longmapsto \texttt{unfold}\{t.\tau\}(e')} \tag{15.9e}$$

$$\frac{\texttt{unfold}\{t.\tau\}(\texttt{gen}\{t.\tau\}(x.e_1; e_2))}{\longmapsto} \tag{15.9f}$$
$$\texttt{map}^+\{t.\tau\}(y.\texttt{gen}\{t.\tau\}(x.e_1; y))([e_2/x]e_1)$$

Rule (15.9c) states that to evaluate the recursor on a value of recursive type, we inductively apply the recursor as guided by the type operator to the value, and then apply the inductive step to the result. Rule (15.9f) is simply the dual of this rule for coinductive types.

Lemma 15.1. *If $e : \tau$ and $e \longmapsto e'$, then $e' : \tau$.*

Proof By rule induction on rules (15.9).   □

Lemma 15.2. *If $e : \tau$, then either e val or there exists e' such that $e \longmapsto e'$.*

Proof By rule induction on rules (15.8).   □

Although a proof of this fact lies beyond our current reach, all programs in **M** terminate.

Theorem 15.3 (Termination for **M**). *If $e : \tau$, then there exists e' val such that $e \longmapsto^* e'$.*

It may, at first, seem surprising that a language with infinite data structures, such as streams, can enjoy such a termination property. But bear in mind that infinite data structures, such as streams, are represented as in a continuing state of creation, and not as a completed whole.

15.4 Solving Type Equations

For a positive type operator $t.\tau$, we may say that the inductive type $\mu(t.\tau)$ and the coinductive type $\nu(t.\tau)$ are both *solutions* (up to isomorphism) of the type equation $t \cong \tau$:

$$\mu(t.\tau) \cong [\mu(t.\tau)/t]\tau$$
$$\nu(t.\tau) \cong [\nu(t.\tau)/t]\tau.$$

Intuitively speaking, this means that every value of an inductive type is the folding of a value of the unfolding of the inductive type, and that, similarly, every value of the unfolding of a coinductive type is the unfolding of a value of the coinductive type itself. It is a good exercise to define functions back and forth between the isomorphic types and to convince yourself informally that they are mutually inverse to one another.

Whereas both are solutions to the same type equation, they are not isomorphic to each other. To see why, consider the inductive type $\mathtt{nat} \triangleq \mu(t.\mathtt{unit} + t)$ and the coinductive type $\mathtt{conat} \triangleq \nu(t.\mathtt{unit} + t)$. Informally, $\mathtt{nat}$ is the smallest (most restrictive) type containing zero, given by $\mathtt{fold}(1 \cdot \langle\rangle)$, and closed under formation of the successor of any other e of type $\mathtt{nat}$, given by $\mathtt{fold}(\mathtt{r} \cdot e)$. Dually, $\mathtt{conat}$ is the largest (most permissive) type of expressions e for which the unfolding, $\mathtt{unfold}(e)$, is either zero, given by $1 \cdot \langle\rangle$, or to the successor of some other e' of type $\mathtt{conat}$, given by $\mathtt{r} \cdot e'$.

Because $\mathtt{nat}$ is defined by the composition of its introduction forms and sum injections, it is clear that only finite natural numbers can be constructed in finite time. Because $\mathtt{conat}$ is defined by the composition of its elimination forms (unfoldings plus case analyses), it is clear that a co-natural number can only be explored to finite depth in finite time—essentially we can only examine some finite number of predecessors of a given co-natural number in a terminating program. Consequently,

1. there is a function $i : \mathtt{nat} \to \mathtt{conat}$ embedding every finite natural number into the type of possibly infinite natural numbers; and

2. there is an "actually infinite" co-natural number ω that is essentially an infinite composition of successors.

Defining the embedding of $\mathtt{nat}$ into $\mathtt{conat}$ is the subject of Exercise **15.1**. The infinite co-natural number ω is defined as follows:

$$\omega \triangleq \mathtt{gen}(x.\mathtt{r} \cdot x; \langle\rangle).$$

One may check that $\mathtt{unfold}\,(\omega) \longmapsto^* \mathtt{r} \cdot \omega$, which means that ω is its own predecessor. The co-natural number ω is larger than any finite natural number in that any finite number of predecessors of ω is non-zero.

Summing up, the mere fact of being a solution to a type equation does not uniquely characterize a type: there can be many different solutions to the same type equation, the natural and the co-natural numbers being good examples of the discrepancy. However, we will show in Part VIII that type equations have unique solutions (up to isomorphism) and that the restriction to polynomial type operators is no longer required. The price we pay for the additional expressive power is that programs are no longer guaranteed to terminate.

15.5 Notes

The language **M** is named after Mendler, on whose work the present treatment is based (Mendler, 1987). Mendler's work is grounded in category theory, specifically the concept of an algebra for a functor (MacLane, 1998; Taylor, 1999). The functorial action of a type constructor (described in Chapter 14) plays a central role. Inductive types are initial algebras and coinductive types are final coalgebras for the functor given by a (polynomial or positive) type operator.

Exercises

15.1. Define a function $i : \mathtt{nat} \to \mathtt{conat}$ that sends every natural number to "itself" in the sense that every finite natural number is sent to its correlate as a co-natural number.
 (a) $\mathtt{unfold}\,(i(\mathtt{z})) \longmapsto^* \mathtt{1} \cdot \langle\rangle$.
 (b) $\mathtt{unfold}\,(i(\mathtt{s}(\overline{n}))) \longmapsto^* \mathtt{r} \cdot i(\overline{n})$.

15.2. Derive the iterator, $\mathtt{iter}\, e \,\{\mathtt{z} \hookrightarrow e_0 \mid \mathtt{s}(x) \hookrightarrow e_1\}$, described in Chapter 9 from the recursor for the inductive type of natural numbers given in Section 15.1.

15.3. Derive the stream generator, $\mathtt{strgen}\, x \,\mathtt{is}\, e \,\mathtt{in}\, \langle\mathtt{hd} \hookrightarrow e_1, \mathtt{tl} \hookrightarrow e_2\rangle$ from the generator for the coinductive stream type given in Section 15.1.

15.4. Consider the type $\mathtt{seq} \triangleq \mathtt{nat} \to \mathtt{nat}$ of infinite sequences of natural numbers. Every stream can be turned into a sequence by the following function:

$$\lambda\,(\mathtt{stream}:s)\,\lambda\,(n:\mathtt{nat})\,\mathtt{hd}(\mathtt{iter}\, n \,\{\mathtt{z} \hookrightarrow s \mid \mathtt{s}(x) \hookrightarrow \mathtt{tl}(x)\}).$$

Show that every sequence can be turned into a stream whose nth element is the nth element of the given sequence.

15.5. The type of lists of natural numbers is defined by the following introduction and elimination forms:

$$\frac{}{\Gamma \vdash \mathtt{nil} : \mathtt{natlist}} \tag{15.10a}$$

$$\frac{\Gamma \vdash e_1 : \texttt{nat} \quad \Gamma \vdash e_2 : \texttt{natlist}}{\Gamma \vdash \texttt{cons}(e_1; e_2) : \texttt{natlist}} \tag{15.10b}$$

$$\frac{\Gamma \vdash e : \texttt{natlist} \quad \Gamma \vdash e_0 : \tau \quad \Gamma x : \texttt{nat}\, y : \tau \vdash e_1 : \tau}{\Gamma \vdash \texttt{rec}\, e\, \{\texttt{nil} \hookrightarrow e_0 \mid \texttt{cons}(x; y) \hookrightarrow e_1\} : \tau} \tag{15.10c}$$

The associated dynamics, whether eager or lazy, can be derived from that of the recursor for the type nat given in Chapter 9. Give a definition of natlist as an inductive type, including the definitions of its associated introduction and elimination forms. Check that they validate the expected dynamics.

15.6. Consider the type itree of possibly infinite binary trees with the following introduction and elimination forms:

$$\frac{\Gamma \vdash e : \texttt{itree}}{\Gamma \vdash \texttt{view}(e) : (\texttt{itree} \times \texttt{itree})\, \texttt{opt}} \tag{15.11a}$$

$$\frac{\Gamma \vdash e : \tau \quad \Gamma x : \tau \vdash e' : (\tau \times \tau)\, \texttt{opt}}{\Gamma \vdash \texttt{itgen}\, x \,\texttt{is}\, e\, \texttt{in}\, e' : \texttt{itree}} \tag{15.11b}$$

Because a possibly infinite tree must be in a state of continual generation, viewing a tree exposes only its top-level structure, an optional pair of possibly infinite trees.[1] If the view is null, the tree is empty, and if it is just(e_1)e_2, then it is non-empty, with children given by e_1 and e_2. To generate an infinite tree, choose a type τ of its state of generation, and provide its current state e and a state transformation e' that, when applied to the current state, announces whether or not generation is complete, and, if not, provides the state for each of the children.

(a) Give a precise dynamics for the itree operations as just described informally. *Hint*: use generic programming!

(b) Reformulate the type itree as a coinductive type, and derive the statics and dynamics of its introduction and elimination forms.

15.7. Exercise **11.5** asked you to define an RS latch as a signal transducer, in which signals are expressed explicitly as functions of time. Here you are asked again to define an RS latch as a signal transducer, but this time with signals expressed as streams of booleans. Under such a representation, time is implicitly represented by the successive elements of the stream. Define an RS latch as a transducer of signals consisting of pairs of booleans.

Note

1 See Chapter 11 for the definition of option types.

PART VII

Variable Types

System F of Polymorphic Types

The languages we have considered so far are all *monomorphic* in that every expression has a unique type, given the types of its free variables, if it has a type at all. Yet it is often the case that essentially the same behavior is required, albeit at several different types. For example, in **T** there is a *distinct* identity function for each type τ, namely $\lambda\,(x:\tau)\,x$, even though the behavior is the same for each choice of τ. Similarly, there is a distinct composition operator for each triple of types, namely

$$\circ_{\tau_1,\tau_2,\tau_3} = \lambda\,(f:\tau_2 \to \tau_3)\,\lambda\,(g:\tau_1 \to \tau_2)\,\lambda\,(x:\tau_1)\,f(g(x)).$$

Each choice of the three types requires a *different* program, even though they all have the same behavior when executed.

Obviously, it would be useful to capture the pattern once and for all, and to instantiate this pattern each time we need it. The expression patterns codify generic (type-independent) behaviors that are shared by all instances of the pattern. Such generic expressions are *polymorphic*. In this chapter, we will study the language **F**, which was introduced by Girard under the name *System F* and by Reynolds under the name *polymorphic typed λ-calculus*. Although motivated by a simple practical problem (how to avoid writing redundant code), the concept of polymorphism is central to an impressive variety of seemingly disparate concepts, including the concept of data abstraction (the subject of Chapter 17), and the definability of product, sum, inductive, and coinductive types considered in the preceding chapters. (Only general recursive types extend the expressive power of the language.)

16.1 Polymorphic Abstraction

The language **F** is a variant of **T** in which we eliminate the type of natural numbers, but add, in compensation, polymorphic types:[1]

Typ	τ	::=	t	t	variable
			$\mathtt{arr}(\tau_1;\tau_2)$	$\tau_1 \to \tau_2$	function
			$\mathtt{all}(t.\tau)$	$\forall(t.\tau)$	polymorphic
Exp	e	::=	x	x	
			$\mathtt{lam}\{\tau\}(x.e)$	$\lambda\,(x:\tau)\,e$	abstraction
			$\mathtt{ap}(e_1;e_2)$	$e_1(e_2)$	application
			$\mathtt{Lam}(t.e)$	$\Lambda(t)\,e$	type abstraction
			$\mathtt{App}\{\tau\}(e)$	$e[\tau]$	type application

A *type abstraction* Lam($t.e$) defines a *generic*, or *polymorphic*, function with *type variable* t standing for an unspecified type within e. A *type application*, or *instantiation* App$\{\tau\}(e)$, applies a polymorphic function to a specified type, which is plugged in for the type variable to obtain the result. The *universal type*, all($t.\tau$), classifies polymorphic functions.

The statics of **F** consists of two judgment forms, the *type formation* judgment,

$$\Delta \vdash \tau \text{ type,}$$

and the *typing judgment*,

$$\Delta\ \Gamma \vdash e : \tau.$$

The hypotheses Δ have the form t type, where t is a variable of sort Typ, and the hypotheses Γ have the form $x : \tau$, where x is a variable of sort Exp.

The rules defining the type formation judgment are as follows:

$$\frac{}{\Delta, t \text{ type} \vdash t \text{ type}} \tag{16.1a}$$

$$\frac{\Delta \vdash \tau_1 \text{ type} \quad \Delta \vdash \tau_2 \text{ type}}{\Delta \vdash \text{arr}(\tau_1; \tau_2) \text{ type}} \tag{16.1b}$$

$$\frac{\Delta, t \text{ type} \vdash \tau \text{ type}}{\Delta \vdash \text{all}(t.\tau) \text{ type}} \tag{16.1c}$$

The rules defining the typing judgment are as follows:

$$\frac{}{\Delta\ \Gamma, x : \tau \vdash x : \tau} \tag{16.2a}$$

$$\frac{\Delta \vdash \tau_1 \text{ type} \quad \Delta\ \Gamma, x : \tau_1 \vdash e : \tau_2}{\Delta\ \Gamma \vdash \text{lam}\{\tau_1\}(x.e) : \text{arr}(\tau_1; \tau_2)} \tag{16.2b}$$

$$\frac{\Delta\ \Gamma \vdash e_1 : \text{arr}(\tau_2; \tau) \quad \Delta\ \Gamma \vdash e_2 : \tau_2}{\Delta\ \Gamma \vdash \text{ap}(e_1; e_2) : \tau} \tag{16.2c}$$

$$\frac{\Delta, t \text{ type } \Gamma \vdash e : \tau}{\Delta\ \Gamma \vdash \text{Lam}(t.e) : \text{all}(t.\tau)} \tag{16.2d}$$

$$\frac{\Delta\ \Gamma \vdash e : \text{all}(t.\tau') \quad \Delta \vdash \tau \text{ type}}{\Delta\ \Gamma \vdash \text{App}\{\tau\}(e) : [\tau/t]\tau'} \tag{16.2e}$$

Lemma 16.1 (Regularity). *If $\Delta\ \Gamma \vdash e : \tau$, and if $\Delta \vdash \tau_i$ type for each assumption $x_i : \tau_i$ in Γ, then $\Delta \vdash \tau$ type.*

Proof By induction on rules (16.2).   ☐

The statics admits the structural rules for a general hypothetical judgment. In particular, we have the following critical substitution property for type formation and expression typing.

Lemma 16.2 (Substitution). *1. If Δ, t type $\vdash \tau'$ type and $\Delta \vdash \tau$ type, then $\Delta \vdash [\tau/t]\tau'$ type.*

2. *If* Δ, t *type* $\Gamma \vdash e' : \tau'$ *and* $\Delta \vdash \tau$ *type, then* $\Delta [\tau/t]\Gamma \vdash [\tau/t]e' : [\tau/t]\tau'$.

3. *If* $\Delta \; \Gamma, x : \tau \vdash e' : \tau'$ *and* $\Delta \; \Gamma \vdash e : \tau$, *then* $\Delta \; \Gamma \vdash [e/x]e' : \tau'$.

The second part of the lemma requires substitution into the context Γ as well as into the term and its type, because the type variable t may occur freely in any of these positions.

Returning to the motivating examples from the introduction, the polymorphic identity function, I, is written

$$\Lambda(t)\lambda(x : t)x;$$

it has the polymorphic type

$$\forall(t.t \to t).$$

Instances of the polymorphic identity are written $I[\tau]$, where τ is some type, and have the type $\tau \to \tau$.

Similarly, the polymorphic composition function, C, is written

$$\Lambda(t_1)\Lambda(t_2)\Lambda(t_3)\lambda(f : t_2 \to t_3)\lambda(g : t_1 \to t_2)\lambda(x : t_1)f(g(x)).$$

The function C has the polymorphic type

$$\forall(t_1.\forall(t_2.\forall(t_3.(t_2 \to t_3) \to (t_1 \to t_2) \to (t_1 \to t_3)))).$$

Instances of C are obtained by applying it to a triple of types, written $C[\tau_1][\tau_2][\tau_3]$. Each such instance has the type

$$(\tau_2 \to \tau_3) \to (\tau_1 \to \tau_2) \to (\tau_1 \to \tau_3).$$

Dynamics

The dynamics of **F** is given as follows:

$$\frac{}{\mathtt{lam}\{\tau\}(x.e) \; \mathsf{val}} \tag{16.3a}$$

$$\frac{}{\mathtt{Lam}(t.e) \; \mathsf{val}} \tag{16.3b}$$

$$\frac{[e_2 \; \mathsf{val}]}{\mathtt{ap}(\mathtt{lam}\{\tau_1\}(x.e); e_2) \longmapsto [e_2/x]e} \tag{16.3c}$$

$$\frac{e_1 \longmapsto e_1'}{\mathtt{ap}(e_1; e_2) \longmapsto \mathtt{ap}(e_1'; e_2)} \tag{16.3d}$$

$$\left[\frac{e_1 \; \mathsf{val} \quad e_2 \longmapsto e_2'}{\mathtt{ap}(e_1; e_2) \longmapsto \mathtt{ap}(e_1; e_2')}\right] \tag{16.3e}$$

$$\overline{\mathrm{App}\{\tau\}(\mathrm{Lam}(t.e)) \longmapsto [\tau/t]e} \tag{16.3f}$$

$$\frac{e \longmapsto e'}{\mathrm{App}\{\tau\}(e) \longmapsto \mathrm{App}\{\tau\}(e')} \tag{16.3g}$$

The bracketed premises and rule are included for a call-by-value interpretation and omitted for a call-by-name interpretation of **F**.

It is a simple matter to prove safety for **F**, using familiar methods.

Lemma 16.3 (Canonical Forms). *Suppose that $e : \tau$ and e val, then*

1. *If $\tau = \mathrm{arr}(\tau_1; \tau_2)$, then $e = \mathrm{lam}\{\tau_1\}(x.e_2)$ with $x : \tau_1 \vdash e_2 : \tau_2$.*
2. *If $\tau = \mathrm{all}(t.\tau')$, then $e = \mathrm{Lam}(t.e')$ with t type $\vdash e' : \tau'$.*

Proof   By rule induction on the statics. $\square$

Theorem 16.4 (Preservation). *If $e : \tau$ and $e \longmapsto e'$, then $e' : \tau$.*

Proof   By rule induction on the dynamics. $\square$

Theorem 16.5 (Progress). *If $e : \tau$, then either e val or there exists e' such that $e \longmapsto e'$.*

Proof   By rule induction on the statics. $\square$

16.2 Polymorphic Definability

The language **F** is astonishingly expressive. Not only are all (lazy) finite products and sums definable in the language, but so are all (lazy) inductive and coinductive types. Their definability is most naturally expressed using definitional equality, which is the least congruence containing the following two axioms:

$$\frac{\Delta\ \Gamma, x : \tau_1 \vdash e_2 : \tau_2 \quad \Delta\ \Gamma \vdash e_1 : \tau_1}{\Delta\ \Gamma \vdash (\lambda(x : \tau)e_2)(e_1) \equiv [e_1/x]e_2 : \tau_2} \tag{16.4a}$$

$$\frac{\Delta, t\ \mathrm{type}\ \Gamma \vdash e : \tau \quad \Delta \vdash \rho\ \mathrm{type}}{\Delta\ \Gamma \vdash \Lambda(t)\,e[\rho] \equiv [\rho/t]e : [\rho/t]\tau} \tag{16.4b}$$

In addition, there are rules omitted here specifying that definitional equality is a congruence relation (that is, an equivalence relation respected by all expression-forming operations).

16.2.1 Products and Sums

The nullary product, or unit, type is definable in **F** as follows:

$$\texttt{unit} \triangleq \forall(r.r \to r)$$

$$\langle\rangle \triangleq \Lambda(r)\lambda\,(x:r)\,x$$

The identity function plays the role of the null tuple, because it is the only closed value of this type.

Binary products are definable in **F** by using encoding tricks similar to those described in Chapter 21 for the untyped λ-calculus:

$$\tau_1 \times \tau_2 \triangleq \forall(r.(\tau_1 \to \tau_2 \to r) \to r)$$

$$\langle e_1, e_2 \rangle \triangleq \Lambda(r)\lambda\,(x:\tau_1 \to \tau_2 \to r)\,x(e_1)(e_2)$$

$$e \cdot 1 \triangleq e[\tau_1](\lambda\,(x:\tau_1)\lambda\,(y:\tau_2)\,x)$$

$$e \cdot \texttt{r} \triangleq e[\tau_2](\lambda\,(x:\tau_1)\lambda\,(y:\tau_2)\,y)$$

The statics given in Chapter 10 is derivable according to these definitions. Moreover, the following definitional equalities are derivable in **F** from these definitions:

$$\langle e_1, e_2 \rangle \cdot 1 \equiv e_1 : \tau_1$$

and

$$\langle e_1, e_2 \rangle \cdot \texttt{r} \equiv e_2 : \tau_2.$$

The nullary sum, or void, type is definable in **F**:

$$\texttt{void} \triangleq \forall(r.r)$$

$$\texttt{abort}\{\rho\}(e) \triangleq e[\rho]$$

Binary sums are also definable in **F**:

$$\tau_1 + \tau_2 \triangleq \forall(r.(\tau_1 \to r) \to (\tau_2 \to r) \to r)$$

$$1 \cdot e \triangleq \Lambda(r)\lambda\,(x:\tau_1 \to r)\lambda\,(y:\tau_2 \to r)\,x(e)$$

$$\texttt{r} \cdot e \triangleq \Lambda(r)\lambda\,(x:\tau_1 \to r)\lambda\,(y:\tau_2 \to r)\,y(e)$$

$$\texttt{case}\,e\,\{1 \cdot x_1 \hookrightarrow e_1 \mid \texttt{r} \cdot x_2 \hookrightarrow e_2\} \triangleq$$

$$e[\rho](\lambda\,(x_1:\tau_1)\,e_1)(\lambda\,(x_2:\tau_2)\,e_2)$$

provided that the types make sense. It is easy to check that the following equivalences are derivable in **F**:

$$\texttt{case}\,1 \cdot d_1\,\{1 \cdot x_1 \hookrightarrow e_1 \mid \texttt{r} \cdot x_2 \hookrightarrow e_2\} \equiv [d_1/x_1]e_1 : \rho$$

and

$$\texttt{case}\,\texttt{r} \cdot d_2\,\{1 \cdot x_1 \hookrightarrow e_1 \mid \texttt{r} \cdot x_2 \hookrightarrow e_2\} \equiv [d_2/x_2]e_2 : \rho.$$

Thus, the dynamic behavior specified in Chapter 11 is correctly implemented by these definitions.

16.2.2 Natural Numbers

As we remarked above, the natural numbers (under a lazy interpretation) are also definable in **F**. The key is the iterator, whose typing rule we recall here for reference:

$$\frac{e_0 : \texttt{nat} \quad e_1 : \tau \quad x : \tau \vdash e_2 : \tau}{\texttt{iter}\{e_1 ; x.e_2\}(e_0) : \tau} .$$

Because the result type τ is arbitrary, this means that if we have an iterator, then we can use it to define a function of type

$$\texttt{nat} \to \forall (t.t \to (t \to t) \to t).$$

This function, when applied to an argument n, yields a polymorphic function that, for any result type, t, given the initial result for z and a transformation from the result for x into the result for s(x), yields the result of iterating the transformation n times, starting with the initial result.

Because the *only* operation we can perform on a natural number is to iterate up to it, we may simply *identify* a natural number, n, with the polymorphic iterate-up-to-n function just described. Thus, we may define the type of natural numbers in **F** by the following equations:

$$\texttt{nat} \triangleq \forall (t.t \to (t \to t) \to t)$$

$$\texttt{z} \triangleq \Lambda(t)\,\lambda\,(z:t)\,\lambda\,(s:t \to t)\,z$$

$$\texttt{s}(e) \triangleq \Lambda(t)\,\lambda\,(z:t)\,\lambda\,(s:t \to t)\,s(e[t](z)(s))$$

$$\texttt{iter}\{e_1;x.e_2\}(e_0) \triangleq e_0[\tau](e_1)(\lambda\,(x:\tau)\,e_2)$$

It is easy to check that the statics and dynamics of the natural numbers type given in Chapter 9 are derivable in **F** under these definitions. The representations of the numerals in **F** are called the *polymorphic Church numerals*.

The encodability of the natural numbers shows that **F** is *at least as expressive* as **T**. But is it *more* expressive? Yes! It is possible to show that the evaluation function for **T** is definable in **F**, even though it is not definable in **T** itself. However, the same diagonal argument given in Chapter 9 applies here, showing that the evaluation function for **F** is not definable in **F**. We may enrich **F** a bit more to define the evaluator for **F**, but as long as all programs in the enriched language terminate, we will once again have an undefinable function, the evaluation function for that extension.

16.3 Parametricity Overview

A remarkable property of **F** is that polymorphic types severely constrain the behavior of their elements. We may prove useful theorems about an expression knowing *only* its type—that is, without ever looking at the code. For example, if i is any expression of type $\forall (t.t \to t)$, then it is the identity function. Informally, when i is applied to a type, τ, and an argument of type τ, it returns a value of type τ. But because τ is not specified until i is called, the function has no choice but to return its argument, which is to say that it is essentially the identity function. Similarly, if b is any expression of type $\forall(t.t \rightarrow t \rightarrow t)$, then b is equivalent to either $\Lambda(t)\lambda(x:t)\lambda(y:t)x$ or $\Lambda(t)\lambda(x:t)\lambda(y:t)y$. Intuitively, when b is applied to two arguments of a given type, the only value it can return is one of the givens.

Properties of a program in **F** that can be proved knowing only its type are called *parametricity properties*. The facts about the functions i and b stated above are examples of parametricity properties. Such properties are sometimes called "free theorems," because they come from typing "for free," without any knowledge of the code itself. It bears repeating that in **F** we prove non-trivial behavioral properties of programs without ever examining the program text. The key to this incredible fact is that we are able to prove a deep property, called *parametricity*, about the language **F**, that then applies to every program written in **F**. One may say that the type system "pre-verifies" programs with respect to a broad range of useful properties, eliminating the need to prove those properties about every program separately. The parametricity theorem for **F** explains the remarkable experience that if a piece of code type checks, then it "just works." Parametricity narrows the space of well-typed programs sufficiently that the opportunities for programmer error are reduced to almost nothing.

So how does the parametricity theorem work? Without getting into too many technical details (but see Chapter 48 for a full treatment), we can give a brief summary of the main idea. Any function $i : \forall(t.t \rightarrow t)$ in **F** enjoys the following property:

> *For any type τ and any property $\mathcal{P}$ of the type τ, then if $\mathcal{P}$ holds of $x : \tau$, then $\mathcal{P}$ holds of $i[\tau](x)$.*

To show that for any type τ, and any x of type τ, the expression $i[\tau](x)$ is equivalent to x, it suffices to fix $x_0 : \tau$, and consider the property $\mathcal{P}_{x_0}$ that holds of $y : \tau$ iff y is equivalent to x_0. Obviously, $\mathcal{P}$ holds of x_0 itself, and hence by the above-displayed property of i, it sends any argument satisfying $\mathcal{P}_{x_0}$ to a result satisfying $\mathcal{P}_{x_0}$, which is to say that it sends x_0 to x_0. Because x_0 is an arbitrary element of τ, it follows that $i[\tau]$ is the identity function, $\lambda(x:\tau)x$, on the type τ, and because τ is itself arbitrary, i is the polymorphic identity function, $\Lambda(t)\lambda(x:t)x$.

A similar argument suffices to show that the function b, defined above, is either $\Lambda(t)\lambda(x:t)\lambda(y:t)x$ or $\Lambda(t)\lambda(x:t)\lambda(y:t)y$. By virtue of its type, the function b enjoys the parametricity property

> *For any type τ and any property $\mathcal{P}$ of τ, if $\mathcal{P}$ holds of $x : \tau$ and of $y : \tau$, then $\mathcal{P}$ holds of $b[\tau](x)(y)$.*

Choose an arbitrary type τ and two arbitrary elements x_0 and y_0 of type τ. Define $\mathcal{Q}_{x_0,y_0}$ to hold of $z : \tau$ iff either z is equivalent to x_0 or z is equivalent to y_0. Clearly $\mathcal{Q}_{x_0,y_0}$ holds of both x_0 and y_0 themselves, so by the quoted parametricity property of b, it follows that $\mathcal{Q}_{x_0,y_0}$ holds of $b[\tau](x_0)(y_0)$, which is to say that it is equivalent to either x_0 or y_0. Since τ, x_0, and y_0 are arbitrary, it follows that b is equivalent to either $\Lambda(t)\lambda(x:t)\lambda(y:t)x$ or $\Lambda(t)\lambda(x:t)\lambda(y:t)y$.

The parametricity theorem for **F** implies even stronger properties of functions such as i and b considered above. For example, the function i of type $\forall(t.t \rightarrow t)$ also satisfies the following condition:

> *If τ and τ' are any two types, and $\mathcal{R}$ is a binary relation between τ and τ', then for any $x : \tau$ and $x' : \tau'$, if $\mathcal{R}$ relates x to x', then $\mathcal{R}$ relates $i[\tau](x)$ to $i[\tau'](x')$.*

Using this property, we may again prove that i is equivalent to the polymorphic identity function. Specifically, if τ is any type and $g : \tau \rightarrow \tau$ is any function on that type, then it follows from the type of i alone that $i[\tau](g(x))$ is equivalent to $g(i[\tau](x))$ for any $x : \tau$. To prove this, simply choose $\mathcal{R}$ to the be graph of the function g, the relation $\mathcal{R}_g$ that holds of x and x' iff x' is equivalent to $g(x)$. The parametricity property of i, when specialized to $\mathcal{R}_g$, states that if x' is equivalent to $g(x)$, then $i[\tau](x')$ is equivalent to $g(i[\tau](x))$, which is to say that $i[\tau](g(x))$ is equivalent to $g(i[\tau](x))$. To show that i is equivalent to the identity function, choose $x_0 : \tau$ arbitrarily, and consider the constant function g_0 on τ that always returns x_0. Because x_0 is equivalent to $g_0(x_0)$, it follows that $i[\tau](x_0)$ is equivalent to x_0, which is to say that i behaves like the polymorphic identity function.

16.4 Notes

System F was introduced by Girard (1972) in the context of proof theory and by Reynolds (1974) in the context of programming languages. The concept of parametricity was originally isolated by Strachey but was not fully developed until the work of Reynolds (1983). The phrase "free theorems" for parametricity theorems was introduced by Wadler (1989).

Exercises

16.1. Give polymorphic definitions and types to the s and k combinators defined in Exercise **3.1**.

16.2. Define in **F** the type bool of *Church booleans*. Define the type bool, and define true and false of this type, and the conditional if e then e_0 else e_1, where e is of this type.

16.3. Define in **F** the inductive type of lists of natural numbers as defined in Chapter 15. *Hint*: Define the representation in terms of the recursor (elimination form) for lists, following the pattern for defining the type of natural numbers.

16.4. Define in **F** an arbitrary inductive type, $\mu(t.\tau)$. *Hint*: generalize your answer to Exercise **16.3**.

16.5. Define the type t list as in Exercise **16.3**, with the element type, t, unspecified. Define the finite set of *elements* of a list l to be those x given by the head of some number of tails of l. Now suppose that $f : \forall(t.t \, \text{list} \rightarrow t \, \text{list})$ is an arbitrary function of the stated type. Show that the elements of $f[\tau](l)$ are a subset of those of l. Thus, f may only permute, replicate, or drop elements from its input list to obtain its output list.

Note

1 Girard's original version of System F included the natural numbers as a basic type.

17 Abstract Types

Data abstraction is perhaps the most important technique for structuring programs. The main idea is to introduce an *interface* that serves as a contract between the *client* and the *implementor* of an abstract type. The interface specifies what the client may rely on for its own work, and, simultaneously, what the implementor must provide to satisfy the contract. The interface serves to isolate the client from the implementor so that each may be developed in isolation from the other. In particular, one implementation can be replaced by another without affecting the behavior of the client, provided that the two implementations meet the same interface and that each simulates the other with respect to the operations of the interface. This property is called *representation independence* for an abstract type.

Data abstraction is formalized by extending the language **F** with *existential types*. Interfaces are existential types that provide a collection of operations acting on an unspecified, or abstract, type. Implementations are packages, the introduction form for existential types, and clients are uses of the corresponding elimination form. It is remarkable that the programming concept of data abstraction is captured so naturally and directly by the logical concept of existential type quantification. Existential types are closely connected with universal types, and hence are often treated together. The superficial reason is that both are forms of type quantification, and hence both require the machinery of type variables. The deeper reason is that existential types are *definable* from universals—surprisingly, data abstraction is actually just a form of polymorphism! Consequently, representation independence is an application of the parametricity properties of polymorphic functions discussed in Chapter 16.

17.1 Existential Types

The syntax of **FE** extends **F** with the following constructs:

Typ	τ	$::=$	$\mathsf{some}(t.\tau)$	$\exists(t.\tau)$	interface
Exp	e	$::=$	$\mathsf{pack}\{t.\tau\}\{\rho\}(e)$	$\mathsf{pack}\,\rho\,\mathsf{with}\,e\,\mathsf{as}\,\exists(t.\tau)$	implementation
			$\mathsf{open}\{t.\tau\}\{\rho\}(e_1; t, x.e_2)$	$\mathsf{open}\,e_1\,\mathsf{as}\,t\,\mathsf{with}\,x{:}\tau\,\mathsf{in}\,e_2$	client

The introduction form $\exists(t.\tau)$ is a *package* of the form $\mathsf{pack}\,\rho\,\mathsf{with}\,e\,\mathsf{as}\,\exists(t.\tau)$, where ρ is a type and e is an expression of type $[\rho/t]\tau$. The type ρ is the *representation type* of the package, and the expression e is the *implementation* of the package. The elimination form is the expression open e_1 as t with x:τ in e_2, which *opens* the package e_1 for use within the *client* e_2 by binding its representation type to t and its implementation to x for use within e_2. Crucially, the typing rules ensure that the client is type-correct independently of the actual representation type used by the implementor, so that it can be varied without affecting the type correctness of the client.

The abstract syntax of the open construct specifies that the type variable t and the expression variable x are bound within the client. They may be renamed at will by α-equivalence without affecting the meaning of the construct, provided, of course, that the names do not conflict with any others in scope. In other words the type t is a "new" type, one that is distinct from all other types, when it is introduced. This principle is sometimes called *generativity* of abstract types: the use of an abstract type by a client "generates" a "new" type within that client. This behavior relies on the identification covnention stated in Chapter 1.

17.1.1 Statics

The statics of **FE** is given by these rules:

$$\frac{\Delta, t \text{ type} \vdash \tau \text{ type}}{\Delta \vdash \text{some}(t.\tau) \text{ type}} \tag{17.1a}$$

$$\frac{\Delta \vdash \rho \text{ type} \quad \Delta, t \text{ type} \vdash \tau \text{ type} \quad \Delta \, \Gamma \vdash e : [\rho/t]\tau}{\Delta \, \Gamma \vdash \text{pack}\{t.\tau\}\{\rho\}(e) : \text{some}(t.\tau)} \tag{17.1b}$$

$$\frac{\Delta \, \Gamma \vdash e_1 : \text{some}(t.\tau) \quad \Delta, t \text{ type } \Gamma, x : \tau \vdash e_2 : \tau_2 \quad \Delta \vdash \tau_2 \text{ type}}{\Delta \, \Gamma \vdash \text{open}\{t.\tau\}\{\tau_2\}(e_1; t, x.e_2) : \tau_2} \tag{17.1c}$$

Rule (17.1c) is complex, so study it carefully! There are two important things to notice:

1. The type of the client, τ_2, must not involve the abstract type t. This restriction prevents the client from attempting to export a value of the abstract type outside of the scope of its definition.

2. The body of the client, e_2, is type checked without knowledge of the representation type, t. The client is, in effect, polymorphic in the type variable t.

Lemma 17.1 (Regularity). *Suppose that* $\Delta \, \Gamma \vdash e : \tau$. *If* $\Delta \vdash \tau_i$ *type for each* $x_i : \tau_i$ *in* Γ, *then* $\Delta \vdash \tau$ *type.*

Proof By induction on rules (17.1), using substitution for expressions and types. □

17.1.2 Dynamics

The dynamics of **FE** is defined by the following rules (including the bracketed material for an eager interpretation, and omitting it for a lazy interpretation):

$$\frac{[e \text{ val}]}{\text{pack}\{t.\tau\}\{\rho\}(e) \text{ val}} \tag{17.2a}$$

$$\left[\frac{e \longmapsto e'}{\text{pack}\{t.\tau\}\{\rho\}(e) \longmapsto \text{pack}\{t.\tau\}\{\rho\}(e')}\right] \tag{17.2b}$$

$$\frac{e_1 \longmapsto e_1'}{\text{open}\{t.\tau\}\{\tau_2\}(e_1; t, x.e_2) \longmapsto \text{open}\{t.\tau\}\{\tau_2\}(e_1'; t, x.e_2)} \tag{17.2c}$$

$$\frac{[e \text{ val}]}{\text{open}\{t.\tau\}\{\tau_2\}(\text{pack}\{t.\tau\}\{\rho\}(e); t, x.e_2) \longmapsto [\rho, e/t, x]e_2} \tag{17.2d}$$

It is important to see that, according to these rules, *there are no abstract types at runtime!* The representation type is propagated to the client by substitution when the package is opened, thereby eliminating the abstraction boundary between the client and the implementor. Thus, data abstraction is a *compile-time discipline* that leaves no traces of its presence at execution time.

17.1.3 Safety

Safety of **FE** is stated and proved by decomposing it into progress and preservation.

Theorem 17.2 (Preservation). *If $e : \tau$ and $e \longmapsto e'$, then $e' : \tau$.*

Proof   By rule induction on $e \longmapsto e'$, using substitution for both expression- and type variables.   □

Lemma 17.3 (Canonical Forms). *If $e : \text{some}(t.\tau)$ and e val, then $e = \text{pack}\{t.\tau\}\{\rho\}(e')$ for some type ρ and some e' such that $e' : [\rho/t]\tau$.*

Proof   By rule induction on the statics, using the definition of closed values.   □

Theorem 17.4 (Progress). *If $e : \tau$, then either e val or there exists e' such that $e \longmapsto e'$.*

Proof   By rule induction on $e : \tau$, using the canonical forms lemma.   □

17.2 Data Abstraction

To illustrate the use of **FE**, we consider an abstract type of queues of natural numbers supporting three operations:

1. Forming the empty queue.
2. Inserting an element at the tail of the queue.
3. Removing the head of the queue, which is assumed non-empty.

This is clearly a bare-bones interface but suffices to illustrate the main ideas of data abstraction. Queue elements are natural numbers, but nothing depends on this choice.

The crucial property of this description is that nowhere do we specify what queues actually *are*, only what we can *do* with them. The behavior of a queue is expressed by the existential type $\exists(t.\tau)$, which serves as the interface of the queue abstraction:

$$\exists(t.\langle \text{emp} \hookrightarrow t, \text{ins} \hookrightarrow \text{nat} \times t \to t, \text{rem} \hookrightarrow t \to (\text{nat} \times t)\,\text{opt}\rangle).$$

The representation type t of queues is *abstract*—all that is known about it is that it supports the operations emp, ins, and rem, with the given types.

An implementation of queues consists of a package specifying the representation type, together with the implementation of the associated operations in terms of that representation. Internally to the implementation, the representation of queues is known and relied upon by the operations. Here is a very simple implementation e_l in which queues are represented as lists:

$$\text{pack natlist with } \langle \text{emp} \hookrightarrow \text{nil}, \text{ins} \hookrightarrow e_i, \text{rem} \hookrightarrow e_r \rangle \text{ as } \exists(t.\tau),$$

where

$$e_i : \text{nat} \times \text{natlist} \to \text{natlist} = \lambda\,(x : \text{nat} \times \text{natlist})\ldots,$$

and

$$e_r : \text{natlist} \to \text{nat} \times \text{natlist} = \lambda\,(x : \text{natlist})\ldots.$$

The elided body of e_i conses the first component of x, the element, onto the second component of x, the queue, and the elided body of e_r reverses its argument, and returns the head element paired with the reversal of the tail. Both of these operations "know" that queues are represented as values of type natlist and are programmed accordingly.

It is also possible to give another implementation e_p of the same interface $\exists(t.\tau)$, but in which queues are represented as pairs of lists, consisting of the "back half" of the queue paired with the reversal of the "front half." This two-part representation avoids the need for reversals on each call and, as a result, achieves amortized constant-time behavior:

$$\text{pack natlist} \times \text{natlist with } \langle \text{emp} \hookrightarrow \langle \text{nil}, \text{nil}\rangle, \text{ins} \hookrightarrow e_i, \text{rem} \hookrightarrow e_r \rangle \text{ as } \exists(t.\tau).$$

In this case, e_i has type

$$\text{nat} \times (\text{natlist} \times \text{natlist}) \to (\text{natlist} \times \text{natlist}),$$

and e_r has type

$$(\mathtt{natlist} \times \mathtt{natlist}) \to \mathtt{nat} \times (\mathtt{natlist} \times \mathtt{natlist}).$$

These operations "know" that queues are represented as values of type $\mathtt{natlist} \times \mathtt{natlist}$ and are implemented accordingly.

The important point is that the *same* client type checks regardless of which implementation of queues we choose, because the representation type is hidden, or *held abstract*, from the client during type checking. Consequently, it cannot rely on whether it is $\mathtt{natlist}$ or $\mathtt{natlist} \times \mathtt{natlist}$ or some other type. That is, the client is *independent* of the representation of the abstract type.

17.3 Definability of Existential Types

The language **FE** is not a proper extension of **F**, because existential types (under a lazy dynamics) are definable in terms of universal types. Why should this be possible? Note that the client of an abstract type is *polymorphic* in the representation type. The typing rule for

$$\mathtt{open}\, e_1 \,\mathtt{as}\, t \,\mathtt{with}\, x{:}\tau \,\mathtt{in}\, e_2 : \tau_2,$$

where $e_1 : \exists(t.\tau)$, specifies that $e_2 : \tau_2$ under the assumptions t type and $x : \tau$. In essence, the client is a polymorphic function of type

$$\forall(t.\tau \to \tau_2),$$

where t may occur in τ (the type of the operations), but not in τ_2 (the type of the result).

This suggests the following encoding of existential types:

$$\exists(t.\tau) \triangleq \forall(u.\forall(t.\tau \to u) \to u)$$

$$\mathtt{pack}\, \rho \,\mathtt{with}\, e \,\mathtt{as}\, \exists(t.\tau) \triangleq \Lambda(u)\, \lambda\, (x : \forall(t.\tau \to u))\, x[\rho](e)$$

$$\mathtt{open}\, e_1 \,\mathtt{as}\, t \,\mathtt{with}\, x{:}\tau \,\mathtt{in}\, e_2 \triangleq e_1[\tau_2](\Lambda(t)\, \lambda\, (x : \tau)\, e_2)$$

An existential is encoded as a polymorphic function taking the overall result type u as argument, followed by a polymorphic function representing the client with result type u, and yielding a value of type u as overall result. Consequently, the open construct simply packages the client as such a polymorphic function, instantiates the existential at the result type, τ_2, and applies it to the polymorphic client. (The translation therefore depends on knowing the overall result type τ_2 of the open construct.) Finally, a package consisting of a representation type ρ and an implementation e is a polymorphic function that, when given the result type u and the client x, instantiates x with ρ and passes to it the implementation e.

17.4 Representation Independence

An important consequence of parametricity is that it ensures that clients are insensitive to the representations of abstract types. More precisely, there is a criterion, *bisimilarity*, for relating two implementations of an abstract type such that the behavior of a client is unaffected by swapping one implementation by another that is bisimilar to it. This principle leads to a simple method for proving the correctness of *candidate* implementation of an abstract type, which is to show that it is bisimilar to an obviously correct *reference* implementation of it. Because the candidate and the reference implementations are bisimilar, no client may distinguish them from one another, and hence if the client behaves properly with the reference implementation, then it must also behave properly with the candidate.

To derive the definition of bisimilarity of implementations, it is helpful to examine the definition of existential types in terms of universals given in Section 17.3. It is immediately clear that the client of an abstract type is polymorphic in the representation of the abstract type. A client c of an abstract type $\exists(t.\tau)$ has type $\forall(t.\tau \to \tau_2)$, where t does not occur free in τ_2 (but may, of course, occur in τ). Applying the parametricity property described informally in Chapter 16 (and developed rigorously in Chapter 48), this says that if R is a bisimulation relation between any two implementations of the abstract type, then the client behaves identically on them. The fact that t does not occur in the result type ensures that the behavior of the client is independent of the choice of relation between the implementations, provided that this relation is preserved by the operations that implement it.

Explaining what is a bisimulation is best done by example. Consider the existential type $\exists(t.\tau)$, where τ is the labeled tuple type

$$\langle \text{emp} \hookrightarrow t, \text{ins} \hookrightarrow \text{nat} \times t \to t, \text{rem} \hookrightarrow t \to (\text{nat} \times t)\,\text{opt}\rangle.$$

This specifies an abstract type of queues. The operations emp, ins, and rem specify, respectively, the empty queue, an insert operation, and a remove operation. For the sake of simplicity, the element type is the type of natural numbers. The result of removal is an optional pair, according to whether the queue is empty or not.

Theorem 48.12 ensures that if ρ and ρ' are any two closed types, and if R is a relation between expressions of these two types, then if the implementations $e : [\rho/x]\tau$ and $e' : [\rho'/x]\tau$ respect R, then $c[\rho]e$ behaves the same as $c[\rho']e'$. It remains to define when two implementations respect the relation R. Let

$$e \triangleq \langle \text{emp} \hookrightarrow e_{\text{m}}, \text{ins} \hookrightarrow e_{\text{i}}, \text{rem} \hookrightarrow e_{\text{r}}\rangle$$

and

$$e' \triangleq \langle \text{emp} \hookrightarrow e'_{\text{m}}, \text{ins} \hookrightarrow e'_{\text{i}}, \text{rem} \hookrightarrow e'_{\text{r}}\rangle.$$

For these implementations to respect R means that the following three conditions hold:

1. The empty queues are related: $R(e_{\text{m}}, e'_{\text{m}})$.
2. Inserting the same element on each of two related queues yields related queues: if $d : \tau$ and $R(q, q')$, then $R(e_{\text{i}}(d)(q), e'_{\text{i}}(d)(q'))$.

3. If two queues are related, then either they are both empty, or their front elements are the same and their back elements are related: if $R(q, q')$, then either

   (a) $e_r(q) \cong \mathtt{null} \cong e'_r(q')$, or

   (b) $e_r(q) \cong \mathtt{just}(\langle d, r \rangle)$ and $e'_r(q') \cong \mathtt{just}(\langle d', r' \rangle)$, with $d \cong d'$ and $R(r, r')$.

If such a relation R exists, then the implementations e and e' are *bisimilar*. The terminology stems from the requirement that the operations of the abstract type preserve the relation: if it holds before an operation is performed, then it must also hold afterwards, and the relation must hold for the initial state of the queue. Thus, each implementation *simulates* the other up to the relationship specified by R.

To see how this works in practice, let us consider informally two implementations of the abstract type of queues defined earlier. For the reference implementation, we choose ρ to be the type $\mathtt{natlist}$, and define the empty queue to be the empty list, define insert to add the given element to the head of the list, and define remove to remove the last element of the list. The code is as follows:

$$t \triangleq \mathtt{natlist}$$

$$\mathtt{emp} \triangleq \mathtt{nil}$$

$$\mathtt{ins} \triangleq \lambda\,(x : \mathtt{nat})\,\lambda\,(q : t)\,\mathtt{cons}(x; q)$$

$$\mathtt{rem} \triangleq \lambda\,(q : t)\,\mathtt{case\ rev}(q)\,\{\mathtt{nil} \hookrightarrow \mathtt{null} \mid \mathtt{cons}(f; qr) \hookrightarrow \mathtt{just}(\langle f, \mathtt{rev}(qr) \rangle)\}.$$

Removing an element takes time linear in the length of the list, because of the reversal.

For the candidate implementation, we choose ρ' to be the type $\mathtt{natlist} \times \mathtt{natlist}$ of pairs of lists $\langle b, f \rangle$ in which b is the "back half" of the queue, and f is the *reversal* of the "front half" of the queue. For this representation, we define the empty queue to be a pair of empty lists, define insert to extend the back with that element at the head, and define remove based on whether the front is empty. If it is non-empty, the head element is removed from it and returned along with the pair consisting of the back and the tail of the front. If it is empty, and the back is not, then we reverse the back, remove the head element, and return the pair consisting of the empty list and the tail of the now-reversed back. The code is as follows:

$$t \triangleq \mathtt{natlist} \times \mathtt{natlist}$$

$$\mathtt{emp} \triangleq \langle \mathtt{nil}, \mathtt{nil} \rangle$$

$$\mathtt{ins} \triangleq \lambda\,(x : \mathtt{nat})\,\lambda\,(\langle bs, fs \rangle : t)\,\langle \mathtt{cons}(x; bs), fs \rangle$$

$$\mathtt{rem} \triangleq \lambda\,(\langle bs, fs \rangle : t)\,\mathtt{case}\ fs\ \{\mathtt{nil} \hookrightarrow e \mid \mathtt{cons}(f; fs') \hookrightarrow \langle bs, fs' \rangle\}, \text{ where}$$

$$e \triangleq \mathtt{case\ rev}(bs)\,\{\mathtt{nil} \hookrightarrow \mathtt{null} \mid \mathtt{cons}(b; bs') \hookrightarrow \mathtt{just}(\langle b, \langle \mathtt{nil}, bs' \rangle \rangle)\}.$$

The cost of the occasional reversal is amortized across the sequence of inserts and removes to show that each operation in a sequence costs unit time overall.

To show that the candidate implementation is correct, we show that it is bisimilar to the reference implementation. To do so, we specify a relation R between the types $\mathtt{natlist}$ and $\mathtt{natlist} \times \mathtt{natlist}$ such that the two implementations satisfy the three simulation conditions given earlier. The required relation states that $R(l, \langle b, f \rangle)$ iff the list l is the list

$app(b)(rev(f))$, where app is the evident append function on lists. That is, thinking of l as the reference representation of the queue, the candidate must ensure that the elements of b followed by the elements of f in reverse order form precisely the list l. It is easy to check that the implementations just described preserve this relation. Having done so, we are assured that the client c behaves the same regardless of whether we use the reference or the candidate. Because the reference implementation is obviously correct (albeit inefficient), the candidate must also be correct in that the behavior of any client is not affected by using it instead of the reference.

17.5 Notes

The connection between abstract types in programming languages and existential types in logic was made by Mitchell and Plotkin (1988). Closely related ideas were already present in Reynolds (1974), but the connection with existential types was not explicitly drawn there. The present formulation of representation independence follows closely Mitchell (1986).

Exercises

17.1. Show that the statics and dynamics of existential types are correctly simulated using the interpretation given in Section 17.3.

17.2. Define in **FE** of the coinductive type of streams of natural numbers as defined in Chapter 15. *Hint*: Define the representation in terms of the generator (introduction form) for streams.

17.3. Define in **FE** an arbitrary coinductive type $\nu(t.\tau)$. *Hint*: generalize your answer to Exercise **17.2**.

17.4. Representation independence for abstract types is a corollary of the parametricity theorem for polymorphic types, using the interpretation of **FE** in **F** given in Section 17.3. Recast the proof of equivalence of the two implementations of queues given in Section 17.4 as an instance of parametricity as defined informally in Chapter 16.

The concept of type quantification naturally leads to the consideration of quantification over *type constructors*, such as list, which are functions mapping types to types. For example, the abstract type of queues of natural numbers considered in Section 17.4 could be generalized to an abstract *type constructor* of queues that does not fix the element type. In the notation that we shall develop in this chapter, such an abstraction is expressed by the existential type $\exists q :: T \to T.\sigma$, where σ is the labeled tuple type

$$\langle \text{emp} \hookrightarrow \forall t :: T.t, \text{ins} \hookrightarrow \forall t :: T.t \times q[t] \to q[t], \text{rem} \hookrightarrow \forall t :: T.q[t] \to (t \times q[t]) \text{opt} \rangle.$$

The existential type quantifies over the *kind* $T \to T$ of type constructors, which map types to types. The operations are polymorphic, or *generic*, in the type of the elements of the queue. Their types involve instances of the abstract queue constructor $q[t]$ representing the abstract type of queues whose elements are of type t. The client instantiates the polymorphic quantifier to specify the element type; the implementations are parametric in this choice (in that their behavior is the same in any case). A package of the existential type given above consists of a representation type constructor and an implementation of the operations in terms of this choice. Possible representations include the constructor $\lambda (u :: T) u \text{ list}$ and the constructor $\lambda (u :: T) u \text{ list} \times u \text{ list}$, both of which have kind $T \to T$. It is easy to check that the implementations of the queue operations given in Section 17.4 carry over to the more general case, almost without change, because they do not rely on the type of the elements of the queue.

The language $\mathbf{F}_\omega$ enriches the language $\mathbf{F}$ with universal and existential quantification over kinds, such as $T \to T$, used in the queues example. The extension accounts for definitional equality of constructors. For example, an implementation of the existential given in the preceding paragraph have to give implementations for the operations in terms of the choice of representation for q. If, say, q is the constructor $\lambda (u :: T) u \text{ list}$, then the ins operation takes a type argument specifying the element type t and a queue of type $(\lambda (u :: T) u \text{ list})[t]$, which should simplify to $t \text{ list}$ by substitution of t for u in the body of the λ-abstraction. Definitional equality of constructors defines the permissible rules of simplification and thereby defines when two types are equal. Equal types should be interchangeable as classifiers, meaning that if e is of type τ and τ is definitionally equal to τ', then e should also have type τ'. In the queues example, any expression of type $t \text{ list}$ should also be of the unsimplified type to which it is definitionally equal.

18.1 Constructors and Kinds

The syntax of kinds of $\mathbf{F}_\omega$ is given by the following grammar:

Kind	κ	$::=$	Type	T	types
			Unit	1	nullary product
			$\mathrm{Prod}(\kappa_1;\kappa_2)$	$\kappa_1 \times \kappa_2$	binary product
			$\mathrm{Arr}(\kappa_1;\kappa_2)$	$\kappa_1 \to \kappa_2$	function

The kinds consist of the kind of types T and the unit kind Unit and are closed under formation of product and function kinds.

The syntax of constructors of $\mathbf{F}_\omega$ is defined by this grammar:

Con	c	$::=$	u	u	variable
			arr	$\to$	function constructor
			$\mathrm{all}\{\kappa\}$	$\forall_\kappa$	universal quantifier
			$\mathrm{some}\{\kappa\}$	$\exists_\kappa$	existential quantifier
			$\mathrm{proj}[\mathrm{l}](c)$	$c \cdot \mathrm{l}$	first projection
			$\mathrm{proj}[\mathrm{r}](c)$	$c \cdot \mathrm{r}$	second projection
			$\mathrm{app}(c_1;c_2)$	$c_1[c_2]$	application
			unit	$\langle\rangle$	null tuple
			$\mathrm{pair}(c_1;c_2)$	$\langle c_1,c_2\rangle$	pair
			$\mathrm{lam}(u.c)$	$\lambda(u)c$	abstraction

The syntax of constructors follows the syntax of kinds in that there are introduction and elimination forms for all kinds. The constants $\to$, $\forall_\kappa$, and $\exists_\kappa$ are the introduction forms for the kind T; there are no elimination forms, because types are only used to classify expressions. We use the meta-variable τ for constructors of kind T, and write $\tau_1 \to \tau_2$ for the application $\to[\tau_1][\tau_2]$, $\forall u :: \kappa.\tau$ for $\forall_\kappa[\lambda(u::\kappa)\tau]$, and similarly for the existential quantifier.

The statics of constructors and kinds of $\mathbf{F}_\omega$ is specified by the judgment

$$\Delta \vdash c :: \kappa$$

which states that the constructor c is well-formed with kind κ. The hypotheses Δ consist of a finite set of assumptions

$$u_1 :: \kappa_1, \ldots, u_n :: \kappa_n,$$

where $n \geq 0$, specifying the kinds of the active constructor variables.

The statics of constructors is defined by the following rules:

$$\frac{}{\Delta, u :: \kappa \vdash u :: \kappa} \tag{18.1a}$$

$$\frac{}{\Delta \vdash \to :: T \to T \to T} \tag{18.1b}$$

$$\frac{}{\Delta \vdash \forall_\kappa :: (\kappa \to T) \to T} \tag{18.1c}$$

$$\frac{}{\Delta \vdash \exists_\kappa :: (\kappa \to T) \to T} \tag{18.1d}$$

$$\frac{\Delta \vdash c :: \kappa_1 \times \kappa_2}{\Delta \vdash c \cdot \mathtt{l} :: \kappa_1} \tag{18.1e}$$

$$\frac{\Delta \vdash c :: \kappa_1 \times \kappa_2}{\Delta \vdash c \cdot \mathtt{r} :: \kappa_2} \tag{18.1f}$$

$$\frac{\Delta \vdash c_1 :: \kappa_2 \to \kappa \quad \Delta \vdash c_2 :: \kappa_2}{\Delta \vdash c_1[c_2] :: \kappa} \tag{18.1g}$$

$$\frac{}{\Delta \vdash \langle\rangle :: 1} \tag{18.1h}$$

$$\frac{\Delta \vdash c_1 :: \kappa_1 \quad \Delta \vdash c_2 :: \kappa_2}{\Delta \vdash \langle c_1, c_2 \rangle :: \kappa_1 \times \kappa_2} \tag{18.1i}$$

$$\frac{\Delta, u :: \kappa_1 \vdash c_2 :: \kappa_2}{\Delta \vdash \lambda(u)\, c_2 :: \kappa_1 \to \kappa_2} \tag{18.1j}$$

The kinds of the three constants specify that they can be used to build constructors of kind T, the kind of types, which, as usual, classify expressions.

18.2 Constructor Equality

The rules of definitional equality for $\mathbf{F}_\omega$ define when two constructors, in particular two types, are interchangeable by differing only by simplifications that can be performed to obtain one from the other. The judgment

$$\Delta \vdash c_1 \equiv c_2 :: \kappa$$

states that c_1 and c_2 are definitionally equal constructors of kind κ. When κ is the kind T, the constructors c_1 and c_2 are *definitionally equal types*.

Definitional equality of constructors is defined by these rules:

$$\frac{\Delta \vdash c :: \kappa}{\Delta \vdash c \equiv c :: \kappa} \tag{18.2a}$$

$$\frac{\Delta \vdash c \equiv c' :: \kappa}{\Delta \vdash c' \equiv c :: \kappa} \tag{18.2b}$$

$$\frac{\Delta \vdash c \equiv c' :: \kappa \quad \Delta \vdash c' \equiv c'' :: \kappa}{\Delta \vdash c \equiv c'' :: \kappa} \tag{18.2c}$$

$$\frac{\Delta \vdash c \equiv c' :: \kappa_1 \times \kappa_2}{\Delta \vdash c \cdot \mathtt{l} \equiv c' \cdot \mathtt{l} :: \kappa_1} \tag{18.2d}$$

$$\frac{\Delta \vdash c \equiv c' :: \kappa_1 \times \kappa_2}{\Delta \vdash c \cdot \mathtt{r} \equiv c' \cdot \mathtt{r} :: \kappa_2} \tag{18.2e}$$

$$\frac{\Delta \vdash c_1 \equiv c_1' :: \kappa_1 \quad \Delta \vdash c_2 \equiv c_2' :: \kappa_2}{\Delta \vdash \langle c_1, c_2 \rangle \equiv \langle c_1', c_2' \rangle :: \kappa_1 \times \kappa_2} \tag{18.2f}$$

$$\frac{\Delta \vdash c_1 :: \kappa_1 \quad \Delta \vdash c_2 :: \kappa_2}{\Delta \vdash \langle c_1, c_2 \rangle \cdot 1 \equiv c_1 :: \kappa_1} \tag{18.2g}$$

$$\frac{\Delta \vdash c_1 :: \kappa_1 \quad \Delta \vdash c_2 :: \kappa_2}{\Delta \vdash \langle c_1, c_2 \rangle \cdot \mathbf{r} \equiv c_2 :: \kappa_2} \tag{18.2h}$$

$$\frac{\Delta \vdash c_1 \equiv c_1' :: \kappa_2 \to \kappa \quad \Delta \vdash c_2 \equiv c_2' :: \kappa_2}{\Delta \vdash c_1[c_2] \equiv c_1'[c_2'] :: \kappa} \tag{18.2i}$$

$$\frac{\Delta, u :: \kappa \vdash c_2 \equiv c_2' :: \kappa_2}{\Delta \vdash \lambda\,(u :: \kappa)\,c_2 \equiv \lambda\,(u :: \kappa)\,c_2' :: \kappa \to \kappa_2} \tag{18.2j}$$

$$\frac{\Delta, u :: \kappa_1 \vdash c_2 :: \kappa_2 \quad \Delta \vdash c_1 :: \kappa_1}{\Delta \vdash (\lambda\,(u :: \kappa)\,c_2)[c_1] \equiv [c_1/u]c_2 :: \kappa_2} \tag{18.2k}$$

In short, definitional equality of constructors is the strongest congruence containing the rules (18.2g), (18.2h), and (18.2k).

18.3 Expressions and Types

The statics of expressions of $\mathbf{F}_\omega$ is defined using two judgment forms:

$$\Delta \vdash \tau \text{ type} \qquad \text{type formation}$$
$$\Delta\,\Gamma \vdash e : \tau \qquad \text{expression formation}$$

Here, as before, Γ is a finite set of hypotheses of the form

$$x_1 : \tau_1, \ldots, x_k : \tau_k$$

such that $\Delta \vdash \tau_i$ type for each $1 \le i \le k$.

The types of $\mathbf{F}_\omega$ are the constructors of kind T:

$$\frac{\Delta \vdash \tau :: \mathrm{T}}{\Delta \vdash \tau \text{ type}} \ . \tag{18.3}$$

This being the only rule for introducing types, the *only* types are the constructors of kind T.

Definitionally equal types classify the same expressions:

$$\frac{\Delta\,\Gamma \vdash e : \tau_1 \quad \Delta \vdash \tau_1 \equiv \tau_2 :: \mathrm{T}}{\Gamma \vdash e : \tau_2} \ . \tag{18.4}$$

This rule ensures that in situations such as that described in the introduction to this chapter, typing is influenced by simplification of types.

The language $\mathbf{F}_\omega$ extends $\mathbf{F}$ to permit universal quantification over arbitrary kinds; the language $\mathbf{FE}_\omega$ extends $\mathbf{F}_\omega$ with existential quantification over arbitrary kinds. The statics of the quantifiers in $\mathbf{FE}_\omega$ is defined by the following rules:

$$\frac{\Delta, u :: \kappa\,\Gamma \vdash e : \tau}{\Delta\,\Gamma \vdash \Lambda(u :: \kappa)\,e : \forall\,u :: \kappa.\tau} \tag{18.5a}$$

$$\frac{\Delta\,\Gamma \vdash e : \forall u :: \kappa.\tau \quad \Delta \vdash c :: \kappa}{\Delta\,\Gamma \vdash e[c] : [c/u]\tau} \tag{18.5b}$$

$$\frac{\Delta \vdash c :: \kappa \quad \Delta, u :: \kappa \vdash \tau\ \text{type} \quad \Delta\,\Gamma \vdash e : [c/u]\tau}{\Delta\,\Gamma \vdash \text{pack}\,c\,\text{with}\,e\,\text{as}\,\exists u :: \kappa.\tau : \exists u :: \kappa.\tau} \tag{18.5c}$$

$$\frac{\Delta\,\Gamma \vdash e_1 : \exists u :: \kappa.\tau \quad \Delta, u :: \kappa\,\Gamma, x : \tau \vdash e_2 : \tau_2 \quad \Delta \vdash \tau_2\ \text{type}}{\Delta\,\Gamma \vdash \text{open}\,e_1\,\text{as}\,u :: \kappa\,\text{with}\,x : \tau\,\text{in}\,e_2 : \tau_2} \tag{18.5d}$$

The dynamics of $\mathbf{FE}_\omega$ is the subject of Exercise **18.2**.

18.4 Notes

The language $\mathbf{F}_\omega$ given here is standard, apart from details of notation. The rule of invariance of typing under definitional equality of types demands that a type checking algorithm must include as a subroutine an algorithm for checking definitional equality. Numerous methods for checking such equivalences are given in the literature, all of which proceed by various means to simplify both sides of an equation, and check whether the results are the same. Another approach, pioneered by Watkins et al. (2008) in another setting, is to avoid definitional equality by maintaining constructors in simplified form. The discussion in the introduction shows that substitution of a simplified constructor into a simplified constructor is not necessarily simplified. The burden is then shifted to defining a form of simplifying substitution whose result is always in simplified form.

Exercises

18.1. Adapt the two implementations of queues given in Chapter 17 to match the signature of queue constructors given in the introduction,

$$\exists q :: \text{T} \to \text{T}.\langle \text{emp} \hookrightarrow \forall t :: \text{T}.t, \text{ins} \hookrightarrow \forall t :: \text{T}.t \times q[t] \to q[t],$$

$$\text{rem} \hookrightarrow \forall t :: \text{T}.q[t] \to (t \times q[t])\,\text{opt}\rangle.$$

Consider the role played by definitional equality in ensuring that both implementations have this type.

18.2. Give an equational dynamics for $\mathbf{FE}_\omega$. What role does definitional equality of constructors play in it? Formulate a transition dynamics for $\mathbf{FE}_\omega$ extended with a type of observable results, say, nat. What role does definitional equality play in the transition dynamics?

PART VIII

Partiality and Recursive Types

We introduced the language **T** as a basis for discussing total computations, those for which the type system guarantees termination. The language **M** generalizes **T** to admit inductive and coinductive types, while preserving totality. In this chapter, we introduce **PCF** as a basis for discussing partial computations, those that may not terminate when evaluated, even when they are well-typed. At first blush, this may seem like a disadvantage, but as we shall see in Chapter 20, it admits greater expressive power than is possible in **T**.

The source of partiality in **PCF** is the concept of *general recursion*, which permits the solution of equations between expressions. The price for admitting solutions to all such equations is that computations may not terminate—the solution to some equations might be undefined (divergent). In **PCF**, the programmer must make sure that a computation terminates; the type system does not guarantee it. The advantage is that the termination proof need not be embedded into the code itself, resulting in shorter programs.

For example, consider the equations

$$f(0) \triangleq 1$$
$$f(n+1) \triangleq (n+1) \times f(n).$$

Intuitively, these equations define the factorial function. They form a system of simultaneous equations in the unknown f, which ranges over functions on the natural numbers. The function we seek is a *solution* to these equations—a specific function $f : \mathbb{N} \to \mathbb{N}$ such that the above conditions are satisfied.

A solution to such a system of equations is a fixed point of an associated functional (higher-order function). To see this, let us re-write these equations in another form:

$$f(n) \triangleq \begin{cases} 1 & \text{if } n = 0 \\ n \times f(n') & \text{if } n = n' + 1. \end{cases}$$

Re-writing yet again, we seek f given by

$$n \mapsto \begin{cases} 1 & \text{if } n = 0 \\ n \times f(n') & \text{if } n = n' + 1. \end{cases}$$

Now define the *functional* F by the equation $F(f) = f'$, where f' is given by

$$n \mapsto \begin{cases} 1 & \text{if } n = 0 \\ n \times f(n') & \text{if } n = n' + 1. \end{cases}$$

Note well that the condition on f' is expressed in terms of f, the argument to the functional F, and not in terms of f' itself! The function f we seek is a *fixed point* of F, a function $f : \mathbb{N} \to \mathbb{N}$ such that $f = F(f)$. In other words e is defined to be *fix*(F), where *fix* is a higher-order operator on functionals F that computes a fixed point for it.

Why should an operator such as F have a fixed point? The key is that functions in **PCF** are *partial*, which means that they may diverge on some (or even all) inputs. Consequently, a fixed point of a functional F is the limit of a series of approximations of the desired solution obtained by iterating F. Let us say that a partial function ϕ on the natural numbers, is an *approximation* to a total function f if $\phi(m) = n$ implies that $f(m) = n$. Let $\bot \colon \mathbb{N} \rightharpoonup \mathbb{N}$ be the totally undefined partial function—$\bot(n)$ is undefined for every $n \in \mathbb{N}$. This is the "worst" approximation to the desired solution f of the recursion equations given above. Given any approximation ϕ of f, we may "improve" it to $\phi' = F(\phi)$. The partial function ϕ' is defined on 0 and on $m + 1$ for every $m \geq 0$ on which ϕ is defined. Continuing, $\phi'' = F(\phi') = F(F(\phi))$ is an improvement on ϕ', and hence a further improvement on ϕ. If we start with $\bot$ as the initial approximation to f, then pass to the limit

$$\lim_{i \geq 0} F^{(i)}(\bot),$$

we will obtain the least approximation to f that is defined for every $m \in \mathbb{N}$, and hence is the function f itself. Turning this around, if the limit exists, it is the solution we seek.

Because this construction works for any functional F, we conclude that *all* such operators have fixed points, and hence that *all* systems of equations such as the one given above have solutions. The solution is given by general recursion, but there is no guarantee that it is a total function (defined on all elements of its domain). For the above example, it happens to be true, because we can prove by induction that this is so, but in general, the solution is a partial function that may diverge on some inputs. It is our task as programmers to ensure that the functions defined by general recursion are total, or at least that we have a grasp of those inputs for which it is well-defined.

19.1 Statics

The syntax of **PCF** is given by the following grammar:

Typ	τ	::=	nat	nat	naturals
			$\mathtt{parr}(\tau_1; \tau_2)$	$\tau_1 \rightharpoonup \tau_2$	partial function
Exp	e	::=	x	x	variable
			z	z	zero
			$\mathtt{s}(e)$	$\mathtt{s}(e)$	successor
			$\mathtt{ifz}\{e_0; x.e_1\}(e)$	$\mathtt{ifz}\, e\, \{\mathtt{z} \hookrightarrow e_0 \mid \mathtt{s}(x) \hookrightarrow e_1\}$	zero test
			$\mathtt{lam}\{\tau\}(x.e)$	$\lambda\,(x : \tau)\, e$	abstraction
			$\mathtt{ap}(e_1; e_2)$	$e_1(e_2)$	application
			$\mathtt{fix}\{\tau\}(x.e)$	$\mathtt{fix}\, x : \tau\, \mathtt{is}\, e$	recursion

The expression $\mathtt{fix}\{\tau\}(x.e)$ is *general recursion*; it is discussed in more detail below. The expression $\mathtt{ifz}\{e_0; x.e_1\}(e)$ branches according to whether e evaluates to $\mathtt{z}$, binding the predecessor to x in the case that it is not.

The statics of **PCF** is inductively defined by the following rules:

$$\frac{}{\Gamma, x : \tau \vdash x : \tau} \tag{19.1a}$$

$$\frac{}{\Gamma \vdash \mathtt{z} : \mathtt{nat}} \tag{19.1b}$$

$$\frac{\Gamma \vdash e : \mathtt{nat}}{\Gamma \vdash \mathtt{s}(e) : \mathtt{nat}} \tag{19.1c}$$

$$\frac{\Gamma \vdash e : \mathtt{nat} \quad \Gamma \vdash e_0 : \tau \quad \Gamma, x : \mathtt{nat} \vdash e_1 : \tau}{\Gamma \vdash \mathtt{ifz}\{e_0; x.e_1\}(e) : \tau} \tag{19.1d}$$

$$\frac{\Gamma, x : \tau_1 \vdash e : \tau_2}{\Gamma \vdash \mathtt{lam}\{\tau_1\}(x.e) : \mathtt{parr}(\tau_1; \tau_2)} \tag{19.1e}$$

$$\frac{\Gamma \vdash e_1 : \mathtt{parr}(\tau_2; \tau) \quad \Gamma \vdash e_2 : \tau_2}{\Gamma \vdash \mathtt{ap}(e_1; e_2) : \tau} \tag{19.1f}$$

$$\frac{\Gamma, x : \tau \vdash e : \tau}{\Gamma \vdash \mathtt{fix}\{\tau\}(x.e) : \tau} \tag{19.1g}$$

Rule (19.1g) reflects the self-referential nature of general recursion. To show that $\mathtt{fix}\{\tau\}(x.e)$ has type τ, we *assume* that it is the case by assigning that type to the variable x, which stands for the recursive expression itself, and checking that the body, e, has type τ under this very assumption.

The structural rules, including in particular substitution, are admissible for the static semantics.

Lemma 19.1. *If $\Gamma, x : \tau \vdash e' : \tau'$, $\Gamma \vdash e : \tau$, then $\Gamma \vdash [e/x]e' : \tau'$.*

19.2 Dynamics

The dynamic semantics of **PCF** is defined by the judgments e val, specifying the closed values, and $e \longmapsto e'$, specifying the steps of evaluation.

The judgment e val is defined by the following rules:

$$\frac{}{\mathtt{z} \text{ val}} \tag{19.2a}$$

$$\frac{[e \text{ val}]}{\mathtt{s}(e) \text{ val}} \tag{19.2b}$$

$$\frac{}{\texttt{lam}\{\tau\}(x.e)\ \textsf{val}} \tag{19.2c}$$

The bracketed premise on rule (19.2b) is included for the *eager* interpretation of the successor operation, and omitted for the *lazy* interpretation. (See Chapter 36 for a further discussion of laziness.)

The transition judgment $e \longmapsto e'$ is defined by the following rules:

$$\left[\frac{e \longmapsto e'}{\texttt{s}(e) \longmapsto \texttt{s}(e')}\right] \tag{19.3a}$$

$$\frac{e \longmapsto e'}{\texttt{ifz}\{e_0; x.e_1\}(e) \longmapsto \texttt{ifz}\{e_0; x.e_1\}(e')} \tag{19.3b}$$

$$\frac{}{\texttt{ifz}\{e_0; x.e_1\}(\texttt{z}) \longmapsto e_0} \tag{19.3c}$$

$$\frac{\texttt{s}(e)\ \textsf{val}}{\texttt{ifz}\{e_0; x.e_1\}(\texttt{s}(e)) \longmapsto [e/x]e_1} \tag{19.3d}$$

$$\frac{e_1 \longmapsto e_1'}{\texttt{ap}(e_1; e_2) \longmapsto \texttt{ap}(e_1'; e_2)} \tag{19.3e}$$

$$\left[\frac{e_1\ \textsf{val} \quad e_2 \longmapsto e_2'}{\texttt{ap}(e_1; e_2) \longmapsto \texttt{ap}(e_1; e_2')}\right] \tag{19.3f}$$

$$\frac{[e_2\ \textsf{val}]}{\texttt{ap}(\texttt{lam}\{\tau\}(x.e); e_2) \longmapsto [e_2/x]e} \tag{19.3g}$$

$$\frac{}{\texttt{fix}\{\tau\}(x.e) \longmapsto [\texttt{fix}\{\tau\}(x.e)/x]e} \tag{19.3h}$$

The bracketed rule (19.3a) is included for an eager interpretation of the successor and omitted otherwise. Bracketed rule (19.3f) and the bracketed premise on rule (19.3g) are included for a call-by-value interpretation, and omitted for a call-by-name interpretation, of function application. Rule (19.3h) implements self-reference by substituting the recursive expression itself for the variable x in its body; this is called *unwinding* the recursion.

Theorem 19.2 (Safety).

1. If $e : \tau$ and $e \longmapsto e'$, then $e' : \tau$.

2. If $e : \tau$, then either e val or there exists e' such that $e \longmapsto e'$.

Proof The proof of preservation is by induction on the derivation of the transition judgment. Consider rule (19.3h). Suppose that $\texttt{fix}\{\tau\}(x.e) : \tau$. By inversion and substitution we have $[\texttt{fix}\{\tau\}(x.e)/x]e : \tau$, as required. The proof of progress proceeds by induction on the derivation of the typing judgment. For example, for rule (19.1g) the result follows because we may make progress by unwinding the recursion. $\qquad\qquad\square$

It is easy to check that if e val, then e is irreducible in that there is no e' such that $e \longmapsto e'$. The safety theorem implies the converse, that an irreducible expression is a value, provided that it is closed and well-typed.

Definitional equality for the call-by-name variant of **PCF**, written $\Gamma \vdash e_1 \equiv e_2 : \tau$, is the strongest congruence containing the following axioms:

$$\frac{}{\Gamma \vdash \mathtt{ifz}\{e_0; x.e_1\}(\mathtt{z}) \equiv e_0 : \tau} \tag{19.4a}$$

$$\frac{}{\Gamma \vdash \mathtt{ifz}\{e_0; x.e_1\}(\mathtt{s}(e)) \equiv [e/x]e_1 : \tau} \tag{19.4b}$$

$$\frac{}{\Gamma \vdash \mathtt{fix}\{\tau\}(x.e) \equiv [\mathtt{fix}\{\tau\}(x.e)/x]e : \tau} \tag{19.4c}$$

$$\frac{}{\Gamma \vdash \mathtt{ap}(\mathtt{lam}\{\tau_1\}(x.e_2); e_1) \equiv [e_1/x]e_2 : \tau} \tag{19.4d}$$

These rules suffice to calculate the value of any closed expression of type nat: if e : nat, then $e \equiv \bar{n}$: nat iff $e \longmapsto^* \bar{n}$.

19.3 Definability

Let us write $\mathtt{fun}\, x(y{:}\tau_1){:}\tau_2 \,\mathtt{is}\, e$ for a recursive function within whose body, $e : \tau_2$, are bound two variables, $y : \tau_1$ standing for the argument and $x : \tau_1 \rightharpoonup \tau_2$ standing for the function itself. The dynamic semantics of this construct is given by the axiom

$$\frac{}{(\mathtt{fun}\, x(y{:}\tau_1){:}\tau_2 \,\mathtt{is}\, e)(e_1) \longmapsto [\mathtt{fun}\, x(y{:}\tau_1){:}\tau_2 \,\mathtt{is}\, e, e_1/x, y]e} \; .$$

That is, to apply a recursive function, we substitute the recursive function itself for x and the argument for y in its body.

Recursive functions are defined in **PCF** using recursive functions, writing

$$\mathtt{fix}\, x : \tau_1 \rightharpoonup \tau_2 \,\mathtt{is}\, \lambda\,(y : \tau_1)\, e$$

for $\mathtt{fun}\, x(y{:}\tau_1){:}\tau_2 \,\mathtt{is}\, e$. We may easily check that the static and dynamic semantics of recursive functions are derivable from this definition.

The primitive recursion construct of **T** is defined in **PCF** using recursive functions by taking the expression

$$\mathtt{rec}\, e\, \{\mathtt{z} \hookrightarrow e_0 \mid \mathtt{s}(x)\, \mathtt{with}\, y \hookrightarrow e_1\}$$

to stand for the application $e'(e)$, where e' is the general recursive function

$$\mathtt{fun}\, f(u{:}\mathtt{nat}){:}\tau \,\mathtt{is}\, \mathtt{ifz}\, u\, \{\mathtt{z} \hookrightarrow e_0 \mid \mathtt{s}(x) \hookrightarrow [f(x)/y]e_1\}.$$

The static and dynamic semantics of primitive recursion are derivable in **PCF** using this expansion.

In general, functions definable in **PCF** are partial in that they may be undefined for some arguments. A partial (mathematical) function, $\phi : \mathbb{N} \rightharpoonup \mathbb{N}$, is *definable* in **PCF** iff there is an expression $e_\phi : \mathtt{nat} \rightharpoonup \mathtt{nat}$ such that $\phi(m) = n$ iff $e_\phi(\overline{m}) \equiv \overline{n} : \mathtt{nat}$. So, for example, if ϕ is the totally undefined function, then e_ϕ is any function that loops without returning when it is applied.

It is informative to classify those partial functions ϕ that are definable in **PCF**. The *partial recursive functions* are defined to be the primitive recursive functions extended with the *minimization* operation: given $\phi(m, n)$, define $\psi(n)$ to be the least $m \geq 0$ such that (1) for $m' < m$, $\phi(m', n)$ is defined and non-zero, and (2) $\phi(m, n) = 0$. If no such m exists, then $\psi(n)$ is undefined.

Theorem 19.3. *A partial function ϕ on the natural numbers is definable in* **PCF** *iff it is partial recursive.*

Proof sketch   Minimization is definable in **PCF**, so it is at least as powerful as the set of partial recursive functions. Conversely, we may, with some tedium, define an evaluator for expressions of **PCF** as a partial recursive function, using Gödel-numbering to represent expressions as numbers. Therefore, **PCF** does not exceed the power of the set of partial recursive functions.   □

Church's Law states that the partial recursive functions coincide with the set of effectively computable functions on the natural numbers—those that can be carried out by a program written in any programming language that is or will ever be defined.[1] Therefore, **PCF** is as powerful as any other programming language with respect to the set of definable functions on the natural numbers.

The universal function ϕ_{univ} for **PCF** is the partial function on the natural numbers defined by

$$\phi_{univ}(\ulcorner e \urcorner)(m) = n \text{ iff } e(\overline{m}) \equiv \overline{n} : \mathtt{nat}.$$

In contrast to **T**, the universal function ϕ_{univ} for **PCF** is partial (might be undefined for some inputs). It is, in essence, an interpreter that, given the code $\ulcorner e \urcorner$ of a closed expression of type $\mathtt{nat} \rightharpoonup \mathtt{nat}$, simulates the dynamic semantics to calculate the result, if any, of applying it to the $\overline{m}$, obtaining $\overline{n}$. Because this process may fail to terminate, the universal function is not defined for all inputs.

By Church's Law, the universal function is definable in **PCF**. In contrast, we proved in Chapter 9 that the analogous function is *not* definable in **T** using the technique of diagonalization. It is instructive to examine why that argument does not apply in the present setting. As in Section 9.4, we may derive the equivalence

$$e_\Delta(\ulcorner e_\Delta \urcorner) \equiv \mathtt{s}(e_\Delta(\ulcorner e_\Delta \urcorner))$$

for **PCF**. But now, instead of concluding that the universal function, e_{univ}, does not exist as we did for **T**, we instead conclude for **PCF** that e_{univ} diverges on the code for e_Δ applied to its own code.

19.4 Finite and Infinite Data Structures

Finite data types (products and sums), including their use in pattern matching and generic programming, carry over verbatim to **PCF**. However, the distinction between the eager and lazy dynamics for these constructs becomes more important. Rather than being a matter of preference, the decision to use an eager or lazy dynamics affects the meaning of a program: the "same" types mean different things in a lazy dynamics than in an eager dynamics. For example, the elements of a product type in an eager language are pairs of values of the component types. In a lazy language, they are instead pairs of unevaluated, possibly divergent, computations of the component types, a very different thing indeed. And similarly for sums.

The situation grows more acute for infinite types such as the type nat of "natural numbers." The scare quotes are warranted, because the "same" type has a very different meaning under an eager dynamics than under a lazy dynamics. In the former case, the type nat is, indeed, the authentic type of natural numbers—the least type containing zero and closed under successor. The principle of mathematical induction is valid for reasoning about the type nat in an eager dynamics. It corresponds to the inductive type nat defined in Chapter 15.

On the other hand, under a lazy dynamics the type nat is no longer the type of natural numbers at all. For example, it includes the value

$$\omega \triangleq \mathtt{fix}\, x : \mathtt{nat}\, \mathtt{is}\, \mathtt{s}(x),$$

which has itself as predecessor! It is, intuitively, an "infinite stack of successors," growing without end. It is clearly not a natural number (it is larger than all of them), so the principle of mathematical induction does not apply. In a lazy setting, nat could be renamed lnat to remind us of the distinction; it corresponds to the type conat defined in Chapter 15.

19.5 Totality and Partiality

The advantage of a total programming language such as **T** is that it ensures, by type checking, that every program terminates, and that every function is total. There is no way to have a well-typed program that goes into an infinite loop. This prohibition may seem appealing, until one considers that the upper bound on the time to termination may be large, so large that it might as well diverge for all practical purposes. But let us grant for the moment that it is a virtue of **T** that it precludes divergence. Why, then, bother with a language such as **PCF** that does not rule out divergence? After all, infinite loops are invariably bugs, so why not rule them out by type checking? The notion seems appealing until one tries to write a program in a language such as **T**.

Consider the computation of the greatest common divisor (gcd) of two natural numbers. It can be programmed in **PCF** by solving the following equations using general recursion:

$$gcd(m, 0) = m$$
$$gcd(0, n) = n$$
$$gcd(m, n) = gcd(m - n, n) \quad \text{if } m > n$$
$$gcd(m, n) = gcd(m, n - m) \quad \text{if } m < n$$

The type of *gcd* defined this way is $(\text{nat} \times \text{nat}) \rightharpoonup \text{nat}$, which suggests that it may not terminate for some inputs. But we may prove by induction on the sum of the pair of arguments that it is, in fact, a total function.

Now consider programming this function in **T**. It is, in fact, programmable using only primitive recursion, but the code to do it is rather painful (try it!). One way to see the problem is that in **T** the only form of looping is one that reduces a natural number by one on each recursive call; it is not (directly) possible to make a recursive call on a smaller number other than the immediate predecessor. In fact, one may code up more general patterns of terminating recursion using only primitive recursion as a primitive, but if you check the details, you will see that doing so comes at a price in performance and program complexity. Program complexity can be mitigated by building libraries that codify standard patterns of reasoning whose cost of development should be amortized over all programs, not just one in particular. But there is still the problem of performance. Indeed, the encoding of more general forms of recursion into primitive recursion means that, deep within the encoding, there must be a "timer" that goes down by ones to ensure that the program terminates. The result will be that programs written with such libraries will be slower than necessary.

But, one may argue, **T** is simply not a serious language. A more serious total programming language would admit sophisticated patterns of control without performance penalty. Indeed, one could easily envision representing the natural numbers in binary, rather than unary, and allowing recursive calls by halving to get logarithmic complexity. Such a formulation is possible, as would be quite a number of analogous ideas that avoid the awkwardness of programming in **T**. Could we not then have a practical language that rules out divergence?

We can, but at a cost. We have already seen one limitation of total programming languages: they are not universal. You cannot write an interpreter for **T** within **T**, and this limitation extends to any total language whatever. If this does not seem important, then consider the *Blum Size Theorem (BST)*, which places another limitation on total languages. Fix *any* total language $\mathcal{L}$ that permits writing functions on the natural numbers. Pick any blowup factor, say 2^{2^n}. The BST states that there is a total function on the natural numbers that is programmable in $\mathcal{L}$, but whose shortest program in $\mathcal{L}$ is larger by the given blowup factor than its shortest program in **PCF**!

The underlying idea of the proof is that *in a total language the proof of termination of a program must be baked into the code itself*, whereas *in a partial language the termination proof is an external verification condition left to the programmer*. There are, and always will be, programs whose termination proof is rather complicated to express, if you fix in advance the means of proving it total. (In **T** it was primitive recursion, but one can be more ambitious, yet still get caught by the BST.) But if you leave room for ingenuity, then programs can be short, because they do not have to embed the proof of their termination in their own running code.

19.6 Notes

The solution to recursion equations described here is based on Kleene's fixed point theorem for complete partial orders, specialized to the approximation ordering of partial functions. The language **PCF** is derived from Plotkin (1977) as a laboratory for the study of semantics of programming languages. Many authors have used PCF as the subject of study of many problems in semantics. It has thereby become the *E. coli* of programming languages.

Exercises

19.1. Consider the problem considered in Section 10.3 of how to define the mutually recursive "even" and "odd" functions. There we gave a solution in terms of primitive recursion. You are, instead, to give a solution in terms of general recursion. *Hint*: consider that a pair of mutually recursive functions is a recursive pair of functions.

19.2. Show that minimization, as explained before the statement of Theorem 19.3, is definable in **PCF**.

19.3. Consider the partial function ϕ_{halts} such that if $e : \text{nat} \rightharpoonup \text{nat}$, then $\phi_{halts}(\ulcorner e \urcorner)$ evaluates to zero iff $e(\ulcorner e \urcorner)$ converges, and evaluates to one otherwise. Prove that ϕ_{halts} is not definable in **PCF**.

19.4. Suppose that we changed the specification of minimization given prior to Theorem 19.3 so that $\psi(n)$ is the least m such that $\phi(m, n) = 0$ and is undefined if no such m exists. Is this "simplified" form of minimization definable in **PCF**?

19.5. Suppose that we wished to define, in the lazy variant of **PCF**, a version of the *parallel or* function specified a function of two arguments that returns z if either of its arguments is z, and s(z) otherwise. That is, we wish to find an expression e satisfying the following properties:

$$e(e_1)(e_2) \longmapsto^* z \text{ if } e_1 \longmapsto^* z$$
$$e(e_1)(e_2) \longmapsto^* z \text{ if } e_2 \longmapsto^* z$$
$$e(e_1)(e_2) \longmapsto^* s(z) \text{ otherwise}$$

Thus, e defines a total function of its two arguments, *even if* one of the arguments diverges. Clearly, such a function cannot be defined in the call-by-value variant of

PCF, but can it be defined in the call-by-name variant? If so, show how; if not, prove that it cannot be, and suggest an extension of **PCF** that would allow it to be defined.

19.6. We appealed to Church's Law to argue that the universal function for **PCF** is definable in **PCF**. See what is behind this claim by considering two aspects of the problem: (1) Gödel-numbering, the representation of abstract syntax by a number; (2) evaluation, the process of interpreting a function on its inputs. Part (1) is a technical issue arising from the limited data structures available in **PCF**. Part (2) is the heart of the matter; explore its implementation in terms of a solution to Part (1).

Note

1 See Chapter 21 for further discussion of Church's Law.

System FPC of Recursive Types

In this chapter, we study **FPC**, a language with products, sums, partial fucntions, and *recursive types*. Recursive types are solutions to type equations $t \cong \tau$ where there is no restriction on where t may occur in τ. Equivalently, a recursive type is a *fixed point* up to isomorphism of the associated unrestricted type operator $t.\tau$. By removing the restrictions on the type operator, we may consider the solution of a type equation such as $t \cong t \rightharpoonup t$, which describes a type that is isomorphic to the type of partial functions defined on itself. If types were sets, such an equation could not be solved, because there are more partial functions on a set than there are elements of that set. But *types are not sets*: they classify *computable* functions, not *arbitrary* functions. With types we may solve such "dubious" type equations, even though we cannot expect to do so with sets. The penalty is that we must admit non-termination. For one thing, type equations involving functions have solutions only if the functions involved are partial.

A benefit of working in the setting of partial functions is that type equations have *unique* solutions (up to isomorphism). Therefore, it makes sense, as we shall do in this chapter, to speak of *the* solution to a type equation. But what about the *distinct* solutions to a type equation given in Chapter 15? These turn out to coincide for any fixed dynamics but give rise to different solutions according to whether the dynamics is eager or lazy (as illustrated in Section 19.4 for the special case of the natural numbers). Under a lazy dynamics (where all constructs are evaluated lazily), recursive types have a coinductive flavor, and the inductive analogs are inaccessible. Under an eager dynamics (where all constructs are evaluated eagerly), recursive types have an inductive flavor. But the coinductive analogs are accessible as well, using function types to selectively impose laziness. It follows that the eager dynamics is *more expressive* than the lazy dynamics, because it is impossible to go the other way around (one cannot define inductive types in a lazy language).

20.1 Solving Type Equations

The language **FPC** has products, sums, and partial functions inherited from the preceding development, extended with the new concept of recursive types. The syntax of recursive types is defined as follows:

Typ	τ	::=	t	t	self-reference
			$\mathtt{rec}(t.\tau)$	$\mathtt{rec}\,t\,\mathtt{is}\,\tau$	recursive type
Exp	e	::=	$\mathtt{fold}\{t.\tau\}(e)$	$\mathtt{fold}(e)$	fold
			$\mathtt{unfold}(e)$	$\mathtt{unfold}(e)$	unfold

The subscript on the concrete syntax of fold is often omitted when it is clear from context.

Recursive types have the same general form as the inductive and coinductive types discussed in Chapter 15, but without restriction on the type operator involved. Recursive type are formed according to the rule:

$$\frac{\Delta, t \text{ type} \vdash \tau \text{ type}}{\Delta \vdash \text{rec}(t.\tau) \text{ type}} \tag{20.1}$$

The statics of folding and unfolding is given by the following rules:

$$\frac{\Gamma \vdash e : [\text{rec}(t.\tau)/t]\tau}{\Gamma \vdash \text{fold}\{t.\tau\}(e) : \text{rec}(t.\tau)} \tag{20.2a}$$

$$\frac{\Gamma \vdash e : \text{rec}(t.\tau)}{\Gamma \vdash \text{unfold}(e) : [\text{rec}(t.\tau)/t]\tau} \tag{20.2b}$$

The dynamics of folding and unfolding is given by these rules:

$$\frac{[e \text{ val}]}{\text{fold}\{t.\tau\}(e) \text{ val}} \tag{20.3a}$$

$$\left[\frac{e \longmapsto e'}{\text{fold}\{t.\tau\}(e) \longmapsto \text{fold}\{t.\tau\}(e')} \right] \tag{20.3b}$$

$$\frac{e \longmapsto e'}{\text{unfold}(e) \longmapsto \text{unfold}(e')} \tag{20.3c}$$

$$\frac{\text{fold}\{t.\tau\}(e) \text{ val}}{\text{unfold}(\text{fold}\{t.\tau\}(e)) \longmapsto e} \tag{20.3d}$$

The bracketed premise and rule are included for an *eager* interpretation of the introduction form, and omitted for a *lazy* interpretation. As mentioned in the introduction, the choice of eager or lazy dynamics affects the meaning of recursive types.

Theorem 20.1 (Safety). *1. If $e : \tau$ and $e \longmapsto e'$, then $e' : \tau$.*
2. If $e : \tau$, then either e val, or there exists e' such that $e \longmapsto e'$.

20.2 Inductive and Coinductive Types

Recursive types may be used to represent inductive types such as the natural numbers. Using an *eager* dynamics for **FPC**, the recursive type

$$\rho = \text{rec } t \text{ is } [\text{z} \hookrightarrow \text{unit}, \text{s} \hookrightarrow t]$$

satisfies the type equation

$$\rho \cong [\text{z} \hookrightarrow \text{unit}, \text{s} \hookrightarrow \rho],$$

and is isomorphic to the type of eager natural numbers. The introduction and elimination forms are defined on ρ by the following equations:[1]

$$z \triangleq \mathtt{fold}(\mathtt{z} \cdot \langle\rangle)$$

$$s(e) \triangleq \mathtt{fold}(\mathtt{s} \cdot e)$$

$$\mathtt{ifz}\, e \,\{\mathtt{z} \hookrightarrow e_0 \mid \mathtt{s}(x) \hookrightarrow e_1\} \triangleq \mathtt{case\, unfold}(e) \,\{\mathtt{z} \cdot \_ \hookrightarrow e_0 \mid \mathtt{s} \cdot x \hookrightarrow e_1\}.$$

It is a good exercise to check that the eager dynamics of natural numbers in **PCF** is correctly simulated by these definitions.

On the other hand, under a lazy dynamics for **FPC**, the same recursive type ρ',

$$\mathtt{rec}\, t \,\mathtt{is}\, [\mathtt{z} \hookrightarrow \mathtt{unit}, \mathtt{s} \hookrightarrow t],$$

satisfies the same type equation,

$$\rho' \cong [\mathtt{z} \hookrightarrow \mathtt{unit}, \mathtt{s} \hookrightarrow \rho'],$$

but is not the type of natural numbers! Rather, it is the type $\mathtt{lnat}$ of lazy natural numbers introduced in Section 19.4. As discussed there, the type ρ' contains the "infinite number" ω, which is of course not a natural number.

Similarly, using an eager dynamics for **FPC**, the type $\mathtt{natlist}$ of lists of natural numbers is defined by the recursive type

$$\mathtt{rec}\, t \,\mathtt{is}\, [\mathtt{n} \hookrightarrow \mathtt{unit}, \mathtt{c} \hookrightarrow \mathtt{nat} \times t],$$

which satisfies the type equation

$$\mathtt{natlist} \cong [\mathtt{n} \hookrightarrow \mathtt{unit}, \mathtt{c} \hookrightarrow \mathtt{nat} \times \mathtt{natlist}].$$

The list introduction operations are given by the following equations:

$$\mathtt{nil} \triangleq \mathtt{fold}(\mathtt{n} \cdot \langle\rangle)$$

$$\mathtt{cons}(e_1; e_2) \triangleq \mathtt{fold}(\mathtt{c} \cdot \langle e_1, e_2 \rangle).$$

A conditional list elimination form is given by the following equation:

$$\mathtt{case}\, e \,\{\mathtt{nil} \hookrightarrow e_0 \mid \mathtt{cons}(x; y) \hookrightarrow e_1\} \triangleq \mathtt{case\, unfold}(e) \,\{\mathtt{n} \cdot \_ \hookrightarrow e_0 \mid \mathtt{c} \cdot \langle x, y \rangle \hookrightarrow e_1\},$$

where we have used pattern-matching syntax to bind the components of a pair for the sake of clarity.

Now consider the *same* recursive type, but in the context of a lazy dynamics for **FPC**. What type is it? If all constructs are lazy, then a value of the recursive type

$$\mathtt{rec}\, t \,\mathtt{is}\, [\mathtt{n} \hookrightarrow \mathtt{unit}, \mathtt{c} \hookrightarrow \mathtt{nat} \times t],$$

has the form $\mathtt{fold}(e)$, where e is an unevaluated computation of the sum type, whose values are injections of unevaluated computations of either the unit type or of the product type $\mathtt{nat} \times t$. And the latter consists of pairs of an unevaluated computation of a (lazy!) natural number, and an unevaluated computation of another value of this type. In particular, this type contains infinite lists whose tails go on without end, as well as finite lists that eventually reach an end. The type is, in fact, a version of the type of infinite streams defined in Chapter 15, rather than a type of finite lists as is the case under an eager dynamics.

It is common in textbooks to depict data structures using "box-and-pointer" diagrams. These work well in the eager setting, provided that no functions are involved. For example, an eager list of eager natural numbers may be depicted using this notation. We may think of fold as an abstract pointer to a tagged cell consisting of either (a) the tag n with no associated data, or (b) the tag c attached to a pair consisting of an authentic natural number and another list, which is an abstract pointer of the same type. But this notation does not scale well to types involving functions, or to languages with a lazy dynamics. For example, the recursive type of "lists" in lazy **FPC** cannot be depicted using boxes and pointers, because of the unevaluated computations occurring in values of this type. It is a mistake to limit one's conception of data structures to those that can be drawn on the blackboard using boxes and pointers or similar informal notations. There is no substitute for a programming language to express data structures fully and accurately.

It is deceiving that the "same" recursive type can have two different meanings according to whether the underlying dynamics is eager or lazy. For example, it is common for lazy languages to use the name "list" for the recursive type of streams, or the name "nat" for the type of lazy natural numbers. This terminology is misleading, considering that such languages do not (and can not) have a proper type of finite lists or a type of natural numbers. *Caveat emptor!*

20.3 Self-Reference

In the general recursive expression $\text{fix}\{\tau\}(x.e)$, the variable x stands for the expression itself. Self-reference is effected by the unrolling transition

$$\text{fix}\{\tau\}(x.e) \longmapsto [\text{fix}\{\tau\}(x.e)/x]e,$$

which substitutes the expression itself for x in its body during execution. It is useful to think of x as an *implicit argument* to e that is instantiated to itself when the expression is used. In many well-known languages this implicit argument has a special name, such as this or self, to emphasize its self-referential interpretation.

Using this intuition as a guide, we may derive general recursion from recursive types. This derivation shows that general recursion may, like other language features, be seen as a manifestation of type structure, instead of as an *ad hoc* language feature. The derivation isolates a type of self-referential expressions given by the following grammar:

Typ	τ	::=	$\text{self}(\tau)$	τ self	self-referential type
Exp	e	::=	$\text{self}\{\tau\}(x.e)$	self x is e	self-referential expression
			$\text{unroll}(e)$	$\text{unroll}(e)$	unroll self-reference

The statics of these constructs is given by the following rules:

$$\frac{\Gamma, x : \text{self}(\tau) \vdash e : \tau}{\Gamma \vdash \text{self}\{\tau\}(x.e) : \text{self}(\tau)} \tag{20.4a}$$

$$\frac{\Gamma \vdash e : \mathtt{self}(\tau)}{\Gamma \vdash \mathtt{unroll}(e) : \tau} \tag{20.4b}$$

The dynamics is given by the following rule for unrolling the self-reference:

$$\frac{}{\mathtt{self}\{\tau\}(x.e) \; \mathsf{val}} \tag{20.5a}$$

$$\frac{e \longmapsto e'}{\mathtt{unroll}(e) \longmapsto \mathtt{unroll}(e')} \tag{20.5b}$$

$$\frac{}{\mathtt{unroll}(\mathtt{self}\{\tau\}(x.e)) \longmapsto [\mathtt{self}\{\tau\}(x.e)/x]e} \tag{20.5c}$$

The main difference, compared to general recursion, is that we distinguish a type of self-referential expressions, instead of having self-reference at every type. However, as we shall see, the self-referential type suffices to implement general recursion, so the difference is a matter of taste.

The type $\mathtt{self}(\tau)$ is definable from recursive types. As suggested earlier, the key is to consider a self-referential expression of type τ to depend on the expression itself. That is, we seek to define the type $\mathtt{self}(\tau)$ so that it satisfies the isomorphism

$$\mathtt{self}(\tau) \cong \mathtt{self}(\tau) \rightharpoonup \tau.$$

We seek a fixed point of the type operator $t.t \rightharpoonup \tau$, where $t \notin \tau$ is a type variable standing for the type in question. The required fixed point is just the recursive type

$$\mathtt{rec}(t.t \rightharpoonup \tau),$$

which we take as the definition of $\mathtt{self}(\tau)$.

The self-referential expression $\mathtt{self}\{\tau\}(x.e)$ is the expression

$$\mathtt{fold}(\lambda\,(x : \mathtt{self}(\tau))\,e).$$

We may check that rule (20.4a) is derivable according to this definition. The expression $\mathtt{unroll}(e)$ is correspondingly the expression

$$\mathtt{unfold}(e)(e).$$

It is easy to check that rule (20.4b) is derivable from this definition. Moreover, we may check that

$$\mathtt{unroll}(\mathtt{self}\{\tau\}(y.e)) \longmapsto^* [\mathtt{self}\{\tau\}(y.e)/y]e.$$

This completes the derivation of the type $\mathtt{self}(\tau)$ of self-referential expressions of type τ.

The self-referential type $\mathtt{self}(\tau)$ can be used to define general recursion for *any* type. We may define $\mathtt{fix}\{\tau\}(x.e)$ to stand for the expression

$$\mathtt{unroll}(\mathtt{self}\{\tau\}(y.[\mathtt{unroll}(y)/x]e))$$

where the recursion at each occurrence of x is unrolled within e. It is easy to check that this verifies the statics of general recursion given in Chapter 19. Moreover, it also validates the dynamics, as shown by the following derivation:

$$\mathtt{fix}\{\tau\}(x.e) = \mathtt{unroll}(\mathtt{self}\{\tau\}(y.[\mathtt{unroll}(y)/x]e))$$
$$\longmapsto^* [\mathtt{unroll}(\mathtt{self}\{\tau\}(y.[\mathtt{unroll}(y)/x]e))/x]e$$
$$= [\mathtt{fix}\{\tau\}(x.e)/x]e.$$

It follows that recursive types can be used to define a non-terminating expression of every type, $\mathtt{fix}\{\tau\}(x.x)$.

20.4 The Origin of State

The concept of *state* in a computation—which will be discussed in Part XIV—has its origins in the concept of recursion, or self-reference, which, as we have just seen, arises from the concept of recursive types. For example, the concept of a *flip-flop* or a *latch* is a circuit built from combinational logic elements (typically, nor or nand gates) that have the characteristic that they maintain an alterable state over time. An RS latch, for example, maintains its output at the logical level of zero or one in response to a signal on the R or S inputs, respectively, after a brief settling delay. This behavior is achieved using *feedback*, which is just a form of self-reference, or recursion: the output of the gate feeds back into its input so as to convey the current state of the gate to the logic that determines its next state.

We can implement an RS latch using recursive types. The idea is to use self-reference to model the passage of time, with the current output being computed from its input and its previous outputs. Specifically, an RS latch is a value of type τ_{rsl} given by

$$\mathtt{rec}\, t \,\mathtt{is}\, \langle X \hookrightarrow \mathtt{bool}, Q \hookrightarrow \mathtt{bool}, N \hookrightarrow t \rangle.$$

The X and Q components of the latch represent its current outputs (of which Q represents the current state of the latch), and the N component represents the next state of the latch. If e is of type τ_{rsl}, then we define $e \,@\, X$ to mean $\mathtt{unfold}(e) \cdot X$, and define $e \,@\, Q$ and $e \,@\, N$ similarly. The expressions $e \,@\, X$ and $e \,@\, Q$ evaluate to the boolean outputs of the latch e, and $e \,@\, N$ evaluates to another latch representing its evolution over time based on these inputs.

For given values r and s, a new latch is computed from an old latch by the recursive function rsl defined as follows:[2]

$$\mathtt{fix}\, rsl \,\mathtt{is}\, \lambda\, (l : \tau_{rsl})\, e_{rsl},$$

where e_{rsl} is the expression

$$\mathtt{fix}\, this \,\mathtt{is}\, \mathtt{fold}(\langle X \hookrightarrow e_{nor}(\langle s, l \,@\, Q \rangle), Q \hookrightarrow e_{nor}(\langle r, l \,@\, X \rangle), N \hookrightarrow rsl(this) \rangle),$$

where e_{nor} is the obvious binary function on booleans. The outputs of the latch are computed in terms of the r and s inputs and the outputs of the previous state of the latch. To get the construction started, we define an initial state of the latch in which the outputs are arbitrarily set to false, and whose next state is determined by applying the recursive function *rsl* to that state:

$$\texttt{fix } this \texttt{ is fold}(\langle \texttt{X} \hookrightarrow \texttt{false}, \texttt{Q} \hookrightarrow \texttt{false}, \texttt{N} \hookrightarrow rsl(this)\rangle).$$

Selection of the N component causes the outputs to be recalculated based on their current values. Notice the role of self-reference in maintaining the state of the latch.

20.5 Notes

The systematic study of recursive types in programming was initiated by Scott (1976, 1982) to give a mathematical model of the untyped λ-calculus. The derivation of recursion from recursive types is an application of Scott's theory. The category-theoretic view of recursive types was developed by Wand (1979) and Smyth and Plotkin (1982). Implementing state using self-reference is fundamental to digital logic (Ward and Halstead, 1990). The example given in Section 20.4 is inspired by Cook (2009) and Abadi and Cardelli (1996). The account of signals as streams (explored in the exercises) is inspired by the pioneering work of Kahn (MacQueen, 2009). The language name **FPC** is taken from Gunter (1992).

Exercises

20.1. Show that the recursive type $D \triangleq \texttt{rec } t \texttt{ is } t \rightharpoonup t$ is non-trivial by interpreting the sk-combinators defined in Exercise **3.1** into it. Specifically, define elements $k : D$ and $s : D$ and a (left-associative) "application" function

$$x : D \, y : D \vdash x \cdot y : D$$

such that
(a) $k \cdot x \cdot y \longmapsto^* x$;
(b) $s \cdot x \cdot y \cdot z \longmapsto^* (x \cdot z) \cdot (y \cdot z)$.

20.2. Recursive types admit the structure of both inductive and coinductive types. Consider the recursive type $\tau \triangleq \texttt{rec } t \texttt{ is } \tau'$ and the associated inductive and coinductive types $\mu(t.\tau')$ and $\nu(t.\tau')$. Complete the following chart consistently with the statics of inductive and coinductive types on the left-hand side and with the statics of recursive types on the right:

$$\texttt{fold}_{t.t \text{ opt}}(e) \triangleq \texttt{fold}(e)$$
$$\texttt{rec}(x.e'; e) \triangleq ?$$
$$\texttt{unfold}_{t.t \text{ opt}}(e) \triangleq \texttt{unfold}(e)$$
$$\texttt{gen}(x.e'; e) \triangleq ?$$

Check that the statics is derivable under these definitions. *Hint*: you will need to use general recursion on the right to fill in the missing cases. You may also find it useful to use generic programming.

Now consider the dynamics of these definitions, under both an eager and a lazy interpretation. What happens in each case?

20.3. Define the type `signal` of *signals* to be the coinductive type of infinite streams of booleans (bits). Define a *signal transducer* to be a function of type `signal` $\rightharpoonup$ `signal`. Combinational logic gates, such as the NOR gate, can be defined as signal transducers. Give a coinductive definition of the type `signal`, and define NOR as a signal transducer. Be sure to take account of the underlying dynamics of **PCF**.

The passage from combinational to digital logic (circuit elements that maintain state) relies on self-reference. For example, an RS latch can be built from NOR two nor gates in this way. Define an RS latch using general recursion and two of the NOR gates just defined.

20.4. The type τ_{rsl} given in Section 20.4 above is the type of streams of pairs of booleans. Give another formulation of an RS latch as a value of type τ_{rsl}, but this time using the coinductive interpretation of the recursive type proposed in Exercise **20.2** (using the lazy dynamics for **FPC**). Expand and simplify this definition using your solution to Exercise **20.2**, and compare it with the formulation given in Section 20.4. *Hint*: the internal state of the stream is a pair of booleans corresponding to the X and Q outputs of the latch.

Notes

1 The "underscore" stands for a variable that does not occur free in e_0.
2 For convenience, we assume that `fold` is evaluated lazily.

PART IX

Dynamic Types

21   The Untyped λ-Calculus

In this chapter, we study the premier example of a uni-typed programming language, the *(untyped) λ-calculus*. This formalism was introduced by Church in the 1930s as a universal language of computable functions. It is distinctive for its austere elegance. The λ-calculus has but one "feature," the higher-order function. Everything is a function, hence every expression may be applied to an argument, which must itself be a function, with the result also being a function. To borrow a turn of phrase, in the λ-calculus it's functions all the way down.

21.1   The λ-Calculus

The abstract syntax of the untyped λ-calculus, called Λ, is given by the following grammar:

$$
\begin{array}{llll}
\text{Exp} & u & ::= & x & x & \text{variable} \\
& & & \lambda(x.u) & \lambda(x)\,u & \text{λ-abstraction} \\
& & & \mathsf{ap}(u_1;u_2) & u_1(u_2) & \text{application}
\end{array}
$$

The statics of Λ is defined by general hypothetical judgments of the form x_1 ok, ..., x_n ok $\vdash u$ ok, stating that u is a well-formed expression involving the variables $x_1, \ldots, x_n$. (As usual, we omit explicit mention of the variables when they can be determined from the form of the hypotheses.) This relation is inductively defined by the following rules:

$$
\frac{}{\Gamma, x \text{ ok} \vdash x \text{ ok}} \tag{21.1a}
$$

$$
\frac{\Gamma \vdash u_1 \text{ ok} \quad \Gamma \vdash u_2 \text{ ok}}{\Gamma \vdash u_1(u_2) \text{ ok}} \tag{21.1b}
$$

$$
\frac{\Gamma, x \text{ ok} \vdash u \text{ ok}}{\Gamma \vdash \lambda(x)\,u \text{ ok}} \tag{21.1c}
$$

The dynamics of Λ is given equationally, rather than via a transition system. Definitional equality for Λ is a judgment of the form $\Gamma \vdash u \equiv u'$, where $\Gamma = x_1$ ok, ..., x_n ok for some $n \geq 0$, and u and u' are terms having at most the variables $x_1, \ldots, x_n$ free. It is inductively defined by the following rules:

$$
\frac{}{\Gamma, u \text{ ok} \vdash u \equiv u} \tag{21.2a}
$$

$$\frac{\Gamma \vdash u \equiv u'}{\Gamma \vdash u' \equiv u} \tag{21.2b}$$

$$\frac{\Gamma \vdash u \equiv u' \quad \Gamma \vdash u' \equiv u''}{\Gamma \vdash u \equiv u''} \tag{21.2c}$$

$$\frac{\Gamma \vdash u_1 \equiv u_1' \quad \Gamma \vdash u_2 \equiv u_2'}{\Gamma \vdash u_1(u_2) \equiv u_1'(u_2')} \tag{21.2d}$$

$$\frac{\Gamma, x \text{ ok} \vdash u \equiv u'}{\Gamma \vdash \lambda(x)u \equiv \lambda(x)u'} \tag{21.2e}$$

$$\frac{\Gamma, x \text{ ok} \vdash u_2 \text{ ok} \quad \Gamma \vdash u_1 \text{ ok}}{\Gamma \vdash (\lambda(x)u_2)(u_1) \equiv [u_1/x]u_2} \tag{21.2f}$$

We often write just $u \equiv u'$ when the variables involved need not be emphasized or are clear from context.

21.2 Definability

Interest in the untyped λ-calculus stems from its surprising expressiveness. It is a *Turing-complete* language in the sense that it has the same capability to express computations on the natural numbers as does any other known programming language. Church's Law states that any conceivable notion of computable function on the natural numbers is equivalent to the λ-calculus. This assertion is true for all *known* means of defining computable functions on the natural numbers. The force of Church's Law is that it postulates that all future notions of computation will be equivalent in expressive power (measured by definability of functions on the natural numbers) to the λ-calculus. Church's Law is therefore a *scientific law* in the same sense as, say, Newton's Law of Universal Gravitation, which predicts the outcome of all future measurements of the acceleration in a gravitational field.[1]

We will sketch a proof that the untyped λ-calculus is as powerful as the language PCF described in Chapter 19. The main idea is to show that the PCF primitives for manipulating the natural numbers are definable in the untyped λ-calculus. In particular, we must show that the natural numbers are definable as λ-terms in such a way that case analysis, which discriminates between zero and non-zero numbers, is definable. The principal difficulty is with computing the predecessor of a number, which requires a bit of cleverness. Finally, we show how to represent general recursion, completing the proof.

The first task is to represent the natural numbers as certain λ-terms, called the *Church numerals*.

$$\overline{0} \triangleq \lambda(b)\lambda(s)b \tag{21.3a}$$

$$\overline{n+1} \triangleq \lambda(b)\lambda(s)s(\overline{n}(b)(s)) \tag{21.3b}$$

It follows that

$$\overline{n}(u_1)(u_2) \equiv u_2(\ldots(u_2(u_1))),$$

the n-fold application of u_2 to u_1. That is, $\overline{n}$ iterates its second argument (the induction step) n times, starting with its first argument (the basis).

Using this definition, it is not difficult to define the basic functions of arithmetic. For example, successor, addition, and multiplication are defined by the following untyped λ-terms:

$$\mathtt{succ} \triangleq \lambda\,(x)\,\lambda\,(b)\,\lambda\,(s)\,s(x(b)(s)) \tag{21.4}$$

$$\mathtt{plus} \triangleq \lambda\,(x)\,\lambda\,(y)\,y(x)(\mathtt{succ}) \tag{21.5}$$

$$\mathtt{times} \triangleq \lambda\,(x)\,\lambda\,(y)\,y(\overline{0})(\mathtt{plus}(x)) \tag{21.6}$$

It is easy to check that $\mathtt{succ}(\overline{n}) \equiv \overline{n+1}$, and that similar correctness conditions hold for the representations of addition and multiplication.

To define $\mathtt{ifz}\{u_0; x.u_1\}(u)$ requires a bit of ingenuity. The key is to define the "cut-off predecessor," $\mathtt{pred}$, such that

$$\mathtt{pred}(\overline{0}) \equiv \overline{0} \tag{21.7}$$

$$\mathtt{pred}(\overline{n+1}) \equiv \overline{n}. \tag{21.8}$$

To compute the predecessor using Church numerals, we must show how to compute the result for $\overline{n+1}$ in terms of its value for $\overline{n}$. At first glance, this seems simple—just take the successor—until we consider the base case, in which we define the predecessor of $\overline{0}$ to be $\overline{0}$. This formulation invalidates the obvious strategy of taking successors at inductive steps, and necessitates some other approach.

What to do? A useful intuition is to think of the computation in terms of a pair of "shift registers" satisfying the invariant that on the nth iteration the registers contain the predecessor of n and n itself, respectively. Given the result for n, namely the pair $(n-1, n)$, we pass to the result for $n+1$ by shifting left and incrementing to obtain $(n, n+1)$. For the base case, we initialize the registers with $(0, 0)$, reflecting the stipulation that the predecessor of zero be zero. To compute the predecessor of n, we compute the pair $(n-1, n)$ by this method, and return the first component.

To make this precise, we must first define a Church-style representation of ordered pairs.

$$\langle u_1, u_2 \rangle \triangleq \lambda\,(f)\,f(u_1)(u_2) \tag{21.9}$$

$$u \cdot \mathtt{l} \triangleq u(\lambda\,(x)\,\lambda\,(y)\,x) \tag{21.10}$$

$$u \cdot \mathtt{r} \triangleq u(\lambda\,(x)\,\lambda\,(y)\,y) \tag{21.11}$$

It is easy to check that under this encoding $\langle u_1, u_2 \rangle \cdot \mathtt{l} \equiv u_1$, and that a similar equivalence holds for the second projection. We may now define the required representation, u_p, of the predecessor function:

$$u'_p \triangleq \lambda\,(x)\,x(\langle \overline{0}, \overline{0} \rangle)(\lambda\,(y)\,\langle y \cdot \mathtt{r}, \mathtt{succ}\,(y \cdot \mathtt{r}) \rangle) \tag{21.12}$$

$$u_p \triangleq \lambda\,(x)\,u'_p(x) \cdot \mathtt{l} \tag{21.13}$$

It is easy to check that this gives us the required behavior. Finally, define $\mathtt{ifz}\{u_0; x.u_1\}(u)$ to be the untyped term

$$u(u_0)(\lambda\,(\_)\,[u_p(u)/x]u_1).$$

This definition gives us all the apparatus of PCF, apart from general recursion. But general recursion is also definable in Λ using a *fixed point combinator*. There are many choices of fixed point combinator, of which the best known is the Y *combinator*:

$$\text{Y} \triangleq \lambda\,(F)\,(\lambda\,(f)\,F(f(f)))(\lambda\,(f)\,F(f(f))).$$

It is easy to check that

$$\text{Y}(F) \equiv F(\text{Y}(F)).$$

Using the Y combinator, we may define general recursion by writing $\text{Y}(\lambda\,(x)\,u)$, where x stands for the recursive expression itself.

Although it is clear that Y as just defined computes a fixed point of its argument, it is probably less clear why it works or how we might have invented it in the first place. The main idea is quite simple. If a function is recursive, it is given an extra first argument, which is arranged at call sites to be the function itself. Whenever we wish to call a self-referential function with an argument, we apply the function first to itself and then to its argument; this protocol is imposed on both the "external" calls to the function and on the "internal" calls that the function may make to itself. For this reason, the first argument is often called this or self, to remind you that it will be, by convention, bound to the function itself.

With this in mind, it is easy to see how to derive the definition of Y. If F is the function whose fixed point we seek, then the function $F' = \lambda\,(f)\,F(f(f))$ is a variant of F in which the self-application convention has been imposed internally by substituting for each occurrence of f in $F(f)$ the self-application $f(f)$. Now check that $F'(F') \equiv F(F'(F'))$, so that $F'(F')$ is the desired fixed point of F. Expanding the definition of F', we have derived that the desired fixed point of F is

$$\lambda\,(f)\,F(f(f))(\lambda\,(f)\,F(f(f))).$$

To finish the derivation, we need only note that nothing depends on the particular choice of F, which means that we can compute a fixed point for F uniformly in F. That is, we may define a *single* function, the term Y as defined above, that computes the fixed point of *any* F.

21.3 Scott's Theorem

Scott's Theorem states that definitional equality for the untyped λ-calculus is undecidable: there is no algorithm to determine whether two untyped terms are definitionally equal. The proof uses the concept of *inseparability*. Any two properties, $\mathcal{A}_0$ and $\mathcal{A}_1$, of λ-terms are *inseparable* if there is no decidable property, $\mathcal{B}$, such that $\mathcal{A}_0\,u$ implies that $\mathcal{B}\,u$ holds, and $\mathcal{A}_1\,u$ implies that $\mathcal{B}\,u$ does *not* hold. We say that a property, $\mathcal{A}$, of untyped terms is *behavioral* iff whenever $u \equiv u'$, then $\mathcal{A}\,u$ iff $\mathcal{A}\,u'$.

The proof of Scott's Theorem decomposes into two parts:

1. For any untyped λ-term u, we may find an untyped term v such that $u(\ulcorner v \urcorner) \equiv v$, where $\ulcorner v \urcorner$ is the Gödel number of v, and $\overline{\ulcorner v \urcorner}$ is its representation as a Church numeral. (See Chapter 9 for a discussion of Gödel-numbering.)
2. Any two non-trivial[2] behavioral properties $\mathcal{A}_0$ and $\mathcal{A}_1$ of untyped terms are inseparable.

Lemma 21.1. *For any u, there exists v such that $u(\overline{\ulcorner v \urcorner}) \equiv v$.*

Proof Sketch   The proof relies on the definability of the following two operations in the untyped λ-calculus:

1. $\mathrm{ap}(\overline{\ulcorner u_1 \urcorner})(\overline{\ulcorner u_2 \urcorner}) \equiv \overline{\ulcorner u_1(u_2) \urcorner}$.
2. $\mathrm{nm}(\overline{n}) \equiv \overline{\ulcorner \overline{n} \urcorner}$.

Intuitively, the first takes the representations of two untyped terms and builds the representation of the application of one to the other. The second takes a numeral for n, and yields the representation of the Church numeral $\overline{n}$. Given these, we may find the required term v by defining $v \triangleq w(\overline{\ulcorner w \urcorner})$, where $w \triangleq \lambda\,(x)\,u(\mathrm{ap}(x)(\mathrm{nm}(x)))$. We have

$$
\begin{aligned}
v &= w(\overline{\ulcorner w \urcorner}) \\
&\equiv u(\mathrm{ap}(\overline{\ulcorner w \urcorner})(\mathrm{nm}(\overline{\ulcorner w \urcorner}))) \\
&\equiv u(\overline{\ulcorner w(\overline{\ulcorner w \urcorner}) \urcorner}) \\
&\equiv u(\overline{\ulcorner v \urcorner}).
\end{aligned}
$$

The definition is very similar to that of $\mathsf{Y}(u)$, except that u takes as input the representation of a term, and we find a v such that, when applied to the representation of v, the term u yields v itself.   □

Lemma 21.2. *Suppose that $\mathcal{A}_0$ and $\mathcal{A}_1$ are two non-trivial behavioral properties of untyped terms. Then there is no untyped term w such that*

1. *For every u, either $w(\overline{\ulcorner u \urcorner}) \equiv \overline{0}$ or $w(\overline{\ulcorner u \urcorner}) \equiv \overline{1}$.*
2. *If $\mathcal{A}_0\,u$, then $w(\overline{\ulcorner u \urcorner}) \equiv \overline{0}$.*
3. *If $\mathcal{A}_1\,u$, then $w(\overline{\ulcorner u \urcorner}) \equiv \overline{1}$.*

Proof   Suppose there is such an untyped term w. Let v be the untyped term

$$
\lambda\,(x)\,\mathtt{ifz}\{u_1;\_.u_0\}(w(x)),
$$

where u_0 and u_1 are chosen such that $\mathcal{A}_0\,u_0$ and $\mathcal{A}_1\,u_1$. (Such a choice must exist by non-triviality of the properties.) By Lemma 21.1 there is an untyped term t such that $v(\overline{\ulcorner t \urcorner}) \equiv t$. If $w(\overline{\ulcorner t \urcorner}) \equiv \overline{0}$, then $t \equiv v(\overline{\ulcorner t \urcorner}) \equiv u_1$, and so $\mathcal{A}_1\,t$, because $\mathcal{A}_1$ is behavioral and $\mathcal{A}_1\,u_1$.

But then $w(\ulcorner t \urcorner) \equiv \overline{1}$ by the defining properties of w, which is a contradiction. Similarly, if $w(\ulcorner t \urcorner) \equiv \overline{1}$, then $\mathcal{A}_0\, t$, and hence $w(\ulcorner t \urcorner) \equiv \overline{0}$, again a contradiction.   □

Corollary 21.3. *There is no algorithm to decide whether $u \equiv u'$.*

Proof For fixed u, the property $\mathcal{E}_u\, u'$ defined by $u' \equiv u$ is a non-trivial behavioral property of untyped terms. So it is inseparable from its negation, and hence is undecidable.   □

21.4 Untyped Means Uni-Typed

The untyped λ-calculus can be faithfully embedded in a typed language with recursive types. Thus, every untyped λ-term has a representation as a typed expression in such a way that execution of the representation of a λ-term corresponds to execution of the term itself. This embedding is *not* a matter of writing an interpreter for the λ-calculus in **FPC**, but rather a direct representation of untyped λ-terms as typed expressions in a language with recursive types.

The key observation is that the *untyped* λ-calculus is really the *uni-typed* λ-calculus. It is not the *absence* of types that gives it its power, but rather that it has *only one* type, the recursive type

$$D \triangleq \mathtt{rec}\, t\, \mathtt{is}\, t \rightharpoonup t.$$

A value of type D is of the form $\mathtt{fold}(e)$ where e is a value of type $D \rightharpoonup D$—a function whose domain and range are both D. Any such function can be regarded as a value of type D by "folding", and any value of type D can be turned into a function by "unfolding". As usual, a recursive type is a solution to a type equation, which in the present case is the equation

$$D \cong D \rightharpoonup D.$$

This isomorphism specifies that D is a type that is isomorphic to the space of partial functions on D itself, which is impossible if types are just sets.

This isomorphism leads to the following translation, of Λ into **FPC**:

$$x^\dagger \triangleq x \tag{21.14a}$$

$$\lambda(x)\, u^\dagger \triangleq \mathtt{fold}(\lambda\,(x : D)\, u^\dagger) \tag{21.14b}$$

$$u_1(u_2)^\dagger \triangleq \mathtt{unfold}(u_1^\dagger)(u_2^\dagger) \tag{21.14c}$$

Note that the embedding of a λ-abstraction is a value, and that the embedding of an application exposes the function being applied by unfolding the recursive type. And so we have

$$\lambda\,(x)\,u_1(u_2)^\dagger = \mathtt{unfold}(\mathtt{fold}(\lambda\,(x:D)\,u_1^\dagger))(u_2^\dagger)$$
$$\equiv \lambda\,(x:D)\,u_1^\dagger(u_2^\dagger)$$
$$\equiv [u_2^\dagger/x]u_1^\dagger$$
$$= ([u_2/x]u_1)^\dagger.$$

The last step, stating that the embedding commutes with substitution, is proved by induction on the structure of u_1. Thus β-reduction is implemented by evaluation of the embedded terms.

Thus, we see that the canonical *untyped* language, Λ, which by dint of terminology stands in opposition to *typed* languages, turns out to be but a typed language after all. Rather than eliminating types, an untyped language consolidates an infinite collection of types into a single recursive type. Doing so renders static type checking trivial, at the cost of incurring dynamic overhead to coerce values to and from the recursive type. In Chapter 22, we will take this a step further by admitting many different types of data values (not just functions), each of which is a component of a "master" recursive type. This generalization shows that so-called *dynamically typed* languages are, in fact, *statically typed*. Thus, this traditional distinction cannot be considered an opposition, because dynamic languages are but particular forms of static languages in which undue emphasis is placed on a single recursive type.

21.5 Notes

The untyped λ-calculus was introduced by Church (1941) as a formalization of the informal concept of a computable function. Unlike the well-known machine models, such as the Turing machine or the random access machine, the λ-calculus codifies mathematical and programming practice. Barendregt (1984) is the definitive reference for all aspects of the untyped λ-calculus; the proof of Scott's theorem is adapted from Barendregt's account. Scott (1980a) gave the first model of the untyped λ-calculus in terms of an elegant theory of recursive types. This construction underlies Scott's apt description of the λ-calculus as "uni-typed," rather than "untyped." The idea to characterize Church's Law as such was communicated to the author, independently of each other, by Robert L. Constable and Mark Lillibridge.

Exercises

21.1. Define an encoding of finite products as defined in Chapter 10 in Λ.

21.2. Define the factorial function in Λ two ways, one without using Y, and one using Y. In both cases, show that your solution, u, has the property that $u(\overline{n}) \equiv \overline{n!}$.

21.3. Define the "Church booleans" in Λ by defining terms `true` and `false` such that
(a) $\texttt{true}(u_1)(u_2) \equiv u_1$.
(b) $\texttt{false}(u_1)(u_2) \equiv u_2$.
What is the encoding of `if` u `then` u_1 `else` u_2?

21.4. Define an encoding of finite sums as defined in Chapter 11 in Λ.

21.5. Define an encoding of finite lists of natural numbers as defined in Chapter 15 in Λ.

21.6. Define an encoding of the infinite streams of natural numbers as defined in Chapter 15 in Λ.

21.7. Show that Λ can be "compiled" to sk-combinators using bracket abstraction (see Exercises **3.4** and **3.5**. Define a translation u^* from Λ into sk combinators such that

$$\text{if } u_1 \equiv u_2, \text{ then } u_1^* \equiv u_2^*.$$

Hint: Define u^* by induction on the structure of u, using the compositional form of bracket abstraction considered in Exercise **3.5**. Show that the translation is itself compositional in that it commutes with substitution:

$$([u_2/x]u_1)^* = [u_2^*/x]u^*.$$

Then proceed by rule induction on rules (21.2) to show the required correctness condition.

Notes

1 It is debatable whether there are any scientific laws in Computer Science. In the opinion of the author Church's Law, which is usually called *Church's Thesis*, is a strong candidate for being a scientific law.

2 A property of untyped terms is *trivial* if it either holds for all untyped terms or never holds for any untyped term.

22 Dynamic Typing

We saw in Chapter 21 that an untyped language is a uni-typed language in which "untyped" terms are just terms of single recursive type. Because all expressions of Λ are well-typed, type safety ensures that no misinterpretation of a value is possible. When spelled out for Λ, type safety follows from there being exactly one class of values, that of functions on values. No application can get stuck, because every value is a function that may be applied to an argument.

This safety property breaks down once more than one class of value is admitted. For example, if the natural numbers are added as a primitive to Λ, then it is possible to incur a run-time error by attempting to apply a number to an argument. One way to manage this is to embrace the possibility, treating class mismatches as checked errors, and weakening the progress theorem as outlined in Chapter 6. Such languages are called *dynamic languages* because an error such as the one described is postponed to run-time, rather than precluded at compile time by type checking. Languages of the latter sort are called *static languages*.

Dynamic languages are often considered in opposition to static languages, but the opposition is illusory. Just as the untyped λ-calculus is uni-typed, so dynamic languages are but special cases of static languages in which there is only one recursive type (albeit with multiple classes of value).

22.1 Dynamically Typed PCF

To illustrate dynamic typing, we formulate a dynamically typed version of **PCF**, called **DPCF**. The abstract syntax of **DPCF** is given by the following grammar:

Exp	d	::=	x	x	variable
			$\mathtt{num}[n]$	$\overline{n}$	numeral
			$\mathtt{zero}$	$\mathtt{zero}$	zero
			$\mathtt{succ}(d)$	$\mathtt{succ}(d)$	successor
			$\mathtt{ifz}\{d_0; x.d_1\}(d)$	$\mathtt{ifz}\,d\,\{\mathtt{zero} \hookrightarrow d_0 \mid \mathtt{succ}(x) \hookrightarrow d_1\}$	zero test
			$\mathtt{fun}(x.d)$	$\lambda\,(x)\,d$	abstraction
			$\mathtt{ap}(d_1; d_2)$	$d_1(d_2)$	application
			$\mathtt{fix}(x.d)$	$\mathtt{fix}\,x\,\mathtt{is}\,d$	recursion

There are two classes of values in **DPCF**, the *numbers*, which have the form $\text{num}[n]$, and the *functions*, which have the form $\text{fun}(x.d)$. The expressions $\texttt{zero}$ and $\texttt{succ}(d)$ are not themselves values, but rather are *constructors* that evaluate to values. General recursion is definable using a fixed point combinator but is taken as primitive here to simplify the analysis of the dynamics in Section 22.3.

As usual, the abstract syntax of **DPCF** is what matters, but we use the concrete syntax to improve readability. However, notational conveniences can obscure important details, such as the tagging of values with their class and the checking of these tags at run-time. For example, the concrete syntax for a number, $\overline{n}$, suggests a "bare" representation, the abstract syntax reveals that the number is labeled with the class num to distinguish it from a function. Correspondingly, the concrete syntax for a function is $\lambda\,(x)\,d$, but its abstract syntax, $\text{fun}(x.d)$, shows that it also sports a class label. The class labels are required to ensure safety by run-time checking, and must not be overlooked when comparing static with dynamic languages.

The statics of **DPCF** is like that of $\boldsymbol{\Lambda}$; it merely checks that there are no free variables in the expression. The judgment

$$x_1 \text{ ok}, \ldots x_n \text{ ok} \vdash d \text{ ok}$$

states that d is a well-formed expression with free variables among those in the hypotheses. If the assumptions are empty, then we write just d ok to mean that d is a closed expression of **DPCF**.

The dynamics of **DPCF** must check for errors that would never arise in a language such as **PCF**. For example, evaluation of a function application must ensure that the value being applied is indeed a function, signaling an error if it is not. Similarly, the conditional branch must ensure that its principal argument is a number, signaling an error if it is not. To account for these possibilities, the dynamics is given by several judgment forms, as summarized in the following chart:

d val	d is a (closed) value
$d \longmapsto d'$	d evaluates in one step to d'
d err	d incurs a run-time error
d is_num n	d is of class num with value n
d isnt_num	d is not of class num
d is_fun $x.d$	d is of class fun with body $x.d$
d isnt_fun	d is not of class fun

The last four judgment forms implement dynamic class checking. They are only relevant when d is already a value. The affirmative class-checking judgments have a second argument that represents the underlying structure of a value; this argument is *not* itself an expression of **DPCF**.

The value judgment d val states that d is a evaluated (closed) expression:

$$\frac{}{\text{num}[n] \text{ val}} \tag{22.1a}$$

$$\frac{}{\text{fun}(x.d) \text{ val}} \tag{22.1b}$$

The affirmative class-checking judgments are defined by the following rules:

$$\frac{}{\text{num}[n] \text{ is\_num } n} \tag{22.2a}$$

$$\frac{}{\text{fun}(x.d) \text{ is\_fun } x.d} \tag{22.2b}$$

The negative class-checking judgments are correspondingly defined by these rules:

$$\frac{}{\text{num}[n] \text{ isnt\_fun}} \tag{22.3a}$$

$$\frac{}{\text{fun}(x.d) \text{ isnt\_num}} \tag{22.3b}$$

The transition judgment $d \longmapsto d'$ and the error judgment d err are defined simultaneously by the following rules:

$$\frac{}{\text{zero} \longmapsto \text{num}[\text{z}]} \tag{22.4a}$$

$$\frac{d \longmapsto d'}{\text{succ}(d) \longmapsto \text{succ}(d')} \tag{22.4b}$$

$$\frac{d \text{ err}}{\text{succ}(d) \text{ err}} \tag{22.4c}$$

$$\frac{d \text{ is\_num } n}{\text{succ}(d) \longmapsto \text{num}[\text{s}(n)]} \tag{22.4d}$$

$$\frac{d \text{ isnt\_num}}{\text{succ}(d) \text{ err}} \tag{22.4e}$$

$$\frac{d \longmapsto d'}{\text{ifz}\{d_0; x.d_1\}(d) \longmapsto \text{ifz}\{d_0; x.d_1\}(d')} \tag{22.4f}$$

$$\frac{d \text{ err}}{\text{ifz}\{d_0; x.d_1\}(d) \text{ err}} \tag{22.4g}$$

$$\frac{d \text{ is\_num } 0}{\text{ifz}\{d_0; x.d_1\}(d) \longmapsto d_0} \tag{22.4h}$$

$$\frac{d \text{ is\_num } n+1}{\text{ifz}\{d_0; x.d_1\}(d) \longmapsto [\text{num}[n]/x]d_1} \tag{22.4i}$$

$$\frac{d \text{ isnt\_num}}{\text{ifz}\{d_0; x.d_1\}(d) \text{ err}} \tag{22.4j}$$

$$\frac{d_1 \longmapsto d_1'}{\text{ap}(d_1; d_2) \longmapsto \text{ap}(d_1'; d_2)} \tag{22.4k}$$

$$\frac{d_1 \text{ err}}{\text{ap}(d_1; d_2) \text{ err}} \tag{22.4l}$$

$$\frac{d_1 \text{ is\_fun } x.d}{\text{ap}(d_1; d_2) \longmapsto [d_2/x]d} \tag{22.4m}$$

$$\frac{d_1 \text{ isnt\_fun}}{\text{ap}(d_1; d_2) \text{ err}} \tag{22.4n}$$

$$\frac{}{\text{fix}(x.d) \longmapsto [\text{fix}(x.d)/x]d} \tag{22.4o}$$

Rule (22.4i) labels the predecessor with the class num to maintain the invariant that variables are bound to expressions of **DPCF**.

Lemma 22.1 (Class Checking). *If d val, then*

1. *either d is_num n for some n, or d isnt_num;*
2. *either d is_fun $x.d'$ for some x and d', or d isnt_fun.*

Proof   By inspection of the rules defining the class-checking judgments.   □

Theorem 22.2 (Progress). *If d ok, then either d val, or d err, or there exists d' such that $d \longmapsto d'$.*

Proof   By induction on the structure of d. For example, if $d = \text{succ}(d')$, then we have by induction either d' val, or d' err, or $d' \longmapsto d''$ for some d''. In the last case, we have by rule (22.4b) that $\text{succ}(d') \longmapsto \text{succ}(d'')$, and in the second-to-last case, we have by rule (22.4c) that $\text{succ}(d')$ err. If d' val, then by Lemma 22.1, either d' is_num n or d' isnt_num. In the former case $\text{succ}(d') \longmapsto \text{num}[\text{s}(n)]$, and in the latter $\text{succ}(d')$ err. The other cases are handled similarly.   □

Lemma 22.3 (Exclusivity). *For any d in **DPCF**, exactly one of the following holds: d val, or d err, or $d \longmapsto d'$ for some d'.*

Proof   By induction on the structure of d, making reference to rules (22.4).   □

22.2 Variations and Extensions

The dynamic language **DPCF** defined in Section 22.1 parallels the static language **PCF** defined in Chapter 19. One discrepancy, however, is in the treatment of natural numbers. Whereas in **PCF** the zero and successor operations are introduction forms for the type nat, in **DPCF** they are elimination forms that act on specially defined numerals. The present formulation uses only a single class of numbers.

One could instead treat zero and $\text{succ}(d)$ as values of separate classes and introduce the obvious class-checking judgments for them. When written in this style, the dynamics of the conditional branch is given as follows:

$$\frac{d \longmapsto d'}{\text{ifz}\{d_0; x.d_1\}(d) \longmapsto \text{ifz}\{d_0; x.d_1\}(d')} \tag{22.5a}$$

$$\frac{d \text{ is\_zero}}{\texttt{ifz}\{d_0; x.d_1\}(d) \longmapsto d_0} \tag{22.5b}$$

$$\frac{d \text{ is\_succ } d'}{\texttt{ifz}\{d_0; x.d_1\}(d) \longmapsto [d'/x]d_1} \tag{22.5c}$$

$$\frac{d \text{ isnt\_zero} \quad d \text{ isnt\_succ}}{\texttt{ifz}\{d_0; x.d_1\}(d) \text{ err}} \tag{22.5d}$$

Notice that the predecessor of a value of the successor class need not be a number, whereas in the previous formulation this possibility does not arise.

DPCF can be extended with structured data similarly. A classic example is to consider a class $\texttt{nil}$, consisting of a "null" value, and a class $\texttt{cons}$, consisting of pairs of values.

Exp d ::=	$\texttt{nil}$	$\texttt{nil}$	null
	$\texttt{cons}(d_1; d_2)$	$\texttt{cons}(d_1; d_2)$	pair
	$\texttt{ifnil}(d; d_0; x, y.d_1)$	$\texttt{ifnil}\, d\, \{\texttt{nil} \hookrightarrow d_0 \mid \texttt{cons}(x; y) \hookrightarrow d_1\}$	
			conditional

The expression $\texttt{ifnil}(d; d_0; x, y.d_1)$ distinguishes the null value from a pair, and signals an error on any other class of value.

Lists (finite sequences) can be encoded using null and pairing. For example, the list consisting of three zeros can berepresented by the value

$$\texttt{cons}(\texttt{zero}; \texttt{cons}(\texttt{zero}; \texttt{cons}(\texttt{zero}; \texttt{nil}))).$$

But what to make of the following value?

$$\texttt{cons}(\texttt{zero}; \texttt{cons}(\texttt{zero}; \texttt{cons}(\texttt{zero}; \lambda\,(x)\,x))).$$

It is not a list, because it does not end with $\texttt{nil}$, but it is a permissible value in the enriched language.

A difficulty with encoding lists using null and pair emerges when defining functions on them. For example, here is a definition of the function $\texttt{append}$ that concatenates two lists:

$$\texttt{fix}\, a\, \texttt{is}\, \lambda\,(x)\,\lambda\,(y)\,\texttt{ifnil}(x; y; x_1, x_2.\texttt{cons}(x_1; a(x_2)(y)))$$

Nothing prevents us from applying this function to any two values, regardless of whether they are lists. If the first argument is not a list, then execution aborts with an error. But because the function does not traverse its second argument, it can be any value at all. For example, we may apply $\texttt{append}$ with a list and a function to obtain the "list" that ends with a λ given above.

It might be argued that the conditional branch that distinguishes null from a pair is inappropriate in **DPCF**, because there are more than just these two classes in the language. One approach that avoids this criticism is to abandon pattern matching on the class of data, replacing it by a general conditional branch that distinguishes null from all other values, and adding to the language *predicates*[1] that test the class of a value and *destructors* that invert the constructors of each class.

We could instead reformulate null and and pairing as follows:

$$
\begin{array}{llll}
\text{Exp} \quad d \quad ::= & \text{cond}(d; d_0; d_1) & \text{cond}(d; d_0; d_1) & \text{conditional} \\
& \text{nil?}(d) & \text{nil?}(d) & \text{nil test} \\
& \text{cons?}(d) & \text{cons?}(d) & \text{pair test} \\
& \text{car}(d) & \text{car}(d) & \text{first projection} \\
& \text{cdr}(d) & \text{cdr}(d) & \text{second projection}
\end{array}
$$

The conditional $\text{cond}(d; d_0; d_1)$ distinguishes d between nil and *all other values*. If d is not nil, the conditional evaluates to d_0, and otherwise evaluates to d_1. In other words, the value nil represents boolean falsehood, and all other values represent boolean truth. The predicates $\text{nil?}(d)$ and $\text{cons?}(d)$ test the class of their argument, yielding nil if the argument is not of the specified class, and yielding some non-nil if so. The destructors $\text{car}(d)$ and $\text{cdr}(d)$ decompose $\text{cons}(d_1; d_2)$ into d_1 and d_2, respectively.[2]

Written in this form, the function append is given by the expression

$$\text{fix } a \text{ is } \lambda\,(x)\,\lambda\,(y)\,\text{cond}(x; \text{cons}(\text{car}(x); a(\text{cdr}(x))(y)); y).$$

The behavior of this formulation of append is no different from the earlier one; the only difference is that instead of dispatching on whether a value is either null or a pair, we instead allow discrimination on any predicate of the value, which includes such checks as special cases.

An alternative, which is not widely used, is to enhance, and not restrict, the conditional branch so that it includes cases for each possible class of value in the language. So in a language with numbers, functions, null, and pairing, the conditional would have four branches. The fourth branch, for pairing, would deconstruct the pair into its constituent parts. The difficulty with this approach is that in realistic languages there are many classes of data, and such a conditional would be rather unwieldy. Moreover, even once we have dispatched on the class of a value, it is nevertheless necessary for the primitive operations associated with that class to admit run-time checks. For example, we may determine that a value d is of the numeric class, but there is no way to propagate this information into the branch of the conditional that then adds d to some other number. The addition operation must still check the class of d, recover the underlying number, and create a new value of numeric class. It is an inherent limitation of dynamic languages that they do not allow values other than classified values.

22.3 Critique of Dynamic Typing

The safety theorem for **DPCF** is an advantage of dynamic over static typing. Unlike static languages, which rule out some candidate programs as ill-typed, every piece of abstract syntax in **DPCF** is well-formed, and hence, by Theorem 22.2, has a well-defined dynamics (albeit one with checked errors). But this convenience is also a disadvantage, because errors that could be ruled out at compile time by type checking are not signaled until run-time.

Consider, for example, the addition function in **DPCF**, whose specification is that, when passed two values of class num, returns their sum, which is also of class num:[3]

$$\mathtt{fun}(x.\mathtt{fix}(p.\mathtt{fun}(y.\mathtt{ifz}\{x; y'.\mathtt{succ}(p(y'))\})))).$$

The addition function may, deceptively, be written in concrete syntax as follows:

$$\lambda(x)\,\mathtt{fix}\,p\,\mathtt{is}\,\lambda(y)\,\mathtt{ifz}\,y\,\{\mathtt{zero} \hookrightarrow x \mid \mathtt{succ}(y') \hookrightarrow \mathtt{succ}(p(y'))\}.$$

It is deceptive, because it obscures the class tags on values, and the operations that check the validity of those tags. Let us now examine the costs of these operations in a bit more detail.

First, note that the body of the fixed point expression is labeled with class fun. The dynamics of the fixed point construct binds p to this function. Consequently, the dynamic class check incurred by the application of p in the recursive call is guaranteed to succeed. But **DPCF** offers no means of suppressing the redundant check, because it cannot express the invariant that p is always bound to a value of class fun.

Second, note that the result of applying the inner λ-abstraction is either x, the argument of the outer λ-abstraction, or the successor of a recursive call to the function itself. The successor operation checks that its argument is of class num, even though this condition is guaranteed to hold for all but the base case, which returns the given x, which can be of any class at all. In principle, we can check that x is of class num once, and note that it is otherwise a loop invariant that the result of applying the inner function is of this class. However, **DPCF** gives us no way to express this invariant; the repeated, redundant tag checks imposed by the successor operation cannot be avoided.

Third, the argument y to the inner function is either the original argument to the addition function, or is the predecessor of some earlier recursive call. But as long as the original call is to a value of class num, then the dynamics of the conditional will ensure that all recursive calls have this class. And again there is no way to express this invariant in **DPCF**, and hence, there is no way to avoid the class check imposed by the conditional branch.

Classification is not free—storage is required for the class label, and it takes time to detach the class from a value each time it is used and to attach a class to a value when it is created. Although the overhead of classification is not asymptotically significant (it slows down the program only by a constant factor), it is nevertheless non-negligible, and should be eliminated when possible. But this is impossible within **DPCF**, because it cannot enforce the restrictions required to express the required invariants. For that we need a static type system.

22.4 Notes

The earliest dynamically typed language is Lisp (McCarthy, 1965), which continues to influence language design a half century after its invention. Dynamic PCF is the core of Lisp, but with a proper treatment of variable binding, correcting what McCarthy himself has described as an error in the original design. Informal discussions of dynamic languages are often complicated by the elision of the dynamic checks that are made explicit here. Although the surface syntax of dynamic PCF is almost the same as that for PCF, minus the type annotations, the underlying dynamics is different. It is for this reason that static PCF cannot be seen as a restriction of dynamic PCF by the imposition of a type system.

Exercises

22.1. Surface syntax can be deceiving; even simple arithmetic expressions do not have the same meaning in **DPCF** that they do in **PCF**. To see why, define the addition function, plus, in **DPCF**, and examine the dynamics of evaluating expressions such as $\text{plus}(\overline{5})(\overline{7})$. Even though this expression might be written as "$5 + 7$" in both static and dynamic languages, they have different meanings.

22.2. Give a precise dynamics to the data structuring primitives described informally in Section 22.2. What class restrictions should cons impose on its arguments? Check the dynamics of the append function when called with two lists as arguments.

22.3. To avoid the difficulties with the representation of lists using cons and nil, introduce a class of lists that are constructed using revised versions of nil and cons that operate on the class of lists. Revisit the dynamics of the append function when redefined using the class of lists.

22.4. Allowing multiple arguments to, and multiple results from, functions is a notorious source of trouble in dynamic languages. The restriction to a single type makes it impossible even to distinguish n things from m things, let alone express more subtle properties of a program. Numerous workarounds have been proposed. Explore the problem yourself by enriching **DPCF** with multi-argument and multi-result functions. Be sure to consider these questions:

(a) If a function is defined with n parameters, what should happen if it is called with more or fewer than n arguments?

(b) What happens if one were to admit functions with a *varying* number of arguments? How would you refer to these arguments within the body of such a function? How does this relate to pattern matching?

(c) What if one wished to admit keyword parameter passing by giving names to the arguments, and allowing them to be passed in any order by associating them with their names?

(d) What notation would you suggest for functions returning multiple results? For example, a division function might return the quotient and the remainder. How might one notate this in the function body? How would a caller access the results individually or collectively?

(e) How would one define the composition of two functions when either or both can take multiple arguments or return multiple results?

Notes

1 Predicates evaluate to the null value to mean that a condition is false, and some non-null value to mean that it is true.

2 The terminology for the projections is archaic, but well-established. It is said that `car` originally stood for "contents of the address register" and that `cdr` stood for "contents of the data register," referring to the details of the original implementation of Lisp.

3 This specification imposes no restrictions on the behavior of addition on arguments that are not classified as numbers, but we could make the further demand that the function abort when applied to arguments that are not classified by `num`.

A *hybrid* language is one that combines static and dynamic typing by enriching a statically typed language with a distinguished type dyn of dynamic values. The dynamically typed language considered in Chapter 22 can be embedded into the hybrid language by viewing a dynamically typed program as a statically typed program of type dyn. Static and dynamic types are not opposed to one another, but may coexist harmoniously. The *ad hoc* device of adding the type dyn to a static language is unnecessary in a language with recursive types, wherein it is definable as a particular recursive type. Thus, one may say that *dynamic typing is a mode of use of static typing*, reconciling an apparent opposition between them.

23.1 A Hybrid Language

Consider the language **HPCF**, which extends **PCF** with the following constructs:

Typ	τ	::=	dyn	dyn	dynamic
Exp	e	::=	new$[l](e)$	$l\,!\,e$	construct
			cast$[l](e)$	$e\,@\,l$	destruct
			inst$[l](e)$	$l\,?\,e$	discriminate
Cls	l	::=	num	num	number
			fun	fun	function

The type dyn is the type of dynamically classified values. The constructor attaches a classifier to a value of a type associated to that classifer, the destructor recovers the value classified with the given classifier, and the discriminator tests the class of a classified value.

The statics of **HPCF** extends that of **PCF** with the following rules:

$$\frac{\Gamma \vdash e : \mathtt{nat}}{\Gamma \vdash \mathtt{new[num]}(e) : \mathtt{dyn}} \tag{23.1a}$$

$$\frac{\Gamma \vdash e : \mathtt{dyn} \rightharpoonup \mathtt{dyn}}{\Gamma \vdash \mathtt{new[fun]}(e) : \mathtt{dyn}} \tag{23.1b}$$

$$\frac{\Gamma \vdash e : \mathtt{dyn}}{\Gamma \vdash \mathtt{cast[num]}(e) : \mathtt{nat}} \tag{23.1c}$$

$$\frac{\Gamma \vdash e : \mathtt{dyn}}{\Gamma \vdash \mathtt{cast[fun]}(e) : \mathtt{dyn} \rightharpoonup \mathtt{dyn}} \tag{23.1d}$$

$$\frac{\Gamma \vdash e : \mathtt{dyn}}{\Gamma \vdash \mathtt{inst[num]}(e) : \mathtt{bool}} \tag{23.1e}$$

$$\frac{\Gamma \vdash e : \mathtt{dyn}}{\Gamma \vdash \mathtt{inst[fun]}(e) : \mathtt{bool}} \tag{23.1f}$$

The statics ensures that classifiers are attached to values of the right type, namely natural numbers for num, and functions on classified values for fun.

The dynamics of **HPCF** extends that of **PCF** with the following rules:

$$\frac{e \ \mathsf{val}}{\mathtt{new[}l\mathtt{]}(e) \ \mathsf{val}} \tag{23.2a}$$

$$\frac{e \longmapsto e'}{\mathtt{new[}l\mathtt{]}(e) \longmapsto \mathtt{new[}l\mathtt{]}(e')} \tag{23.2b}$$

$$\frac{e \longmapsto e'}{\mathtt{cast[}l\mathtt{]}(e) \longmapsto \mathtt{cast[}l\mathtt{]}(e')} \tag{23.2c}$$

$$\frac{\mathtt{new[}l\mathtt{]}(e) \ \mathsf{val}}{\mathtt{cast[}l\mathtt{]}(\mathtt{new[}l\mathtt{]}(e)) \longmapsto e} \tag{23.2d}$$

$$\frac{\mathtt{new[}l'\mathtt{]}(e) \ \mathsf{val} \quad l \neq l'}{\mathtt{cast[}l\mathtt{]}(\mathtt{new[}l'\mathtt{]}(e)) \ \mathsf{err}} \tag{23.2e}$$

$$\frac{e \longmapsto e'}{\mathtt{inst[}l\mathtt{]}(e) \longmapsto \mathtt{inst[}l\mathtt{]}(e')} \tag{23.2f}$$

$$\frac{\mathtt{new[}l\mathtt{]}(e) \ \mathsf{val}}{\mathtt{inst[}l\mathtt{]}(\mathtt{new[}l\mathtt{]}(e)) \longmapsto \mathtt{true}} \tag{23.2g}$$

$$\frac{\mathtt{new[}l\mathtt{]}(e) \ \mathsf{val} \quad l \neq l'}{\mathtt{inst[}l'\mathtt{]}(\mathtt{new[}l\mathtt{]}(e)) \longmapsto \mathtt{false}} \tag{23.2h}$$

Casting compares the class of the object to the required class, returning the underlying object if these coincide, and signaling an error otherwise.[1]

Lemma 23.1 (Canonical Forms). *If $e : \mathtt{dyn}$ and e val, then $e = \mathtt{new[}l\mathtt{]}(e')$ for some class l and some e' val. If $l = \mathtt{num}$, then $e' : \mathtt{nat}$, and if $l = \mathtt{fun}$, then $e' : \mathtt{dyn} \rightharpoonup \mathtt{dyn}$.*

Proof   By rule induction on the statics of **HPCF**.   □

Theorem 23.2 (Safety). *The language **HPCF** is safe:*

1. If $e : \tau$ and $e \longmapsto e'$, then $e' : \tau$.

2. If $e : \tau$, then either e val, or e err, or $e \longmapsto e'$ for some e'.

Proof Preservation is proved by rule induction on the dynamics, and progress is proved by rule induction on the statics, making use of the canonical forms lemma. The opportunities for run-time errors are the same as those for **DPCF**—a well-typed cast might fail at run-time if the class of the cast does not match the class of the value.   □

In a language such as **FPC** (Chapter 20) with recursive types, there is no need to add dyn as a primitive type. Instead, it is defined to be type

$$\mathtt{rec}\, t \,\mathtt{is}\, [\mathtt{num} \hookrightarrow \mathtt{nat}, \mathtt{fun} \hookrightarrow t \rightharpoonup t]. \tag{23.3}$$

The introduction and elimination forms for this definition of dyn are definable as follows:[2]

$$\mathtt{new}[\mathtt{num}](e) \triangleq \mathtt{fold}(\mathtt{num} \cdot e) \tag{23.4}$$

$$\mathtt{new}[\mathtt{fun}](e) \triangleq \mathtt{fold}(\mathtt{fun} \cdot e) \tag{23.5}$$

$$\mathtt{cast}[\mathtt{num}](e) \triangleq \mathtt{case}\,\mathtt{unfold}(e)\,\{\mathtt{num} \cdot x \hookrightarrow x \mid \mathtt{fun} \cdot x \hookrightarrow \mathtt{error}\} \tag{23.6}$$

$$\mathtt{cast}[\mathtt{fun}](e) \triangleq \mathtt{case}\,\mathtt{unfold}(e)\,\{\mathtt{num} \cdot x \hookrightarrow \mathtt{error} \mid \mathtt{fun} \cdot x \hookrightarrow x\}. \tag{23.7}$$

These definition simply decompose the class operations for dyn into recursive unfoldings and case analyses on values of a sum type.

23.2 Dynamic as Static Typing

The language **DPCF** of Chapter 22 can be embedded into **HPCF** by a simple translation that makes explicit the class checking in the dynamics of **DPCF**. Specifically, we may define a translation $d^\dagger$ of expressions of **DPCF** into expressions of **HPCF** according to the following static correctness criterion:

Theorem 23.3. *If* x_1 *ok*, ..., x_n *ok* $\vdash$ d *ok according to the statics of* **DPCF***, then* $x_1 : \mathtt{dyn}, \ldots, x_n : \mathtt{dyn} \vdash d^\dagger : \mathtt{dyn}$ *in* **HPCF***.*

The proof of Theorem 23.3 is given by induction on the structure of d based on the following translation:

$$x^\dagger \triangleq x$$

$$\mathtt{num}[n]^\dagger \triangleq \mathtt{new}[\mathtt{num}](\overline{n})$$

$$\mathtt{zero}^\dagger \triangleq \mathtt{new}[\mathtt{num}](\mathtt{z})$$

$$\mathtt{succ}(d)^\dagger \triangleq \mathtt{new}[\mathtt{num}](\mathtt{s}(\mathtt{cast}[\mathtt{num}](d^\dagger)))$$

$$\mathtt{ifz}\{d_0; x.d_1\}(d)^\dagger \triangleq \mathtt{ifz}\{d_0^\dagger; x.[\mathtt{new}[\mathtt{num}](x)/x]d_1^\dagger\}(\mathtt{cast}[\mathtt{num}](d^\dagger))$$

$$(\mathtt{fun}(x.d))^\dagger \triangleq \mathtt{new}[\mathtt{fun}](\lambda\,(x : \mathtt{dyn})\,d^\dagger)$$

$$(\mathtt{ap}(d_1; d_2))^\dagger \triangleq \mathtt{cast}[\mathtt{fun}](d_1^\dagger)(d_2^\dagger)$$

$$\mathtt{fix}(x.d) \triangleq \mathtt{fix}\{\mathtt{dyn}\}(x.d^\dagger)$$

A rigorous proof of correctness of this translation requires methods like those in Chapter 47.

23.3 Optimization of Dynamic Typing

The language **HPCF** combines static and dynamic typing by enriching **PCF** with the type dyn of classified values. It is, for this reason, called a *hybrid* language. Unlike a purely dynamic type system, a hybrid type system can express invariants that are crucial to the optimization of programs in **HPCF**.

Consider the addition function in **DPCF** given in Section 22.3, which we transcribe here for convenience:

$$\lambda \, (x) \, \texttt{fix} \, p \, \texttt{is} \, \lambda \, (y) \, \texttt{ifz} \, y \, \{\texttt{zero} \hookrightarrow x \mid \texttt{succ}(y') \hookrightarrow \texttt{succ}(p(y'))\}.$$

It is a value of type dyn in **HPCF** given as follows:

$$\texttt{fun} \, ! \, \lambda \, (x : \texttt{dyn}) \, \texttt{fix} \, p : \texttt{dyn} \, \texttt{is} \, \texttt{fun} \, ! \, \lambda \, (y : \texttt{dyn}) \, e_{x,p,y}, \qquad (23.8)$$

within which the fragment

$$x : \texttt{dyn}, \, p : \texttt{dyn}, \, y : \texttt{dyn} \vdash e_{x,p,y} : \texttt{dyn}$$

stands for the expression

$$\texttt{ifz} \, (y \, @ \, \texttt{num}) \, \{\texttt{zero} \hookrightarrow x \mid \texttt{succ}(y') \hookrightarrow \texttt{num} \, ! \, (\texttt{s}((p \, @ \, \texttt{fun})(\texttt{num} \, ! \, y') \, @ \, \texttt{num}))\}.$$

The embedding into **HPCF** makes explicit the run-time checks that are implicit in the dynamics of **DPCF**.

Careful examination of the embedded formulation of addition reveals a great deal of redundancy and overhead that can be eliminated in the statically typed version. Eliminating this redundancy requires a static type discipline, because the intermediate computations involve values of a type other than dyn. This transformation shows that the freedoms offered by dynamic languages accruing from the absence of types are, instead, limitations on their expressive power arising from the restriction to a single type.

The first redundancy arises from the use of recursion in a dynamic language. In the above example, we use recursion to define the inner loop p of the computation. The value p is, by definition, a λ-abstraction, which is explicitly tagged as a function. Yet the call to p within the loop checks at run-time whether p is in fact a function before applying it. Because p is an internally defined function, all of its call sites are under the control of the addition function, which means that there is no need for such pessimism at calls to p, provided that we change its type to dyn $\rightharpoonup$ dyn, which directly expresses the invariant that p is a function acting on dynamic values.

Performing this transformation, we obtain the following reformulation of the addition function that eliminates this redundancy:

$$\texttt{fun} \, ! \, \lambda \, (x : \texttt{dyn}) \, \texttt{fun} \, ! \, \texttt{fix} \, p : \texttt{dyn} \rightharpoonup \texttt{dyn} \, \texttt{is} \, \lambda \, (y : \texttt{dyn}) \, e'_{x,p,y},$$

where $e'_{x,p,y}$ is the expression

$$\texttt{ifz} \, (y \, @ \, \texttt{num}) \, \{\texttt{zero} \hookrightarrow x \mid \texttt{succ}(y') \hookrightarrow \texttt{num} \, ! \, (\texttt{s}(p(\texttt{num} \, ! \, y') \, @ \, \texttt{num}))\}.$$

We have "hoisted" the function class label out of the loop and suppressed the cast inside the loop. Correspondingly, the type of p has changed to dyn $\rightharpoonup$ dyn.

Next, note that the variable y of type dyn is cast to a number on each iteration of the loop before it is tested for zero. Because this function is recursive, the bindings of y arise in one of two ways: at the initial call to the addition function, and on each recursive call. But the recursive call is made on the predecessor of y, which is a true natural number that is labeled with num at the call site, only to be removed by the class check at the conditional on the next iteration. This observation suggests that we hoist the check on y outside of the loop, and avoid labeling the argument to the recursive call. Doing so changes the type of the function, however, from dyn $\rightharpoonup$ dyn to nat $\rightharpoonup$ dyn. Consequently, further changes are required to ensure that the entire function remains well-typed.

Before doing so, let us make another observation. The result of the recursive call is checked to ensure that it has class num, and, if so, the underlying value is incremented and labeled with class num. If the result of the recursive call came from an earlier use of this branch of the conditional, then obviously the class check is redundant, because we know that it must have class num. But what if the result came from the other branch of the conditional? In that case, the function returns x, which need not be of class num because it is provided by the caller of the function. However, we may reasonably insist that it is an error to call addition with a non-numeric argument. This restriction can be enforced by replacing x in the zero branch of the conditional by x @ num.

Combining these optimizations we obtain the inner loop e''_x defined as follows:

$$\text{fix } p : \text{nat} \rightharpoonup \text{nat is } \lambda\, (y : \text{nat})\, \text{ifz } y\, \{\text{zero} \hookrightarrow x \,@\, \text{num} \mid \text{succ}(y') \hookrightarrow \text{s}(p(y'))\}.$$

It has the type nat $\rightharpoonup$ nat, and runs without class checks when applied to a natural number.

Finally, recall that the goal is to define a version of addition that works on values of type dyn. Thus, we need a value of type dyn $\rightharpoonup$ dyn, but what we have at hand is a function of type nat $\rightharpoonup$ nat. It can be converted to the needed form by pre-composing with a cast to num and post-composing with a coercion to num:

$$\text{fun}\,!\,\lambda\,(x : \text{dyn})\,\text{fun}\,!\,\lambda\,(y : \text{dyn})\,\text{num}\,!\,(e''_x(y \,@\, \text{num})).$$

The innermost λ-abstraction converts the function e''_x from type nat $\rightharpoonup$ nat to type dyn $\rightharpoonup$ dyn by composing it with a class check that ensures that y is a natural number at the initial call site, and applies a label to the result to restore it to type dyn.

The outcome of these transformations is that the inner loop of the computation runs at "full speed," without any manipulation of tags on functions or numbers. But the outermost form of addition remains; it is a value of type dyn encapsulating a curried function that takes two arguments of type dyn. Doing so preserves the correctness of all calls to addition, which pass and return values of type dyn, while optimizing its execution during the computation. Of course, we could strip the class tags from the addition function, changing its type from dyn to the more descriptive dyn $\rightharpoonup$ dyn $\rightharpoonup$ dyn, but this imposes the obligation on the caller to treat addition not as a value of type dyn, but rather as a function that must be applied to two successive values of type dyn whose class is num. As long as the call sites to addition are under programmer control, there is no obstacle to effecting this transformation. It is only when there are external call sites, not directly under programmer control, that there is any need to package addition as a value of type dyn. Applying this principle generally, we see that dynamic typing is only of marginal utility—it is used only at the margins of a system where uncontrolled calls arise. Internally to a system there is no benefit, and considerable drawback, to restricting attention to the type dyn.

23.4 Static versus Dynamic Typing

There have been many attempts by advocates of dynamic typing to distinguish dynamic from static languages. It is useful to consider the supposed distinctions from the present viewpoint.

1. *Dynamic languages associate types with values, whereas static languages associate types to variables.* Dynamic languages associate *classes*, not *types*, to values by tagging them with identifiers such as num and fun. This form of classification amounts to a use of recursive sum types within a statically typed language, and hence cannot be seen as a distinguishing feature of dynamic languages. Moreover, static languages assign types to expressions, not just variables. Because dynamic languages are just particular static languages (with a single type), the same can be said of dynamic languages.

2. *Dynamic languages check types at run-time, whereas static language check types at compile time.* Dynamic languages are just as surely statically typed as static languages, albeit for a degenerate type system with only one type. As we have seen, dynamic languages do perform class checks at run-time, but so too do static languages that admit sum types. The difference is only the extent to which we must use classification: always in a dynamic language, only as necessary in a static language.

3. *Dynamic languages support heterogeneous collections, whereas static languages support homogeneous collections.* The purpose of sum types is to support heterogeneity, so that any static language with sums admits heterogeneous data structures. A typical example is a list such as

$$\mathrm{cons}(\mathrm{num}[1]; \mathrm{cons}(\mathrm{fun}(x.x); \mathrm{nil}))$$

(written in abstract syntax for emphasis). It is sometimes said that such a list is not representable in a static language, because of the disparate nature of its components. Whether in a static *or* a dynamic language, lists are *type* homogeneous, but can be *class* heterogeneous. All elements of the above list are of type dyn; the first is of class num, and the second is of class fun.

Thus, the seeming opposition between static and dynamic typing is an illusion. The question is not *whether* to have static typing, but rather how best to embrace it. Confining one's attention to a single recursive type seems pointlessly restrictive. Indeed, many so-called untyped languages have implicit concessions to there being more than one type. The classic example is the ubiquitous concept of "multi-argument functions," which are a concession to the existence of products of the type of values (with pattern matching). It is then a short path to considering "multi-result functions," and other *ad hoc* language features that amount to admitting a richer and richer static type discipline.

23.5 Notes

Viewing dynamic languages as static languages with recursive types was first proposed by Dana Scott (Scott, 1980b), who also suggested glossing "untyped" as "uni-typed." Most modern statically typed languages, such as Java or Haskell or OCaml or SML, include a type similar to dyn, or admit recursive types with which to define it. For this reason one might expect that the opposition between dynamic and static typing would fade away, but industrial and academic trends suggest otherwise.

Exercises

23.1. Consider the extensions to **DPCF** described in Section 22.2 to admit null and pairing and their associated operations. Extend the statics and dynamics of **HPCF** to account for these extensions, and give a translation of the null and pairing operations described informally in Chapter 22 in terms of this extension to **HPCF**.

23.2. Continue the interpretation of the null and pairing operations in **HPCF** given in Exercise **23.1** to provide an interpretation in **FPC**. Specifically, define the expanded dyn as a recursive type and give a direct implementation of the null and pairing primitives in terms of this recursive type.

23.3. Consider the append function defined in Chapter 22 using nil and cons to represent lists:

$$\texttt{fix}\, a\, \texttt{is}\, \lambda\,(x)\, \lambda\,(y)\, \texttt{cond}(x; \texttt{cons}(\texttt{car}(x); a(\texttt{cdr}(x))(y)); y).$$

Rewrite append in **HPCF** using the definitions given in Exercise **23.1**. Then optimize the implementation to eliminate unnecessary overhead while ensuring that append still has type dyn.

Notes

1 The judgment e err signals a checked error that is to be treated as described in Section 6.3.
2 The expression error aborts the computation with an error; this can be accomplished using exceptions, which are the subject of Chapter 29.

PART X

Subtyping

Structural Subtyping

A *subtype* relation is a pre-order (reflexive and transitive relation) on types that validates the *subsumption principle*:

> if τ' *is a subtype of* τ, *then a value of type* τ' *may be provided when a value of type* τ *is required.*

The subsumption principle relaxes the strictures of a type system to allow values of one type to be treated as values of another.

Experience shows that the subsumption principle, although useful as a general guide, can be tricky to apply correctly in practice. The key to getting it right is the principle of introduction and elimination. To see whether a candidate subtyping relationship is sensible, it suffices to consider whether every *introduction* form of the subtype can be safely manipulated by every *elimination* form of the supertype. A subtyping principle makes sense only if it passes this test; the proof of the type safety theorem for a given subtyping relation ensures that this is the case.

A good way to get a subtyping principle wrong is to think of a type merely as a set of values (generated by introduction forms) and to consider whether every value of the subtype can also be considered to be a value of the supertype. The intuition behind this approach is to think of subtyping as akin to the subset relation in ordinary mathematics. But, as we shall see, this can lead to serious errors, because it fails to take account of the elimination forms that are applicable to the supertype. It is not enough to think only of the introduction forms; subtyping is a matter of *behavior*, not *containment*.

24.1 Subsumption

A *subtyping judgment* has the form $\tau' <: \tau$, and states that τ' is a subtype of τ. At the least we demand that the following *structural rules* of subtyping be admissible:

$$\overline{\tau <: \tau} \tag{24.1a}$$

$$\frac{\tau'' <: \tau' \quad \tau' <: \tau}{\tau'' <: \tau} \tag{24.1b}$$

In practice, we either tacitly include these rules as primitive or prove that they are admissible for a given set of subtyping rules.

The point of a subtyping relation is to enlarge the set of well-typed programs, which is accomplished by the *subsumption rule*:

$$\frac{\Gamma \vdash e : \tau' \quad \tau' <: \tau}{\Gamma \vdash e : \tau} \tag{24.2}$$

In contrast to most other typing rules, the rule of subsumption is *not* syntax-directed, because it does not constrain the form of e. That is, the subsumption rule can be applied to *any* form of expression. In particular, to show that $e : \tau$, we have two choices: either apply the rule appropriate to the particular form of e, or apply the subsumption rule, checking that $e : \tau'$ and $\tau' <: \tau$.

24.2 Varieties of Subtyping

In this section, we will informally explore several different forms of subtyping in the context of extensions of the language **FPC** introduced in Chapter 20.

Numeric Types

We begin with an informal discussion of numeric types such as are common in many programming languages. Our mathematical experience suggests subtyping relationships among numeric types. For example, in a language with types int, rat, and real, representing the integers, the rationals, and the reals, it is tempting to postulate the subtyping relationships

$$\text{int} <: \text{rat} <: \text{real}$$

by analogy with the set containments

$$\mathbb{Z} \subseteq \mathbb{Q} \subseteq \mathbb{R}.$$

But are these subtyping relationships sensible? The answer depends on the representations and interpretations of these types. Even in mathematics, the containments just mentioned are usually not true—or are true only in a rough sense. For example, the set of rational numbers can be considered to consist of ordered pairs (m, n), with $n \neq 0$ and $\gcd(m, n) = 1$, representing the ratio m/n. The set $\mathbb{Z}$ of integers can be isomorphically embedded within $\mathbb{Q}$ by identifying $n \in \mathbb{Z}$ with the ratio $n/1$. Similarly, the real numbers are often represented as convergent sequences of rationals, so that strictly speaking the rationals are not a subset of the reals, but rather can be embedded in them by choosing a canonical representative (a particular convergent sequence) of each rational.

For mathematical purposes, it is entirely reasonable to overlook fine distinctions such as that between $\mathbb{Z}$ and its embedding within $\mathbb{Q}$. Ignoring the difference is justified because the operations on rationals restrict to the embedding in the expected way: if we add two integers thought of as rationals in the canonical way, then the result is the rational associated with their sum. And similarly for the other operations, provided that we take some care in defining them to ensure that it all works out properly. For the purposes of computing, however, we must also take account of algorithmic efficiency and the finiteness of machine representations. For example, what are often called "real numbers" in a programming language are, of course, floating point numbers, a finite subset of the rational numbers. Not every rational can be exactly represented as a floating point number, nor does floating point arithmetic restrict to rational arithmetic, even when its arguments are exactly represented as floating point numbers.

Product Types

Product types give rise to a form of subtyping based on the subsumption principle. The only elimination form applicable to a value of product type is a projection. Under mild assumptions about the dynamics of projections, we may consider one product type to be a subtype of another by considering whether the projections applicable to the supertype can be validly applied to values of the subtype.

Consider a context in which a value of type $\tau = \langle \tau_j \rangle_{j \in J}$ is required. The statics of finite products (rules (10.3)) ensures that the only operation we may perform on a value of type τ, other than to bind it to a variable, is to take the jth projection from it for some $j \in J$ to obtain a value of type τ_j. Now suppose that e is of type τ'. For the projection $e \cdot j$ to be well-formed, then τ' is a finite product type $\langle \tau'_i \rangle_{i \in I}$ such that $j \in I$. Moreover, for the projection to be of type τ_j, it is enough to require that $\tau'_j = \tau_j$. Because $j \in J$ is arbitrary, we arrive at the following subtyping rule for finite product types:

$$\frac{J \subseteq I}{\prod_{i \in I} \tau_i <: \prod_{j \in J} \tau_j} .$$

(24.3)

This rule sufices for the required subtyping, but not necessary; we will consider a more liberal form of this rule in Section 24.3. The justification for rule (24.3) is that we may evaluate $e \cdot i$ regardless of the actual form of e, provided only that it has a field indexed by $i \in I$.

Sum Types

By an argument dual to the one given for finite product types, we may derive a related subtyping rule for finite sum types. If a value of type $\sum_{j \in J} \tau_j$ is required, the statics of sums (rules (11.3)) ensures that the only non-trivial operation that we may perform on that value is a J-indexed case analysis. If we provide a value of type $\sum_{i \in I} \tau'_i$ instead, no difficulty will arise so long as $I \subseteq J$ and each τ'_i is equal to τ_i. If the containment is strict, some cases cannot arise, but this does not disrupt safety.

$$\frac{I \subseteq J}{\sum_{i \in I} \tau_i <: \sum_{j \in J} \tau_j} .$$

(24.4)

Note well the reversal of the containment as compared to rule (24.3).

Dynamic Types

A popular form of subtyping is associated with the type dyn introduced in Chapter 23. The type dyn provides no information about the class of a value of this type. One might argue that it is whole the point of dynamic typing to suppress this information statically, making it available only dynamically. On the other hand, it is not much trouble to introduce subtypes of dyn that specify the class of a value, relying on subsumption to "forget" the class when it cannot be determined statically.

Working in the context of Chapter 23 this amounts to introduce two new types, dyn[num] and dyn[fun], governed by the following two subtyping axioms:

$$\frac{\rule{3cm}{0.4pt}}{\mathtt{dyn[num]} <: \mathtt{dyn}} \tag{24.5a}$$

$$\frac{\rule{3cm}{0.4pt}}{\mathtt{dyn[fun]} <: \mathtt{dyn}} \tag{24.5b}$$

Of course, in a richer language with more classes of dynamic values, one would correspondingly introduce more such subtypes of dyn, one for each additional class. As a matter of notation, the type dyn is frequently spelled object, and its class-specific subtypes dyn[num] and dyn[fun], are often written as num and fun, respectively. But doing so invites confusion between the separate concepts of *class* and *type*, as discussed in detail in Chapters 22 and 23.

The class-specific subtypes of dyn come into play by reformulating the typing rules for introducing values of type dyn to note the class of the created value:

$$\frac{\Gamma \vdash e : \mathtt{nat}}{\Gamma \vdash \mathtt{new[num]}(e) : \mathtt{dyn[num]}} \tag{24.6a}$$

$$\frac{\Gamma \vdash e : \mathtt{dyn} \rightharpoonup \mathtt{dyn}}{\Gamma \vdash \mathtt{new[fun]}(e) : \mathtt{dyn[fun]}} \tag{24.6b}$$

Thus, in this formulation, classified values "start life" with class-specific types, because in those cases it is statically apparent what is the class of the introduced value. Subsumption is used to weaken the type to dyn in those cases where no static prediction can be made—for example, when the branches of a conditional evaluate to dynamic values of different classes it is necessary to weaken the type of the branches to dyn.

The advantage of such a subtyping mechanism is that we can express more precise types, such as the type dyn[num] $\rightharpoonup$ dyn[num] of functions mapping a value of type dyn with class num to another such value. This typing is more precise than, say, dyn $\rightharpoonup$ dyn, which merely classifies functions that act on dynamically typed values. In this way, weak invariants can be expressed and enforced, but only insofar as it is possible to track the classes of the values involved in a computation. Subtyping is not nearly a powerful enough mechanism for practical situations, rendering the additional specificity not worth the effort of including it. (A more powerful approach is developed in Chapter 25.)

24.3 Variance

In addition to basic subtyping principles such as those considered in Section 24.2, it is also important to consider the effect of subtyping on type constructors. A type constructor *covariant* in an argument if subtyping in that argument is preserved by the constructor. It is *contravariant* if subtyping in that argument is reversed by the constructor. It is *invariant* in an argument if subtyping for the constructed type is not affected by subtyping in that argument.

Product and Sum Types

Finite product types are *covariant* in each field. For if e is of type $\prod_{i \in I} \tau_i'$, and the projection $e \cdot j$ is to be of type τ_j, then it suffices to require that $j \in I$ and $\tau_j' <: \tau_j$.

$$\frac{(\forall i \in I)\ \tau_i' <: \tau_i}{\prod_{i \in I} \tau_i' <: \prod_{i \in I} \tau_i} \tag{24.7}$$

It is implicit in this rule that the dynamics of projection cannot be sensitive to the precise type of any of the fields of a value of finite product type.

Finite sum types are also covariant, because each branch of a case analysis on a value of the supertype expects a value of the corresponding summand, for which it suffices to provide a value of the corresponding subtype summand:

$$\frac{(\forall i \in I)\ \tau_i' <: \tau_i}{\sum_{i \in I} \tau_i' <: \sum_{i \in I} \tau_i} \tag{24.8}$$

Partial Function Types

The variance of the function type constructors is a bit more subtle. We will work here with the partial function types, but the same considerations apply to the total function type. Let us consider first the variance of the function type in its range. Suppose that $e : \tau_1 \rightharpoonup \tau_2'$. Then if $e_1 : \tau_1$, then $e(e_1) : \tau_2'$, and if $\tau_2' <: \tau_2$, then $e(e_1) : \tau_2$ as well.

$$\frac{\tau_2' <: \tau_2}{\tau_1 \rightharpoonup \tau_2' <: \tau_1 \rightharpoonup \tau_2} \tag{24.9}$$

Every function that delivers a value of type τ_2' also delivers a value of type τ_2, provided that $\tau_2' <: \tau_2$. Thus, the function type constructor is covariant in its range.

Now let us consider the variance of the function type in its domain. Suppose again that $e : \tau_1 \rightharpoonup \tau_2$. Then e can be applied to any value of type τ_1 to obtain a value of type τ_2. Hence, by the subsumption principle, it can be applied to any value of a subtype τ_1' of τ_1, and it will still deliver a value of type τ_2. Consequently, we may just as well think of e as having type $\tau_1' \rightharpoonup \tau_2$.

$$\frac{\tau_1' <: \tau_1}{\tau_1 \rightharpoonup \tau_2 <: \tau_1' \rightharpoonup \tau_2} \qquad (24.10)$$

The function type is contravariant in its domain position. Note well the reversal of the subtyping relation in the premise as compared to the conclusion of the rule!

Combining these rules we obtain the following general principle of contra- and covariance for function types:

$$\frac{\tau_1' <: \tau_1 \quad \tau_2' <: \tau_2}{\tau_1 \rightharpoonup \tau_2' <: \tau_1' \rightharpoonup \tau_2} \qquad (24.11)$$

Beware of the reversal of the ordering in the domain!

Recursive Types

The language **FPC** has a partial function types, which behave the same under subtyping as total function types, sums and products, which behave as described above, and recursive types, which introduce some subtleties that have been the source of error in language design. To gain some intuition, consider the type of labeled binary trees with natural numbers at each node,

$$\text{rec } t \text{ is } [\text{empty} \hookrightarrow \text{unit}, \text{binode} \hookrightarrow \langle \text{data} \hookrightarrow \text{nat}, \text{lft} \hookrightarrow t, \text{rht} \hookrightarrow t \rangle],$$

and the type of "bare" binary trees, without data attached to the nodes,

$$\text{rec } t \text{ is } [\text{empty} \hookrightarrow \text{unit}, \text{binode} \hookrightarrow \langle \text{lft} \hookrightarrow t, \text{rht} \hookrightarrow t \rangle].$$

Is either a subtype of the other? Intuitively, we might expect the type of labeled binary trees to be a *subtype* of the type of bare binary trees, because any use of a bare binary tree can simply ignore the presence of the label.

Now consider the type of bare "two-three" trees with two sorts of nodes, those with two children, and those with three:

$$\text{rec } t \text{ is } [\text{empty} \hookrightarrow \text{unit}, \text{binode} \hookrightarrow \tau_2, \text{trinode} \hookrightarrow \tau_3],$$

where

$$\tau_2 \triangleq \langle \text{lft} \hookrightarrow t, \text{rht} \hookrightarrow t \rangle, \text{ and}$$
$$\tau_3 \triangleq \langle \text{lft} \hookrightarrow t, \text{mid} \hookrightarrow t, \text{rht} \hookrightarrow t \rangle.$$

What subtype relationships should hold between this type and the preceding two tree types? Intuitively the type of bare two-three trees should be a *supertype* of the type of bare binary trees, because any use of a two-three tree proceeds by three-way case analysis, which covers both forms of binary tree.

To capture the pattern illustrated by these examples, we need a subtyping rule for recursive types. It is tempting to consider the following rule:

$$\frac{t \text{ type} \vdash \tau' <: \tau}{\text{rec } t \text{ is } \tau' <: \text{rec } t \text{ is } \tau} \text{ ??} \qquad (24.12)$$

That is, to check whether one recursive type is a subtype of the other, we simply compare their bodies, with the bound variable treated as an argument. Notice that by reflexivity of subtyping, we have $t <: t$, and hence we may use this fact in the derivation of $\tau' <: \tau$.

Rule (24.12) validates the intuitively plausible subtyping between labeled binary tree and bare binary trees just described. Deriving this requires checking that the subtyping relationship

$$\langle \text{data} \hookrightarrow \text{nat}, \text{lft} \hookrightarrow t, \text{rht} \hookrightarrow t \rangle <: \langle \text{lft} \hookrightarrow t, \text{rht} \hookrightarrow t \rangle,$$

holds generically in t, which is evidently the case.

Unfortunately, Rule (24.12) also underwrites *incorrect* subtyping relationships, as well as some correct ones. As an example of what goes wrong, consider the recursive types

$$\tau' = \text{rec } t \text{ is } \langle a \hookrightarrow t \rightharpoonup \text{nat}, b \hookrightarrow t \rightharpoonup \text{int} \rangle$$

and

$$\tau = \text{rec } t \text{ is } \langle a \hookrightarrow t \rightharpoonup \text{int}, b \hookrightarrow t \rightharpoonup \text{int} \rangle.$$

We assume for the sake of the example that $\text{nat} <: \text{int}$, so that by using rule (24.12) we may derive $\tau' <: \tau$, which is incorrect. Let $e : \tau'$ be the expression

$$\text{fold}(\langle a \hookrightarrow \lambda (x : \tau') 4, b \hookrightarrow \lambda (x : \tau') q((\text{unfold}(x) \cdot a)(x)) \rangle),$$

where $q : \text{nat} \rightharpoonup \text{nat}$ is the discrete square root function. Because $\tau' <: \tau$, it follows that $e : \tau$ as well, and hence

$$\text{unfold}(e) : \langle a \hookrightarrow \tau \rightharpoonup \text{int}, b \hookrightarrow \tau \rightharpoonup \text{int} \rangle.$$

Now let $e' : \tau$ be the expression

$$\text{fold}(\langle a \hookrightarrow \lambda (x : \tau) \text{-4}, b \hookrightarrow \lambda (x : \tau) 0 \rangle).$$

(The important point about e' is that the a method returns a negative number; the b method is of no significance.) To finish the proof, observe that

$$(\text{unfold}(e) \cdot b)(e') \longmapsto^* q(-4),$$

which is a stuck state. We have derived a well-typed program that "gets stuck," refuting type safety!

Rule (24.12) is therefore incorrect. But what has gone wrong? The error lies in the choice of a single variable to stand for both recursive types, which does not correctly model self-reference. In effect, we are treating two distinct recursive types as if they were equal while checking their bodies for a subtyping relationship. But this is clearly wrong! It fails to take account of the self-referential nature of recursive types. On the left side, the bound variable stands for the subtype, whereas on the right the bound variable stands for the super-type. Confusing them leads to the unsoundness just illustrated.

As is often the case with self-reference, the solution is to *assume* what we are trying to prove, and check that this assumption can be maintained by examining the bodies of the recursive types. To do so, we use hypothetical judgments of the form $\Delta \vdash \tau' <: \tau$, where Δ consists of hypotheses t type and $t <: \tau$ that declares a fresh type variable t that is not otherwise declared in Δ. Using such hypothetical judgments, we may state the correct rule for subtyping recursive types as follows:

$$\frac{\Delta, t \text{ type}, t' \text{ type}, t' <: t \vdash \tau' <: \tau \quad \Delta, t' \text{ type} \vdash \tau' \text{ type} \quad \Delta, t \text{ type} \vdash \tau \text{ type}}{\Delta \vdash \text{rec } t' \text{ is } \tau' <: \text{rec } t \text{ is } \tau}.$$

(24.13)

That is, to check whether $\text{rec } t' \text{ is } \tau' <: \text{rec } t \text{ is } \tau$, we assume that $t' <: t$, because t' and t stand for the corresponding recursive types, and check that $\tau' <: \tau$ under this assumption. It is instructive to check that the unsound subtyping example given above is not derivable using this rule: the subtyping assumption is at odds with the contravariance of the function type in its domain.

Quantified Types

Consider extending **FPC** with the universal and existential quantified types discussed in Chapters 16 and 17. The variance principles for the quantifiers state that they are uniformly covariant in the quantified types:

$$\frac{\Delta, t \text{ type} \vdash \tau' <: \tau}{\Delta \vdash \forall(t.\tau') <: \forall(t.\tau)}$$

(24.14a)

$$\frac{\Delta, t \text{ type} \vdash \tau' <: \tau}{\Delta \vdash \exists(t.\tau') <: \exists(t.\tau)}$$

(24.14b)

Consequently, we may derive the principle of substitution:

Lemma 24.1. *If* $\Delta, t \text{ type} \vdash \tau_1 <: \tau_2$, *and* $\Delta \vdash \tau \text{ type}$, *then* $\Delta \vdash [\tau/t]\tau_1 <: [\tau/t]\tau_2$.

Proof By induction on the subtyping derivation.   □

It is easy to check that the above variance principles for the quantifiers are consistent with the principle of subsumption. For example, a package of the subtype $\exists(t.\tau')$ consists of a representation type ρ and an implementation e of type $[\rho/t]\tau'$. But if $t \text{ type} \vdash \tau' <: \tau$, we have by substitution that $[\rho/t]\tau' <: [\rho/t]\tau$, and hence e is also an implementation of type $[\rho/t]\tau$. So the package is also of the supertype.

It is natural to extend subtyping to the quantifiers by allowing quantification over all subtypes of a specified type; this is called *bounded quantification*.

$$\frac{}{\Delta, t \text{ type}, t <: \tau \vdash t <: \tau}$$

(24.15a)

$$\frac{\Delta \vdash \tau :: \text{T}}{\Delta \vdash \tau <: \tau}$$

(24.15b)

$$\frac{\Delta \vdash \tau'' <: \tau' \quad \Delta \vdash \tau' <: \tau}{\Delta \vdash \tau'' <: \tau}$$

(24.15c)

$$\frac{\Delta \vdash \tau_1' <: \tau_1 \quad \Delta, t \text{ type}, t <: \tau_1' \vdash \tau_2 <: \tau_2'}{\Delta \vdash \forall t <: \tau_1.\tau_2 <: \forall t <: \tau_1'.\tau_2'} \tag{24.15d}$$

$$\frac{\Delta \vdash \tau_1 <: \tau_1' \quad \Delta, t \text{ type}, t <: \tau_1 \vdash \tau_2 <: \tau_2'}{\Delta \vdash \exists t <: \tau_1.\tau_2 <: \exists t <: \tau_1'.\tau_2'} \tag{24.15e}$$

Rule (24.15d) states that the universal quantifier is contravariant in its bound, whereas rule (24.15e) states that the existential quantifier is covariant in its bound.

24.4 Dynamics and Safety

There is a subtle assumption in the definition of product subtyping in Section 24.2, namely that the *same* projection operation from an I-tuple applies also to a J-tuple, provided $J \supseteq I$. But this need not be the case. One could represent I-tuples differently from J-tuples at will, so that the meaning of the projection at position $i \in I \subseteq J$ is different in the two cases. Nothing rules out this possibility, yet product subtyping relies on it not being the case. From this point of view, product subtyping is not well-justified, but one may instead consider that subtyping limits possible implementations to ensure that it makes sense.

Similar considerations apply to sum types. An J-way case analysis need not be applicable to an I-way value of sum type, even when $I \subseteq J$ and all the types in common agree. For example, one might represent values of a sum type with a "small" index set in a way that is not applicable for a "large" index set. In that case, the "large" case analysis would not make sense on a value of "small" sum type. Here again we may consider either that subtyping is not justified, or that it imposes limitations on the implementation that are not otherwise forced.

These considerations merit careful consideration of the safety of languages with subtyping. As an illustrative case we consider the safety of **FPC** enriched with product subtyping. The main concern is that the subsumption rule obscures the "true" type of a value, complicating the canonical forms lemma. Moreover, we assume that the same projection makes sense for a wider tuple than a narrower one, provided that it is within range.

Lemma 24.2 (Structurality).

1. *The tuple subtyping relation is reflexive and transitive.*
2. *The typing judgment $\Gamma \vdash e : \tau$ is closed under weakening and substitution.*

Proof

1. Reflexivity is proved by induction on the structure of types. Transitivity is proved by induction on the derivations of the judgments $\tau'' <: \tau'$ and $\tau' <: \tau$ to obtain a derivation of $\tau'' <: \tau$.
2. By induction on rules (10.3), augmented by rule (24.2). □

Lemma 24.3 (Inversion).

1. *If $e \cdot j : \tau$, then $e : \prod_{i \in I} \tau_i$, $j \in I$, and $\tau_j <: \tau$.*
2. *If $\langle e_i \rangle_{i \in I} : \tau$, then $\prod_{i \in I} \tau_i' <: \tau$ where $e_i : \tau_i'$ for each $i \in I$.*
3. *If $\tau' <: \prod_{j \in J} \tau_j$, then $\tau' = \prod_{i \in I} \tau_i'$ for some I and some types τ_i' for $i \in I$.*
4. *If $\prod_{i \in I} \tau_i' <: \prod_{j \in J} \tau_j$, then $J \subseteq I$ and $\tau_j' <: \tau_j$ for each $j \in J$.*

Proof By induction on the subtyping and typing rules, paying special attention to rule (24.2).   □

Theorem 24.4 (Preservation). *If $e : \tau$ and $e \longmapsto e'$, then $e' : \tau$.*

Proof By induction on rules (10.4). For example, consider rule (10.4d), so that $e = \langle e_i \rangle_{i \in I} \cdot k$ and $e' = e_k$. By Lemma 24.3, we have $\langle e_i \rangle_{i \in I} : \prod_{j \in J} \tau_j$, with $k \in J$ and $\tau_k <: \tau$. By another application of Lemma 24.3 for each $i \in I$, there exists τ_i' such that $e_i : \tau_i'$ and $\prod_{i \in I} \tau_i' <: \prod_{j \in J} \tau_j$. By Lemma 24.3 again, we have $J \subseteq I$ and $\tau_j' <: \tau_j$ for each $j \in J$. But then $e_k : \tau_k$, as desired. The remaining cases are similar.   □

Lemma 24.5 (Canonical Forms). *If e val and $e : \prod_{j \in J} \tau_j$, then e is of the form $\langle e_i \rangle_{i \in I}$, where $J \subseteq I$, and $e_j : \tau_j$ for each $j \in J$.*

Proof By induction on rules (10.3) augmented by rule (24.2).   □

Theorem 24.6 (Progress). *If $e : \tau$, then either e val or there exists e' such that $e \longmapsto e'$.*

Proof By induction on rules (10.3) augmented by rule (24.2). The rule of subsumption is handled by appeal to the inductive hypothesis on the premise of the rule. Rule (10.4d) follows from Lemma 24.5.   □

24.5 Notes

Subtyping is perhaps the most widely misunderstood concept in programming languages. Subtyping is principally a convenience, akin to type inference, that makes some programs simpler to write. But the subsumption rule cuts both ways. Inasmuch as it allows the implicit passage from τ' to τ when τ' is a subtype of τ, it also weakens the meaning of a type assertion $e : \tau$ to mean that e has some type contained in the type τ. Subsumption precludes expressing the requirement that e has *exactly* the type τ, or that two expressions jointly have the *same* type. And it is just this weakness that creates so many of the difficulties with subtyping.

Much has been written about subtyping, often in relation to object-oriented programming. Standard ML (Milner et al., 1997) is one of the first languages to make use of subtyping, in two forms, called *enrichment* and *realization*. The former corresponds to product subtyping, and the latter to the "forgetful" subtyping associated with type definitions (see Chapter 43). The first systematic studies of subtyping include those by Mitchell (1984), Reynolds (1980), and Cardelli (1988). Pierce (2002) give a thorough account of subtyping, especially of recursive and polymorphic types and proves that subtyping for bounded impredicative universal quantification is undecidable.

Exercises

24.1. Check the variance of the type

$$(\texttt{unit} \rightharpoonup \tau) \times (\tau \rightharpoonup \texttt{unit}).$$

When viewed as a constructor with argument τ, is it covariant or contravariant? Give a precise proof or counterexample in each case.

24.2. Consider the two recursive types,

$$\rho_1 \triangleq \mathsf{rec}\, t \,\mathsf{is}\, \langle \texttt{eq} \hookrightarrow (t \rightharpoonup \texttt{bool}) \rangle,$$

and

$$\rho_2 \triangleq \mathsf{rec}\, t \,\mathsf{is}\, \langle \texttt{eq} \hookrightarrow (t \rightharpoonup \texttt{bool}), \texttt{f} \hookrightarrow \texttt{bool} \rangle.$$

It is clear that ρ_1 could not be a subtype of ρ_2, because, viewed as a product after unrolling, a value of the former type lacks a component that a value of the latter has. But is ρ_2 a subtype of ρ_1? If so, prove it by exhibiting a derivation of this fact using the rules given in Section 24.3. If not, give a counterexample showing that the suggested subtyping would violate type safety.

24.3. Another approach to the dynamics of subtyping that ensures safety, but gives subsumption dynamic significance, associates a witness, called a *coercion*, to each subtyping relation, and inserts a coercion wherever subsumption is used. More precisely,

   (a) Assign to each valid subtyping $\tau <: \tau'$ a coercion function $\chi : \tau \rightharpoonup \tau'$ that transforms a value of type τ into a value of type τ'.
   (b) Interpret the subsumption rule as implicit coercion. Specifically, when $\tau <: \tau'$ is witnessed by $\chi : \tau \rightharpoonup \tau'$, applying subsumption to $e : \tau$ inserts an application of χ to obtain $\chi(e) : \tau'$.

Formulate this idea precisely for the case of a subtype relation generated by "width" subtyping for products, and the variance principles for product, sum, and function types. Your solution should make clear that it evades the tacit projection assumption mentioned above.

But there may be more than one coercion $\chi : \tau \rightharpoonup \tau'$ corresponding to the subtyping $\tau <: \tau'$. The meaning of a program would then depend on which coercion is chosen when subsumption is used. If there is exactly one coercion for each subtyping relation, it is said to be *coherent*. Is your coercion interpretation of product subtyping coherent? (A proper treatment of coherence requires expression equivalence, which is discussed in Chapter 47.)

25   Behavioral Typing

In Chapter 23, we demonstrated that dynamic typing is but a mode of use of static typing, one in which dynamically typed values are of type dyn, a particular recursive sum type. A value of type dyn is always of the form $\text{new}[c](e)$, where c is its *class* and e is its underlying value. Importantly, the class c determines the type of the underlying value of a dynamic value. The type system of the hybrid language is rather weak in that every dynamically classified value has the same type, and there is no mention of the class in its type. To correct this shortcoming it is common to enrich the type system of the hybrid language to capture such information, for example, as described in Section 24.2.

In such a situation, subtyping is used to resolve a fundamental tension between *structure* and *behavior* in the design of type systems. On the one hand, types determine the structure of a programming language and, on the other, serve a behavioral specifications of expressions written in that language. Subtyping attempts to resolve this tension, unsuccessfully, by allowing certain forms of retyping. Although subtyping works reasonably well for small examples, things get far more complicated when we wish to specify the deep structure of a value, say, that it is of a class c and its underlying value is of another class d whose underlying value is a natural number. There is no limit to the degree of specificity one may wish in such descriptions, which gives rise to endless variations on type systems to accommodate various special situations.

Another resolution of the tension between structure and behavior in typing is to separate these aspects by distinguishing *types* from *type refinements*. Type refinements specify the execution behavior of an expression of a particular type using specifications that capture whatever properties are of interest, limited only by the difficulty of proving that a program satisfies the specification given by a refinement.

Certain limited forms of behavioral specifications can express many useful properties of programs while remaining mechanically checkable. These include the fundamental behavioral properties determined by the type itself but can be extended to include sharper conditions than just these structural properties. In this chapter, we will consider a particular notion of refinement tailored to the hybrid language of Chapter 23. It is based on two basic principles:

1. Type constructors, such as product, sum, and function space, act on refinements of their component types to induce a refinement on the compound type formed by those constructors.

2. It is useful to track the class of a value of type dyn and to assign multiple refinements to specify distinct behaviors of expressions involving values of dynamic type.

We will formulate a system of refinements based on these principles that ensures that a well-refined program cannot incur a run-time error arising from the attempt to cast a value to a class other than its own.

25.1 Statics

We will develop a system of refinements for the extension with sums and products of the language **HPCF** defined in Chapter 23 in which there are but two classes of values of type dyn, namely num and fun.[1] The syntax of refinements ϕ is given by the following grammar:

Ref	ϕ	::=	$\texttt{true}\{\tau\}$	$\top_\tau$	truth
			$\texttt{and}\{\tau\}(\phi_1;\phi_2)$	$\phi_1 \wedge_\tau \phi_2$	conjunction
			$\texttt{new}[\texttt{num}](\phi)$	$\texttt{num}\,!\,\phi$	dynamic number
			$\texttt{new}[\texttt{fun}](\phi)$	$\texttt{fun}\,!\,\phi$	dynamic function
			$\texttt{prod}(\phi_1;\phi_2)$	$\phi_1 \times \phi_2$	product
			$\texttt{sum}(\phi_1;\phi_2)$	$\phi_1 + \phi_2$	sum
			$\texttt{parr}(\phi_1;\phi_2)$	$\phi_1 \rightharpoonup \phi_2$	function

Informally, a refinement is a *predicate* specifying a property of the values of some type. Equivalently, one may think of a refinement as a *subset* of the values of a type, those that satisfy the specified property. To expose the dependence of refinements on types, the syntax of truth and conjunction is parameterized by the type whose values they govern. In most cases, the underlying type is clear from context, in which case it is omitted. Note that the syntax of the product, sum, and function refinements is exactly the same as the syntax of the types they govern, but they are refinements, not types.

The judgment $\phi \sqsubseteq \tau$ means that ϕ is a refinement of the type τ. It is defined by the following rules:

$$\frac{}{\top \sqsubseteq \tau} \tag{25.1a}$$

$$\frac{\phi_1 \sqsubseteq \tau \quad \phi_2 \sqsubseteq \tau}{\phi_1 \wedge \phi_2 \sqsubseteq \tau} \tag{25.1b}$$

$$\frac{\phi \sqsubseteq \texttt{nat}}{\texttt{num}\,!\,\phi \sqsubseteq \texttt{dyn}} \tag{25.1c}$$

$$\frac{\phi \sqsubseteq \texttt{dyn} \rightharpoonup \texttt{dyn}}{\texttt{fun}\,!\,\phi \sqsubseteq \texttt{dyn}} \tag{25.1d}$$

$$\frac{\phi_1 \sqsubseteq \tau_1 \quad \phi_2 \sqsubseteq \tau_2}{\phi_1 \times \phi_2 \sqsubseteq \tau_1 \times \tau_2} \tag{25.1e}$$

$$\frac{\phi_1 \sqsubseteq \tau_1 \quad \phi_2 \sqsubseteq \tau_2}{\phi_1 + \phi_2 \sqsubseteq \tau_1 + \tau_2} \tag{25.1f}$$

$$\frac{\phi_1 \sqsubseteq \tau_1 \quad \phi_2 \sqsubseteq \tau_2}{\phi_1 \rightharpoonup \phi_2 \sqsubseteq \tau_1 \rightharpoonup \tau_2} \tag{25.1g}$$

It is easy to see that each refinement refines a unique type, the *underlying type* of that refinement. The concrete syntax num ! ϕ and fun ! ϕ is both concise and commonplace, but, beware, it tends to obscure the critical distinctions between types, classes, and refinements.

The *refinement satisfaction* judgment, $e \in_\tau \phi$, where $e : \tau$ and $\phi \sqsubseteq \tau$, states that the well-typed expression e exhibits the behavior specified by ϕ. The hypothetical form,

$$x_1 \in_{\tau_1} \phi_1, \ldots, x_n \in_{\tau_n} \phi_n \vdash e \in_\tau \phi,$$

constrains the expressions that may be substituted for a variable to satisfy its associated refinement type (which could be the trivial refinement $\top$, that imposes no constraints). We write Φ for such a finite sequence of refinement assumptions on variables, called a *refinement context*. Each such Φ determines a typing context Γ given by $x_1 : \tau_1, \ldots, x_n : \tau_n$, specifying only the types of the variables involved. We often write Φ_Γ to state that Γ is the unique typing context determined by Φ in this way.

The definition of the refinement satisfaction judgment makes use of an auxiliary judgment, $\phi_1 \leq_\tau \phi_2$, where $\phi_1 \sqsubseteq \tau$ and $\phi_2 \sqsubseteq \tau$, which we shall often just write as $\phi_1 \leq \phi_2$ when τ is clear from context. This judgment is called *refinement entailment*. It states that the refinement ϕ_1 is *at least as strong as*, or *no weaker than*, the refinement ϕ_2. Informally, this means that if $e : \tau$ satisfies ϕ_1, then it must also satisfy ϕ_2. According to this interpretation, refinement entailment is reflexive and transitive. The refinement $\top$, which holds of any well-typed expression, is greater than (entailed by) any other refinement, and the conjunction of two refinements, $\phi_1 \wedge \phi_2$ is the meet (greatest lower bound) of ϕ_1 and ϕ_2. Because no value can be of two different classes, the conjunction of num ! ϕ_1 and fun ! ϕ_2 entails any refinement all. Finally, refinement entailment satisfies the same variance principles given for subtyping in Section 24.3.

$$\frac{\phi \sqsubseteq \tau}{\phi \leq_\tau \phi} \tag{25.2a}$$

$$\frac{\phi_1 \leq_\tau \phi_2 \quad \phi_2 \leq_\tau \phi_3}{\phi_1 \leq_\tau \phi_3} \tag{25.2b}$$

$$\frac{\phi \sqsubseteq \tau}{\phi \leq_\tau \top} \tag{25.2c}$$

$$\frac{\phi_1 \sqsubseteq \tau \quad \phi_2 \sqsubseteq \tau}{\phi_1 \wedge \phi_2 \leq_\tau \phi_1} \tag{25.2d}$$

$$\frac{\phi_1 \sqsubseteq \tau \quad \phi_2 \sqsubseteq \tau}{\phi_1 \wedge \phi_2 \leq_\tau \phi_2} \tag{25.2e}$$

$$\frac{\phi \leq_\tau \phi_1 \quad \phi \leq_\tau \phi_2}{\phi \leq_\tau \phi_1 \wedge \phi_2} \tag{25.2f}$$

$$\overline{\mathtt{num}\,!\,\phi_1 \wedge \mathtt{fun}\,!\,\phi_2 \leq_{\mathrm{dyn}} \phi} \tag{25.2g}$$

$$\frac{\phi \leq_{\mathrm{nat}} \phi'}{\mathtt{num}\,!\,\phi \leq_{\mathrm{dyn}} \mathtt{num}\,!\,\phi'} \tag{25.2h}$$

$$\frac{\phi \leq_{\mathrm{dyn}\to\mathrm{dyn}} \phi'}{\mathtt{fun}\,!\,\phi \leq_{\mathrm{dyn}} \mathtt{fun}\,!\,\phi'} \tag{25.2i}$$

$$\frac{\phi_1 \leq_{\tau_1} \phi_1' \quad \phi_2 \leq_{\tau_2} \phi_2'}{\phi_1 \times \phi_2 \leq_{\tau_1 \times \tau_2} \phi_1' \times \phi_2'} \tag{25.2j}$$

$$\frac{\phi_1 \leq_{\tau_1} \phi_1' \quad \phi_2 \leq_{\tau_2} \phi_2'}{\phi_1 + \phi_2 \leq_{\tau_1 + \tau_2} \phi_1' + \phi_2'} \tag{25.2k}$$

$$\frac{\phi_1' \leq_{\tau_1} \phi_1 \quad \phi_2 \leq_{\tau_2} \phi_2'}{\phi_1 \rightharpoonup \phi_2 \leq_{\tau_1 \to \tau_2} \phi_1' \rightharpoonup \phi_2'} \tag{25.2l}$$

For the sake of brevity, we usually omit the type subscripts from refinements and the refinement entailment relation.

We are now in a position to define the refinement satisfaction judgment, $\Phi_\Gamma \vdash e \in_\tau \phi$, in which we assume that $\Gamma \vdash e : \tau$. When such a satisfaction judgment holds, we say that e is *well-refined*, a property that can be stated only for expressions that are *well-typed*. The goal is to ensure that well-refined expressions do not incur (checked) run-time errors. In the present setting refinements rule out casting a value of class c to a class $c' \neq c$. The formulation of satisfaction, though simple-minded, will involve many important ideas.

To simplify the exposition, it is best to present the rules in groups, rather than all at once. The first group consists of the rules that pertain to expressions independently of their types.

$$\overline{\Phi_\Gamma, x \in_\tau \phi \vdash x \in_\tau \phi} \tag{25.3a}$$

$$\frac{\Phi \vdash e \in_\tau \phi' \quad \phi' \leq_\tau \phi}{\Phi \vdash e \in_\tau \phi} \tag{25.3b}$$

$$\frac{\Phi \vdash e \in_\tau \phi_1 \quad \Phi \vdash e \in_\tau \phi_2}{\Phi \vdash e \in_\tau \phi_1 \wedge \phi_2} \tag{25.3c}$$

$$\frac{\Phi, x \in_\tau \phi \vdash e \in_\tau \phi}{\Phi \vdash \mathtt{fix}\,x : \tau\,\mathtt{is}\,e \in_\tau \phi} \tag{25.3d}$$

Rule (25.3a) expresses the obvious principle that if a variable is *assumed* to satisfy a refinement ϕ, then of course it *does* satisfy that refinement. As usual, the principle of substitution is admissible. It states that if a variable is assumed to satisfy ϕ, then we may substitute for it any expression that does satisfy that refinement, and the resulting instance will continue to satisfy the same refinement it had before the substitution.

Rule (25.3b) is analogous to the subsumption principle given in Chapter 24, although here it has a subtly different meaning. Specifically, if an expression e satisfies a refinement

ϕ', and ϕ' is stronger than some refinement ϕ (as determined by rules (25.2)), then e must also satisfy the refinement ϕ. This inference is simply a matter of logic: the judgment $\phi' \leq \phi$ states that ϕ' logically entails ϕ.

Rule (25.3c) expresses the logical meaning of conjunction. If an expression e satisfies both ϕ_1 and ϕ_2, then it also satisfies $\phi_1 \wedge \phi_2$. Rule (25.3b) ensures that the converse holds as well, noting that by rules (25.2d) and (25.2e) a conjunction is stronger than either of its conjuncts. Similarly, the same rule ensures that if e satisfies ϕ, then it also satisfies $\top$, but we *do not* postulate that every well-typed expression satisfies $\top$, for that would defeat the goal of ensuring that well-refined expressions do not incur a run-time fault.

Rule (25.3d) states that refinements are closed under general recursion (formation of fixed points). To show that $\mathtt{fix}\, x : \tau\, \mathtt{is}\, e$ satisfies a refinement ϕ, it suffices to show that e satisfies ϕ, under the assumption that x, which stands for the recursive expression itself, satisfies ϕ. It is thus obvious that non-terminating expressions, such as $\mathtt{fix}\, x : \tau\, \mathtt{is}\, x$, satisfy any refinement at all. In particular, such a divergent expression does not incur a run-time error, the guarantee we are after with the present system of refinements.

The second group concerns the type dyn of classified values.

$$\frac{\Phi \vdash e \in_{\mathtt{nat}} \phi}{\Phi \vdash \mathtt{num}\,!\, e \in_{\mathtt{dyn}} \mathtt{num}\,!\, \phi} \tag{25.4a}$$

$$\frac{\Phi \vdash e \in_{\mathtt{dyn} \rightharpoonup \mathtt{dyn}} \phi}{\Phi \vdash \mathtt{fun}\,!\, e \in_{\mathtt{dyn}} \mathtt{fun}\,!\, \phi} \tag{25.4b}$$

$$\frac{\Phi \vdash e \in_{\mathtt{dyn}} \mathtt{num}\,!\, \phi}{\Phi \vdash e\, @\, \mathtt{num} \in_{\mathtt{nat}} \phi} \tag{25.4c}$$

$$\frac{\Phi \vdash e \in_{\mathtt{dyn} \rightharpoonup \mathtt{dyn}} \mathtt{fun}\,!\, \phi}{\Phi \vdash e\, @\, \mathtt{fun} \in_{\mathtt{dyn} \rightharpoonup \mathtt{dyn}} \phi} \tag{25.4d}$$

$$\frac{\Phi \vdash e \in_{\mathtt{dyn}} \top}{\Phi \vdash \mathtt{num}\,?\, e \in_{\mathtt{bool}} \top} \tag{25.4e}$$

$$\frac{\Phi \vdash e \in_{\mathtt{dyn}} \top}{\Phi \vdash \mathtt{fun}\,?\, e \in_{\mathtt{bool}} \top} \tag{25.4f}$$

Rules (25.4a) and (25.4b) state that a newly created value of class c satisfies the refinement of the type dyn stating this fact, provided that the underlying value satisfies the given refinement ϕ of the type associated to that class (nat for num and dyn $\rightharpoonup$ dyn for fun).

Rules (25.4c) and (25.4d) state that a value of type dyn may only be safely cast to a class c if the value is known statically to be of this class. This condition is stated in the premises of these rules, which require the class of the cast value to be known and suitable for the cast. The result of a well-refined cast satisfies the refinement given to its underlying value. It is important to realize that in the quest to avoid run-time faults, it is not possible to cast a value whose only known refinement is $\top$, which imposes no restrictions on it. This limitation is burdensome, because in many situations it is not possible to determine statically what is the class of a value. We will return to this critical point shortly.

Rules (25.4e) and (25.4f) compute a boolean based on the class of its argument. We shall have more to say about this in Section 25.2.

The third group of rules govern nullary and binary product types.

$$\frac{}{\Phi \vdash \langle\rangle \in_{\mathtt{unit}} \top} \tag{25.5a}$$

$$\frac{\Phi \vdash e_1 \in_{\tau_1} \phi_1 \quad \Phi \vdash e_2 \in_{\tau_2} \phi_2}{\Phi \vdash \langle e_1, e_2 \rangle \in_{\tau_1 \times \tau_2} \phi_1 \times \phi_2} \tag{25.5b}$$

$$\frac{\Phi \vdash e \in_{\tau_1 \times \tau_2} \phi_1 \times \phi_2}{\Phi \vdash e \cdot \mathtt{l} \in_{\tau_1} \phi_1} \tag{25.5c}$$

$$\frac{\Phi \vdash e \in_{\tau_1 \times \tau_2} \phi_1 \times \phi_2}{\Phi \vdash e \cdot \mathtt{r} \in_{\tau_1} \phi_1} \tag{25.5d}$$

Rule (25.5a) states the obvious: the null-tuple is well-refined by the trivial refinement. Because unit contains only one element, little else can be said about it. Rule (25.5b) states that a pair satisfies a product of refinements if each component satisfies the corresponding refinement. Rules (25.5c) and (25.5d) state the converse.

The fourth group of rules govern nullary and binary sum types.

$$\frac{\Phi \vdash e \in_{\mathtt{void}} \phi'}{\Phi \vdash e \in_{\mathtt{void}} \phi} \tag{25.6a}$$

$$\frac{\Phi \vdash e_1 \in_{\tau_1} \phi_1}{\Phi \vdash \mathtt{l} \cdot e_1 \in_{\tau_1 + \tau_2} \phi_1 + \phi_2} \tag{25.6b}$$

$$\frac{\Phi \vdash e_2 \in_{\tau_2} \phi_2}{\Phi \vdash \mathtt{r} \cdot e_2 \in_{\tau_1 + \tau_2} \phi_1 + \phi_2} \tag{25.6c}$$

$$\frac{\Phi \vdash e \in_{\tau_1 + \tau_2} \phi_1 + \phi_2 \quad \Phi, x_1 \in_{\tau_1} \phi_1 \vdash e_1 \in_{\tau} \phi \quad \Phi, x_2 \in_{\tau_2} \phi_2 \vdash e_2 \in_{\tau} \phi}{\Phi \vdash \mathtt{case}\, e\, \{\mathtt{l} \cdot x_1 \hookrightarrow e_1 \mid \mathtt{r} \cdot x_2 \hookrightarrow e_2\} \in_{\tau} \phi} \tag{25.6d}$$

Rule (25.6a) states that if an expression of type void satisfies *some* refinement (and hence is error-free), then it satisfies *every* refinement (of type void), because there are no values of this type, and hence, being error-free, must diverge.

Rules (25.6b) and (25.6c) are similarly motivated. If e_1 satisfies ϕ_1, then $\mathtt{l} \cdot e_1$ satisfies $\phi_1 + \phi_2$ *for any* refinement ϕ_2, precisely because the latter refinement is irrelevant to the injection. Similarly, the right injection is independent of the refinement of the left summand.

Rule (25.6d) is in some respects the most interesting rule of all, one that we shall have occasion to revise shortly. The salient feature of this rule is that it propagates refinement information about the injected value into the corresponding branch by stating an assumption about the bound variable of each branch. But it *does not* propagate any information into the branches about what is known about e in each branch, namely that in the first branch e must be of the form $\mathtt{l} \cdot e_1$, and in the second branch, e must be of the form $\mathtt{r} \cdot e_2$.

The failure to propagate this information may seem harmless, but it is, in fact, quite restrictive. To see why, consider the special case of the type bool, which is defined in Section 11.3.2 to be unit + unit. The conditional expression if e then e_1 else e_2 is defined to be a case analysis in which there is no associated data to pass into the branches of the conditional. So, within the then branch e_1 it is not known statically that e is in fact true, nor is it known within the else branch e_2 that e is in fact false.

The fifth group of rules governs the function type.

$$\frac{\Phi, x \in_{\tau_1} \phi_1 \vdash e_2 \in_{\tau_2} \phi_2}{\Phi \vdash \lambda(x : \tau_1) e_2 \in_{\tau_1 \to \tau_2} \phi_1 \rightharpoonup \phi_2} \tag{25.7a}$$

$$\frac{\Phi \vdash e_1 \in_{\tau_2 \to \tau} \phi_2 \rightharpoonup \phi \quad e_2 \in_{\tau_2} \phi_2}{\Phi \vdash e_1(e_2) \in_{\tau} \phi} \tag{25.7b}$$

Rule (25.7a) states that a λ-abstraction satisfies a function refinement if its body satisfies the range refinement, under the assumption that its argument satisfies the domain refinement. This is only to be expected.

Rule (25.7b) states the converse. If an expression of function type satisfies a function refinement, and it is applied to an argument satisfying the domain refinement, then the application must satisfy the range refinement.

The last group of rules govern the type nat:

$$\frac{}{\Phi \vdash z \in_{\mathsf{nat}} \top} \tag{25.8a}$$

$$\frac{\Phi \vdash e \in_{\mathsf{nat}} \top}{\Phi \vdash s(e) \in_{\mathsf{nat}} \top} \tag{25.8b}$$

$$\frac{\Phi \vdash e \in_{\mathsf{nat}} \top \quad \Phi \vdash e_0 \in_{\tau} \phi \quad \Phi, x \in_{\mathsf{nat}} \top \vdash e_1 \in_{\tau} \phi}{\Phi \vdash \mathsf{ifz}\, e\, \{\mathsf{z} \hookrightarrow e_0 \mid \mathsf{s}(x) \hookrightarrow e_1\} \in_{\tau} \phi} \tag{25.8c}$$

These rules are completely unambitious: they merely restate the typing rules as refinement rules that impose no requirements and make no guarantees of any properties of the natural numbers. One could envision adding refinements of the natural numbers, for instance stating that a natural number is known to be zero or non-zero, for example.

To get a feel for the foregoing rules, it is useful to consider some simple examples. First, we may combine rules (25.3b) and (25.4a) to derive the judgment

$$\mathsf{num} \,!\, \overline{n} \in_{\mathsf{dyn}} \top$$

for any natural number n. That is, we may "forget" the class of a value by applying subsumption and appealing to rule (25.2c). Second, such reasoning is essential in stating refinement satisfaction for a boolean conditional (or, more generally, any case analysis). For example, the following judgment is directly derivable without subsumption:

$$\Phi, x \in_{\mathsf{bool}} \top \vdash \mathsf{if}\, x \,\mathsf{then}\, (\mathsf{num} \,!\, \mathsf{z})\, \mathsf{else}\, (\mathsf{num} \,!\, \mathsf{s}(\mathsf{z})) \in_{\mathsf{dyn}} \mathsf{num} \,!\, \top.$$

But the following judgment is only derivable because we may weaken knowledge of the class of a value in each branch to a common refinement, in this case the weakest refinement of all:

$$\Phi, x \in_{\mathsf{bool}} \top \vdash \mathsf{if}\, x \,\mathsf{then}\, (\mathsf{num} \,!\, \mathsf{z})\, \mathsf{else}\, (\mathsf{fun} \,!\, (\lambda(y : \mathsf{dyn})\, y)) \in_{\mathsf{dyn}} \top.$$

In general conditionals attenuate the information we have about a value, except in those cases where the same information is known about both branches. Conditionals are the main source of lossiness in checking refinement satisfaction.

Conjunction refinements are used to express multiple properties of a single expression. For example, the identity function on the type dyn satisfies the conjunctive refinement

$$(\text{num}\ !\ \top \rightharpoonup \text{num}\ !\ \top) \wedge (\text{fun}\ !\ \top \rightharpoonup \text{fun}\ !\ \top).$$

The occurrences of $\top$ in the first conjunct refine the type nat, whereas the occurrences in the second conjunct refine the type dyn $\rightharpoonup$ dyn. It is a good exercise to check that $\lambda\,(x : \text{dyn})\,x$ satisfies the above refinement of the type dyn $\rightharpoonup$ dyn.

25.2 Boolean Blindness

Let us consider a very simple example that exposes a serious disease suffered by many programming languages, a condition called *boolean blindness*. Suppose that x is a variable of type dyn with refinement $\top$, and consider the expression

$$\text{if}\,(\text{num}\ ?\ x)\,\text{then}\,x\,@\,\text{num}\,\text{else}\,z.$$

Although it is clear that this expression has type nat, it is nevertheless *ill-refined* (satisfies no refinement), even though it does not incur a run-time error. Specifically, within the then branch, we as programmers know that x is a value of class num, but this fact is not propagated into the then branch by rules (25.6) (of which the boolean conditional is a special case). Consequently, rule (25.4c) does not apply (formally we do not know enough about x to cast it safely), so the expression is ill-refined. The branches of the conditional are "blind" both to the outcome and to the meaning of the boolean value computed by the test whether x is of class num.

Boolean blindness is endemic among programming languages. The difficulty is that a boolean carries exactly one bit of information, which is not sufficient to capture the *meaning* of that bit. A *boolean*, which is (literally) a bit of data, ought to be distinguished from a *proposition*, which expresses a fact. Taken by itself, a boolean conveys no information other than its value, whereas a proposition expresses the reasoning that goes into ensuring that a piece of code is correct. In terms of the above example knowing that num $?\ x$ evaluates dynamically to the boolean true is not connected statically with the fact that the class of x is num or not. That information lives elsewhere, in the specification of the class test primitive. The question is how to connect the boolean value returned by the class test with relevant facts about whether the class of x is num or not.

Because the purpose of a type refinement system is precisely to capture such facts in a form that can be stated and verified, one may suspect that the difficulty with the foregoing example is that the system of refinements under consideration is too weak to capture the property that we need to ensure that run-time faults do not occur. The example shows that something more is needed if type refinement is to be useful, so we first consider what might be involved in enriching the definition of refinement satisfaction to ensure that the proper connections are made. The matter boils down to two issues:

1. Propagating that num $?x$ returned true into the then branch, and that it returned false into the else branch.
2. Connecting facts about the return value of a test to facts about the value being tested.

These are, in the present context, distinct aspects of the problem. Let us consider them in turn. The upshot of the discussion will be to uncover a design flaw in casting and to suggest an alternative formulation that does not suffer from boolean blindness.

To address the problem as stated, we first need to enrich the language of refinements to include true $\sqsubseteq$ bool and false $\sqsubseteq$ bool, stating that a boolean is either true or false, respectively. That way we can hope to express facts about boolean-valued expressions as refinement judgments. But what is the refinement rule for the boolean conditional? As a first guess one might consider something like the following:

$$\frac{\Phi, e \in_{\text{bool}} \text{true} \vdash e_1 \in_\tau \phi \quad \Phi, e \in_{\text{bool}} \text{false} \vdash e_2 \in_\tau \phi}{\Phi \vdash \text{if } e \text{ then } e_1 \text{ else } e_2 \in_\tau \phi} \tag{25.9}$$

Such a rule is a bit unusual in that it introduces a hypothesis about an expression, rather than a variable, but let us ignore that for the time being and press on.

Having re-formulated the refinement rule for the conditional, we immediately run into another problem: how to deduce that $x \in_{\text{dyn}}$ num $! \top$, which is required for casting, from the assumption that num $?x \in_{\text{bool}}$ true? One way to achieve this is by modifying the refinement rule for the conditional to account for the special case in which the boolean expression is *literally* num $?e$ for some e. If it is, then we propagate into the then branch the additional assumption $e \in_{\text{dyn}}$ num $! \top$, but if it is not, then no fact about the class of e is propagated into the else branch.[2] This change is enough to ensure that the example under consideration is well-refined. But what if the boolean on which we are conditioning is not literally num$?e$, but merely *implies* the test would return true? How then are we to make the connection between such expressions and relevant facts about the class of e? Clearly, there is no end to the special cases we could consider to restore vision to refinements, but there is no unique best solution.

All is not lost, however! The foregoing analysis suggests that the fault lies not in our refinements, but in our language design. The sole source of run-time errors is the "naked cast" that attempts to extract the underlying natural number from a value of type dyn—and signals a run-time error if it cannot do so because the class of the value is not num. The boolean-valued test for the class of a value seems to provide a way to avoid these errors. But, as we have just seen, the true cause of the problem is the attempt to separate the test from the cast. We may, instead, combine these into a single form, say

$$\text{ifofcl}[\text{num}](e;x_0.e_0;e_1),$$

that tests whether the class of e is num, and, if so, passes the underlying number to e_0 by substituting it for x_0, and otherwise evaluates e_1. No run-time error is possible, and hence no refinements are needed to ensure that it cannot occur.

But does this not mean that type refinements are pointless? Not at all. It simply means that in some cases verification methods, such as type refinements, are needed solely to remedy a language design flaw, and not provide a useful tool for programmers to help express and verify the correctness of their programs. We may still wish to express invariants such as the property that a particular function maps values of class c into values of class c', simply for the purpose of stating a programmer's intention. Or we may enrich the system of refinements to track properties such as whether a number is even or odd, and to state conditions such as that a given function maps evens to odds and odds to evens. There is no limit, in principle, to the variations and extensions to help ensure that programs behave as expected.

25.3 Refinement Safety

The judgment $\Phi_\Gamma \vdash a \in_\tau \phi$ presupposes that $\Gamma \vdash e : \tau$, so by adapting the proofs given earlier, we may type preservation and progress for well-typed terms.

Theorem 25.1 (Type Safety). *Suppose that $e : \tau$ for closed e.*

1. If $e \longmapsto e'$, then $e' : \tau$.
2. Either e err, or e val, or there exists e' such that $e \longmapsto e'$.

The proof of progress requires a canonical forms lemma, which for the type dyn is stated as follows:

Lemma 25.2 (Canonical Forms). *Suppose that $e : \mathrm{dyn}$ and e val. Then either $e = \mathrm{num} \, ! \, e'$ or $e = \mathrm{fun} \, ! \, e'$ for some e'.*

The expression e' would also be a value under an eager dynamics but need not be under a lazy dynamics. The proof of Lemma 25.2 proceeds as usual, by analyzing the typing rules for values.

The goal of the refinement system introduced in Section 25.1 is to ensure that errors cannot arise in a well-refined program. To show this, we first show that the dynamics preserves refinements.

Lemma 25.3. *Suppose that e val and $e \in_{\mathrm{dyn}} \phi$. If $\phi \leq \mathrm{num} \, ! \, \phi'$, then $e = \mathrm{num} \, ! \, e'$, where $e' \in_{nat} \phi'$, and if $\phi \leq \mathrm{fun} \, ! \, \phi'$, then $e = \mathrm{fun} \, ! \, e'$, where $e' \in_{\mathrm{dyn} \to \mathrm{dyn}} \phi'$.*

Proof The proof requires Lemma 25.2 to characterize the possible values of dyn, and an analysis of the refinement satisfaction rules. The lemma accommodates rule (25.3b), which appeals to the transitivity of refinement entailment. □

Theorem 25.4 (Refinement Preservation). *If $e \in_\tau \phi$ and $e \longmapsto e'$, then $e' \in_\tau \phi$.*

Proof We know by the preceding theorem that $e' : \tau$. To show that $e' \in_\tau \phi$ we proceed by induction on the definition of refinement satisfaction given in Section 25.1. The type-independent group, rules (25.3), are all easily handled, apart from the rule for fixed points, which requires an appeal to a substitution lemma, just as in Theorem 19.2. The remaining groups are all handled easily, bearing in mind that an incorrect expression cannot make a transition.   □

Theorem 25.5 (Refinement Error-Freedom). *If $e \in_\tau \phi$, then $\neg(e\ err)$.*

Proof By induction on the definition of refinement satisfaction. The only interesting cases are rules (25.4c) and (25.4d), which are handled by appeal to Lemma 25.3 in the case that the cast expression is a value.   □

Corollary 25.6 (Refinement Safety). *If $e \in_\tau \phi$, then either $e\ val$ or there exists e' such that $e' \in_\tau \phi$ and $e \longmapsto e'$. In particular, $\neg(e\ err)$.*

Proof By Theorems 25.1, 25.4, and 25.5.   □

25.4 Notes

The distinction between types and refinements is fundamental; yet, the two are often conflated. Types determine the structure of a programming language, including its statics and dynamics; refinements specify the behavior of well-typed programs. In full generality, the satisfaction judgment $e \in_\tau \phi$ need not be decidable, whereas it is sensible to insist that the typing judgment $e : \tau$ be decidable. The refinement system presented in this chapter is decidable, but one may consider many notions of refinement that are not. For example, one may postulate that if $e \in_\tau \phi$ and that e' is indistinguishable from e by any program in the language,[3] then $e' \in_\tau \phi$. In contrast such a move is not sensible in a type system, because the dynamics is derived from the statics by the inversion principle. Therefore, refinement is necessarily posterior to typing.

The syntactic formulation of type refinements considered in this chapter was originally given by Freeman and Pfenning (1991) and extended by Davies and Pfenning (2000), Davies (2005), Xi and Pfenning (1998), Dunfield and Pfenning (2003), and Mandelbaum et al. (2003). A more general semantic formulation of type refinement was given explicitly by Denney (1998) in the style of the realizability interpretation of type theory on which NuPRL (Constable, 1986) is based. (See the survey by van Oosten (2002) for the history of the realizability interpretations of constructive logic.)

Exercises

25.1. Show that if $\phi_1 \leq \phi_1'$ and $\phi_2 \leq \phi_2'$, then $\phi_1 \wedge \phi_2 \leq \phi_1' \wedge \phi_2'$.

25.2. Show that $\phi \leq \phi'$ iff for every ϕ'', if $\phi'' \leq \phi$, then $\phi'' \leq \phi'$. (This property of entailment is an instance of the more general *Yoneda Lemma* in category theory.)

25.3. Extend the system of refinements to recursive types by introducing a refinement $\text{fold}(\phi)$ that classifies values of recursive type $\text{rec } t \text{ is } \tau$ in terms of a refinement of the unfolding of that recursive type.

25.4. Consider the following two forms of refinement for sum types, *summand refinements*:

$$\frac{\phi_1 \sqsubseteq \tau_1}{1 \cdot \phi_1 \sqsubseteq \tau_1 + \tau_2} \tag{25.10a}$$

$$\frac{\phi_2 \sqsubseteq \tau_2}{\text{r} \cdot \phi_2 \sqsubseteq \tau_1 + \tau_2} \tag{25.10b}$$

Informally, $1 \cdot \phi_1$ classifies expressions of type $\tau_1 + \tau_2$ that lie within the left summand and whose underlying value satisfies ϕ_1, and similarly for $\text{r} \cdot \phi_2$.

(a) State entailment rules governing summand refinements.

(b) State refinement rules assigning summand refinements to the introduction forms of a sum type.

(c) Give rules for the case analysis construct using summand refinements to allow unreachable branches to be disregarded during refinement checking.

(d) Modify rule (25.6d) so that the information "learned" by examining the value of e at execution time is propagated into the appropriate branch of the case analysis.

Check the importance of this extension to the prospects for a cure for Boolean blindness.

25.5. Using the preceding exercise, derive the refinements $\text{num} ! \phi$ and $\text{fun} ! \phi$ from the other refinement rules, including the refinement $\text{fold}(\phi)$ considered in Exercise **25.3**.

25.6. Show that the addition function (23.8), a value of type dyn, satisfies the refinement

$$\text{fun} ! (\text{num} ! \top \rightharpoonup \text{fun} ! (\text{num} ! \top \rightharpoonup \text{num} ! \top)),$$

stating that

(a) It is itself a value of class fun.

(b) The so-classified function maps a value of class num to a result, if any, of class fun.

(c) The so-classified function maps a value of class num to a result, if any, of class num.

This description exposes the hidden complexity in the superficial simplicity of a uni-typed language.

25.7. Revisit the optimization process of the addition function carried out in Section 23.3 in view of your answer to Exercise **25.6**. Show that the validity of the optimizations is guaranteed by the satisfaction of the stated type refinement for addition.

Notes

1 Of course, in a richer language, there would be more classes than just these two, each with an associated type of the underlying data that it classifies.
2 For the special case of there being exactly two classes, we could propagate that the class of e is `fun` into the `else` branch, but this approach does not generalize.
3 See Chapter 47 for a precise definition and development of this concept.

PART XI

Dynamic Dispatch

26   Classes and Methods

It often arises that the values of a type are partitioned into a variety of *classes*, each classifying data with distinct internal structure. A simple example is provided by the type of points in the plane, which are classified according to whether they are represented in cartesian or polar form. Both are represented by a pair of real numbers, but in the cartesian case, these are the x and y coordinates of the point, whereas in the polar case, these are its distance r from the origin and its angle θ with the polar axis. A classified value is an *object*, or *instance*, of its class. The class determines the type of the classified data, the *instance type* of the class; the classified data itself is the *instance data* of the object.

Methods are functions that act on classified values. The behavior of a method is determined by the class of its argument. The method *dispatches* on the class of the argument.[1] Because the selection is made at run-time, it is called *dynamic dispatch*. For example, the squared distance of a point from the origin is calculated differently according to whether the point is represented in cartesian or polar form. In the former case, the required distance is $x^2 + y^2$, whereas in the latter it is simply r^2. Similarly, the quadrant of a cartesian point can be determined by examining the sign of its x and y coordinates, and the quadrant of a polar point can be calculated by taking the integral part of the angle θ divided by $\pi/2$.

Dynamic dispatch is often described in terms of a particular implementation strategy, which we will call the *class-based* organization. In this organization, each object is represented by a vector of methods specialized to the class of that object. We may equivalently use a *method-based* organization in which each method branches on the class of an object to determine its behavior. Regardless of the organization used, the fundamental idea is that (a) objects are classified and (b) methods dispatch on the class of an object. The class-based and method-based organizations are interchangeable and, in fact, related by a natural duality between sum and product types. We explain this symmetry by focusing first on the behavior of each method on each object, which is given by a *dispatch matrix*. From this, we derive both a class-based and a method-based organization in such a way that their equivalence is obvious.

26.1 The Dispatch Matrix

Because each method acts by dispatch on the class of its argument, we may envision the entire system of classes and methods as a *dispatch matrix* e_{dm} whose rows are classes, whose columns are methods, and whose (c, d)-entry defines the behavior of method d

acting on an argument of class c, expressed as a function of the instance data of the object. Thus, the dispatch matrix has a type of the form

$$\prod_{c \in C} \prod_{d \in D} (\tau^c \rightharpoonup \rho_d),$$

where C is the set of class names, D is the set of method names, τ^c is the instance type associated with class c, and ρ_d is the result type of method d. The instance type is the same for all methods acting on a given class, and the result type is the same for all classes acted on by a given method.

As an illustrative example, let us consider the type of points in the plane classified into two classes, cart and pol, that corresponds to the cartesian and polar representations. The instance data for a cartesian point has the type

$$\tau^{\text{cart}} = \langle \text{x} \hookrightarrow \text{float}, \text{y} \hookrightarrow \text{float} \rangle,$$

and the instance data for a polar point has the type

$$\tau^{\text{pol}} = \langle \text{r} \hookrightarrow \text{float}, \text{th} \hookrightarrow \text{float} \rangle.$$

Consider two methods acting on points, dist and quad, which compute, respectively, the squared distance of a point from the origin and the quadrant of a point. The squared distance method is given by the tuple $e_{\text{dist}} = \langle \text{cart} \hookrightarrow e_{\text{dist}}^{\text{cart}}, \text{pol} \hookrightarrow e_{\text{dist}}^{\text{pol}} \rangle$ of type

$$\langle \text{cart} \hookrightarrow \tau^{\text{cart}} \rightharpoonup \rho_{\text{dist}}, \text{pol} \hookrightarrow \tau^{\text{pol}} \rightharpoonup \rho_{\text{dist}} \rangle,$$

where $\rho_{\text{dist}} = \text{float}$ is the result type,

$$e_{\text{dist}}^{\text{cart}} = \lambda \, (u : \tau^{\text{cart}}) \, (u \cdot \text{x})^2 + (u \cdot \text{y})^2$$

is the squared distance computation for a cartesian point, and

$$e_{\text{dist}}^{\text{pol}} = \lambda \, (v : \tau^{\text{pol}}) \, (v \cdot \text{r})^2$$

is the squared distance computation for a polar point. Similarly, the quadrant method is given by the tuple $e_{\text{quad}} = \langle \text{cart} \hookrightarrow e_{\text{quad}}^{\text{cart}}, \text{pol} \hookrightarrow e_{\text{quad}}^{\text{pol}} \rangle$ of type

$$\langle \text{cart} \hookrightarrow \tau^{\text{cart}} \rightharpoonup \rho_{\text{quad}}, \text{pol} \hookrightarrow \tau^{\text{pol}} \rightharpoonup \rho_{\text{quad}} \rangle,$$

where $\rho_{\text{quad}} = [\text{I}, \text{II}, \text{III}, \text{IV}]$ is the type of quadrants, and $e_{\text{quad}}^{\text{cart}}$ and $e_{\text{quad}}^{\text{pol}}$ are expressions that compute the quadrant of a point in rectangular and polar forms, respectively.

Now let $C = \{\, \text{cart}, \text{pol} \,\}$ and let $D = \{\, \text{dist}, \text{quad} \,\}$, and define the dispatch matrix e_{dm} to be the value of type

$$\prod_{c \in C} \prod_{d \in D} (\tau^c \rightharpoonup \rho_d)$$

such that, for each class c and method d,

$$e_{\text{dm}} \cdot c \cdot d \longmapsto^* e_d^c.$$

That is, the entry in the dispatch matrix e_{dm} for class c and method d defines the behavior of that method acting on an object of that class.

Dynamic dispatch is an abstraction given by the following components:

- An abstract type t_{obj} of *objects*, which are classified by the classes on which the methods act.
- An operation $new[c](e)$ of type t_{obj} that creates an object of the class c with instance data given by the expression e of type τ^c.
- An operation $e \Leftarrow d$ of type ρ_d that invokes method d on the object given by the expression e of type t_{obj}.

These operations must satisfy the defining characteristic of dynamic dispatch,

$$(new[c](e)) \Leftarrow d \longmapsto^* e_d^c(e),$$

which states that invoking method d on an object of class c with instance data e amounts to applying e_d^c, the code in the dispatch matrix for class c and method d to the instance data e.

In other words, dynamic dispatch is an *abstract type* with interface given by the existential type

$$\exists (t_{obj}.\langle new \hookrightarrow \prod_{c \in C} \tau^c \rightharpoonup t_{obj}, snd \hookrightarrow \prod_{d \in D} t_{obj} \rightharpoonup \rho_d \rangle). \tag{26.1}$$

There are two main ways to implement this abstract type. The *class-based* organization, defines objects as tuples of methods and creates objects by specializing the methods to the given instance data. The *method-based* organization creates objects by tagging the instance data with the class and defines methods by examining the class of the object. These two organizations are isomorphic to one another and hence can be interchanged at will. Nevertheless, many languages favor one representation over the other, asymmetrizing an inherently symmetric situation.

The abstract type (26.1) calls attention to shortcoming of dynamic dispatch, namely that a message can be sent to exactly one object at a time. This viewpoint seems natural in certain cases, such as discrete event simulation in the language Simula-67. But often it is essential to act on several classes of object at once. For example, the multiplication of a vector by a scalar combines the elements of a field and a commutative monoid; there is no natural way to associate scalar multiplication with either the field or the monoid, nor any way to anticipate that particular combination. Moreover, the multiplication is not performed by checking at run-time that one has a scalar and a vector in hand, for there is nothing inherent in a scalar or a vector that marks them as such. The right tool for handling such situations is a module system (Chapters 44 and 45), not dynamic dispatch. The two mechanisms serve different purposes and complement each other.

The same example serves to refute a widely held fallacy, namely that the values of an abstract type cannot be heterogeneous. It is sometimes said that an abstract type of complex numbers must commit to a single representation, say, rectangular, and cannot accommodate multiple representations. This is a fallacy. Although it is true that an abstract type defines a single type, it is wrong to say that only one representation of objects is possible. The abstract type can be implemented as a sum, and the operations may correspondingly dispatch on the summand to compute the result. Dynamic dispatch is a mode of use of data abstraction, and therefore cannot be opposed to it.

26.2 Class-Based Organization

The class-based organization starts with the observation that the dispatch matrix can be reorganized to "factor out" the instance data for each method acting on that class to obtain the *class vector* e_{cv} of type

$$\tau_{cv} \triangleq \prod_{c \in C} (\tau^c \rightharpoonup (\prod_{d \in D} \rho_d)).$$

Each entry of the class vector consists of a *constructor* that determines the result of each of the methods when acting on given instance data.

An object has the type $\rho = \prod_{d \in D} \rho_d$ consisting of the product of the result types of the methods. For example, in the case of points in the plane, the type ρ is the product type

$$\langle \text{dist} \hookrightarrow \rho_{\text{dist}}, \text{quad} \hookrightarrow \rho_{\text{quad}} \rangle.$$

Each component specifies the result of the methods acting on that object.

The message send operation $e \Leftarrow d$ is just the projection $e \cdot d$. So, in the case of points in the plane, $e \Leftarrow \text{dist}$ is the projection $e \cdot \text{dist}$, and similarly $e \Leftarrow \text{quad}$ is the projection $e \cdot \text{quad}$.

The class-based organization combines the implementation of each class into a *class vector* e_{cv} a tuple of type τ_{cv}, consisting of the *constructor* of type $\tau^c \rightharpoonup \rho$ for each class $c \in C$. The class vector is defined by $e_{cv} = \langle c \hookrightarrow e^c \rangle_{c \in C}$, where for each $c \in C$ the expression e^c is

$$\lambda (u : \tau^c) \langle d \hookrightarrow e_{\text{dm}} \cdot c \cdot d(u) \rangle_{d \in D}.$$

For example, the constructor for the class cart is the function e^{cart} given by the expression

$$\lambda (u : \tau^{\text{cart}}) \langle \text{dist} \hookrightarrow e_{\text{dm}} \cdot \text{cart} \cdot \text{dist}(u), \text{quad} \hookrightarrow e_{\text{dm}} \cdot \text{cart} \cdot \text{quad}(u) \rangle.$$

Similarly, the constructor for the class pol is the function e^{pol} given by the expression

$$\lambda (u : \tau^{\text{pol}}) \langle \text{dist} \hookrightarrow e_{\text{dm}} \cdot \text{pol} \cdot \text{dist}(u), \text{quad} \hookrightarrow e_{\text{dm}} \cdot \text{pol} \cdot \text{quad}(u) \rangle.$$

The class vector e_{cv} in this case is the tuple $\langle \text{cart} \hookrightarrow e^{\text{cart}}, \text{pol} \hookrightarrow e^{\text{pol}} \rangle$ of type $\langle \text{cart} \hookrightarrow \tau^{\text{cart}} \rightharpoonup \rho, \text{pol} \hookrightarrow \tau^{\text{pol}} \rightharpoonup \rho \rangle$.

An object of a class is obtained by applying the constructor for that class to the instance data:

$$\text{new}[c](e) \triangleq e_{cv} \cdot c(e).$$

For example, a cartesian point is obtained by writing $\text{new}[\text{cart}](\langle \text{x} \hookrightarrow x_0, \text{y} \hookrightarrow y_0 \rangle)$, which is defined by the expression

$$e_{cv} \cdot \text{cart}(\langle \text{x} \hookrightarrow x_0, \text{y} \hookrightarrow y_0 \rangle).$$

Similarly, a polar point is obtained by writing $\mathtt{new[pol]}(\mathtt{r} \hookrightarrow r_0, \mathtt{th} \hookrightarrow \theta_0)$, which is defined by the expression

$$e_{\mathsf{cv}} \cdot \mathtt{pol}(\langle \mathtt{r} \hookrightarrow r_0, \mathtt{th} \hookrightarrow \theta_0 \rangle).$$

It is easy to check for this organization of points that, for each class c and method d, we may derive

$$(\mathtt{new[c]}(e)) \Leftarrow d \longmapsto^* (e_{\mathsf{cv}} \cdot c(e)) \cdot d$$
$$\longmapsto^* e_{\mathsf{dm}} \cdot c \cdot d(e).$$

That is, the message send evokes the behavior of the given method on the instance data of the given object.

26.3 Method-Based Organization

The method-based organization starts with the *transpose* of the dispatch matrix, which has the type

$$\prod_{d \in D} \prod_{c \in C} (\tau^c \rightharpoonup \rho_d).$$

By observing that each row of the transposed dispatch matrix determines a method, we obtain the *method vector* e_{mv} of type

$$\tau_{\mathsf{mv}} \triangleq \prod_{d \in D} \left(\sum_{c \in C} \tau^c \right) \rightharpoonup \rho_d.$$

Each entry of the method vector consists of a *dispatcher* that determines the result as a function of the instance data associated with a given object.

An object is a value of type $\tau = \sum_{c \in C} \tau^c$, the sum over the classes of the instance types. For example, the type of points in the plane is the sum type

$$[\mathtt{cart} \hookrightarrow \tau^{\mathtt{cart}}, \mathtt{pol} \hookrightarrow \tau^{\mathtt{pol}}].$$

Each point is labeled with its class, specifying its representation as having either cartesian or polar form.

An object of a class c is just the instance data labeled with its class to form an element of the object type:

$$\mathtt{new[c]}(e) \triangleq c \cdot e.$$

For example, a cartesian point with coordinates x_0 and y_0 is given by the expression

$$\mathtt{new[cart]}(\langle \mathtt{x} \hookrightarrow x_0, \mathtt{y} \hookrightarrow y_0 \rangle) \triangleq \mathtt{cart} \cdot \langle \mathtt{x} \hookrightarrow x_0, \mathtt{y} \hookrightarrow y_0 \rangle.$$

Similarly, a polar point with distance r_0 and angle θ_0 is given by the expression

$$\mathtt{new[pol]}(\langle \mathtt{r} \hookrightarrow r_0, \mathtt{th} \hookrightarrow \theta_0 \rangle) \triangleq \mathtt{pol} \cdot \langle \mathtt{r} \hookrightarrow r_0, \mathtt{th} \hookrightarrow \theta_0 \rangle.$$

The method-based organization consolidates the implementation of each method into the *method vector* e_{mv} of type τ_{mv} defined by $\langle d \hookrightarrow e_d \rangle_{d \in D}$, where for each $d \in D$ the expression $e_d : \tau \rightharpoonup \rho_d$ is

$$\lambda\,(this : \tau)\,\mathsf{case}\,this\,\{c \cdot u \hookrightarrow e_{\mathsf{dm}} \cdot c \cdot d(u)\}_{c \in C}.$$

Each entry in the method vector is a *dispatch function* that defines the action of that method on each class of object.

In the case of points in the plane, the method vector has the product type

$$\langle \mathsf{dist} \hookrightarrow \tau \rightharpoonup \rho_{\mathsf{dist}}, \mathsf{quad} \hookrightarrow \tau \rightharpoonup \rho_{\mathsf{quad}} \rangle.$$

The dispatch function for the dist method has the form

$$\lambda\,(this : \tau)\,\mathsf{case}\,this\,\{\mathsf{cart} \cdot u \hookrightarrow e_{\mathsf{dm}} \cdot \mathsf{cart} \cdot \mathsf{dist}(u) \mid \mathsf{pol} \cdot v \hookrightarrow e_{\mathsf{dm}} \cdot \mathsf{pol} \cdot \mathsf{dist}(v)\},$$

and the dispatch function for the quad method has the similar form

$$\lambda\,(this : \tau)\,\mathsf{case}\,this\,\{\mathsf{cart} \cdot u \hookrightarrow e_{\mathsf{dm}} \cdot \mathsf{cart} \cdot \mathsf{quad}(u) \mid \mathsf{pol} \cdot v \hookrightarrow e_{\mathsf{dm}} \cdot \mathsf{pol} \cdot \mathsf{quad}(v)\}.$$

The *message send* operation $e \Leftarrow d$ applies the dispatch function for method d to the object e:

$$e \Leftarrow d \triangleq e_{\mathsf{mv}} \cdot d(e).$$

Thus, we have, for each class c and method d

$$(\mathtt{new}[c](e)) \Leftarrow d \longmapsto^* e_{\mathsf{mv}} \cdot d(c \cdot e)$$
$$\longmapsto^* e_{\mathsf{dm}} \cdot c \cdot d(e)$$

The result is, of course, the same as for the class-based organization.

26.4 Self-Reference

It is often useful to allow methods to create new objects or to send messages to objects. It is not possible to do so using the simple dispatch matrix described in Section 26.1, for the simple reason that there is no provision for self-reference within its entries. This deficiency may be remedied by changing the type of the entries of the dispatch matrix to account for sending messages and creating objects, as follows:

$$\prod_{c \in C} \prod_{d \in D} \forall (t_{\mathsf{obj}}.\tau_{\mathsf{cv}} \rightharpoonup \tau_{\mathsf{mv}} \rightharpoonup \tau^c \rightharpoonup \rho_d).$$

The type variable t_{obj} represents the abstract object type.[2] The types τ_{cv} and τ_{mv}, are, respectively, the type of the class and method vectors, defined in terms of the abstract type of objects t_{obj}. They are defined by the equations

$$\tau_{\mathsf{cv}} \triangleq \prod_{c \in C} (\tau^c \rightharpoonup t_{\mathsf{obj}})$$

and

$$\tau_{\mathsf{mv}} \triangleq \prod_{d \in D} (t_{\mathsf{obj}} \rightharpoonup \rho_d).$$

The component of the class vector corresponding to a class c is a constructor that builds a value of the abstract object type t_{obj} from the instance data for c. The component of the method vector corresponding to a method d is a dispatcher that yields a result of type ρ_d when applied to a value of the abstract object type t_{obj}.

In accordance with the revised type of the dispatch matrix, the behavior associated to class c and method d has the form

$$\Lambda(t_{\mathsf{obj}}) \lambda (cv : \tau_{\mathsf{cv}}) \lambda (mv : \tau_{\mathsf{mv}}) \lambda (u : \tau^c) e_d^c.$$

The arguments cv and mv are used to create new objects and to send messages to objects. Within the expression e_d^c, an object of class c' with instance data e' is created by writing $cv \cdot c'(e')$, which selects the appropriate constructor from the class vector cv and applies it to the given instance data. The class c' may well be the class c itself; this is one form of self-reference within e_d^c. Similarly, within e_d^c a method d' is invoked on e' by writing $mv \cdot d'(e')$. The method d' may well be the method d itself; this is another aspect of self-reference within e_d^c.

To account for self-reference in the method-based organization, the method vector e_{mv} will be defined to have the self-referential type $[\tau / t_{\mathsf{obj}}] \tau_{\mathsf{mv}}$ self in which the object type τ is, as before, the sum of the instance types of the classes, $\sum_{c \in C} \tau^c$. The method vector is defined by the following equation:

$$e_{\mathsf{mv}} \triangleq \mathtt{self}\ mv\ \mathtt{is}\ \langle d \hookrightarrow \lambda (this : \tau)\ \mathtt{case}\ this\ \{c \cdot u \hookrightarrow e_{\mathsf{dm}} \cdot c \cdot d[\tau](e'_{\mathsf{cv}})(e'_{\mathsf{mv}})(u)\}_{c \in C}\rangle_{d \in D},$$

where

$$e'_{\mathsf{cv}} \triangleq \langle c \hookrightarrow \lambda (u : \tau^c) c \cdot u \rangle_{c \in C} : [\tau / t_{\mathsf{obj}}] \tau_{\mathsf{cv}}$$

and

$$e'_{\mathsf{mv}} \triangleq \mathtt{unroll}(mv) : [\tau / t_{\mathsf{obj}}] \tau_{\mathsf{mv}}.$$

Object creation is defined by the equation

$$\mathtt{new}[c](e) \triangleq c \cdot e : \tau$$

and message send is defined by the equation

$$e \Leftarrow d \triangleq \mathtt{unroll}(e_{\mathsf{mv}}) \cdot d(e) : \rho_d.$$

To account for self-reference in the class-based organization, the class vector e_{cv} will be defined to have the type $[\rho / t_{\mathsf{obj}}] \tau_{\mathsf{cv}}$ self in which the object type ρ is, as before, the product of the result types of the methods $\prod_{d \in D} \rho_d$. The class vector is defined by the following equation:

$$e_{cv} \triangleq \texttt{self } cv \texttt{ is } \langle c \hookrightarrow \lambda\,(u:\tau^c)\,\langle d \hookrightarrow e_{dm} \cdot c \cdot d[\rho](e''_{cv})(e''_{mv})(u)\rangle_{d \in D}\rangle_{c \in C},$$

where

$$e''_{cv} \triangleq \texttt{unroll}(cv) : [\rho/t_{obj}]\tau_{cv}$$

and

$$e''_{mv} \triangleq \langle d \hookrightarrow \lambda\,(this:\rho)\,this \cdot d\rangle_{d \in D} : [\rho/t_{obj}]\tau_{mv}.$$

Object creation is defined by the equation

$$\texttt{new}[c](e) \triangleq \texttt{unroll}(e_{cv}) \cdot c(e) : \rho,$$

and message send is defined by the equation

$$e \Leftarrow d \triangleq e \cdot d : \rho_d.$$

The symmetries between the two organizations are striking. They are a reflection of the fundamental symmetries between sum and product types.

26.5 Notes

The term "object-oriented" means many things to many people, but certainly dynamic dispatch, the action of methods on instances of classes, is one of its central concepts. These characteristic features emerge from the more general concepts of sum, product, and function types, which are useful, alone and in combination, in a wider variety of circumstances. A bias towards either a class- or method-based organization seems misplaced in view of the inherent symmetries of the situation. The dynamic dispatch abstraction given by the type (26.1) admits either form of implementation, as demonstrated in Sections 26.2 and 26.3. The literature on object-oriented programming, of which dynamic dispatch is a significant aspect, is extensive. Abadi and Cardelli (1996) and Pierce (2002) give a thorough account of much of this work.

Exercises

26.1. Consider the possibility that some methods may only be defined on instances of some classes, so that a message send operation may result in a "not understood" error at run-time. Use the type τ opt defined in Section 11.3.4 to rework the dispatch matrix to account for "not understood" errors. Reformulate the class- and method-based implementations of dynamic dispatch using the revised dispatch matrix representation. Proceed in two stages. In the first stage, ignore the possibility of self-reference so that the behavior associated to a method on an instance of a particular class cannot incur a "not understood" error. In the second stage, use your solution to the first stage to further rework the dispatch matrix and the implementations of dynamic dispatch to account for the behavior of a method to include incurring a "not understood" error.

26.2. Type refinements can be used to ensure the absence of specified "not understood" errors that may otherwise arise in the context of Exercise **26.1**. To do so, begin by specifying, for each $c \in C$, a subset $D_c \subseteq D$ of methods that must be well-defined on instances of class c. This definition determines, for each $d \in D$, the set $C_d \triangleq \{ c \in C \mid d \in D_c \}$ of classes on which method d must be well-defined. Using summand refinements for the type τ opt, define the type refinement

$$\phi_{\mathsf{dm}} \triangleq \prod_{c \in C} (\prod_{d \in D_c} \mathsf{just}(\top_{\tau^c} \rightharpoonup \top_{\rho_d})) \times (\prod_{d \in D \setminus D_c} \top_{(\tau^c \rightharpoonup \rho_d) \, \mathsf{opt}}),$$

which refines the type of dispatch matrix to within a permutation of its columns.[3] It specifies that if $d \in D_c$, then the dispatch matrix entry for class c and method d must be present and imposes no restriction on any other entry. Assume that $e_{\mathsf{dm}} \in_{\tau_{\mathsf{dm}}} \phi_{\mathsf{dm}}$, as expected. Assume a method-based organization in which the object type t_{obj} is the sum over all classes of their instance types.

(a) Define the refinements $\mathtt{inst}[c]$ and $\mathtt{admits}[d]$ of t_{obj} stating that $e \in t_{\mathsf{obj}}$ is an instance of class $c \in C$ and that e admits method $d \in D$, respectively. Show that if $d \in D_c$, then $\mathtt{inst}[c] \leq \mathtt{admits}[d]$, which is to say that any instance of class c admits any method d for that class.

(b) Define $\phi_{\mathsf{cv}} \sqsubseteq \tau_{\mathsf{cv}}$ and $\phi_{\mathsf{mv}} \sqsubseteq \tau_{\mathsf{mv}}$ in terms of $\mathtt{inst}[c]$ and $\mathtt{admits}[d]$ so that $e_{\mathsf{cv}} \in_{\tau_{\mathsf{cv}}} \phi_{\mathsf{cv}}$ and $e_{\mathsf{mv}} \in_{\tau_{\mathsf{mv}}} \phi_{\mathsf{mv}}$. Remember to use the class and method vectors derived in Exercise **26.1**.

(c) Referring to the definitions of object creation and message send and of the class- and method vectors derived in Exercise **26.1**, conclude that if message $d \in D_c$ is sent to an instance of $c \in C$, then no "not understood" error can arise at run-time in a well-refined program.

26.3. Using self-reference, set up a dispatch matrix in which two methods may call one another mutually recursively when invoked on an instance of a class. Specifically, let num be a class of numbers with instance type $\tau^{\mathtt{num}} = \mathtt{nat}$, and let ev and od be two methods with result type $\rho_{\mathsf{ev}} = \rho_{\mathsf{od}} = \mathtt{bool}$. Define the dispatch entries for methods ev and od for the class num so that they determine, by laborious mutual recursion, whether the instance datum is an even or an odd natural number.

26.4. Generalize the account of self-reference to admit constructors whose arguments may involve objects and methods whose results may involve objects. Specifically, allow the abstract object type t_{obj} to occur in the instance type τ^c of a class c or in the result type ρ_d of a method d. Rework the development in Section 26.4 to account for this generalization. *Hint*: Use recursive types as described in Chapter 20.

Notes

1 More generally, we may dispatch on the class of multiple arguments simultaneously. We concentrate on single dispatch for the sake of simplicity.
2 The variable t_{obj} is chosen not to occur in any τ^c or ρ_d. This restriction can be relaxed; see Exercise **26.4**.
3 Working up to such a permutation is a notational convenience and can be avoided at the expense of some clarity in the presentation.

Inheritance

In this chapter, we build on Chapter 26 and consider the process of defining the dispatch matrix that determines the behavior of each method on each class. A common strategy is to build the dispatch matrix incrementally by adding new classes or methods to an existing dispatch matrix. To add a class requires that we define the behavior of each method on objects of that class, and to define a method requires that we define the behavior of that method on objects of the classes. The definition of these behaviors can be given by any means available in the language. However, it is often suggested that a useful means of defining a new class is to *inherit* the behavior of another class on some methods, and to *override* its behavior on others, resulting in an amalgam of the old and new behaviors. The new class is often called a *subclass* of the old class, which is then called the *superclass*. Similarly, a new method can be defined by inheriting the behavior of another method on some classes, and overriding the behavior on others. By analogy, we may call the new method a *sub-method* of a given *super-method*. For the sake of clarity, we restrict attention to the non-self-referential case in the following development.

27.1 Class and Method Extension

We begin by extending a given dispatch matrix, e_{dm}, of type

$$\prod_{c \in C} \prod_{d \in D} (\tau^c \to \rho_d)$$

with a new class $c^* \notin C$ and a new method $d^* \notin D$ to obtain a new dispatch matrix e_{dm}^* of type

$$\prod_{c \in C^*} \prod_{d \in D^*} (\tau^c \to \rho_d),$$

where $C^* = C \cup \{c^*\}$ and $D^* = D \cup \{d^*\}$.

To add a new class c^* to the dispatch matrix, we must specify the following information:[1]

1. The instance type τ^{c^*} of the new class c^*.
2. The behavior $e_d^{c^*}$ of each method $d \in D$ on an object of the new class c^*, a function of type $\tau^{c^*} \to \rho_d$.

These data determine a new dispatch matrix e^*_{dm} such that the following conditions are satisfied:

1. For each $c \in C$ and $d \in D$, the behavior $e^*_{dm} \cdot c \cdot d$ is the same as the behavior $e_{dm} \cdot c \cdot d$.
2. For each $d \in D$, the behavior $e^*_{dm} \cdot c^* \cdot d$ is given by $e^{c^*}_d$.

To define c^* as a subclass of some class $c \in C$ means to define the behavior $e^{c^*}_d$ to be e^c_d for some (perhaps many) $d \in D$. It is sensible to inherit a method d in this way only if the subtype relationship

$$\tau^c \to \rho_d <: \tau^{c^*} \to \rho_d$$

is valid, which will be the case if $\tau^{c^*} <: \tau^c$. This subtyping condition ensures that the inherited behavior can be invoked on the instance data of the new class.

Similarly, to add a new method d^* to the dispatch matrix, we must specify the following information:

1. The result type ρ_{d^*} of the new method d^*.
2. The behavior $e^c_{d^*}$ of the new method d^* on an object of each class $c \in C$, a function of type $\tau^c \to \rho_{d^*}$.

These data determine a new dispatch matrix e^*_{dm} such that the following conditions are satisfied:

1. For each $c \in C$ and $d \in D$, the behavior $e^*_{dm} \cdot c \cdot d$ is the same as $e_{dm} \cdot c \cdot d$.
2. The behavior $e^*_{dm} \cdot c \cdot d^*$ is given by $e^c_{d^*}$.

To define d^* as a sub-method of some $d \in D$ means to define the behavior $e^c_{d^*}$ to be e^c_d for some (perhaps many) classes $c \in C$. This definition is only sensible if the subtype relationship

$$\tau^c \to \rho_d <: \tau^c \to \rho_{d^*}$$

holds, which is the case if $\rho_d <: \rho_{d^*}$. This subtyping relationship ensures that the result of the old behavior suffices for the new behavior.

We will now consider how inheritance relates to the method- and class-based organizations of dynamic dispatch considered in Chapter 26.

27.2 Class-Based Inheritance

Recall that the class-based organization given in Chapter 26 consists of a class vector e_{cv} of type

$$\tau_{cv} \triangleq \prod_{c \in C} (\tau^c \to \rho),$$

where the object type ρ is the finite product type $\prod_{d \in D} \rho_d$. The class vector consists of a tuple of constructors that specialize the methods to a given object of each class.

Let us consider the effect of adding a new class c^* as described in Section 27.1. The new class vector e_{cv}^* has type

$$\tau_{cv}^* \triangleq \prod_{c \in C^*} (\tau^c \to \rho).$$

There is an isomorphism, written $(\ )^\dagger$, between τ_{cv}^* and the type

$$\tau_{cv} \times (\tau^{c^*} \to \rho),$$

which can be used to define the new class vector e_{cv}^* as follows:

$$\langle e_{cv}, \lambda\, (u : \tau^{c^*}) \langle d \hookrightarrow e_d^{c^*}(u) \rangle_{d \in D} \rangle^\dagger.$$

This definition makes clear that the old class vector e_{cv} is reused intact in the new class vector, which extends the old class vector with a new constructor.

Although the object type ρ is the same both before and after the extension with the new class, the behavior of an object of class c^* may differ arbitrarily from that of any other object, even that of the superclass from which it inherits its behavior. So, knowing that c^* inherits from c tells us nothing about the behavior of its objects, but only about the means by which the class is defined. Inheritance carries no semantic significance but is only a record of the history of how a class is defined.

Now let us consider the effect of adding a new method d^* as described in Section 27.1. The new class vector e_{cv}^* has type

$$\tau_{cv}^* \triangleq \prod_{c \subset C} (\tau^c \to \rho^*),$$

where ρ^* is the product type $\prod_{d \in D^*} \rho_d$. There is an isomorphism, written $(\ )^\ddagger$, between ρ^* and the type $\rho \times \rho_{d^*}$, where ρ is the old object type. Using this the new class vector e_{cv}^* is defined by

$$\langle c \hookrightarrow \lambda\, (u : \tau^c) \langle \langle d \hookrightarrow ((e_{cv} \cdot c)(u)) \cdot d \rangle_{d \in D}, e_{d^*}^c(u) \rangle^\ddagger \rangle_{c \in C}.$$

Observe that each constructor must be re-defined to account for the new method, but the definition makes use of the old class vector for the definitions of the old methods.

By this construction, the new object type ρ^* is a subtype of the old object type ρ. Consequently, any objects with the new method can be used in situations expecting an object without the new method, as might be expected. To avoid redefining old classes when a new method is introduced, we may restrict inheritance so that new methods are only added to new subclasses. Subclasses may then have more methods than super-classes, and objects of the subclass can be provided when an object of the superclass is required.

27.3 Method-Based Inheritance

The method-based organization is dual to that of the class-based organization. Recall that the method-based organization given in Chapter 26 consists of a method vector e_{mv} of type

$$\tau_{\mathrm{mv}} \triangleq \prod_{d \in D} \tau \rightarrow \rho_d,$$

where the instance type τ is the sum type $\sum_{c \in C} \tau^c$. The method vector consists of a tuple of functions that dispatch on the class of the object to determine their behavior.

Let us consider the effect of adding a new method d^* as described in Section 27.1. The new method vector e_{mv}^* has type

$$\tau_{\mathrm{mv}}^* \triangleq \prod_{d \in D^*} \tau \rightarrow \rho_d.$$

There is an isomorphism, written $(\ )^{\ddagger}$, between τ_{mv}^* and the type

$$\tau_{\mathrm{mv}} \times (\tau \rightarrow \rho_{d^*}).$$

Using this isomorphism, the new method vector e_{mv}^* is defined as

$$\langle e_{\mathrm{mv}}, \lambda\, (\mathit{this} : \tau)\, \mathsf{case}\, \mathit{this}\, \{c \cdot u \hookrightarrow e_{d^*}^c(u)\}_{c \in C} \rangle^{\ddagger}.$$

The old method vector is re-used intact, extended with a dispatch function for the new method.

The object type does not change under the extension with a new method, but because $\rho^* <: \rho$, there is no difficulty using a new object in a context expecting an old object—the added method is ignored.

Finally, let us consider the effect of adding a new class c^* as described in Section 27.1. The new method vector, e_{mv}^*, has the type

$$\tau_{\mathrm{mv}}^* \triangleq \prod_{d \in D} \tau^* \rightarrow \rho_d,$$

where τ^* is the new object type $\sum_{c \in C^*} \tau^c$, which is a super-type of the old object type τ. There is an isomorphism, written $(\ )^{\dagger}$, between τ^* and the sum type $\tau + \tau^{c^*}$, which we may use to define the new method vector e_{mv}^* as follows:

$$\langle d \hookrightarrow \lambda\, (\mathit{this} : \tau^*)\, \mathsf{case}\, \mathit{this}^{\dagger}\, \{\mathbf{l} \cdot u \hookrightarrow (e_{\mathrm{mv}} \cdot d)(u) \mid \mathbf{r} \cdot u \hookrightarrow e_d^{c^*}(u)\} \rangle_{d \in D}.$$

Every method must be redefined to account for the new class, but the old method vector is reused.

27.4 Notes

Abadi and Cardelli (1996) and Pierce (2002) provide thorough accounts of the interaction of inheritance and subtyping. Liskov and Wing (1994) discuss it from a behavioral perspective. They propose to require that subclasses respect the behavior of the superclass when inheritance is used.

Exercises

27.1. Consider the case of extending a dispatch matrix with self-reference by a new class c^* in which a method d is inherited from an existing class c. What requirements ensure that such an inheritance is properly defined? What happens if we extend a self-referential dispatch matrix with a new method, d^* that inherits its behavior on class c from another method d?

27.2. Consider the example of two mutually recursive methods given in Exercise **26.3**. Suppose that num∗ is a new class with instance type $\tau^{\texttt{num}*} <: \tau^{\texttt{num}}$ that inherits the ev method from num, but defines its own version of the od method. What happens when message ev is sent to an instance of num∗? Will the revised od method ever be invoked?

27.3. *Method specialization* consists of defining a new class by inheriting methods from another class or classes, while redefining some of the methods that the inherited methods might invoke. The behavior of the inherited methods on instances of the new class is altered to the extent that they invoke a method that is specialized to the new class. Reconsider Exercise **26.3** in light of Exercise **27.2**, seeking to ensure that the specialization of od is invoked when the inherited method ev is invoked on instances of the new class.

    (a) Redefine the class num along the following lines. The instance data of num is an object admitting methods ev and od. The class num admits these methods and simply hands them off to the instance object.

    (b) The classes zero or of succ admit both the ev and od methods and are defined using message send to effect mutual recursion as necessary.

    (c) Define a subclass succ∗ of succ that overrides the od method. Show that ev on an instance of succ∗ correctly invokes the overridden od method.

Note

1 The extension with a new method will be considered separately for the sake of clarity.

PART XII

Control Flow

28 Control Stacks

Structural dynamics is convenient for proving properties of languages, such as a type safety theorem, but is less convenient as a guide for implementation. A structural dynamics defines a transition relation using rules that determine where to apply the next instruction without spelling out how to find where the instruction lies within an expression. To make this process explicit, we introduce a mechanism, called a *control stack*, that records the work that remains to be done after an instruction is executed. Using a stack eliminates the need for premises on the transition rules so that the transition system defines an *abstract machine* whose steps are determined by information explicit in its state, much as a concrete computer does.

In this chapter, we develop an abstract machine **K** for evaluating expressions in **PCF**. The machine makes explicit the context in which primitive instruction steps are executed, and the process by which the results are propagated to determine the next step of execution. We prove that **K** and **PCF** are equivalent in the sense that both achieve the same outcomes for the same expressions.

28.1 Machine Definition

A state s of the stack machine **K** for **PCF** consists of a *control stack* k and a closed expression e. States take one of two forms:

1. An *evaluation* state of the form $k \triangleright e$ corresponds to the evaluation of a closed expression e on a control stack k.
2. A *return* state of the form $k \triangleleft e$, where e val, corresponds to the evaluation of a stack k on a closed value e.

As an aid to memory, note that the separator "points to" the focal entity of the state, the expression in an evaluation state and the stack in a return state.

The control stack represents the context of evaluation. It records the "current location" of evaluation, the context into which the value of the current expression is returned. Formally, a control stack is a list of *frames*:

$$\frac{}{\epsilon \text{ stack}} \tag{28.1a}$$

$$\frac{f \text{ frame} \quad k \text{ stack}}{k;f \text{ stack}} \tag{28.1b}$$

The frames of the **K** machine are inductively defined by the following rules:

$$\frac{}{\text{s}(-) \text{ frame}} \tag{28.2a}$$

$$\frac{}{\text{ifz}\{e_0; x.e_1\}(-) \text{ frame}} \tag{28.2b}$$

$$\frac{}{\text{ap}(-; e_2) \text{ frame}} \tag{28.2c}$$

The frames correspond to search rules in the dynamics of **PCF**. Thus, instead of relying on the structure of the transition derivation to keep a record of pending computations, we make an explicit record of them in the form of a frame on the control stack.

The transition judgment between states of the **PCF** machine is inductively defined by a set of inference rules. We begin with the rules for natural numbers, using an eager semantics for the successor.

$$\frac{}{k \vartriangleright \text{z} \longmapsto k \vartriangleleft \text{z}} \tag{28.3a}$$

$$\frac{}{k \vartriangleright \text{s}(e) \longmapsto k;\text{s}(-) \vartriangleright e} \tag{28.3b}$$

$$\frac{}{k;\text{s}(-) \vartriangleleft e \longmapsto k \vartriangleleft \text{s}(e)} \tag{28.3c}$$

To evaluate z, we simply return it. To evaluate $\text{s}(e)$, we push a frame on the stack to record the pending successor and evaluate e; when that returns with e', we return $\text{s}(e')$ to the stack.

Next, we consider the rules for case analysis.

$$\frac{}{k \vartriangleright \text{ifz}\{e_0; x.e_1\}(e) \longmapsto k;\text{ifz}\{e_0; x.e_1\}(-) \vartriangleright e} \tag{28.4a}$$

$$\frac{}{k;\text{ifz}\{e_0; x.e_1\}(-) \vartriangleleft \text{z} \longmapsto k \vartriangleright e_0} \tag{28.4b}$$

$$\frac{}{k;\text{ifz}\{e_0; x.e_1\}(-) \vartriangleleft \text{s}(e) \longmapsto k \vartriangleright [e/x]e_1} \tag{28.4c}$$

The test expression is evaluated, recording the pending case analysis on the stack. Once the value of the test expression is determined, the zero or non-zero branch of the condition is evaluated, substituting the predecessor in the latter case.

Finally, we give the rules for functions, which are evaluated by-name, and the rule for general recursion.

$$\frac{}{k \vartriangleright \text{lam}\{\tau\}(x.e) \longmapsto k \vartriangleleft \text{lam}\{\tau\}(x.e)} \tag{28.5a}$$

$$\frac{}{k \vartriangleright \text{ap}(e_1; e_2) \longmapsto k;\text{ap}(-; e_2) \vartriangleright e_1} \tag{28.5b}$$

$$\frac{}{k;\mathtt{ap}(-;e_2) \lhd \mathtt{lam}\{\tau\}(x.e) \longmapsto k \rhd [e_2/x]e} \tag{28.5c}$$

$$\frac{}{k \rhd \mathtt{fix}\{\tau\}(x.e) \longmapsto k \rhd [\mathtt{fix}\{\tau\}(x.e)/x]e} \tag{28.5d}$$

It is important that evaluation of a general recursion requires no stack space.

The initial and final states of the **K** machine are defined by the following rules:

$$\frac{}{\epsilon \rhd e \ \text{initial}} \tag{28.6a}$$

$$\frac{e \ \text{val}}{\epsilon \lhd e \ \text{final}} \tag{28.6b}$$

28.2 Safety

To define and prove safety for the **PCF** machine requires that we introduce a new typing judgment, $k \lhd\!: \tau$, which states that the stack k expects a value of type τ. This judgment is inductively defined by the following rules:

$$\frac{}{\epsilon \lhd\!: \tau} \tag{28.7a}$$

$$\frac{k \lhd\!: \tau' \quad f : \tau \rightsquigarrow \tau'}{k;f \lhd\!: \tau} \tag{28.7b}$$

This definition makes use of an auxiliary judgment, $f : \tau \rightsquigarrow \tau'$, stating that a frame f transforms a value of type τ to a value of type τ'.

$$\frac{}{\mathtt{s}(-) : \mathtt{nat} \rightsquigarrow \mathtt{nat}} \tag{28.8a}$$

$$\frac{e_0 : \tau \quad x : \mathtt{nat} \vdash e_1 : \tau}{\mathtt{ifz}\{e_0; x.e_1\}(-) : \mathtt{nat} \rightsquigarrow \tau} \tag{28.8b}$$

$$\frac{e_2 : \tau_2}{\mathtt{ap}(-;e_2) : \mathtt{parr}(\tau_2;\tau) \rightsquigarrow \tau} \tag{28.8c}$$

The states of the **PCF** machine are well-formed if their stack and expression components match:

$$\frac{k \lhd\!: \tau \quad e : \tau}{k \rhd e \ \text{ok}} \tag{28.9a}$$

$$\frac{k \lhd\!: \tau \quad e : \tau \quad e \ \text{val}}{k \lhd e \ \text{ok}} \tag{28.9b}$$

We leave the proof of safety of the **PCF** machine as an exercise.

Theorem 28.1 (Safety). *1. If s ok and $s \longmapsto s'$, then s' ok.*

2. If s ok, then either s final or there exists s' such that $s \longmapsto s'$.

28.3 Correctness of the K Machine

Does evaluation of an expression e using the **K** machine yield the same result as does the structural dynamics of **PCF**? The answer to this question can be derived from the following facts.

Completeness If $e \longmapsto^* e'$, where e' val, then $\epsilon \triangleright e \longmapsto^* \epsilon \triangleleft e'$.

Soundness If $\epsilon \triangleright e \longmapsto^* \epsilon \triangleleft e'$, then $e \longmapsto^* e'$ with e' val.

To prove completeness a plausible first step is to consider a proof by induction on the definition of multi-step transition, which reduces the theorem to the following two lemmas:

1. If e val, then $\epsilon \triangleright e \longmapsto^* \epsilon \triangleleft e$.
2. If $e \longmapsto e'$, then, for every v val, if $\epsilon \triangleright e' \longmapsto^* \epsilon \triangleleft v$, then $\epsilon \triangleright e \longmapsto^* \epsilon \triangleleft v$.

The first can be proved easily by induction on the structure of e. The second requires an inductive analysis of the derivation of $e \longmapsto e'$ that gives rise to two complications. The first complication is that we cannot restrict attention to the empty stack, for if e is, say, $ap(e_1; e_2)$, then the first step of the **K** machine is

$$\epsilon \triangleright ap(e_1; e_2) \longmapsto \epsilon;ap(-; e_2) \triangleright e_1.$$

To handle such situations, we consider the evaluation of e_1 on any stack, not just the empty stack.

Specifically, we prove that if $e \longmapsto e'$ and $k \triangleright e' \longmapsto^* k \triangleleft v$, then $k \triangleright e \longmapsto^* k \triangleleft v$. Reconsider the case $e = ap(e_1; e_2)$, $e' = ap(e_1'; e_2)$, with $e_1 \longmapsto e_1'$. We are given that $k \triangleright ap(e_1'; e_2) \longmapsto^* k \triangleleft v$, and we are to show that $k \triangleright ap(e_1; e_2) \longmapsto^* k \triangleleft v$. It is easy to show that the first step of the former derivation is

$$k \triangleright ap(e_1'; e_2) \longmapsto k;ap(-; e_2) \triangleright e_1'.$$

We would like to apply induction to the derivation of $e_1 \longmapsto e_1'$, but to do so, we need a value v_1 such that $e_1' \longmapsto^* v_1$, which is not at hand.

We therefore consider the value of each sub-expression of an expression. This information is given by the evaluation dynamics described in Chapter 7, which has the property that $e \Downarrow e'$ iff $e \longmapsto^* e'$ and e' val.

Lemma 28.2. *If $e \Downarrow v$, then for every k stack, $k \triangleright e \longmapsto^* k \triangleleft v$.*

The desired result follows by the analog of Theorem 7.2 for **PCF**, which states that $e \Downarrow v$ iff $e \longmapsto^* v$.

To prove soundness, we note that it is awkward to reason inductively about a multi-step transition from $\epsilon \triangleright e \longmapsto^* \epsilon \triangleleft v$. The intermediate steps could involve alternations of evaluation and return states. Instead, we consider a **K** machine state to encode an expression, and show that the machine transitions are simulated by the transitions of the structural dynamics.

To do so, we define a judgment, $s \leftrightarrowtail e$, stating that state s "unravels to" expression e. It will turn out that for initial states, $s = \epsilon \rhd e$, and final states, $s = \epsilon \lhd e$, we have $s \leftrightarrowtail e$. Then we show that if $s \longmapsto^* s'$, where s' final, $s \leftrightarrowtail e$, and $s' \leftrightarrowtail e'$, then e' val and $e \longmapsto^* e'$. For this, it is enough to show the following two facts:

1. If $s \leftrightarrowtail e$ and s final, then e val.
2. If $s \longmapsto s'$, $s \leftrightarrowtail e$, $s' \leftrightarrowtail e'$, and $e' \longmapsto^* v$, where v val, then $e \longmapsto^* v$.

The first is quite simple, we need only note that the unraveling of a final state is a value. For the second, it is enough to prove the following lemma.

Lemma 28.3. *If* $s \longmapsto s'$, $s \leftrightarrowtail e$, *and* $s' \leftrightarrowtail e'$, *then* $e \longmapsto^* e'$.

Corollary 28.4. $e \longmapsto^* \overline{n}$ *iff* $\epsilon \rhd e \longmapsto^* \epsilon \lhd \overline{n}$.

28.3.1 Completeness

Proof of Lemma 28.2   The proof is by induction on an evaluation dynamics for **PCF**.
   Consider the evaluation rule

$$\frac{e_1 \Downarrow \mathtt{lam}\{\tau_2\}(x.e) \quad [e_2/x]e \Downarrow v}{\mathtt{ap}(e_1; e_2) \Downarrow v} \tag{28.10}$$

For an arbitrary control stack k, we are to show that $k \rhd \mathtt{ap}(e_1; e_2) \longmapsto^* k \lhd v$. Applying both of the inductive hypotheses in succession, interleaved with steps of the **K** machine, we obtain

$$\begin{aligned} k \rhd \mathtt{ap}(e_1; e_2) &\longmapsto k;\mathtt{ap}(-; e_2) \rhd e_1 \\ &\longmapsto^* k;\mathtt{ap}(-; e_2) \lhd \mathtt{lam}\{\tau_2\}(x.e) \\ &\longmapsto k \rhd [e_2/x]e \\ &\longmapsto^* k \lhd v. \end{aligned}$$

The other cases of the proof are handled similarly.   □

28.3.2 Soundness

The judgment $s \leftrightarrowtail e'$, where s is either $k \rhd e$ or $k \lhd e$, is defined in terms of the auxiliary judgment $k \bowtie e = e'$ by the following rules:

$$\frac{k \bowtie e = e'}{k \rhd e \leftrightarrowtail e'} \tag{28.11a}$$

$$\frac{k \bowtie e = e'}{k \lhd e \leftrightarrowtail e'} \tag{28.11b}$$

In words, to unravel a state, we wrap the stack around the expression to form a complete program. The unraveling relation is inductively defined by the following rules:

$$\frac{}{\epsilon \bowtie e = e} \tag{28.12a}$$

$$\frac{k \bowtie \mathrm{s}(e) = e'}{k;\mathrm{s}(-) \bowtie e = e'} \tag{28.12b}$$

$$\frac{k \bowtie \mathtt{ifz}\{e_0; x.e_1\}(e) = e'}{k;\mathtt{ifz}\{e_0; x.e_1\}(-) \bowtie e = e'} \tag{28.12c}$$

$$\frac{k \bowtie \mathrm{ap}(e_1; e_2) = e}{k;\mathrm{ap}(-; e_2) \bowtie e_1 = e} \tag{28.12d}$$

These judgments both define total functions.

Lemma 28.5. *The judgment $s \hookrightarrow e$ relates every state s to a unique expression e, and the judgment $k \bowtie e = e'$ relates every stack k and expression e to a unique expression e'.*

We are therefore justified in writing $k \bowtie e$ for the unique e' such that $k \bowtie e = e'$.

The following lemma is crucial. It states that unraveling preserves the transition relation.

Lemma 28.6. *If $e \longmapsto e'$, $k \bowtie e = d$, $k \bowtie e' = d'$, then $d \longmapsto d'$.*

Proof The proof is by rule induction on the transition $e \longmapsto e'$. The inductive cases, where the transition rule has a premise, follow easily by induction. The base cases, where the transition is an axiom, are proved by an inductive analysis of the stack k.

For an example of an inductive case, suppose that $e = \mathrm{ap}(e_1; e_2)$, $e' = \mathrm{ap}(e_1'; e_2)$, and $e_1 \longmapsto e_1'$. We have $k \bowtie e = d$ and $k \bowtie e' = d'$. It follows from rules (28.12) that $k;\mathrm{ap}(-; e_2) \bowtie e_1 = d$ and $k;\mathrm{ap}(-; e_2) \bowtie e_1' = d'$. So by induction $d \longmapsto d'$, as desired.

For an example of a base case, suppose that $e = \mathrm{ap}(\mathtt{lam}\{\tau_2\}(x.e); e_2)$ and $e' = [e_2/x]e$ with $e \longmapsto e'$ directly. Assume that $k \bowtie e = d$ and $k \bowtie e' = d'$; we are to show that $d \longmapsto d'$. We proceed by an inner induction on the structure of k. If $k = \epsilon$, the result follows immediately. Consider, say, the stack $k = k';\mathrm{ap}(-; c_2)$. It follows from rules (28.12) that $k' \bowtie \mathrm{ap}(e; c_2) = d$ and $k' \bowtie \mathrm{ap}(e'; c_2) = d'$. But by the structural dynamics $\mathrm{ap}(e; c_2) \longmapsto \mathrm{ap}(e'; c_2)$, so by the inner inductive hypothesis we have $d \longmapsto d'$, as desired. $\qquad\square$

We may now complete the proof of Lemma 28.3.

Proof of Lemma 28.3 The proof is by case analysis on the transitions of the **K** machine. In each case, after unraveling, the transition will correspond to zero or one transitions of the **PCF** structural dynamics.

Suppose that $s = k \triangleright \mathrm{s}(e)$ and $s' = k;\mathrm{s}(-) \triangleright e$. Note that $k \bowtie \mathrm{s}(e) = e'$ iff $k;\mathrm{s}(-) \bowtie e = e'$, from which the result follows immediately.

Suppose that $s = k$;$\mathtt{ap(lam\{\tau\}}(x.e_1); -) \lhd e_2$ and $s' = k \rhd [e_2/x]e_1$. Let e' be such that k;$\mathtt{ap(lam\{\tau\}}(x.e_1); -) \bowtie e_2 = e'$ and let e'' be such that $k \bowtie [e_2/x]e_1 = e''$. Observe that $k \bowtie \mathtt{ap(lam\{\tau\}}(x.e_1); e_2) = e'$. The result follows from Lemma 28.6.

$\square$

28.4 Notes

The abstract machine considered here is typical of a wide class of machines that make control flow explicit in the state. The prototype is the SECD machine (Landin, 1965), which is a linearization of a structural operational semantics (Plotkin, 1981). The advantage of a machine model is that the explicit treatment of control is needed for languages that allow the control state to be manipulated (see Chapter 30 for a prime example). The disadvantage is that the control state of the computation must be made explicit, necessitating rules for manipulating it that are left implicit in a structural dynamics.

Exercises

28.1. Give the proof of Theorem 28.1 for conditional expressions.

28.2. Formulate a call-by-value variant of the **PCF** machine.

28.3. Analyze the worst-case asymptotic complexity of executing each instruction of the **K** machine.

28.4. Refine the proof of Lemma 28.2 by bounding the number of machine steps taken for each step of the **PCF** dynamics.

Exceptions

Exceptions effect a non-local transfer of control from the point at which the exception is *raised* to an enclosing *handler* for that exception. This transfer interrupts the normal flow of control in a program in response to unusual conditions. For example, exceptions can be used to signal an error condition, or to signal the need for special handling in unusual circumstances. We could use conditionals to check for and process errors or unusual conditions, but using exceptions is often more convenient, particularly because the transfer to the handler is conceptually direct and immediate, rather than indirect via explicit checks.

In this chapter, we will consider two extensions of **PCF** with exceptions. The first, **FPCF**, enriches **PCF** with the simplest form of exception, called a *failure*, with no associated data. A failure can be intercepted and turned into a success (or another failure!) by transferring control to another expression. The second, **XPCF**, enriches **PCF** with *exceptions*, with associated data that is passed to an exception handler that intercepts it. The handler may analyze the associated data to determine how to recover from the exceptional condition. A key choice is to decide on the type of the data associated to an exception.

29.1 Failures

The syntax of **FPCF** is defined by the following extension of the grammar of **PCF**:

$$\text{Exp} \quad e \quad ::= \quad \begin{array}{lll} \texttt{fail} & \texttt{fail} & \text{signal a failure} \\ \texttt{catch}(e_1;e_2) & \texttt{catch}\,e_1\,\texttt{ow}\,e_2 & \text{catch a failure} \end{array}$$

The expression `fail` aborts the current evaluation, and the expression $\texttt{catch}(e_1;e_2)$ catches any failure in e_1 by evaluating e_2 instead. Either e_1 or e_2 may themselves abort, or they may diverge or return a value as usual in **PCF**.

The statics of **FPCF** is given by these rules:

$$\frac{}{\Gamma \vdash \texttt{fail} : \tau} \tag{29.1a}$$

$$\frac{\Gamma \vdash e_1 : \tau \quad \Gamma \vdash e_2 : \tau}{\Gamma \vdash \texttt{catch}(e_1;e_2) : \tau} \tag{29.1b}$$

A failure can have any type, because it never returns. The two expressions in a `catch` expression must have the same type, because either might determine the value of that expression.

The dynamics of **FPCF** is given using a technique called *stack unwinding*. Evaluation of a catch pushes a frame of the form $\text{catch}(-; e)$ onto the control stack that awaits the arrival of a failure. Evaluation of a fail expression pops frames from the control stack until it reaches a frame of the form $\text{catch}(-; e)$, at which point the frame is removed from the stack and the expression e is evaluated. Failure propagation is expressed by a state of the form $k \blacktriangleleft$, which extends the two forms of state considered in Chapter 28 to express failure propagation.

The **FPCF** machine extends the **PCF** machine with the following additional rules:

$$\frac{}{k \triangleright \text{fail} \longmapsto k \blacktriangleleft} \tag{29.2a}$$

$$\frac{}{k \triangleright \text{catch}(e_1; e_2) \longmapsto k; \text{catch}(-; e_2) \triangleright e_1} \tag{29.2b}$$

$$\frac{}{k; \text{catch}(-; e_2) \triangleleft v \longmapsto k \triangleleft v} \tag{29.2c}$$

$$\frac{}{k; \text{catch}(-; e_2) \blacktriangleleft \longmapsto k \triangleright e_2} \tag{29.2d}$$

$$\frac{(f \neq \text{catch}(-; e))}{k; f \blacktriangleleft \longmapsto k \blacktriangleleft} \tag{29.2e}$$

Evaluating fail propagates a failure up the stack. The act of failing itself, fail, will, of course, give rise to a failure. Evaluating $\text{catch}(e_1; e_2)$ consists of pushing the handler on the control stack and evaluating e_1. If a value reaches to the handler, the handler is removed and the value is passed to the surrounding frame. If a failure reaches the handler, the stored expression is evaluated with the handler removed from the control stack. Failures propagate through all frames other than the catch frame.

The initial and final states of the **FPCF** machine are defined by the following rules:

$$\frac{}{\epsilon \text{ initial}} \tag{29.3a}$$

$$\frac{e \text{ val}}{\epsilon \triangleleft e \text{ final}} \tag{29.3b}$$

$$\frac{}{\epsilon \blacktriangleleft \text{ final}} \tag{29.3c}$$

The definition of stack typing given in Chapter 28 can be extended to account for the new forms of frame so that safety can be proved in the same way as before. The only difference is that the statement of progress must be weakened to take account of failure: a well-typed expression is either a value, or may take a step, or may signal failure.

Theorem 29.1 (Safety for **FPCF**). *1. If s ok and $s \longmapsto s'$, then s' ok.*

2. If s ok, then either s final or there exists s' such that $s \longmapsto s'$.

29.2 Exceptions

The language **XPCF** enriches **FPCF** with *exceptions*, failures to which a value is attached. The syntax of **XPCF** extends that of **PCF** with the following forms of expression:

Exp e ::=   raise(e)   raise(e)   raise an exception
              try(e_1; $x.e_2$)   try e_1 ow $x \hookrightarrow e_2$ handle an exception

The argument to raise is evaluated to determine the value passed to the handler. The expression try(e_1; $x.e_2$) binds a variable x in the handler e_2. The associated value of the exception is bound to that variable within e_2, should an exception be raised when e_1 is evaluated.

The statics of exceptions extends the statics of failures to account for the type of the value carried with the exception:

$$\frac{\Gamma \vdash e : \tau_{\text{exn}}}{\Gamma \vdash \text{raise}(e) : \tau} \tag{29.4a}$$

$$\frac{\Gamma \vdash e_1 : \tau \quad \Gamma, x : \tau_{\text{exn}} \vdash e_2 : \tau}{\Gamma \vdash \text{try}(e_1; x.e_2) : \tau} \tag{29.4b}$$

The type τ_{exn} is some fixed, but as yet unspecified, type of exception values. (The choice of τ_{exn} is discussed in Section 29.3.)

The dynamics of **XPCF** is similar to that of **FPCF**, except that the failure state $k \blacktriangleleft$ is replaced by the exception state $k \blacktriangleleft e$ which passes an exception value e to the stack k. There is only one notion of exception, but the associated value can be used to identify the source of the exception. We use a by-value interpretation to avoid the problem of *imprecise exceptions* that arises under a by-name interpretation.

The stack frames of the **PCF** machine are extended to include raise($-$) and try($-$; $x.e_2$). These are used in the following rules:

$$\frac{}{k \triangleright \text{raise}(e) \longmapsto k;\text{raise}(-) \triangleright e} \tag{29.5a}$$

$$\frac{}{k;\text{raise}(-) \triangleleft e \longmapsto k \blacktriangleleft e} \tag{29.5b}$$

$$\frac{}{k \triangleright \text{try}(e_1; x.e_2) \longmapsto k;\text{try}(-; x.e_2) \triangleright e_1} \tag{29.5c}$$

$$\frac{}{k;\text{try}(-; x.e_2) \triangleleft e \longmapsto k \triangleleft e} \tag{29.5d}$$

$$\frac{}{k;\text{try}(-; x.e_2) \blacktriangleleft e \longmapsto k \triangleright [e/x]e_2} \tag{29.5e}$$

$$\frac{(f \neq \text{try}(-; x.e_2))}{k;f \blacktriangleleft e \longmapsto k \blacktriangleleft e} \tag{29.5f}$$

The main difference compared to rules (29.2) is that an exception passes a values to the stack, whereas a failure does not.

The initial and final states of the **XPCF** machine are defined by the following rules:

$$\frac{}{\epsilon \triangleright e \text{ initial}} \tag{29.6a}$$

$$\frac{e \text{ val}}{\epsilon \triangleleft e \text{ final}} \tag{29.6b}$$

$$\frac{}{\epsilon \blacktriangleleft e \text{ final}} \tag{29.6c}$$

Theorem 29.2 (Safety for **XPCF**). *1. If s ok and s $\longmapsto$ s', then s' ok.*
2. If s ok, then either s final or there exists s' such that s $\longmapsto$ s'.

29.3 Exception Values

The statics of **XPCF** is parameterized by the type τ_{exn} of values associated to exceptions. The choice of τ_{exn} is important because it determines how the source of an exception is identified in a program. If τ_{exn} is the one-element type unit, then exceptions degenerate to failures, which are unable to identify their source. Thus, τ_{exn} must have more than one value to be useful.

This fact suggests that τ_{exn} should be a finite sum. The classes of the sum identify the sources of exceptions, and the classified value carries information about the particular instance. For example, τ_{exn} might be a sum type of the form

$$[\text{div} \hookrightarrow \text{unit}, \text{fnf} \hookrightarrow \text{string}, \ldots].$$

Here the class div might represent an arithmetic fault, with no associated data, and the class fnf might represent a "file not found" error, with associated data being the name of the file that was not found.

Using a sum means that an exception handler can dispatch on the class of the exception value to identify its source and cause. For example, we might write

```
handle e₁ ow x ↪
  match x {
     div ⟨⟩ ↪ e_div
   | fnf s ↪ e_fnf }
```

to handle the exceptions specified by the above sum type. Because the exception and its associated data are coupled in a sum type, there is no possibility of misinterpreting the data associated to one exception as being that of another.

The disadvantage of choosing a finite sum for τ_{exn} is that it specifies a *closed world* of possible exception sources. All sources must be identified for the entire program, which impedes modular development and evolution. A more modular approach admits an *open world* of exception sources that can be introduced as the program evolves and even as it executes. A generalization of finite sums, called *dynamic classification*, defined in Chapter 33, is required for an open world. (See that Chapter for further discussion.)

When τ_{exn} is a type of classified values, its classes are often called *exceptions*, so that one may speak of "the fnf exception" in the above example. This terminology is harmless, and all but unavoidable, but it invites confusion between two separate ideas:

1. Exceptions as a *control mechanism* that allows the course of evaluation to be altered by raising and handling exceptions.
2. Exceptions as a *data value* associated with such a deviation of control that allows the source of the deviation to be identified.

As a control mechanism, exceptions can be eliminated using explicit *exception passing*. A computation of type τ that may raise an exception is interpreted as an exception-free computation of type $\tau + \tau_{\text{exn}}$; see Exercise **29.5** for more on this method.

29.4 Notes

Various forms of exceptions were considered in Lisp (Steele, 1990). The original formulation of ML (Gordon et al., 1979) as a metalanguage for mechanized logic used failures to implement backtracking proof search. Most modern languages now have exceptions, but differ in the forms of data that may be associated with them.

Exercises

29.1. Prove Theorem 29.2. Are any properties of τ_{exn} required for the proof?

29.2. Give an evaluation dynamics for **XPCF** using the following judgment forms:
   - Normal evaluation: $e \Downarrow v$, where $e : \tau$, $v : \tau$, and v val.
   - Exceptional evaluation: $e \Uparrow v$, where $e : \tau$, and $v : \tau_{\text{exn}}$, and v val.

   The first states that e evaluates normally to value v, the second that e raises an exception with value v.

29.3. Give a structural operational dynamics to **XPCF** by inductively defining the following judgment forms:
   - $e \longmapsto e'$, stating that expression e transitions to expression e';
   - e val, stating that expression e is a value.

Ensure that $e \Downarrow v$ iff $e \longmapsto^* v$, and $e \Uparrow v$ iff $e \longmapsto^* \mathtt{raise}(v)$, where v val in both cases.

29.4. The closed world assumption on exceptions amounts to choosing the type of exception values to be a finite sum type shared by the entire program. Under such an assumption, it is possible to track exceptions by placing an upper bound on the possible classes of an exception value.

Type refinements (defined in Chapter 25) can be used for exception tracking in a closed-world setting. Define *finite sum refinements* by the rule

$$\frac{X' \subseteq X \quad (\forall x \in X')\, \phi_x \sqsubseteq \tau_x}{[\phi_x]_{x \in X'} \sqsubseteq [\tau_x]_{x \in X}} .$$

In particular, the refinement $\emptyset$ is the vacuous sum refinement [] satisfied by no value. Entailment of finite sum refinements is defined by the rule

$$\frac{X' \subseteq X'' \quad (\forall x \in X')\, \phi_x \le \phi'_x}{[\phi_x]_{x \in X'} \le [\phi'_x]_{x \in X''}} .$$

So, in particular, $\emptyset \le \phi$ for all sum refinements ϕ of τ_{exn}. Entailment weakens knowledge of the class of a value of sum type, which is crucial to their application to exception tracking.

The goal of this exercise is to develop a system of type refinements for the modal formulation of exceptions in **MPCF** using sum refinements to perform exception tracking.

(a) Define the command refinement judgment $m \in_\tau \phi \,\mathsf{ow}\, \chi$, where $m \mathbin{\dot\sim} \tau, \phi \sqsubseteq \tau$, and $\chi \sqsubseteq \tau_{\mathsf{exn}}$, to mean that if m returns e, then $e \in_\tau \phi$, and if m raises e, then $e \in_{\tau_{\mathsf{exn}}} \chi$.

(b) Define satisfaction and entailment for the expression refinement $\mathtt{cmd}(\phi; \chi) \sqsubseteq \mathtt{cmd}(\tau)$, where $\phi \sqsubseteq \tau$ and $\chi \sqsubseteq \tau_{\mathsf{exn}}$. This refinement classifies encapsulated commands that satisfy the stated value and exception refinements in the sense of the preceding problem.

29.5. Show that exceptions in **MPCF** can be eliminated by a translation into **PCF** enriched with sum types by what is called the *exception-passing style* transformation. Each command $m \mathbin{\dot\sim} \tau$ of **MPCF** is translated to a pure expression $\widehat{m}$ of type $\widehat{\tau} + \tau_{\mathsf{exn}}$ whose value is either $\mathtt{l} \cdot e$, where $e : \tau$, for normal return, or $\mathtt{r} \cdot e$, where $e : \tau_{\mathsf{exn}}$, for an exceptional return. The command translation is extended to an expression translation $\widehat{e}$ that replaces occurrences of $\mathtt{cmd}(m)$ by $\widehat{m}$. The corresponding type translation, $\widehat{\tau}$, replaces $\mathtt{cmd}(\tau)$ by $\widehat{\tau} + \tau_{\mathsf{exn}}$. Define the command translation from **MPCF** to **PCF** enriched with sums, and show that it has the required type and correctly simulates the behavior of exceptions.

30 Continuations

The semantics of many control constructs (such as exceptions and coroutines) can be expressed in terms of *reified* control stacks, a representation of a control stack as a value that can be reactivated at any time, *even if* control has long since returned past the point of reification. Reified control stacks of this kind are called *continuations*; they are values that can be passed and returned at will in a computation. Continuations never "expire", and it is always sensible to reinstate a continuation without compromising safety. Thus continuations support unlimited "time travel" — we can go back to a previous step of the computation, then return to some point in its future.

Why are continuations useful? Fundamentally, they are representations of the control state of a computation at a given time. Using continuations we can "checkpoint" the control state of a program, save it in a data structure, and return to it later. In fact this is precisely what is necessary to implement *threads* (concurrently executing programs) — the thread scheduler suspends a program for later execution from where it left off.

30.1 Overview

We will consider the extension **KPCF** of **PCF** with the type $cont(\tau)$ of continuations accepting values of type τ. The introduction form for $cont(\tau)$ is $letcc\{\tau\}(x.e)$, which binds the *current continuation* (that is, the current control stack) to the variable x, and evaluates the expression e. The corresponding elimination form is $throw\{\tau\}(e_1; e_2)$, which restores the value given by e_1 to the control stack given by e_2.

To illustrate the use of these primitives, consider the problem of multiplying the first n elements of an infinite sequence q of natural numbers, where q is represented by a function of type $nat \rightharpoonup nat$. If zero occurs among the first n elements, we would like to effect an "early return" with the value zero, without further multiplication. This problem can be solved using exceptions, but we will solve it with continuations to show how they are used.

Here is the solution in **PCF**, without short-cutting:

```
fix ms is
  λ q : nat ⇀ nat.
    λ n : nat.
      case n {
        z ↪ s(z)
        | s(n') ↪ (q z) × (ms (q ∘ succ) n')
      }
```

The recursive call composes q with the successor function to shift the sequence by one step.

Here is the solution in **KPCF**, with short-cutting:

```
λ q : nat ⇀ nat.
  λ n : nat.
    letcc ret : nat cont in
      let ms be
        fix ms is
          λ q : nat ⇀ nat.
            λ n : nat.
              case n {
                z ↪ s(z)
              | s(n') ↪
                case q z {
                  z ↪ throw z to ret
                | s(n'') ↪ (q z) × (ms (q ∘ succ) n')
                }
              }
      in
        ms q n
```

The letcc binds the return point of the function to the variable ret for use within the main loop of the computation. If an element is zero, control is thrown to ret, effecting an early return with the value zero.

To take another example, given that k has type τ cont and f has type $\tau' \rightharpoonup \tau$, return k' of type return a continuation k' of type τ' cont such that throwing a value v' of type τ' to k' throws the value of $f(v')$ to k. Thus, we seek to define a function compose of type

$$(\tau' \rightharpoonup \tau) \rightharpoonup \tau \text{ cont} \rightharpoonup \tau' \text{ cont}.$$

The continuation we seek is the one in effect at the point of the ellipsis in the expression throw $f(\ldots)$ to k. It is the continuation that, when given a value v', applies f to it, and throws the result to k. We can seize this continuation using letcc by writing

```
throw f(letcc x:τ' cont in ...) to k
```

The desired continuation is bound to x, but how can we return it as the result of compose? We use the same idea as for short-circuit multiplication, writing

```
letcc ret:τ' cont cont in
  throw (f (letcc r in throw r to ret)) to k
```

as the body of compose. Note that the type of ret is τ cont cont, that of a continuation that expects to be thrown a continuation!

30.2 Continuation Dynamics

The syntax of **KPCF** is as follows:

Type	τ	::=	$\mathtt{cont}(\tau)$	τ cont	continuation
Expr	e	::=	$\mathtt{letcc}\{\tau\}(x.e)$	$\mathtt{letcc}\,x\,\mathtt{in}\,e$	mark
			$\mathtt{throw}\{\tau\}(e_1;e_2)$	$\mathtt{throw}\,e_1\,\mathtt{to}\,e_2$	goto
			$\mathtt{cont}(k)$	$\mathtt{cont}(k)$	continuation

The expression $\mathtt{cont}(k)$ is a reified control stack, which arises during evaluation.

The statics of **KPCF** is defined by the following rules:

$$\frac{\Gamma, x : \mathtt{cont}(\tau) \vdash e : \tau}{\Gamma \vdash \mathtt{letcc}\{\tau\}(x.e) : \tau} \tag{30.1a}$$

$$\frac{\Gamma \vdash e_1 : \tau_1 \quad \Gamma \vdash e_2 : \mathtt{cont}(\tau_1)}{\Gamma \vdash \mathtt{throw}\{\tau\}(e_1;e_2) : \tau} \tag{30.1b}$$

The result type of a $\mathtt{throw}$ expression is arbitrary because it does not return to the point of the call.

The statics of continuation values is given by the following rule:

$$\frac{k : \tau}{\Gamma \vdash \mathtt{cont}(k) : \mathtt{cont}(\tau)} \tag{30.2}$$

A continuation value $\mathtt{cont}(k)$ has type $\mathtt{cont}(\tau)$ exactly if it is a stack accepting values of type τ.

To define the dynamics of **KPCF**, we extend the **PCF** machine with two forms of stack frame:

$$\frac{}{\mathtt{throw}\{\tau\}(-;e_2)\ \mathsf{frame}} \tag{30.3a}$$

$$\frac{e_1\ \mathsf{val}}{\mathtt{throw}\{\tau\}(e_1;-)\ \mathsf{frame}} \tag{30.3b}$$

Every reified control stack is a value:

$$\frac{k\ \mathsf{stack}}{\mathtt{cont}(k)\ \mathsf{val}} \tag{30.4}$$

The transition rules of the **PCF** machine governing continuations are as follows:

$$\frac{}{k \triangleright \mathtt{cont}(k) \longmapsto k \triangleleft \mathtt{cont}(k)} \tag{30.5a}$$

$$\frac{}{k \triangleright \mathtt{letcc}\{\tau\}(x.e) \longmapsto k \triangleright [\mathtt{cont}(k)/x]e} \tag{30.5b}$$

$$\frac{}{k \triangleright \mathtt{throw}\{\tau\}(e_1;e_2) \longmapsto k;\mathtt{throw}\{\tau\}(-;e_2) \triangleright e_1} \tag{30.5c}$$

$$\frac{e_1 \text{ val}}{k;\texttt{throw}\{\tau\}(-;e_2) \triangleleft e_1 \longmapsto k;\texttt{throw}\{\tau\}(e_1;-) \triangleright e_2} \qquad (30.5\text{d})$$

$$\frac{e \text{ val}}{k;\texttt{throw}\{\tau\}(e;-) \triangleleft \texttt{cont}(k') \longmapsto k' \triangleleft e} \qquad (30.5\text{e})$$

Evaluation of a letcc expression duplicates the control stack; evaluation of a throw expression destroys the current control stack.

The safety of **KPCF** is proved by extending the safety proof for the **K** machine given in Chapter 28.

We need only add typing rules for the two new forms of frame, which are as follows:

$$\frac{e_2 : \texttt{cont}(\tau)}{\texttt{throw}\{\tau'\}(-;e_2) : \tau \rightsquigarrow \tau'} \qquad (30.6\text{a})$$

$$\frac{e_1 : \tau \quad e_1 \text{ val}}{\texttt{throw}\{\tau'\}(e_1;-) : \texttt{cont}(\tau) \rightsquigarrow \tau'} \qquad (30.6\text{b})$$

The rest of the definitions remain as in Chapter 28.

Lemma 30.1 (Canonical Forms). *If $e : \texttt{cont}(\tau)$ and e val, then $e = \texttt{cont}(k)$ for some k such that $k : \tau$.*

Theorem 30.2 (Safety). *1. If s ok and $s \longmapsto s'$, then s' ok.*
2. If s ok, then either s final or there exists s' such that $s \longmapsto s'$.

30.3 Coroutines from Continuations

The distinction between a routine and a subroutine is the distinction between a manager and a worker. The routine calls the subroutine to do some work, and the subroutine returns to the routine when its work is done. The relationship is asymmetric in that there is a distinction between the *caller*, the main routine, and the *callee*, the subroutine. It is useful to consider a symmetric situation in which two routines each call the other to do some work. Such a pair of routines are called *coroutines*; their relationship to one another is symmetric, not hierarchical.

A subroutine is implemented by having the caller pass to the callee a continuation representing the work to be done once the subroutine finishes. When it does, it throws the return value to that continuation, without the possibility of return. A coroutine is implemented by having two routines each call each other as subroutines by providing a continuation when control is ceded from one to the other. The only tricky part is how the entire process gets started.

Consider the type of each routine of the pair. A routine is a continuation accepting two arguments, data to be passed to the routine when it is resumed and a continuation to be resumed when the routine has finished its task. The datum represents the state of the computation, and the continuation is a coroutine that accepts arguments of the same form. Thus, the type of a coroutine must satisfy the type isomorphism

$$\tau \, \texttt{coro} \cong (\tau \times \tau \, \texttt{coro}) \, \texttt{cont}.$$

Therefore, we define $\tau \, \texttt{coro}$ to be the recursive type

$$\tau \, \texttt{coro} \triangleq \texttt{rec} \, t \, \texttt{is} \, (\tau \times t) \, \texttt{cont}.$$

Up to isomorphism, the type $\tau \, \texttt{coro}$ is the type of continuations that accept a value of type τ, representing the state of the coroutine, and the partner coroutine, a value of the same type.

A coroutine r passes control to another coroutine r' by evaluating the expression $\texttt{resume}(\langle s, r' \rangle)$, where s is the current state of the computation. Doing so creates a new coroutine whose entry point is the return point (calling site) of $\texttt{resume}$. Therefore, the type of $\texttt{resume}$ is

$$\tau \times \tau \, \texttt{coro} \rightharpoonup \tau \times \tau \, \texttt{coro}.$$

The definition of $\texttt{resume}$ is as follows:

$$\lambda \, (\langle s, r' \rangle : \tau \times \tau \, \texttt{coro}) \, \texttt{letcc} \, k \, \texttt{in} \, \texttt{throw} \, \langle s, \texttt{fold}(k) \rangle \, \texttt{to} \, \texttt{unfold}(r').$$

When applied, $\texttt{resume}$ seizes the current continuation and passes the state, s, and the seized continuation (packaged as a coroutine) to the called coroutine.

Because the state is explicitly passed from one routine to the other, a coroutine is a state transformation function that, when activated with the current state, determines the next state of the computation. A system of coroutines is created by establishing a joint exit point to which the result of the system is thrown and creating a pair of coroutines that transform the state and pass control to the partner routine. If either routine wishes to terminate the computation, it does so by throwing a result value to their common exit point. Thus, a coroutine is a function of type

$$(\tau', \tau) \, \texttt{rout} \triangleq \tau' \, \texttt{cont} \rightharpoonup \tau \rightharpoonup \tau,$$

where τ' is the result type and τ is the state type of the system of coroutines.

To set up a system of coroutines we define a function $\texttt{run}$ that, given two routines, creates a function of type $\tau \rightharpoonup \tau'$ that, when applied to the initial state, computes a result of type τ'. The computation consists of a cooperating pair of routines that share a common exit point. The definition of $\texttt{run}$ begins as follows:

$$\lambda \, (\langle r_1, r_2 \rangle) \, \lambda \, (s_0) \, \texttt{letcc} \, x_0 \, \texttt{in} \, \texttt{let} \, r_1' \, \texttt{be} \, r_1(x_0) \, \texttt{in} \, \texttt{let} \, r_2' \, \texttt{be} \, r_2(x_0) \, \texttt{in} \dots$$

Given two routines, $\texttt{run}$ establishes their common exit point and passes this continuation to both routines. By throwing to this continuation, either routine may terminate the computation with a result of type τ'. The body of the run function continues as follows:

$$\mathtt{rep}(r_2')(\mathtt{letcc}\, k \,\mathtt{in}\, \mathtt{rep}(r_1')(\langle s_0, \mathtt{fold}(k)\rangle))$$

The auxiliary function rep creates an infinite loop that transforms the state and passes control to the other routine:

$$\lambda\,(t)\,\mathtt{fix}\, l \,\mathtt{is}\, \lambda\,(\langle s, r\rangle)\, l(\mathtt{resume}(\langle t(s), r\rangle)).$$

The system is initialized by starting routine r_1 with the initial state, and arranging that, when it cedes control to its partner, it starts routine r_2 with the resulting state. At that point, the system is bootstrapped: each routine will resume the other on each iteration of the loop.

A good example of coroutining is the interleaving of input and output in a computation. This is done by coroutining between a *producer* routine and a *consumer* routine. The producer emits the next element of the input, if any, and passes control to the consumer, removing that element from the input. The consumer processes the next data item, and returns control to the producer, with the result of processing attached to the output. For simplicity input and output are modeled as lists of type $\tau_i\, \mathtt{list}$ and $\tau_o\, \mathtt{list}$, respectively, which are passed back and forth between the routines. The routines exchange messages according to the following protocol. The message $\mathtt{OK}(\langle i, o\rangle)$ is sent from the consumer to producer to acknowledge receipt of the previous message, and to pass back the current state of the input and output channels. The message $\mathtt{EMIT}(\langle e, \langle i, o\rangle\rangle)$, where e is a value of type $\tau_i\, \mathtt{opt}$, is sent from the producer to the consumer to emit the next value (if any) from the input, and to pass the current state of the input and output channels to the consumer.

Here is an implementation of the producer/consumer coroutines. The type τ of the state maintained by the routines is the labeled sum type

$$[\mathtt{OK} \hookrightarrow \tau_i\, \mathtt{list} \times \tau_o\, \mathtt{list}, \mathtt{EMIT} \hookrightarrow \tau_i\, \mathtt{opt} \times (\tau_i\, \mathtt{list} \times \tau_o\, \mathtt{list})].$$

The above type specifies the message protocol between the producer and the consumer described in the preceding paragraph.

The producer P is defined by the expression

$$\lambda\,(x_0)\,\lambda\,(msg)\,\mathtt{case}\, msg\,\{b_1 \mid b_2 \mid b_3\},$$

where the first branch b_1 is

$$\mathtt{OK}\cdot\langle \mathtt{nil}, os\rangle \hookrightarrow \mathtt{EMIT}\cdot\langle \mathtt{null}, \langle \mathtt{nil}, os\rangle\rangle$$

and the second branch b_2 is

$$\mathtt{OK}\cdot\langle \mathtt{cons}(i; is), os\rangle \hookrightarrow \mathtt{EMIT}\cdot\langle \mathtt{just}(i), \langle is, os\rangle\rangle,$$

and the third branch b_3 is

$$\mathtt{EMIT}\cdot\_ \hookrightarrow \mathtt{error}.$$

In words, if the input is exhausted, the producer emits the value null, along with the current channel state. Otherwise, it emits $\mathtt{just}(i)$, where i is the first remaining input and removes that element from the passed channel state. The producer cannot see an EMIT message and signals an error if it should occur.

The consumer C is defined by the expression

$$\lambda\,(x_0)\,\lambda\,(msg)\,\mathtt{case}\,msg\,\{b_1' \mid b_2' \mid b_3'\},$$

where the first branch b_1' is

$$\mathtt{EMIT}\cdot\langle\mathtt{null},\langle\_,os\rangle\rangle\hookrightarrow\mathtt{throw}\,os\,\mathtt{to}\,x_0,$$

the second branch b_2' is

$$\mathtt{EMIT}\cdot\langle\mathtt{just}(i),\langle is,os\rangle\rangle\hookrightarrow\mathtt{OK}\cdot\langle is,\mathtt{cons}(f(i);os)\rangle,$$

and the third branch b_3' is

$$\mathtt{OK}\cdot\_\hookrightarrow\mathtt{error}.$$

The consumer dispatches on the emitted datum. If it is absent, the output channel state is passed to x_0 as the overall value of the computation. If it is present, the function f (unspecified here) of type $\tau_i\rightharpoonup\tau_o$ is applied to transform the input to the output, and the result is added to the output channel. If the message OK is received, the consumer signals an error, as the producer never produces such a message.

The initial state s_0 has the form $\mathtt{OK}\cdot\langle is,os\rangle$, where is and os are the initial input and output channel state, respectively. The computation is created by the expression

$$\mathtt{run}(\langle P,C\rangle)(s_0),$$

which sets up the coroutines as described earlier.

Although it is relatively easy to visualize and implement coroutines involving only two partners, it is more complex and less useful to consider a similar pattern of control among $n\geq 2$ participants. In such cases, it is more common to structure the interaction as a collection of n routines, each of which is a coroutine of a central *scheduler*. When a routine resumes its partner, it passes control to the scheduler, which determines which routine to execute next, again as a coroutine of itself. When structured as coroutines of a scheduler, the individual routines are called *threads*. A thread *yields* control by resuming its partner, the scheduler, which then determines which thread to execute next as a coroutine of itself. This pattern of control is called *cooperative multi-threading*, because it is based on voluntary yields, rather than forced suspensions by a scheduler.

30.4 Notes

Continuations are a ubiquitous notion in programming languages. Reynolds (1993) provides an excellent account of the multiple discoveries of continuations. The formulation given here is inspired by Felleisen and Hieb (1992), who pioneered the development of linguistic theories of control and state.

Exercises

30.1. Type safety for **KPCF** follows almost directly from Theorem 28.1. Isolate the key observations required to extend the proof to include continuation types.

30.2. Exhibit a closed **KPCF** expression of each of the following types:

(a) $\tau + (\tau\ \mathtt{cont})$.

(b) $\tau\ \mathtt{cont}\ \mathtt{cont} \to \tau$.

(c) $(\tau_2\ \mathtt{cont} \to \tau_1\ \mathtt{cont}) \to (\tau_1 \to \tau_2)$.

(d) $(\tau_1 + \tau_2)\ \mathtt{cont} \to (\tau_1\ \mathtt{cont} \times \tau_2\ \mathtt{cont})$.

Hint: you will need to use `letcc` and `throw`.

30.3. The type `stream` of infinite streams of natural numbers defined in Chapter 15 can be implemented using continuations. Define `stream` to be the recursive type satisfying the isomorphism

$$\mathtt{stream} \cong (\mathtt{nat} \times \mathtt{stream})\ \mathtt{cont}\ \mathtt{cont}.$$

To examine the front of the stream, throw to it a continuation expecting a natural number and another stream. When passed such a continuation, the stream throws to it the next number in the stream, paired with another stream (that is, another continuation) representing the stream of numbers following that number. Define the introduction and elimination forms for streams defined in Chapter 15 using this representation.

PART XIII

Symbolic Data

31 Symbols

A *symbol* is an atomic datum with no internal structure. Whereas a variable is given meaning by substitution, a symbol is given meaning by a family of operations indexed by symbols. A symbol is just a name, or index, for a family of operations. Many different interpretations may be given to symbols according to the operations we choose to consider, giving rise to concepts such as fluid binding, dynamic classification, mutable storage, and communication channels. A type is associated to each symbol whose interpretation depends on the particular application. For example, in the case of mutable storage, the type of a symbol constrains the contents of the cell named by that symbol to values of that type.

In this chapter, we consider two constructs for computing with symbols. The first is a means of *declaring* new symbols for use within a specified *scope*. The expression $\text{new } a \sim \rho \text{ in } e$ introduces a "new" symbol a with associated type ρ for use within e. The declared symbol a is "new" in the sense that it is bound by the declaration within e and so may be renamed at will to ensure that it differs from any finite set of active symbols. Whereas the statics determines the scope of a declared symbol, its range of significance, or *extent*, is determined by the dynamics. There are two different dynamic interpretations of symbols, the *scoped* and the *free* (short for *scope-free*) dynamics. The scoped dynamics limits the extent of the symbol to its scope; the lifetime of the symbol is restricted to the evaluation of its scope. Alternatively, under the free dynamics the extent of a symbol exceeds its scope, extending to the entire computation of which it is a part. We may say that in the free dynamics a symbol "escapes its scope," but it is more accurate to say that its scope widens to encompass the rest of the computation.

The second construct associated with symbols is the concept of a *symbol reference*, an expression whose purpose is to refer to a particular symbol. Symbol references are values of a type ρ sym and are written 'a for some symbol a with associated type ρ. The elimination form for the type ρ sym is a conditional branch that determines whether a symbol reference refers to a statically specified symbol. The statics of the elimination form ensures that, in the positive case, the type associated to the referenced symbol is manifested, whereas in the negative case, no type information can be gleaned from the test.

31.1 Symbol Declaration

We will consider here an extension **SPCF** of **PCF** with the means to allocate new symbols. This capability will be used in later chapters that use symbols for other purposes. Here we will only be concerned with symbol allocation, and the introduction and elimination of symbols as values of a type of plain symbols.

The syntax for symbol declaration in **SPCF** is given by the following grammar:

$$\text{Exp} \quad e \quad ::= \quad \text{new}\{\tau\}(a.e) \quad \text{new } a \sim \tau \text{ in } e \quad \text{generation}$$

The statics of symbol declaration makes use of a *signature*, or *symbol context*, that associates a type to each of a finite set of symbols. We use the letter Σ to range over signatures, which are finite sets of pairs $a \sim \tau$, where a is a symbol and τ is a type. The typing judgment $\Gamma \vdash_\Sigma e : \tau$ is parameterized by a signature Σ associating types to symbols. In effect, there is an infinite family of typing judgments, one for each choice of Σ. The expression new $a \sim \tau$ in e shifts from one instance of the family to another by adding a new symbol to Σ.

The statics of symbol declaration makes use of a judgment, τ mobile, whose definition depends on whether the dynamics is scoped. In a scoped dynamics, mobility is defined so that the computed value of a mobile type cannot depend on any symbol. By constraining the scope of a declaration to have mobile type, we can, under this interpretation, ensure that the extent of a symbol is confined to its scope. In a free dynamics, every type is deemed mobile, because the dynamics ensures that the scope of a symbol is widened to accommodate the possibility that the value returned from the scope of a declaration may depend on the declared symbol. The term "mobile" reflects the informal idea that symbols may or may not be "moved" from the scope of their declaration according to the dynamics given to them. A free dynamics allows symbols to be moved freely, whereas a scoped dynamics limits their range of motion.

The statics of symbol declaration itself is given by the following rule:

$$\frac{\Gamma \vdash_{\Sigma, a \sim \rho} e : \tau \quad \tau \text{ mobile}}{\Gamma \vdash_\Sigma \text{new}\{\rho\}(a.e) : \tau} \tag{31.1}$$

As mentioned, the condition on τ ensures that the returned value does not escape its scope, if any.

31.1.1 Scoped Dynamics

The scoped dynamics of symbol declaration is given by a transition judgment of the form $e \underset{\Sigma}{\longmapsto} e'$ indexed by a signature Σ specifying the active symbols of the transition. Either e or e' may involve the symbols declared in Σ, but no others.

$$\frac{e \underset{\Sigma, a \sim \rho}{\longmapsto} e'}{\text{new}\{\rho\}(a.e) \underset{\Sigma}{\longmapsto} \text{new}\{\rho\}(a.e')} \tag{31.2a}$$

$$\frac{e \text{ val}_\Sigma}{\text{new}\{\rho\}(a.e) \underset{\Sigma}{\longmapsto} e} \tag{31.2b}$$

Rule (31.2a) specifies that evaluation takes place within the scope of the declaration of a symbol. Rule (31.2b) specifies that the declared symbol is "forgotten" once its scope has been evaluated.

The definition of the judgment τ mobile must be chosen to ensure that the following *mobility condition* is satisfied:

If τ mobile, $\vdash_{\Sigma, a \sim \rho} e : \tau$, and $e\ val_{\Sigma, a \sim \rho}$, then $\vdash_\Sigma e : \tau$ and $e\ val_\Sigma$.

For example, in the presence of symbol references (see Section 31.2 below), a function type cannot be deemed mobile, because a function may contain a reference to a local symbol. The type nat may only be deemed mobile if the successor is evaluated eagerly, for otherwise a symbol reference may occur within a value of this type, invalidating the condition.

Theorem 31.1 (Preservation). *If $\vdash_\Sigma e : \tau$ and $e \underset{\Sigma}{\mapsto} e'$, then $\vdash_\Sigma e' : \tau$.*

Proof By induction on the dynamics of symbol declaration. Rule (31.2a) follows by induction, applying rule (31.1). Rule (31.2b) follows from the condition on mobility. □

Theorem 31.2 (Progress). *If $\vdash_\Sigma e : \tau$, then either $e \underset{\Sigma}{\mapsto} e'$, or $e\ val_\Sigma$.*

Proof There is only one rule to consider, rule (31.1). By induction, we have either $e \underset{\Sigma, a \sim \rho}{\longmapsto} e'$, in which case rule (31.2a) applies, or $e\ val_{\Sigma, a \sim \rho}$, in which case by the mobility condition we have $e\ val_\Sigma$, and hence rule (31.2b) applies. □

31.1.2 Scope-Free Dynamics

The scope-free dynamics of symbols is defined by a transition system between states of the form $\nu\,\Sigma\,\{e\}$, where Σ is a signature and e is an expression over this signature. The judgment $\nu\,\Sigma\,\{e\} \longmapsto \nu\,\Sigma'\,\{e'\}$ states that evaluation of e relative to symbols Σ results in the expression e' in the extension Σ' of Σ.

$$\frac{}{\nu\,\Sigma\,\{\,\mathtt{new}\{\rho\}(a.e)\,\} \longmapsto \nu\,\Sigma, a \sim \rho\,\{e\}} \tag{31.3}$$

Rule (31.3) specifies that symbol generation enriches the signature with the newly introduced symbol by extending the signature for all future transitions.

All other rules of the dynamics are changed to account for the allocated symbols. For example, the dynamics of function application cannot be inherited from Chapter 19 but is reformulated as follows:

$$\frac{\nu\,\Sigma\,\{e_1\} \longmapsto \nu\,\Sigma'\,\{e_1'\}}{\nu\,\Sigma\,\{e_1(e_2)\} \longmapsto \nu\,\Sigma'\,\{e_1'(e_2)\}} \tag{31.4a}$$

$$\frac{}{\nu\,\Sigma\,\{\,\lambda(x:\tau)\,e(e_2)\,\} \longmapsto \nu\,\Sigma\,\{[e_2/x]e\}} \tag{31.4b}$$

These rules shuffle around the signature to account for symbol declarations within the constituent expressions of the application. Similar rules are required for all other constructs of **SPCF**.

Theorem 31.3 (Preservation). *If $\nu\,\Sigma\,\{e\} \longmapsto \nu\,\Sigma'\,\{e'\}$ and $\vdash_\Sigma e : \tau$, then $\Sigma' \supseteq \Sigma$ and $\vdash_{\Sigma'} e' : \tau$.*

Proof There is only one rule to consider, rule (31.3), which is handled by inversion of rule (31.1).   □

Theorem 31.4 (Progress). *If $\vdash_\Sigma e : \tau$, then either $e\ \mathrm{val}_\Sigma$ or $\nu\,\Sigma\,\{e\} \longmapsto \nu\,\Sigma'\,\{e'\}$ for some Σ' and e'.*

Proof Immediate, by rule (31.3).   □

31.2 Symbol References

Symbols are not themselves values, but they may be used to form values. One useful example is provided by the type $\tau\ \mathrm{sym}$ of *symbol references*. A value of this type has the form $'a$, where a is a symbol in the signature. To compute with a reference, we may branch according to whether it is a reference to a specified symbol. The syntax of symbol references is given by the following grammar:

Typ	τ	$::=$	$\mathrm{sym}(\tau)$	$\tau\ \mathrm{sym}$	symbols
Exp	e		$\mathrm{quote}[a]$	$'a$	reference
			$\mathrm{is}[a]\{t.\tau\}(e;e_1;e_2)$	if e is a then e_1 ow e_2	comparison

The expression $\mathrm{quote}[a]$ is a reference to the symbol a, a value of type $\mathrm{sym}(\tau)$. The expression $\mathrm{is}[a]\{t.\tau\}(e;e_1;e_2)$ compares the value of e, which is a reference to some symbol b, with the given symbol a. If b is a, the expression evaluates to e_1, and otherwise to e_2.

31.2.1 Statics

The typing rules for symbol references are as follows:

$$\frac{}{\Gamma \vdash_{\Sigma,a\sim\rho} \mathrm{quote}[a] : \mathrm{sym}(\rho)} \tag{31.5a}$$

$$\frac{\Gamma \vdash_{\Sigma,a\sim\rho} e : \mathrm{sym}(\rho') \quad \Gamma \vdash_{\Sigma,a\sim\rho} e_1 : [\rho/t]\tau \quad \Gamma \vdash_{\Sigma,a\sim\rho} e_2 : [\rho'/t]\tau}{\Gamma \vdash_{\Sigma,a\sim\rho} \mathrm{is}[a]\{t.\tau\}(e;e_1;e_2) : [\rho'/t]\tau} \tag{31.5b}$$

Rule (31.5a) is the introduction rule for the type $\mathrm{sym}(\rho)$. It states that if a is a symbol with associated type ρ, then $\mathrm{quote}[a]$ is an expression of type $\mathrm{sym}(\rho)$. Rule (31.5b) is the elimination rule for the type $\text{sym}(\rho)$. The type associated to the given symbol a need not be the same as the type of the symbol referred to by the expression e. If e evaluates to a reference to a, then these types will coincide, but if it refers to another symbol, $b \neq a$, then these types may well differ.

With this in mind, consider rule (31.5b). *A priori* there is a discrepancy between the type ρ of a and the type ρ' of the symbol referred to by e. This discrepancy is mediated by the type operator $t.\tau$.[1] Regardless of the outcome of the comparison, the overall type of the expression is $[\rho'/t]\tau$. If e evaluates to the symbol a, then we "learn" that the types ρ' and ρ coincide, because the specified and referenced symbol coincide. This coincidence is reflected by the type $[\rho/t]\tau$ for e_1. If e evaluates to some other symbol, $a' \neq a$, then the comparison evaluates to e_2, which is required to have type $[\rho'/t]\tau$; no further information about the type of the symbol is acquired in this branch.

31.2.2 Dynamics

The (scoped) dynamics of symbol references is given by the following rules:

$$\frac{}{\text{quote}[a] \ \text{val}_{\Sigma,a\sim\rho}} \tag{31.6a}$$

$$\frac{}{\text{is}[a]\{t.\tau\}(\text{quote}[a]; e_1; e_2) \underset{\Sigma,a\sim\rho}{\longmapsto} e_1} \tag{31.6b}$$

$$\frac{(a \neq a')}{\text{is}[a]\{t.\tau\}(\text{quote}[a']; e_1; e_2) \underset{\Sigma,a\sim\rho,a'\sim\rho'}{\longmapsto} e_2} \tag{31.6c}$$

$$\frac{e \underset{\Sigma,a\sim\rho}{\longmapsto} e'}{\text{is}[a]\{t.\tau\}(e; e_1; e_2) \underset{\Sigma,a\sim\rho}{\longmapsto} \text{is}[a]\{t.\tau\}(e'; e_1; e_2)} \tag{31.6d}$$

Rules (31.6b) and (31.6c) specify that $\text{is}[a]\{t.\tau\}(e; e_1; e_2)$ branches according to whether the value of e is a reference to the symbol a.

31.2.3 Safety

To ensure that the mobility condition is satisfied, it is important that symbol reference types *not* be deemed mobile.

Theorem 31.5 (Preservation). *If* $\vdash_\Sigma e : \tau$ *and* $e \underset{\Sigma}{\longmapsto} e'$, *then* $\vdash_\Sigma e' : \tau$.

Proof By rule induction on rules (31.6). The most interesting case is rule (31.6b). When the comparison is positive, the types ρ and ρ' must be the same, because each symbol has at most one associated type. Therefore, e_1, which has type $[\rho'/t]\tau$, also has type $[\rho/t]\tau$, as required. $\qquad\square$

Lemma 31.6 (Canonical Forms). *If $\vdash_\Sigma e : \texttt{sym}(\rho)$ and $e\ val_\Sigma$, then $e = \texttt{quote}[a]$ for some a such that $\Sigma = \Sigma', a \sim \rho$.*

Proof By rule induction on rules (31.5), taking account of the definition of values. $\square$

Theorem 31.7 (Progress). *Suppose that $\vdash_\Sigma e : \tau$. Then either $e\ val_\Sigma$, or there exists e' such that $e \underset{\Sigma}{\mapsto} e'$.*

Proof By rule induction on rules (31.5). For example, consider rule (31.5b), in which we have that $\texttt{is}[a]\{t.\tau\}(e; e_1; e_2)$ has some type τ and that $e : \texttt{sym}(\rho)$ for some ρ. By induction either rule (31.6d) applies, or else we have that $e\ val_\Sigma$, in which case we are assured by Lemma 31.6 that e is $\texttt{quote}[a]$ for some symbol b of type ρ declared in Σ. But then progress is assured by rules (31.6b) and (31.6c), because equality of symbols is decidable (either a is b or it is not). $\qquad\square$

31.3 Notes

The concept of a symbol in a programming language was considered by McCarthy in the original formulation of Lisp (McCarthy, 1965). Unfortunately, symbols were not clearly distinguished from variables, leading to unexpected behaviors (see Chapter 32). The present account of symbols was influenced by Pitts and Stark (1993) on the declaration of names in the π-calculus (Milner, 1999). The associated type of a symbol may be used for applications that associate information with the symbol, such as its fluid binding (see Chapter 32) or its string representation (its "print name" in Lisp jargon).

Exercises

31.1. The elimination form for symbol references given in Section 31.2 is "one-sided" in the sense that one may compare a reference to an unknown symbol to a known symbol with a known type. An alternative elimination form provides an *equality test* on symbol references. Formulate such a variation.

31.2. A list of type $(\tau\ \texttt{sym} \times \tau)\,\texttt{list}$ is called an *association list*. Using your solution to Exercise **31.1** define a function $\texttt{find}$ that sends an association list to a mapping of type $\tau\ \texttt{sym} \rightharpoonup \tau\ \texttt{opt}$.

31.3. It would be more efficient to represent an association list by a balanced tree associating values to symbols, but to do so would require a total ordering on symbols (at least among the symbols with the same associated type). What obstacles arise when introducing a linear ordering on symbols?

31.4. In Lisp a *symbolic expression*, or *s-expression*, or *sexpr*, may be thought of as a value of the recursive type

$$\texttt{sexpr} \triangleq \texttt{rec}\, s \,\texttt{is}\, [\texttt{sym} \hookrightarrow \texttt{sym}(s)\,;\texttt{nil} \hookrightarrow \texttt{unit}\,;\texttt{cons} \hookrightarrow s \times s].$$

It is customary to write $\text{cons}(e_0; e_1)$ for $\texttt{fold}(\texttt{cons} \cdot \langle e_0, e_1 \rangle)$, where $e_0 : \texttt{sexpr}$ and $e_1 : \texttt{sexpr}$, and to write $\texttt{nil}$ for $\texttt{fold}(\texttt{nil} \cdot \langle \rangle)$. The *list notation* $(e_0, \ldots, e_{n-1})$ is then used as shorthand for the s-expression

$$\text{cons}(e_0; \ldots \text{cons}(e_{n-1}; \texttt{nil}) \ldots).$$

Because lists involving symbols arise often, it is customary to extend the quotation notation from symbols to general s-expressions so that one need not quote each symbol contained within it. Give the definition of this extension, and work out its meaning for the special case of lists described above.

31.5. Considering symbol allocation to be an effect, give a modal formulation of **SPCF** along the lines of **MPCF** described in Chapter 29. Consider both a scoped and a scope-free extent for symbols.

Note

1 See Chapter 14 for a discussion of type operators.

32 Fluid Binding

In this chapter, we return to the concept of dynamic scoping of variables that was criticized in Chapter 8. There it was observed that dynamic scoping is problematic for at least two reasons. One is that renaming of bound variables is not respected; another is that dynamic scope is not type safe. These violations of the expected behavior of variables is intolerable, because they are at variance with mathematical practice and because they compromise modularity.

It is possible, however, to recover a type-safe analog of dynamic scoping by divorcing it from the concept of a variable, and instead introducing a new mechanism, called *fluid binding*. Fluid binding associates to a symbol (and not a variable) a value of a specified type within a specified scope. The identification principle for bound variables is retained, type safety is not compromised, yet some of the benefits of dynamic scoping are preserved.

32.1 Statics

To account for fluid binding, we enrich **SPCF** defined in Chapter 31 with these constructs to obtain **FSPCF**:

$$\text{Exp} \quad e \quad ::= \quad \begin{array}{lll} \text{put}[a](e_1; e_2) & \text{put } e_1 \text{ for } a \text{ in } e_2 & \text{binding} \\ \text{get}[a] & \text{get } a & \text{retrieval} \end{array}$$

The expression $\text{get}[a]$ evaluates to the value of the current binding of a, if it has one, and is stuck otherwise. The expression $\text{put}[a](e_1; e_2)$ binds the symbol a to the value e_1 for the duration of the evaluation of e_2, at which point the binding of a reverts to what it was prior to the execution. The symbol a is not bound by the put expression but is instead a parameter of it.

The statics of **FSPCF** is defined by judgments of the form

$$\Gamma \vdash_\Sigma e : \tau,$$

much as in Chapter 31, except that here the signature associates a type to each symbol, instead of just declaring the symbol to be in scope. Thus, Σ is here defined to be a finite set of declarations of the form $a \sim \tau$ such that no symbol is declared more than once in the same signature. Note that the association of a type to a symbol is *not* a typing assumption. In particular, the signature Σ enjoys no structural properties and cannot be considered as a form of hypothesis as defined in Chapter 3.

The following rules govern the new expression forms:

$$\overline{\Gamma \vdash_{\Sigma, a \sim \tau} \mathsf{get}[a] : \tau} \tag{32.1a}$$

$$\frac{\Gamma \vdash_{\Sigma, a \sim \tau_1} e_1 : \tau_1 \quad \Gamma \vdash_{\Sigma, a \sim \tau_1} e_2 : \tau_2}{\Gamma \vdash_{\Sigma, a \sim \tau_1} \mathsf{put}[a](e_1; e_2) : \tau_2} \tag{32.1b}$$

Rule (32.1b) specifies that the symbol a is a parameter of the expression that must be declared in Σ.

32.2 Dynamics

The dynamics of **FSPCF** relies on a stack-like allocation of symbols in **SPCF** and maintains an association of values to symbols that tracks this stack-like allocation discipline. To do so, we define a family of transition judgments of the form $e \overset{\mu}{\underset{\Sigma}{\longmapsto}} e'$, where Σ is as in the statics, and μ is a finite function mapping some subset of the symbols declared in Σ to values of the right type. If μ is defined for some symbol a, then it has the form $\mu' \otimes a \hookrightarrow e$ for some μ' and value e. If μ is undefined for some symbol a, we may regard it as having the form $\mu' \otimes a \hookrightarrow \bullet$. We will write $a \hookrightarrow \_$ to stand for either $a \hookrightarrow \bullet$ or $a \hookrightarrow e$ for some expression e.

The dynamics of **FSPCF** is defined by the following rules:

$$\overline{\mathsf{get}[a] \overset{\mu \otimes a \hookrightarrow e}{\underset{\Sigma, a \sim \tau}{\longmapsto}} e} \tag{32.2a}$$

$$\frac{e_1 \overset{\mu}{\underset{\Sigma, a \sim \tau}{\longmapsto}} e_1'}{\mathsf{put}[a](e_1; e_2) \overset{\mu}{\underset{\Sigma, a \sim \tau}{\longmapsto}} \mathsf{put}[a](e_1'; e_2)} \tag{32.2b}$$

$$\frac{e_1 \, \mathsf{val}_{\Sigma, a \sim \tau} \quad e_2 \overset{\mu \otimes a \hookrightarrow e_1}{\underset{\Sigma, a \sim \tau}{\longmapsto}} e_2'}{\mathsf{put}[a](e_1; e_2) \overset{\mu \otimes a \hookrightarrow \_}{\underset{\Sigma, a \sim \tau}{\longmapsto}} \mathsf{put}[a](e_1; e_2')} \tag{32.2c}$$

$$\frac{e_1 \, \mathsf{val}_{\Sigma, a \sim \tau} \quad e_2 \, \mathsf{val}_{\Sigma, a \sim \tau}}{\mathsf{put}[a](e_1; e_2) \overset{\mu}{\underset{\Sigma, a \sim \tau}{\longmapsto}} e_2} \tag{32.2d}$$

Rule (32.2a) specifies that $\mathsf{get}[a]$ evaluates to the current binding of a, if any. Rule (32.2b) specifies that the binding for the symbol a is evaluated before the binding is created. Rule (32.2c) evaluates e_2 in an environment where the symbol a is bound to the value e_1, regardless of whether or not a is already bound in the environment. Rule (32.2d) eliminates the fluid binding for a once evaluation of the extent of the binding has completed.

According to the dynamics of **FSPCF** given by rules (32.2), there is no transition of the form $\mathrm{get}[a] \underset{\Sigma}{\overset{\mu}{\mapsto}} e$ if $\mu(a) = \bullet$. The judgment e unbound$_\Sigma$ states that execution of e will lead to such a "stuck" state and is inductively defined by the following rules:

$$\frac{\mu(a) = \bullet}{\mathrm{get}[a] \text{ unbound}_\mu} \tag{32.3a}$$

$$\frac{e_1 \text{ unbound}_\mu}{\mathrm{put}[a](e_1; e_2) \text{ unbound}_\mu} \tag{32.3b}$$

$$\frac{e_1 \text{ val}_\Sigma \quad e_2 \text{ unbound}_\mu}{\mathrm{put}[a](e_1; e_2) \text{ unbound}_\mu} \tag{32.3c}$$

In a larger language, it would also be necessary to include error propagation rules of the sort discussed in Chapter 6.

32.3 Type Safety

We first define the auxiliary judgment $\mu : \Sigma$ by the following rules:

$$\overline{\emptyset : \emptyset} \tag{32.4a}$$

$$\frac{\vdash_\Sigma e : \tau \quad \mu : \Sigma}{\mu \otimes a \hookrightarrow e : \Sigma, a \sim \tau} \tag{32.4b}$$

$$\frac{\mu : \Sigma}{\mu \otimes a \hookrightarrow \bullet : \Sigma, a \sim \tau} \tag{32.4c}$$

These rules specify that, if a symbol is bound to a value, then that value must be of the type associated to the symbol by Σ. No demand is made in the case that the symbol is unbound (equivalently, bound to a "black hole").

Theorem 32.1 (Preservation). *If $e \underset{\Sigma}{\overset{\mu}{\mapsto}} e'$, where $\mu : \Sigma$ and $\vdash_\Sigma e : \tau$, then $\vdash_\Sigma e' : \tau$.*

Proof   By rule induction on rules (32.2). Rule (32.2a) is handled by the definition of $\mu : \Sigma$. Rule (32.2b) follows by induction. Rule (32.2d) is handled by inversion of rules (32.1). Finally, rule (32.2c) is handled by inversion of rules (32.1) and induction.   □

Theorem 32.2 (Progress). *If $\vdash_\Sigma e : \tau$ and $\mu : \Sigma$, then either e val$_\Sigma$, or e unbound$_\mu$, or there exists e' such that $e \underset{\Sigma}{\overset{\mu}{\mapsto}} e'$.*

Proof   By induction on rules (32.1). For rule (32.1a), we have $\Sigma \vdash a \sim \tau$ from the premise of the rule, and hence, because $\mu : \Sigma$, we have either $\mu(a) = \bullet$ or $\mu(a) = e$ for some e such that $\vdash_\Sigma e : \tau$. In the former case, we have e unbound$_\mu$, and in the latter, we have $\mathrm{get}[a] \underset{\Sigma}{\overset{\mu}{\mapsto}} e$. For rule (32.1b), we have by induction that either e_1 val$_\Sigma$ or e_1 unbound$_\mu$, or

$e_1 \overset{\mu}{\underset{\Sigma}{\mapsto}} e_1'$. In the latter two cases, we may apply rule (32.2b) or rule (32.3b), respectively. If e_1 val$_\Sigma$, we apply induction to obtain that either e_2 val$_\Sigma$, in which case rule (32.2d) applies; e_2 unbound$_\mu$, in which case rule (32.3c) applies; or $e_2 \overset{\mu}{\underset{\Sigma}{\mapsto}} e_2'$, in which case rule (32.2c) applies. $\square$

32.4 Some Subtleties

The value of put e_1 for a in e_2 is the value of e_2, calculated in a context where a is bound to the value of e_1. If e_2 is of a basic type, such as nat, then the reversion of the binding of a cannot influence the meaning of the result.[1]

But what if the type of put e_1 for a in e_2 is a function type, so that the returned value is a λ-abstraction? The body of the returned λ may refer to the binding of a, which is reverted upon return from the put. For example, consider the expression

$$\text{put } 17 \text{ for } a \text{ in } \lambda\, (x : \text{nat})\, x + \text{get } a, \tag{32.5}$$

which has type nat $\to$ nat, given that a is a symbol of type nat. Let us assume, for the sake of discussion, that a is unbound at the point at which this expression is evaluated. Evaluating the put binds a to the number 17 and returns the function $\lambda\, (x : \text{nat})\, x + \text{get } a$. But because a is reverted to its unbound state upon exiting the put, applying this function to an argument will result in an error, unless a binding for a is given. Thus, if f is bound to the result of evaluating (32.5), then the expression

$$\text{put } 21 \text{ for } a \text{ in } f(7) \tag{32.6}$$

will evaluate to 28, whereas evaluation of $f(7)$ in the absence of a surrounding binding for a will incur an error.

Contrast this with the similar expression

$$\text{let } y \text{ be } 17 \text{ in } \lambda\, (x : \text{nat})\, x + y, \tag{32.7}$$

where we have replaced the fluid-bound symbol a by a statically bound variable y. This expression evaluates to $\lambda\, (x : \text{nat})\, x + 17$, which adds 17 to its argument when applied. There is no possibility of an unbound symbol arising at execution time, because variables are interpreted by substitution.

One way to think about this situation is to consider that fluid-bound symbols serve as an alternative to passing extra arguments to a function to specialize its value when it is called. To see this, let e stand for the value of expression (32.5), a λ-abstraction whose body is dependent on the binding of the symbol a. To use this function safely, it is necessary that the programmer provide a binding for a prior to calling it. For example, the expression

$$\text{put } 7 \text{ for } a \text{ in } (e(9))$$

evaluates to 16, and the expression

$$\text{put } 8 \text{ for } a \text{ in } (e(9))$$

evaluates to 17. Writing just $e(9)$, without a surrounding binding for a, results in a run-time error attempting to retrieve the binding of the unbound symbol a.

This behavior can be simulated by adding an argument to the function value that will be bound to the current binding of the symbol a at the point where the function is called. Instead of using fluid binding, we would provide an extra argument at each call site, writing

$$e'(7)(9)$$

and

$$e'(8)(9),$$

respectively, where e' is the λ-abstraction

$$\lambda(y:\mathtt{nat})\lambda(x:\mathtt{nat})x + y.$$

Adding arguments can be cumbersome, though, especially when several call sites provide the same binding for a. Using fluid binding, we may write

$$\mathtt{put}\,7\,\mathtt{for}\,a\,\mathtt{in}\,\langle e(8), e(9)\rangle,$$

whereas using an extra argument we must write

$$\langle e'(7)(8), e'(7)(9)\rangle.$$

However, such redundancy can be reduced by factoring out the common part, writing

$$\mathtt{let}\,f\,\mathtt{be}\,e'(7)\,\mathtt{in}\,\langle f(8), f(9)\rangle.$$

The awkwardness of this simulation is usually taken as an argument in favor of including fluid binding in a language. The drawback, which is often perceived as an advantage, is that nothing in the type of a function reveals its dependency on the binding of a symbol. It is therefore quite easy to forget that such a binding is required, leading to run-time failures that might better be caught at compile time.

32.5 Fluid References

The $\mathtt{get}$ and $\mathtt{put}$ operations for fluid binding are indexed by a symbol that must be given as part of the syntax of the operator. It is sometimes useful to defer until run-time the choice of fluid on which a $\mathtt{get}$ or $\mathtt{put}$ acts. *References* to fluids allow the name of the fluid to be a value. References come equipped with analogs of the $\mathtt{get}$ and $\mathtt{put}$ primitives, but for a dynamically determined symbol.

We may extend **FSPCF** with fluid references by adding the following syntax:

Typ	τ	$::=$	$\mathtt{fluid}(\tau)$	$\tau\,\mathtt{fluid}$	fluid
Exp	e	$::=$	$\mathtt{fl}[a]$	$\&\,a$	reference
			$\mathtt{getfl}(e)$	$\mathtt{getfl}\,e$	retrieval
			$\mathtt{putfl}(e; e_1; e_2)$	$\mathtt{putfl}\,e\,\mathtt{is}\,e_1\,\mathtt{in}\,e_2$	binding

The expression $\mathtt{fl}[a]$ is the symbol a considered as a value of type $\mathtt{fluid}(\tau)$. The expressions $\mathtt{getfl}(e)$ and $\mathtt{putfl}(e; e_1; e_2)$ are analogs of the $\mathtt{get}$ and $\mathtt{put}$ operations for fluid-bound symbols.

The statics of these constructs is given by the following rules:

$$\frac{}{\Gamma \vdash_{\Sigma, a \sim \tau} \mathtt{fl}[a] : \mathtt{fluid}(\tau)} \tag{32.8a}$$

$$\frac{\Gamma \vdash_{\Sigma} e : \mathtt{fluid}(\tau)}{\Gamma \vdash_{\Sigma} \mathtt{getfl}(e) : \tau} \tag{32.8b}$$

$$\frac{\Gamma \vdash_{\Sigma} e : \mathtt{fluid}(\tau) \quad \Gamma \vdash_{\Sigma} e_1 : \tau \quad \Gamma \vdash_{\Sigma} e_2 : \tau_2}{\Gamma \vdash_{\Sigma} \mathtt{putfl}(e; e_1; e_2) : \tau_2} \tag{32.8c}$$

Because we are using a scoped dynamics, references to fluids cannot be deemed mobile.

The dynamics of references consists of resolving the referent and deferring to the underlying primitives acting on symbols.

$$\frac{}{\mathtt{fl}[a] \ \mathsf{val}_{\Sigma, a \sim \tau}} \tag{32.9a}$$

$$\frac{e \overset{\mu}{\underset{\Sigma}{\mapsto}} e'}{\mathtt{getfl}(e) \overset{\mu}{\underset{\Sigma}{\mapsto}} \mathtt{getfl}(e')} \tag{32.9b}$$

$$\frac{}{\mathtt{getfl}(\mathtt{fl}[a]) \overset{\mu}{\underset{\Sigma}{\mapsto}} \mathtt{get}[a]} \tag{32.9c}$$

$$\frac{e \overset{\mu}{\underset{\Sigma}{\mapsto}} e'}{\mathtt{putfl}(e; e_1; e_2) \overset{\mu}{\underset{\Sigma}{\mapsto}} \mathtt{putfl}(e'; e_1; e_2)} \tag{32.9d}$$

$$\frac{}{\mathtt{putfl}(\mathtt{fl}[a]; e_1; e_2) \overset{\mu}{\underset{\Sigma}{\mapsto}} \mathtt{put}[a](e_1; e_2)} \tag{32.9e}$$

32.6 Notes

Dynamic binding arose in early dialects of Lisp from not distinguishing variables from symbols. When separated, variables retain their substitutive meaning, and symbols give rise to a separate concept of fluid binding. Allen (1978) discusses the implementation of fluid binding. The present formulation here draws on Nanevski (2003).

Exercises

32.1. *Deep binding* is an implementation of fluid binding where the value associated to a symbol is stored on the control stack as part of a put frame, and is retrieved by finding the most recent such association. Define a stack machine for **FSPCF** that implements deep binding by extending the **FPCF** machine. Be sure to consider new as well as put and get. Attempting to get the binding for an unbound symbol signals a failure; otherwise, its most recent binding is returned. Where do the issues discussed in Section 32.4 arise? *Hint:* you will need to introduce an auxiliary judgment $k \geq k'\ ?\ a$, which searches for the binding of the symbol a on the stack k', returning its value (or failure) to the stack k.

32.2. *Shallow binding* is an implementation of fluid binding that maintains a mapping sending each active symbol to a *stack* of values, the topmost being the active binding for that symbol. Define a stack machine for **FSPCF** that maintains such a mapping to facilitate access to the binding of a symbol. *Hint:* use evaluation states of the form $k \parallel \mu \triangleright e$, where μ is a mapping each symbol a allocated on k to a stack of values, the topmost element of which, if any, is the current binding of a. Use similar forms of return and fail states, and ensure that the mapping invariant is maintained.

32.3. Exception handlers can be implemented by combining fluid binding with continuations (Chapter 30). Reserve a single fluid-bound symbol hdlr that is always bound to the active exception handler, which is represented by a continuation accepting a value of type τ_{exn}. Raising an exception consists of throwing an exception value to this continuation. When entering the scope of a handler, a continuation representing the "otherwise" clause is put as the binding of hdlr. Give a precise formulation of exception handling based on this summary. *Hint:* it is important to ensure that the current handler is maintained for both normal and exceptional returns.

Note

1 As long as the successor is evaluated eagerly; if not, the following examples are adaptable to situations where the value of e_2 is a lazily evaluated number.

33 Dynamic Classification

In Chapters 11 and 26, we investigated the use of sums for classifying values of disparate type. Every value of a classified type is labeled with a symbol that determines the type of the instance data. A classified value is decomposed by pattern matching against a known class, which reveals the type of the instance data. Under this representation, the possible classes of an object are determined *statically* by its type. However, it is sometimes useful to allow the possible classes of data value to be determined *dynamically*.

Dynamic generation of classes has many applications, most of which derive from the guarantee that a newly allocated class is distinct from all others that have been or ever will be generated. In this regard a dynamic class is a "secret" whose disclosure can be used to limit the flow of information in a program. In particular, a dynamically classified value is opaque unless its identity has been disclosed by its creator. Thus, dynamic classification can be used to ensure that an exception reaches only its intended handler, or that a message on a communication channel reaches only the intended recipient.

33.1 Dynamic Classes

A dynamic class is a symbol is generated at run-time. A classified value consists of a symbol of type τ together with a value of that type. To compute with a classified value, it is compared with a known class. If the value is of this class, the underlying instance data are passed to the positive branch; otherwise, the negative branch is taken, where it is matched against other known classes.

33.1.1 Statics

The syntax of dynamic classification is given by the following grammar:

Typ	τ	::=	clsfd	clsfd	classified
Exp	e	::=	$\text{in}[a](e)$	$a \cdot e$	instance
			$\text{isin}[a](e; x.e_1; e_2)$	$\text{match } e \text{ as } a \cdot x \hookrightarrow e_1 \text{ ow} \hookrightarrow e_2$	comparison

The expression $\text{in}[a](e)$ is a classified value with class a and underlying value e. The expression $\text{isin}[a](e; x.e_1; e_2)$ checks whether the class of the value given by e is a. If so, the classified value is passed to e_1; if not, the expression e_2 is evaluated instead.

The statics of dynamic classification is defined by these rules:

$$\frac{\Gamma \vdash_{\Sigma, a \sim \tau} e : \tau}{\Gamma \vdash_{\Sigma, a \sim \tau} in[a](e) : \texttt{clsfd}} \tag{33.1a}$$

$$\frac{\Gamma \vdash_{\Sigma, a \sim \tau} e : \texttt{clsfd} \quad \Gamma, x : \tau \vdash_{\Sigma, a \sim \tau} e_1 : \tau' \quad \Gamma \vdash_{\Sigma, a \sim \tau} e_2 : \tau'}{\Gamma \vdash_{\Sigma, a \sim \tau} isin[a](e; x.e_1; e_2) : \tau'} \tag{33.1b}$$

The typing judgment is indexed by a signature associating a type to each symbol. Here the type governs the instance data associated to each symbol.

33.1.2 Dynamics

To maximize the flexibility in using dynamic classification, we will consider a free dynamics for symbol generation. Within this framework, the dynamics of classification is given by the following rules:

$$\frac{e \ \mathsf{val}_\Sigma}{in[a](e) \ \mathsf{val}_\Sigma} \tag{33.2a}$$

$$\frac{\nu \Sigma \{ e \} \longmapsto \nu \Sigma' \{ e' \}}{\nu \Sigma \{ in[a](e) \} \longmapsto \nu \Sigma' \{ in[a](e') \}} \tag{33.2b}$$

$$\frac{e \ \mathsf{val}_\Sigma}{\nu \Sigma \{ isin[a](in[a](e); x.e_1; e_2) \} \longmapsto \nu \Sigma \{ [e/x]e_1 \}} \tag{33.2c}$$

$$\frac{e' \ \mathsf{val}_\Sigma \quad (a \neq a')}{\nu \Sigma \{ isin[a](in[a'](e'); x.e_1; e_2) \} \longmapsto \nu \Sigma \{ e_2 \}} \tag{33.2d}$$

$$\frac{\nu \Sigma \{ e \} \longmapsto \nu \Sigma' \{ e' \}}{\nu \Sigma \{ isin[a](e; x.e_1; e_2) \} \longmapsto \nu \Sigma' \{ isin[a](e'; x.e_1; e_2) \}} \tag{33.2e}$$

Throughout, if the states involved are well-formed, then there will be a declaration $a \sim \tau$ for some type τ in Σ.

The dynamics of the elimination form for the type $\texttt{clsfd}$ relies on *disequality* of names (specifically, rule (33.2d)). Because disequality is not preserved under substitution, it is not sensible to consider any language construct whose dynamics relies on such a substitution. To see what goes wrong, consider the expression

$$\texttt{match}\, b \cdot \langle \rangle \,\texttt{as}\, a \cdot \_ \hookrightarrow \texttt{true}\, \texttt{ow} \hookrightarrow \texttt{match}\, b \cdot \langle \rangle \,\texttt{as}\, b \cdot \_ \hookrightarrow \texttt{false}\, \texttt{ow} \hookrightarrow \texttt{true}.$$

This expression evaluates to $\texttt{false}$, because the outer conditional is on the class a, which is *a priori* different from b. However, if we substitute b for a in this expression, we obtain

$$\texttt{match}\, b \cdot \langle \rangle \,\texttt{as}\, b \cdot \_ \hookrightarrow \texttt{true}\, \texttt{ow} \hookrightarrow \texttt{match}\, b \cdot \langle \rangle \,\texttt{as}\, b \cdot \_ \hookrightarrow \texttt{false}\, \texttt{ow} \hookrightarrow \texttt{true},$$

which evaluate to $\texttt{true}$, because now the outer conditional governs the evaluation.

33.1.3 Safety

Theorem 33.1 (Safety).

1. *If $\vdash_\Sigma e : \tau$ and $\nu \Sigma \{ e \} \longmapsto \nu \Sigma' \{ e' \}$, then $\Sigma' \supseteq \Sigma$ and $\vdash_{\Sigma'} e' : \tau$.*
2. *If $\vdash_\Sigma e : \tau$, then either e val_Σ or $\nu \Sigma \{ e \} \longmapsto \nu \Sigma' \{ e' \}$ for some e' and Σ'.*

Proof   Similar to the safety proofs given in Chapters 11 and 31.   □

33.2 Class References

The type $\mathtt{cls}(\tau)$ has as values references to classes.

Typ	τ	$::=$	$\mathtt{cls}(\tau)$	$\tau\,\mathtt{cls}$	class reference
Exp	e	$::=$	$\mathtt{cls}[a]$	$\&\,a$	reference
			$\mathtt{mk}(e_1; e_2)$	$\mathtt{mk}(e_1; e_2)$	instance
			$\mathtt{isof}(e_0; e_1; x.e_2; e_3)$	$\mathtt{isof}(e_0; e_1; x.e_2; e_3)$	dispatch

The statics of these constructs is given by the following rules:

$$\frac{}{\Gamma \vdash_{\Sigma, a \sim \tau} \mathtt{cls}[a] : \mathtt{cls}(\tau)} \tag{33.3a}$$

$$\frac{\Gamma \vdash_\Sigma e_1 : \mathtt{cls}(\tau) \quad \Gamma \vdash_\Sigma e_2 : \tau}{\Gamma \vdash_\Sigma \mathtt{mk}(e_1; e_2) : \mathtt{clsfd}} \tag{33.3b}$$

$$\frac{\Gamma \vdash_\Sigma e_0 : \mathtt{cls}(\tau) \quad \Gamma \vdash_\Sigma e_1 : \mathtt{clsfd} \quad \Gamma, x : \tau \vdash_\Sigma e_2 : \tau' \quad \Gamma \vdash_\Sigma e_3 : \tau'}{\Gamma \vdash_\Sigma \mathtt{isof}(e_0; e_1; x.e_2; e_3) : \tau'} \tag{33.3c}$$

The corresponding dynamics is given by these rules:

$$\frac{\nu \Sigma \{ e_1 \} \longmapsto \nu \Sigma' \{ e_1' \}}{\nu \Sigma \{ \mathtt{mk}(e_1; e_2) \} \longmapsto \nu \Sigma' \{ \mathtt{mk}(e_1'; e_2) \}} \tag{33.4a}$$

$$\frac{e_1\,\mathsf{val}_\Sigma \quad \nu \Sigma \{ e_2 \} \longmapsto \nu \Sigma' \{ e_2' \}}{\nu \Sigma \{ \mathtt{mk}(e_1; e_2) \} \longmapsto \nu \Sigma' \{ \mathtt{mk}(e_1; e_2') \}} \tag{33.4b}$$

$$\frac{e\,\mathsf{val}_\Sigma}{\nu \Sigma \{ \mathtt{mk}(\mathtt{cls}[a]; e) \} \longmapsto \nu \Sigma \{ \mathtt{in}[a](e) \}} \tag{33.4c}$$

$$\frac{\nu \Sigma \{ e_0 \} \longmapsto \nu \Sigma' \{ e_0' \}}{\nu \Sigma \{ \mathtt{isof}(e_0; e_1; x.e_2; e_3) \} \longmapsto \nu \Sigma' \{ \mathtt{isof}(e_0'; e_1; x.e_2; e_3) \}} \tag{33.4d}$$

$$\frac{}{\nu \Sigma \{ \mathtt{isof}(\mathtt{cls}[a]; e_1; x.e_2; e_3) \} \longmapsto \nu \Sigma \{ \mathtt{isin}[a](e_1; x.e_2; e_3) \}} \tag{33.4e}$$

Rules (33.4d) and (33.4e) specify that the first argument is evaluated to determine the target class, which is then used to check whether the second argument, a classified data value, is of the target class. This formulation is a two-stage process in which e_0 determines the pattern against which to match the classified value of e_1.

33.3 Definability of Dynamic Classes

The type clsfd can be defined in terms of symbolic references, product types, and existential types by the type expression

$$\texttt{clsfd} \triangleq \exists(t.t \texttt{ sym} \times t).$$

The introduction form $\texttt{in}[a](e)$, in which a is a symbol with associated type is τ and e is an expression of type τ, is defined to be the package

$$\texttt{pack } \tau \texttt{ with } \langle 'a, e \rangle \texttt{ as } \exists(t.t \texttt{ sym} \times t). \tag{33.5}$$

The elimination form $\texttt{isin}[a](e; x.e_1; e_2)$, of some type τ', and where the type associated to a is τ, is defined in terms of symbol comparison (see Chapter 31), together with existential and product elimination, and function types. By rule (33.1b), the type of e is clsfd, which is now the existential type (33.5). Similarly, the branches both have the overall type τ', and within e_1 the variable x has type τ. The elimination form for the type clsfd is defined to be

$$\texttt{open } e \texttt{ as } t \texttt{ with } \langle x, y \rangle{:}t \texttt{ sym} \times t \texttt{ in } (e_{body}(y)),$$

where e_{body} is an expression to be defined shortly. It opens the package e which is an element of the type (33.5), decomposing it into a type t a symbol reference x of type t sym, and an associated value y of type t. The expression e_{body} will turn out to have the type $t \rightharpoonup \tau'$ so that the application to y will be type correct.

The expression e_{body} compares the symbolic reference x to the symbol a of type τ, yielding a value of type $t \rightharpoonup \tau'$. The expression e_{body} is

$$\texttt{is}[a]\{u.u \rightharpoonup \tau'\}(x; e_1'; e_2'),$$

where, as specified by rule (31.5b), e_1' has type $[\tau/u](u \rightharpoonup \tau') = \tau \rightharpoonup \tau'$, and e_2' has type $[t/u](u \rightharpoonup \tau') = t \rightharpoonup \tau'$. The expression e_1' "knows" that the abstract type t is τ, the type associated to the symbol a, because the comparison is positive. On the other hand, e_2' does not "learn" anything about the type t.

It remains to choose the expressions e_1' and e_2'. In the case of a positive comparison, we wish to pass the classified value to the expression e_1 by substitution for the variable x. We therefore define e_1' to be the expression

$$\lambda(x : \tau) e_1 : \tau \rightharpoonup \tau'.$$

In the case of a negative comparison, no value is propagated to e_2. We therefore define e_2' to be the expression

$$\lambda(\_ : t) e_2 : t \rightharpoonup \tau'.$$

We may then check that the statics and dynamics given in Section 33.1 are derivable under these definitions.

33.4 Applications of Dynamic Classification

Dynamic classification has a number of interesting applications in programming. The most obvious is to generalize dynamic dispatch (Chapter 26) to support computation over a dynamically extensible type of heterogeneous values. Introducing a new class requires introducing a new row in the dispatch matrix defining the behavior of the methods on the newly defined class. To allow for this, the rows of the matrix must be indexed by class references, rather than by classes, so that it is accessible without knowing statically the class.

Another application is to use dynamic classification as a form of "perfect encryption" that ensures that classified values can neither be constructed nor deconstructed without knowing the class in question. Abstract encryption of this form can be used to ensure privacy of communication among the parties in a computation. One example of such a scenario is in channel-based communication, as will be considered in Chapter 40. Another, less obvious, application is to ensure that an exception value may only be received by the intended handler, and no other.

33.4.1 Classifying Secrets

Dynamic classification can be used to enforce *confidentiality* and *integrity* of data values in a program. A value of type clsfd may only be constructed by *sealing* it with some class a and may only be deconstructed by a case analysis that includes a branch for a. By controlling which parties in a multi-party interaction have access to the classifier a we may control how classified values are created (ensuring their *integrity*) and how they are inspected (ensuring their *confidentiality*). Any party that lacks access to a cannot decipher a value classified by a, nor may it create a classified value with this class. Because classes are dynamically generated symbols, they offer an absolute confidentiality guarantee among parties in a computation.[1]

Consider the following simple protocol for controlling the integrity and confidentiality of data in a program. A fresh symbol a is introduced, and we return a pair of functions of type

$$(\tau \rightharpoonup \texttt{clsfd}) \times (\texttt{clsfd} \rightharpoonup \tau \texttt{ opt}),$$

called the *constructor* and *destructor* functions for that class, which is accomplished by writing

```
new a ~ τ in
  ⟨ λ(x : τ)a · x,
    λ(x : clsfd)match x as a · y ↪ just(y)ow ↪ null ⟩.
```

The first function creates a value classified by a, and the second function recovers the instance data of a value classified by a. Outside of the scope of the declaration, the symbol a is an unguessable secret.

To enforce the *integrity* of a value of type τ, it suffices to ensure that only trusted parties have access to the constructor. To enforce the *confidentiality* of a value of type τ it suffices to ensure that only trusted parties have access to the destructor. Ensuring the integrity of a value amounts to associating an invariant to it that is maintained by the trusted parties that may create an instance of that class. Ensuring the confidentiality of a value amounts to propagating the invariant to parties that may decipher it.

33.4.2 Exception Values

Exception handling is a communication between two agents, one that may raise an exception, and one that may handle it. We wish to ensure that an exception can be caught only by a designated handler, without fear that any intervening handler may intercept it. This secrecy property can be ensured by using dynamic class allocation. A new class is declared, with the ability to create an instance given only to the raising agent and the ability to match an instance given only to the handler. The exception value cannot be intercepted by any other handler, because no other handler is capable of matching it. This property is crucial to "black box" composition of programs from components. Without dynamic classification one can never be sure that alien code cannot intercept an exception intended for a handler within one's own code, or *vice versa*.

With this in mind, let us now reconsider the choice of the type τ_{exn} of exception values specified in Chapter 29. There we distinguished the *closed-world* assumption, which amounts to defining τ_{exn} to be a finite sum type known to the whole program, from the *open-world* assumption, which is realized by defining τ_{exn} to be the type clsfd of dynamically classified values. This choice supports modularity and evolution by allowing fresh exceptions (classes) to be allocated at will, avoiding the need for an up-front agreement on the forms of exception. Another perspective is that dynamic classification treats an exception as a shared secret between the handler and the raiser of that exception. When an exception value is raised, it can only be intercepted and analyzed by a handler that can match the value against the specified class. It is only by using dynamic classification that one can gain control over the flow of information in a program that uses exceptions. Without it, an unintended handler can intercept an exception that was not intended for it, disrupting the logic of the program.

33.5 Notes

Dynamic classification appears in Standard ML (Milner et al., 1997) as the type exn. The usefulness of the type exn is obscured by its too-close association with the exception mechanism. The π-calculus (Milner, 1999) popularized using "name generation" and "channel passing" to control the connectivity and information flow in a process network. In Chapter 40, we shall make explicit that this aspect of the π-calculus is an application of dynamic classification.

Exercises

33.1. Consider the following *open-world named exception* mechanism, which is typical of the exception mechanism found in many languages.

exception a of τ in e	declare an exception a of type τ in e
raise a with e	raise exception a with value e
try e ow $a_1(x_1) \hookrightarrow e_1 \mid \ldots \mid a_n(x_n) \hookrightarrow e_n \mid x \hookrightarrow e'$	handle exceptions $a_1, \ldots, a_n$

Exceptions are declared by name, specifying the type of their associated values. Each execution of an exception declaration generates a *fresh* exception. An exception is raised by specifying the exception name and a value to associate with it. The handler intercepts any finite number of named exceptions, passing their associated values to handlers and otherwise propagates the exception to the default handler.

The following rules define the statics of these constructs:

$$\frac{\Gamma \vdash_{\Sigma, a \sim \tau} e : \tau'}{\Gamma \vdash_{\Sigma} \text{exception } a \text{ of } \tau \text{ in } e : \tau'} \tag{33.6a}$$

$$\frac{\Sigma \vdash a \sim \tau \quad \Gamma \vdash_{\Sigma} e : \tau}{\Gamma \vdash_{\Sigma} \text{raise } a \text{ with } e : \tau'} \tag{33.6b}$$

$$\frac{\Sigma \vdash a_1 \sim \tau_1 \quad \ldots \quad \Sigma \vdash a_n \sim \tau_n \quad \Gamma \vdash_{\Sigma} e : \tau'}{\Gamma, x_1 : \tau_1 \vdash_{\Sigma} e_1 : \tau' \quad \ldots \quad \Gamma, x_n : \tau_n \vdash e_n : \tau' \quad \Gamma, x : \tau_{\text{exn}} \vdash e' : \tau'}{\Gamma \vdash_{\Sigma} \text{try } e \text{ ow } a_1(x_1) \hookrightarrow e_1 \mid \ldots \mid a_n(x_n) \hookrightarrow e_n \mid x \hookrightarrow e' : \tau'} \tag{33.6c}$$

Give an implementation of named exceptions in terms of dynamic classification and general value-passing exceptions (Chapter 29).

33.2. Show that dynamic classification with dynamic classes can be implemented in the combination of **FPC** and **FE**$_\omega$ enriched with references to free assignables, and with no modal separation (so as to permit benign effects). Specifically, provide a package of the following higher-kind existential type:

$$\tau \triangleq \exists\, clsfd :: \text{T}.\exists\, class :: \text{T} \to \text{T}.\langle \text{new} \hookrightarrow \tau_{\text{new}}, \text{mk} \hookrightarrow \tau_{\text{mk}}, \text{isof} \hookrightarrow \tau_{\text{isof}} \rangle.$$

where

$$\tau_{\text{new}} \triangleq \forall(t.cls[t])$$

$$\tau_{\text{mk}} \triangleq \forall(t.(cls[t] \times t) \to clsfd)$$

$$\tau_{\text{isof}} \triangleq \forall(t.\forall(u.(cls[t] \times clsfd \times (t \to u) \times u) \to u)).$$

These operations correspond to the mechanisms of dynamic classification described earlier in this chapter. *Hint:* Define $cls[t]$ to be t opt ref, and define $clsfd$ so that a classified value is represented by an encapsulated assignment to its class. Creating a new class allocates a reference, creating a classified value creates an encapsulated assignment, and testing for a class is implemented by assigning to the target class, then running the classified value, and seeing whether the contents of the target class has changed.

33.3. Open-world named exceptions obstruct exception tracking (as described in Exercise **29.4**).

(a) Show that it is not computable to track the exact set of exception names that might be raised by an expression.

(b) Show that it is impossible to finitely bound set of exceptions that can be thrown by an expression. *Hint*: Show that there are expressions for which any such upper bound is inaccurate.

33.4. Exercise **33.3** may seem disappointing, until you realize that whereas *positive* exception tracking is impossible under the open-world assumption, *negative* exception tracking is not only possible, but more desirable. It is often more useful to know that a specified exception *cannot* be raised than it is to know that it *can*. Negative exception tracking can be expressed using *exclusion refinements* of the form $\overline{X}$, where X is a finite set of dynamic classes. Informally, a value satisfies such a refinement only if its class is not among those in the set X. Define a system of exclusion refinements by defining entailment and satisfaction for them. Be sure to state refinement rules for class allocation and for the introduction and elimination forms for the type `clsfd`.

Note

---

1 Of course, this guarantee is for programs written in conformance with the statics given here. If the abstraction imposed by the type system is violated, no guarantees of confidentiality can be made.

PART XIV

Mutable State

34

Modernized Algol

Modernized Algol, or **MA**, is an imperative, block-structured programming language based on the classic language Algol. **MA** extends **PCF** with a new syntactic sort of *commands* that act on *assignables* by retrieving and altering their contents. Assignables are introduced by *declaring* them for use within a specified scope; this is the essence of block structure. Commands are combined by sequencing and are iterated using recursion.

MA maintains a careful separation between *pure* expressions, whose meaning does not depend on any assignables, and *impure* commands, whose meaning is given in terms of assignables. The segregation of pure from impure ensures that the evaluation order for expressions is not constrained by the presence of assignables in the language, so that they can be manipulated just as in **PCF**. Commands, on the other hand, have a constrained execution order, because the execution of one may affect the meaning of another.

A distinctive feature of **MA** is that it adheres to the *stack discipline*, which means that assignables are allocated on entry to the scope of their declaration, and deallocated on exit, using a conventional stack discipline. Stack allocation avoids the need for more complex forms of storage management, at the cost of reducing the expressive power of the language.

34.1 Basic Commands

The syntax of the language **MA** of modernized Algol distinguishes pure *expressions* from impure *commands*. The expressions include those of **PCF** (as described in Chapter 19), augmented with one construct, and the commands are those of a simple imperative programming language based on assignment. The language maintains a sharp distinction between *variables* and *assignables*. Variables are introduced by λ-abstraction and are given meaning by substitution. Assignables are introduced by a declaration and are given meaning by assignment and retrieval of their *contents*, which is, for the time being, restricted to natural numbers. Expressions evaluate to values, and have no effect on assignables. Commands are executed for their effect on assignables, and return a value. Composition of commands not only sequences their execution order, but also passes the value returned by the first to the second before it is executed. The returned value of a command is, for the time being, restricted to the natural numbers. (But see Section 34.3 for the general case.)

The syntax of **MA** is given by the following grammar, from which we have omitted repetition of the expression syntax of **PCF** for the sake of brevity.

Typ	τ	::=	cmd	cmd	command
Exp	e	::=	$\text{cmd}(m)$	$\text{cmd}\,m$	encapsulation
Cmd	m	::=	$\text{ret}(e)$	$\text{ret}\,e$	return
			$\text{bnd}(e; x.m)$	$\text{bnd}\,x \leftarrow e \,;\, m$	sequence
			$\text{dcl}(e; a.m)$	$\text{dcl}\,a := e\,\text{in}\,m$	new assignable
			$\text{get}[a]$	$@\,a$	fetch
			$\text{set}[a](e)$	$a := e$	assign

The expression $\text{cmd}(m)$ consists of the unevaluated command m thought of as a value of type cmd. The command $\text{ret}(e)$ returns the value of the expression e without having any effect on the assignables. The command $\text{bnd}(e; x.m)$ evaluates e to an encapsulated command, then this command is executed for its effects on assignables, with its value substituted for x in m. The command $\text{dcl}(e; a.m)$ introduces a new assignable, a, for use within the command m whose initial contents is given by the expression e. The command $\text{get}[a]$ returns the current contents of the assignable a and the command $\text{set}[a](e)$ changes the contents of the assignable a to the value of e, and returns that value.

34.1.1 Statics

The statics of **MA** consists of two forms of judgment:

1. Expression typing: $\Gamma \vdash_\Sigma e : \tau$.
2. Command formation: $\Gamma \vdash_\Sigma m$ ok.

The context Γ specifies the types of variables, as usual, and the signature Σ consists of a finite set of assignables. As with other uses of symbols, the signature cannot be interpreted as a form of typing hypothesis (it enjoys no structural properties of entailment), but must be considered as an index of a family of judgments, one for each choice of Σ.

The statics of **MA** is inductively defined by the following rules:

$$\frac{\Gamma \vdash_\Sigma m \text{ ok}}{\Gamma \vdash_\Sigma \text{cmd}(m) : \text{cmd}} \tag{34.1a}$$

$$\frac{\Gamma \vdash_\Sigma e : \text{nat}}{\Gamma \vdash_\Sigma \text{ret}(e) \text{ ok}} \tag{34.1b}$$

$$\frac{\Gamma \vdash_\Sigma e : \text{cmd} \quad \Gamma, x : \text{nat} \vdash_\Sigma m \text{ ok}}{\Gamma \vdash_\Sigma \text{bnd}(e; x.m) \text{ ok}} \tag{34.1c}$$

$$\frac{\Gamma \vdash_\Sigma e : \text{nat} \quad \Gamma \vdash_{\Sigma,a} m \text{ ok}}{\Gamma \vdash_\Sigma \text{dcl}(e; a.m) \text{ ok}} \tag{34.1d}$$

$$\frac{}{\Gamma \vdash_{\Sigma,a} \mathtt{get}[a] \ \mathsf{ok}} \tag{34.1e}$$

$$\frac{\Gamma \vdash_{\Sigma,a} e : \mathtt{nat}}{\Gamma \vdash_{\Sigma,a} \mathtt{set}[a](e) \ \mathsf{ok}} \tag{34.1f}$$

Rule (34.1a) is the introduction rule for the type cmd, and rule (34.1c) is the corresponding elimination form. Rule (34.1d) introduces a new assignable for use within a specified command. The name a of the assignable is bound by the declaration, and so may be renamed to satisfy the implicit constraint that it not already occur in Σ. Rule (34.1e) states that the command to retrieve the contents of an assignable a returns a natural number. Rule (34.1f) states that we may assign a natural number to an assignable.

34.1.2 Dynamics

The dynamics of **MA** is defined in terms of a *memory* μ a finite function assigning a numeral to each of a finite set of assignables.

The dynamics of expressions consists of these two judgment forms:

1. $e \ \mathsf{val}_\Sigma$, stating that e is a value relative to Σ.
2. $e \underset{\Sigma}{\mapsto} e'$, stating that the expression e steps to the expression e'.

These judgments are inductively defined by the following rules, together with the rules defining the dynamics of **PCF** (see Chapter 19). It is important, however, that the successor operation be given an *eager*, instead of *lazy*, dynamics so that a closed value of type nat is a numeral (for reasons that will be explained in Section 34.3).

$$\frac{}{\mathtt{cmd}(m) \ \mathsf{val}_\Sigma} \tag{34.2a}$$

Rule (34.2a) states that an encapsulated command is a value.

The dynamics of commands is defined in terms of states $m \parallel \mu$, where μ is a memory mapping assignables to values, and m is a command. There are two judgments governing such states:

1. $m \parallel \mu \ \mathsf{final}_\Sigma$. The state $m \parallel \mu$ is complete.
2. $m \parallel \mu \underset{\Sigma}{\mapsto} m' \parallel \mu'$. The state $m \parallel \mu$ steps to the state $m' \parallel \mu'$; the set of active assignables is given by the signature Σ.

These judgments are inductively defined by the following rules:

$$\frac{e \ \mathsf{val}_\Sigma}{\mathtt{ret}(e) \parallel \mu \ \mathsf{final}_\Sigma} \tag{34.3a}$$

$$\frac{e \underset{\Sigma}{\mapsto} e'}{\mathtt{ret}(e) \parallel \mu \underset{\Sigma}{\mapsto} \mathtt{ret}(e') \parallel \mu} \tag{34.3b}$$

$$\frac{e \underset{\Sigma}{\mapsto} e'}{\text{bnd}(e; x.m) \parallel \mu \underset{\Sigma}{\mapsto} \text{bnd}(e'; x.m) \parallel \mu} \tag{34.3c}$$

$$\frac{e \text{ val}_\Sigma}{\text{bnd}(\text{cmd}(\text{ret}(e)); x.m) \parallel \mu \underset{\Sigma}{\mapsto} [e/x]m \parallel \mu} \tag{34.3d}$$

$$\frac{m_1 \parallel \mu \underset{\Sigma}{\mapsto} m_1' \parallel \mu'}{\text{bnd}(\text{cmd}(m_1); x.m_2) \parallel \mu \underset{\Sigma}{\mapsto} \text{bnd}(\text{cmd}(m_1'); x.m_2) \parallel \mu'} \tag{34.3e}$$

$$\frac{}{\text{get}[a] \parallel \mu \otimes a \hookrightarrow e \underset{\Sigma,a}{\longmapsto} \text{ret}(e) \parallel \mu \otimes a \hookrightarrow e} \tag{34.3f}$$

$$\frac{e \underset{\Sigma,a}{\longmapsto} e'}{\text{set}[a](e) \parallel \mu \underset{\Sigma,a}{\longmapsto} \text{set}[a](e') \parallel \mu} \tag{34.3g}$$

$$\frac{e \text{ val}_{\Sigma,a}}{\text{set}[a](e) \parallel \mu \otimes a \hookrightarrow \_ \underset{\Sigma,a}{\longmapsto} \text{ret}(e) \parallel \mu \otimes a \hookrightarrow e} \tag{34.3h}$$

$$\frac{e \underset{\Sigma}{\mapsto} e'}{\text{dcl}(e; a.m) \parallel \mu \underset{\Sigma}{\mapsto} \text{dcl}(e'; a.m) \parallel \mu} \tag{34.3i}$$

$$\frac{e \text{ val}_\Sigma \quad m \parallel \mu \otimes a \hookrightarrow e \underset{\Sigma,a}{\longmapsto} m' \parallel \mu' \otimes a \hookrightarrow e'}{\text{dcl}(e; a.m) \parallel \mu \underset{\Sigma}{\mapsto} \text{dcl}(e'; a.m') \parallel \mu'} \tag{34.3j}$$

$$\frac{e \text{ val}_\Sigma \quad e' \text{ val}_{\Sigma,a}}{\text{dcl}(e; a.\text{ret}(e')) \parallel \mu \underset{\Sigma}{\mapsto} \text{ret}(e') \parallel \mu} \tag{34.3k}$$

Rule (34.3a) specifies that a `ret` command is final if its argument is a value. Rules (34.3c) to (34.3e) specify the dynamics of sequential composition. The expression e must, by virtue of the type system, evaluate to an encapsulated command, which is executed to find its return value, which is then substituted into the command m before executing it.

Rules (34.3i) to (34.3k) define the concept of *block structure* in a programming language. Declarations adhere to the *stack discipline* in that an assignable is allocated during evaluation of the body of the declaration, and deallocated after evaluation of the body is complete. Therefore, the lifetime of an assignable can be identified with its scope, and hence we may visualize the dynamic lifetimes of assignables as being nested inside one another, in the same way as their static scopes are nested inside one another. The stack-like behavior of assignables is a characteristic feature of what are known as *Algol-like languages*.

34.1.3 Safety

The judgment $m \parallel \mu \; \text{ok}_\Sigma$ is defined by the rule

$$\frac{\vdash_\Sigma m \; \text{ok} \quad \mu : \Sigma}{m \parallel \mu \; \text{ok}_\Sigma} \tag{34.4}$$

where the auxiliary judgment $\mu : \Sigma$ is defined by the rule

$$\frac{\forall a \in \Sigma \quad \exists e \quad \mu(a) = e \text{ and } e \; \text{val}_\emptyset \text{ and } \vdash_\emptyset e : \text{nat}}{\mu : \Sigma} \tag{34.5}$$

That is, the memory must bind a number to each assignable in Σ.

Theorem 34.1 (Preservation).

1. *If $e \underset{\Sigma}{\mapsto} e'$ and $\vdash_\Sigma e : \tau$, then $\vdash_\Sigma e' : \tau$.*
2. *If $m \parallel \mu \underset{\Sigma}{\mapsto} m' \parallel \mu'$, with $\vdash_\Sigma m \; \text{ok}$ and $\mu : \Sigma$, then $\vdash_\Sigma m' \; \text{ok}$ and $\mu' : \Sigma$.*

Proof Simultaneously, by induction on rules (34.2) and (34.3).

Consider rule (34.3j). Assume that $\vdash_\Sigma \text{dcl}(e; a.m) \; \text{ok}$ and $\mu : \Sigma$. By inversion of typing we have $\vdash_\Sigma e : \text{nat}$ and $\vdash_{\Sigma,a} m \; \text{ok}$. Because $e \; \text{val}_\Sigma$ and $\mu : \Sigma$, we have $\mu \otimes a \hookrightarrow e : \Sigma, a$. By induction, we have $\vdash_{\Sigma,a} m' \; \text{ok}$ and $\mu' \otimes a \hookrightarrow e' : \Sigma, a$, from which the result follows immediately.

Consider rule (34.3k). Assume that $\vdash_\Sigma \text{dcl}(e; a.\text{ret}(e')) \; \text{ok}$ and $\mu : \Sigma$. By inversion we have $\vdash_\Sigma e : \text{nat}$, and $\vdash_{\Sigma,a} \text{ret}(e') \; \text{ok}$, and so $\vdash_{\Sigma,a} e' : \text{nat}$. But because $e' \; \text{val}_{\Sigma,a}$, and e' is a numeral, and we also have $\vdash_\Sigma e' : \text{nat}$, as required. $\qquad\square$

Theorem 34.2 (Progress).

1. *If $\vdash_\Sigma e : \tau$, then either $e \; \text{val}_\Sigma$, or there exists e' such that $e \underset{\Sigma}{\mapsto} e'$.*
2. *If $\vdash_\Sigma m \; \text{ok}$ and $\mu : \Sigma$, then either $m \parallel \mu \; \text{final}_\Sigma$ or $m \parallel \mu \underset{\Sigma}{\mapsto} m' \parallel \mu'$ for some μ' and m'.*

Proof Simultaneously, by induction on rules (34.1). Consider rule (34.1d). By the first inductive hypothesis we have either $e \underset{\Sigma}{\mapsto} e'$ or $e \; \text{val}_\Sigma$. In the former case, rule (34.3i) applies. In the latter, we have by the second inductive hypothesis,

$$m \parallel \mu \otimes a \hookrightarrow e \; \text{final}_{\Sigma,a} \quad \text{or} \quad m \parallel \mu \otimes a \hookrightarrow e \underset{\Sigma,a}{\longmapsto} m' \parallel \mu' \otimes a \hookrightarrow e'.$$

In the former case, we apply rule (34.3k), and in the latter, rule (34.3j). $\qquad\square$

34.2 Some Programming Idioms

The language **MA** is designed to expose the elegant interplay between the execution of an expression for its value and the execution of a command for its effect on assignables. In this section we show how to derive several standard idioms of imperative programming in **MA**.

We define the *sequential composition* of commands, written $\{x \leftarrow m_1 ; m_2\}$, to stand for the command $\mathtt{bnd}\, x \leftarrow \mathtt{cmd}\,(m_1) ; m_2$. Binary composition readily generalizes to an n-ary form by defining

$$\{x_1 \leftarrow m_1 ; \dots x_{n-1} \leftarrow m_{n-1} ; m_n\},$$

to stand for the iterated composition

$$\{x_1 \leftarrow m_1 ; \dots \{x_{n-1} \leftarrow m_{n-1} ; m_n\}\}.$$

We sometimes write just $\{m_1 ; m_2\}$ for the composition $\{\_ \leftarrow m_1 ; m_2\}$ where the returned value from m_1 is ignored; this generalizes in the obvious way to an n-ary form.

A related idiom, the command $\mathtt{do}\, e$, executes an encapsulated command and returns its result. By definition, $\mathtt{do}\, e$ stands for the command $\mathtt{bnd}\, x \leftarrow e ; \mathtt{ret}\, x$.

The *conditional* command $\mathtt{if}\,(m)\, m_1 \,\mathtt{else}\, m_2$ executes either m_1 or m_2 according to whether the result of executing m is zero or not:

$$\{x \leftarrow m ; \mathtt{do}\,(\mathtt{ifz}\, x \,\{\mathtt{z} \hookrightarrow \mathtt{cmd}\, m_1 \mid \mathtt{s}(\_) \hookrightarrow \mathtt{cmd}\, m_2\})\}.$$

The returned value of the conditional is the value returned by the selected command.

The *while loop* command $\mathtt{while}\,(m_1)\, m_2$ repeatedly executes the command m_2 while the command m_1 yields a non-zero number. It is defined as follows:

$$\mathtt{do}\,(\mathtt{fix}\, loop : \mathtt{cmd}\,\mathtt{is}\,\mathtt{cmd}\,(\mathtt{if}\,(m_1)\,\{\mathtt{ret}\,\mathtt{z}\}\,\mathtt{else}\,\{m_2 ; \mathtt{do}\, loop\})).$$

This command runs the self-referential encapsulated command that, when executed, first executes m_1, branching on the result. If the result is zero, the loop returns zero (arbitrarily). If the result is non-zero, the command m_2 is executed and the loop is repeated.

A *procedure* is a function of type $\tau \rightharpoonup \mathtt{cmd}$ that takes an argument of some type τ and yields an unexecuted command as result. Many procedures have the form $\lambda\,(x : \tau)\,\mathtt{cmd}\, m$, which we abbreviate to $\mathtt{proc}\,(x : \tau)\, m$. A *procedure call* is the composition of a function application with the activation of the resulting command. If e_1 is a procedure and e_2 is its argument, then the procedure call $\mathtt{call}\, e_1(e_2)$ is defined to be the command $\mathtt{do}\,(e_1(e_2))$, which immediately runs the result of applying e_1 to e_2.

As an example, here is a procedure of type nat $\rightharpoonup$ cmd that returns the factorial of its argument:

```
proc (x:nat) {
  dcl r := 1 in
  dcl a := x in
  { while ( @ a ) {
      y ← @ r
    ; z ← @ a
    ; r := (x-z+1)× y
    ; a := z-1
    }
    ; x ← @ r
    ; ret x
  }
}
```

The loop maintains the invariant that the contents of r is the factorial of x minus the contents of a. Initialization makes this invariant true, and it is preserved by each iteration of the loop, so that upon completion of the loop the assignable a contains 0 and r contains the factorial of x, as required.

34.3 Typed Commands and Typed Assignables

So far we have restricted the type of the returned value of a command, and the contents of an assignable, to be nat. Can this restriction be relaxed, while adhering to the stack discipline?

The key to admitting returned and assignable values of other types may be uncovered by a close examination of the proof of Theorem 34.1. For the proof to go through, it is crucial that values of type nat, the type of assignables and return values, cannot contain an assignable, for otherwise the embedded assignable would escape the scope of its declaration. This property is self-evidently true for eagerly evaluated natural numbers but fails when they are evaluated lazily. Thus, the safety of **MA** hinges on the evaluation order for the successor operation, in contrast to most other situations where either interpretation is also safe.

When extending **MA** to admit assignables and returned values of other types, it is necessary to pay close attention to whether assignables can be embedded in a value of a candidate type. For example, if return values of procedure type are allowed, then the following command violates safety:

$$dcl\, a := z\ in\ \{ret\,(proc\,(x : nat)\,\{a := x\})\}.$$

This command, when executed, allocates a new assignable a and returns a procedure that, when called, assigns its argument to a. But this makes no sense, because the assignable a

is deallocated when the body of the declaration returns, but the returned value still refers to it. If the returned procedure is called, execution will get stuck in the attempt to assign to a.

A similar example shows that admitting assignables of procedure type is also unsound. For example, suppose that b is an assignable whose contents are of type $\text{nat} \rightharpoonup \text{cmd}$, and consider the command

$$\text{dcl } a := z \text{ in } \{b := \text{proc}(x : \text{nat}) \text{cmd}(a := x) ; \text{ret } z\}.$$

We assign to b a procedure that uses a locally declared assignable a and then leaves the scope of the declaration. If we then call the procedure stored in b, execution will get stuck attempting to assign to the non-existent assignable a.

To admit declarations that return values other than nat and to admit assignables with contents of types other than nat, we must rework the statics of **MA** to record the returned type of a command and to record the type of the contents of each assignable. First, we generalize the finite set Σ of active assignables to assign a mobile type to each active assignable so that Σ has the form of a finite set of assumptions of the form $a \sim \tau$, where a is an assignable. Second, we replace the judgment $\Gamma \vdash_\Sigma m$ ok by the more general form $\Gamma \vdash_\Sigma m \mathbin{\dot\sim} \tau$, stating that m is a well-formed command returning a value of type τ. Third, the type cmd is generalized to $\text{cmd}(\tau)$, which is written in examples as τ cmd, to specify the return type of the encapsulated command.

The statics given in Section 34.1.1 is generalized to admit typed commands and typed assignables as follows:

$$\frac{\Gamma \vdash_\Sigma m \mathbin{\dot\sim} \tau}{\Gamma \vdash_\Sigma \text{cmd}(m) : \text{cmd}(\tau)} \tag{34.6a}$$

$$\frac{\Gamma \vdash_\Sigma e : \tau}{\Gamma \vdash_\Sigma \text{ret}(e) \mathbin{\dot\sim} \tau} \tag{34.6b}$$

$$\frac{\Gamma \vdash_\Sigma e : \text{cmd}(\tau) \quad \Gamma, x : \tau \vdash_\Sigma m \mathbin{\dot\sim} \tau'}{\Gamma \vdash_\Sigma \text{bnd}(e; x.m) \mathbin{\dot\sim} \tau'} \tag{34.6c}$$

$$\frac{\Gamma \vdash_\Sigma e : \tau \quad \tau \text{ mobile} \quad \Gamma \vdash_{\Sigma, a \sim \tau} m \mathbin{\dot\sim} \tau' \quad \tau' \text{ mobile}}{\Gamma \vdash_\Sigma \text{dcl}(e; a.m) \mathbin{\dot\sim} \tau'} \tag{34.6d}$$

$$\frac{}{\Gamma \vdash_{\Sigma, a \sim \tau} \text{get}[a] \mathbin{\dot\sim} \tau} \tag{34.6e}$$

$$\frac{\Gamma \vdash_{\Sigma, a \sim \tau} e : \tau}{\Gamma \vdash_{\Sigma, a \sim \tau} \text{set}[a](e) \mathbin{\dot\sim} \tau} \tag{34.6f}$$

Apart from the generalization to track returned types and content types, the most important change is that in rule (34.6d) both the type of a declared assignable and the return type of the declaration is required to be *mobile*. The definition of the judgment τ mobile is guided by the following *mobility condition*:

$$\text{if } \tau \text{ mobile}, \ \vdash_\Sigma e : \tau \text{ and } e \text{ val}_\Sigma, \text{ then } \vdash_\emptyset e : \tau \text{ and } e \text{ val}_\emptyset. \tag{34.7}$$

That is, a value of mobile type may not depend on any active assignables.

As long as the successor operation is evaluated eagerly, the type nat is mobile:

$$\frac{}{\mathtt{nat\ mobile}} \tag{34.8}$$

Similarly, a product of mobile types may safely be deemed mobile, if pairs are evaluated eagerly:

$$\frac{\tau_1 \text{ mobile} \quad \tau_2 \text{ mobile}}{\tau_1 \times \tau_2 \text{ mobile}} \tag{34.9}$$

And the same goes for sums, if the injections are evaluated eagerly:

$$\frac{\tau_1 \text{ mobile} \quad \tau_2 \text{ mobile}}{\tau_1 + \tau_2 \text{ mobile}} \tag{34.10}$$

In each of these cases, laziness defeats mobility, because values may contain suspended computations that depend on an assignable. For example, if the successor operation for the natural numbers were evaluated lazily, then $s(e)$ would be a value for any expression e including one that refers to an assignable a.

Because the body of a procedure may involve an assignable, no procedure type is mobile, nor is any command type. What about function types other than procedure types? We may think they are mobile, because a pure expression cannot depend on an assignable. Although this is the case, the mobility condition need not hold. For example, consider the following value of type $\mathtt{nat} \rightharpoonup \mathtt{nat}$:

$$\lambda\,(x : \mathtt{nat})\,(\lambda\,(\_ : \tau\ \mathtt{cmd})\,\mathtt{z})(\mathtt{cmd}\,\{@\,a\}).$$

Although the assignable a is not actually needed to compute the result, it nevertheless occurs in the value, violating the mobility condition.

The mobility restriction on the statics of declarations ensures that the type associated to an assignable is always mobile. We may therefore assume, without loss of generality, that the types associated to the assignables in the signature Σ are mobile.

Theorem 34.3 (Preservation for Typed Commands).

1. *If* $e \underset{\Sigma}{\longmapsto} e'$ *and* $\vdash_\Sigma e : \tau$, *then* $\vdash_\Sigma e' : \tau$.
2. *If* $m \parallel \mu \underset{\Sigma}{\longmapsto} m' \parallel \mu'$, *with* $\vdash_\Sigma m \mathrel{\dot{\sim}} \tau$ *and* $\mu : \Sigma$, *then* $\vdash_\Sigma m' \mathrel{\dot{\sim}} \tau$ *and* $\mu' : \Sigma$.

Theorem 34.4 (Progress for Typed Commands).

1. *If* $\vdash_\Sigma e : \tau$, *then either* $e \ \mathit{val}_\Sigma$, *or there exists* e' *such that* $e \underset{\Sigma}{\longmapsto} e'$.
2. *If* $\vdash_\Sigma m \mathrel{\dot{\sim}} \tau$ *and* $\mu : \Sigma$, *then either* $m \parallel \mu \ \mathit{final}_\Sigma$ *or* $m \parallel \mu \underset{\Sigma}{\longmapsto} m' \parallel \mu'$ *for some* μ' *and* m'.

The proofs of Theorems 34.3 and 34.4 follows very closely the proof of Theorems 34.1 and 34.2. The main difference is that we appeal to the mobility condition to ensure that returned values and stored values are independent of the active assignables.

34.4 Notes

Modernized Algol is a derivative of Reynolds's Idealized Algol (Reynolds, 1981). In contrast to Reynolds's formulation, Modernized Algol maintains a separation between computations that depend on the memory and those that do not, and does not rely on call-by-name for function application, but rather has a type of encapsulated commands that can be used where call-by-name would otherwise be required. The modal distinction between expressions and commands was present in the original formulation of Algol 60 but is developed here in light of the concept of monadic effects introduced by Moggi (1989). Its role in functional programming was emphasized by Wadler (1992). The modal separation in **MA** is adapted directly from Pfenning and Davies (2001), which stresses the connection to lax modal logic.

What are called *assignables* here are invariably called *variables* elsewhere. The distinction between variables and assignables is blurred in languages that allow assignables as forms of expression. (Indeed, Reynolds himself[1] regards this as a defining feature of Algol, in opposition to the formulation given here.) In **MA**, we choose to make the distinction between variables, which are given meaning by substitution, and assignables, which are given meaning by mutation. Drawing this distinction requires new terminology; the term *assignable* seems apt for the imperative programming concept.

The concept of mobility of a type was introduced in the ML5 language for distributed computing (Murphy et al., 2004), with the similar meaning that a value of a mobile type cannot depend on local resources. Here the mobility restriction is used to ensure that the language adheres to the stack discipline.

Exercises

34.1. Originally, Algol had both *scalar* assignables, whose contents are atomic values, and *array* assignables, which is a finite sequence of scalar assignables. Like scalar assignables, array assignables are stack-allocated. Extend **MA** with array assignables, ensuring that the language remains type safe, but allowing that computation may abort if a non-existent array element is accessed.

34.2. Consider carefully the behavior of assignable declarations within recursive procedures, as in the following expression

$$\texttt{fix } p \texttt{ is } \lambda \, (p : \tau) \, \texttt{dcl } a := e \texttt{ in } \texttt{cmd}(m)$$

of type $\tau \rightharpoonup \rho \texttt{ cmd}$ for some ρ. Because p is recursive, the body m of the procedure may call itself during its execution, causing the *same* declaration to be executed more than once. Explain the dynamics of getting and setting a in such a situation.

34.3. Originally, Algol considered assignables as expressions that stand for their contents in memory. Thus, if a is an assignable containing a number, one could write expressions such as $a + a$ that would evaluate to twice the contents of a. Moreover, one could write commands such as $a := a + a$ to double the contents of a. These conventions encouraged programmers to think of assignables as variables, quite the opposite of their separation in **MA**. This convention, combined with an over-emphasis on concrete syntax, led to a conundrum about the different roles of a in the above assignment command: its meaning on the left of the assignment is different from its meaning on the right. These came to be called the *left-*, or *l-value*, and the *right-*, or *r-value* of the assignable a, corresponding to its position in the assignment statement. When viewed as abstract syntax, though, there is no ambiguity to be explained: the assignment operator is indexed by its target assignable, instead of taking as argument an expression that happens to be an assignable, so that the command is $\mathtt{set}[a](a + a)$, not $\mathtt{set}(a; a + a)$.

This still leaves the puzzle of how to regard assignables as forms of expression. As a first cut, reformulate the dynamics of **MA** to account for this. Reformulate the dynamics of expressions in terms of the judgments $e \parallel \mu \underset{\Sigma}{\mapsto} e' \parallel \mu'$ and $e \parallel \mu$ final that allow evaluation of e to depend on the contents of the memory. Each use of an assignable as an expression should require one access to the memory. Then prove *memory invariance*:: if $e \parallel \mu \underset{\Sigma}{\mapsto} e' \parallel \mu'$, then $\mu' = \mu$.

A natural generalization is to allow any sequence of commands to be considered as an expression, if they are all *passive* in the sense that no assignments are allowed. Write do $\{m\}$, where m is a passive command, for a *passive block* whose evaluation consists of executing the command m on the current memory, using its return value as the value of the expression. Observe that memory invariance holds for passive blocks.

The use of an assignable a as an expression may now be rendered as the passive block do $\{@\,a\}$. More complex uses of assignables as expressions admit several different interpretations using passive blocks. For example, an expression such as $a + a$ might be rendered in one of two ways:

(a) do $\{@\,a\} + $ do $\{@\,a\}$, or

(b) let x be do $\{@\,a\}$ in $x + x$.

The latter formulation accesses a only once, but uses its value twice. Comment on there being two different interpretations of $a + a$.

34.4. Recursive procedures in Algol are *declared* using a command of the form proc $p(x : \tau) : \rho$ is m in m', which is governed by the typing rule

$$\frac{\Gamma, p : \tau \rightharpoonup \rho \,\mathtt{cmd}, x : \tau \vdash_\Sigma m \mathbin{\dot{\sim}} \rho \quad \Gamma, p : \tau \rightharpoonup \rho \,\mathtt{cmd} \vdash_\Sigma m' \mathbin{\dot{\sim}} \tau'}{\Gamma \vdash_\Sigma \mathtt{proc}\ p(x : \tau) : \rho\ \mathtt{is}\ m\ \mathtt{in}\ m' \mathbin{\dot{\sim}} \tau'} . \tag{34.11}$$

From the present viewpoint, it is peculiar to insist on declaring procedures at all, because they are simply values of procedure type, and even more peculiar to insist that they be confined for use within a command. One justification for this limitation, though, is that Algol included a peculiar feature, called an *own variable*[2] that was declared for use within the procedure, but whose state persisted across calls to the procedure. One application would be to a procedure that generated pseudo-random numbers based on a stored seed that influenced the behavior of successive calls to it. Give a formulation in **MA** of the extended declaration

$$\text{proc } p(x : \tau) : \rho \text{ is } \{\text{own } a := e \text{ in } m\} \text{ in } m'$$

where a is declared as an "own" of the procedure p. Contrast the meaning of the foregoing declaration with the following one:

$$\text{proc } p(x : \tau) : \rho \text{ is } \{\text{dcl } a := e \text{ in } m\} \text{ in } m'.$$

34.5. A natural generalization of own assignables is to allow the creation of many such scenarios for a single procedure (or mutually recursive collection of procedures), with each instance creating its own persistent state. This ability motivated the concept of a *class* in Simula-67 as a collection of procedures, possibly mutually recursive, that shared common persistent state. Each instance of a class is called an *object* of that class; calls to its constituent procedures mutate the private persistent state. Formulate this 1967 precursor of imperative object-oriented programming in the context of **MA**.

34.6. There are several ways to formulate an abstract machine for **MA** that accounts for both the *control stack*, which sequences execution (as described in Chapter 28 for **PCF**), and the *data stack*, which records the contents of the assignables. A *consolidated stack* combines these two separate concepts into one, whereas *separated stacks* keeps the memory separate from the control stack, much as we have done in the structural dynamics given by rules (34.3). In either case, the storage required for an assignable is deallocated when exiting the scope of that assignable, a key benefit of the stack discipline for assignables in **MA**.

With a modal separation between expressions and commands, it is natural to use a structural dynamics for expressions (given by the transition and value judgments, $e \longmapsto e'$ and e val), and a stack machine dynamics for commands.

(a) Formulate a consolidated stack machine where both assignables and stack frames are recorded on the same stack. Consider states $k \rhd_\Sigma m$, where $\vdash_\Sigma k \lhd: \tau$ and $\vdash_\Sigma m \mathrel{\dot\sim} \tau$, and $k \lhd_\Sigma e$, where $\vdash_\Sigma k \lhd: \tau$ and $\vdash_\Sigma e : \tau$. Comment on the implementation methods required for a consolidated stack.

(b) Formulate a separated stack machine where the memory is maintained separately from the control stack. Consider states of the form $\mu \parallel k \rhd_\Sigma m$, where $\mu : \Sigma$, $\vdash_\Sigma k \lhd: \tau$, and $\vdash_\Sigma m \mathrel{\dot\sim} \tau$, and of the form $\mu \parallel k \lhd_\Sigma e$, where $\vdash_\Sigma k \lhd: \tau$, $\vdash_\Sigma e : \tau$, and e val.

Notes

1 Personal communication, 2012.
2 That is to say, an *own assignable*.

35

Assignable References

A *reference* to an assignable a is a value, written $\&a$, of *reference type* that determines the assignable a. A reference to an assignable provides the *capability* to get or set the contents of that assignable, even if the assignable itself is not in scope when it is used. Two references can be compared for equality to test whether they govern the same underlying assignable. If two references are equal, then setting one will affect the result of getting the other; if they are not equal, then setting one cannot influence the result of getting from the other. Two references that govern the same underlying assignable are *aliases*. Aliasing complicates reasoning about programs that use references, because any two references may refer to the assignable.

Reference types are compatible with both a scoped and a scope-free allocation of assignables. When assignables are scoped, the range of significance of a reference type is limited to the scope of the assignable to which it refers. Reference types are therefore immobile, so that they cannot be returned from the body of a declaration, nor stored in an assignable. Although ensuring adherence to the stack discipline, this restriction precludes using references to create mutable data structures, those whose structure can be altered during execution. Mutable data structures have a number of applications in programming, including improving efficiency (often at the expense of expressiveness) and allowing cyclic (self-referential) structures to be created. Supporting mutability requires that assignables be given a scope-free dynamics, so that their lifetime persists beyond the scope of their declaration. Consequently, all types are mobile, so that a value of any type may be stored in an assignable or returned from a command.

35.1 Capabilities

The commands $\mathsf{get}[a]$ and $\mathsf{set}[a](e)$ in **MA** operate on statically specified assignable a. Even to write these commands requires that the assignable a be in scope where the command occurs. But suppose that we wish to define a procedure that, say, updates an assignable to double its previous value, and returns the previous value. We can write such a procedure for any given assignable, a, but what if we wish to write a generic procedure that works for any given assignable?

One way to do this is give the procedure the *capability* to get and set the contents of some caller-specified assignable. Such a capability is a pair consisting of a *getter* and a *setter* for that assignable. The getter for an assignable a is a command that, when executed, returns the contents of a. The setter for an assignable a is a procedure that, when applied to a value of suitable type, assigns that value to a. Thus, a capability for an assignable a containing a value of type τ is a value of type

$$\tau \text{ cap} \triangleq \tau \text{ cmd} \times (\text{nat} \rightharpoonup \text{nat cmd}).$$

A capability for getting and setting an assignable a containing a value of type τ is given by the pair

$$\langle \text{cmd}(@\,a), \text{proc}(x : \tau)\, a := x \rangle$$

of type τ cap. Because a capability type is a product of a command type and a procedure type, no capability type is mobile. Thus, a capability cannot be returned from a command, nor stored into an assignable. This is as it should be, for otherwise we would violate the stack discipline for allocating assignables.

The proposed generic doubling procedure is programmed using capabilities as follows:

$$\text{proc}\,(\langle get, set \rangle : \text{nat cmd} \times (\text{nat} \rightharpoonup \text{nat cmd}))\,\{x \leftarrow \text{do } get\,; y \leftarrow \text{do }(set(x + x))\,; \text{ret } x\}.$$

The procedure is called with the capability to access an assignable a. When executed, it invokes the getter to obtain the contents of a, and then invokes the setter to assign to a, returning the previous value. Observe that the assignable a need not be accessible by this procedure; the capability given by the caller comprises the commands required to get and set a.

35.2 Scoped Assignables

A weakness of using a capability to give indirect access to an assignable is that there is no guarantee that a given getter/setter pair are in fact the capability for a particular assignable. For example, we might pair the getter for a with the setter for b, leading to unexpected behavior. There is nothing in the type system that prevents creating such mismatched pairs.

To avoid this, we introduce the concept of a *reference* to an assignable. A reference is a value from which we may obtain the capability to get and set a particular assignable. Moreover, two references can be tested for equality to see whether they act on the same assignable.[1] The *reference type* $\text{ref}(\tau)$ has as values references to assignables of type τ. The introduction and elimination forms for this type are given by the following syntax chart:

Typ	τ	::=	$\text{ref}(\tau)$	τ ref	assignable
Exp	e	::=	$\text{ref}[a]$	$\&a$	reference
Cmd	m	::=	$\text{getref}(e)$	$*e$	contents
			$\text{setref}(e_1; e_2)$	$e_1 *= e_2$	update

The statics of reference types is defined by the following rules:

$$\frac{}{\Gamma \vdash_{\Sigma,a \sim \tau} \text{ref}[a] : \text{ref}(\tau)} \tag{35.1a}$$

$$\frac{\Gamma \vdash_\Sigma e : \mathtt{ref}(\tau)}{\Gamma \vdash_\Sigma \mathtt{getref}(e) \mathbin{\dot\sim} \tau} \tag{35.1b}$$

$$\frac{\Gamma \vdash_\Sigma e_1 : \mathtt{ref}(\tau) \quad \Gamma \vdash_\Sigma e_2 : \tau}{\Gamma \vdash_\Sigma \mathtt{setref}(e_1; e_2) \mathbin{\dot\sim} \tau} \tag{35.1c}$$

Rule (35.1a) specifies that the name of any active assignable is an expression of type $\mathtt{ref}(\tau)$.

The dynamics of reference types defers to the corresponding operations on assignables, and does not alter the underlying dynamics of assignables:

$$\frac{}{\mathtt{ref}[a] \; \mathsf{val}_{\Sigma, a \sim \tau}} \tag{35.2a}$$

$$\frac{e \underset{\Sigma}{\longmapsto} e'}{\mathtt{getref}(e) \parallel \mu \underset{\Sigma}{\longmapsto} \mathtt{getref}(e') \parallel \mu} \tag{35.2b}$$

$$\frac{}{\mathtt{getref}(\mathtt{ref}[a]) \parallel \mu \underset{\Sigma, a \sim \tau}{\longmapsto} \mathtt{get}[a] \parallel \mu} \tag{35.2c}$$

$$\frac{e_1 \underset{\Sigma}{\longmapsto} e_1'}{\mathtt{setref}(e_1; e_2) \parallel \mu \underset{\Sigma}{\longmapsto} \mathtt{setref}(e_1'; e_2) \parallel \mu} \tag{35.2d}$$

$$\frac{}{\mathtt{setref}(\mathtt{ref}[a]; e) \parallel \mu \underset{\Sigma, a \sim \tau}{\longmapsto} \mathtt{set}[a](e) \parallel \mu} \tag{35.2e}$$

A reference to an assignable is a value. The $\mathtt{getref}$ and $\mathtt{setref}$ operations on references defer to the corresponding operations on assignables once the referent has been resolved.

Because references give rise to capabilities, the reference type is immobile. As a result, references cannot be stored in assignables or returned from commands. The immobility of references ensures safety, as can be seen by extending the safety proof given in Chapter 34.

As an example of using references, the generic doubling procedure discussed in the preceding section is programmed using references as follows:

$$\mathtt{proc}\,(r : \mathtt{nat}\,\mathtt{ref})\,\{x \leftarrow *r \mathbin{;} r \mathbin{*}= x + x \mathbin{;} \mathtt{ret}\,x\}.$$

Because the argument is a reference, rather than a capability, there is no possibility that the getter and setter refer to different assignables.

The ability to pass references to procedures comes at a price, because any two references might refer to the same assignable (if they have the same type). Consider a procedure that, when given two references x and y, adds twice the contents of y to the contents of x. One way to write this code creates no complications:

$$\lambda\,(x : \mathtt{nat}\,\mathtt{ref})\,\lambda\,(y : \mathtt{nat}\,\mathtt{ref})\,\mathtt{cmd}\,\{x' \leftarrow *x \mathbin{;} y' \leftarrow *y \mathbin{;} x \mathbin{*}= x' + y' + y'\}.$$

Even if x and y refer to the same assignable, the effect will be to set the contents of the assignable referenced by x to the sum of its original contents and twice the contents of the assignable referenced by y.

But now consider the following seemingly equivalent implementation of this procedure:

$$\lambda\,(x : \mathtt{nat\ ref})\,\lambda\,(y : \mathtt{nat\ ref})\,\mathtt{cmd}\,\{x\ \mathrel{+}= y\ ;\ x\ \mathrel{+}= y\},$$

where $x \mathrel{+}= y$ is the command

$$\{x' \leftarrow *\,x\ ;\ y' \leftarrow *\,y\ ;\ x *= x' + y'\}$$

that adds the contents of y to the contents of x. The second implementation works right, as long as x and y do not refer to the same assignable. If they do refer to a common assignable a, with contents n, the result is that a is to set $4 \times n$, instead of the intended $3 \times n$. The second get of y is affected by the first set of x.

In this case, it is clear how to avoid the problem: use the first implementation, rather than the second. But the difficulty is not in fixing the problem once it has been discovered, but in noticing the problem in the first place. Wherever references (or capabilities) are used, the problems of interference lurk. Avoiding them requires very careful consideration of all possible aliasing relationships among all of the references in play. The problem is that the number of possible aliasing relationships among n references grows combinatorially in n.

35.3 Free Assignables

Although it is interesting to note that references and capabilities are compatible with the stack discipline, for references to be useful requires that this restriction be relaxed. With immobile references it is impossible to build data structures containing references, or to return references from procedures. To allow this, we must arrange that the lifetime of an assignable extend beyond its scope. In other words, we must give up stack allocation for heap allocation. Assignables that persist beyond their scope of declaration are called *scope-free*, or just *free*, assignables. When all assignables are free, every type is mobile and so any value, including a reference, may be used in a data structure.

Supporting free assignables amounts to changing the dynamics so that allocation of assignables persists across transitions. We use transition judgments of the form

$$\nu\,\Sigma\,\{m \parallel \mu\} \longmapsto \nu\,\Sigma'\,\{m' \parallel \mu'\}.$$

Execution of a command may allocate new assignables, may alter the contents of existing assignables, and may give rise to a new command to be executed at the next step. The rules defining the dynamics of free assignables are as follows:

$$\frac{e\ \mathsf{val}_\Sigma}{\nu\,\Sigma\,\{\mathtt{ret}(e) \parallel \mu\}\ \mathsf{final}} \tag{35.3a}$$

$$\frac{e \underset{\Sigma}{\longmapsto} e'}{\nu\,\Sigma\,\{\mathtt{ret}(e) \parallel \mu\} \longmapsto \nu\,\Sigma\,\{\mathtt{ret}(e') \parallel \mu\}} \tag{35.3b}$$

$$\frac{e \underset{\Sigma}{\longmapsto} e'}{\nu\,\Sigma\,\{\mathtt{bnd}(e; x.m) \parallel \mu\} \longmapsto \nu\,\Sigma\,\{\mathtt{bnd}(e'; x.m) \parallel \mu\}} \tag{35.3c}$$

$$\frac{e \text{ val}_\Sigma}{\nu\, \Sigma\, \{\, \text{bnd}(\text{cmd}(\text{ret}(e)); x.m) \parallel \mu \,\} \longmapsto \nu\, \Sigma\, \{\, [e/x]m \parallel \mu \,\}} \tag{35.3d}$$

$$\frac{\nu\, \Sigma\, \{\, m_1 \parallel \mu \,\} \longmapsto \nu\, \Sigma'\, \{\, m_1' \parallel \mu' \,\}}{\nu\, \Sigma\, \{\, \text{bnd}(\text{cmd}(m_1); x.m_2) \parallel \mu \,\} \longmapsto \nu\, \Sigma'\, \{\, \text{bnd}(\text{cmd}(m_1'); x.m_2) \parallel \mu' \,\}} \tag{35.3e}$$

$$\frac{}{\nu\, \Sigma, a \sim \tau\, \{\, \text{get}[a] \parallel \mu \otimes a \hookrightarrow e \,\} \longmapsto \nu\, \Sigma, a \sim \tau\, \{\, \text{ret}(e) \parallel \mu \otimes a \hookrightarrow e \,\}} \tag{35.3f}$$

$$\frac{e \underset{\Sigma}{\mapsto} e'}{\nu\, \Sigma\, \{\, \text{set}[a](e) \parallel \mu \,\} \longmapsto \nu\, \Sigma\, \{\, \text{set}[a](e') \parallel \mu \,\}} \tag{35.3g}$$

$$\frac{e \text{ val}_{\Sigma, a \sim \tau}}{\nu\, \Sigma, a \sim \tau\, \{\, \text{set}[a](e) \parallel \mu \otimes a \hookrightarrow \_ \,\} \longmapsto \nu\, \Sigma, a \sim \tau\, \{\, \text{ret}(e) \parallel \mu \otimes a \hookrightarrow e \,\}} \tag{35.3h}$$

$$\frac{e \underset{\Sigma}{\mapsto} e'}{\nu\, \Sigma\, \{\, \text{dcl}(e; a.m) \parallel \mu \,\} \longmapsto \nu\, \Sigma\, \{\, \text{dcl}(e'; a.m) \parallel \mu \,\}} \tag{35.3i}$$

$$\frac{e \text{ val}_\Sigma}{\nu\, \Sigma\, \{\, \text{dcl}(e; a.m) \parallel \mu \,\} \longmapsto \nu\, \Sigma, a \sim \tau\, \{\, m \parallel \mu \otimes a \hookrightarrow e \,\}} \tag{35.3j}$$

The language **RMA** extends **MA** with references to free assignables. Its dynamics is similar to that of references to scoped assignables given earlier.

$$\frac{e \underset{\Sigma}{\mapsto} e'}{\nu\, \Sigma\, \{\, \text{getref}(e) \parallel \mu \,\} \longmapsto \nu\, \Sigma\, \{\, \text{getref}(e') \parallel \mu \,\}} \tag{35.4a}$$

$$\frac{}{\nu\, \Sigma\, \{\, \text{getref}(\text{ref}[a]) \parallel \mu \,\} \longmapsto \nu\, \Sigma\, \{\, \text{get}[a] \parallel \mu \,\}} \tag{35.4b}$$

$$\frac{e_1 \underset{\Sigma}{\mapsto} e_1'}{\nu\, \Sigma\, \{\, \text{setref}(e_1; e_2) \parallel \mu \,\} \longmapsto \nu\, \Sigma\, \{\, \text{setref}(e_1'; e_2) \parallel \mu \,\}} \tag{35.4c}$$

$$\frac{}{\nu\, \Sigma\, \{\, \text{setref}(\text{ref}[a]; e_2) \parallel \mu \,\} \longmapsto \nu\, \Sigma\, \{\, \text{set}[a](e_2) \parallel \mu \,\}} \tag{35.4d}$$

The expressions cannot alter or extend the memory, only commands may do so.

As an example of using **RMA**, consider the command $\text{newref}[\tau](e)$ defined by

$$\text{dcl}\, a := e \text{ in ret } (\&a). \tag{35.5}$$

This command allocates a fresh assignable and returns a reference to it. Its static and dynamics are derived from the foregoing rules as follows:

$$\frac{\Gamma \vdash_\Sigma e : \tau}{\Gamma \vdash_\Sigma \text{newref}[\tau](e) \mathrel{\dot\sim} \text{ref}(\tau)} \tag{35.6}$$

$$\frac{e \underset{\Sigma}{\mapsto} e'}{\nu \, \Sigma \, \{\, \texttt{newref}[\tau](e) \parallel \mu \,\} \longmapsto \nu \, \Sigma \, \{\, \texttt{newref}[\tau](e') \parallel \mu \,\}} \tag{35.7a}$$

$$\frac{e \, \mathrm{val}_\Sigma}{\nu \, \Sigma \, \{\, \texttt{newref}[\tau](e) \parallel \mu \,\} \longmapsto \nu \, \Sigma, a \sim \tau \, \{\, \texttt{ret}(\texttt{ref}[a]) \parallel \mu \otimes a \hookrightarrow e \,\}} \tag{35.7b}$$

Oftentimes, the command $\texttt{newref}[\tau](e)$ is taken as primitive, and the declaration command is omitted. In that case, all assignables are accessed by reference, and no direct access to assignables is provided.

35.4 Safety

Although the proof of safety for references to scoped assignables presents few difficulties, the safety for free assignables is tricky. The main difficulty is to account for cyclic dependencies within data structures. The contents of one assignable may contain a reference to itself, or a reference to another assignable that contains a reference to it, and so forth. For example, consider the following procedure e of type $\texttt{nat} \rightharpoonup \texttt{nat cmd}$:

$$\texttt{proc}\,(x:\texttt{nat})\,\{\texttt{if}\,(x)\,\texttt{ret}\,(1)\,\texttt{else}\,\{f \leftarrow @\,a \,;\, y \leftarrow f(x-1) \,;\, \texttt{ret}\,(x * y)\}\}.$$

Let μ be a memory of the form $\mu' \otimes a \hookrightarrow e$ in which the contents of a contains, via the body of the procedure, a reference to a itself. Indeed, if the procedure e is called with a non-zero argument, it will "call itself" by indirect reference through a.

Cyclic dependencies complicate the definition of the judgment $\mu : \Sigma$. It is defined by the following rule:

$$\frac{\vdash_\Sigma m \mathbin{\overset{.}{\sim}} \tau \quad \vdash_\Sigma \mu : \Sigma}{\nu \, \Sigma \, \{\, m \parallel \mu \,\} \, \texttt{ok}} \tag{35.8}$$

The first premise of the rule states that the command m is well-formed relative to Σ. The second premise states that the memory μ conforms to Σ, *relative to all of* Σ so that cyclic dependencies are permitted. The judgment $\vdash_{\Sigma'} \mu : \Sigma$ is defined as follows:

$$\frac{\forall a \sim \tau \in \Sigma \quad \exists e \quad \mu(a) = e \text{ and } \vdash_{\Sigma'} e : \tau}{\vdash_{\Sigma'} \mu : \Sigma} \tag{35.9}$$

Theorem 35.1 (Preservation).

1. If $\vdash_\Sigma e : \tau$ and $e \underset{\Sigma}{\mapsto} e'$, then $\vdash_\Sigma e' : \tau$.

2. If $\nu \, \Sigma \, \{\, m \parallel \mu \,\}$ ok and $\nu \, \Sigma \, \{\, m \parallel \mu \,\} \longmapsto \nu \, \Sigma' \, \{\, m' \parallel \mu' \,\}$, then $\nu \, \Sigma' \, \{\, m' \parallel \mu' \,\}$ ok.

Proof Simultaneously, by induction on transition. We prove the following stronger form of the second statement:

If $\nu \, \Sigma \, \{\, m \parallel \mu \,\} \longmapsto \nu \, \Sigma' \, \{\, m' \parallel \mu' \,\}$, where $\vdash_\Sigma m \mathbin{\overset{.}{\sim}} \tau$, $\vdash_\Sigma \mu : \Sigma$, then Σ' extends Σ, and $\vdash_{\Sigma'} m' \mathbin{\overset{.}{\sim}} \tau$, and $\vdash_{\Sigma'} \mu' : \Sigma'$.

Consider the transition

$$\nu \, \Sigma \, \{ \, \mathtt{dcl}(e;a.m) \parallel \mu \, \} \longmapsto \nu \, \Sigma, a \sim \rho \, \{ \, m \parallel \mu \otimes a \hookrightarrow e \, \}$$

where $e \, \mathsf{val}_\Sigma$. By assumption and inversion of rule (34.6d), we have $\vdash_\Sigma e : \rho$, $\vdash_{\Sigma,a\sim\rho} m \mathrel{\dot{\sim}} \tau$, and $\vdash_\Sigma \mu : \Sigma$. But because extension of Σ with a fresh assignable does not affect typing, we also have $\vdash_{\Sigma,a\sim\rho} \mu : \Sigma$ and $\vdash_{\Sigma,a\sim\rho} e : \rho$, from which it follows by rule (35.9) that $\vdash_{\Sigma,a\sim\rho} \mu \otimes a \hookrightarrow e : \Sigma, a \sim \rho$.

The other cases follow a similar pattern and are left as an exercise for the reader.   □

Theorem 35.2 (Progress).

1. *If $\vdash_\Sigma e : \tau$, then either $e \, \mathsf{val}_\Sigma$ or there exists e' such that $e \underset{\Sigma}{\longmapsto} e'$.*

2. *If $\nu \, \Sigma \, \{ \, m \parallel \mu \, \}$ ok then either $\nu \, \Sigma \, \{ \, m \parallel \mu \, \}$ final or $\nu \, \Sigma \, \{ \, m \parallel \mu \, \} \longmapsto \nu \, \Sigma' \, \{ \, m' \parallel \mu' \, \}$ for some Σ', μ', and m'.*

Proof Simultaneously, by induction on typing. For the second statement, we prove the stronger form

> If $\vdash_\Sigma m \mathrel{\dot{\sim}} \tau$ and $\vdash_\Sigma \mu : \Sigma$, then either $\nu \, \Sigma \, \{ \, m \parallel \mu \, \}$ final, or $\nu \, \Sigma \, \{ \, m \parallel \mu \, \} \longmapsto \nu \, \Sigma' \, \{ \, m' \parallel \mu' \, \}$ for some Σ', μ', and m'.

Consider the typing rule

$$\frac{\Gamma \vdash_\Sigma e : \rho \quad \Gamma \vdash_{\Sigma,a\sim\rho} m \mathrel{\dot{\sim}} \tau}{\Gamma \vdash_\Sigma \mathtt{dcl}(e;a.m) \mathrel{\dot{\sim}} \tau}$$

We have by the first inductive hypothesis that either $e \, \mathsf{val}_\Sigma$ or $e \underset{\Sigma}{\longmapsto} e'$ for some e'. In the latter case, we have by rule (35.3i)

$$\nu \, \Sigma \, \{ \, \mathtt{dcl}(e;a.m) \parallel \mu \, \} \longmapsto \nu \, \Sigma \, \{ \, \mathtt{dcl}(e';a.m) \parallel \mu \, \}.$$

In the former case, we have by rule (35.3j) that

$$\nu \, \Sigma \, \{ \, \mathtt{dcl}(e;a.m) \parallel \mu \, \} \longmapsto \nu \, \Sigma, a \sim \rho \, \{ \, m \parallel \mu \otimes a \hookrightarrow e \, \}.$$

Now consider the typing rule

$$\frac{}{\Gamma \vdash_{\Sigma,a\sim\tau} \mathtt{get}[a] \mathrel{\dot{\sim}} \tau}$$

By assumption $\vdash_{\Sigma,a\sim\tau} \mu : \Sigma, a \sim \tau$, and hence there exists $e \, \mathsf{val}_{\Sigma,a\sim\tau}$ such that $\mu = \mu' \otimes a \hookrightarrow e$ and $\vdash_{\Sigma,a\sim\tau} e : \tau$. By rule (35.3f)

$$\nu \, \Sigma, a \sim \tau \, \{ \, \mathtt{get}[a] \parallel \mu' \otimes a \hookrightarrow e \, \} \longmapsto \nu \, \Sigma, a \sim \tau \, \{ \, \mathtt{ret}(e) \parallel \mu' \otimes a \hookrightarrow e \, \},$$

as required. The other cases are handled similarly.   □

35.5 Benign Effects

The modal separation between commands and expressions ensures that the meaning of an expression does not depend on the (ever-changing) contents of assignables. Although this is helpful in many, perhaps most, situations, it also precludes programming techniques that use storage effects to implement purely functional behavior. A prime example is memoization. Externally, a suspended computation behaves exactly like the underlying computation; internally, an assignable is associated with the computation that stores the result of any evaluation of the computation for future use. Other examples are self-adjusting data structures, which use state to improve their efficiency without changing their functional behavior. For example, a splay tree is a binary search tree that uses mutation internally to re-balance the tree as elements are inserted, deleted, and retrieved, so that lookup takes time proportional to the logarithm of the number of elements.

These are examples of *benign storage effects*, uses of mutation in a data structure to improve efficiency without disrupting its functional behavior. One class of examples are self-adjusting data structures that reorganize themselves during one use to improve efficiency of later uses. Another class of examples are memoized, or lazy, data structures, which are discussed in Chapter 36. Benign effects such as these are impossible to implement if a strict separation between expressions and commands is maintained. For example, a self-adjusting tree involves mutation but is a value just like any other, and this cannot be achieved in **MA**. Although several special-case techniques are known, the most general solution is to do away with the modal distinction, coalescing expressions and commands into a single syntactic category. The penalty is that the type system no longer ensures that an expression of type τ denotes a value of that type; it might also have storage effects during its evaluation. The benefit is that one may freely use benign effects, but it is up to the programmer to ensure that they truly are benign.

The language **RPCF** extends **PCF** with references to free assignables. The following rules define the statics of the distinctive features of **RPCF**:

$$\frac{\Gamma \vdash_\Sigma e_1 : \tau_1 \quad \Gamma \vdash_{\Sigma, a \sim \tau_1} e_2 : \tau_2}{\Gamma \vdash_\Sigma \mathtt{dcl}(e_1; a.e_2) : \tau_2} \tag{35.10a}$$

$$\frac{}{\Gamma \vdash_{\Sigma, a \sim \tau} \mathtt{get}[a] : \tau} \tag{35.10b}$$

$$\frac{\Gamma \vdash_{\Sigma, a \sim \tau} e : \tau}{\Gamma \vdash_{\Sigma, a \sim \tau} \mathtt{set}[a](e) : \tau} \tag{35.10c}$$

Correspondingly, the dynamics of **RPCF** is given by transitions of the form

$$\nu \Sigma \{ e \parallel \mu \} \longmapsto \nu \Sigma' \{ e' \parallel \mu' \},$$

where e is an expression and not a command. The rules defining the dynamics are very similar to those for **RMA**, but with commands and expressions integrated into a single category.

To illustrate the concept of a benign effect, consider the technique of *back-patching* to implement recursion. Here is an implementation of the factorial function that uses an assignable to implement recursive calls:

```
dcl a := λn:nat.0 in
  { f ← a := λn:nat.ifz(n, 1, n'.n×(@a)(n'))
  ; ret(f)
  }
```

This declaration returns a function of type nat ⇀ nat that is obtained by (a) allocating a free assignable initialized arbitrarily with a function of this type, (b) defining a λ-abstraction in which each "recursive call" consists of retrieving and applying the function stored in that assignable, (c) assigning this function to the assignable, and (d) returning that function. The result is a function on the natural numbers, even though it uses state in its implementation.

Backpatching is not expressible in **RMA**, because it relies on assignment. Let us attempt to recode the previous example in **RMA**:

```
dcl a := proc(n:nat){ret 0} in
  { f ← a := ...
  ; ret(f)
  },
```

where the elided procedure assigned to *a* is given by

```
proc(n:nat) {if (ret(n)) {ret(1)} else {f←@a; x←f(n-1); ret(n×x)}}.
```

The difficulty is that what we have is a command, not an expression. Moreover, the result of the command is of the procedure type nat ⇀ (nat cmd) and not of the function type nat ⇀ nat. Consequently, we cannot use the factorial procedure in an expression but have to execute it as a command using code such as this:

```
{ f ← fact; x ← f(n); ret(x) }.
```

35.6 Notes

Reynolds (1981) uses capabilities to provide indirect access to assignables; references are just an abstract form of capability. References are often permitted only for free assignables, but with mobility restrictions one may also have references to scoped assignables. The proof of safety of free references outlined here follows those given by Wright and Felleisen (1994) and Harper (1994).

Benign effects are central to the distinction between Haskell, which provides an Algol-like separation between commands and expressions, and ML, which integrates evaluation with execution. The choice between them is classic trade-off, with neither superior to the other in all respects.

Exercises

35.1. Consider scoped array assignables as described in Exercise **34.1**. Extend the treatment of array assignables in Exercise **34.1**, to account for array assignable references.

35.2. References to scope-free assignables are often used to implement recursive data structures such as mutable lists and trees. Examine such data structures in the context of **RMA** enriched with sum, product, and recursive types.

Give six different types that could be considered a type of linked lists, according to the following characteristics:

(a) A mutable list may only be updated *in toto* by replacing it with another (immutable) list.

(b) A mutable list can be altered in one of two ways, to make it empty, or to change both its head and tail element simultaneously. The tail element is any other such mutable list, so circularities may arise.

(c) A mutable list is, permanently, either empty or non-empty. If not, both its head and tail can be modified simultaneously.

(d) A mutable list is, permanently, either empty or non-empty. If not, its tail, but not its head, can be set to another such list.

(e) A mutable list is, permanently, either empty or non-empty. If not, either its head or its tail elements can be modified independently.

(f) A mutable list can be altered to become either empty or non-empty. If it is non-empty, either it head, or its tail, can be modified independently of one another.

Discuss the merits and deficiencies of each representation.

Note

1 The getter and setter do not suffice to define equality, because not all types admit a test for equality. When they do, and when there are at least two distinct values of their type, we can determine whether they are aliases by assigning to one and checking whether the contents of the other is changed.

36 Lazy Evaluation

Lazy evaluation comprises a variety of methods to *defer* evaluation of an expression until it is required, and to *share* the results of any such evaluation among all uses of a deferred computation. Laziness is not merely an implementation device, but it also affects the *meaning* of a program.

One form of laziness is the *by-need* evaluation strategy for function application. Recall from Chapter 8 that the by-name evaluation order passes the argument to a function in unevaluated form so that it is only evaluated if it is actually used. But because the argument is replicated by substitution, it might be evaluated more than once. By-need evaluation ensures that the argument to a function is evaluated at most once, by ensuring that all copies of an argument share the result of evaluating any one copy.

Another form of laziness is the concept of a *lazy data structure*. As we have seen in Chapters 10, 11, and 20, we may choose to defer evaluation of the components of a data structure until they are actually required, and not when the data structure is created. But if a component is required more than once, then the same computation will, without further provision, be repeated on each use. To avoid this, the deferred portions of a data structure are shared so an access to one will propagate its result to all occurrences of the same computation.

Yet another form of laziness arises from the concept of general recursion considered in Chapter 19. Recall that the dynamics of general recursion is given by unrolling, which replicates the recursive computation on each use. It would be preferable to share the results of such computation across unrollings. A lazy implementation of recursion avoids such replications by sharing those results.

Traditionally, languages are biased towards either eager or lazy evaluation. Eager languages use a by-value dynamics for function applications, and evaluate the components of data structures when they are created. Lazy languages adopt the opposite strategy, preferring a by-name dynamics for functions, and a lazy dynamics for data structures. The overhead of laziness is reduced by managing sharing to avoid redundancy. Experience has shown, however, that the distinction is better drawn at the level of types. It is important to have both lazy and eager types, so that the programmer controls the use of laziness, rather than having it enforced by the language dynamics.

36.1 PCF By-Need

We begin by considering a lazy variant of **PCF**, called **LPCF**, in which functions are called by name, and the successor operator is evaluated lazily. Under a lazy interpretation variables are bound to unevaluated expressions, and the argument to the successor left unevaluated: any successor is a value, regardless of whether the predecessor is or not. By-name function application replicates the unevaluated argument by substitution, which means that there can arise many copies of the same expression, each evaluated separately, if at all. By-need evaluation uses a device called *memoization* to share all such copies of an argument and to ensure that if it is evaluated at all, its value is stored so that all other uses of it will avoid re-computation. Computations are named during evaluation, and are accessed by a level of indirection using this name to index the memo table, which records the expression and, if it is every evaluated, its value.

The dynamics of **LPCF** is based on a transition system with states of the form $\nu \Sigma \{ e \parallel \mu \}$, where Σ is a finite set of hypotheses $a_1 \sim \tau_1, \ldots, a_n \sim \tau_n$ associating types to symbols, e is an expression that can involve the symbols in Σ, and μ maps each symbol declared in Σ to either an expression or a special symbol, $\bullet$, called the *black hole*. (The role of the black hole is explained below.) As a notational convenience, we use a bit of legerdemain with the concrete syntax similar to that used in Chapter 34. Specifically, the concrete syntax for the expression $\mathtt{via}(a)$, which fetches the contents of the assignable a, is $@\, a$.

The dynamics of **LPCF** is given by he following two forms of judgment:

1. e val$_\Sigma$, stating that e is a value that can involve the symbols in Σ.
2. $\nu \Sigma \{ e \parallel \mu \} \longmapsto \nu \Sigma' \{ e' \parallel \mu' \}$, stating that one step of evaluation of the expression e relative to memo table μ with the symbols declared in Σ results in the expression e' relative to the memo table μ' with symbols declared in Σ'.

The dynamics is defined so that the active symbols grow during evaluation. The memo table may be altered destructively during execution to show progress in the evaluation of the expression associated with a symbol.

The judgment e val$_\Sigma$ expressing that e is a closed value is defined by the following rules:

$$\frac{}{\mathtt{z} \ \mathsf{val}_\Sigma} \tag{36.1a}$$

$$\frac{}{\mathtt{s}(@\, a) \ \mathsf{val}_{\Sigma, a \sim \mathtt{nat}}} \tag{36.1b}$$

$$\frac{}{\lambda\, (x : \tau)\, e \ \mathsf{val}_\Sigma} \tag{36.1c}$$

Rules (36.1a) through (36.1c) specify that z is a value, any expression of the form $\mathtt{s}(@\, a)$, where a is a symbol, is a value, and that any λ-abstraction, possibly containing symbols, is a value. It is important that symbols themselves are not values, rather they stand for (possibly unevaluated) expressions as specified by the memo table. The expression $@\, a$, which is short for $\mathtt{via}(a)$, is *not* a value. Rather, it is accessed to obtain, and possibly update, the binding of the symbol a in memory.

The initial and final states of evaluation are defined as follows:

$$\frac{}{\nu\,\emptyset\,\{\,e\parallel\emptyset\,\}\;\mathsf{initial}} \tag{36.2a}$$

$$\frac{e\;\mathsf{val}_\Sigma}{\nu\,\Sigma\,\{\,e\parallel\mu\,\}\;\mathsf{final}} \tag{36.2b}$$

Rule (36.2a) specifies that an initial state consists of an expression evaluated relative to an empty memo table. Rule (36.2b) specifies that a final state has the form $\nu\,\Sigma\,\{\,e\parallel\mu\,\}$, where e is a value relative to Σ.

The transition judgment for the dynamics of **LPCF** is defined by the following rules:

$$\frac{e\;\mathsf{val}_{\Sigma,a\sim\tau}}{\nu\,\Sigma,a\sim\tau\,\{\,@\,a\parallel\mu\otimes a\hookrightarrow e\,\}\longmapsto\nu\,\Sigma,a\sim\tau\,\{\,e\parallel\mu\otimes a\hookrightarrow e\,\}} \tag{36.3a}$$

$$\frac{\nu\,\Sigma,a\sim\tau\,\{\,e\parallel\mu\otimes a\hookrightarrow\bullet\,\}\longmapsto\nu\,\Sigma',a\sim\tau\,\{\,e'\parallel\mu'\otimes a\hookrightarrow\bullet\,\}}{\nu\,\Sigma,a\sim\tau\,\{\,@\,a\parallel\mu\otimes a\hookrightarrow e\,\}\longmapsto\nu\,\Sigma',a\sim\tau\,\{\,@\,a\parallel\mu'\otimes a\hookrightarrow e'\,\}} \tag{36.3b}$$

$$\frac{}{\nu\,\Sigma\,\{\,\mathsf{s}(e)\parallel\mu\,\}\longmapsto\nu\,\Sigma,a\sim\mathsf{nat}\,\{\,\mathsf{s}(@\,a)\parallel\mu\otimes a\hookrightarrow e\,\}} \tag{36.3c}$$

$$\frac{\nu\,\Sigma\,\{\,e\parallel\mu\,\}\longmapsto\nu\,\Sigma'\,\{\,e'\parallel\mu'\,\}}{\nu\,\Sigma\,\{\,\mathtt{ifz}\,e\,\{\mathsf{z}\hookrightarrow e_0\mid\mathsf{s}(x)\hookrightarrow e_1\}\parallel\mu\,\}\longmapsto\nu\,\Sigma'\,\{\,\mathtt{ifz}\,e'\,\{\mathsf{z}\hookrightarrow e_0\mid\mathsf{s}(x)\hookrightarrow e_1\}\parallel\mu'\,\}} \tag{36.3d}$$

$$\frac{}{\nu\,\Sigma\,\{\,\mathtt{ifz}\,\mathsf{z}\,\{\mathsf{z}\hookrightarrow e_0\mid\mathsf{s}(x)\hookrightarrow e_1\}\parallel\mu\,\}\longmapsto\nu\,\Sigma\,\{\,e_0\parallel\mu\,\}} \tag{36.3e}$$

$$\frac{}{\left\{\begin{array}{c}\nu\,\Sigma,a\sim\mathsf{nat}\,\{\,\mathtt{ifz}\,\mathsf{s}(@\,a)\,\{\mathsf{z}\hookrightarrow e_0\mid\mathsf{s}(x)\hookrightarrow e_1\}\parallel\mu\otimes a\hookrightarrow e\,\}\\\longmapsto\\\nu\,\Sigma,a\sim\mathsf{nat}\,\{\,[@\,a/x]e_1\parallel\mu\otimes a\hookrightarrow e\,\}\end{array}\right\}} \tag{36.3f}$$

$$\frac{\nu\,\Sigma\,\{\,e_1\parallel\mu\,\}\longmapsto\nu\,\Sigma'\,\{\,e_1'\parallel\mu'\,\}}{\nu\,\Sigma\,\{\,e_1(e_2)\parallel\mu\,\}\longmapsto\nu\,\Sigma'\,\{\,e_1'(e_2)\parallel\mu'\,\}} \tag{36.3g}$$

$$\frac{}{\left\{\begin{array}{c}\nu\,\Sigma\,\{\,(\lambda\,(x:\tau)\,e)(e_2)\parallel\mu\,\}\\\longmapsto\\\nu\,\Sigma,a\sim\tau\,\{\,[@\,a/x]e\parallel\mu\otimes a\hookrightarrow e_2\,\}\end{array}\right\}} \tag{36.3h}$$

$$\frac{}{\nu\,\Sigma\,\{\,\mathtt{fix}\,x:\tau\,\mathtt{is}\,e\parallel\mu\,\}\longmapsto\nu\,\Sigma,a\sim\tau\,\{\,@\,a\parallel\mu\otimes a\hookrightarrow[@\,a/x]e\,\}} \tag{36.3i}$$

Rule (36.3a) governs a symbol whose associated expression is a value; the value of the symbol is the value associated to that symbol in the memo table. Rule (36.3b) specifies that if the expression associated to a symbol is not a value, then it is evaluated "in place" until such time as rule (36.3a) applies. This is achieved by switching the focus of evaluation to the associated expression, while at the same time associating the *black hole* to that symbol. The black hole represents the absence of a value for that symbol, so that any attempt to use it during evaluation of its associated expression cannot make progress. The black hole signals a circular dependency that, if not caught using a black hole, would initiate an infinite regress.

Rule (36.3c) specifies that evaluation of $s(e)$ allocates a fresh symbol a for the expression e, and yields the value $s(@\, a)$. The value of e is not determined until such time as the predecessor is required in a later computation, implementing a lazy dynamics for the successor. Rule (36.3f), which governs a conditional branch on a successor, substitutes $@\, a$ for the variable x when computing the predecessor of a non-zero number, ensuring that all occurrences of x share the same predecessor computation.

Rule (36.3g) specifies that the value of the function position of an application must be determined before the application can be executed. Rule (36.3h) specifies that to evaluate an application of a λ-abstraction we allocate a fresh symbol a for the argument, and substitute $@\, a$ for the argument variable of the function. The argument is evaluated only if it is needed in the later computation, and then that value is shared among all occurrences of the argument variable in the body of the function.

General recursion is implemented by rule (36.3i). Recall from Chapter 19 that the expression $\mathtt{fix}\, x{:}\tau\ \mathtt{is}\ e$ stands for the solution of the recursion equation $x = e$. Rule (36.3i) computes this solution by associating a fresh symbol a with the body e substituting $@\, a$ for x within e to effect the self-reference. It is this substitution that permits a named expression to depend on its own name. For example, the expression $\mathtt{fix}\, x{:}\tau\ \mathtt{is}\ x$ associates the expression a to a in the memo table, and returns $@\, a$. The next step of evaluation is stuck, because it seeks to evaluate $@\, a$ with a bound to the black hole. In contrast, an expression such as $\mathtt{fix}\, f : \tau' \rightharpoonup \tau\ \mathtt{is}\ \lambda\,(x : \tau')\, e$ does not get stuck, because the self-reference is "hidden" within the λ-abstraction, and hence need not be evaluated to determine the value of the binding.

36.2 Safety of PCF By-Need

We write $\Gamma \vdash_\Sigma e : \tau$ to mean that e has type τ under the assumptions Γ, treating symbols declared in Σ as expressions of their associated type. The rules are as in Chapter 19, extended with the following rule for symbols:

$$\frac{}{\Gamma \vdash_{\Sigma,a\sim\tau} @\, a : \tau} \tag{36.4}$$

This rule states that the demand for the binding of a symbol, $@\, a$, is a form of expression. It is a "delayed substitution" that lazily replaces a demand for a by its binding.

The judgment $\nu \Sigma \{ e \parallel \mu \}$ ok is defined by the following rules:

$$\frac{\vdash_\Sigma e : \tau \quad \vdash_\Sigma \mu : \Sigma}{\nu \Sigma \{ e \parallel \mu \} \text{ ok}} \tag{36.5a}$$

$$\frac{\forall a \sim \tau \in \Sigma \quad \mu(a) = e \neq \bullet \implies \vdash_{\Sigma'} e : \tau}{\vdash_{\Sigma'} \mu : \Sigma} \tag{36.5b}$$

Rule (36.5b) permits self-reference through the memo table by allowing the expression associated to a symbol a to contain occurrences of @ a. A symbol that is bound to the "black hole" is considered to be of any type.

Theorem 36.1 (Preservation). *If* $\nu \Sigma \{ e \parallel \mu \} \longmapsto \nu \Sigma' \{ e' \parallel \mu' \}$ *and* $\nu \Sigma \{ e \parallel \mu \}$ *ok,* *then* $\nu \Sigma' \{ e' \parallel \mu' \}$ *ok.*

Proof We prove by induction on rules (36.3) that if $\nu \Sigma \{ e \parallel \mu \} \longmapsto \nu \Sigma' \{ e' \parallel \mu' \}$ and $\vdash_\Sigma \mu : \Sigma$ and $\vdash_\Sigma e : \tau$, then $\Sigma' \supseteq \Sigma$ and $\vdash_{\Sigma'} \mu' : \Sigma'$ and $\vdash_{\Sigma'} e' : \tau$.

Consider rule (36.3b), for which we have $e = e' = @\, a$, $\mu = \mu_0 \otimes a \hookrightarrow e_0$, $\mu' = \mu_0' \otimes a \hookrightarrow e_0'$, and

$$\nu \Sigma, a \sim \tau \{ e_0 \parallel \mu_0 \otimes a \hookrightarrow \bullet \} \longmapsto \nu \Sigma', a \sim \tau \{ e_0' \parallel \mu_0' \otimes a \hookrightarrow \bullet \}.$$

Assume that $\vdash_{\Sigma, a \sim \tau} \mu : \Sigma, a \sim \tau$. It follows that $\vdash_{\Sigma, a \sim \tau} e_0 : \tau$ and $\vdash_{\Sigma, a \sim \tau} \mu_0 : \Sigma$, and hence that

$$\vdash_{\Sigma, a \sim \tau} \mu_0 \otimes a \hookrightarrow \bullet : \Sigma, a \sim \tau.$$

We have by induction that $\Sigma' \supseteq \Sigma$ and $\vdash_{\Sigma', a \sim \tau} e_0' : \tau'$ and

$$\vdash_{\Sigma', a \sim \tau} \mu_0 \otimes a \hookrightarrow \bullet : \Sigma, a \sim \tau.$$

But then

$$\vdash_{\Sigma', a \sim \tau} \mu' : \Sigma', a \sim \tau,$$

which suffices for the result.

Consider rule (36.3g), so that e is the application $e_1(e_2)$ and

$$\nu \Sigma \{ e_1 \parallel \mu \} \longmapsto \nu \Sigma' \{ e_1' \parallel \mu' \}.$$

Suppose that $\vdash_\Sigma \mu : \Sigma$ and $\vdash_\Sigma e : \tau$. By inversion of typing $\vdash_\Sigma e_1 : \tau_2 \rightharpoonup \tau$ for some type τ_2 such that $\vdash_\Sigma e_2 : \tau_2$. By induction $\Sigma' \supseteq \Sigma$ and $\vdash_{\Sigma'} \mu' : \Sigma'$ and $\vdash_{\Sigma'} e_1' : \tau_2 \rightharpoonup \tau$. By weakening we have $\vdash_{\Sigma'} e_2 : \tau_2$, so that $\vdash_{\Sigma'} e_1'(e_2) : \tau$, which is enough for the result. $\quad\square$

The statement of the progress theorem allows for the occurrence of a black hole, representing a checkable form of non-termination. The judgment $\nu \Sigma \{ e \parallel \mu \}$ loops, stating that e diverges by virtue of encountering the black hole, is defined by the following rules:

$$\frac{}{\nu \Sigma, a \sim \tau \{ @\, a \parallel \mu \otimes a \hookrightarrow \bullet \} \text{ loops}} \tag{36.6a}$$

$$\frac{\nu \Sigma, a \sim \tau \{ e \parallel \mu \otimes a \hookrightarrow \bullet \} \text{ loops}}{\nu \Sigma, a \sim \tau \{ @\, a \parallel \mu \otimes a \hookrightarrow e \} \text{ loops}} \tag{36.6b}$$

$$\frac{\nu\,\Sigma\,\{\,e\,\|\,\mu\,\}\ \text{loops}}{\nu\,\Sigma\,\{\,\mathtt{ifz}\,e\,\{\mathtt{z}\hookrightarrow e_0\mid\mathtt{s}(x)\hookrightarrow e_1\}\,\|\,\mu\,\}\ \text{loops}} \tag{36.6c}$$

$$\frac{\nu\,\Sigma\,\{\,e_1\,\|\,\mu\,\}\ \text{loops}}{\nu\,\Sigma\,\{\,e_1(e_2)\,\|\,\mu\,\}\ \text{loops}} \tag{36.6d}$$

There are other ways of forming an infinite loop. The looping judgment simply codifies those cases in which the looping behavior is a self-dependency, which is mediated by a black hole.

Theorem 36.2 (Progress). *If $\nu\,\Sigma\,\{\,e\,\|\,\mu\,\}$ ok, then either $\nu\,\Sigma\,\{\,e\,\|\,\mu\,\}$ final, or $\nu\,\Sigma\,\{\,e\,\|\,\mu\,\}$ loops, or there exists μ' and e' such that $\nu\,\Sigma\,\{\,e\,\|\,\mu\,\}\longmapsto\nu\,\Sigma'\{\,e'\,\|\,\mu'\,\}$.*

Proof We proceed by induction on the derivations of $\vdash_\Sigma e : \tau$ and $\vdash_\Sigma \mu : \Sigma$ implicit in the derivation of $\nu\,\Sigma\,\{\,e\,\|\,\mu\,\}$ ok.

Consider rule (19.1a), where the symbol a is declared in Σ. Thus, $\Sigma = \Sigma_0, a \sim \tau$ and $\vdash_\Sigma \mu : \Sigma$. It follows that $\mu = \mu_0 \otimes a \hookrightarrow e_0$ with $\vdash_\Sigma \mu_0 : \Sigma_0$ and $\vdash_\Sigma e_0 : \tau$. Note that $\vdash_\Sigma \mu_0 \otimes a \hookrightarrow \bullet : \Sigma$. Applying induction to the derivation of $\vdash_\Sigma e_0 : \tau$, we consider three cases:

1. $\nu\,\Sigma\,\{\,e_0\,\|\,\mu\otimes a\hookrightarrow\bullet\,\}$ final. By inversion of rule (36.2b) we have e_0 val$_\Sigma$, and hence by rule (36.3a) we obtain $\nu\,\Sigma\,\{\,@\,a\,\|\,\mu\,\}\longmapsto\nu\,\Sigma\,\{\,e_0\,\|\,\mu\,\}$.
2. $\nu\,\Sigma\,\{\,e_0\,\|\,\mu_0\otimes a\hookrightarrow\bullet\,\}$ loops. By applying rule (36.6b) we obtain $\nu\,\Sigma\,\{\,@\,a\,\|\,\mu\,\}$ loops.
3. $\nu\,\Sigma\,\{\,e_0\,\|\,\mu_0\otimes a\hookrightarrow\bullet\,\}\longmapsto\nu\,\Sigma'\{\,e_0'\,\|\,\mu_0'\otimes a\hookrightarrow\bullet\,\}$. By applying rule (36.3b) we obtain

$$\nu\,\Sigma\,\{\,@\,a\,\|\,\mu\otimes a\hookrightarrow e_0\,\}\longmapsto\nu\,\Sigma'\{\,@\,a\,\|\,\mu'\otimes a\hookrightarrow e_0'\,\}. \qquad\square$$

36.3 FPC By-Need

The language **LFPC** is **FPC** but with a by-need dynamics. For example, the dynamics of product types in **LFPC** is given by the following rules:

$$\frac{}{\langle\,@\,a_1,\,@\,a_2\,\rangle\ \text{val}_{\Sigma,a_1\sim\tau_1,a_2\sim\tau_2}} \tag{36.7a}$$

$$\left\{\begin{array}{c}\nu\,\Sigma\,\{\,\langle e_1,e_2\rangle\,\|\,\mu\,\}\\[4pt]\longmapsto\\[4pt]\nu\,\Sigma,a_1\sim\tau_1,a_2\sim\tau_2\,\{\,\langle\,@\,a_1,\,@\,a_2\,\rangle\,\|\,\mu\otimes a_1\hookrightarrow e_1\otimes a_2\hookrightarrow e_2\,\}\end{array}\right\} \tag{36.7b}$$

$$\frac{\nu\,\Sigma\,\{\,e\,\|\,\mu\,\}\longmapsto\nu\,\Sigma'\{\,e'\,\|\,\mu'\,\}}{\nu\,\Sigma\,\{\,e\cdot 1\,\|\,\mu\,\}\longmapsto\nu\,\Sigma'\{\,e'\cdot 1\,\|\,\mu'\,\}} \tag{36.7c}$$

$$\frac{\nu \, \Sigma \, \{ e \parallel \mu \} \text{ loops}}{\nu \, \Sigma \, \{ e \cdot 1 \parallel \mu \} \text{ loops}} \tag{36.7d}$$

$$\left\{ \begin{array}{c} \nu \, \Sigma, a_1 \sim \tau_1, a_2 \sim \tau_2 \, \{ \langle @ \, a_1, @ \, a_2 \rangle \cdot 1 \parallel \mu \} \\ \longmapsto \\ \nu \, \Sigma, a_1 \sim \tau_1, a_2 \sim \tau_2 \, \{ @ \, a_1 \parallel \mu \} \end{array} \right\} \tag{36.7e}$$

$$\frac{\nu \, \Sigma \, \{ e \parallel \mu \} \longmapsto \nu \, \Sigma' \, \{ e' \parallel \mu' \}}{\nu \, \Sigma \, \{ e \cdot \mathbf{r} \parallel \mu \} \longmapsto \nu \, \Sigma' \, \{ e' \cdot \mathbf{r} \parallel \mu' \}} \tag{36.7f}$$

$$\frac{\nu \, \Sigma \, \{ e \parallel \mu \} \text{ loops}}{\nu \, \Sigma \, \{ e \cdot \mathbf{r} \parallel \mu \} \text{ loops}} \tag{36.7g}$$

$$\left\{ \begin{array}{c} \nu \, \Sigma, a_1 \sim \tau_1, a_2 \sim \tau_2 \, \{ \langle @ \, a_1, @ \, a_2 \rangle \cdot \mathbf{r} \parallel \mu \} \\ \longmapsto \\ \nu \, \Sigma, a_1 \sim \tau_1, a_2 \sim \tau_2 \, \{ @ \, a_2 \parallel \mu \} \end{array} \right\} \tag{36.7h}$$

A pair is considered a value only if its arguments are symbols (rule (36.7a)), which are introduced when the pair is created (rule (36.7b)). The first and second projections evaluate to one or the other symbol in the pair, inducing a demand for the value of that component (rules (36.7e) and (36.7h)).

Similar ideas can be used to give a by-need dynamics to sums and recursive types.

36.4 Suspension Types

The dynamics of **LFPC** outlined in the previous section imposes a by-need interpretation on every type. A more flexible approach is to isolate the machinery of by-need evaluation by introducing a type τ susp of memoized computations, called *suspensions*, of a value of type τ to an eager variant of **FPC**. Doing so allows the programmer to choose the extent to which a by-need dynamics is imposed.

Informally, the type τ susp has as introduction form susp $x : \tau$ is e representing a suspended, self-referential, computation, e, of type τ. It has as elimination form the operation force(e) that evaluates the suspended computation presented by e, records the value in a memo table, and returns that value as result. Using suspension types, we can construct lazy types at will. For example, the type of lazy pairs with components of type τ_1 and τ_2 is expressible as the type

$$\tau_1 \text{ susp} \times \tau_2 \text{ susp}$$

and the type of by-need functions with domain τ_1 and range τ_2 is expressible as the type

$$\tau_1 \text{ susp} \rightharpoonup \tau_2.$$

We may also express more complex combinations of eagerness and laziness, such as the type of "lazy lists" consisting of computations that, when forced, evaluate either to the empty list, or a non-empty list consisting of a natural number and another lazy list:

$$\mathtt{rec}\, t \,\mathtt{is}\, (\mathtt{unit} + (\mathtt{nat} \times t))\,\mathtt{susp}.$$

Contrast this preceding type with this one:

$$\mathtt{rec}\, t \,\mathtt{is}\, (\mathtt{unit} + (\mathtt{nat} \times t\,\mathtt{susp})).$$

Values of the latter type are the empty list and a pair consisting of a natural number and a computation of another such value.

The language **SFPC** extends **FPC** with a type of suspensions:

Typ	τ	$::=$	$\mathtt{susp}(\tau)$	$\tau\,\mathtt{susp}$	suspension
Exp	e	$::=$	$\mathtt{susp}\{\tau\}(x.e)$	$\mathtt{susp}\,x : \tau\,\mathtt{is}\,e$	delay
			$\mathtt{force}(e)$	$\mathtt{force}(e)$	force
			$\mathtt{lcell}[a]$	$\mathtt{lcell}[a]$	indirection

Suspended computations are potentially self-referential; the bound variable x refers to the suspension itself. The expression $\mathtt{lcell}[a]$ is a reference to the suspension named a.

The statics of **SFPC** is given using a judgment of the form $\Gamma \vdash_\Sigma e : \tau$, where Σ assigns types to the names of suspensions. It is defined by the following rules:

$$\frac{\Gamma, x : \mathtt{susp}(\tau) \vdash_\Sigma e : \tau}{\Gamma \vdash_\Sigma \mathtt{susp}\{\tau\}(x.e) : \mathtt{susp}(\tau)} \tag{36.8a}$$

$$\frac{\Gamma \vdash_\Sigma e : \mathtt{susp}(\tau)}{\Gamma \vdash_\Sigma \mathtt{force}(e) : \tau} \tag{36.8b}$$

$$\frac{}{\Gamma \vdash_{\Sigma, a \sim \tau} \mathtt{lcell}[a] : \mathtt{susp}(\tau)} \tag{36.8c}$$

Rule (36.8a) checks that the expression, e, has type τ under the assumption that x, which stands for the suspension itself, has type $\mathtt{susp}(\tau)$.

The dynamics of **SFPC** is eager, with memoization confined to the suspension type as described by the following rules:

$$\frac{}{\mathtt{lcell}[a]\,\mathtt{val}_{\Sigma, a \sim \tau}} \tag{36.9a}$$

$$\left\{ \begin{array}{c} \nu\,\Sigma\,\{\,\mathtt{susp}\{\tau\}(x.e) \parallel \mu\,\} \\ \longmapsto \\ \nu\,\Sigma, a \sim \tau\,\{\,\mathtt{lcell}[a] \parallel \mu \otimes a \hookrightarrow [\mathtt{lcell}[a]/x]e\,\} \end{array} \right\} \tag{36.9b}$$

$$\frac{\nu\,\Sigma\,\{\,e \parallel \mu\,\} \longmapsto \nu\,\Sigma'\,\{\,e' \parallel \mu'\,\}}{\nu\,\Sigma\,\{\,\mathtt{force}(e) \parallel \mu\,\} \longmapsto \nu\,\Sigma'\,\{\,\mathtt{force}(e') \parallel \mu'\,\}} \tag{36.9c}$$

$$\frac{e \ \text{val}_{\Sigma, a \sim \tau}}{\left\{ \begin{array}{c} \nu \, \Sigma, a \sim \tau \, \{ \, \texttt{force}(\texttt{lcell}[a]) \parallel \mu \otimes a \hookrightarrow e \, \} \\ \longmapsto \\ \nu \, \Sigma, a \sim \tau \, \{ \, e \parallel \mu \otimes a \hookrightarrow e \, \} \end{array} \right\}} \tag{36.9d}$$

$$\frac{\begin{array}{c} \nu \, \Sigma, a \sim \tau \, \{ \, e \parallel \mu \otimes a \hookrightarrow \bullet \, \} \\ \longmapsto \\ \nu \, \Sigma', a \sim \tau \, \{ \, e' \parallel \mu' \otimes a \hookrightarrow \bullet \, \} \end{array}}{\left\{ \begin{array}{c} \nu \, \Sigma, a \sim \tau \, \{ \, \texttt{force}(\texttt{lcell}[a]) \parallel \mu \otimes a \hookrightarrow e \, \} \\ \longmapsto \\ \nu \, \Sigma', a \sim \tau \, \{ \, \texttt{force}(\texttt{lcell}[a]) \parallel \mu' \otimes a \hookrightarrow e' \, \} \end{array} \right\}} \tag{36.9e}$$

Rule (36.9a) specifies that a reference to a suspension is a value. Rule (36.9b) specifies that evaluation of a delayed computation consists of allocating a fresh symbol for it in the memo table, and returning a reference to that suspension. Rules (36.9c) to (36.9e) specify that demanding the value of a suspension forces evaluation of the suspended computation, which is then stored in the memo table and returned as the result.

36.5 Notes

The by-need dynamics given here is inspired by Ariola and Felleisen (1997) but with the difference that by-need cells are regarded as assignables, rather than variables. Doing so maintains the principle that variables are given meaning by substitution. In contrast, by-need cells are a form of assignable to which at most one assignment is ever done.

Exercises

36.1. Recall from Chapter 20 that, under a lazy interpretation, the recursive type

$$\texttt{rec} \, t \, \texttt{is} \, [\texttt{z} \hookrightarrow \texttt{unit}, \texttt{s} \hookrightarrow t]$$

contains the "infinite number" $\omega \triangleq \texttt{fix} \, x : \texttt{nat} \, \texttt{is} \, \texttt{s}(x)$. Contrast the behavior of ω under the by-need interpretation given in this chapter with that by-name interpretation given in Chapters 19 and 20.

36.2. In **LFPC** the putative recursive type of "lists" of natural numbers,

$$\texttt{rec} \, t \, \texttt{is} \, [\texttt{nil} \hookrightarrow \texttt{unit}, \texttt{cons} \hookrightarrow \texttt{nat} \times t],$$

is, rather, the type of finite or infinite streams of natural numbers. To prove this, exhibit the stream of all natural numbers as an element of this type.

36.3. Complete the definition of **LFPC** by giving the by-need dynamics for unit, void, sum, and recursive types.

36.4. **LFPC** can be interpreted into **SFPC**. Complete the following chart defining the interpretation, $\widehat{\tau}$, of the type τ:

$$\text{unit} \triangleq \ldots$$

$$\tau_1 \times \tau_2 \triangleq \ldots$$

$$\text{void} \triangleq \ldots$$

$$\tau_1 + \tau_2 \triangleq \ldots$$

$$\text{rec}\, t \,\text{is}\, \tau \triangleq \ldots.$$

Hint: Characterize the *values* of the lazy types in the left column, and express those values as eager types in the right column, using suspensions where necessary.

PART XV

Parallelism

37

Nested Parallelism

Parallel computation seeks to reduce the running times of programs by allowing many computations to be carried out simultaneously. For example, if we wish to add two numbers, each given by a complex computation, we may consider evaluating the addends simultaneously, then computing their sum. The ability to exploit parallelism is limited by the dependencies among parts of a program. Obviously, if one computation depends on the result of another, then we have no choice but to execute them sequentially so that we may propagate the result of the first to the second. Consequently, the fewer dependencies among sub-computations, the greater the opportunities for parallelism.

In this chapter, we discuss the language **PPCF**, which is the extension of **PCF** with *nested parallelism*. Nested parallelism has a hierarchical structure arising from *forking* two (or more) parallel computations, then *joining* these computations to combine their results before proceeding. Nested parallelism is also known as *fork-join parallelism*. We will consider two forms of dynamics for nested parallelism. The first is a structural dynamics in which a single transition on a compound expression may involve multiple transitions on its constituent expressions. The second is a cost dynamics (introduced in Chapter 7) that focuses attention on the sequential and parallel complexity (also known as the *work* and the *depth*, or *span*) of a parallel program by associating a *series-parallel graph* with each computation.

37.1 Binary Fork-Join

The syntax of **PPCF** extends that of **PCF** with the following construct:

Exp e ::= $\mathtt{par}(e_1; e_2; x_1.x_2.e)$ $\mathtt{par}\, x_1 = e_1 \,\mathtt{and}\, x_2 = e_2 \,\mathtt{in}\, e$ parallel let

The variables x_1 and x_2 are bound only within e, and not within e_1 or e_2, which ensures that they are not mutually dependent and hence can be evaluated simultaneously. The variable bindings represent a fork of two parallel computations e_1 and e_2, and the body e represents their join.

The static of **PPCF** enriches that of **PCF** with the following rule for parallel let:

$$\frac{\Gamma \vdash e_1 : \tau_1 \quad \Gamma \vdash e_2 : \tau_2 \quad \Gamma, x_1 : \tau_1, x_2 : \tau_2 \vdash e : \tau}{\Gamma \vdash \mathtt{par}(e_1; e_2; x_1.x_2.e) : \tau} \tag{37.1}$$

The *sequential structural dynamics* of **PPCF** is defined by a transition judgment of the form $e \mapsto_{\text{seq}} e'$ defined by these rules:

$$\frac{e_1 \mapsto_{\text{seq}} e_1'}{\text{par}(e_1; e_2; x_1.x_2.e) \mapsto_{\text{seq}} \text{par}(e_1'; e_2; x_1.x_2.e)} \tag{37.2a}$$

$$\frac{e_1 \text{ val} \quad e_2 \mapsto_{\text{seq}} e_2'}{\text{par}(e_1; e_2; x_1.x_2.e) \mapsto_{\text{seq}} \text{par}(e_1; e_2'; x_1.x_2.e)} \tag{37.2b}$$

$$\frac{e_1 \text{ val} \quad e_2 \text{ val}}{\text{par}(e_1; e_2; x_1.x_2.e) \mapsto_{\text{seq}} [e_1, e_2/x_1, x_2]e} \tag{37.2c}$$

The *parallel structural dynamics* of **PPCF** is given by a transition judgment of the form $e \mapsto_{\text{par}} e'$, defined as follows:

$$\frac{e_1 \mapsto_{\text{par}} e_1' \quad e_2 \mapsto_{\text{par}} e_2'}{\text{par}(e_1; e_2; x_1.x_2.e) \mapsto_{\text{par}} \text{par}(e_1'; e_2'; x_1.x_2.e)} \tag{37.3a}$$

$$\frac{e_1 \mapsto_{\text{par}} e_1' \quad e_2 \text{ val}}{\text{par}(e_1; e_2; x_1.x_2.e) \mapsto_{\text{par}} \text{par}(e_1'; e_2; x_1.x_2.e)} \tag{37.3b}$$

$$\frac{e_1 \text{ val} \quad e_2 \mapsto_{\text{par}} e_2'}{\text{par}(e_1; e_2; x_1.x_2.e) \mapsto_{\text{par}} \text{par}(e_1; e_2'; x_1.x_2.e)} \tag{37.3c}$$

$$\frac{e_1 \text{ val} \quad e_2 \text{ val}}{\text{par}(e_1; e_2; x_1.x_2.e) \mapsto_{\text{par}} [e_1, e_2/x_1, x_2]e} \tag{37.3d}$$

The parallel dynamics abstracts away from any limitations on processing capacity; such limitations are considered in Section 37.4.

The *implicit parallelism theorem* states that the sequential and the parallel dynamics coincide. Consequently, we need never be concerned with the *semantics* of a parallel program (its meaning is given by the sequential dynamics), but only with its *efficiency*. As a practical matter, this means that a program can be developed on a sequential platform, even if it is meant to run on a parallel platform, because the behavior is not affected by whether we execute it using a sequential or a parallel dynamics. Because the sequential dynamics is deterministic (every expression has at most one value), the implicit parallelism theorem implies that the parallel dynamics is also deterministic. For this reason, the implicit parallelism theorem is also known as the *deterministic parallelism theorem*. This terminology emphasizes the distinction between *deterministic parallelism*, the subject of this chapter, from *non-deterministic concurrency*, the subject of Chapters 39 and 40.

A proof of the implicit parallelism theorem can be given by giving an evaluation dynamics $e \Downarrow v$ in the style of Chapter 7, and showing that

$$e \mapsto_{\text{par}}^* v \quad \text{iff} \quad e \Downarrow v \quad \text{iff} \quad e \mapsto_{\text{seq}}^* v$$

(where v is a closed expression such that v val). The most important rule of the evaluation dynamics is for the evaluation of a parallel `let`:

$$\frac{e_1 \Downarrow v_1 \quad e_2 \Downarrow v_2 \quad [v_1, v_2/x_1, x_2]e \Downarrow v}{\mathtt{par}(e_1; e_2; x_1.x_2.e) \Downarrow v} \tag{37.4}$$

The other rules are easily derived from the structural dynamics of **PCF** as in Chapter 7.

It is possible to show that the sequential dynamics of **PPCF** agrees with its evaluation dynamics by extending the proof of Theorem 7.2.

Lemma 37.1. *For all v val, $e \mapsto^*_{seq} v$ if, and only if, $e \Downarrow v$.*

Proof It suffices to show that if $e \mapsto_{seq} e'$ and $e' \Downarrow v$, then $e \Downarrow v$, and that if $e_1 \mapsto^*_{seq} v_1$ and $e_2 \mapsto^*_{seq} v_2$ and $[v_1, v_2/x_1, x_2]e \mapsto^*_{seq} v$, then

$$\mathtt{par}\, x_1 = e_1 \,\mathtt{and}\, x_2 = e_2 \,\mathtt{in}\, e \mapsto^*_{seq} v. \qquad \square$$

By a similar argument, we may show that the parallel dynamics also agrees with the evaluation dynamics, and hence with the sequential dynamics.

Lemma 37.2. *For all v val, $e \mapsto^*_{par} v$ if, and only if, $e \Downarrow v$.*

Proof It suffices to show that if $e \mapsto_{par} e'$ and $e' \Downarrow v$, then $e \Downarrow v$, and that if $e_1 \mapsto^*_{par} v_1$ and $e_2 \mapsto^*_{par} v_2$ and $[v_1, v_2/x_1, x_2]e \mapsto^*_{par} v$, then

$$\mathtt{par}\, x_1 = e_1 \,\mathtt{and}\, x_2 = e_2 \,\mathtt{in}\, e \mapsto^*_{par} v.$$

The proof of the first is by induction on the parallel dynamics. The proof of the second proceeds by simultaneous induction on the derivations of $e_1 \mapsto^*_{par} v_1$ and $e_2 \mapsto^*_{par} v_2$. If $e_1 = v_1$ with v_1 val and $e_2 = v_2$ with v_2 val, then the result follows immediately from the third premise. If $e_2 = v_2$ but $e_1 \mapsto_{par} e'_1 \mapsto^*_{par} v_1$, then by induction we have that $\mathtt{par}\, x_1 = e'_1 \,\mathtt{and}\, x_2 = v_2 \,\mathtt{in}\, e \mapsto^*_{par} v$, and hence the result follows by an application of rule (37.3b). The symmetric case follows similarly by an application of rule (37.3c), and in the case that both e_1 and e_2 transition, the result follows by induction and rule (37.3a). $\square$

Theorem 37.3 (Implicit Parallelism). *The sequential and parallel dynamics coincide: for all v val, $e \mapsto^*_{seq} v$ iff $e \mapsto^*_{par} v$.*

Proof By Lemmas 37.1 and 37.2. $\square$

The implicit parallelism theorem states that parallelism does not affect the semantics of a program, only the efficiency of its execution. Correctness is not affected by parallelism, only efficiency.

37.2 Cost Dynamics

In this section, we define a *parallel cost dynamics* that assigns a *cost graph* to the evaluation of a **PPCF** expression. Cost graphs are defined by the following grammar:

$$
\text{Cost} \quad c \quad ::= \quad
\begin{array}{ll}
\mathbf{0} & \text{zero cost} \\
\mathbf{1} & \text{unit cost} \\
c_1 \otimes c_2 & \text{parallel combination} \\
c_1 \oplus c_2 & \text{sequential combination}
\end{array}
$$

A cost graph is a *series-parallel* ordered directed acyclic graph, with a designated *source* node and *sink* node. For $\mathbf{0}$ the graph consists of one node and no edges, with the source and sink both being the node itself. For $\mathbf{1}$ the graph consists of two nodes and one edge directed from the source to the sink. For $c_1 \otimes c_2$, if g_1 and g_2 are the graphs of c_1 and c_2, respectively, then the graph has two extra nodes, a source node with two edges to the source nodes of g_1 and g_2, and a sink node, with edges from the sink nodes of g_1 and g_2 to it. The children of the source are ordered according to the sequential evaluation order. Finally, for $c_1 \oplus c_2$, where g_1 and g_2 are the graphs of c_1 and c_2, the graph has as source node the source of g_1, as sink node the sink of g_2, and an edge from the sink of g_1 to the source of g_2.

The intuition behind a cost graph is that nodes represent subcomputations of an overall computation, and edges represent *sequentiality constraints*, stating that one computation depends on the result of another, and hence cannot be started before the one on which it depends completes. The product of two graphs represents *parallelism opportunities* in which there are no sequentiality constraints between the two computations. The assignment of source and sink nodes reflects the overhead of *forking* two parallel computations and *joining* them after they have both completed. At the structural level, we note that only the root has no ancestors, and only the final node of the cost graph has no descendents. Interior nodes may have one or two descendents, the former representing a sequential dependency, and the latter representing a *fork point*. Such nodes may have one or two ancestors, the former corresponding to a sequential dependency and the latter representing a *join point*.

We associate with each cost graph two numeric measures, the *work*, $wk(c)$, and the *depth*, $dp(c)$. The work is defined by the following equations:

$$
wk(c) =
\begin{cases}
0 & \text{if } c = \mathbf{0} \\
1 & \text{if } c = \mathbf{1} \\
wk(c_1) + wk(c_2) & \text{if } c = c_1 \otimes c_2 \\
wk(c_1) + wk(c_2) & \text{if } c = c_1 \oplus c_2
\end{cases}
\tag{37.5}
$$

The depth is defined by the following equations:

$$
dp(c) =
\begin{cases}
0 & \text{if } c = \mathbf{0} \\
1 & \text{if } c = \mathbf{1} \\
\max(dp(c_1), dp(c_2)) & \text{if } c = c_1 \otimes c_2 \\
dp(c_1) + dp(c_2) & \text{if } c = c_1 \oplus c_2
\end{cases}
\tag{37.6}
$$

Informally, the work of a cost graph determines the total number of computation steps represented by the cost graph, and thus corresponds to the *sequential complexity* of the computation. The depth of the cost graph determines the *critical path length*, the length of the longest dependency chain within the computation, which imposes a lower bound on the *parallel complexity* of a computation. The critical path length is a lower bound on the number of steps required to complete the computation.

In Chapter 7 we introduced *cost dynamics* to assign time complexity to computations. The proof of Theorem 7.7 shows that $e \Downarrow^k v$ iff $e \longmapsto^k v$. That is, the step complexity of an evaluation of e to a value v is just the number of transitions required to derive $e \longmapsto^* v$. Here we use cost graphs as the measure of complexity, then relate these cost graphs to the structural dynamics given in Section 37.1.

The judgment $e \Downarrow^c v$, where e is a closed expression, v is a closed value, and c is a cost graph specifies the cost dynamics. By definition we arrange that $e \Downarrow^0 e$ when e val. The cost assignment for `let` is given by the following rule:

$$\frac{e_1 \Downarrow^{c_1} v_1 \quad e_2 \Downarrow^{c_2} v_2 \quad [v_1, v_2/x_1, x_2]e \Downarrow^c v}{\mathtt{par}(e_1; e_2; x_1.x_2.e) \Downarrow^{(c_1 \otimes c_2) \oplus 1 \oplus c} v} \tag{37.7}$$

The cost assignment specifies that, under ideal conditions, e_1 and e_2 are evaluated in parallel, and that their results are passed to e. The cost of fork and join is implicit in the parallel combination of costs, and assign unit cost to the substitution because we expect it to be implemented by a constant-time mechanism for updating an environment. The cost dynamics of other language constructs is specified in a similar way, using only sequential combination to isolate the source of parallelism to the `let` construct.

Two simple facts about the cost dynamics are important to keep in mind. First, the cost assignment does not influence the outcome.

Lemma 37.4. $e \Downarrow v$ iff $e \Downarrow^c v$ for some c.

Proof From right to left, erase the cost assignments to construct an evaluation derivation. From left to right, decorate the evaluation derivations with costs as determined by the rules defining the cost dynamics. ☐

Second, the cost of evaluating an expression is uniquely determined.

Lemma 37.5. If $e \Downarrow^c v$ and $e \Downarrow^{c'} v$, then c is c'.

Proof By induction on the derivation of $e \Downarrow^c v$. ☐

The link between the cost dynamics and the structural dynamics is given by the following theorem, which states that the work cost is the sequential complexity, and the depth cost is the parallel complexity, of the computation.

Theorem 37.6. If $e \Downarrow^c v$, then $e \mapsto^w_{seq} v$ and $e \mapsto^d_{par} v$, where $w = wk(c)$ and $d = dp(c)$. Conversely, if $e \mapsto^w_{seq} v$, then there exists c such that $e \Downarrow^c v$ with $wk(c) = w$, and if $e \mapsto^d_{par} v'$, then there exists c' such that $e \Downarrow^{c'} v'$ with $dp(c') = d$.

Proof The first part is proved by induction on the derivation of $e \Downarrow^c v$, the interesting case being rule (37.7). By induction, we have $e_1 \mapsto^{w_1}_{seq} v_1$, $e_2 \mapsto^{w_2}_{seq} v_2$, and $[v_1, v_2/x_1, x_2]e \mapsto^w_{seq} v$, where $w_1 = wk(c_1)$, $w_2 = wk(c_2)$, and $w = wk(c)$. By pasting together derivations, we get a derivation

$$\mathtt{par}(e_1; e_2; x_1.x_2.e) \mapsto^{w_1}_{seq} \mathtt{par}(v_1; e_2; x_1.x_2.e)$$
$$\mapsto^{w_2}_{seq} \mathtt{par}(v_1; v_2; x_1.x_2.e)$$
$$\mapsto_{seq} [v_1, v_2/x_1, x_2]e$$
$$\mapsto^w_{seq} v.$$

Noting that $wk((c_1 \otimes c_2) \oplus \mathbf{1} \oplus c) = w_1 + w_2 + 1 + w$ completes the proof. Similarly, we have by induction that $e_1 \mapsto^{d_1}_{par} v_1$, $e_2 \mapsto^{d_2}_{par} v_2$, and $[v_1, v_2/x_1, x_2]e \mapsto^d_{par} v$, where $d_1 = dp(c_1)$, $d_2 = dp(c_2)$, and $d = dp(c)$. Assume, without loss of generality, that $d_1 \leq d_2$ (otherwise simply swap the roles of d_1 and d_2 in what follows). We may paste together derivations as follows:

$$\mathtt{par}(e_1; e_2; x_1.x_2.e) \mapsto^{d_1}_{par} \mathtt{par}(v_1; e'_2; x_1.x_2.e)$$
$$\mapsto^{d_2-d_1}_{par} \mathtt{par}(v_1; v_2; x_1.x_2.e)$$
$$\mapsto_{par} [v_1, v_2/x_1, x_2]e$$
$$\mapsto^d_{par} v.$$

Calculating $dp((c_1 \otimes c_2) \oplus \mathbf{1} \oplus c) = \max(d_1, d_2) + 1 + d$ completes the proof.

Turning to the second part, it suffices to show that if $e \mapsto_{seq} e'$ with $e' \Downarrow^{c'} v$, then $e \Downarrow^c v$ with $wk(c) = wk(c') + 1$, and if $e \mapsto_{par} e'$ with $e' \Downarrow^{c'} v$, then $e \Downarrow^c v$ with $dp(c) = dp(c') + 1$.

Suppose that $e = \mathtt{par}(e_1; e_2; x_1.x_2.e_0)$ with e_1 val and e_2 val. Then $e \mapsto_{seq} e'$, where $e = [e_1, e_2/x_1, x_2]e_0$ and there exists c' such that $e' \Downarrow^{c'} v$. But then $e \Downarrow^c v$, where $c = (\mathbf{0} \otimes \mathbf{0}) \oplus \mathbf{1} \oplus c'$, and a simple calculation shows that $wk(c) = wk(c') + 1$, as required. Similarly, $e \mapsto_{par} e'$ for e' as above, and hence $e \Downarrow^c v$ for some c such that $dp(c) = dp(c') + 1$, as required.

Suppose that $e = \mathtt{par}(e_1; e_2; x_1.x_2.e_0)$ and $e \mapsto_{seq} e'$, where $e' = \mathtt{par}(e'_1; e_2; x_1.x_2.e_0)$ and $e_1 \mapsto_{seq} e'_1$. From the assumption that $e' \Downarrow^{c'} v$, we have by inversion that $e'_1 \Downarrow^{c'_1} v_1$, $e_2 \Downarrow^{c'_2} v_2$, and $[v_1, v_2/x_1, x_2]e_0 \Downarrow^{c'_0} v$, with $c' = (c'_1 \otimes c'_2) \oplus \mathbf{1} \oplus c'_0$. By induction there exists c_1 such that $wk(c_1) = 1 + wk(c'_1)$ and $e_1 \Downarrow^{c_1} v_1$. But then $e \Downarrow^c v$, with $c = (c_1 \otimes c'_2) \oplus \mathbf{1} \oplus c'_0$.

By a similar argument, suppose that $e = \mathtt{par}(e_1; e_2; x_1.x_2.e_0)$ and $e \mapsto_{par} e'$, where $e' = \mathtt{par}(e'_1; e'_2; x_1.x_2.e_0)$ and $e_1 \mapsto_{par} e'_1$, $e_2 \mapsto_{par} e'_2$, and $e' \Downarrow^{c'} v$. Then by inversion $e'_1 \Downarrow^{c'_1} v_1$, $e'_2 \Downarrow^{c'_2} v_2$, $[v_1, v_2/x_1, x_2]e_0 \Downarrow^{c_0} v$. But then $e \Downarrow^c v$, where $c = (c_1 \otimes c_2) \oplus \mathbf{1} \oplus c_0$, $e_1 \Downarrow^{c_1} v_1$ with $dp(c_1) = 1 + dp(c'_1)$, $e_2 \Downarrow^{c_2} v_2$ with $dp(c_2) = 1 + dp(c'_2)$, and $[v_1, v_2/x_1, x_2]e_0 \Downarrow^{c_0} v$. Calculating, we get

$$dp(c) = \max(dp(c'_1) + 1, dp(c'_2) + 1) + 1 + dp(c_0)$$
$$= \max(dp(c'_1), dp(c'_2)) + 1 + 1 + dp(c_0)$$
$$= dp((c'_1 \otimes c'_2) \oplus \mathbf{1} \oplus c_0) + 1$$
$$= dp(c') + 1,$$

which completes the proof. $\square$

Corollary 37.7. *If $e \mapsto^w_{seq} v$ and $e \mapsto^d_{par} v'$, then v is v' and $e \Downarrow^c v$ for some c such that $wk(c) = w$ and $dp(c) = d$.*

37.3 Multiple Fork-Join

So far we have confined attention to binary fork/join parallelism induced by the parallel `let` construct. A generalizaton, called *data parallelism*, allows the simultaneous creation of any number of tasks that compute on the components of a data structure. The main example is a *sequence* of values of a specified type. The primitive operations on sequences are a natural source of unbounded parallelism. For example, we may consider a parallel map construct that applies a given function to every element of a sequence simultaneously, forming a sequence of the results.

We will consider here a simple language of sequence operations to illustrate the main ideas.

Typ	τ	$::=$	$\mathtt{seq}(\tau)$	$\tau\,\mathtt{seq}$	sequence
Exp	e	$::=$	$\mathtt{seq}(e_0,\ldots,e_{n-1})$	$[e_0,\ldots,e_{n-1}]$	sequence
			$\mathtt{len}(e)$	$\lvert e\rvert$	size
			$\mathtt{sub}(e_1;e_2)$	$e_1[e_2]$	element
			$\mathtt{tab}(x.e_1;e_2)$	$\mathtt{tab}(x.e_1;e_2)$	tabulate
			$\mathtt{map}(x.e_1;e_2)$	$[e_1 \mid x \in e_2]$	map
			$\mathtt{cat}(e_1;e_2)$	$\mathtt{cat}(e_1;e_2)$	concatenate

The expression $\mathtt{seq}(e_0,\ldots,e_{n-1})$ evaluates to an n-sequence whose elements are given by the expressions $e_0,\ldots,e_{n-1}$. The operation $\mathtt{len}(e)$ returns the number of elements in the sequence given by e. The operation $\mathtt{sub}(e_1;e_2)$ retrieves the element of the sequence given by e_1 at the index given by e_2. The tabulate operation, $\mathtt{tab}(x.e_1;e_2)$, yields the sequence of length given by e_2 whose ith element is given by $[i/x]e_1$. The operation $\mathtt{map}(x.e_1;e_2)$ computes the sequence whose ith element is given by $[e/x]e_1$, where e is the ith element of the sequence given by e_2. The operation $\mathtt{cat}(e_1;e_2)$ concatenates two sequences of the same type.

The statics of these operations is given by the following typing rules:

$$\frac{\Gamma \vdash e_0 : \tau \quad \ldots \quad \Gamma \vdash e_{n-1} : \tau}{\Gamma \vdash \mathtt{seq}(e_0,\ldots,e_{n-1}) : \mathtt{seq}(\tau)} \tag{37.8a}$$

$$\frac{\Gamma \vdash e : \mathtt{seq}(\tau)}{\Gamma \vdash \mathtt{len}(e) : \mathtt{nat}} \tag{37.8b}$$

$$\frac{\Gamma \vdash e_1 : \mathtt{seq}(\tau) \quad \Gamma \vdash e_2 : \mathtt{nat}}{\Gamma \vdash \mathtt{sub}(e_1;e_2) : \tau} \tag{37.8c}$$

$$\frac{\Gamma, x : \mathtt{nat} \vdash e_1 : \tau \quad \Gamma \vdash e_2 : \mathtt{nat}}{\Gamma \vdash \mathtt{tab}(x.e_1;e_2) : \mathtt{seq}(\tau)} \tag{37.8d}$$

$$\frac{\Gamma \vdash e_2 : \mathtt{seq}(\tau) \quad \Gamma, x : \tau \vdash e_1 : \tau'}{\Gamma \vdash \mathtt{map}(x.e_1; e_2) : \mathtt{seq}(\tau')} \tag{37.8e}$$

$$\frac{\Gamma \vdash e_1 : \mathtt{seq}(\tau) \quad \Gamma \vdash e_2 : \mathtt{seq}(\tau)}{\Gamma \vdash \mathtt{cat}(e_1; e_2) : \mathtt{seq}(\tau)} \tag{37.8f}$$

The cost dynamics of these constructs is defined by the following rules:

$$\frac{e_0 \Downarrow^{c_0} v_0 \quad \cdots \quad e_{n-1} \Downarrow^{c_{n-1}} v_{n-1}}{\mathtt{seq}(e_0, \ldots, e_{n-1}) \Downarrow^{\otimes_{i=0}^{n-1} c_i} \mathtt{seq}(v_0, \ldots, v_{n-1})} \tag{37.9a}$$

$$\frac{e \Downarrow^c \mathtt{seq}(v_0, \ldots, v_{n-1})}{\mathtt{len}(e) \Downarrow^{c \oplus 1} \mathtt{num}[n]} \tag{37.9b}$$

$$\frac{e_1 \Downarrow^{c_1} \mathtt{seq}(v_0, \ldots, v_{n-1}) \quad e_2 \Downarrow^{c_2} \mathtt{num}[i] \quad (0 \leq i < n)}{\mathtt{sub}(e_1; e_2) \Downarrow^{c_1 \oplus c_2 \oplus 1} v_i} \tag{37.9c}$$

$$\frac{e_2 \Downarrow^c \mathtt{num}[n] \quad [\mathtt{num}[0]/x]e_1 \Downarrow^{c_0} v_0 \quad \cdots \quad [\mathtt{num}[n-1]/x]e_1 \Downarrow^{c_{n-1}} v_{n-1}}{\mathtt{tab}(x.e_1; e_2) \Downarrow^{c \oplus \otimes_{i=0}^{n-1} c_i} \mathtt{seq}(v_0, \ldots, v_{n-1})} \tag{37.9d}$$

$$\frac{e_2 \Downarrow^c \mathtt{seq}(v_0, \ldots, v_{n-1}) \quad [v_0/x]e_1 \Downarrow^{c_0} v_0' \quad \cdots \quad [v_{n-1}/x]e_1 \Downarrow^{c_{n-1}} v_{n-1}'}{\mathtt{map}(x.e_1; e_2) \Downarrow^{c \oplus \otimes_{i=0}^{n-1} c_i} \mathtt{seq}(v_0', \ldots, v_{n-1}')} \tag{37.9e}$$

$$\frac{e_1 \Downarrow^{c_1} \mathtt{seq}(v_0, \ldots, v_{m-1}) \quad e_2 \Downarrow^{c_2} \mathtt{seq}(v_0', \ldots, v_{n-1}')}{\mathtt{cat}(e_1; e_2) \Downarrow^{c_1 \oplus c_2 \oplus \otimes_{i=0}^{m+n} 1} \mathtt{seq}(v_0, \ldots, v_{m-1}, v_0', \ldots, v_{n-1}')} \tag{37.9f}$$

The cost dynamics for sequence operations is validated by introducing a sequential and parallel cost dynamics and extending the proof of Theorem 37.6 to cover this extension.

37.4 Bounded Implementations

Theorem 37.6 states that the cost dynamics accurately models the dynamics of the parallel `let` construct, whether executed sequentially or in parallel. The theorem validates the cost dynamics from the point of view of the dynamics of the language, and permits us to draw conclusions about the asymptotic complexity of a parallel program that abstracts away from the limitations imposed by a concrete implementation. Chief among these is the restriction to a fixed number, $p > 0$, of processors on which to schedule the workload. Besides limiting the available parallelism this also imposes some synchronization overhead that must be taken into account. A *bounded implementation* is one for which we may establish an asymptotic bound on the execution time once these overheads are taken into account.

A bounded implementation must take account of the limitations and capabilities of the hardware on which the program is run. Because we are only interested in asymptotic upper bounds, it is convenient to formulate an abstract machine model, and to show that the primitives of the language can be implemented on this model with guaranteed time (and space) bounds. One example of such a model is the *shared-memory multiprocessor*, or *SMP*, model. The basic assumption of the SMP model is that there are some fixed $p > 0$ processors coordinated by an interconnect that permits constant-time access to any object in memory shared by all p processors.[1] An SMP is assumed to provide a constant-time synchronization primitive with which to control simultaneous access to a memory cell. There are a variety of such primitives, any of which are enough to provide a parallel fetch-and-add instruction that allows each processor to get the current contents of a memory cell and update it by adding a fixed constant in a single atomic operation—the interconnect serializes any simultaneous accesses by more than one processor.

Building a bounded implementation of parallelism involves two major tasks. First, we must show that the primitives of the language can be implemented efficiently on the abstract machine model. Second, we must show how to schedule the workload across the processors to minimize execution time by maximizing parallelism. When working with a low-level machine model such as an SMP, both tasks involve a fair bit of technical detail to show how to use low-level machine instructions, including a synchronization primitive, to implement the language primitives and to schedule the workload. Collecting these together, we may then give an asymptotic bound on the time complexity of the implementation that relates the abstract cost of the computation to cost of implementing the workload on a p-way multiprocessor. The prototypical result of this kind is *Brent's Theorem*.

Theorem 37.8. *If $e \Downarrow^c v$ with $wk(c) = w$ and $dp(c) = d$, then e can be evaluated on a p-processor SMP in time $O(\max(w/p, d))$.*

The theorem tells us that we can never execute a program in fewer steps than its depth d and that, at best, we can divide the work up evenly into w/p rounds of execution by the p processors. Note that if $p = 1$ then the theorem establishes an upper bound of $O(w)$ steps, the sequential complexity of the computation. Moreover, if the work is proportional to the depth, then we are unable to exploit parallelism, and the overall time is proportional to the work alone.

Theorem 37.8 motivates consideration of a useful figure of merit, the *parallelizability ratio*, which is the ratio w/d of work to depth. If $w/d \gg p$, then the program is *parallelizable*, because then $w/p \gg d$, and we may therefore reduce running time by using p processors at each step. If the parallelizability ratio is a constant, then d will dominate w/p, and we will have little opportunity to exploit parallelism to reduce running time. It is not known, in general, whether a problem admits a parallelizable solution. The best we can say, on present knowledge, is that there are algorithms for some problems that have a high degree of parallelizability, and there are problems for which no such algorithm is known. It is a difficult problem in complexity theory to analyze which problems are parallelizable, and which are not.

Proving Brent's Theorem for an SMP would take us much too far afield for the present purposes. Instead, we shall prove a Brent-type Theorem for an abstract machine, the **P** machine. The machine is unrealistic in that it is defined at a very high level of abstraction. But it is designed to match well the cost semantics given earlier in this chapter. In particular, there are mechanisms that account for both sequential and parallel dependencies in a computation.

At the highest level, the state of the **P** machine consists of a global task graph whose structure corresponds to a "diagonal cut" through the cost graph of the overall computation. Nodes immediately above the cut are eligible to be executed, higher ancestors having already been completed, and whose immediate descendents are waiting for their ancestors to complete. Further descendents in the full task graph are tasks yet to be created, once the immediate descendents are finished. The **P** machine discards completed tasks, and future tasks beyond the immediate dependents are only created as execution proceeds. Thus, it is only those nodes next to the cut line through the cost graph that are represented in the **P** machine state.

The *global state* of the **P** machine is a configuration of the form $\nu \Sigma \{ \mu \}$, where Σ is degenerated to just a finite set of (pairwise distinct) *task names* and μ is a finite mapping the task names in Σ to *local states*, representing the state of an individual task. A *local state* is either a closed **PCF** expression, or one of two special *join points* that implement the sequential and parallel dependencies of a task on one or two ancestors, respectively.[2] Thus, when expanded out, a global state has the form

$$\nu\, a_1, \ldots, a_n \{ a_1 \hookrightarrow s_1 \otimes \ldots \otimes a_n \hookrightarrow s_n \},$$

where $n \geq 1$, and each s_i is a local state. The ordering of the tasks in a state, like the order of declarations in the signature, is not significant.

A **P** machine state transition has the form $\nu \Sigma \{ \mu \} \longmapsto \nu \Sigma' \{ \mu' \}$. There are two forms of such transitions, the *global* and the *local*. A global step selects as many tasks as are available, up to a pre-specified parameter $p > 0$, which represents the number of processors available at each round. (Such a scheduler is *greedy* in the sense that it never fails to execute an available task, up to the specified limit for each round.) A task is *finished* if it consists of a closed **PCF** value, or is a join point whose dependents are not yet finished; otherwise, a task is *available*, or *ready*. A ready task is always capable of taking a local step consisting of either a step of **PCF**, expressed in the setting of the **P** machine, or a *synchronization* step that manages the join-point logic. Because the **P** machine employs a greedy scheduler, it must complete execution in time proportional to $\max(w/p, d)$ steps by doing up to p steps of work at a time, insofar as it is possible within the limits of the depth of the computation. We thus get a *Brent-type Theorem* for the abstract machine that illustrates more sophisticated Brent-type Theorems for other models, such as the **PRAM**, that are used in the analysis of parallel algorithms.

The local transitions of the **P** machine corresponding to the steps of **PCF** itself are illustrated by the following example rules for application; the others follow a similar pattern.[3]

$$\frac{\neg(e_1\ \mathsf{val})}{\nu\, a \{ a \hookrightarrow e_1(e_2) \} \longmapsto_{loc} \nu\, a\, a_1 \{ a \hookrightarrow \mathtt{join}[a_1](x_1.x_1(e_2)) \otimes a_1 \hookrightarrow e_1 \}} \tag{37.10a}$$

$$\frac{e_1\ \mathsf{val}}{\nu\, a \{ a \hookrightarrow e_1(e_2) \} \longmapsto_{loc} \nu\, a\, a_2 \{ a \hookrightarrow \mathtt{join}[a_2](x_2.e_1(x_2)) \otimes a_2 \hookrightarrow e_2 \}} \tag{37.10b}$$

$$\frac{e_1 \text{ val} \quad e_2 \text{ val}}{\nu\, a_1\, a_2 \{a_1 \hookrightarrow \text{join}[a_2](x_2.e_1(x_2)) \otimes a_2 \hookrightarrow e_2\} \longmapsto_{loc} \nu\, a_1 \{a_1 \hookrightarrow [e_2/x_2]e_1\}} \quad (37.10\text{c})$$

$$\frac{e_2 \text{ val}}{\nu\, a \{a \hookrightarrow (\lambda\,(x : \tau_2)\,e)(e_2)\} \longmapsto_{loc} \nu\, a \{a \hookrightarrow [e_2/x]e\}} \quad (37.10\text{d})$$

Rules (37.10a) and (37.10b) create create tasks for the evaluation of the function and argument of an expression. Rule (37.10c) propagates the result of evaluation of the function or argument of an application to the appropriate application expression. This rule mediates between the first two rules and rule (37.10d), which effects a β-reduction in-place.

The local transitions of the **P** machine corresponding to binary fork and join are as follows:

$$\left\{\begin{array}{c} \nu\, a \{a \hookrightarrow \text{par}(e_1; e_2; x_1.x_2.e)\} \\ \longmapsto_{loc} \\ \nu\, a_1, a_2, a \{a_1 \hookrightarrow e_1 \otimes a_2 \hookrightarrow e_2 \otimes a \hookrightarrow \text{join}[a_1; a_2](x_1; x_2.e)\} \end{array}\right\} \quad (37.11\text{a})$$

$$\frac{e_1 \text{ val} \quad e_2 \text{ val}}{\left\{\begin{array}{c} \nu\, a_1, a_2, a \{a_1 \hookrightarrow e_1 \otimes a_2 \hookrightarrow e_2 \otimes a \hookrightarrow \text{join}[a_1; a_2](x_1; x_2.e)\} \\ \longmapsto_{loc} \\ \nu\, a \{a \hookrightarrow [e_1, e_2/x_1, x_2]e\} \end{array}\right\}} \quad (37.11\text{b})$$

Rule (37.11a) creates two parallel tasks on which the executing task depends. The expression $\text{join}[a_1; a_2](x_1; x_2.e)$ is blocked on tasks a_1 and a_2, so that no local step applies to it. Rule (37.11b) synchronizes a task with the tasks on which it depends once their execution has completed; those tasks are no longer required, and are eliminated from the state.

Each global transition is the simultaneous execution of one step of computation on as many as $p \geq 1$ processors.

$$\nu\, \Sigma_1\, a_1 \{\mu_1 \otimes a_1 \hookrightarrow s_1\} \longmapsto_{loc} \nu\, \Sigma'_1\, a_1 \{\mu'_1 \otimes a_1 \hookrightarrow s'_1\}$$

$$\cdots$$

$$\frac{\nu\, \Sigma_n\, a_n \{\mu_n \otimes a_n \hookrightarrow s_n\} \longmapsto_{loc} \nu\, \Sigma'_n\, a_n \{\mu'_n \otimes a_n \hookrightarrow s'_n\}}{\left\{\begin{array}{c} \nu\, \Sigma_0\, \Sigma_1\, a_1\, \ldots\, \Sigma_n\, a_n \{\mu_0 \otimes \mu_1 \otimes a_1 \hookrightarrow s_1 \otimes \ldots \otimes \mu_n \otimes a_n \hookrightarrow s_n\} \\ \longmapsto_{glo} \\ \nu\, \Sigma_0\, \Sigma'_1\, a_1\, \ldots\, \Sigma'_n\, a_n \{\mu_0 \otimes \mu'_1 \otimes a_1 \hookrightarrow s'_1 \otimes \ldots \otimes \mu'_n \otimes a_n \hookrightarrow s'_n\} \end{array}\right\}} \quad (37.12)$$

At each global step, some number $1 \leq n \leq p$ of ready tasks are scheduled for execution, where n is maximal among the number of ready tasks. Because no two distinct tasks may depend on the same task, we may partition the n tasks so that each scheduled task is grouped with the tasks on which it depends as necessary for any local join step. Any local fork step adds two fresh tasks to the state resulting from the global transition; any local join step eliminates two tasks whose execution has completed. A subtle point is that it is implicit in our name binding conventions that the names of any created tasks are *globally unique*, even though they are *locally created*. In implementation terms, this requires a synchronization step among the processors to ensure that task names are not accidentally reused among the parallel tasks.

The proof of a Brent-type Theorem for the **P** machine is now obvious. We need only ensure that the parameter n of rule (37.12) is chosen as large as possible at each step, limited only by the parameter p and the number of ready tasks. A scheduler with this property is *greedy*; it never allows a processor to go idle if work remains to be done. Consequently, if there are always p available tasks at each global step, then the evaluation will complete in w/p steps, where w is the work complexity of the program. If, at some stage, fewer than p tasks are available, then performance degrades according to the sequential dependencies among the sub-computations. In the limiting case, the **P** machine must take at least d steps, where d is the depth of the computation.

37.5 Scheduling

The global transition relation of the **P** machine defined in Section 37.4 affords wide latitude in the choice of tasks that are advanced by taking a local transition. Doing so abstracts from implementation details that are irrelevant to the proof of the Brent-type Theorem given later in that section, the only requirement being that the number of tasks chosen be as large as possible up to the specified bound p, representing the number of available processors. When taking into account factors not considered here, it is necessary to specify the scheduling policy more precisely—for example, different scheduling policies may have asymptotically different space requirements. The overall idea is to consider scheduling a computation on p processors as a *p-way parallel traversal* of its cost graph, visiting up to p nodes at a time in an order consistent with the dependency ordering. In this section, we will consider one such traversal, *p-way parallel depth-first-search*, or *p-DFS*, which specializes to the familiar depth-first traversal in the case that $p = 1$.

Recall that the depth first-search of a directed graph maintain a stack of unvisited nodes, which is initialized with the start node. At each round, a node is popped from the stack and visited, and then its unvisited children are pushed on the stack (in reverse order in the case of ordered graphs), completing that round. The traversal terminates when the stack is empty. When viewed as a scheduling strategy, visiting a node of a cost graph consists of scheduling the work associated with that node on a processor. The job of such as scheduler is to do the work of the computation in depth-first order, visiting the children of a node from left to right, consistently with the sequential dynamics (which would, in particular, treat a parallel binding as two sequential bindings). Notice that because a cost graph is directed acyclic, there are no "back edges" arising from the traversal, and because it is series-parallel in structure, there are no "cross edges." Thus, all children of a node are unvisited, and no task is considered more than once.

Although evocative, viewing scheduling as graph traversal invites one to imagine that the cost graph is given explicitly as a data structure, which is not at all the case. Instead, the graph is created dynamically as the sub-computations are executed. At each round, the computation associated with a node may *complete* (when it has achieved its value), *continue* (when more work is yet to be done), or *fork* (when it generates parallel sub-computations with a specified join point). Once a computation has completed and its value has been passed to the associated join point, its node in the cost graph is discarded. Furthermore, the children of a node only come into existence as a result of its execution, according to whether it completes (no children), continues (one child), or forks (two children). Thus, one may envision that the cost graph "exists" as a cut through the abstract cost graph representing pending tasks that have not yet been activated by the traversal.

A parallel depth-first search works much the same way, except that as many as p nodes are visited at each round, constrained only by the presence of unvisited (yet-to-be-scheduled) nodes. One might naively think that this simply means popping up to p nodes from the stack on each round, visiting them all simultaneously, and pushing their dependents on the stack in reverse order, just as for conventional depth-first search. But a moment's thought reveals that this is not correct. Because the cost graphs are ordered, the visited nodes form a sequence determined by the left-to-right ordering of the children of a node. If a node completes, it has no children and is removed from its position in the sequence in the next round. If a node continues, it has one child that occupies the same relative position as its parent in the next round. And if a node forks two children, they are inserted into the sequence after the predecessor, and immediately prior to that node, related to each other by the left-to-right ordering of the children. The task associated to the visited node itself becomes the join point of the immediately preceding pair of tasks, with which it will synchronize when they complete. Thus, the visited sequence of $k \leq p$ nodes becomes, on the next round, anywhere from 0 (if all nodes completes) to $3 \times k$ nodes (if each node forks). These are placed into consideration, in the specified order, for the next round to ensure that they are processed in depth-first order. Importantly, the data structure maintaining the unvisited nodes of the graph is not a simple pushdown stack, because of the "in-place" replacement of each visited node by zero, one, or two nodes in between its predecessor and successor in the sequential ordering of the visited nodes.

Consider a variant of the **P** machine in which the order of the tasks is significant. A task is *finished* if it is a value, *blocked* if it is a join, and *ready* otherwise. Local transitions remain the same as in Section 37.4, bearing in mind that the ordering is significant. A global transition, however, consists of making a local transition on each of the first $k \leq p$ ready tasks.[4] After this selection, the global state is depicted as follows:

$$\nu \, \Sigma_0 \, a_1 \, \Sigma_1 \, \ldots \, a_k \, \Sigma_k \, \Sigma \, \{ \, \mu_0 \otimes a_1 \hookrightarrow e_1 \otimes \mu_1 \otimes \ldots a_k \hookrightarrow e_k \otimes \mu \, \}$$

where each μ_i consists of finished or blocked tasks, and each e_i is ready. A schedule is greedy If $k < p$ only when no task in μ is ready.

After a local transition is made on each of the k selected tasks, the resulting global state has the form

$$\nu \, \Sigma_0 \Sigma_1' \, a_1 \, \Sigma_1 \, \ldots \, \Sigma_k' \, a_k \, \Sigma_k \, \Sigma \, \{ \, \mu_0 \otimes \mu_1' \otimes a_1 \hookrightarrow e_1' \otimes \mu_1 \otimes \ldots \mu_k' \otimes a_k \hookrightarrow e_k' \otimes \mu \, \}$$

where each μ_i' represents the newly created task(s) of the local transition on task $a_i \hookrightarrow e_i$, and each e_i' is the expression resulting from the transition on that task. Next, all possible synchronizations are made by replacing each occurrence of an adjacent triple of the form

$$a_{i,1} \hookrightarrow e_1 \otimes a_{i,2} \hookrightarrow e_2 \otimes a_i \hookrightarrow \mathtt{join}[a_{i,1}; a_{i,2}](x_1; x_2.e)$$

(with e_1 and e_2 finished) by the task $a_i \hookrightarrow [e_1, e_2/x_1, x_2]e$. Doing so propagates the values of tasks $a_{i,1}$ and $a_{i,2}$ to the join point, enabling the computation to continue. The two finished tasks are removed from the state, and the join point is no longer blocked.

37.6 Notes

Parallelism is a high-level programming concept that increases efficiency by carrying out multiple computations simultaneously when they are mutually independent. Parallelism does not change the meaning of a program, but only how fast it is executed. The cost semantics specifies the number of steps required to execute a program sequentially and with maximal parallelism. A bounded implementation provides a bound on the number of steps when the number of processors is limited, limiting the degree of parallelism that can be realized. This formulation of parallelism was introduced by Blelloch (1990). The concept of a cost semantics and the idea of a bounded implementation studied here are derived from Blelloch and Greiner (1995, 1996).

Exercises

37.1. Consider extending **PPCF** with exceptions, as described in Chapter 29, under the assumption that τ_{exn} has at least two exception values. Give a sequential and a parallel structural dynamics to parallel let in such a way that determinacy continues to hold.

37.2. Give a matching cost semantics to **PPCF** extended with exceptions (described in Exercise **37.1**) by inductively defining the following two judgments:
(a) $e \Downarrow^c v$, stating that e evaluates to value v with cost c;
(b) $e \Uparrow^c v$, stating that e raises the value v with cost c.
The analog of Theorem 37.6 remains valid for the dynamics. In particular, if $e \Uparrow^c v$, then both $e \mapsto^w_{\mathsf{seq}} \mathtt{raise}(v)$, where $w = wk(c)$, and $e \mapsto^d_{\mathsf{par}} \mathtt{raise}(v)$, where $d = dp(c)$, and conversely.

37.3. Extend the **P** machine to admit exceptions to match your solution to Exercise **37.2**. Argue that the revised machine supports a Brent-type validation of the cost semantics.

37.4. Another way to express the dynamics of **PPCF** enriched with exceptions is by rewriting $\mathtt{par}(e_1; e_2; x_1.x_2.e)$ into another such parallel binding, $\mathtt{par}(e_1'; e_2'; x_1'.x_2'.e')$, which implements the correct dynamics to ensure determinacy. *Hint*: Extend **XPCF** with sums (Chapter 11), using them to record the outcome of each parallel sub-computation (e_1' derived from e_1, and e_2' derived from e_2), and then check the outcomes (e' derived from e) in such a way to ensure determinacy.

Notes

1 A slightly weaker assumption is that each access may require up to $\lg p$ time to account for the overhead of synchronization, but we shall neglect this refinement in the present, simplified account.
2 The use of join points for each sequential dependency is profligate but aligns the machine with the cost semantics. Realistically, individual tasks manage sequential dependencies without synchronization, by using local control stacks as in Chapter 28.
3 Here and elsewhere typing information is omitted from Σ, because it is not relevant to the dynamics.
4 Thus, the local transition given by rule (37.11b) is never applicable; the dynamics of joins will be described shortly.

38

Futures and Speculations

A *future* is a computation that is performed before it is value is needed. Like a suspension, a future represents a value that is to be determined later. Unlike a suspension, a future is always evaluated, regardless of whether its value is required. In a sequential setting, futures are of little interest; a future of type τ is just an expression of type τ. In a parallel setting, however, futures are of interest because they provide a means of initiating a parallel computation whose result is not needed until later, by which time it will have been completed.

The prototypical example of the use of futures is to implementing *pipelining*, a method for overlapping the stages of a multistage computation to the fullest extent possible. Pipelining minimizes the latency caused by one stage waiting for a previous stage to complete by allowing the two stages to execute in parallel until an explicit dependency arises. Ideally, the computation of the result of an earlier stage is finished by the time a later stage needs it. At worst, the later stage is delayed until the earlier stage completes, incurring what is known as a *pipeline stall*.

A *speculation* is a delayed computation whose result might be needed for the overall computation to finish. The dynamics for speculations executes suspended computations in parallel with the main thread of computation, without regard to whether the value of the speculation is needed by the main thread. If the value of the speculation is needed, then such a dynamics pays off, but if not, the effort to compute it is wasted.

Futures are *work efficient* in that the overall work done by a computation involving futures is no more than the work done by a sequential execution. Speculations, in contrast, are *work inefficient* in that speculative execution might be in vain—the overall computation may involve more steps than the work needed to compute the result. For this reason, speculation is a risky strategy for exploiting parallelism. It can make use of available resources, but perhaps only at the expense of doing more work than necessary!

38.1 Futures

The syntax of futures is given by the following grammar:

Typ	τ	::=	$\mathtt{fut}(\tau)$	$\tau\,\mathtt{fut}$	future
Exp	e	::=	$\mathtt{fut}(e)$	$\mathtt{fut}(e)$	future
			$\mathtt{fsyn}(e)$	$\mathtt{fsyn}(e)$	synchronize
			$\mathtt{fcell}[a]$	$\mathtt{fcell}[a]$	indirection

The type τ fut is the type of futures of type τ. Futures are introduced by the expression fut(e), which schedules e for evaluation and returns a reference to it. Futures are eliminated by the expression fsyn(e), which synchronizes with the future referred to by e, returning its value. Indirect references to future values are represented by fcell[a], indicating a future value to be stored at a.

38.1.1 Statics

The statics of futures is given by the following rules:

$$\frac{\Gamma \vdash e : \tau}{\Gamma \vdash \mathtt{fut}(e) : \mathtt{fut}(\tau)} \tag{38.1a}$$

$$\frac{\Gamma \vdash e : \mathtt{fut}(\tau)}{\Gamma \vdash \mathtt{fsyn}(e) : \tau} \tag{38.1b}$$

These rules are unsurprising, because futures add no new capabilities to the language beyond providing an opportunity for parallel evaluation.

38.1.2 Sequential Dynamics

The sequential dynamics of futures is easily defined. Futures are evaluated eagerly; synchronization returns the value of the future.

$$\frac{e \; \mathsf{val}}{\mathtt{fut}(e) \; \mathsf{val}} \tag{38.2a}$$

$$\frac{e \longmapsto e'}{\mathtt{fut}(e) \longmapsto \mathtt{fut}(e')} \tag{38.2b}$$

$$\frac{e \longmapsto e'}{\mathtt{fsyn}(e) \longmapsto \mathtt{fsyn}(e')} \tag{38.2c}$$

$$\frac{e \; \mathsf{val}}{\mathtt{fsyn}(\mathtt{fut}(e)) \longmapsto e} \tag{38.2d}$$

Under a sequential dynamics futures have little purpose: they introduce a pointless level of indirection.

38.2 Speculations

The syntax of (non-recursive) speculations is given by the following grammar:[1]

Typ	τ	::=	spec(τ)	τ spec	speculation
Exp	e	::=	spec(e)	spec(e)	speculate
			ssyn(e)	ssyn(e)	synchronize
			scell[a]	scell[a]	indirection

The type τ spec is the type of speculations of type τ. The introduction form spec(e) creates a computation that can be speculatively evaluated, and the elimination form ssyn(e) synchronizes with a speculation. A reference to the result of a speculative computation stored at a is written scell[a].

38.2.1 Statics

The statics of speculations is given by the following rules:

$$\frac{\Gamma \vdash e : \tau}{\Gamma \vdash \text{spec}(e) : \text{spec}(\tau)} \tag{38.3a}$$

$$\frac{\Gamma \vdash e : \text{spec}(\tau)}{\Gamma \vdash \text{ssyn}(e) : \tau} \tag{38.3b}$$

Thus, the statics for speculations as given by rules (38.3) is equivalent to the statics for futures given by rules (38.1).

38.2.2 Sequential Dynamics

The definition of the sequential dynamics of speculations is like that of futures, except that speculations are values.

$$\frac{}{\text{spec}(e) \text{ val}} \tag{38.4a}$$

$$\frac{e \longmapsto e'}{\text{ssyn}(e) \longmapsto \text{ssyn}(e')} \tag{38.4b}$$

$$\frac{}{\text{ssyn}(\text{spec}(e)) \longmapsto e} \tag{38.4c}$$

Under a sequential dynamics speculations are simply a re-formulation of suspensions.

38.3 Parallel Dynamics

Futures are only interesting insofar as they admit a parallel dynamics that allows the computation of the future to go ahead concurrently with some other computation. In this section, we give a parallel dynamics of futures and speculation in which the creation, execution, and synchronization of tasks is made explicit. The parallel dynamics of futures and speculations is *identical*, except for the termination condition. Whereas futures require that all tasks are completed before termination, speculations may be abandoned before they are completed. For the sake of concision we will give the parallel dynamics of futures, remarking only where alterations are made for the parallel dynamics of speculations.

The parallel dynamics of futures relies on a modest extension to the language given in Section 38.1 to introduce *names* for tasks. Let Σ be a finite mapping assigning types to names. As mentioned earlier, the expression $\mathtt{fcell}[a]$ is a value referring to the outcome of task a. The statics of this expression is given by the following rule:[2]

$$\frac{}{\Gamma \vdash_{\Sigma, a \sim \tau} \mathtt{fcell}[a] : \mathtt{fut}(\tau)} \tag{38.5}$$

Rules (38.1) carry over in the obvious way with Σ recording the types of the task names.

States of the parallel dynamics have the form $\nu \Sigma \{ e \parallel \mu \}$, where e is the *focus* of evaluation, and μ records the active parallel futures (or speculations). Formally, μ is a finite mapping assigning expressions to the task names declared in Σ. A state is well-formed according to the following rule:

$$\frac{\vdash_\Sigma e : \tau \quad (\forall a \in dom(\Sigma)) \vdash_\Sigma \mu(a) : \Sigma(a)}{\nu \Sigma \{ e \parallel \mu \} \, \mathsf{ok}} \tag{38.6}$$

As discussed in Chapter 35, this rule admits self-referential and mutually referential futures. A more refined condition could as well be given that avoids circularities; we leave this as an exercise for the reader.

The parallel dynamics is divided into two phases, the *local* phase, which defines the basic steps of evaluation of an expression, and the *global* phase, which executes all possible local steps in parallel. The local dynamics of futures is defined by the following rules:[3]

$$\frac{}{\mathtt{fcell}[a] \, \mathsf{val}_{\Sigma, a \sim \tau}} \tag{38.7a}$$

$$\frac{}{\nu \Sigma \{ \mathtt{fut}(e) \parallel \mu \} \longmapsto_{loc} \nu \Sigma, a \sim \tau \{ \mathtt{fcell}[a] \parallel \mu \otimes a \hookrightarrow e \}} \tag{38.7b}$$

$$\frac{\nu \Sigma \{ e \parallel \mu \} \longmapsto_{loc} \nu \Sigma' \{ e' \parallel \mu' \}}{\nu \Sigma \{ \mathtt{fsyn}(e) \parallel \mu \} \longmapsto_{loc} \nu \Sigma' \{ \mathtt{fsyn}(e') \parallel \mu' \}} \tag{38.7c}$$

$$\frac{e' \, \mathsf{val}_{\Sigma, a \sim \tau}}{\left\{ \begin{array}{c} \nu \Sigma, a \sim \tau \{ \mathtt{fsyn}(\mathtt{fcell}[a]) \parallel \mu \otimes a \hookrightarrow e' \} \\ \longmapsto_{loc} \\ \nu \Sigma, a \sim \tau \{ e' \parallel \mu \otimes a \hookrightarrow e' \} \end{array} \right\}} \tag{38.7d}$$

Rule (38.7b) activates a future named a executing the expression e and returns a reference to it. Rule (38.7d) synchronizes with a future whose value has been determined. Note that a local transition always has the form

$$\nu \Sigma \{ e \parallel \mu \} \longmapsto_{loc} \nu \Sigma \, \Sigma' \{ e' \parallel \mu \otimes \mu' \}$$

where Σ' is either empty or declares the type of a single symbol, and μ' is either empty or of the form $a \hookrightarrow e'$ for some expression e'.

A global step of the parallel dynamics consists of at most one local step for the focal expression and one local step for each of up to p futures, where $p > 0$ is a fixed parameter representing the number of processors.

$$\mu = \mu_0 \otimes a_1 \hookrightarrow e_1 \otimes \ldots \otimes a_n \hookrightarrow e_n$$

$$\mu'' = \mu_0 \otimes a_1 \hookrightarrow e_1' \otimes \ldots \otimes a_n \hookrightarrow e_n'$$

$$\nu \Sigma \{ e \parallel \mu \} \longmapsto_{loc}^{0,1} \nu \Sigma \Sigma' \{ e' \parallel \mu \otimes \mu' \}$$

$$\frac{(\forall 1 \le i \le n \le p) \quad \nu \Sigma \{ e_i \parallel \mu \} \longmapsto_{loc} \nu \Sigma \Sigma_i' \{ e_i' \parallel \mu \otimes \mu_i' \}}{\left\{ \begin{array}{c} \nu \Sigma \{ e \parallel \mu \} \\ \longmapsto_{glo} \\ \nu \Sigma \Sigma' \Sigma_1' \ldots \Sigma_n' \{ e' \parallel \mu'' \otimes \mu' \otimes \mu_1' \otimes \ldots \otimes \mu_n' \} \end{array} \right\}} \tag{38.8a}$$

Rule (38.8a) allows the focus expression to take either zero or one step because it might be blocked awaiting the completion of evaluation of a parallel future (or synchronizing with a speculation). The futures allocated by the local steps of execution are consolidated in the result of the global step. We assume without loss of generality that the names of the new futures in each local step are pairwise disjoint so that the combination makes sense. In implementation terms, satisfying this disjointness assumption means that the processors must synchronize their access to memory.

The initial state of a computation, for futures or speculations, is defined by the rule

$$\frac{}{\nu \varnothing \{ e \parallel \varnothing \} \text{ initial}} \tag{38.9}$$

For futures, a state is final only if the focus and all parallel futures have completed evaluation:

$$\frac{e \text{ val}_\Sigma \quad \mu \text{ val}_\Sigma}{\nu \Sigma \{ e \parallel \mu \} \text{ final}} \tag{38.10a}$$

$$\frac{(\forall a \in dom(\Sigma)) \ \mu(a) \text{ val}_\Sigma}{\mu \text{ val}_\Sigma} \tag{38.10b}$$

For speculations, a state is final only if the focus is a value, regardless of whether any other speculations have completed:

$$\frac{e \text{ val}_\Sigma}{\nu \Sigma \{ e \parallel \mu \} \text{ final}} \tag{38.11}$$

All futures must terminate to ensure that the work performed in parallel matches that performed sequentially; no future is created whose value is not needed according to the sequential semantics. In contrast, speculations can be abandoned when their values are not needed.

38.4 Pipelining with Futures

Pipelining is an interesting example of the use of parallel futures. Consider a situation in which a *producer* builds a list whose elements represent units of work, and a *consumer* traverses the work list and acts on each element of that list. The elements of the work list can be thought of as "instructions" to the consumer, which maps a function over that list to carry out those instructions. An obvious sequential implementation first builds the work list, then traverses it to perform the work indicated by the list. This strategy works well provided that the elements of the list can be produced quickly, but if each element needs a lot of computation, it would be preferable to overlap production of the next list element with execution of the previous unit of work, which can be programmed using futures.

Let flist be the recursive type $\mathtt{rec}\,t\,\mathtt{is}\,\mathtt{unit} + (\mathtt{nat} \times t\,\mathtt{fut})$, whose elements are nil, defined to be $\mathtt{fold}(1 \cdot \langle\rangle)$, and $\mathtt{cons}(e_1, e_2)$, defined to be $\mathtt{fold}(\mathtt{r} \cdot \langle e_1, \mathtt{fut}(e_2)\rangle)$. The producer is a recursive function that generates a value of type flist:

```
fix produce : (nat → nat opt) → nat → flist is
  λ f. λ i.
    case f(i) {
      null ↪ nil
    | just x ↪ cons(x, fut (produce f (i+1)))
    }
```

On each iteration the producer generates a parallel future to produce the tail. The future continues to execute after the producer returns so that its evaluation overlaps with subsequent computation.

The consumer folds an operation over the work list as follows:

```
fix consume : ((nat×nat)→nat) → nat → flist → nat is
  λ g. λ a. λ xs.
    case xs {
      nil ↪ a
    | cons (x, xs) ↪ consume g (g (x, a)) (fsyn xs)
    }
```

The consumer synchronizes with the tail of the work list just at the point where it makes a recursive call and hence needs the head element of the tail to continue processing. At this point, the consumer will block, if necessary, to await computation of the tail before continuing the recursion.

Speculations arise naturally in lazy languages. But although they provide opportunities for parallelism, they are not, in general, *work efficient*: a speculation might be evaluated even though its value is never needed. An alternative is to combine suspensions (see Chapter 36) with futures so that the programmer may specify which suspensions ought to be evaluated in parallel. The notion of a *spark* is designed to achieve this. A spark evaluates a computation in parallel only for its effect on suspensions that are likely to be needed later. Specifically, we may define

$$\mathtt{spark}(e_1; e_2) \triangleq \mathtt{letfut}\,\_\,\mathtt{be}\,\mathtt{force}(e_1)\,\mathtt{in}\,e_2,$$

where $e_1 : \tau_1\,\mathtt{susp}$ and $e_2 : \tau_2$.[4] The expression $\mathtt{force}(e_1)$ is evaluated in parallel, forcing the evaluation of e_1, in hopes that it will have completed evaluation before its value is needed by e_2.

As an example, consider the type strm of streams of numbers defined by the recursive type $rec\, t$ is $(unit + (nat \times t))$ susp. Elements of this type are suspended computations that, when forced, either signals the end of stream, or produces a number and another such stream. Suppose that s is such a stream, and assume that we know, for reasons of its construction, that it is finite. We wish to compute map$(f)(s)$ for some function f, and to overlap this computation with the production of the stream elements. We will make use of a function mapforce that forces successive elements of the input stream, but yields no useful output. The computation

$$letfut\, \_ \, be\, map(force)(s)\, in\, map(f)(s)$$

forces the elements of the stream in parallel with the computation of map$(f)(s)$, with the intention that all suspensions in s are forced before their values are needed by the main computation.

38.5 Notes

Futures were introduced by Friedman and Wise (1976), and featured in the MultiLisp language (Halstead, 1985) for parallel programming. A similar concept is proposed by Arvind et al. (1986) under the name "I-structures." The formulation given here is derived from Greiner and Blelloch (1999). Sparks were introduced by Trinder et al. (1998).

Exercises

38.1. Use futures to define letfut x be e_1 in e_2, a parallel let in which e_2 is evaluated in parallel with e_1 up to the point that e_2 needs the value of x.

38.2. Use futures to encode binary nested parallelism by giving a definition of par$(e_1; e_2; x_1.x_2.e)$. *Hint*: Only one future is needed if you are careful.

Notes

1 We confine ourselves to the non-recursive case to ease the comparison with futures.
2 A similar rule applies to scell$[a]$ in the case of speculations.
3 These rules are augmented by a reformulation of the dynamics of the other constructs of the language phrased in terms of the present notion of state.
4 The expression evaluates e_1 simultaneously with e_2, up to the point that the value of x is needed. Its definition in terms of futures is the subject of Exercise **38.1**.

PART XVI

Concurrency and Distribution

39

Process Calculus

So far we have studied the statics and dynamics of programs in isolation, without regard to their interaction with each other or the world. But to extend this analysis to even the most rudimentary forms of input and output requires that we consider external agents that interact with the program. After all, the purpose of a computer is, ultimately, to interact with a person!

To extend our investigations to interactive systems, we develop a small language, called **PiC**, which is derived from a variety of similar formalisms, called *process calculi*, that give an abstract formulation of interaction among independent agents. The development will be carried out in stages, starting with simple action models, then extending to interacting concurrent processes, and finally to synchronous and asynchronous communication. The calculus consists of two main syntactic categories, *processes* and *events*. The basic form of process is one that awaits the arrival of an event. Processes are formed by concurrent composition, replication, and declaration of a channel. The basic forms of event are signaling on a channel and querying a channel; these are later generalized to sending and receiving data on a channel. Events are formed from send and receive events by finite non-deterministic choice.

39.1 Actions and Events

Concurrent interaction is based on *events*, which specify the *actions* that a process can take. Two processes interact by taking two complementary actions, a *signal* and a *query* on a *channel*. The processes synchronize when one signals on a channel that the other is querying, after which they continue to interact with other processes.

To begin with, we will focus on *sequential processes*, which simply await the arrival of one of several possible actions, known as an event.

Proc	P	::=	await(E)	$\$E$	synchronize
Evt	E	::=	null	$\mathbf{0}$	null
			or($E_1; E_2$)	$E_1 + E_2$	choice
			que[a](P)	$?a; P$	query
			sig[a](P)	$!a; P$	signal

The variable a ranges over symbols serving as *channels* that mediate communication among the processes.

We will not distinguish between events that differ only up to *structural congruence*, which is defined to be the strongest equivalence relation closed under these rules:

$$\frac{E \equiv E'}{\$\,E \equiv \$\,E'} \tag{39.1a}$$

$$\frac{E_1 \equiv E_1' \quad E_2 \equiv E_2'}{E_1 + E_2 \equiv E_1' + E_2'} \tag{39.1b}$$

$$\frac{P \equiv P'}{?a;P \equiv ?a;P'} \tag{39.1c}$$

$$\frac{P \equiv P'}{!a;P \equiv !a;P'} \tag{39.1d}$$

$$\frac{}{E + \mathbf{0} \equiv E} \tag{39.1e}$$

$$\frac{}{E_1 + E_2 \equiv E_2 + E_1} \tag{39.1f}$$

$$\frac{}{E_1 + (E_2 + E_3) \equiv (E_1 + E_2) + E_3} \tag{39.1g}$$

Imposing structural congruence on sequential processes enables us to think of an event as having the form

$$!a;P_1 + \cdots + ?a;Q_1 + \cdots$$

consisting of a sum of signal and query events, with the sum of no events being the null event **0**.

An illustrative example of Milner's is a simple vending machine that may take in a 2p coin, then optionally either allow a request for a cup of tea, or take another 2p coin, then allow a request for a cup of coffee.

$$V = \$\,(?2\mathrm{p};\$\,(!\mathtt{tea};V + ?2\mathrm{p};\$\,(!\mathtt{cof};V))) \tag{39.2}$$

As the example indicates, we allow recursive definitions of processes, with the understanding that a defined identifier may always be replaced with its definition wherever it occurs. (Later we will show how to avoid reliance on recursive definitions.)

Because the computation occurring within a process is suppressed, sequential processes have no dynamics on their own, but only through their interaction with other processes. For the vending machine to work, there must be another process (you) who initiates the events expected by the machine, causing both your state (the coins in your pocket) and its state (as just described) to change as a result.

39.2 Interaction

Processes become interesting when they are allowed to interact with one another to achieve a common goal. To account for interaction, we enrich the language of processes with *concurrent composition*:

$$
\begin{array}{lllll}
\text{Proc} & P & ::= & \texttt{await}(E) & \$\, E & \text{synchronize} \\
& & & \texttt{stop} & \mathbf{1} & \text{inert} \\
& & & \texttt{conc}(P_1; P_2) & P_1 \otimes P_2 & \text{composition}
\end{array}
$$

The process $\mathbf{1}$ represents the inert process, and the process $P_1 \otimes P_2$ represents the concurrent composition of P_1 and P_2. We may identify $\mathbf{1}$ with $\$\,\mathbf{0}$, the process that awaits the event that will never occur, but we prefer to treat the inert process as a primitive concept.

We will identify processes up to structural congruence, the strongest equivalence relation closed under these rules:

$$
\frac{}{P \otimes \mathbf{1} \equiv P} \tag{39.3a}
$$

$$
\frac{}{P_1 \otimes P_2 \equiv P_2 \otimes P_1} \tag{39.3b}
$$

$$
\frac{}{P_1 \otimes (P_2 \otimes P_3) \equiv (P_1 \otimes P_2) \otimes P_3} \tag{39.3c}
$$

$$
\frac{P_1 \equiv P_1' \quad P_2 \equiv P_2'}{P_1 \otimes P_2 \equiv P_1' \otimes P_2'} \tag{39.3d}
$$

Up to structural congruence every process has the form

$$
\$\, E_1 \otimes \ldots \otimes \$\, E_n
$$

for some $n \geq 0$, it being understood that when $n = 0$ this stands for the null process $\mathbf{1}$.

Interaction between processes consists of synchronization of two complementary actions. The dynamics of interaction is defined by two forms of judgment. The transition judgment $P \longmapsto P'$ states that the process P evolves to the process P' as a result of a single step of computation. The family of transition judgments, $P \overset{\alpha}{\mapsto} P'$, where α is an *action*, states that the process P may evolve to the process P' as long as the action α is permissible in the context in which the transition occurs. As a notational convenience, we often regard the unlabeled transition to be the labeled transition corresponding to the special silent action.

The possible actions are given by the following grammar:

$$
\begin{array}{llllll}
\text{Act} & \alpha & ::= & \texttt{que}[a] & a\,? & \text{query} \\
& & & \texttt{sig}[a] & a\,! & \text{signal} \\
& & & \texttt{sil} & \varepsilon & \text{silent}
\end{array}
$$

The *query action a ?* and the *signal action a !* are complementary, and the *silent action ε*, is self-complementary. We define the *complementary* action to α to be the action $\overline{\alpha}$ given by the equations $\overline{a\,?} = a\,!$, $\overline{a\,!} = a\,?$, and $\overline{\varepsilon} = \varepsilon$.

$$\frac{\rule{4cm}{0.4pt}}{\$\,(!a;P + E) \overset{a\,!}{\longmapsto} P} \tag{39.4a}$$

$$\frac{\rule{4cm}{0.4pt}}{\$\,(?a;P + E) \overset{a\,?}{\longmapsto} P} \tag{39.4b}$$

$$\frac{P_1 \overset{\alpha}{\longmapsto} P_1'}{P_1 \otimes P_2 \overset{\alpha}{\longmapsto} P_1' \otimes P_2} \tag{39.4c}$$

$$\frac{P_1 \overset{\alpha}{\longmapsto} P_1' \quad P_2 \overset{\overline{\alpha}}{\longmapsto} P_2'}{P_1 \otimes P_2 \longmapsto P_1' \otimes P_2'} \tag{39.4d}$$

Rules (39.4a) and (39.4b) specify that any of the events on which a process is synchronizing may occur. Rule (39.4d) synchronizes two processes that take complementary actions.

As an example, let us consider the vending machine V, given by Equation (39.2), interacting with the user process U defined as follows:

$$U = \$\,!2p;\$\,!2p;\$\,?\mathtt{cof};\mathbf{1}.$$

Here is a trace of the interaction between V and U:

$$V \otimes U \longmapsto \$\,(!\mathtt{tea};V + ?2p;\$\,!\mathtt{cof};V) \otimes \$\,!2p;\$\,?\mathtt{cof};\mathbf{1}$$
$$\longmapsto \$\,!\mathtt{cof};V \otimes \$\,?\mathtt{cof};\mathbf{1}$$
$$\longmapsto V$$

These steps are justified by the following pairs of labeled transitions:

$$U \overset{2p\,!}{\longmapsto} U' = \$\,!2p;\$\,?\mathtt{cof};\mathbf{1}$$
$$V \overset{2p\,?}{\longmapsto} V' = \$\,(!\mathtt{tea};V + ?2p;\$\,!\mathtt{cof};V)$$

$$U' \overset{2p\,!}{\longmapsto} U'' = \$\,?\mathtt{cof};\mathbf{1}$$
$$V' \overset{2p\,?}{\longmapsto} V'' = \$\,!\mathtt{cof};V$$

$$U'' \overset{\mathtt{cof}\,?}{\longmapsto} \mathbf{1}$$
$$V'' \overset{\mathtt{cof}\,!}{\longmapsto} V$$

We have suppressed uses of structural congruence in the foregoing derivation to avoid clutter, but it is important to see its role in managing the non-deterministic choice of events by a process.

39.3 Replication

Some presentations of process calculi forego reliance on defining equations for processes in favor of a *replication* construct, which we write as $*P$. This process stands for as many concurrently executing copies of P as needed. Implicit replication can be expressed by the structural congruence

$$*P \equiv P \otimes *P. \tag{39.5}$$

Understood as a principle of structural congruence, this rule hides the steps of process creation and gives no hint as to how often it should be applied. We could alternatively build replication into the dynamics to model the details of replication more closely:

$$*P \longmapsto P \otimes *P. \tag{39.6}$$

Because there is no constraint on the use of this rule, it can at any time create a new copy of the replicated process P. It is also possible to tie its use to send and receive events so that replication is causal, rather than spontaneous.

So far we have used recursive process definitions to define processes that interact repeatedly according to some protocol. Rather than take recursive definition as a primitive notion, we may instead use replication to model repetition. We do so by introducing an "activator" process that is used to cause the replication. Consider the recursive definition $X = P(X)$, where P is a process expression that may refer to itself as X. Such a self-referential process can be simulated by defining the activator process

$$A = *\$(?a;P(\$(!a;\mathbf{1}))),$$

in which we have replaced occurrences of X within P by an initiator process that signals the event a to the activator. Note that the activator A is structurally congruent to the process $A' \otimes A$, where A' is the process

$$\$(?a;P(\$(!a;\mathbf{1}))).$$

To start process P, we concurrently compose the activator A with an initiator process, $\$(!a;\mathbf{1})$. Note that

$$A \otimes \$(!a;\mathbf{1}) \longmapsto A \otimes P(\$!a;\mathbf{1}),$$

which starts the process P while maintaining a running copy of the activator, A.

As an example, let us consider Milner's vending machine, written using replication, instead of recursive process definition:

$$V_0 = \$(!v;\mathbf{1}) \tag{39.7}$$

$$V_1 = *\$(?v;V_2) \tag{39.8}$$

$$V_2 = \$(?2\mathsf{p};\$(!\mathsf{tea};V_0 + ?2\mathsf{p};\$(!\mathsf{cof};V_0))) \tag{39.9}$$

The process V_1 is a replicated server that awaits a signal on channel v to create another instance of the vending machine. The recursive calls are replaced by signals along v to re-start the machine. The original machine V is simulated by the concurrent composition $V_0 \otimes V_1$.

This example motivates replacing spontaneous replication by *replicated synchronization*, which is defined by the following rules:

$$\frac{}{*\$(!a;P + E) \xrightarrow{a!} P \otimes *\$(!a;P + E)} \tag{39.10a}$$

$$\frac{}{*\$(?a;P + E) \xrightarrow{a?} P \otimes *\$(?a;P + E)} \tag{39.10b}$$

The process $*\$(E)$ is to be regarded not as a composition of replication and synchronization, but as the inseparable combination of these two constructs. The advantage is that the replication occurs only as needed, precisely when a synchronization with another process is possible, avoiding the need "guess" when replication is needed.

39.4 Allocating Channels

It is often useful (particularly once we have introduced inter-process communication) to introduce new channels within a process, and not assume that all channels of interaction are given *a priori*. To allow for this, we enrich the syntax of processes with channel declaration:

$$\text{Proc} \quad P \quad ::= \quad \text{new}(a.P) \quad \nu a.P \quad \text{new channel}$$

The channel a is bound within the process P. To simplify notation, we sometimes write $\nu a_1, \ldots, a_k.P$ for the iterated declaration $\nu a_1 \ldots \nu a_k.P$.

We then extend structural congruence with the following rules:

$$\frac{P =_\alpha P'}{P \equiv P'} \tag{39.11a}$$

$$\frac{P \equiv P'}{\nu a.P \equiv \nu a.P'} \tag{39.11b}$$

$$\frac{a \notin P_2}{(\nu a.P_1) \otimes P_2 \equiv \nu a.(P_1 \otimes P_2)} \tag{39.11c}$$

$$\frac{}{\nu a.\nu b.P \equiv \nu b.\nu a.P} \tag{39.11d}$$

$$\frac{(a \notin P)}{\nu a.P \equiv P} \tag{39.11e}$$

Rule (39.11c), called *scope extrusion*, will be especially important in Section 39.6. Rule (39.11e) states that channels are de-allocated once they are no longer in use.

To account for the scopes of channels, we extend the statics of **PiC** with a *signature* Σ comprising a finite set of active channels. The judgment $\vdash_\Sigma P$ proc states that a process P is well-formed relative to the channels declared in the signature Σ.

$$\frac{}{\vdash_\Sigma \mathbf{1} \text{ proc}} \tag{39.12a}$$

$$\frac{\vdash_\Sigma P_1 \text{ proc} \quad \vdash_\Sigma P_2 \text{ proc}}{\vdash_\Sigma P_1 \otimes P_2 \text{ proc}} \tag{39.12b}$$

$$\frac{\vdash_\Sigma E \text{ event}}{\vdash_\Sigma \$ E \text{ proc}} \tag{39.12c}$$

$$\frac{\vdash_{\Sigma,a} P \text{ proc}}{\vdash_\Sigma \nu a.P \text{ proc}} \tag{39.12d}$$

The foregoing rules make use of an auxiliary judgment, $\vdash_\Sigma E$ event, stating that E is a well-formed event relative to Σ.

$$\frac{}{\vdash_\Sigma \mathbf{0} \text{ event}} \tag{39.13a}$$

$$\frac{\vdash_{\Sigma,a} P \text{ proc}}{\vdash_{\Sigma,a} ?a;P \text{ event}} \tag{39.13b}$$

$$\frac{\vdash_{\Sigma,a} P \text{ proc}}{\vdash_{\Sigma,a} !a;P \text{ event}} \tag{39.13c}$$

$$\frac{\vdash_\Sigma E_1 \text{ event} \quad \vdash_\Sigma E_2 \text{ event}}{\vdash_\Sigma E_1 + E_2 \text{ event}} \tag{39.13d}$$

The judgment $\vdash_\Sigma \alpha$ action states that α is a well-formed action relative to Σ:

$$\frac{}{\vdash_{\Sigma,a} a\,? \text{ action}} \tag{39.14a}$$

$$\frac{}{\vdash_{\Sigma,a} a\,! \text{ action}} \tag{39.14b}$$

$$\frac{}{\vdash_\Sigma \varepsilon \text{ action}} \tag{39.14c}$$

The dynamics of the current fragment of **PiC** is correspondingly generalized to keep track of the set of active channels. The judgment $P \xmapsto[\Sigma]{\alpha} P'$ states that P transitions to P' with action α relative to channels Σ. The dynamics of this extension is obtained by indexing the transitions by the signature, and adding a rule for channel declaration.

$$\frac{}{\$\,(!a;P + E) \xmapsto[\Sigma,a]{a\,!} P} \tag{39.15a}$$

$$\frac{}{\$\,(?a;P + E) \xmapsto[\Sigma,a]{a\,?} P} \tag{39.15b}$$

$$\frac{P_1 \overset{\alpha}{\underset{\Sigma}{\mapsto}} P_1'}{P_1 \otimes P_2 \overset{\alpha}{\underset{\Sigma}{\mapsto}} P_1' \otimes P_2} \tag{39.15c}$$

$$\frac{P_1 \overset{\alpha}{\underset{\Sigma}{\mapsto}} P_1' \quad P_2 \overset{\overline{\alpha}}{\underset{\Sigma}{\mapsto}} P_2'}{P_1 \otimes P_2 \underset{\Sigma}{\mapsto} P_1' \otimes P_2'} \tag{39.15d}$$

$$\frac{P \overset{\alpha}{\underset{\Sigma,a}{\mapsto}} P' \quad \vdash_\Sigma \alpha \text{ action}}{\nu\, a.P \overset{\alpha}{\underset{\Sigma}{\mapsto}} \nu\, a.P'} \tag{39.15e}$$

Rule (39.15e) ensures that no process may interact with $\nu\, a.P$ along the channel a by using the identification convention to choose $a \notin \Sigma$.

Consider again the definition of the vending machine using replication instead of recursion. The channel v used to initialize the machine is private to the machine itself. The process $V = \nu\, v.(V_0 \otimes V_1)$ declares a new channel v for use by V_0 and V_1, which are defined essentially as before. The interaction of the user process U with V begins as follows:

$$(\nu\, v.(V_0 \otimes V_1)) \otimes U \underset{\Sigma}{\mapsto} (\nu\, v.V_2) \otimes U \equiv \nu\, v.(V_2 \otimes U).$$

The interaction continues within the scope of the declaration, which ensures that v does not occur within U.

39.5 Communication

Synchronization coordinates the execution of two processes that take the complementary actions of signaling and querying a common channel. *Synchronous communication* generalizes synchronization to pass a data value betwen two synchronizing processes, one of which is the *sender* of the value and the other its *receiver*. The type of the data is immaterial to the communication.

To account for interprocess communication, we enrich the language of processes to include *variables*, as well as *channels*, in the formalism. Variables range, as always, over types, and are given meaning by substitution. Channels, on the other hand, are assigned types that classify the data carried on that channel and are given meaning by send and receive events that generalize the signal and query events considered in Section 39.2. The abstract syntax of communication events is given by the following grammar:

$$\text{Evt} \quad E \quad ::= \quad \begin{array}{lll} \texttt{snd}[a](e;P) & !\,a(e\,;P) & \text{send} \\ \texttt{rcv}[a](x.P) & ?\,a(x.P) & \text{receive} \end{array}$$

The event $\texttt{rcv}[a](x.P)$ represents the receipt of a value x on the channel a, passing x to the process P. The variable x is bound within P. The event $\texttt{snd}[a](e;P)$ represents the transmission of e on a and continuing with P.

We modify the syntax of declarations to account for the type of value sent on a channel.

$$\text{Proc} \quad P \quad ::= \quad \text{new}\{\tau\}(a.P) \quad \nu\, a \sim \tau.P \quad \text{typed channel}$$

The process $\text{new}[\tau](a.P)$ introduces a new channel a with associated type τ for use within the process P. The channel a is bound within P.

The statics is extended to account for the type of a channel. The judgment $\Gamma \vdash_\Sigma P$ proc states that P is a well-formed process involving the channels declared in Σ and the variables declared in Γ. It is inductively defined by the following rules, wherein we assume that the typing judgment $\Gamma \vdash_\Sigma e : \tau$ is given separately.

$$\frac{}{\Gamma \vdash_\Sigma \mathbf{1} \text{ proc}} \tag{39.16a}$$

$$\frac{\Gamma \vdash_\Sigma P_1 \text{ proc} \quad \Gamma \vdash_\Sigma P_2 \text{ proc}}{\Gamma \vdash_\Sigma P_1 \otimes P_2 \text{ proc}} \tag{39.16b}$$

$$\frac{\Gamma \vdash_{\Sigma, a \sim \tau} P \text{ proc}}{\Gamma \vdash_\Sigma \nu\, a \sim \tau.P \text{ proc}} \tag{39.16c}$$

$$\frac{\Gamma \vdash_\Sigma E \text{ event}}{\Gamma \vdash_\Sigma \$\, E \text{ proc}} \tag{39.16d}$$

Rules (39.16) make use of the auxiliary judgment $\Gamma \vdash_\Sigma E$ event, stating that E is a well-formed event relative to Γ and Σ, which is defined as follows:

$$\frac{}{\Gamma \vdash_\Sigma \mathbf{0} \text{ event}} \tag{39.17a}$$

$$\frac{\Gamma \vdash_\Sigma E_1 \text{ event} \quad \Gamma \vdash_\Sigma E_2 \text{ event}}{\Gamma \vdash_\Sigma E_1 + E_2 \text{ event}} \tag{39.17b}$$

$$\frac{\Gamma, x : \tau \vdash_{\Sigma, a \sim \tau} P \text{ proc}}{\Gamma \vdash_{\Sigma, a \sim \tau} ?\, a(x.P) \text{ event}} \tag{39.17c}$$

$$\frac{\Gamma \vdash_{\Sigma, a \sim \tau} e : \tau \quad \Gamma \vdash_{\Sigma, a \sim \tau} P \text{ proc}}{\Gamma \vdash_{\Sigma, a \sim \tau} !\, a(e\, ; P) \text{ event}} \tag{39.17d}$$

Rule (39.17d) makes use of a typing judgment for expressions that ensures that the type of a channel is respected by communication.

The dynamics of communication extends that of synchronization by enriching send and receive actions with the value sent or received.

$$\text{Act} \quad \alpha \quad ::= \quad \begin{array}{lll} \text{rcv}[a](e) & a\, ?\, e & \text{receive} \\ \text{snd}[a](e) & a\, !\, e & \text{send} \\ \text{sil} & \varepsilon & \text{silent} \end{array}$$

Complementarity is defined as before, by switching the orientation of an action: $\overline{a\, ?\, e} = a!e$, $\overline{a\, !\, e} = a\, ?\, e$, and $\overline{\varepsilon} = \varepsilon$.

The statics ensures that the expression associated with these actions is a value of a type suitable for the channel:

$$\frac{\vdash_{\Sigma,a\sim\tau} e : \tau \quad e \; \mathsf{val}_{\Sigma,a\sim\tau}}{\vdash_{\Sigma,a\sim\tau} a \; ! \; e \; \mathsf{action}} \tag{39.18a}$$

$$\frac{\vdash_{\Sigma,a\sim\tau} e : \tau \quad e \; \mathsf{val}_{\Sigma,a\sim\tau}}{\vdash_{\Sigma,a\sim\tau} a \; ? \; e \; \mathsf{action}} \tag{39.18b}$$

$$\frac{}{\vdash_{\Sigma} \varepsilon \; \mathsf{action}} \tag{39.18c}$$

The dynamics is defined by replacing the synchronization rules (39.15a) and (39.15b) with the following communication rules:

$$\frac{e \xmapsto[\Sigma,a\sim\tau]{} e'}{\$(!\,a(e\,;P)+E) \xmapsto[\Sigma,a\sim\tau]{} \$(!\,a(e'\,;P)+E)} \tag{39.19a}$$

$$\frac{e \; \mathsf{val}_{\Sigma,a\sim\tau}}{\$(!\,a(e\,;P)+E) \xmapsto[\Sigma,a\sim\tau]{a!e} P} \tag{39.19b}$$

$$\frac{e \; \mathsf{val}_{\Sigma,a\sim\tau}}{\$(?\,a(x.P)+E) \xmapsto[\Sigma,a\sim\tau]{a?e} [e/x]P} \tag{39.19c}$$

Rule (39.19c) is non-deterministic in that it "guesses" the value e to be received along channel a. Rules (39.19) make reference to the dynamics of expressions, which is left unspecified because nothing depends on it.

Using synchronous communication, both the sender and the receiver of a message are blocked until the interaction is completed. Therefore the sender must be notified whenever a message is received, which means that there must be an implicit reply channel from receiver to sender that carries the notification. This means that synchronous communication can be decomposed into a simpler *asynchronous send* operation, which sends a message on a channel without waiting for its receipt, together with *channel passing* to send an acknowledgment channel along with the message data.

Asynchronous communication is defined by removing the synchronous send event from the process calculus and adding a new form of process that simply sends a message on a channel. The syntax of asynchronous send is as follows:

$$\text{Proc} \quad P \quad ::= \quad \mathsf{asnd}[a](e) \quad !\,a(e) \quad \text{send}$$

The process $\mathsf{asnd}[a](e)$ sends the message e on channel a and then terminates immediately. Without the synchronous send event, every event is, up to structural congruence, a choice of zero or more read events. The statics of asynchronous send is given by the following rule:

$$\frac{\Gamma \vdash_{\Sigma,a\sim\tau} e : \tau}{\Gamma \vdash_{\Sigma,a\sim\tau} !\,a(e) \; \mathsf{proc}} \tag{39.20}$$

The dynamics is given similarly:

$$\frac{e \text{ val}_\Sigma}{!\,a(e) \xmapsto[\Sigma]{a!e} 1} \tag{39.21}$$

The rule for communication remains unchanged. A pending asynchronous send is essentially a buffer holding the value to be sent once a receiver is available.

39.6 Channel Passing

An interesting case of interprocess communication arises when one process passes *channel reference*, a form of value, to another along a common channel. The receiving process need not have any direct access to the channel referred to by the reference. It merely operates on it using send and receive operations that act on channel references instead of fixed channels. Doing so allows for new patterns of communication to be established among processes. For example, two processes, P and Q, may share a channel a along which they may send and receive messages. If the scope of a is confined to these processes, then no other process R may communicate on that channel; it is, in effect, a *private* channel between P and Q.

The following process expression illustrates such a situation:

$$(\nu\, a \sim \tau.(P \otimes Q)) \otimes R.$$

The process R is excluded from the scope of the channel a, which however includes both P and Q. The processes P and Q may communicate with each other on channel a, but R has no access to this channel. If P and Q wish to allow R to communicate along a, they may do so by sending a reference to a to R along some channel b known to all three processes. Thus, we have the following situation:

$$\nu\, b \sim \tau \text{ chan.}((\nu\, a \sim \tau.(P \otimes Q)) \otimes R).$$

Assuming that P initiates the inclusion of R into its communication with Q along a, it has the form $\$\,(!\,b(\&\, a\,;\, P'))$. The process R correspondingly takes the form $\$\,(?\, b(x.R'))$. The system of processes therefore has the form

$$\nu\, b \sim \tau \text{ chan.}(\nu\, a \sim \tau.(\$\,(!\,b(\&\, a\,;\, P')) \otimes Q) \otimes \$\,(?\, b(x.R'))).$$

Sending a reference to a to R would seem to violate the scope of a. The communication of the reference would seem to escape the scope of the referenced channel, which would be nonsensical. It is here that the concept of scope extrusion, introduced in Section 39.4 comes into play:

$$\nu\, b \sim \tau \text{ chan.}\nu\, a \sim \tau.(\$\,(!\,b(\&\, a\,;\, P')) \otimes Q \otimes \$\,(?\, b(x.R'))).$$

The scope of a expands to encompass R, preparing the ground for communication between P and R, resulting in

$$\nu\, b \sim \tau\, \mathsf{chan}.\nu\, a \sim \tau.(P' \otimes Q \otimes [\&\, a/x]R').$$

The reference to the channel a is substituted for the variable x within R'.

The process R may now communicate with P and Q by sending and receiving messages along the channel reference substituted for the variable x. For this, we use dynamic forms of send and receive in which the channel on which to communicate is determined by evaluation of an expression. For example, to send a message e of type τ along the channel referred to by x, the process R' would have the form

$$\$\,(!!\,(x\,;e\,;R'')).$$

Similarly, to receive along the referenced channel, the process R' would have the form

$$\$\,(??\,(x\,;y.R'')).$$

In both cases, the dynamic communication forms evolve to the static communication forms once the referenced channel has been determined.

The syntax of channel reference types is given by the following grammar:

Typ	τ	$::=$	$\mathsf{chan}(\tau)$	$\tau\ \mathsf{chan}$	channel type
Exp	e	$::=$	$\mathsf{chref}[a]$	$\&\,a$	reference
Evt	E	$::=$	$\mathsf{sndref}(e_1;e_2;P)$	$!!\,(e_1\,;e_2\,;P)$	send
			$\mathsf{rcvref}(e;x.P)$	$??\,(e\,;x.P)$	receive

The events $\mathsf{sndref}(e_1;e_2;P)$ and $\mathsf{rcvref}(e;x.P)$ are dynamic versions of the events $\mathsf{snd}[a](e;P)$ and $\mathsf{rcv}[a](x.P)$ in which the channel reference is determined dynamically by evaluation of an expression.

The statics of channel references is given by the following rules:

$$\frac{}{\Gamma \vdash_{\Sigma,a\sim\tau} \&\, a : \tau\ \mathsf{chan}} \tag{39.22a}$$

$$\frac{\Gamma \vdash_\Sigma e_1 : \tau\ \mathsf{chan} \quad \Gamma \vdash_\Sigma e_2 : \tau \quad \Gamma \vdash_\Sigma P\ \mathsf{proc}}{\Gamma \vdash_\Sigma\, !!\,(e_1\,;e_2\,;P)\ \mathsf{event}} \tag{39.22b}$$

$$\frac{\Gamma \vdash_\Sigma e : \tau\ \mathsf{chan} \quad \Gamma, x : \tau \vdash_\Sigma P\ \mathsf{proc}}{\Gamma \vdash_\Sigma\, ??\,(e\,;x.P)\ \mathsf{event}} \tag{39.22c}$$

Because channel references are forms of expression, events must be evaluated to determine the channel to which they refer.

$$\frac{E \xmapsto[\Sigma,a\sim\tau]{} E'}{\$\,(E) \xmapsto[\Sigma,a\sim\tau]{} \$\,(E')} \tag{39.23a}$$

$$\frac{e\ \mathsf{val}_{\Sigma,a\sim\tau}}{\$\,(!!\,(\&\,a\,;e\,;P)+E) \xmapsto[\Sigma,a\sim\tau]{} \$\,(!\,a(e\,;P)+E)} \tag{39.23b}$$

$$\frac{e \ \mathsf{val}_{\Sigma,a\sim\tau}}{\$ \, (??\,(\&\, a\;;\, x.P) + E) \xmapsto[\Sigma,a\sim\tau]{} \$ \, (?\, a(x.P) + E)} \tag{39.23c}$$

Events must similarly be evaluated; see Chapter 40 for guidance on how to formulate such a dynamics.

39.7 Universality

The process calculus **PiC** developed in this chapter is *universal* in the sense that the untyped λ-calculus can be encoded within it. Consequently, via this encoding, the same functions on the natural numbers are definable in **PiC** as are definable in Λ and hence, by Church's Law, any known programming language. This claim is remarkable because **PiC** has so few capabilities that one might suspect that it is too weak to be a useful programming language. The key to seeing that **PiC** is universal is to note that communication allows processes to send and receive values of an arbitrary type. So long as recursive and channel reference types are available, then it is a purely technical matter to show that Λ is encodable within it. After all, what makes Λ universal is that its one type is a recursive type (see Chapter 21), so it is natural to guess that with messages of recursive type available then **PiC** would be universal. And indeed it is.

To prove universality it suffices to give an encoding of the untyped λ-calculus under a call-by-name dynamics into **PiC**. To motivate the translation, consider a call-by-name stack machine for evaluating λ-terms. A stack is a composition of frames, each of which have the form $-(e_2)$ corresponding to the evaluation of the function part of an application. A stack is represented in **PiC** by a reference to a channel that expects an expression (the function to apply) and another channel reference (the stack on which to evaluate the result of the application). A λ-term is represented by a reference to a channel that expects a stack on which the expression is evaluated.

Let κ be the type of continuations. It should be isomorphic to the type of references to channels that carry a pair of values, an argument, whose type is a reference to a channel carrying a continuation, and another continuation to which to deliver the result of the application. Thus, we seek to have the following type isomorphism:

$$\kappa \cong (\kappa \ \mathtt{chan} \times \kappa) \, \mathtt{chan}.$$

The solution is a recursive type, as described in Chapter 20. Thus, just as for Λ itself, the key to the universality of **PiC** is the use of the recursive type κ.

We now give the translation of Λ into **PiC**. For the sake of the induction, the translation of a Λ expression u is given relative to a variable of type κ, representing the continuation to which the result will be sent. The representation is given by the following equations:

$$x \ @ \ k \triangleq \, !!\,(x\;;\,k)$$

$$\lambda\,(x)\,u \ @ \ k \triangleq \, \$\,??\,(\mathtt{unfold}(k)\;;\,\langle x, k'\rangle.u \ @ \ k')$$

$$u_1(u_2) \ @ \ k \triangleq$$

$$\nu\, a_1 \sim \kappa \ \mathtt{chan} \times \kappa.(u_1 \ @ \ \mathtt{fold}(\&\, a_1)) \otimes \nu\, a \sim \kappa.*\,\$\,?\, a(k_2.u_2 \ @ \ k_2) \otimes !\,a_1(\langle\&\, a, k\rangle)$$

We use pattern matching on pairs for the sake of readability. Only asynchronous sends are needed.

The use of static and dynamic communication operations in the translation merits close consideration. The call site of a λ-term is determined dynamically; we cannot predict at translation time the continuation of the term. In particular, the binding of a variable can be used at several call sites, corresponding to uses of that variable. On the other hand, the channel associated to an argument is determined statically. The server associated to the variable listens on a statically determined channel for a continuation, which is determined dynamically.

As a check on the correctness of the representation, consider the following derivation:

$$(\lambda\,(x)\,x)(y)\,@\,k \longmapsto^*$$
$$\nu\,a_1 \sim \tau.(\$\,?\,a_1(\langle x,k'\rangle.!!\,(x\,;\,k'))) \otimes \nu\,a \sim \kappa.*\,\$\,?\,a(k_2.!!\,(y\,;\,k_2)) \otimes\,!\,a_1(\langle \& \,a,k\rangle)$$
$$\longmapsto^* \nu\,a \sim \kappa.*\,\$\,?\,a(k_2.!!\,(y\,;\,k_2)) \otimes\,!\,a(k)$$
$$\longmapsto^* \nu\,a \sim \kappa.*\,\$\,?\,a(k_2.!!\,(y\,;\,k_2)) \otimes\,!!\,(y\,;\,k)$$

Apart from the idle server process listening on channel a, this is just the translation $y\,@\,k$. (Using the methods to be developed in detail in Chapter 49, we may show that the result of the computation step is "bisimilar" to the translation of $y\,@\,k$, and hence equivalent to it for all purposes.)

39.8 Notes

Process calculi as models of concurrency and interaction were introduced and extensively developed by Hoare (1978) and Milner (1999). Milner's original formulation, CCS, was introduced to model pure synchronization, whereas Hoare's, CSP, included value-passing. CCS was extended to become the π-calculus (Milner, 1999), which includes channel-passing. Dozens upon dozens of variations and extensions of CSP, CCS, and the π-calculus have been considered in the literature and continue to be a subject of intensive study. (See Engberg and Nielsen (2000) for an account of some of the critical developments in the area.)

The process calculus considered here is derived from the π-calculus as presented in Milner (1999). The overall line of development, and the vending machine example and the λ-calculus encoding, are adapted from Milner (1999). The distinction drawn here between static and dynamic events (that is, those that are given syntactically versus those that arise by evaluation) flows naturally from the distinction between variables and channels. It is possible to formulate **PiC** using only channel references, suppressing any mention of channels themselves. The present formulation coheres with the formulation of assignables and assignable references in Chapters 34 and 35. The concept of dynamic events is taken one step further in Concurrent ML (Reppy, 1999), wherein events are values of an event type (see also Chapter 40).

Exercises

39.1. Booleans can be represented in the process calculus similarly to the way in they are represented in Λ (Chapter 21), called the *Milner booleans*. Specifically, a boolean can be represented by a channel carrying a pair of channel references that are signaled (sent a trivial value) to indicate whether the boolean is true or false. Give a definition of processes corresponding to truth, falsehood, and conditional branch between two processes, each parameterized by a channel a representing the boolean.

39.2. Define the sequential composition $P \, ; Q$ of processes P and Q in **PiC**. *Hint*: Define an auxiliary translation $P \rhd p$, where p is a channel value, such that $P \rhd p$ behaves like P, but sends the unit value on p just before termination.

39.3. Consider again an RS latch, which was the subject of Exercises **11.4**, **15.7**, and **20.3**. Implement an RS latch as a process $L(i, o)$ that takes a pair of booleans as input on channel i, representing the R and S inputs to the latch, and outputs a pair of booleans on channel o, representing the outputs Q and Z, with Q being the output of interest. Consider the following input processes:

$$I(i) \triangleq *\,!\,i(\langle \texttt{false}, \texttt{false} \rangle)$$

$$I_{reset}(i) \triangleq \,!\,i(\langle \texttt{true}, \texttt{false} \rangle)\,;\,I_{reset}$$

$$I_{set}(i) \triangleq \,!\,i(\langle \texttt{true}, \texttt{false} \rangle)\,;\,I_{set}$$

The first quiesces the inputs by holding both R and S at $\texttt{false}$ forever. The second asserts the R input (only), and then quiesces; the third asserts the S input (only), and then quiesces.

    Show that the process $L(i, o) \otimes I_{reset}(i)$ evolves to a process capable of taking the action $o\,!\,\langle \texttt{false}, \texttt{false} \rangle$ and is then forever capable of evolving to a process taking the same action. Similarly, show that $L(i, o) \otimes I_{set}(i)$ evolves to a process capable of taking the action $o\,!\,\langle \texttt{true}, \texttt{false} \rangle$, and is then forever capable of evolving to a process taking the same action.

39.4. Some versions of process calculus to note have a distinction between events and processes. They instead consider the *non-deterministic choice* $P_1 + P_2$ of two processes, which is defined by the following silent transition rules:

$$\frac{}{P_1 + P_2 \underset{\Sigma}{\mapsto} P_1} \tag{39.24a}$$

$$\frac{}{P_1 + P_2 \underset{\Sigma}{\mapsto} P_2} \tag{39.24b}$$

Thus, $P_1 + P_2$ may spontaneously evolve into either P_1 or P_2, without interacting with any other process. Show that non-deterministic choice is definable in the asynchronous process calculus in such a way that the given transitions are possible.

39.5. In the asynchronous process, calculus events are finite sums of inputs, called an *input choice*, of the form

$$? a_1(x_1.P_1) + \cdots + ? a_n(x_n.P_n).$$

The behavior of the process

$$P \triangleq \$ (? a_1(x_1.P_1) + \cdots + ? a_n(x_n.P_n))$$

is tantalizingly close to that of the concurrent composition of processes receiving on a single channel,

$$Q \triangleq \$? a_1(x_1.P_1) \otimes \ldots \otimes \$? a_n(x_n.P_n).$$

The processes P and Q are similar in that both may synchronize with a concurrently executing sender on any of the specified receive channels. They are different in that P abandons the other receives once one has synchronized with a sender, whereas Q leaves the other choices available for further synchronization. So a receive-only choice can be defined in terms of the concurrent composition of single-choice receives by arranging that the other choices are deactivated once one has been chosen. Show that this is the case. *Hint*: Associate a Milner boolean (Exercise **39.1**) with each choice group that limits synchronization to at most one sender.

39.6. The *polyadic π-calculus* is a process calculus in which all channels are constrained to carry values of the recursive type π satisfying the isomorphism

$$\pi \cong \sum_{n \in \mathbb{N}} \underbrace{\pi \text{ chan} \times \ldots \times \pi \text{ chan}}_{n}.$$

Thus, a message value has the form

$$n \cdot \underbrace{\langle \& a_1, \ldots, \& a_n \rangle}_{n}$$

in which the tag n indicates the size of the tuple of channel references associated with it. Show that the encoding of Λ given in Section 39.7 can be given using only channels of type π, proving the universality of the polyadic π-calculus.

40

Concurrent Algol

In this chapter, we integrate concurrency into the framework of Modernized Algol described in Chapter 34. The resulting language, called Concurrent Algol, or **CA**, illustrates the integration of the mechanisms of the process calculus described in Chapter 39 into a practical programming language. To avoid distracting complications, we drop assignables from Modernized Algol entirely. (There is no loss of generality, however, because free assignables are definable in Concurrent Algol using processes as cells.)

The process calculus described in Chapter 39 is intended as a self-standing model of concurrent computation. When viewed in the context of a programming language, however, it is possible to streamline the machinery to take full advantage of types that are in any case required for other purposes. In particular the concept of a *channel*, which features prominently in Chapter 39, is identified with the concept of a *dynamic class* as described in Chapter 33. More precisely, we take *broadcast communication* of dynamically classified values as the basic synchronization mechanism of the language. Being dynamically classified, messages consist of a *payload* tagged with a *class*, or *channel*. The type of the channel determines the type of the payload. Importantly, only those processes that have access to the channel may decode the message; all others must treat it as inscrutable data that can be passed around but not examined. In this way, we can model not only the mechanisms described in Chapter 39 but also formulate an abstract account of encryption and decryption in a network using the methods described in Chapter 39.

Concurrent Algol features a modal separation between commands and expressions like in Modernized Algol. It is also possible to combine these two levels (so as to allow benign concurrency effects), but we do not develop this approach in detail here.

40.1 Concurrent Algol

The syntax of **CA** is obtained by removing assignables from **MA**, and adding a syntactic level of *processes* to represent the global state of a program:

Typ	τ	::=	$\mathtt{cmd}(\tau)$	$\tau\ \mathtt{cmd}$	commands
Exp	e	::=	$\mathtt{cmd}(m)$	$\mathtt{cmd}\ m$	command
Cmd	m	::=	$\mathtt{ret}\ e$	$\mathtt{ret}\ e$	return
			$\mathtt{bnd}(e; x.m)$	$\mathtt{bnd}\ x \leftarrow e\ ;\ m$	sequence
Proc	p	::=	$\mathtt{stop}$	$\mathbf{1}$	idle
			$\mathtt{run}(m)$	$\mathtt{run}(m)$	atomic
			$\mathtt{conc}(p_1; p_2)$	$p_1 \otimes p_2$	concurrent
			$\mathtt{new}[\tau](a.p)$	$\nu\, a \sim \tau.p$	new channel

The process $\mathrm{run}(m)$ is an atomic process executing the command m. The other forms of process are adapted from Chapter 39. If Σ has the form $a_1 \sim \tau_1, \ldots, a_n \sim \tau_n$, then we sometimes write $\nu \Sigma\{p\}$ for the iterated form $\nu a_1 \sim \tau_1 \ldots \nu a_n \sim \tau_n.p$.

The statics of **CA** is given by these judgments:

$$\Gamma \vdash_\Sigma e : \tau \qquad \text{expression typing}$$
$$\Gamma \vdash_\Sigma m \mathbin{\dot{\sim}} \tau \qquad \text{command typing}$$
$$\Gamma \vdash_\Sigma p \text{ proc} \qquad \text{process formation}$$
$$\Gamma \vdash_\Sigma \alpha \text{ action} \qquad \text{action formation}$$

The expression and command typing judgments are essentially those of **MA**, augmented with the constructs described below.

Process formation is defined by the following rules:

$$\frac{}{\vdash_\Sigma \mathbf{1} \text{ proc}} \tag{40.1a}$$

$$\frac{\vdash_\Sigma m \mathbin{\dot{\sim}} \tau}{\vdash_\Sigma \mathrm{run}(m) \text{ proc}} \tag{40.1b}$$

$$\frac{\vdash_\Sigma p_1 \text{ proc} \quad \vdash_\Sigma p_2 \text{ proc}}{\vdash_\Sigma p_1 \otimes p_2 \text{ proc}} \tag{40.1c}$$

$$\frac{\vdash_{\Sigma,a\sim\tau} p \text{ proc}}{\vdash_\Sigma \nu a \sim \tau.p \text{ proc}} \tag{40.1d}$$

Processes are identified up to structural congruence, as described in Chapter 39.

Action formation is defined by the following rules:

$$\frac{}{\vdash_\Sigma \varepsilon \text{ action}} \tag{40.2a}$$

$$\frac{\vdash_\Sigma e : \mathtt{clsfd} \quad e \text{ val}_\Sigma}{\vdash_\Sigma e \,! \text{ action}} \tag{40.2b}$$

$$\frac{\vdash_\Sigma e : \mathtt{clsfd} \quad e \text{ val}_\Sigma}{\vdash_\Sigma e \,? \text{ action}} \tag{40.2c}$$

Messages are values of the type $\mathtt{clsfd}$ defined in Chapter 33.

The dynamics of **CA** is defined by transitions between processes, which represent the state of the computation. More precisely, the judgment $p \xmapsto[\Sigma]{\alpha} p'$ states that the process p evolves in one step to the process p' while undertaking action α.

$$\frac{m \xRightarrow[\Sigma]{\alpha} \nu \Sigma'\{m' \otimes p\}}{\mathrm{run}(m) \xmapsto[\Sigma]{\alpha} \nu \Sigma'\{\mathrm{run}(m') \otimes p\}} \tag{40.3a}$$

$$\frac{e \text{ val}_\Sigma}{\mathrm{run}(\mathtt{ret}\, e) \xmapsto[\Sigma]{\varepsilon} \mathbf{1}} \tag{40.3b}$$

$$\frac{p_1 \xmapsto[\Sigma]{\alpha} p_1'}{p_1 \otimes p_2 \xmapsto[\Sigma]{\alpha} p_1' \otimes p_2} \tag{40.3c}$$

$$\frac{p_1 \xmapsto[\Sigma]{\alpha} p_1' \quad p_2 \xmapsto[\Sigma]{\bar{\alpha}} p_2'}{p_1 \otimes p_2 \xmapsto[\Sigma]{\varepsilon} p_1' \otimes p_2'} \tag{40.3d}$$

$$\frac{p \xmapsto[\Sigma, a \sim \tau]{\alpha} p' \quad \vdash_\Sigma \alpha \text{ action}}{\nu\, a \sim \tau.p \xmapsto[\Sigma]{\alpha} \nu\, a \sim \tau.p'} \tag{40.3e}$$

Rule (40.3a) states that a step of execution of the atomic process $\mathrm{run}(m)$ consists of a step of execution of the command m, which may allocate some set Σ' of symbols or create a concurrent process p. This rule implements scope extrusion for classes (channels) by expanding the scope of the channel declaration to the context in which the command m occurs. Rule (40.3b) states that a completed command evolves to the inert (stopped) process; processes are executed solely for their effect, and not for their value.

Executing a command in **CA** may, in addition to evolving to another command, allocate a new channel or may spawn a new process. More precisely, the judgment[1]

$$m \xRightarrow[\Sigma]{\alpha} \nu\, \Sigma' \{ m' \otimes p' \}$$

states that the command m transitions to the command m' while creating new channels Σ' and new processes p'. The action α specifies the interactions of which m is capable when executed. As a notational convenience, we drop mention of the new channels or processes when either are trivial.

The following rules define the execution of the basic forms of command inherited from **MA**:

$$\frac{e \xmapsto[\Sigma]{} e'}{\mathrm{ret}\, e \xRightarrow[\Sigma]{\varepsilon} \mathrm{ret}\, e'} \tag{40.4a}$$

$$\frac{m_1 \xRightarrow[\Sigma]{\alpha} \nu\, \Sigma' \{ m_1' \otimes p' \}}{\mathrm{bnd}\, x \leftarrow \mathrm{cmd}\, m_1 \, ; m_2 \xRightarrow[\Sigma]{\alpha} \nu\, \Sigma' \{ \mathrm{bnd}\, x \leftarrow \mathrm{cmd}\, m_1' \, ; m_2 \otimes p' \}} \tag{40.4b}$$

$$\frac{e \, \mathrm{val}_\Sigma}{\mathrm{bnd}\, x \leftarrow \mathrm{cmd}\, (\mathrm{ret}\, e) \, ; m_2 \xRightarrow[\Sigma]{\varepsilon} [e/x]m_2} \tag{40.4c}$$

$$\frac{e_1 \xmapsto[\Sigma]{} e_1'}{\mathrm{bnd}\, x \leftarrow e_1 \, ; m_2 \xRightarrow[\Sigma]{\varepsilon} \mathrm{bnd}\, x \leftarrow e_1' \, ; m_2} \tag{40.4d}$$

These rules are supplemented by rules governing communication and synchronization among processes in the next two sections.

40.2 Broadcast Communication

In this section, we consider a very general form of process synchronization called *broadcast*. Processes emit and accept messages of type clsfd, the type of dynamically classified values considered in Chapter 33. A message consists of a *channel*, which is its class, and a *payload*, which is a value of the type associated with the channel (class). Recipients may pattern match against a message to determine whether it is of a given class, and, if so, recover the associated payload. No process that lacks access to the class of a message may recover the payload of that message. (See Section 33.4.1 for a discussion of how to enforce confidentiality and integrity restrictions using dynamic classification.)

The syntax of the commands pertinent to broadcast communication is given by the following grammar:

$$
\begin{array}{llllll}
\text{Cmd} & m & ::= & \text{spawn}(e) & \text{spawn}(e) & \text{spawn} \\
& & & \text{emit}(e) & \text{emit}(e) & \text{emit message} \\
& & & \text{acc} & \text{acc} & \text{accept message} \\
& & & \text{newch}\{\tau\} & \text{newch} & \text{new channel}
\end{array}
$$

The command spawn(e) spawns a process that executes the encapsulated command given by e. The commands emit(e) and acc emit and accept messages, which are classified values whose class is the channel on which the message is sent. The command newch[τ] returns a reference to a fresh class carrying values of type τ.

The statics of broadcast communication is given by the following rules:

$$
\frac{\Gamma \vdash_\Sigma e : \text{cmd(unit)}}{\Gamma \vdash_\Sigma \text{spawn}(e) \mathrel{\dot{\sim}} \text{unit}}
\tag{40.5a}
$$

$$
\frac{\Gamma \vdash_\Sigma e : \text{clsfd}}{\Gamma \vdash_\Sigma \text{emit}(e) \mathrel{\dot{\sim}} \text{unit}}
\tag{40.5b}
$$

$$
\frac{}{\Gamma \vdash_\Sigma \text{acc} \mathrel{\dot{\sim}} \text{clsfd}}
\tag{40.5c}
$$

$$
\frac{}{\Gamma \vdash_\Sigma \text{newch}\{\tau\} \mathrel{\dot{\sim}} \text{cls}(\tau)}
\tag{40.5d}
$$

Execution of these commands is defined as follows:

$$
\frac{}{\text{spawn}(\text{cmd}(m)) \xRightarrow[\Sigma]{\varepsilon} \text{ret} \langle\rangle \otimes \text{run}(m)}
\tag{40.6a}
$$

$$
\frac{e \underset{\Sigma}{\mapsto} e'}{\text{spawn}(e) \xRightarrow[\Sigma]{\varepsilon} \text{spawn}(e')}
\tag{40.6b}
$$

$$\frac{e \; \mathsf{val}_\Sigma}{\mathtt{emit}(e) \overset{e\,!}{\underset{\Sigma}{\Rightarrow}} \mathtt{ret} \; \langle \rangle} \tag{40.6c}$$

$$\frac{e \underset{\Sigma}{\mapsto} e'}{\mathtt{emit}(e) \overset{\varepsilon}{\underset{\Sigma}{\Rightarrow}} \mathtt{emit}(e')} \tag{40.6d}$$

$$\frac{e \; \mathsf{val}_\Sigma}{\mathtt{acc} \overset{e\,?}{\underset{\Sigma}{\Rightarrow}} \mathtt{ret}\, e} \tag{40.6e}$$

$$\frac{}{\mathtt{newch}\{\tau\} \overset{\varepsilon}{\underset{\Sigma}{\Rightarrow}} \nu\, a \sim \tau\, \{\, \mathtt{ret}\, (\&\, a)\,\}} \tag{40.6f}$$

Rule (40.6c) specifies that $\mathtt{emit}(e)$ has the effect of emitting the message e. Correspondingly, rule (40.6e) specifies that $\mathtt{acc}$ may accept (any) message that is being sent.

As usual, the preservation theorem for **CA** ensures that well-typed programs remain well-typed during execution. The proof of preservation requires a lemma about command execution.

Lemma 40.1. *If $m \overset{\alpha}{\underset{\Sigma}{\Rightarrow}} \nu\, \Sigma'\, \{m' \otimes p'\}$, $\vdash_\Sigma m \overset{\centerdot}{\sim} \tau$, then $\vdash_\Sigma \alpha$ action, $\vdash_{\Sigma\,\Sigma'} m' \overset{\centerdot}{\sim} \tau$, and $\vdash_{\Sigma\,\Sigma'} p'$ proc.*

Proof   By induction on rules (40.4).   □

With this in hand, the proof of preservation goes along familiar lines.

Theorem 40.2 (Preservation). *If $\vdash_\Sigma p$ proc and $p \underset{\Sigma}{\mapsto} p'$, then $\vdash_\Sigma p'$ proc.*

Proof   By induction on transition, appealing to Lemma 40.1 for the crucial steps.   □

Typing does not, however, guarantee progress with respect to unlabeled transition, for the simple reason that there may be no other process with which to communicate. By extending progress to labeled transitions, we may state that this is the *only* way for process execution to get stuck. But some care must be taken to account for allocating new channels.

Theorem 40.3 (Progress). *If $\vdash_\Sigma p$ proc, then either $p \equiv 1$, or $p \equiv \nu\, \Sigma'\{p'\}$ such that $p' \overset{\alpha}{\underset{\Sigma\,\Sigma'}{\longmapsto}} p''$ for some $\vdash_{\Sigma\,\Sigma'} p''$ and some $\vdash_{\Sigma\,\Sigma'} \alpha$ action.*

Proof   By induction on rules (40.1) and (40.5).   □

The progress theorem says that no process can get stuck for any reason other than the inability to communicate with another process. For example, a process that receives on a channel for which there is no sender is "stuck," but this does not violate Theorem 40.3.

40.3 Selective Communication

Broadcast communication provides no means of restricting acceptance to messages of a particular class (that is, of messages on a particular channel). Using broadcast communication, we may restrict attention to a particular channel a of type τ by running the following command:

$$\texttt{fix}\ loop : \tau\ \texttt{cmd}\ \texttt{is}\ \{x \leftarrow \texttt{acc}\ ; \texttt{match}\ x\ \texttt{as}\ a \cdot y \hookrightarrow \texttt{ret}\ y\ \texttt{ow} \hookrightarrow \texttt{emit}(x)\ ; \texttt{do}\ loop\}$$

This command is always capable of receiving a broadcast message. When one arrives, it is examined to see whether it is classified by a. If so, the underlying classified value is returned; otherwise, the message is re-broadcast so that another process may consider it. *Polling* consists of repeatedly executing the above command until a message of channel a is successfully accepted, if ever it is.

Polling is evidently impractical in most situations. An alternative is to change the language to allow for *selective communication*. Rather than accept any broadcast message, we may confine attention to messages sent only on certain channels. The type $\texttt{event}(\tau)$ of *events* consists of a finite choice of accepts, all of whose payloads are of type τ.

Typ	τ	::=	$\texttt{event}(\tau)$	τ event	events
Exp	e	::=	$\texttt{rcv}[a]$	$?a$	selective read
			$\texttt{never}\{\tau\}$	never	null
			$\texttt{or}(e_1; e_2)$	e_1 or e_2	choice
			$\texttt{wrap}(e_1; x.e_2)$	e_1 as x in e_2	post-composition
Cmd	m	::=	$\texttt{sync}(e)$	$\texttt{sync}(e)$	synchronize

Events in **CA** are similar to those of the asynchronous process calculus described in Chapter 39. The chief difference is that post-composition is considered as a general operation on events, instead of one tied to the receive event itself.

The statics of event expressions is given by the following rules:

$$\frac{\Sigma \vdash a \sim \tau}{\Gamma \vdash_{\Sigma} \texttt{rcv}[a] : \texttt{event}(\tau)} \tag{40.7a}$$

$$\frac{}{\Gamma \vdash_{\Sigma} \texttt{never}\{\tau\} : \texttt{event}(\tau)} \tag{40.7b}$$

$$\frac{\Gamma \vdash_{\Sigma} e_1 : \texttt{event}(\tau) \quad \Gamma \vdash_{\Sigma} e_2 : \texttt{event}(\tau)}{\Gamma \vdash_{\Sigma} \texttt{or}(e_1; e_2) : \texttt{event}(\tau)} \tag{40.7c}$$

$$\frac{\Gamma \vdash_{\Sigma} e_1 : \texttt{event}(\tau_1) \quad \Gamma, x : \tau_1 \vdash_{\Sigma} e_2 : \tau_2}{\Gamma \vdash_{\Sigma} \texttt{wrap}(e_1; x.e_2) : \texttt{event}(\tau_2)} \tag{40.7d}$$

The corresponding dynamics is defined by these rules:

$$\frac{\Sigma \vdash a \sim \tau}{\text{rcv}[a] \ \text{val}_\Sigma} \tag{40.8a}$$

$$\frac{}{\text{never}\{\tau\} \ \text{val}_\Sigma} \tag{40.8b}$$

$$\frac{e_1 \ \text{val}_\Sigma \quad e_2 \ \text{val}_\Sigma}{\text{or}(e_1 ; e_2) \ \text{val}_\Sigma} \tag{40.8c}$$

$$\frac{e_1 \underset{\Sigma}{\mapsto} e_1'}{\text{or}(e_1 ; e_2) \underset{\Sigma}{\mapsto} \text{or}(e_1' ; e_2)} \tag{40.8d}$$

$$\frac{e_1 \ \text{val}_\Sigma \quad e_2 \underset{\Sigma}{\mapsto} e_2'}{\text{or}(e_1 ; e_2) \underset{\Sigma}{\mapsto} \text{or}(e_1 ; e_2')} \tag{40.8e}$$

$$\frac{e_1 \underset{\Sigma}{\mapsto} e_1'}{\text{wrap}(e_1 ; x.e_2) \underset{\Sigma}{\mapsto} \text{wrap}(e_1' ; x.e_2')} \tag{40.8f}$$

$$\frac{e_1 \ \text{val}_\Sigma}{\text{wrap}(e_1 ; x.e_2) \ \text{val}_\Sigma} \tag{40.8g}$$

Event values are identified up to structural congruence as described in Chapter 39.

The statics of the synchronization command is given by the following rule:

$$\frac{\Gamma \vdash_\Sigma e : \text{event}(\tau)}{\Gamma \vdash_\Sigma \text{sync}(e) \mathbin{\dot\sim} \tau} \tag{40.9a}$$

The type of the event determines the type of value returned by the synchronization command.

Execution of a synchronization command depends on the event.

$$\frac{e \underset{\Sigma}{\mapsto} e'}{\text{sync}(e) \underset{\Sigma}{\overset{\varepsilon}{\Rightarrow}} \text{sync}(e')} \tag{40.10a}$$

$$\frac{e \ \text{val}_\Sigma \quad \vdash_\Sigma e : \tau \quad \Sigma \vdash a \sim \tau}{\text{sync}(\text{rcv}[a]) \underset{\Sigma}{\overset{a \cdot e \, ?}{\Longrightarrow}} \text{ret}(e)} \tag{40.10b}$$

$$\frac{\text{sync}(e_1) \underset{\Sigma}{\overset{\alpha}{\Rightarrow}} m_1}{\text{sync}(\text{or}(e_1 ; e_2)) \underset{\Sigma}{\overset{\alpha}{\Rightarrow}} m_1} \tag{40.10c}$$

$$\frac{\text{sync}(e_2) \overset{\alpha}{\underset{\Sigma}{\Rightarrow}} m_2}{\text{sync}(\text{or}(e_1; e_2)) \overset{\alpha}{\underset{\Sigma}{\Rightarrow}} m_2} \tag{40.10d}$$

$$\frac{\text{sync}(e_1) \overset{\alpha}{\underset{\Sigma}{\Rightarrow}} m_1}{\text{sync}(\text{wrap}(e_1; x.e_2)) \overset{\alpha}{\underset{\Sigma}{\Rightarrow}} \text{bnd}(\text{cmd}(m_1); x.\text{ret}(e_2))} \tag{40.10e}$$

Rule (40.10b) states that an acceptance on a channel a may synchronize only with messages classified by a. When combined with structural congruence, rules (40.10c) and (40.10d) state that either event between two choices may engender an action. Rule (40.10e) yields the command that performs the command m_1 resulting from the action α taken by the event e_1, then returns e_2 with x bound to the return value of m_1.

Selective communication and dynamic events can be used together to implement a communication protocol in which a channel reference is passed on a channel in order to establish a communication path with the recipient. Let a be a channel carrying values of type $\text{cls}(\tau)$, and let b be a channel carrying values of type τ, so that $\& b$ can be passed as a message along channel a. A process that wishes to accept a channel reference on a and then accept on that channel has the form

$$\{x \leftarrow \text{sync}(?a) ; y \leftarrow \text{sync}(??x) ; \ldots\}.$$

The event $?a$ specifies a selective receipt on channel a. Once the value x is accepted, the event $??x$ specifies a selective receipt on the channel referenced by x. So, if $\& b$ is sent along a, then the event $?? \& b$ evaluates to $?b$, which accepts selectively on channel b, even though the receiving process may have no direct access to the channel b itself.

40.4 Free Assignables as Processes

Scope-free assignables are definable in **CA** by associating to each assignable a server process that sets and gets the contents of the assignable. To each assignable a of type τ is associated a server that selectively accepts a message on channel a with one of two forms:

1. $\text{get} \cdot (\& b)$, where b is a channel of type τ. This message requests that the contents of a be sent on channel b.

2. $\text{set} \cdot (\langle e, \& b \rangle)$, where e is a value of type τ, and b is a channel of type τ. This message requests that the contents of a be set to e, and that the new contents be transmitted on channel b.

In other words, a is a channel of type τ_{srvr} given by

$$[\text{get} \hookrightarrow \tau \, \text{cls}, \text{set} \hookrightarrow \tau \times \tau \, \text{cls}].$$

The server selectively accepts on channel a, then dispatches on the class of the message to satisfy the request.

The server associated with the assignable a of type τ maintains the contents of a using recursion. When called with the current contents of the assignable, the server selectively accepts on channel a, dispatching on the associated request, and calling itself recursively with the (updated, if necessary) contents:

$$\lambda\,(u : \tau_{srvr}\,\text{cls})\,\text{fix}\,srvr : \tau \rightharpoonup \text{void}\,\text{cmd}\,\text{is}\,\lambda\,(x : \tau)\,\text{cmd}\,\{y \leftarrow \text{sync}(??\,u)\,;\,e_{(40.12)}\}. \tag{40.11}$$

The server is a procedure that takes an argument of type τ, the current contents of the assignable, and yields a command that never terminates, because it restarts the server loop after each request. The server selectively accepts a message on channel a, and dispatches on it as follows:

$$\text{case}\,y\,\{\text{get}\cdot z \hookrightarrow e_{(40.13)}\,|\,\text{set}\cdot\langle x', z\rangle \hookrightarrow e_{(40.14)}\}. \tag{40.12}$$

A request to get the contents of the assignable a is served as follows:

$$\{\_ \leftarrow \text{emit}(\text{mk}(z; x))\,;\,\text{do}\,srvr(x)\} \tag{40.13}$$

A request to set the contents of the assignable a is served as follows:

$$\{\_ \leftarrow \text{emit}(\text{mk}(z; x'))\,;\,\text{do}\,srvr(x')\} \tag{40.14}$$

The type τ ref is defined to be τ_{srvr} cls, the type of channels (classes) to servers providing a cell containing a value of type τ. A new free assignable is created by the command ref e_0, which is defined to be

$$\{x \leftarrow \text{newch}\,;\,\_ \leftarrow \text{spawn}(e_{(40.11)}(x)(e_0))\,;\,\text{ret}\,x\}. \tag{40.15}$$

A channel carrying a value of type τ_{srvr} is allocated to serve as the name of the assignable, and a new server is spawned that accepts requests on that channel, with initial value e_0 of type τ_0.

The commands $*\,e_0$ and $e_0 *= e_1$ send a message to the server to get and set the contents of an assignable. The code for $*\,e_0$ is as follows:

$$\{x \leftarrow \text{newch}\,;\,\_ \leftarrow \text{emit}(\text{mk}(e_0; \text{get}\cdot x))\,;\,\text{sync}(??\,(x))\} \tag{40.16}$$

A channel is allocated for the return value, the server is contacted with a get message specifying this channel, and the result of receiving on this channel is returned. Similarly, the code for $e_0 *= e_1$ is as follows:

$$\{x \leftarrow \text{newch}\,;\,\_ \leftarrow \text{emit}(\text{mk}(e_0; \text{set}\cdot\langle e_1, x\rangle))\,;\,\text{sync}(??\,(x))\} \tag{40.17}$$

40.5 Notes

Concurrent Algol is a synthesis of process calculus and Modernized Algol; is essentially an "Algol-like" formulation of Concurrent ML (Reppy, 1999). The design is influenced by Parallel Algol (Brookes, 2002). Much work on concurrent interaction takes communication channels as a basic concept, but see Linda (Gelernter, 1985) for an account similar to the one suggested here.

Exercises

40.1. In Section 40.2 channels are allocated using the command newch, which returns a channel reference. Alternatively one may extend **CA** with a means of declaring channels just as assignables are declared in **MA**. Formulate the syntax, statics, and dynamics of such a construct, and derive newch using this extension.

40.2. Extend selective communication (Section 40.3) to account for channel references, which give rise to a new form of event. Give the syntax, statics, and semantics of this extension.

40.3. Adapt the implementation of an RS latch given in Exercise **39.3** to **CA**.

Note

1 The right-hand side of this judgment is a triple consisting of Σ', m', and p', not a process expression comprising these parts.

41

Distributed Algol

A *distributed* computation is one that takes place at many *sites*, each of which controls some *resources* at that site. For example, the sites might be nodes on a network, and a resource might be a device or sensor at that site, or a database controlled by that site. Only programs that execute at a particular site may access the resources situated at that site. Consequently, command execution always takes place at a particular site, called the *locus of execution*. Access to resources at a remote site from a local site is achieved by moving the locus of execution to the remote site, running code to access the local resource, and returning a value to the local site.

In this chapter, we consider the language **DA**, which extends Concurrent Algol with a *spatial* type system that mediates access to resources on a network. The type safety theorem ensures that all accesses to a resource controlled by a site are through a program executing at that site, even though references to local resources can be freely passed around to other sites on the network. The main idea is that channels and events are *located* at a particular site, and that synchronization on an event can only occur at the proper site for that event. Issues of concurrency, which are temporal, are thereby separated from those of distribution, which are spatial.

The concept of location in **DA** is sufficiently abstract that it admits another useful interpretation that can be useful in computer security settings. The "location" of a computation can be considered to be the *principal* on whose behalf the computation is executing. From this point of view, a local resource is one that is accessible to a particular principal, and a mobile computation is one that can be executed by any principal. Movement from one location to another may then be interpreted as executing a piece of code on behalf of another principal, returning its result to the principal that initiated the transfer.

41.1 Statics

The statics of **DA** is inspired by the *possible worlds* interpretation of modal logic. Under that interpretation the truth of a proposition is considered relative to a *world*, which determines the state of affairs described by that proposition. A proposition may be true in one world, and false in another. For example, one may use possible worlds to model counter-factual reasoning, where one postulates that certain facts that happen to be true in this, the *actual*, world, might be otherwise in some other, *possible*, world. For instance, in the actual world you, the reader, are reading this book, but in a possible world you may never have taken up the study of programming languages at all. Of course not everything is possible: there is no possible world in which $2 + 2$ is other than 4, for example. Moreover, once a commitment has been made to one counter-factual, others are ruled out. We say that one world is *accessible* from another when the first is a sensible counter-factual relative to the first. So, for example, one may consider that relative to a possible world in which you are the king, there is no further possible world in which someone else is also the king (there being only one sovereign).

In **DA**, we shall interpret possible worlds as sites on a network, with accessibility between worlds expressing network connectivity. We postulate that every site is connected to itself (reflexivity); that if one site is reachable from another, then the second is also reachable from the first (symmetry); and that if a site is reachable from a reachable site, then this site is itself reachable from the first (transitivity). From the point of view of modal logics, the type system of **DA** is derived from the logic **S5**, for which accessibility is an equivalence relation.

The syntax of **DA** derives from that of **CA**. The following grammar summarizes the important changes:

$$
\begin{array}{llllll}
\text{Typ} & \tau & ::= & \text{cmd}[w](\tau) & \tau\,\text{cmd}[w] & \text{commands} \\
           &   &   & \text{event}[w](\tau) & \tau\,\text{event}[w] & \text{events} \\
\text{Cmd} & m & ::= & \text{at}[w](m) & \text{at } w \text{ do } m & \text{change site}
\end{array}
$$

The command and event types are indexed by the site w at which they make sense. The command $\text{at}[w](m)$ changes the locus of execution from one site to another.

A signature Σ in **DA** consists of a finite set of declarations of the form $a \sim \tau \ @ \ w$, where τ is a type and w is a site. Such a declaration specifies that a is a channel at site w carrying a payload of type τ. We may think of a signature Σ as a family of signatures Σ_w one for each world w, containing the declarations of the channels at that world. Partitioning channels in this way corresponds to the idea that channels are located at a particular site. They may be handled passively at other sites, but their only active role is at the site at which they are declared.

The statics of **DA** is given by the following judgment forms:

$$
\begin{array}{ll}
\Gamma \vdash_\Sigma e : \tau & \text{expression typing} \\
\Gamma \vdash_\Sigma m \overset{.}{\sim} \tau \ @ \ w & \text{command typing} \\
\Gamma \vdash_\Sigma p \ \text{proc} \ @ \ w & \text{process formation} \\
\Gamma \vdash_\Sigma \alpha \ \text{action} \ @ \ w & \text{action formation}
\end{array}
$$

The expression typing judgment is independent of the site, expressing the requirement that the values of a type be meaningful at any site. On the other hand, commands can only be executed at a particular site, because their meaning depends on the resources at a site. Processes are similarly confined to execution at a site. Actions are site-specific; there is no inter-site synchronization.

The expressions of the command and event types of **DA** are defined by the following rules:

$$\frac{\Gamma \vdash_\Sigma m \mathrel{\dot\sim} \tau @ w}{\Gamma \vdash_\Sigma \mathtt{cmd}(m) : \mathtt{cmd}[w](\tau)} \tag{41.1a}$$

$$\frac{}{\Gamma \vdash_\Sigma \mathtt{never}[\tau] : \mathtt{event}[w](\tau)} \tag{41.1b}$$

$$\frac{\Sigma \vdash a \sim \tau @ w}{\Gamma \vdash_\Sigma \mathtt{rcv}[a] : \mathtt{event}[w](\tau)} \tag{41.1c}$$

$$\frac{\Gamma \vdash_\Sigma e_1 : \mathtt{event}[w](\tau) \quad \Gamma \vdash_\Sigma e_2 : \mathtt{event}[w](\tau)}{\Gamma \vdash_\Sigma \mathtt{or}(e_1; e_2) : \mathtt{event}[w](\tau)} \tag{41.1d}$$

$$\frac{\Gamma \vdash_\Sigma e_1 : \mathtt{event}[w](\tau_1) \quad \Gamma, x : \tau_1 \vdash_\Sigma e_2 : \tau_2}{\Gamma \vdash_\Sigma \mathtt{wrap}(e_1; x.e_2) : \mathtt{event}[w](\tau_2)} \tag{41.1e}$$

Rule (41.1a) states that the type of an encapsulated command records the site at which the command is executed. Rules (41.1b) to (41.1e) specify that events are attached to a site because channels are. Communication among processes is confined to a site; there is no inter-site synchronization.

The statics of the commands of **DA** is given by the following rules:

$$\frac{\Gamma \vdash_\Sigma e : \tau}{\Gamma \vdash_\Sigma \mathtt{ret}(e) \mathrel{\dot\sim} \tau @ w} \tag{41.2a}$$

$$\frac{\Gamma \vdash_\Sigma e_1 : \tau_1 \, \mathtt{cmd} @ w \quad \Gamma, x : \tau_1 \vdash_\Sigma m_2 \mathrel{\dot\sim} \tau_2 @ w}{\Gamma \vdash_\Sigma \mathtt{bnd}(e_1; x.m_2) \mathrel{\dot\sim} \tau_2 @ w} \tag{41.2b}$$

$$\frac{\Gamma \vdash_\Sigma e : \mathtt{cmd}[w](\mathtt{unit})}{\Gamma \vdash_\Sigma \mathtt{spawn}(e) \mathrel{\dot\sim} \mathtt{unit} @ w} \tag{41.2c}$$

$$\frac{\Gamma \vdash_\Sigma e : \tau \quad \Sigma \vdash a \sim \tau @ w}{\Gamma \vdash_\Sigma \mathtt{snd}[a](e) \mathrel{\dot\sim} \mathtt{unit} @ w} \tag{41.2d}$$

$$\frac{\Gamma \vdash_\Sigma e : \mathtt{event}[w](\tau)}{\Gamma \vdash_\Sigma \mathtt{sync}(e) \mathrel{\dot\sim} \tau @ w} \tag{41.2e}$$

$$\frac{\Gamma \vdash_\Sigma m' \mathrel{\dot\sim} \tau' @ w'}{\Gamma \vdash_\Sigma \mathtt{at}[w'](m') \mathrel{\dot\sim} \tau' @ w} \tag{41.2f}$$

Rule (41.2a) states that an expression may be returned at any site, because its meaning is independent of the site. Rule (41.2b) ensures that the sequential composition of commands is allowed only within a site, and not across sites. Rule (41.2e) states that the sync command returns a value of the same type as that of the event, and can be executed only at the site to which the given event pertains. Rule (41.2d) states that a message can be sent along a channel available at the site from which it is sent. Finally, rule (41.2f) states that to execute a command at a site w' requires that the command pertain to that site. The returned value is then passed to the original site.

Process formation is defined as follows:

$$\frac{}{\vdash_\Sigma \mathbf{1} \text{ proc } @ \ w} \tag{41.3a}$$

$$\frac{\vdash_\Sigma m \mathbin{\dot\sim} \mathsf{unit} \ @ \ w}{\vdash_\Sigma \mathsf{run}(m) \text{ proc } @ \ w} \tag{41.3b}$$

$$\frac{\vdash_\Sigma p_1 \text{ proc } @ \ w \quad \vdash_\Sigma p_2 \text{ proc } @ \ w}{\vdash_\Sigma p_1 \otimes p_2 \text{ proc } @ \ w} \tag{41.3c}$$

$$\frac{\vdash_{\Sigma, a \sim \tau @ w} p \text{ proc } @ \ w}{\vdash_\Sigma \nu \, a \sim \tau . p \text{ proc } @ \ w} \tag{41.3d}$$

These rules state that processes are sited. In particular, an atomic process consists of a command suitable for the site at which the process is run, and a new channel is allocated at the site of the process that allocates it.

Action formation is defined as follows:

$$\frac{}{\vdash_\Sigma \varepsilon \text{ action } @ \ w} \tag{41.4a}$$

$$\frac{\vdash_\Sigma e : \tau \quad e \ \mathsf{val}_\Sigma \quad \Sigma \vdash a \sim \tau \ @ \ w}{\vdash_\Sigma a \cdot e \, ! \text{ action } @ \ w} \tag{41.4b}$$

$$\frac{\vdash_\Sigma e : \tau \quad e \ \mathsf{val}_\Sigma \quad \Sigma \vdash a \sim \tau \ @ \ w}{\vdash_\Sigma a \cdot e \, ? \text{ action } @ \ w} \tag{41.4c}$$

Messages are values of type `clsfd` and are meaningful only at the site at which the channel is allocated. Locality of actions corresponds to confinement of communication to a single site.

41.2 Dynamics

The dynamics of **DA** is a labeled transition judgment between processes at a site. Thus, the judgment

$$p \xmapsto[\Sigma]{\alpha \, @ \, w} p'$$

states that at site w the process p steps to the process p', engendering the action α. It is defined by the following rules:

$$\frac{m \xmapsto[\Sigma]{\alpha \, @ \, w} \nu \, \Sigma' \{ m' \otimes p \}}{\mathsf{run}(m) \xmapsto[\Sigma]{\alpha \, @ \, w} \nu \, \Sigma' \{ \mathsf{run}(m') \otimes p \}} \tag{41.5a}$$

$$\frac{e \ \mathsf{val}_\Sigma}{\mathsf{run}(\mathsf{ret} \, e) \xmapsto[\Sigma]{\varepsilon \, @ \, w} \mathbf{1}} \tag{41.5b}$$

$$\frac{p_1 \xmapsto[\Sigma]{\alpha \,@\, w} p_1'}{p_1 \otimes p_2 \xmapsto[\Sigma]{\alpha \,@\, w} p_1' \otimes p_2} \tag{41.5c}$$

$$\frac{p_1 \xmapsto[\Sigma]{\alpha \,@\, w} p_1' \quad p_2 \xmapsto[\Sigma]{\bar{\alpha} \,@\, w} p_2'}{p_1 \otimes p_2 \xmapsto[\Sigma]{\varepsilon \,@\, w} p_1' \otimes p_2'} \tag{41.5d}$$

$$\frac{p \xmapsto[\Sigma, a \sim \tau \,@\, w]{\alpha \,@\, w} p' \quad \vdash_\Sigma \alpha \text{ action } @ \ w}{v \, a \sim \tau . p \xmapsto[\Sigma]{\alpha \,@\, w} v \, a \sim \tau . p'} \tag{41.5e}$$

These rules are like rules (40.3), but for the sensitivity to the site at which execution takes place. The site comes into play in rules (41.5a) and (41.5e).

Rule (41.5a) makes use of the command execution judgment

$$m \xRightarrow[\Sigma]{\alpha \,@\, w} v \, \Sigma' \{ m' \otimes p \},$$

which states that the command m when executed at site w may engender the action α and in the process create new channels, Σ', and a new process p. (The result of the transition is not a process expression, but a triple comprising the newly allocated channels, the newly created processes, and a new command.)

Command execution is defined by the following rules:

$$\frac{}{\mathtt{spawn(cmd}(m)) \xRightarrow[\Sigma]{\varepsilon \,@\, w} \mathtt{ret}(\langle\rangle) \otimes \mathtt{run}(m)} \tag{41.6a}$$

$$\frac{e \ \mathsf{val}_\Sigma \quad \vdash_\Sigma e : \tau \quad \Sigma \vdash a \sim \tau \ @ \ w}{\mathtt{snd}[a](e) \xRightarrow[\Sigma]{a \cdot e \,! \,@\, w} \mathtt{ret} \ \langle\rangle} \tag{41.6b}$$

$$\frac{e \ \mathsf{val}_\Sigma \quad \vdash_\Sigma e : \tau \quad \Sigma \vdash a \sim \tau \ @ \ w}{\mathtt{sync(rcv}[a]) \xRightarrow[\Sigma]{a \cdot e \,? \,@\, w} \mathtt{ret}(e)} \tag{41.6c}$$

$$\frac{\mathtt{sync}(e_1) \xRightarrow[\Sigma]{\alpha \,@\, w} m_1}{\mathtt{sync(or}(e_1; e_2)) \xRightarrow[\Sigma]{\alpha \,@\, w} m_1} \tag{41.6d}$$

$$\frac{\mathtt{sync}(e_2) \xRightarrow[\Sigma]{\alpha \,@\, w} m_2}{\mathtt{sync(or}(e_1; e_2)) \xRightarrow[\Sigma]{\alpha \,@\, w} m_2} \tag{41.6e}$$

$$\frac{\mathtt{sync}(e_1) \xRightarrow[\Sigma]{\alpha \,@\, w} m_1}{\mathtt{sync(wrap}(e_1; x.e_2)) \xRightarrow[\Sigma]{\alpha \,@\, w} \mathtt{bnd(cmd}(m_1); x.\mathtt{ret}(e_2))} \tag{41.6f}$$

$$m \xrightarrow[\Sigma]{\alpha @ w'} \nu \Sigma' \{ m' \otimes p' \}$$
$$\overline{ \mathsf{at}[w'](m) \xrightarrow[\Sigma]{\alpha @ w} \nu \Sigma' \{ \mathsf{at}[w'](m') \otimes p' \} }$$

(41.6g)

$$\frac{e \ \mathsf{val}_\Sigma}{\mathsf{at}[w'](\mathsf{ret}(e)) \xrightarrow[\Sigma]{\varepsilon @ w} \mathsf{ret}(e)}$$

(41.6h)

Rule (41.6a) states that new processes created at a site stay at that site—the new process executes the given command at the current site. Rule (41.6b) specifies that a send generates an event specific to the site at which it occurs. Rules (41.6c) to (41.6f) specify that receive events occur only for channels allocated at the execution site. Rules (41.6g) and (41.6h) state that the command $\mathsf{at}[w'](m)$ is executed at site w by executing m at site w', and returning the result to the site w.

41.3 Safety

The safety theorem for **DA** ensures that synchronization on a channel may only occur at the site on which the channel resides, even though channel references may be propagated from one site to another during a computation. By the time the reference is resolved and synchronization is attempted, the computation will be executing at the right site.

Lemma 41.1 (Execution). *If* $m \xrightarrow[\Sigma]{\alpha @ w} \nu \Sigma' \{ m' \otimes p' \}$, *and* $\vdash_\Sigma m \mathrel{\dot{\sim}} \tau @ w$, *then* $\vdash_\Sigma \alpha \ action @ w$, $\vdash_{\Sigma \Sigma'} m' \mathrel{\dot{\sim}} \tau @ w$, *and* $\vdash_{\Sigma \Sigma'} p' \ proc @ w$.

Proof By induction on rules (41.6). □

Theorem 41.2 (Preservation). *If* $p \xrightarrow[\Sigma @ w]{\alpha} p'$ *and* $\vdash_\Sigma p \ proc @ w$, *then* $\vdash_\Sigma p' \ proc @ w$.

Proof By induction on the statics of **DA**, appealing to Lemma 41.1 for atomic processes. □

The progress theorem states that the only impediment to execution of a well-typed program is synchronizing on an event that never occurs.

Theorem 41.3 (Progress). *If* $\vdash_\Sigma p \ proc @ w$, *then either* $p \equiv \mathbf{1}$ *or there exists* α *and* p' *such that* $p \xrightarrow[\Sigma @ w]{\alpha} p'$.

Proof By induction on the dynamics of **DA**. □

41.4 Notes

The use of a spatial modality to express locality and mobility constraints in a distributed program was introduced in the experimental language ML5 (Murphy et al., 2004). Some languages for distributed computing consolidate concurrency with distribution by allowing cross-site interaction. The idea of **DA** is to separate temporal from spatial considerations, limiting synchronization to a single site, but allowing movement of the locus of execution from one site to another.

Exercises

41.1. The definition of **DA** given in this chapter has no means of allocating new channels, or sending and receiving on them. Remedy this shortcoming by adding a command to create channel references. Give the statics and dynamics of this extension, and of any associated extensions needed to account for it. *Hint*: the type of channel references, $chan[w](\tau)$, should be indexed by the site of the channel to which the reference refers.

41.2. Given a channel reference $e : chan[w'](\tau)$, it is sensible to send a message asynchronously from site w along this channel by providing a payload $e' : \tau$. It is also possible to implement a synchronous remote send (also known as a *remote procedure call*) that sends a message $e' : \tau$ on a remote channel $e : chan[w'](\tau)$ and returns a result of type τ' in response to the message. Implement both of these capabilities in **DA**. *Hint*: Implement synchronous communication using a reply channel as described in Chapter 39.

PART XVII

Modularity

42 Modularity and Linking

Modularity is the most important technique for controlling the complexity of programs. Programs are decomposed into separate *components* with precisely specified, and tightly controlled, interactions. The pathways for interaction among components determine dependencies that constrain the process by which the components are integrated, or *linked*, to form a complete system. Different systems may use the same components, and a single system may use multiple instances of a single component. Sharing of components amortizes the cost of their development across systems and helps limit errors by limiting coding effort.

Modularity is not limited to programming languages. In mathematics, the proof of a theorem is decomposed into a collection of definitions and lemmas. References among the lemmas determine a dependency relation that constrains their integration to form a complete proof of the main theorem. Of course, one person's theorem is another person's lemma; there is no intrinsic limit on the depth and complexity of the hierarchies of results in mathematics. Mathematical structures are themselves composed of separable parts, for example, a ring comprises a group and a monoid structure on the same underlying set.

Modularity arises from the structural properties of the hypothetical and general judgments. Dependencies among components are expressed by free variables whose typing assumptions state the presumed properties of the component. Linking amounts to substitution to discharge the hypothesis.

42.1 Simple Units and Linking

Decomposing a program into units amounts to exploiting the transitivity of the hypothetical judgment (see Chapter 3). The decomposition may be described as an interaction between two parties, the *client* and the *implementor*, mediated by an agreed-upon contract, an *interface*. The client *assumes* that the implementor upholds the contract, and the implementor *guarantees* that the contract will be upheld. The assumption made by the client amounts to a declaration of its dependence on the implementor discharged by *linking* the two parties accordng to their agreed-upon contract.

The interface that mediates the interaction between a client and an implementor is a *type*. Linking is the implementation of the composite structural rules of substitution and transitivity:

$$\frac{\Gamma \vdash e_{impl} : \tau_{intf} \quad \Gamma, x : \tau_{intf} \vdash e_{client} : \tau_{client}}{\Gamma \vdash [e_{impl}/x]e_{client} : \tau_{client}} \tag{42.1}$$

The type τ_{intf} is the interface type. It defines the operations provided by the implementor e_{impl} and relied upon by the client e_{client}. The free variable x expresses the dependency of e_{client} on e_{impl}. That is, the client accesses the implementation by using the variable x.

The interface type τ_{intf} is the contract between the client and the implementor. It determines the properties of the implementation on which the client may depend and, at the same time, determines the obligations that the implementor must fulfill. The simplest form of interface type is a finite product type of the form $\langle f_1 \hookrightarrow \tau_1, \ldots, f_n \hookrightarrow \tau_n \rangle$, specifying a component with components f_i of type τ_i. Such a type is an *application program interface*, or *API*, because it determines the operations that the client (application) may expect from the implementor. A more advanced form of interface is one that defines an abstract type of the form $\exists (t.\langle f_1 \hookrightarrow \tau_1, \ldots, f_n \hookrightarrow \tau_n \rangle)$, which defines an abstract type t representing the internal state of an "abstract machine" whose "instruction set" consists of the operations $f_1, \ldots, f_n$ whose types may involve t. Being abstract, the type t is not revealed to the client but is known only to the implementor.[1]

Conceptually, linking is just substitution, but practically this can be implemented in many ways. One method is *separate compilation*. The expressions e_{client} and e_{impl}, the *source modules*, are translated (compiled) into another, lower-level, language, resulting in *object modules*. Linking consists of performing the required substitution at the level of the object language in such a way that the result corresponds to translating $[e_{impl}/x]e_{client}$. Another method, *separate checking*, shifts the requirement for translation to the linker. The client and implementor units are checked for type correctness with respect to the interface but are not translated into lower-level form. Linking then consists of translating the composite program as a whole, often resulting in a more efficient outcome than would be possible when compiling separately.

The foregoing are all forms of *static linking* because the program is composed before it is executed. Another method, *dynamic linking*, defers program composition until run-time, so that a component is loaded only if it is actually required during execution. This might seem to involve executing programs with free variables, but it does not. Each client implemented by a *stub* that forwards accesses to a stored implementation (typically, in an ambient file system). The difficulty with dynamic linking is that it refers to components by name (say, a path in a file system), and the binding of that name may change at any time, wreaking havoc on program behavior.

42.2 Initialization and Effects

Linking resolves the dependencies among the components of a program by substitution. This view is valid so long as the components are given by pure expressions, those that evaluate to a value without inducing any effects. For in such cases, there is no problem with the replication, or complete omission, of a component arising from repeated, or absent, uses of a variable representing it. But what if the expression defining the implementation of a component has an effect when evaluated? At a minimum replication of the component implies replication of its effects. Worse, effects introduce *implicit dependencies* among components that are not apparent from their types. For example, if each of two components mutates a shared assignable, the order in which they are linked with a client program affects the behavior of the whole.

This may raise doubts about the treatment of linking as substitution, but on closer inspection it becomes clear that implicit dependencies are naturally expressed by the modal distinction between expressions and commands introduced in Chapter 34. Specifically, a component that may have an effect when executed does not have type τ_{intf} of implementations of the interface type, but rather the type τ_{intf} cmd of encapsulated commands that, when executed, have effects and yield implementations. Being encapsulated, a value of this type is itself free of effects, but it may have effects when evaluated.

The distinction between the types τ_{intf} and τ_{intf} cmd is mediated by the sequencing command introduced in Chapter 34. For the sake of generality, let us assume that the client is itself an encapsulated command of type τ_{client} cmd, so that it may itself have effects when executed, and may serve as a component of a yet larger system. Assuming that the client refers to the encapsulated implementation by the variable x, the command

$$\text{bnd}\, x \leftarrow x \,;\, \text{do}\, e_{client}$$

first determines the implementation of the interface by running the encapsulated command x then running the client code with the result bound to x. The implicit dependencies of the client on the implementor are made explicit by the sequencing command, which ensures that the implementor's effects occur prior to those of the client, precisely because the client depends on the implementor for its execution.

More generally, to manage such interactions in a large program it is common to isolate an *initialization procedure* whose role is to stage the effects engendered by the various components according to some policy or convention. Rather than attempt to survey all possible policies, let us just note that the upshot of such conventions is that the initialization procedure is a command of the form

$$\{x_1 \leftarrow x_1 \,;\, \ldots x_n \leftarrow x_n \,;\, m_{main}\},$$

where $x_1, \ldots, x_n$ represent the components of the system and m_{main} is the main (startup) routine. After linking the initialization procedure has the form

$$\{x_1 \leftarrow e_1 \,;\, \ldots x_n \leftarrow e_n \,;\, m_{main}\},$$

where $e_1, \ldots, e_n$ are the encapsulated implementations of the linked components. When the initialization procedure is executed, it results in the substitution

$$[v_1, \ldots, v_n / x_1, \ldots, x_n] m_{main},$$

where the expressions $v_1, \ldots, v_n$ represent the values resulting from executing $e_1, \ldots, e_n$, respectively, and the implicit effects have occurred in the order specified by the initializer.

42.3 Notes

The relationship between the structural properties of entailment and the practical problem of separate development was implicit in much early work on programming languages but became explicit once the correspondence between propositions and types was developed. There are many indications of this correspondence in sources such as *Proofs and Types* (Girard, 1989) and *Intuitionistic Type Theory* (Martin-Löf, 1984), but it was first made explicit by Cardelli (1997).

Note

1 See Chapters 17 and 48 for a discussion of type abstraction.

43

Singleton Kinds and Subkinding

The expression $\text{let } e_1 : \tau \text{ be } x \text{ in } e_2$ is a form of abbreviation mechanism by which we may bind e_1 to the variable x for use within e_2. In the presence of function types, this expression is definable as the application $(\lambda (x : \tau) e_2)(e_1)$, which accomplishes the same thing. It is natural to consider an analogous form of let expression, which binds a type to a type variable within a scope. Using $\text{def } t \text{ is } \tau \text{ in } e$ to bind the type variable t to τ within the expression e, we may write expressions such as

$$\text{def } t \text{ is nat} \times \text{nat in } \lambda (x : t) \, \mathsf{s}(x \cdot 1),$$

which introduces a *type abbreviation* within an expression. To ensure that this expression is well-typed, the type variable t is to be *synonymous* with the type $\text{nat} \times \text{nat}$, for otherwise the body of the λ-abstraction is not type correct.

Following the pattern of the expression-level let, we might guess that $\text{def } t \text{ is } \tau \text{ in } e$ abbreviates the polymorphic instantiation $\Lambda(t) \, e[\tau]$, which binds t to τ within e. Doing so captures the dynamics of type abbreviation, but it fails to adhere to the intended statics. The difficulty is that, according to this interpretation of type definitions, the expression e is type-checked in the absence of any knowledge of the binding of t, rather than in the knowledge that t is synonymous with τ. Thus, in the above example, the expression $\mathsf{s}(x \cdot 1)$ would fail to type check, unless the binding of t were exposed.

Interpreting type definition in terms of type abstraction and type application fails. One solution is to consider type abbreviation to be a primitive notion with the following statics:

$$\frac{\Gamma \vdash [\tau/t]e : \tau'}{\Gamma \vdash \text{def } t \text{ is } \tau \text{ in } e : \tau'} \tag{43.1}$$

This formulation would solve the problem of type abbreviation, but in an *ad hoc* way. Is there a more general solution?

There is, by introducing *singleton kinds*, which classify type constructors by revealing their identity. Singletons n the type definition problem but play a crucial role in the design of module systems (as described in Chapters 44 and 45.)

43.1 Overview

The central organizing principle of type theory is *compositionality*. To ensure that a program can be decomposed into separable parts, we ensure that the composition of a program from constituent parts is mediated by the types of those parts. Put in other terms, the only thing that one part of a program "knows" about another is its type. For example, the formation rule for addition of natural numbers depends only on the type of its arguments (both have type nat), and not on their specific form or value. But in the case of a type abbreviation of the form def t is τ in e, the principle of compositionality dictates that the only thing that e "knows" about the type variable t is its kind, namely T, and not its binding, namely τ. The proposed representation of type abbreviation as the combination of type abstraction and type application meets this requirement, but it does not have the intended meaning!

We could, as suggested in the introduction, abandon the core principles of type theory, and introduce type abbreviations as a primitive notion. But there is no need to do so. Instead, we need a kind for t that captures its identity; such a kind is called a *singleton kind*. Informally, the kind $S(\tau)$ is the kind of types that are definitionally equal to τ. That is, up to definitional equality, this kind has only one inhabitant, namely τ. Consequently, if $u :: S(\tau)$ is a variable of singleton kind, then within its scope, the variable u is synonymous with τ. Thus, we may represent def t is τ in e by $\Lambda(t :: S(\tau)) e[\tau]$, which correctly propagates the identity of t, namely τ, to e during type checking.

The formalization of singleton kinds requires some more machinery at the constructor and kind level. First, we capture the idea that a constructor of singleton kind is *a fortiori* a constructor of kind T and hence is a type. Otherwise, a variable u of singleton kind cannot be used as a type, even though it is explicitly defined to be one! To avoid this problem, we introduce a *subkinding* relation $\kappa_1 <:: \kappa_2$. The fundamental axiom of subkinding is $S(\tau) <:: T$, stating that every constructor of singleton kind is a type. Second, we account for constructors occurring within kinds. A singleton kind is a *dependent kind* in that its meaning depends on a constructor. Put another way, $S(\tau)$ is a *family of kinds* indexed by constructors of kind T. Products and functions are generalized to *dependent products* and *dependent functions* of families. The dependent product kind, $\Sigma u :: \kappa_1.\kappa_2$, classifies pairs $\langle c_1, c_2 \rangle$ such that $c_1 :: \kappa_1$, as might be expected, and $c_2 :: [c_1/u]\kappa_2$, in which the kind of the second component is sensitive to the first component itself, and not just its kind. The dependent function kind, $\Pi u :: \kappa_1.\kappa_2$, classifies functions that, when applied to a constructor $c_1 :: \kappa_1$, results in a constructor of kind $[c_1/u]\kappa_2$. Note that the kind of the result is sensitive to the argument, and not just to its kind.

Third, it is useful to consider singletons not just of kind T, but also of higher kinds. To support this, we introduce *higher singletons*, written $S(c :: \kappa)$, where κ is a kind and c is a constructor of kind κ. These are definable in terms of the basic form of singleton kinds using dependent function and product kinds.

43.2 Singletons

A singleton kind has the form $S(c)$, where c is a constructor. The singleton classifies all constructors that are equivalent to the constructor c. For the time being, we consider singleton kinds in the context of the language $\mathbf{F}_\omega$ described in Chapter 18, which includes a kind of types and is closed under product and function kinds. In Section 43.3, we will enrich the language of kinds in a way that will ensure that the product and function kinds of $\mathbf{F}_\omega$ are definable.

The statics of singletons uses the following judgment forms:

$$\Delta \vdash \kappa \text{ kind} \qquad\qquad \text{kind formation}$$
$$\Delta \vdash \kappa_1 \equiv \kappa_2 \qquad\qquad \text{kind equivalence}$$
$$\Delta \vdash c :: \kappa \qquad\qquad \text{constructor formation}$$
$$\Delta \vdash c_1 \equiv c_2 :: \kappa \qquad \text{constructor equivalence}$$
$$\Delta \vdash \kappa_1 <:: \kappa_2 \qquad\qquad \text{subkinding}$$

These judgments are defined simultaneously by a collection of rules, including the following:

$$\frac{\Delta \vdash c :: \text{Type}}{\Delta \vdash \text{S}(c) \text{ kind}} \tag{43.2a}$$

$$\frac{\Delta \vdash c :: \text{Type}}{\Delta \vdash c :: \text{S}(c)} \tag{43.2b}$$

$$\frac{\Delta \vdash c :: \text{S}(d)}{\Delta \vdash c \equiv d :: \text{Type}} \tag{43.2c}$$

$$\frac{\Delta \vdash c :: \kappa_1 \quad \Delta \vdash \kappa_1 <:: \kappa_2}{\Delta \vdash c :: \kappa_2} \tag{43.2d}$$

$$\frac{\Delta \vdash c :: \text{Type}}{\Delta \vdash \text{S}(c) <:: \text{Type}} \tag{43.2e}$$

$$\frac{\Delta \vdash c \equiv d :: \text{Type}}{\Delta \vdash \text{S}(c) \equiv \text{S}(d)} \tag{43.2f}$$

$$\frac{\Delta \vdash \kappa_1 \equiv \kappa_2}{\Delta \vdash \kappa_1 <:: \kappa_2} \tag{43.2g}$$

$$\frac{\Delta \vdash \kappa_1 <:: \kappa_2 \quad \Delta \vdash \kappa_2 <:: \kappa_3}{\Delta \vdash \kappa_1 <:: \kappa_3} \tag{43.2h}$$

Omitted for brevity are rules stating that constructor and kind equivalence are reflexive, symmetric, transitive, and preserved by kind and constructor formation.

Rule (43.2b) expresses the principle of "self-recognition," which states that every constructor c of kind Type also has the kind $\text{S}(c)$. By rule (43.2c), any constructor of kind $\text{S}(c)$ is definitionally equal to c. Consequently, self-recognition expresses the reflexivity of constructor equivalence. Rule (43.2e) is just the subsumption principle re-stated at the level of constructors and kinds. Rule (43.2f) states that the singleton kind respects equivalence of its constructors, so that equivalent constructors determine the same singletons. Rules (43.2g) and (43.2h) state that the subkinding relation is a pre-order that respects kind equivalence.

To see these rules in action, let us consider a few illustrative examples. First, consider the behavior of variables of singleton kind. Suppose that $\Delta \vdash u :: \text{S}(c)$ is such a variable. Then, by rule (43.2c), we may deduce that $\Delta \vdash u \equiv c :: \text{T}$. Thus, declaring u with a singleton kind defines it to be the constructor specified by its kind.

Taking this a step further, the existential type $\exists\, u :: S(c).\tau$ is the type of packages whose representation type is (equivalent to) c—it is an abstract type whose identity is revealed by assigning it a singleton kind. By the general principles of equivalence, we have that the type $\exists\, u :: S(c).\tau$ is equivalent to the type $\exists\, \_ :: S(c).[c/u]\tau$, wherein we have propagated the equivalence of u and c into the type τ. On the other hand, we may also "forget" the definition of u, because the subtyping

$$\exists\, u :: S(c).\tau <: \exists\, u :: T.\tau$$

is derivable using the following variance rule for existential types over a kind:

$$\frac{\Delta \vdash \kappa_1 <:: \kappa_2 \quad \Delta, u :: \kappa_1 \vdash \tau_1 <: \tau_2}{\Delta \vdash \exists\, u :: \kappa_1.\tau_1 <: \exists\, u :: \kappa_2.\tau_2} \tag{43.3}$$

Similarly, we may derive the subtyping

$$\forall\, u :: T.\tau <: \forall\, u :: S(c).\tau$$

from the following variance rule for universals over a kind:

$$\frac{\Delta \vdash \kappa_2 <:: \kappa_1 \quad \Delta, u :: \kappa_2 \vdash \tau_1 <: \tau_2}{\Delta \vdash \forall\, u :: \kappa_1.\tau_1 <: \forall\, u :: \kappa_2.\tau_2} \tag{43.4}$$

Informally, the displayed subtyping states that a polymorphic function that may be applied to *any* type is one that may only be applied to a particular type c.

These examples show that singleton kinds express the idea of a scoped definition of a type variable in a way that is not tied to an *ad hoc* definition mechanism but arises naturally from general principles of binding and scope. We will see in Chapters 44 and 45 more advanced uses of singletons to manage the interaction among program modules.

43.3 Dependent Kinds

Although it is perfectly possible to add singleton kinds to the framework of higher kinds introduced in Chapter 18, to do so would be to short-change the expressiveness of the language. Using higher kinds, we can express the kind of constructors that, when applied to a type, yield a specific type, say int, as result, namely $T \to S(int)$. But we cannot express the kind of constructors that, when applied to a type, yield *that very type* as result, for there is no way for the result kind to refer to the argument of the function. Similarly, using product kinds we can express the kind of pairs whose first component is int and whose second component is an arbitrary type, namely $S(int) \times T$. But we cannot express the kind of pairs whose second component is equivalent to its first component, for there is no way for the kind of the second component to make reference to the first component itself.

To express such concepts requires that product and function kinds be generalized so that the kind of the second component of a pair may mention the first component of that pair, or the kind of the result of a function may mention the argument to which it is applied. Such kinds are called *dependent kinds* because they involve kinds that mention, or depend upon, constructors (of kind T). The syntax of dependent kinds is given by the following grammar:

Kind	κ	::=	$S(c)$	$S(c)$	singleton
			$\Sigma(\kappa_1; u.\kappa_2)$	$\Sigma\, u :: \kappa_1.\kappa_2$	dependent product
			$\Pi(\kappa_1; u.\kappa_2)$	$\Pi\, u :: \kappa_1.\kappa_2$	dependent function
Con	c	::=	u	u	variable
			$\mathtt{pair}(c_1; c_2)$	$\langle c_1, c_2 \rangle$	pair
			$\mathtt{proj[l]}(c)$	$c \cdot \mathtt{l}$	first projection
			$\mathtt{proj[r]}(c)$	$c \cdot \mathtt{r}$	second projection
			$\mathtt{lam}\{\kappa\}(u.c)$	$\lambda\,(u :: \kappa)\,c$	abstraction
			$\mathtt{app}(c_1; c_2)$	$c_1[c_2]$	application

As a notational convenience, when there is no dependency in a kind we write $\kappa_1 \times \kappa_2$ for $\Sigma\, \_ :: \kappa_1.\kappa_2$, and $\kappa_1 \to \kappa_2$ for $\Pi\, \_ :: \kappa_1.\kappa_2$, where the "blank" stands for an irrelevant variable.

The dependent product kind $\Sigma\, u :: \kappa_1.\kappa_2$ classifies pairs $\langle c_1, c_2 \rangle$ of constructors in which c_1 has kind κ_1 and c_2 has kind $[c_1/u]\kappa_2$. For example, the kind $\Sigma\, u :: T.S(u)$ classifies pairs $\langle c, c \rangle$, where c is a constructor of kind T. More generally, this kind classifies pairs of the form $\langle c_1, c_2 \rangle$ where c_1 and c_2 are equivalent but not necessarily identical, constructors. The dependent function kind $\Pi\, u :: \kappa_1.\kappa_2$ classifies constructors c that, when applied to a constructor c_1 of kind κ_1, yields a constructor of kind $[c_1/u]\kappa_2$. For example, the kind $\Pi\, u :: T.S(u)$ classifies constructors that, when applied to a constructor c, yields a constructor equivalent to c; a constructor of this kind is essentially the identity function. We may, of course, combine these to form kinds such as

$$\Pi\, u :: T \times T.S(u \cdot \mathtt{r}) \times S(u \cdot \mathtt{l}),$$

which classifies functions that swap the components of a pair of types. (Such examples suggest that the behavior of a constructor may be pinned down precisely using dependent kinds. We shall see in Section 43.4 that this is the case.)

The formation, introduction, and elimination rules for the product kind are as follows:

$$\frac{\Delta \vdash \kappa_1 \text{ kind} \quad \Delta, u :: \kappa_1 \vdash \kappa_2 \text{ kind}}{\Delta \vdash \Sigma\, u :: \kappa_1.\kappa_2 \text{ kind}} \tag{43.5a}$$

$$\frac{\Delta \vdash c_1 :: \kappa_1 \quad \Delta \vdash c_2 :: [c_1/u]\kappa_2}{\Delta \vdash \langle c_1, c_2 \rangle :: \Sigma\, u :: \kappa_1.\kappa_2} \tag{43.5b}$$

$$\frac{\Delta \vdash c :: \Sigma\, u :: \kappa_1.\kappa_2}{\Delta \vdash c \cdot \mathtt{l} :: \kappa_1} \tag{43.5c}$$

$$\frac{\Delta \vdash c :: \Sigma\, u :: \kappa_1.\kappa_2}{\Delta \vdash c \cdot \mathtt{r} :: [c \cdot \mathtt{l}/u]\kappa_2} \tag{43.5d}$$

In rule (43.5a), note that the variable u may occur in the kind κ_2 by appearing in a singleton kind. Correspondingly, rules (43.5b), (43.5c), and (43.5d) substitute a constructor for this variable.

The following equivalence axioms govern the constructors associated with the dependent product kind:

$$\frac{\Delta \vdash c_1 :: \kappa_1 \quad \Delta \vdash c_2 :: \kappa_2}{\Delta \vdash \langle c_1, c_2 \rangle \cdot \mathbf{1} \equiv c_1 :: \kappa_1} \tag{43.6a}$$

$$\frac{\Delta \vdash c_1 :: \kappa_1 \quad \Delta \vdash c_2 :: \kappa_2}{\Delta \vdash \langle c_1, c_2 \rangle \cdot \mathbf{r} \equiv c_2 :: \kappa_2} \tag{43.6b}$$

The subkinding rule for the dependent product kind specifies that it is covariant in both positions:

$$\frac{\Delta \vdash \kappa_1 <:: \kappa_1' \quad \Delta, u :: \kappa_1 \vdash \kappa_2 <:: \kappa_2'}{\Delta \vdash \Sigma\, u :: \kappa_1.\kappa_2 <:: \Sigma\, u :: \kappa_1'.\kappa_2'} \tag{43.7}$$

The congruence rule for equivalence of dependent product kinds is formally similar:

$$\frac{\Delta \vdash \kappa_1 \equiv \kappa_1' \quad \Delta, u :: \kappa_1 \vdash \kappa_2 \equiv \kappa_2'}{\Delta \vdash \Sigma\, u :: \kappa_1.\kappa_2 \equiv \Sigma\, u :: \kappa_1'.\kappa_2'} \tag{43.8}$$

Notable consequences of these rules include the subkindings

$$\Sigma\, u :: S(\mathtt{int}).S(u) <:: \Sigma\, u :: \mathsf{T}.S(u)$$

and

$$\Sigma\, u :: \mathsf{T}.S(u) <:: \mathsf{T} \times \mathsf{T},$$

and the equivalence

$$\Sigma\, u :: S(\mathtt{int}).S(u) \equiv S(\mathtt{int}) \times S(\mathtt{int}).$$

Subkinding is used to "forget" information about the identity of the components of a pair, and equivalence is used to propagate such information within a kind.

The formation, introduction, and elimination rules for dependent function kinds are as follows:

$$\frac{\Delta \vdash \kappa_1 \ \mathsf{kind} \quad \Delta, u :: \kappa_1 \vdash \kappa_2 \ \mathsf{kind}}{\Delta \vdash \Pi\, u :: \kappa_1.\kappa_2 \ \mathsf{kind}} \tag{43.9a}$$

$$\frac{\Delta, u :: \kappa_1 \vdash c :: \kappa_2}{\Delta \vdash \lambda\,(u :: \kappa_1)\,c :: \Pi\, u :: \kappa_1.\kappa_2} \tag{43.9b}$$

$$\frac{\Delta \vdash c :: \Pi\, u :: \kappa_1.\kappa_2 \quad \Delta \vdash c_1 :: \kappa_1}{\Delta \vdash c[c_1] :: [c_1/u]\kappa_2} \tag{43.9c}$$

Rule (43.9b) specifies that the result kind of a λ-abstraction depends uniformly on the argument u. Correspondingly, rule (43.9c) specifies that the kind of an application is obtained by substitution of the argument into the result kind of the function itself.

The following rule of equivalence governs the constructors associated with the dependent product kind:

$$\frac{\Delta, u :: \kappa_1 \vdash c :: \kappa_2 \quad \Delta \vdash c_1 :: \kappa_1}{\Delta \vdash (\lambda\,(u :: \kappa_1)\,c)[c_1] \equiv [c_1/u]c :: \kappa_2} \tag{43.10}$$

The subkinding rule for the dependent function kind specifies that it is contravariant in its domain and covariant in its range:

$$\frac{\Delta \vdash \kappa_1' <:: \kappa_1 \quad \Delta, u :: \kappa_1' \vdash \kappa_2 <:: \kappa_2'}{\Delta \vdash \Pi u :: \kappa_1.\kappa_2 <:: \Pi u :: \kappa_1'.\kappa_2'} \tag{43.11}$$

The equivalence rule is similar, except that the symmetry of equivalence obviates a choice of variance:

$$\frac{\Delta \vdash \kappa_1 \equiv \kappa_1' \quad \Delta, u :: \kappa_1 \vdash \kappa_2 \equiv \kappa_2'}{\Delta \vdash \Pi u :: \kappa_1.\kappa_2 \equiv \Pi u :: \kappa_1'.\kappa_2'} \tag{43.12}$$

Rule (43.11) gives rise to the subkinding

$$\Pi u :: \mathtt{T}.\mathtt{S}(\mathtt{int}) <:: \Pi u :: \mathtt{S}(\mathtt{int}).\mathtt{T},$$

which illustrates the co- and contravariance of the dependent function kind. In particular, a function that takes any type and delivers the type int is also a function that takes the type int and delivers a type. Rule (43.12) gives rise to the equivalence

$$\Pi u :: \mathtt{S}(\mathtt{int}).\mathtt{S}(u) \equiv \mathtt{S}(\mathtt{int}) \to \mathtt{S}(\mathtt{int}),$$

which propagates information about the argument into the range kind. Combining these two rules we may derive the subkinding

$$\Pi u :: \mathtt{T}.\mathtt{S}(u) <:: \mathtt{S}(\mathtt{int}) \to \mathtt{S}(\mathtt{int}).$$

Intuitively, a constructor function that yields its argument is, in particular, a constructor function that may only be applied to int and yields int. Formally, by contravariance we have the subkinding

$$\Pi u :: \mathtt{T}.\mathtt{S}(u) <:: \Pi u :: \mathtt{S}(\mathtt{int}).\mathtt{S}(u),$$

and by sharing propagation we may derive the indicated superkind.

43.4 Higher Singletons

Although singletons are restricted to constructors of kind T, we may use dependent product and function kinds to define singletons of every kind. Specifically, we wish to define the kind $\mathtt{S}(c :: \kappa)$, where c is of kind κ, that classifies constructors equivalent to c. When $\kappa = \mathtt{T}$, this is, of course, just $\mathtt{S}(c)$; the problem is to define singletons for the higher kinds $\Sigma u :: \kappa_1.\kappa_2$ and $\Pi u :: \kappa_1.\kappa_2$.

Suppose that $c :: \kappa_1 \times \kappa_2$. The singleton kind $\mathtt{S}(c :: \kappa_1 \times \kappa_2)$ classifies constructors equivalent to c. If we assume, inductively, that singletons are defined for κ_1 and κ_2, then we need only note that c is equivalent to $\langle c \cdot \mathtt{l}, c \cdot \mathtt{r} \rangle$. For then, the singleton $\mathtt{S}(c :: \kappa_1 \times \kappa_2)$ can be defined to be $\mathtt{S}(c \cdot \mathtt{l} :: \kappa_1) \times \mathtt{S}(c \cdot \mathtt{r} :: \kappa_2)$. Similarly, suppose that $c :: \kappa_1 \to \kappa_2$. Using the equivalence of c and $\lambda (u :: \kappa_1 \to \kappa_2) c[u]$, we may define $\mathtt{S}(c :: \kappa_1 \to \kappa_2)$ to be $\Pi u :: \kappa_1.\mathtt{S}(c[u] :: \kappa_2)$.

In general, the kind $S(c :: \kappa)$ is defined by induction on the structure of κ by the following kind equivalences:

$$\frac{\Delta \vdash c :: S(c')}{\Delta \vdash S(c :: S(c')) \equiv S(c)} \tag{43.13a}$$

$$\frac{\Delta \vdash c :: \Sigma\, u :: \kappa_1.\kappa_2}{\Delta \vdash S(c :: \Sigma\, u :: \kappa_1.\kappa_2) \equiv \Sigma\, u :: S(c \cdot 1 :: \kappa_1).S(c \cdot r :: \kappa_2)} \tag{43.13b}$$

$$\frac{\Delta \vdash c :: \Pi\, u :: \kappa_1.\kappa_2}{\Delta \vdash S(c :: \Pi\, u :: \kappa_1.\kappa_2) \equiv \Pi\, u :: \kappa_1.S(c[u] :: \kappa_2)} \tag{43.13c}$$

The sensibility of these equations relies on rule (43.2c) together with the following principles of constructor equivalence, called *extensionality principles*:

$$\frac{\Delta \vdash c :: \Sigma\, u :: \kappa_1.\kappa_2}{\Delta \vdash c \equiv \langle c \cdot 1, c \cdot r \rangle :: \Sigma\, u :: \kappa_1.\kappa_2} \tag{43.14a}$$

$$\frac{\Delta \vdash c :: \Pi\, u :: \kappa_1.\kappa_2}{\Delta \vdash c \equiv \lambda\, (u :: \kappa_1)\, c[u] :: \Pi\, u :: \kappa_1.\kappa_2} \tag{43.14b}$$

Rule (43.2c) states that the only constructors of kind $S(c')$ are those equivalent to c', and rules (43.14a) and (43.14b) state that the only members of the dependent product and function types are, respectively, pairs and λ-abstractions of the right kinds.

Finally, the following *self-recognition* rules are required to ensure that rule (43.2b) extends to higher kinds.

$$\frac{\Delta \vdash c \cdot 1 :: \kappa_1 \quad \Delta \vdash c \cdot r :: [c \cdot 1/u]\kappa_2}{\Delta \vdash c :: \Sigma\, u :: \kappa_1.\kappa_2} \tag{43.15a}$$

$$\frac{\Delta, u :: \kappa_1 \vdash c[u] :: \kappa_2}{\Delta \vdash c :: \Pi\, u :: \kappa_1.\kappa_2} \tag{43.15b}$$

An illustrative case arises when u is a constructor variable of kind $\Sigma\, v :: T.S(v)$. We may derive that $u \cdot 1 :: S(u \cdot 1)$ using rule (43.2b). We may also derive $u \cdot r :: S(u \cdot 1)$ using rule (43.5d). Therefore, by rule (43.15a), we may derive $u :: \Sigma\, v :: S(u \cdot 1).S(u \cdot 1)$, which is a subkind of $\Sigma\, v :: T.S(v)$. This more precise kind is a correct kinding for u, because the first component of u is $u \cdot 1$, and the second component of u is equivalent to the first component, and hence is also $u \cdot 1$. But without rule (43.15a), it is impossible to derive this fact.

The point of introducing higher singletons is to ensure that every constructor can be classified by a kind that determines it up to definitional equality. Viewed as extending singleton types, we would expect that higher singletons enjoy similar properties.

Theorem 43.1. *If $\Delta \vdash c :: \kappa$, then $\Delta \vdash S(c :: \kappa) <:: \kappa$ and $\Delta \vdash c :: S(c :: \kappa)$.*

The proof of this theorem is beyond the scope of this text.

43.5 Notes

Singleton kinds were introduced by Stone and Harper (2006) to isolate the concept of type sharing that arises in the ML module system (Milner et al., 1997; Harper and Lillibridge, 1994; Leroy, 1994). The meta-theory of singleton kinds is surprisingly intricate. The main source of complexity arises from constructor-indexed families of kinds. If $u :: \kappa \vdash c' :: \kappa'$, and if $c_1 :: \kappa$ and $c_2 : \kappa$ are distinct but equivalent, then so are the instances $[c_1/u]\kappa'$ and $[c_2/u]\kappa'$. Managing kind equivalence raises significant technical difficulties in the proofs.

Exercises

43.1. Show that rules (43.5c) and (43.5d) are inter-derivable with the following two rules:

$$\frac{\Delta \vdash c :: \kappa_1 \times \kappa_2}{\Delta \vdash c \cdot \mathbf{1} :: \kappa_1} \tag{43.16a}$$

$$\frac{\Delta \vdash c :: \kappa_1 \times \kappa_2}{\Delta \vdash c \cdot \mathbf{r} :: \kappa_2}. \tag{43.16b}$$

43.2. Show that rule (43.9c) is inter-derivable with the rule

$$\frac{\Delta \vdash c :: \kappa_1 \to \kappa_2 \quad \Delta \vdash c_1 :: \kappa_1}{\Delta \vdash c[c_1] :: \kappa_2}. \tag{43.17}$$

43.3. It is useful to *modify* a kind κ by imposing on κ a definition of one of its components.

A component of a kind is specified by a *simple path* consisting of a finite, possibly empty, sequence of symbols $\mathbf{1}$ and $\mathbf{r}$ thought of as a tree address within a kind. The *path projection* $c \cdot p$ of a constructor c of kind κ by a path p is inductively defined by these equations:

$$c \cdot \varepsilon \triangleq c$$
$$c \cdot (\mathbf{1}\, p) \triangleq (c \cdot \mathbf{1}) \cdot p$$
$$c \cdot (\mathbf{r}\, p) \triangleq (c \cdot \mathbf{r}) \cdot p$$

If $\Delta, u :: \kappa \vdash c :: \kappa_{\mathbf{r}}$, then the patched kind $\kappa\{\mathbf{r} := c\}$ is the kind $\kappa_1 \times \mathsf{S}(c :: \kappa_{\mathbf{r}})$. It has the property that

$$\Delta, u :: \kappa\{\mathbf{r} := c\} \vdash u \cdot \mathbf{r} \equiv c :: \kappa_{\mathbf{r}}.$$

Define $\Delta \vdash \kappa\{p := c\}$ kind, where $\Delta \vdash \kappa$ kind, $\Delta, u :: \kappa \vdash u \cdot p :: \kappa_p$, and $\Delta \vdash c :: \kappa_c$, to be such that $\Delta \vdash \kappa\{p := c\} <:: \kappa$ and $\Delta, u :: \kappa\{p := c\} \vdash u \cdot p \equiv c :: \kappa_c$.

43.4. Patching is used to constrain a component of a kind to be equivalent to a specified constructor. A *sharing specification* imposed on a kind ensures that a definitional equality holds of any constructor of that kind. Informally, the kind $u :: \kappa / u \cdot p \equiv u \cdot q$ is a subkind κ' of κ such that

$$\Delta, u :: \kappa' \vdash u \cdot p \equiv u \cdot q :: \kappa''. \tag{43.18}$$

For example, the kind $u :: T \times T / u \cdot 1 \equiv u \cdot r$ classifiers pairs of types whose left and right components are definitionally equal.

Suppose that $\Delta \vdash \kappa$ kind is a well-formed kind and that $\Delta, u :: \kappa \vdash u \cdot p :: \kappa_p$ and $\Delta, u :: \kappa \vdash u \cdot q :: \kappa_q$ are well-formed paths. Define $\Delta \vdash u :: \kappa / p \equiv q$ kind to be the kind κ' specified by Equation (43.18). *Hint*: Make use of the answer to Exercise **43.3**.

44

Type Abstractions and Type Classes

An interface is a contract that specifies the rights of a client and the responsibilities of an implementor. Being a specification of behavior, an interface is a type. In principle, any type may serve as an interface, but in practice it is usual to structure code into *modules* consisting of separable and reusable components. An interface specifies the behavior of a module expected by a client and imposed on the implementor. It is the fulcrum balancing the tension between separation and integration. As a rule, a module ought to have a well-defined behavior that can be understood separately, but it is equally important that it be easy to combine modules to form an integrated whole.

A fundamental question is, what is the type of a module? That is, what form should an interface take? One long-standing idea is that an interface is a labeled tuple of functions and procedures with specified types. The types of the fields of the tuple are often called *function headers*, because they summarize the call and return types of each function. Using interfaces of this form is called *procedural abstraction*, because it limits the dependencies between modules to a specified set of procedures. We may think of the fields of the tuple as being the instruction set of a virtual machine. The client makes use of these instructions in its code, and the implementor agrees to provide their implementations.

The problem with procedural abstraction is that it does not provide as much insulation as one might like. For example, a module that implements a dictionary must expose in the types of its operations the exact representation of the tree as, say, a recursive type (or, in more rudimentary languages, a pointer to a structure that itself may contain such pointers). Yet the client ought not depend on this representation: the purpose of abstraction is to get rid of pointers. The solution, as discussed in Chapter 17, is to extend the abstract machine metaphor to allow the internal state of the machine to be hidden from the client. In the case of a dictionary, the representation of the dictionary as a binary search tree is hidden by existential quantification. This concept is called *type abstraction*, because the type of the underlying data (state of the abstract machine) is hidden.

Type abstraction is a powerful method for limiting the dependencies among the modules that constitute a program. It is very useful in many circumstances but is not universally applicable. It is often useful to expose, rather than to obscure, type information across a module boundary. A typical example is the implementation of a dictionary, which is a mapping from keys to values. To use, say, a binary search tree to implement a dictionary, we require that the key type admit a total ordering with which keys can be compared. The dictionary abstraction does not depend on the exact type of the keys but only requires that the key type be constrained to provide a comparison operation. A *type class* is a specification of such a requirement. The class of comparable types, for example, specifies a type t together with an operation leq of type $(t \times t) \to$ bool with which to compare them. Superficially, such a specification looks like a type abstraction, because it specifies a type and one or more operations on it, but with the important difference that the type t is not hidden from the client. For if it were, the client would only be able to compare keys using leq but would have no means of obtaining keys to compare. A type class, in contrast to a type abstraction, is not intended to be an exhaustive specification of the operations on a type, but rather a constraint on its behavior expressed by demanding that certain operations, such as comparison, be available, without limiting the other operations that might be defined on it.

Type abstractions and type classes are the extremal cases of a general concept of module type that we shall discuss in detail in this chapter. The crucial idea is the *controlled revelation* of type information across module boundaries. Type abstractions are opaque; type classes are transparent. These are both instances of *translucency*, which arises from combining existential types (Chapter 17), subtyping (Chapter 24), and singleton kinds and subkinding (Chapter 43). Unlike in Chapter 17, however, we will distinguish the types of modules, which are called *signatures*, from the types of ordinary values. The distinction is not essential, but it will be helpful to keep the two concepts separate at the outset, deferring discussion of how to ease the segregation once the basic concepts are in place.

44.1 Type Abstraction

Type abstraction is captured by a form of existential type quantification similar to that described in Chapter 17. For example, a dictionary with keys of type τ_{key} and values of type τ_{val} implements the signature σ_{dict} defined by $[\![t :: \mathsf{T} ; \tau_{\mathsf{dict}}]\!]$, where τ_{dict} is the labeled tuple type

$$\langle \mathtt{emp} \hookrightarrow t \,,\, \mathtt{ins} \hookrightarrow \tau_{\mathsf{key}} \times \tau_{\mathsf{val}} \times t \to t \,,\, \mathtt{fnd} \hookrightarrow \tau_{\mathsf{key}} \times t \to \tau_{\mathsf{val}} \, \mathtt{opt} \rangle.$$

The type variable t occurring in τ_{dict} and bound by σ_{dict} is the abstract type of dictionaries on which are defined three operations emp, ins, and fnd with the specified types. The type τ_{val} is immaterial to the discussion, because the dictionary operations impose no restrictions on the values that are associated to keys. However, it is important that the type τ_{key} be some fixed type, such as str, equipped with a suite of operations, such as comparison. Observe that the signature σ_{dict} merely specifies that a dictionary is a value of some type that admits the operations emp, ins, and fnd with the types given by τ_{dict}.

An implementation of the signature σ_{dict} is a *structure* M_{dict} of the form $[\![\rho_{\mathsf{dict}} ; e_{\mathsf{dict}}]\!]$, where ρ_{dict} is some concrete representation of dictionaries, and e_{dict} is a labeled tuple of type $[\rho_{\mathsf{dict}}/t]\tau_{\mathsf{dict}}$ of the general form

$$\langle \mathtt{emp} \hookrightarrow \ldots \,,\, \mathtt{ins} \hookrightarrow \ldots \,,\, \mathtt{fnd} \hookrightarrow \ldots \rangle.$$

The elided parts implement the dictionary operations in terms of the chosen representation type ρ_{dict}, making use of the comparison operation that we assume is available of values of type τ_{key}. For example, the type ρ_{dict} might be a recursive type defining a balanced binary search tree, such as a red-black tree. The dictionary operations work on the underlying representation of the dictionary as such a tree, just as would a package of existential type (see Chapter 17). The supposition about τ_{key} is temporary and is lifted in Section 44.2.

To ensure that the representation of the dictionary is hidden from a client, the structure M_{dict} is *sealed* with the signature σ_{dict} to obtain the module

$$M_{\mathsf{dict}} \mathbin{\uparrow} \sigma_{\mathsf{dict}}.$$

The effect of sealing is to ensure that the *only* information about M_{dict} that propagates to the client is given by σ_{dict}. In particular, because σ_{dict} only specifies that the type t have kind T, no information about the choice of t as ρ_{dict} in M_{dict} is made available to the client.

A module is a *two-phase* object consisting of a *static part* and a *dynamic part*. The static part is a constructor of a specified kind; the dynamic part is a value of a specified type. There are two elimination forms that extract the static and dynamic parts of a module. These are, respectively, a form of constructor and a form of expression. More precisely, the constructor $M \cdot \mathsf{s}$ stands for the static part of M, and the expression $M \cdot \mathsf{d}$ stands for its dynamic part. According to the inversion principle, if a module M has introduction form, then $M \cdot \mathsf{s}$ should be equivalent to the static part of M. So, for example, $M_{\mathsf{dict}} \cdot \mathsf{s}$ should be equivalent to ρ_{dict}.

But consider the static part of a sealed module, which has the form $(M_{\mathsf{dict}} \mathbin{\uparrow} \sigma_{\mathsf{dict}}) \cdot \mathsf{s}$. Because sealing hides the representation of an abstract type, this constructor should not be equivalent to ρ_{dict}. If M'_{dict} is another implementation of σ_{dict}, should $(M_{\mathsf{dict}} \mathbin{\uparrow} \sigma_{\mathsf{dict}}) \cdot \mathsf{s}$ be equivalent to $(M'_{\mathsf{dict}} \mathbin{\uparrow} \sigma_{\mathsf{dict}}) \cdot \mathsf{s}$? To ensure reflexivity of type equivalence, this equation should hold when M and M' are equivalent modules. But this violates representation independence for abstract types by making equivalence of abstract types sensitive to their implementation.

It would seem, then, that there is a contradiction between two very fundamental concepts, type equivalence and representation independence. The way out of this conundrum is to *disallow* reference to the static part of a sealed module: the type expression $M \mathbin{\uparrow} \sigma \cdot \mathsf{s}$ is deemed ill-formed. More generally, the formation of $M \cdot \mathsf{s}$ is disallowed unless M is a *module value*, whose static part is always manifest. An explicit structure is a module value, as is any module variable (provided that module variables are bound by-value).

One effect of this restriction is that sealed modules must be bound to a variable before they are used. Because module variables are bound by-value, doing so has the effect of imposing abstraction at the binding site. In fact, we may think of sealing as a kind of computational effect that "occurs" at the binding site, much as the bind operation in Algol discussed in Chapter 34 engenders the effects induced by an encapsulated command. As a consequence two bindings of the same sealed module result in two abstract types. The type system willfully ignores the identity of the two occurrences of the same module in order to ensure that their representations can be changed independently of one another without disrupting the behavior of any client code (because the client cannot rely on their identity, it must regard them as different).

44.2 Type Classes

Type abstraction is an essential tool for limiting dependencies among modules in a program. The signature of a type abstraction determines all that is known about a module by a client; no other uses of the values of an abstract type are permissible. A complementary tool is to use a signature to partially specify the capabilities of a module. Such a signature is a *type class*, or a *view*; an *instance* of the type class is an implementation of it. Because the signature of a type class only constrains the minimum capabilities of an unknown module, there must be some other means of working with values of that type. The way to achieve this is to expose, rather than to hide, the identity of the static part of a module. In this sense, type classes are the "opposite" of type abstractions, but we shall see below that there is a smooth progression between them, mediated by a subsignature judgment.

Let us consider the implementation of dictionaries as a client of the implementation of its keys. To implement a dictionary using a binary search tree, the only requirement is that keys come equipped with a total ordering given by a comparison operation. This requirement can be expressed by a signature σ_{ord} given by

$$[\![t :: \mathsf{T} \,; \langle \mathtt{leq} \hookrightarrow (t \times t) \to \mathtt{bool} \rangle]\!] .$$

Because a given type can be ordered in many ways, it is essential that the ordering be packaged with the type to determine a type of keys.

The implementation of dictionaries as binary search trees takes the form

$$X : \sigma_{\mathsf{ord}} \vdash M^X_{\mathsf{bstdict}} : \sigma^X_{\mathsf{dict}}.$$

Here σ^X_{dict} is the signature $[\![t :: \mathsf{T} \,; \tau^X_{\mathsf{dict}}]\!]$, whose body, τ^X_{dict}, is the tuple type

$$\langle \mathtt{emp} \hookrightarrow t \,, \mathtt{ins} \hookrightarrow X \cdot \mathsf{s} \times \tau_{\mathsf{val}} \times t \to t \,, \mathtt{fnd} \hookrightarrow X \cdot \mathsf{s} \times t \to \tau_{\mathsf{val}} \, \mathtt{opt} \rangle,$$

and M^X_{bstdict} is a structure (not given explicitly here) that implements the dictionary operations using binary search trees.[1] Within M^X_{bstdict}, the static and dynamic parts of the module X are accessed by writing $X \cdot \mathsf{s}$ and $X \cdot \mathsf{d}$, respectively. In particular, the comparison operation on keys is accessed by the projection $X \cdot \mathsf{d} \cdot \mathtt{leq}$.

The declared signature of the module variable X expresses a constraint on the capabilities of a key type by specifying an upper bound on its signature in the subsignature ordering. So any module bound to X must provide a type of keys and a comparison operation on that type, but nothing else is assumed of it. Because this is all we know about the unknown module X, the dictionary implementation is constrained to rely only on these specified capabilities, and no others. When linking with a module defining X, the implementation need not be sealed with this signature but must instead have a signature that is no larger than it in the subsignature relation. Indeed, the signature σ_{ord} is useless for sealing, as is easily seen by example. Suppose that $M_{\mathsf{natord}} : \sigma_{\mathsf{ord}}$ is an instance of the class of ordered types under the usual ordering. If we seal M_{natord} with σ_{ord} by writing

$$M_{\mathsf{natord}} \uparrow \sigma_{\mathsf{ord}},$$

the resulting module is *useless*, because we would then have no way to create values of the key type.

We see, then, that a type class is a description (or view) of a pre-existing type and is not a means of introducing a new type. Rather than obscure the identity of the static part of M_{natord}, we wish to propagate its identity as nat while specifying a comparison with which to order them. Type identity propagation is achieved using singleton kinds (as described in Chapter 43). Specifically, the most precise, or *principal*, signature of a structure is the one that exposes its static part using a singleton kind. In the case of the module M_{natord}, the principal signature is the signature σ_{natord} given by

$$[\![t :: S(\text{nat}) ; \text{leq} \hookrightarrow (t \times t) \to \text{bool}]\!],$$

which, by the rules of equivalence (defined formally in Section 44.3), is equivalent to the signature

$$[\![\_ :: S(\text{nat}) ; \text{leq} \hookrightarrow (\text{nat} \times \text{nat}) \to \text{bool}]\!].$$

The derivation of such an equivalence is called *equivalence propagation*, because it propagates the identity of the type t into its scope.

The dictionary implementation M^X_{bstdict} expects a module X with signature σ_{ord}, but the module M_{natord} provides the signature σ_{natord}. Applying the rules of subkinding given in Chapter 43, together with the covariance principle for signatures, we obtain the subsignature relationship

$$\sigma_{\text{natord}} <: \sigma_{\text{ord}}.$$

By the subsumption principle, a module of signature σ_{natord} may be provided when a module of signature σ_{ord} is required. Therefore, M_{natord} may be linked to X in M^X_{bstdict}.

Combining subtyping with sealing provides a smooth gradation between type classes and type abstractions. The principal signature for M^X_{bstdict} is the signature ρ^X_{dict} given by

$$[\![t :: S(\tau^X_{\text{bst}}) ; \langle \text{emp} \hookrightarrow t , \text{ins} \hookrightarrow X \cdot s \times \tau_{\text{val}} \times t \to t , \text{fnd} \hookrightarrow X \cdot s \times t \to \tau_{\text{val}} \text{ opt} \rangle]\!],$$

where τ^X_{bst} is the type of binary search trees with keys given by the module X of signature σ_{ord}. This signature is a subsignature of σ^X_{dict} given earlier, so that the sealed module

$$M^X_{\text{bstdict}} \upharpoonright \sigma^X_{\text{dict}}$$

is well-formed and has type σ^X_{dict}, which hides the representation type of the dictionary abstraction.

After linking X to M_{natord}, the signature of the dictionary is specialized by propagating the identity of the static part of M_{natord} using the subsignature judgment. As remarked earlier, the dictionary implementation satisfies the typing

$$X : \sigma_{\text{ord}} \vdash M^X_{\text{bstdict}} : \sigma^X_{\text{dict}}.$$

But because $\sigma_{\text{natord}} <: \sigma_{\text{ord}}$, we have, by contravariance, that

$$X : \sigma_{\text{natord}} \vdash M^X_{\text{bstdict}} : \sigma^X_{\text{dict}}.$$

is also a valid typing judgment. If $X : \sigma_{\text{natord}}$, then $X \cdot \text{s}$ is equivalent to nat, because it has kind $S(\text{nat})$, so that the typing

$$X : \sigma_{\text{natord}} \vdash M^X_{\text{bstdict}} : \sigma_{\text{natdict}}$$

is also valid. The closed signature σ_{natdict} is given explicitly by

$$[\![\, t :: \text{T} \,; \langle \text{emp} \hookrightarrow t \,, \text{ins} \hookrightarrow \text{nat} \times \tau_{\text{val}} \times t \to t \,, \text{fnd} \hookrightarrow \text{nat} \times t \to \tau_{\text{val}}\, \text{opt} \rangle]\!] \,.$$

The representation of dictionaries is hidden, but the representation of keys as natural numbers is not. The dependency on X has been eliminated by replacing all occurrences of $X \cdot \text{s}$ within σ^X_{dict} by the type nat. Having derived this typing we may link X with $M_{\textit{natord}}$ as described in Chapter 42 to obtain a composite module, M_{natdict}, of signature σ_{natdict}, in which keys are natural numbers ordered as specified by M_{natord}.

It is convenient to exploit subtyping for labeled tuple types to avoid creating an *ad hoc* module specifying the standard ordering on the natural numbers. Instead we can extract the required module directly from the implementation of the abstract type of numbers using subsumption. As an illustration, let X_{nat} be a module variable of signature σ_{nat}, which has the form

$$[\![\, t :: \text{T} \,; \langle \text{zero} \hookrightarrow t \,, \text{succ} \hookrightarrow t \to t \,, \text{leq} \hookrightarrow (t \times t) \to \text{bool} \,, \dots \rangle]\!]$$

The fields of the tuple provide all and only the operations that are available on the abstract type of natural numbers. Among them is the comparison operation leq, which is required by the dictionary module. Applying the subtyping rules for labeled tuples given in Chapter 24, together with the covariance of signatures, we obtain the subsignature relationship

$$\sigma_{\text{nat}} <: \sigma_{\text{ord}},$$

so that by subsumption the variable X_{nat} may be linked to the variable X postulated by the dictionary implementation. Subtyping takes care of extracting the required leq field from the abstract type of natural numbers, demonstrating that the natural numbers are an instance of the class of ordered types. Of course, this approach only works if we wish to order the natural numbers in the natural way provided by the abstract type. If, instead, we wish to use another ordering, then we must construct instances of σ_{ord} "by hand" to define the appropriate ordering.

44.3 A Module Language

The module language **Mod** formalizes the ideas outlined in the preceding section. The syntax is divided into five levels: expressions classified by types, constructors classified by kinds, and modules classified by signatures. The expression and type level consists of various language mechanisms described earlier in this book, including at least product, sum, and partial function types. The constructor and kind level is as described in Chapters 18 and 43, with singleton and dependent kinds. The following grammar summarizes the syntax of modules.

Sig	σ	::=	$\mathrm{sig}\{\kappa\}(t.\tau)$	$[\![t :: \kappa ; \tau]\!]$	signature
Mod	M	::=	X	X	variable
			$\mathrm{str}(c;e)$	$[\![c ; e]\!]$	structure
			$\mathrm{seal}\{\sigma\}(M)$	$M \uparrow \sigma$	seal
			$\mathrm{let}\{\sigma\}(M_1; X.M_2)$	$(\mathrm{let}\ X\ \mathrm{be}\ M_1\ \mathrm{in}\ M_2) : \sigma$	definition
Con	c	::=	$\mathrm{stat}(M)$	$M \cdot \mathrm{s}$	static part
Exp	e	::=	$\mathrm{dyn}(M)$	$M \cdot \mathrm{d}$	dynamic part

The statics of **Mod** consists of the following forms of judgment:

$\Gamma \vdash \sigma$ sig	well-formed signature
$\Gamma \vdash \sigma_1 \equiv \sigma_2$	equivalent signatures
$\Gamma \vdash \sigma_1 <: \sigma_2$	subsignature
$\Gamma \vdash M : \sigma$	well-formed module
$\Gamma \vdash M$ val	module value
$\Gamma \vdash e$ val	expression value

Rather than segregate hypotheses into zones, we instead admit the following three forms of hypothesis groups:

$X : \sigma, X$ val	module value variable
$u :: \kappa$	constructor variable
$x : \tau, x$ val	expression value variable

It is important that module and expression variables are always regarded as values to ensure that type abstraction is properly enforced. Correspondingly, each module and expression variable appears in Γ paired with the hypothesis that it is a value. As a notational convenience, we will not explicitly state the value hypotheses associated with module and expression variables, under the convention that all such variables implicitly come paired with such an assumption.

The following rules define the formation, equivalence, and subsignature judgments.

$$\frac{\Gamma \vdash \kappa\ \mathrm{kind} \quad \Gamma, u :: \kappa \vdash \tau\ \mathrm{type}}{\Gamma \vdash [\![u :: \kappa ; \tau]\!]\ \mathrm{sig}} \tag{44.1a}$$

$$\frac{\Gamma \vdash \kappa_1 \equiv \kappa_2 \quad \Gamma, u :: \kappa_1 \vdash \tau_1 \equiv \tau_2}{\Gamma \vdash [\![u :: \kappa_1 ; \tau_1]\!] \equiv [\![u :: \kappa_2 ; \tau_2]\!]} \tag{44.1b}$$

$$\frac{\Gamma \vdash \kappa_1 <:: \kappa_2 \quad \Gamma, u :: \kappa_1 \vdash \tau_1 <: \tau_2}{\Gamma \vdash [\![u :: \kappa_1 ; \tau_1]\!] <: [\![u :: \kappa_2 ; \tau_2]\!]} \tag{44.1c}$$

Most important, signatures are covariant in both the kind and type positions: subkinding and subtyping are preserved by the formation of a signature. It follows from rule (44.1b) that

$$[\![u :: \mathrm{S}(c) ; \tau]\!] \equiv [\![\_ :: \mathrm{S}(c) ; [c/u]\tau]\!]$$

and, further, it follows from rule (44.1c) that

$$\llbracket \_ :: \mathsf{S}(c) \,;\, [c/u]\tau \rrbracket <: \llbracket \_ :: \mathsf{T} \,;\, [c/u]\tau \rrbracket$$

and so

$$\llbracket u :: \mathsf{S}(c) \,;\, \tau \rrbracket <: \llbracket \_ :: \mathsf{T} \,;\, [c/u]\tau \rrbracket.$$

It is also the case that

$$\llbracket u :: \mathsf{S}(c) \,;\, \tau \rrbracket <: \llbracket u :: \mathsf{T} \,;\, \tau \rrbracket.$$

But the two supersignatures of $\llbracket u :: \mathsf{S}(c) \,;\, \tau \rrbracket$ are *incomparable* with respect to the subsignature judgment.

The statics of expressions of **Mod** is given by the following rules:

$$\frac{}{\Gamma, X : \sigma \vdash X : \sigma} \tag{44.2a}$$

$$\frac{\Gamma \vdash c :: \kappa \quad \Gamma \vdash e : [c/u]\tau}{\Gamma \vdash \llbracket c \,;\, e \rrbracket : \llbracket u :: \kappa \,;\, \tau \rrbracket} \tag{44.2b}$$

$$\frac{\Gamma \vdash \sigma \; \mathsf{sig} \quad \Gamma \vdash M : \sigma}{\Gamma \vdash M \uparrow \sigma : \sigma} \tag{44.2c}$$

$$\frac{\Gamma \vdash \sigma \; \mathsf{sig} \quad \Gamma \vdash M_1 : \sigma_1 \quad \Gamma, X : \sigma_1 \vdash M_2 : \sigma}{\Gamma \vdash (\mathtt{let}\, X \, \mathtt{be}\, M_1 \, \mathtt{in}\, M_2) : \sigma : \sigma} \tag{44.2d}$$

$$\frac{\Gamma \vdash M : \sigma \quad \Gamma \vdash \sigma <: \sigma'}{\Gamma \vdash M : \sigma'} \tag{44.2e}$$

In rule (44.2b), it is always possible to choose κ to be the most specific kind of c in the subkind ordering, which uniquely determines c up to constructor equivalence. For such a choice, the signature $\llbracket u :: \kappa \,;\, \tau \rrbracket$ is equivalent to $\llbracket \_ :: \kappa \,;\, [c/u]\tau \rrbracket$, which propagates the identity of the static part of the module expression into the type of its dynamic part. Rule (44.2c) is used together with the subsumption (rule (44.2e)) to ensure that M has the specified signature.

The need for a signature annotation on a module definition is a manifestation of the *avoidance problem*. Rule (44.2d) would be perfectly sensible were the signature σ omitted from the syntax of the definition. However, omitting this information greatly complicates type checking. If σ were omitted from the syntax of the definition, the type checker would be required to find a signature σ for the body of the definition that *avoids* the module variable X. Inductively, we may suppose that we have found a signature σ_1 for the module M_1, and a signature σ_2 for the module M_2, under the assumption that X has signature σ_1. To find a signature for an unadorned definition, we must find a supersignature σ of σ_2 that avoids X. To ensure that all possible choices of σ are accounted for, we seek the least (most precise) such signature with respect to the subsignature relation; this is called the *principal signature* of a module. The problem is that there may not be a least supersignature of a given signature that avoids a specified variable. (Consider the example above of a signature with two incomparable supersignatures. The example can be chosen so that the supersignatures avoid a variable X that occurs in the subsignature.) Consequently, modules do not have principal signatures, a significant complication for type checking. To avoid this problem, we insist that the avoiding supersignature σ be given by the programmer so that the type checker is not required to find one.

Modules give rise to a new form of constructor expression, $M \cdot \mathsf{s}$, and a new form of value expression, $M \cdot \mathsf{d}$. These operations, respectively, extract the static and dynamic parts of the module M. Their formation rules are as follows:

$$\frac{\Gamma \vdash M \text{ val} \quad \Gamma \vdash M : [\![u :: \kappa \,; \tau]\!]}{\Gamma \vdash M \cdot \mathsf{s} :: \kappa} \tag{44.3a}$$

$$\frac{\Gamma \vdash M : [\![\_ :: \kappa \,; \tau]\!]}{\Gamma \vdash M \cdot \mathsf{d} : \tau} \tag{44.3b}$$

Rule (44.3a) requires that the module expression M be a value according to the following rules:

$$\frac{}{\Gamma, X : \sigma, X \text{ val} \vdash X \text{ val}} \tag{44.4a}$$

$$\frac{\Gamma \vdash e \text{ val}}{\Gamma \vdash [\![c \,; e]\!] \text{ val}} \tag{44.4b}$$

(It is not strictly necessary to insist that the dynamic part of a structure be a value for the structure to itself be a value.)

Rule (44.3a) specifies that only structure values have well-defined static parts, and hence precludes reference to the static part of a sealed structure, which is not a value. This property ensures representation independence for abstract types, as discussed in Section 44.1. For if $M \cdot \mathsf{s}$ were admissible when M is a sealed module, it would be a type whose identity depends on the underlying implementation, in violation of the abstraction principle. Module variables are, on the other hand, values, so that if $X : [\![t :: \mathsf{T} \,; \tau]\!]$ is a module variable, then $X \cdot \mathsf{s}$ is a well-formed type. What this means in practice is that sealed modules must be bound to variables before they can be used. It is for this reason that we include definitions among module expressions.

Rule (44.3b) requires that the signature of the module, M, be non-dependent, so that the result type, τ, does not depend on the static part of the module. This independence may not always be the case. For example, if M is a sealed module, say, $N \upharpoonright [\![t :: \mathsf{T} \,; t]\!]$ for some module N, then projection $M \cdot \mathsf{d}$ is ill-formed. For if it were well-formed, its type would be $M \cdot \mathsf{s}$, which would violate representation independence for abstract types. But if M is a module value, then it is always possible to derive a non-dependent signature for it, provided that we include the following rule of *self-recognition*:

$$\frac{\Gamma \vdash M : [\![u :: \kappa \,; \tau]\!] \quad \Gamma \vdash M \text{ val}}{\Gamma \vdash M : [\![u :: \mathsf{S}(M \cdot \mathsf{s} :: \kappa) \,; \tau]\!]} \tag{44.5}$$

This rule propagates the identity of the static part of a module value into its signature. The dependency of the type of the dynamic part on the static part is then eliminable by sharing propagation.

The following rule of constructor equivalence states that a type projection from a module value is eliminable:

$$\frac{\Gamma \vdash [\![c\,;e]\!] : [\![t :: \kappa\,;\tau]\!] \quad \Gamma \vdash [\![c\,;e]\!] \text{ val}}{\Gamma \vdash [\![c\,;e]\!] \cdot \mathsf{s} \equiv c :: \kappa} \tag{44.6}$$

The requirement that the expression e be a value, which is implicit in the second premise of the rule, is not strictly necessary but does no harm. A consequence is that apparent dependencies of closed constructors (or kinds) on modules may always be eliminated. In particular, the identity of the constructor $[\![c\,;e]\!] \cdot \mathsf{s}$ is independent of e, as would be expected if representation independence is to be assured.

The dynamics of modules is given as follows:

$$\frac{e \longmapsto e'}{[\![c\,;e]\!] \longmapsto [\![c\,;e']\!]} \tag{44.7a}$$

$$\frac{e \text{ val}}{[\![c\,;e]\!] \cdot \mathsf{d} \longmapsto e} \tag{44.7b}$$

There is no need to evaluate constructors at run-time, because the dynamics of expressions does not depend on their types. It is not difficult to prove type safety for this dynamics relative to the foregoing statics.

44.4 First- and Second-Class

It is common to draw a distinction between *first-class* and *second-class* modules based on whether signatures are types, and hence whether modules are just a form of expression like any other. When modules are first-class, their values can depend on the state of the world at run-time. When modules are second-class signatures are a separate form of classifier from types, and module expressions may not be used in the same way as ordinary expressions. For example, it may not be possible to compute a module based on the phase of the moon.

Superficially, it seems as though first-class modules are uniformly superior to second-class modules, because you can do more with them. But on closer examination, we see that the "less is more" principle applies here as well, much as in the distinction between dynamic and static languages discussed in Chapters 22 and 23. In particular, if modules are first-class, then one must adopt a "pessimistic" attitude towards expressions that compute them, precisely because they represent fully general, even state-dependent, computations. One consequence is that it is difficult, or even impossible, to track the identity of the static part of a module during type checking. A general module expression need not have a well-defined static component, precluding its use in type expressions. Second-class modules, on the other hand, can be permissive with the use of the static components of modules in types, precisely because the range of possible computations is reduced. In this respect, second-class modules are more powerful than first-class, despite initial impressions. More importantly, a second-class module system can always be enriched to *allow* first-class modules, without *requiring* that they be first-class. Thus, we have the best of both worlds: the flexibility of first-class modules and the precision of second-class modules. In short, you pay for only what you use: if you use first-class capabilities, you should expect to pay a cost, but if you do not, you should not be taxed on the unrealized gain.

First-class modules are added to **Mod** in the following way. First, enrich the type system with existential types, as described in Chapter 17, so that "first-class modules" are just packages of existential type. A second-class module M of signature $[\![t :: \kappa \; ; \tau]\!]$ is made first-class by forming the package pack $M \cdot$ s with $M \cdot$ d as $\exists(t.\tau)$ of type $\exists t :: \kappa.\tau$ consisting of the static and dynamic parts of M. Second, to allow packages to act like modules, we introduce the module expression open e that opens the contents of a package as a module:

$$\frac{\Gamma \vdash e : \exists t :: \kappa.\tau}{\Gamma \vdash \mathsf{open}\, e : [\![t :: \kappa \; ; \tau]\!]} \tag{44.8}$$

Because the package e is an arbitrary expression of existential type, the module expression open e may not be regarded as a value, and hence does not have a well-defined static part. Instead, we must generally bind it to a variable before it is used, mimicking the composite behavior of the existential elimination form given in Chapter 17.

44.5 Notes

The use of dependent types to express modularity was first proposed by MacQueen (1986). Later studies extended this proposal to model the *phase distinction* between compile- and run-time (Harper et al., 1990) and to account for type abstraction as well as type classes (Harper and Lillibridge, 1994; Leroy, 1994). The avoidance problem was first isolated by Castagna and Pierce (1994) and by Harper and Lillibridge (1994). It has come to play a central role in subsequent work on modules, such as Lillibridge (1997) and Dreyer (2005). The self-recognition rule was introduced by Harper and Lillibridge (1994) and by Leroy (1994). That rule was later identified as a manifestation of higher-order singletons (Stone and Harper, 2006). A consolidation of these ideas is used as the foundation for a mechanization of the meta-theory of modules (Lee et al., 2007). A thorough summary of the main issues in module system design is given in Dreyer (2005).

The presentation given here focuses attention on the type structure required to support modularity. An alternative formulation uses *elaboration*, a translation of modularity constructs into more primitive notions, such as polymorphism and higher-order functions. *The Definition of Standard ML* (Milner et al., 1997) pioneered the elaboration approach. Building on earlier work of Russo, a more rigorous type-theoretic formulation was given by Rossberg et al. (2010). The advantage of the elaboration-based approach is that it can make do with a simpler type theory as the target language but at the expense of making the explanation of modularity more complex.

Exercises

44.1. Consider the type abstraction σ_{set} of *finite sets* of elements of type τ_{elt} given by the following equations:

$$\sigma_{\text{set}} \triangleq [\![t :: \mathrm{T} \,;\, \tau_{\text{set}}]\!]$$

$$\tau_{\text{set}} \triangleq \langle \text{emp} \hookrightarrow t \,,\, \text{ins} \hookrightarrow \tau_{\text{elt}} \times t \to t \,,\, \text{mem} \hookrightarrow \tau_{\text{elt}} \times t \to \text{bool} \rangle.$$

Define an implementation

$$\Gamma, D : \sigma_{\text{dict}} \vdash M_{\text{set}} : \sigma_{\text{set}}$$

of finite sets of elements in terms of a dictionary whose key and value types are chosen appropriately.

44.2. Fix an ordered type τ_{nod} of *nodes*, and consider the type abstraction σ_{grph} of *finite graphs* given by the following equations:

$$\sigma_{\text{grph}} \triangleq [\![t_{\text{grph}} :: \mathrm{T} \,;\, [\![t_{\text{edg}} :: \mathrm{S}(\tau_{\text{edg}}) \,;\, \tau_{\text{grph}}]\!]]\!]$$

$$\tau_{\text{edg}} \triangleq \tau_{\text{nod}} \times \tau_{\text{nod}}$$

$$\tau_{\text{grph}} \triangleq \langle \text{emp} \hookrightarrow t_{\text{grph}} \,,\, \text{ins} \hookrightarrow \tau_{\text{edg}} \times t_{\text{grph}} \to t_{\text{grph}} \,,\, \text{mem} \hookrightarrow \tau_{\text{edg}} \times t_{\text{grph}} \to \text{bool} \rangle.$$

The signature σ_{grph} is translucent, with both opaque and transparent type components: graphs themselves are abstract, but edges are pairs of nodes.

Define an implementation

$$N : \sigma_{\text{ord}}, S : \sigma_{\text{nodset}}, D : \sigma_{\text{nodsetdict}} \vdash M_{\text{grph}} : \sigma_{\text{grph}}$$

in terms of an implementation of nodes, sets of nodes, and a dictionary mapping nodes to sets of nodes. Represent the graph by a dictionary assigning to each node the set of nodes incident upon it. Define the node type τ_{nod} to be the type $N \cdot \text{s}$, and choose the signatures of the set and dictionary abstractions appropriately in terms of this choice of node type.

44.3. Define *signature modification*, a variant of kind modification defined in Exercise **43.3**, in which a definition of a constructor component can be imposed on a signature. Let P stand for a composition of static and dynamic projections of the form $\cdot\, \text{d} \ldots \cdot \text{d} \cdot \text{s}$, so that $X \cdot P$ stands for $X \cdot \text{d} \ldots \cdot \text{d} \cdot \text{s}$. Assume that $\Gamma \vdash \sigma$ sig, $\Gamma, X : \sigma \vdash X \cdot P :: \kappa$, and $\Gamma \vdash c :: \kappa$. Define signature $\sigma\{P := c\}$ such that $\Gamma \vdash \sigma\{P := c\} <: \sigma$ and $\Gamma, X : \sigma\{P := c\} \vdash X \cdot P \equiv c :: \kappa$.

44.4. The signature σ_{grph} is a subsignature (instance) of the type class

$$\sigma_{\text{grphcls}} \triangleq [\![t_{\text{grph}} :: \mathrm{T} \,;\, [\![t_{\text{edg}} :: \mathrm{T} \,;\, \tau_{\text{grph}}]\!]]\!]$$

in which the definition of t_{edg} has been made explicit as the product of two nodes.

Check that $\Gamma \vdash \sigma_{\text{grph}} \equiv \sigma_{\text{grphcls}}\{\cdot\, \text{d} \cdot \text{s} := \tau_{\text{nod}} \times \tau_{\text{nod}}\}$, so that the former can be defined as the latter.

Note

1 Here and elsewhere in this chapter and the next, the superscript X serves as a reminder that the module variable X may occur free in the annotated module or signature.

To be adequately expressive, it is essential that a module system support module *hierarchies*. Hierarchical structure arises naturally in programming, both as an organizational device for partitioning of a large program into manageable pieces, and as a localization device that allows one type abstraction or type class to be layered on top of another. In such a scenario, the lower layer plays an auxiliary role relative to the upper layer, and we may think of the upper layer as being abstracted over the lower in the sense that any implementation of the lower layer induces an instance of the upper layer corresponding to that instance. The pattern of dependency of one abstraction on another is captured by an *abstraction* mechanism that allows the implementation of one abstraction to be considered a function of the implementation of another. Hierarchies and abstraction work in tandem to offer an expressive language for organizing programs.

45.1 Hierarchy

It is common in modular programming to layer a type class or a type abstraction on top of a type class. For example, the class of *equality types*, which are those that admit a boolean equivalence test, is described by the signature σ_{eq} defined as follows:

$$[\![t :: \text{T} \, ; \, \langle \text{eq} \hookrightarrow (t \times t) \to \text{bool} \rangle]\!] .$$

Instances of this class consist of a type together with a binary equality operation defined on it. Such instances are modules with a subsignature of σ_{eq}; the signature σ_{nateq} given by

$$[\![t :: \text{S}(\text{nat}) \, ; \, \langle \text{eq} \hookrightarrow (t \times t) \to \text{bool} \rangle]\!]$$

is one example. A module value of this signature has the form

$$[\![\text{nat} \, ; \, \langle \text{eq} \hookrightarrow \ldots \rangle]\!] ,$$

where the elided expression implements an equivalence relation on the natural numbers. All other instance values of the class σ_{eq} have a similar form, differing in the choice of type, and/or the choice of comparison operation.

The class of *ordered types* are an extension of the class of equality types with a binary operation for the (strict) comparison of two elements of that type. One way to formulate this is as the signature

$$[\![t :: \text{T} \, ; \, \langle \text{eq} \hookrightarrow (t \times t) \to \text{bool}, \text{lt} \hookrightarrow (t \times t) \to \text{bool} \rangle]\!] ,$$

which is a subsignature of σ_{eq} according to the rules of subtyping given in Chapter 24. This relationship amounts to the requirement that every ordered type is *a fortiori* an equality type.

This situation is well and good, but it would be even better if there were a way to incrementally extend the equality type class to the ordered type class without having to rewrite the signature as we have done in the foregoing example. Instead, we would like to *layer* the comparison aspect on top of an equality type class to obtain the ordered type class. For this, we use a *hierarchical signature* σ_{eqord} of the form

$$\sum X : \sigma_{\text{eq}} \cdot \sigma_{\text{ord}}^X.$$

In this signature, we write σ_{ord}^X for the signature

$$[\![t :: \text{S}(X \cdot \text{s}) \,; \langle \text{lt} \hookrightarrow (t \times t) \to \text{bool}\rangle]\!],$$

which refers to the static part of X, namely the type on which the equality relation is defined. The notation σ_{ord}^X emphasizes that this signature has a free module variable X occurring within it, and hence is only meaningful in a context in which X has been declared.

A value of the signature σ_{eqord} is a pair of modules, $\langle M_{\text{eq}} \,; M_{\text{ord}}\rangle$, in which M_{eq} comprises a type equipped with an equality relation on it, and the second comprises a type equipped with an ordering relation on it. Crucially, the second type is constrained by the singleton kind in σ_{ord}^X to be the *same* as the first type. Such a constraint is a *sharing specification*. The process of drawing out of the consequences of a sharing specification is called *sharing propagation*.

Sharing propagation is achieved by combining subkinding (as described in Chapter 43) with subtyping for signatures. For example, a particular ordering M_{natord} of the natural numbers is a module with signature

$$\sum X : \sigma_{\text{nateq}} \cdot \sigma_{\text{ord}}^X.$$

By covariance of the hierarchical signature, this signature is a subsignature of σ_{eqord}, so that by subsumption, we may regard M_{natord} as a module of the latter signature. The static part of the subsignature is a singleton, so we may apply the rules of sharing propagation given in Chapter 43 to show that the subsignature is equivalent to the signature

$$\sum X : \sigma_{\text{nateq}} \cdot \sigma_{\text{natord}},$$

where σ_{natord} is the closed signature

$$[\![t :: \text{S}(\text{nat}) \,; \langle \text{lt} \hookrightarrow (t \times t) \to \text{bool}\rangle]\!].$$

Notice that sharing propagation has replaced the type $X \cdot \text{s}$ in the signature with nat, eliminating the dependency on the module variable X. After another round of sharing propagation, this signature is equivalent to the signature ρ_{natord} given by

$$[\![\_ :: \text{S}(\text{nat}) \,; \langle \text{lt} \hookrightarrow (\text{nat} \times \text{nat}) \to \text{bool}\rangle]\!].$$

Here we have replaced both occurrences of t in the type of the comparison operation with nat as a consequence of the kind of t. The net effect is to propagate the identity of the static part of M_{natord} to the signature of the second component of M_{natord}.

Although its value is a pair, which seems symmetric, a module of signature σ_{eqord} is asymmetric in that the signature of the second component is dependent on the first component itself. The dependence is displayed by the occurrence of the module variable X in the signature σ_{ord}. Thus, for $\langle M_{\mathrm{eq}} \, ; M_{\mathrm{ord}} \rangle$ to be a well-formed module of signature σ_{eqord}, the first component M_{eq} must have signature σ_{eq}, which is meaningful independently of the other component of the pair. On the other hand, the second component, M_{ord}, must have signature σ_{eq}^{X}, with the understanding that X stands for the module M_{eq}. In general, this signature is not meaningful independently of M_{eq} itself, and hence it may not be possible to handle M_{ord} independently of M_{eq}.

Turning this the other way around, if M is *any* module of signature σ_{eqord}, then it is always sensible to project it onto its first coordinate to obtain a module $M \cdot 1$ of signature σ_{eq}. But it is not always sensible to project it onto its second coordinate, because it may not be possible to give a signature to $M \cdot 2$ in the case that the dependency on the first component cannot be resolved statically. This problem can arise if the $M \cdot 1$ is a sealed module, whose static part cannot be formed in order to ensure representation independence. In such a situation, the dependence of the signature $\sigma_{\mathrm{ord}}^{X}$ on the module variable X cannot be eliminated, and so no signature can be given to the second projection. For this reason, the first component of a module hierarchy is a *submodule* of the hierarchy, whereas the second component may or may not be a submodule of it. Put in other terms, the second component of a hierarchy is "projectible" exactly when the dependence of its signature on the first component is eliminable by sharing propagation. That is, we may know enough about the first component statically to ensure that an independent type for the second component can be given. In that case, the second component can be considered to be a submodule of the pair; otherwise, the second is inseparable from the first, and therefore cannot be projected from the pair.

Consider a module M_{natord} of signature σ_{natord}, which, we noted earlier, is a subsignature of σ_{eqord}. The first projection $M_{\mathrm{natord}} \cdot 1$ is a well-formed module of closed signature σ_{eq} and, hence, is a submodule of M_{natord}. The situation is less clear for the second projection, $M_{\mathrm{natord}} \cdot 2$, because its signature, $\sigma_{\mathrm{ord}}^{X}$, depends on the first component via the variable X. However, we noted above that the signature σ_{natord} is equivalent to the signature

$$\sum {}_- : \sigma_{\mathrm{nateq}} \cdot \rho_{\mathrm{natord}}$$

in which the dependency on X is eliminated by sharing propagation. This, too, is a valid signature for M_{natord}, and hence, the second projection $M_{\mathrm{natord}} \cdot 2$ is a well-formed module of closed signature ρ_{natord}. Otherwise, if the *only* signature available for M_{natord} were σ_{eqord}, then the second projection would be ill-formed—the second component would not be separable from the first, and hence could not be considered a submodule of the pair.

The hierarchical dependency of the signature of the second component of a pair on the first component gives rise to a useful alternative interpretation of a hierarchical module signature as describing a *family of modules* given by the second component thought of as being indexed by the first component. In the case at hand, the collection of modules of the signature σ_{eqord} gives rise to a family of modules of signature $\sigma_{\mathrm{ord}}^{X}$, where X ranges over σ_{eq}. That is, to each choice, M_{eq}, of signature σ_{eq}, we associate the collection of choices M_{ord} coherent with the first choice in accordance with the sharing constraint in $\sigma_{\mathrm{ord}}^{X}$, taking X to be M_{ord}. This collection is the *fiber over* M_{eq}, and the collection of modules of signature σ_{eqord} is *fibered over* σ_{eq} (by the first projection).

The preceding example illustrates the layering of one type class on top of another. It is also useful to layer a type abstraction over a type class. A good example is given by a dictionary abstraction in which the type of keys is an instance of the class of ordered types but is otherwise unspecified. The signature σ_{keydict} of such a dictionary is given as follows:

$$\sum K : \sigma_{\text{eqord}} \cdot \sigma^K_{\text{dict}},$$

where σ_{eqord} is the signature of ordered equality types (in either of the two forms discussed above), and σ^K_{dict} is the signature of dictionaries of some type τ given as follows:

$$[\![t :: \mathtt{T} \, ; \, \langle \mathtt{emp} \hookrightarrow t, \mathtt{ins} \hookrightarrow K \cdot \mathtt{s} \times \tau \times t \to t, \mathtt{fnd} \hookrightarrow K \cdot \mathtt{s} \times t \to \tau \, \mathtt{opt} \rangle]\!].$$

The $\mathtt{ins}$ and $\mathtt{fnd}$ operations make use of the type $K \cdot \mathtt{s}$ of keys given by the submodule of the dictionary module. We may think of σ_{keydict} as specifying a family of dictionary modules, one for each choice of the ordered type of keys. Regardless of the interpretation, an implementation of the signature σ_{keydict} consists of a two-level hierarchy of the form $\langle M_1 \, ; \, M_2 \rangle$, where M_1 specifies the key type and its ordering, and M_2 implements the dictionary for keys of this type in terms of this ordering.

45.2 Abstraction

The signature σ_{keydict} describes a family of dictionary modules indexed by a module of ordered keys. Such modules evaluate to pairs consisting of the ordered type of keys together with the dictionary *per se*, specialized to that choice of keys. Although it is possible that the code of the dictionary operations differs for each choice of keys, it is more often the case that the *same* implementation can be used for *all* choices of keys, the only difference being that references to, say, $X \cdot \mathtt{lt}$ refers to a different function for each choice of key module X.

Such a uniform implementation of dictionaries is given by an *abstracted module*, or *functor*. A functor is a module expressed as a function of an unknown module of specified signature. The uniform dictionary module would be expressed as a functor abstracted over the module implementing keys, which is to say as a λ-abstraction

$$M_{\text{dictfun}} \triangleq \lambda \, Z : \sigma_{\text{eqord}} \cdot M^Z_{\text{keydict}}.$$

Here M^Z_{keydict} is the generic implementation of dictionaries in terms of an unspecified module Z of signature σ_{eqord}. The signature of Z expresses the requirement that the dictionary implementation relies on the keys being an ordered type but makes no other requirement on it.

A functor is a form of module and hence has a signature as well, a *functor signature*. The signature σ_{dictfun} of the functor M^Z_{keydict} has the form

$$\prod Z : \sigma_{\text{eqord}} \cdot \rho^Z_{\text{keydict}},$$

which specifies that its *domain* is the signature, σ_{eqord}, of ordered types, and whose *range* is a signature ρ^Z_{keydict} that depends on the module Z. Using a mild extension of the notation introduced in Exercise **44.3**, we may define

$$\rho_{\text{keydict}} \triangleq \sigma_{\text{keydict}}\{\cdot 1 \cdot 1 \cdot \mathsf{s} := Z \cdot 1 \cdot \mathsf{s}\}.$$

This definition ensures that the required sharing constraint between the key type in the result of the functor and the key type given as its argument.

The dictionary functor M_{dictfun} defines a generic implementation of dictionaries in terms of an ordered type of keys. An instance of the dictionary for a specific choice of keys is obtained by *applying*, or *instantiating*, it with a module of its domain signature σ_{eqord}. For example, because M_{natord}, the type of natural numbers ordered in the usual way, is such a module, we may form the instance $M_{\text{dictfun}}(M_{\text{natord}})$ to obtain a dictionary with numeric keys. By choosing other modules of signature σ_{eqord}, we may obtain corresponding instances of the dictionary functor. More generally, if M is any module of signature σ_{dictfun}, then it is a functor that we may apply it to any module M_{key} of signature σ_{eqord} to obtain the instance $M(M_{\text{key}})$.

But what is the signature of such an instance, and how may it be deduced? Recall that the result signature of σ_{dictfun} is dependent on the argument itself and not just its signature. It is therefore not immediately clear what signature to assign to the instance; the dependency on the argument must be resolved in order to obtain a signature that makes sense independently of the argument. The situation is broadly similar to the problem of computing the signature of the second component of a hierarchical module, and similar methods are used to resolve the dependencies, namely to exploit subtyping for signatures specialize the result signature according to the argument.

Let us consider an illustrative example. Note that by contravariance of subtyping for functor signatures, we may *weaken* a functor signature by *strengthening* its domain signature. In the case of the signature σ_{dictfun} of the dictionary functor, we may obtain a supersignature $\sigma_{\text{natdictfun}}$ by strengthening its domain to require that the key type be the type of natural numbers:

$$\prod Z : \sigma_{\text{natord}} \cdot \rho^Z_{\text{keydict}}.$$

Fixing Z to be a module variable of the specialized signature σ_{natord}, the range signature ρ^Z_{keydict} is given by the modification

$$\sigma_{\text{keydict}}\{\cdot 1 \cdot 1 \cdot \mathsf{s} := Z \cdot 1 \cdot \mathsf{s}\}.$$

By sharing propagation, this is equivalent to the closed signature, ρ_{natdict}, given by

$$\sigma_{\text{keydict}}\{\cdot 1 \cdot 1 \cdot \mathsf{s} := \mathtt{nat}\},$$

because we may derive the equivalence of $Z \cdot 1 \cdot \mathsf{s}$ and $\mathtt{nat}$ once the signature of Z is specialized to σ_{natord}.

Now by subsumption if M is a module of signature σ_{dictfun}, then M is also a module of the supersignature

$$\prod Z : \sigma_{\text{natord}} \cdot \rho^Z_{\text{keydict}}.$$

We have just shown that the latter signature is equivalent to the non-dependent functor signature

$$\prod\nolimits_{-} : \sigma_{\mathsf{natord}} \cdot \rho_{\mathsf{natdict}}.$$

The range is now given independently of the argument, so we may deduce that if M_{natkey} has signature σ_{natord}, then the application $M(M_{\mathsf{natkey}})$ has the signature ρ_{natdict}.

The crucial point is that the dependence of the range signature on the domain signature is eliminated by propagating knowledge about the type components of the argument itself. Absent this knowledge, the functor application cannot be regarded as well-formed, much as the second projection from a hierarchy cannot be admitted if the dependency of its signature on the first component cannot be eliminated. If the argument to the functor is a value, then it is always possible to find a signature for it that maximizes the propagation of type sharing information so that the dependency of the range on the argument can always be eliminated.

45.3 Hierarchy and Abstraction

In this section, we sketch the extension of the module language introduced in Chapter 44 to account for module hierarchies and module abstraction.

The syntax of **Mod** is enriched with the following clauses:

Sig	σ	::=	$\mathsf{sub}(\sigma_1;X.\sigma_2)$	$\sum X : \sigma_1 \cdot \sigma_2$	hierarchy
			$\mathsf{fun}(\sigma_1;X.\sigma_2)$	$\prod X : \sigma_1 \cdot \sigma_2$	functor
Mod	M	::=	$\mathsf{sub}(M_1;M_2)$	$\langle M_1 ; M_2 \rangle$	hierarchy
			$\mathsf{fst}(M)$	$M \cdot 1$	first component
			$\mathsf{snd}(M)$	$M \cdot 2$	second component
			$\mathsf{fun}\{\sigma\}(X.M)$	$\lambda X : \sigma \cdot M$	functor
			$\mathsf{app}(M_1;M_2)$	$M_1(M_2)$	instance

The syntax of signatures is extended to include hierarchies and functors, and the syntax of modules is correspondingly extended with introduction and elimination forms for these signatures.

The judgment M projectible states that the module, M, is *projectible* in the sense that its constituent types may be referenced by compositions of projections, including the static part of a structure. This judgment is inductively defined by the following rules:

$$\frac{}{\Gamma, X : \sigma \vdash x \text{ projectible}} \tag{45.1a}$$

$$\frac{\Gamma \vdash M_1 \text{ projectible} \quad \Gamma \vdash M_2 \text{ projectible}}{\Gamma \vdash \langle M_1 ; M_2 \rangle \text{ projectible}} \tag{45.1b}$$

$$\frac{\Gamma \vdash M \text{ projectible}}{\Gamma \vdash M \cdot 1 \text{ projectible}} \tag{45.1c}$$

$$\frac{\Gamma \vdash M \text{ projectible}}{\Gamma \vdash M \cdot 2 \text{ projectible}} \tag{45.1d}$$

All module variables are considered projectible, even though this condition is only relevant for hierarchies of basic structures. Because the purpose of sealing is to hide the representation of an abstract type, no sealed module is considered projectible. Furthermore, no functor is projectible, because there is no concept of projection for a functor. More importantly, no functor instance is projectible, which ensures that any two instances of the same functor define distinct abstract types. Functors are therefore *generative*. (See Section 45.4 for a discussion of an alternative treatment of functors.)

The signature formation judgment is extended to include these rules:

$$\frac{\Gamma \vdash \sigma_1 \text{ sig} \quad \Gamma, X : \sigma_1 \vdash \sigma_2 \text{ sig}}{\Gamma \vdash \sum X : \sigma_1 \cdot \sigma_2 \text{ sig}} \tag{45.2a}$$

$$\frac{\Gamma \vdash \sigma_1 \text{ sig} \quad \Gamma, X : \sigma_1 \vdash \sigma_2 \text{ sig}}{\Gamma \vdash \prod X : \sigma_1 \cdot \sigma_2 \text{ sig}} \tag{45.2b}$$

Signature equivalence is defined to be compatible with the two new forms of signature:

$$\frac{\Gamma \vdash \sigma_1 \equiv \sigma_1' \quad \Gamma, X : \sigma_1 \vdash \sigma_2 \equiv \sigma_2'}{\Gamma \vdash \sum X : \sigma_1 \cdot \sigma_2 \equiv \sum X : \sigma_1' \cdot \sigma_2'} \tag{45.3a}$$

$$\frac{\Gamma \vdash \sigma_1 \equiv \sigma_1' \quad \Gamma, X : \sigma_1 \vdash \sigma_2 \equiv \sigma_2'}{\Gamma \vdash \prod X : \sigma_1 \cdot \sigma_2 \equiv \prod X : \sigma_1' \cdot \sigma_2'} \tag{45.3b}$$

The subsignature judgment is augmented with the following rules:

$$\frac{\Gamma \vdash \sigma_1 <: \sigma_1' \quad \Gamma, X : \sigma_1 \vdash \sigma_2 <: \sigma_2'}{\Gamma \vdash \sum X : \sigma_1 \cdot \sigma_2 <: \sum X : \sigma_1' \cdot \sigma_2'} \tag{45.4a}$$

$$\frac{\Gamma \vdash \sigma_1' <: \sigma_1 \quad \Gamma, X : \sigma_1' \vdash \sigma_2 <: \sigma_2'}{\Gamma \vdash \prod X : \sigma_1 \cdot \sigma_2 <: \prod X : \sigma_1' \cdot \sigma_2'} \tag{45.4b}$$

Rule (45.4a) specifies that the hierarchical signature is covariant in both positions, whereas rule (45.4b) specifies that the functor signature is contravariant in its domain and covariant in its range.

The statics of module expressions is extended by the following rules:

$$\frac{\Gamma \vdash M_1 : \sigma_1 \quad \Gamma \vdash M_2 : \sigma_2}{\Gamma \vdash \langle M_1 \, ; M_2 \rangle : \sum {}_- : \sigma_1 \cdot \sigma_2} \tag{45.5a}$$

$$\frac{\Gamma \vdash M : \sum X : \sigma_1 \cdot \sigma_2}{\Gamma \vdash M \cdot 1 : \sigma_1} \tag{45.5b}$$

$$\frac{\Gamma \vdash M : \sum {}_- : \sigma_1 \cdot \sigma_2}{\Gamma \vdash M \cdot 2 : \sigma_2} \tag{45.5c}$$

$$\frac{\Gamma, X : \sigma_1 \vdash M_2 : \sigma_2}{\Gamma \vdash \lambda\, X : \sigma_1 \cdot M_2 : \prod X : \sigma_1 \cdot \sigma_2} \tag{45.5d}$$

$$\frac{\Gamma \vdash M_1 : \prod {}_- : \sigma_2 \cdot \sigma \quad \Gamma \vdash M_2 : \sigma_2}{\Gamma \vdash M_1\,(M_2) : \sigma} \tag{45.5e}$$

Rule (45.5a) states that an explicit module hierarchy is given a signature in which there is no dependency of the signature of the second component on the first component (indicated here by the underscore in place of the module variable). A dependent signature can be given to a hierarchy by sealing, which makes it into a non-value, even if the components are values. Rule (45.5b) states that the first projection is defined for general hierarchical signatures. On the other hand, rule (45.5c) restricts the second projection to non-dependent hierarchies, as discussed in the preceding section. Similarly, rule (45.5e) restricts instantiation to functors whose types are non-dependent, forcing any dependencies to be resolved using the subsignature relation and sharing propagation before application.

The self-recognition rules given in Chapter 44 are extended to account for the formation of hierarchical module value by the following rules:

$$\frac{\Gamma \vdash M \text{ projectible} \quad \Gamma \vdash M : \sum X : \sigma_1 \cdot \sigma_2 \quad \Gamma \vdash M \cdot 1 : \sigma_1'}{\Gamma \vdash M : \sum X : \sigma_1' \cdot \sigma_2} \tag{45.6a}$$

$$\frac{\Gamma \vdash M \text{ projectible} \quad \Gamma \vdash M : \sum {}_- : \sigma_1 \cdot \sigma_2 \quad \Gamma \vdash M \cdot 2 : \sigma_2'}{\Gamma \vdash M : \sum {}_- : \sigma_1 \cdot \sigma_2'} \tag{45.6b}$$

Rules (45.6a) and (45.6b) allow the specialization of the signature of a hierarchical module value to express that its constructor components are equivalent to their projections from the module itself.

45.4 Applicative Functors

In the module language just described, functors are regarded as generative in the sense that any two instances, even with arguments, are considered to "generate" distinct abstract types. Generativity is achieved by treating a functor application $M\,(M_1)$ to be non-projectible, so that if it defines an abstract type in the result, that type cannot be referenced without first binding the application to a variable. Any two such bindings are necessarily to distinct variables X and Y, and so the abstract types $X \cdot \mathsf{s}$ and $Y \cdot \mathsf{s}$ are distinct, regardless of their bindings.

The justification for this design decision merits careful consideration. By treating functors as generative, we are ensuring that a client of the functor cannot in any way rely on the implementation of that functor. That is, we are extending the principle of representation independence for abstract types to functors in a natural way. A consequence of this policy is that the module language is compatible with extensions such as a *conditional module* that branches on an arbitrary dynamic condition that might even depend on external conditions such as the phase of the moon! A functor with such an implementation *must* be considered generative, because the abstract types arising from any instance cannot be regarded as well-defined until the moment when the application is evaluated, which amounts to the point at which it is bound to a variable. By regarding all functors as generative we are, in effect, maximizing opportunities to exploit changes of representation without disrupting the behavior of clients of the functor, a bedrock principle of modular decomposition.

But because the module language considered in the preceding section does not include anything so powerful as a conditional module, we might consider that the restriction to generative functors is too severe and can be usefully relaxed. One such alternative is the concept of an *applicative* functor. An applicative functor is one for which instances by values are regarded as projectible:[1]

$$\frac{M \text{ projectible} \quad M_1 \text{ val}}{M(M_1) \text{ projectible}} \tag{45.7}$$

It is important that, because of this rule, applicative functors are *not compatible* with conditional modules. Thus, a module language based on applicative functors is inherently restricted as compared to one based on generative functors.

The benefit of considering a functor instance to be projectible is that we may form types such as $(M(M_1)) \cdot s$, which projects the static part of the instance. But this raises the question. When are two such type expressions equivalent? The difficulty is that the answer to this question depends on the functor argument. For suppose that F is an applicative functor variable. Under what conditions should $(F(M_1)) \cdot s$ and $(F(M_2)) \cdot s$ be regarded as the same type? In the case of generative functors, we did not face this question, because the instances are not projectible, but for applicative functors the question cannot be dodged, but must be addressed. We will return to this point in a moment, after considering one further complication that raises a similar issue.

The difficulty is that the body of an applicative functor cannot be sealed to impose abstraction, and, according to the rules given in the preceding section, no sealed module is projectible. Because sealing is the only means of imposing abstraction, we must relax this condition and allow sealed projectible modules to be projectible:

$$\frac{M \text{ projectible}}{M \upharpoonright \sigma \text{ projectible}} \tag{45.8}$$

Thus, we may form type expressions of the form $(M \upharpoonright \sigma) \cdot s$, which project the static part of a sealed module. And once again we are faced with the issue that the equivalence of two such types must involve the equivalence of the sealed modules themselves, in seeming violation of representation independence.

Summarizing, if we are to treat functors as applicative, then some compromise of the principle of representation independence for abstract types is required. We must define equivalence for the static parts of sealed modules, and doing so requires at least checking whether the underlying modules are identical. Because the underlying modules have both static and dynamic parts, this means comparing their executable code for equivalence during type checking. More significantly, because the formation of a client may depend on the equivalence of two modules, we cannot change the representation of a sealed module without fear of disrupting the typing or behavior of the client. But such a dependency undermines the very purpose of having a module system in the first place!

45.5 Notes

Module hierarchies and functors in the form discussed here were introduced by Milner et al. (1997), which also employed the reading of a module hierarchy as an indexed family of modules. The theory of hierarchies and functors was first studied by Harper and Lillibridge (1994) and Leroy (1994), building on earlier work by Mitchell and Plotkin (1988) on existential types. The concept of an applicative functor was introduced by Leroy (1995) and is central to the module system of O'Caml (2012).

Exercises

45.1. Consider the following signature σ_{orddict} of dictionaries equipped with their type of ordered keys and their type of values:

$$\sigma_{\text{orddict}} \triangleq \sum K : \sigma_{\text{ord}} \cdot \sum V : \sigma_{\text{typ}} \cdot \sigma_{\text{dict}}^{K,V}$$

$$\sigma_{\text{dict}}^{K,V} \triangleq [\![t :: \mathsf{T} \, ; \, \langle \mathsf{emp} \hookrightarrow t, \mathsf{ins} \hookrightarrow K \cdot \mathsf{s} \times V \cdot \mathsf{s} \times t \to t, \mathsf{fnd} \hookrightarrow K \cdot \mathsf{s} \times t \to V \cdot \mathsf{s} \, \mathsf{opt} \rangle]\!]$$

$$\sigma_{\text{typ}} \triangleq [\![t :: \mathsf{T} \, ; \, \mathsf{unit}]\!].$$

Define a functor $M_{\text{orddictfun}}$ that implements a dictionary in terms of an ordered type of keys and a type of values. It should have signature

$$\sigma_{\text{orddictfun}} \triangleq \prod \langle K \, ; V \rangle : \sum \_ : \sigma_{\text{ord}} \cdot \sigma_{\text{typ}} \cdot \sigma_{\text{dict}}^{K,V},$$

where

$$\sigma_{\text{dict}}^{K,V} \triangleq \sigma_{\text{orddict}} \{ \cdot 1 \cdot \mathsf{s} := K \cdot \mathsf{s} \} \{ \cdot 2 \cdot 1 \cdot \mathsf{s} := V \cdot \mathsf{s} \}.$$

45.2. Define a signature σ_{ordset} of finite sets that comes equipped with its own ordered type of elements. Define the signature σ_{setfun} of a functor that implements this set abstraction in terms of an instance of the class of ordered types. Be sure to propagate type sharing information! Give a functor M_{setfun} with signature σ_{setfun} implementing the finite set abstraction in terms of a given ordered element type. *Hint:* use the dictionary functor M_{dictfun} from Exercise **45.1**.

45.3. Define a signature σ_{ordgrph} of graphs that comes equipped with an ordered type of nodes. Define the signature of a functor that implements graphs in terms of an ordered type of nodes. Define a functor with this signature that implements graphs in terms of an ordered types of nodes. *Hint*: use the functor M_{dictfun} from Exercise **45.1** and the functor M_{setfun} of Exercise **45.2**.

Note

1 We may also consider functor abstractions to be projectible, but because all variables are projectible.

PART XVIII

Equational Reasoning

Equality for System **T**

The beauty of functional programming is that equality of expressions in a functional language corresponds follows the familiar patterns of mathematical reasoning. For example, in the language **T** of Chapter 9 in which we can express addition as the function plus, the expressions

$$\lambda\,(x:\mathtt{nat})\,\lambda\,(y:\mathtt{nat})\,\mathtt{plus}(x)(y)$$

and

$$\lambda\,(x:\mathtt{nat})\,\lambda\,(y:\mathtt{nat})\,\mathtt{plus}(y)(x)$$

are equal. In other words, the addition function *as programmed in* **T** is commutative.

Commutativity of addition may seem self-evident, but *why* is it true? What does it mean for two expressions to be equal? These two expressions are not *definitionally* equal; their equality requires proof and is not merely a matter of calculation. Yet the two expressions are interchangeable because they given the same result when applied to the same number. In general, two functions are *logically equivalent* if they give equal results for equal arguments. Because this is all that matters about a function, we may expect that logically equivalent functions are interchangeable in any program. Thinking of the programs in which these functions occur as *observations* of their behavior, these functions are said to be *observationally equivalent*. The main result of this chapter is that observational and logical equivalence coincide for a variant of **T** in which the successor is evaluated eagerly, so that a value of type nat is a numeral.

46.1 Observational Equivalence

When are two expressions equal? Whenever we cannot tell them apart! It may seem tautological to say so, but it is not, because it all depends on what we consider to be a means of telling expressions apart. What "experiment" are we permitted to perform on expressions in order to distinguish them? What counts as an observation that, if different for two expressions, is a sure sign that they are different?

If we permit ourselves to consider the syntactic details of the expressions, then very few expressions could be considered equal. For example, if it is significant that an expression contains, say, more than one function application, or that it has an occurrence of λ-abstraction, then very few expressions would come out as equivalent. But such considerations seem silly, because they conflict with the intuition that the significance of an expression lies in its contribution to the *outcome* of a computation, and not to the process of obtaining that outcome. In short, if two expressions make the same contribution to the outcome of a complete program, then they ought to be regarded as equal.

We must fix what we mean by a complete program. Two considerations inform the definition. First, the dynamics of **T** is defined only for expressions without free variables, so a complete program should clearly be a *closed* expression. Second, the outcome of a computation should be *observable*, so that it is evident whether the outcome of two computations differs or not. We define a *complete program* to be a closed expression of type nat and define the *observable behavior* of the program to be the numeral to which it evaluates.

An *experiment* on, or *observation* about, an expression is any means of using that expression within a complete program. We define an *expression context* to be an expression with a "hole" in it serving as a place-holder for another expression. The hole is permitted to occur anywhere, including within the scope of a binder. The bound variables within whose scope the hole lies are *exposed to capture* by the expression context. A *program context* is a closed expression context of type nat—that is, it is a complete program with a hole in it. The meta-variable C stands for any expression context.

Replacement is the process of filling a hole in an expression context C with an expression e which is written $C\{e\}$. Importantly, the free variables of e that are exposed by C are *captured* by replacement (which is why replacement is not a form of substitution, which is defined so as to avoid capture). If C is a program context, then $C\{e\}$ is a complete program iff all free variables of e are captured by the replacement. For example, if $C = \lambda (x : \text{nat}) \circ$, and $e = x + x$, then

$$C\{e\} = \lambda (x : \text{nat}) x + x.$$

The free occurrences of x in e are captured by the λ-abstraction as a result of the replacement of the hole in C by e.

We sometimes write $C\{\circ\}$ to emphasize the occurrence of the hole in C. Expression contexts are closed under *composition* in that, if C_1 and C_2 are expression contexts, then so is

$$C\{\circ\} \triangleq C_1\{C_2\{\circ\}\},$$

and we have $C\{e\} = C_1\{C_2\{e\}\}$. The *trivial*, or *identity*, expression context is the "bare hole," written $\circ$, for which $\circ\{e\} = e$.

The statics of expressions of **T** is extended to expression contexts by defining the typing judgment

$$C : (\Gamma \triangleright \tau) \rightsquigarrow (\Gamma' \triangleright \tau')$$

so that if $\Gamma \vdash e : \tau$, then $\Gamma' \vdash C\{e\} : \tau'$. This judgment is inductively defined by a collection of rules derived from the statics of **T** (see rules (9.1)). Some representative rules are as follows:

$$\overline{} \quad \circ : (\Gamma \triangleright \tau) \rightsquigarrow (\Gamma \triangleright \tau) \qquad (46.1a)$$

$$\frac{\mathcal{C} : (\Gamma \triangleright \tau) \rightsquigarrow (\Gamma' \triangleright \mathsf{nat})}{\mathsf{s}(\mathcal{C}) : (\Gamma \triangleright \tau) \rightsquigarrow (\Gamma' \triangleright \mathsf{nat})} \qquad (46.1b)$$

$$\frac{\mathcal{C} : (\Gamma \triangleright \tau) \rightsquigarrow (\Gamma' \triangleright \mathsf{nat}) \quad \Gamma' \vdash e_0 : \tau' \quad \Gamma', x : \mathsf{nat}, y : \tau' \vdash e_1 : \tau'}{\mathsf{rec}\, \mathcal{C} \{\mathsf{z} \hookrightarrow e_0 \mid \mathsf{s}(x)\,\mathsf{with}\, y \hookrightarrow e_1\} : (\Gamma \triangleright \tau) \rightsquigarrow (\Gamma' \triangleright \tau')} \qquad (46.1c)$$

$$\frac{\Gamma' \vdash e : \mathsf{nat} \quad \mathcal{C}_0 : (\Gamma \triangleright \tau) \rightsquigarrow (\Gamma' \triangleright \tau') \quad \Gamma', x : \mathsf{nat}, y : \tau' \vdash e_1 : \tau'}{\mathsf{rec}\, e \{\mathsf{z} \hookrightarrow \mathcal{C}_0 \mid \mathsf{s}(x)\,\mathsf{with}\, y \hookrightarrow e_1\} : (\Gamma \triangleright \tau) \rightsquigarrow (\Gamma' \triangleright \tau')} \qquad (46.1d)$$

$$\frac{\Gamma' \vdash e : \mathsf{nat} \quad \Gamma' \vdash e_0 : \tau' \quad \mathcal{C}_1 : (\Gamma \triangleright \tau) \rightsquigarrow (\Gamma', x : \mathsf{nat}, y : \tau' \triangleright \tau')}{\mathsf{rec}\, e \{\mathsf{z} \hookrightarrow e_0 \mid \mathsf{s}(x)\,\mathsf{with}\, y \hookrightarrow \mathcal{C}_1\} : (\Gamma \triangleright \tau) \rightsquigarrow (\Gamma' \triangleright \tau')} \qquad (46.1e)$$

$$\frac{\mathcal{C}_2 : (\Gamma \triangleright \tau) \rightsquigarrow (\Gamma', x : \tau_1 \triangleright \tau_2)}{\lambda\, (x : \tau_1)\, \mathcal{C}_2 : (\Gamma \triangleright \tau) \rightsquigarrow (\Gamma' \triangleright \tau_1 \rightarrow \tau_2)} \qquad (46.1f)$$

$$\frac{\mathcal{C}_1 : (\Gamma \triangleright \tau) \rightsquigarrow (\Gamma' \triangleright \tau_2 \rightarrow \tau') \quad \Gamma' \vdash e_2 : \tau_2}{\mathcal{C}_1(e_2) : (\Gamma \triangleright \tau) \rightsquigarrow (\Gamma' \triangleright \tau')} \qquad (46.1g)$$

$$\frac{\Gamma' \vdash e_1 : \tau_2 \rightarrow \tau' \quad \mathcal{C}_2 : (\Gamma \triangleright \tau) \rightsquigarrow (\Gamma' \triangleright \tau_2)}{e_1(\mathcal{C}_2) : (\Gamma \triangleright \tau) \rightsquigarrow (\Gamma' \triangleright \tau')} \qquad (46.1h)$$

Lemma 46.1. *If $\mathcal{C} : (\Gamma \triangleright \tau) \rightsquigarrow (\Gamma' \triangleright \tau')$, then $\Gamma' \subseteq \Gamma$, and if $\Gamma \vdash e : \tau$, then $\Gamma' \vdash \mathcal{C}\{e\} : \tau'$.*

Contexts are closed under composition, with the trivial context acting as an identity for it.

Lemma 46.2. *If $\mathcal{C} : (\Gamma \triangleright \tau) \rightsquigarrow (\Gamma' \triangleright \tau')$, and $\mathcal{C}' : (\Gamma' \triangleright \tau') \rightsquigarrow (\Gamma'' \triangleright \tau'')$, then $\mathcal{C}'\{\mathcal{C}\{\circ\}\} : (\Gamma \triangleright \tau) \rightsquigarrow (\Gamma'' \triangleright \tau'')$.*

Lemma 46.3. *If $\mathcal{C} : (\Gamma \triangleright \tau) \rightsquigarrow (\Gamma' \triangleright \tau')$ and $x \notin \mathrm{dom}(\Gamma)$, then $\mathcal{C} : (\Gamma, x : \tau'' \triangleright \tau) \rightsquigarrow (\Gamma', x : \tau'' \triangleright \tau')$.*

Proof By induction on rules (46.1). ∎

A *complete program* is a closed expression of type nat.

Definition 46.4. *Two complete programs, e and e', are Kleene equal, written $e \simeq e'$, iff there exists $n \geq 0$ such that $e \longmapsto^* \overline{n}$ and $e' \longmapsto^* \overline{n}$.*

Kleene equality is obviously reflexive and symmetric; transitivity follows from determinacy of evaluation. Closure under converse evaluation follows similarly. It is immediate from the definition that $\overline{0} \not\simeq \overline{1}$.

Definition 46.5. *Suppose that* $\Gamma \vdash e : \tau$ *and* $\Gamma \vdash e' : \tau$ *are two expressions of the same type. Two such expressions are* observationally equivalent, *written* $\Gamma \vdash e \cong e' : \tau$, *iff* $C\{e\} \simeq C\{e'\}$ *for every program context* $C : (\Gamma \rhd \tau) \rightsquigarrow (\emptyset \rhd \text{nat})$.

In other words, for all possible experiments, the outcome of an experiment on e is the same as the outcome on e', which is an equivalence relation. For the sake of brevity, we often write $e \cong_\tau e'$ for $\emptyset \vdash e \cong e' : \tau$.

A family of equivalence relations $\Gamma \vdash e_1 \,\mathcal{E}\, e_2 : \tau$ is a *congruence* iff it is preserved by all contexts. That is,

$$\text{if } \Gamma \vdash e \,\mathcal{E}\, e' : \tau, \text{ then } \Gamma' \vdash C\{e\} \,\mathcal{E}\, C\{e'\} : \tau'$$

for every expression context $C : (\Gamma \rhd \tau) \rightsquigarrow (\Gamma' \rhd \tau')$. Such a family of relations is *consistent* iff $\emptyset \vdash e \,\mathcal{E}\, e' : \text{nat}$ implies $e \simeq e'$.

Theorem 46.6. *Observational equivalence is the coarsest consistent congruence on expressions.*

Proof Consistency follows from the definition by noting that the trivial context is a program context. Observational equivalence is clearly an equivalence relation. To show that it is a congruence, we need only observe that type-correct composition of a program context with an arbitrary expression context is again a program context. Finally, it is the coarsest such equivalence relation, for if $\Gamma \vdash e \,\mathcal{E}\, e' : \tau$ for some consistent congruence $\mathcal{E}$, and if $C : (\Gamma \rhd \tau) \rightsquigarrow (\emptyset \rhd \text{nat})$, then by congruence $\emptyset \vdash C\{e\} \,\mathcal{E}\, C\{e'\} : \text{nat}$, and hence by consistency $C\{e\} \simeq C\{e'\}$. $\qquad\square$

A *closing substitution* γ for the typing context $\Gamma = x_1 : \tau_1, \ldots, x_n : \tau_n$ is a finite function assigning closed expressions $e_1 : \tau_1, \ldots, e_n : \tau_n$ to $x_1, \ldots, x_n$, respectively. We write $\hat{\gamma}(e)$ for the substitution $[e_1, \ldots, e_n/x_1, \ldots, x_n]e$, and write $\gamma : \Gamma$ to mean that if $x : \tau$ occurs in Γ, then there exists a closed expression e such that $\gamma(x) = e$ and $e : \tau$. We write $\gamma \cong_\Gamma \gamma'$, where $\gamma : \Gamma$ and $\gamma' : \Gamma$, to express that $\gamma(x) \cong_{\Gamma(x)} \gamma'(x)$ for each x declared in Γ.

Lemma 46.7. *If* $\Gamma \vdash e \cong e' : \tau$ *and* $\gamma : \Gamma$, *then* $\hat{\gamma}(e) \cong_\tau \hat{\gamma}(e')$. *Moreover, if* $\gamma \cong_\Gamma \gamma'$, *then* $\hat{\gamma}(e) \cong_\tau \widehat{\gamma'}(e)$ *and* $\hat{\gamma}(e') \cong_\tau \widehat{\gamma'}(e')$.

Proof Let $C : (\emptyset \rhd \tau) \rightsquigarrow (\emptyset \rhd \text{nat})$ be a program context; we are to show that $C\{\hat{\gamma}(e)\} \simeq C\{\hat{\gamma}(e')\}$. Because C has no free variables, this is equivalent to showing that $\hat{\gamma}(C\{e\}) \simeq \hat{\gamma}(C\{e'\})$. Let $\mathcal{D}$ be the context

$$\lambda(x_1 : \tau_1) \ldots \lambda(x_n : \tau_n)\, C\{\circ\}(e_1)\ldots(e_n),$$

where $\Gamma = x_1 : \tau_1, \ldots, x_n : \tau_n$ and $\gamma(x_1) = e_1, \ldots, \gamma(x_n) = e_n$. By Lemma 46.3 we have $C : (\Gamma \rhd \tau) \rightsquigarrow (\Gamma \rhd \text{nat})$, from which it follows that $\mathcal{D} : (\Gamma \rhd \tau) \rightsquigarrow (\emptyset \rhd \text{nat})$. Because $\Gamma \vdash e \cong e' : \tau$, we have $\mathcal{D}\{e\} \simeq \mathcal{D}\{e'\}$. But by construction $\mathcal{D}\{e\} \simeq \hat{\gamma}(C\{e\})$, and $\mathcal{D}\{e'\} \simeq \hat{\gamma}(C\{e'\})$, so $\hat{\gamma}(C\{e\}) \simeq \hat{\gamma}(C\{e'\})$. Because C is arbitrary, it follows that $\hat{\gamma}(e) \cong_\tau \hat{\gamma}(e')$.

Defining $\mathcal{D}'$ like $\mathcal{D}$, but based on γ', rather than γ, we may also show that $\mathcal{D}'\{e\} \simeq \mathcal{D}'\{e'\}$, and hence $\widehat{\gamma'}(e) \cong_\tau \widehat{\gamma'}(e')$. Now if $\gamma \cong_\Gamma \gamma'$, then by congruence we have $\mathcal{D}\{e\} \cong_{\text{nat}} \mathcal{D}'\{e\}$, and $\mathcal{D}\{e'\} \cong_{\text{nat}} \mathcal{D}'\{e'\}$. It follows that $\mathcal{D}\{e\} \cong_{\text{nat}} \mathcal{D}'\{e'\}$, and so, by consistency of observational equivalence, we have $\mathcal{D}\{e\} \simeq \mathcal{D}'\{e'\}$, which is to say that $\hat{\gamma}(e) \cong_\tau \widehat{\gamma'}(e')$. $\square$

Theorem 46.6 licenses the principle of *proof by coinduction*: to show that $\Gamma \vdash e \cong e' : \tau$, it is enough to exhibit a consistent congruence $\mathcal{E}$ such that $\Gamma \vdash e \, \mathcal{E} \, e' : \tau$. It can be difficult to construct such a relation. In the next section, we will provide a general method for doing so that exploits types.

46.2 Logical Equivalence

The key to simplifying reasoning about observational equivalence is to exploit types. Informally, we may classify the uses of expressions of a type into two broad categories, the *passive* and the *active* uses. The passive uses are those that manipulate expressions without inspecting them. For example, we may pass an expression of type τ to a function that simply returns it. The active uses are those that operate on the expression itself; these are the elimination forms associated with the type of that expression. For the purposes of distinguishing two expressions, it is only the active uses that matter; the passive uses manipulate expressions at arm's length, affording no opportunities to distinguish one from another.

Logical equivalence is therefore defined as follows.

Definition 46.8. Logical equivalence *is a family of relations* $e \sim_\tau e'$ *between closed expressions of type* τ. *It is defined by induction on* τ *as follows:*

$$e \sim_{\text{nat}} e' \quad \textit{iff} \quad e \simeq e'$$

$$e \sim_{\tau_1 \to \tau_2} e' \quad \textit{iff} \quad \textit{if } e_1 \sim_{\tau_1} e_1', \textit{ then } e(e_1) \sim_{\tau_2} e'(e_1')$$

The definition of logical equivalence at type nat licenses the following principle of *proof by nat-induction*. To show that $\mathcal{E}\,(e, e')$ whenever $e \sim_{\text{nat}} e'$, it is enough to show that

1. $\mathcal{E}\,(\overline{0}, \overline{0})$, and
2. if $\mathcal{E}\,(\overline{n}, \overline{n})$, then $\mathcal{E}\,(\overline{n+1}, \overline{n+1})$.

This assertion is justified by mathematical induction on $n \geq 0$, where $e \longmapsto^* \overline{n}$ and $e' \longmapsto^* \overline{n}$ by the definition of Kleene equivalence.

Lemma 46.9. *Logical equivalence is symmetric and transitive: if* $e \sim_\tau e'$, *then* $e' \sim_\tau e$, *and if* $e \sim_\tau e'$ *and* $e' \sim_\tau e''$, *then* $e \sim_\tau e''$.

Proof Simultaneously, by induction on the structure of τ. If $\tau = $ nat, the result is immediate. If $\tau = \tau_1 \rightarrow \tau_2$, then we may assume that logical equivalence is symmetric and transitive at types τ_1 and τ_2. For symmetry, assume that $e \sim_\tau e'$; we wish to show $e' \sim_\tau e$. Assume that $e'_1 \sim_{\tau_1} e_1$; it suffices to show that $e'(e'_1) \sim_{\tau_2} e(e_1)$. By induction we have that $e_1 \sim_{\tau_1} e'_1$. Therefore, by assumption $e(e_1) \sim_{\tau_2} e'(e'_1)$, and hence by induction $e'(e'_1) \sim_{\tau_2} e(e_1)$. For transitivity, assume that $e \sim_\tau e'$ and $e' \sim_\tau e''$; we are to show $e \sim_\tau e''$. Suppose that $e_1 \sim_{\tau_1} e''_1$; it is enough to show that $e(e_1) \sim_\tau e''(e''_1)$. By symmetry and transitivity, we have $e_1 \sim_{\tau_1} e_1$, so by assumption $e(e_1) \sim_{\tau_2} e'(e_1)$. We also have by assumption $e'(e_1) \sim_{\tau_2} e''(e''_1)$. By transitivity, we have $e'(e_1) \sim_{\tau_2} e''(e''_1)$, which suffices for the result. □

Logical equivalence is extended to open terms by substitution of related closed terms to obtain related results. If γ and γ' are two substitutions for Γ, we define $\gamma \sim_\Gamma \gamma'$ to hold iff $\gamma(x) \sim_{\Gamma(x)} \gamma'(x)$ for every variable, x, such that $\Gamma \vdash x : \tau$. *Open logical equivalence*, written $\Gamma \vdash e \sim e' : \tau$, is defined to mean that $\hat{\gamma}(e) \sim_\tau \widehat{\gamma'}(e')$ whenever $\gamma \sim_\Gamma \gamma'$.

Lemma 46.10. *Open logical equivalence is symmetric and transitive.*

Proof Follows from Lemma 46.9 and the definition of open logical equivalence. □

At this point, we are "two thirds of the way" to justifying the use of the name "open logical equivalence." The remaining third, reflexivity, is established in the next section.

46.3 Logical and Observational Equivalence Coincide

In this section, we prove the coincidence of observational and logical equivalence.

Lemma 46.11 (Converse Evaluation). *Suppose that $e \sim_\tau e'$. If $d \longmapsto e$, then $d \sim_\tau e'$, and if $d' \longmapsto e'$, then $e \sim_\tau d'$.*

Proof By induction on the structure of τ. If $\tau = $ nat, then the result follows from the closure of Kleene equivalence under converse evaluation. If $\tau = \tau_1 \rightarrow \tau_2$, then suppose that $e \sim_\tau e'$, and $d \longmapsto e$. To show that $d \sim_\tau e'$, we assume $e_1 \sim_{\tau_1} e'_1$ and show $d(e_1) \sim_{\tau_2} e'(e'_1)$. It follows from the assumption that $e(e_1) \sim_{\tau_2} e'(e'_1)$. Noting that $d(e_1) \longmapsto e(e_1)$, the result follows by induction. □

Lemma 46.12 (Consistency). *If $e \sim_{nat} e'$, then $e \simeq e'$.*

Proof Immediate, from Definition 46.8. □

Theorem 46.13 (Reflexivity). *If $\Gamma \vdash e : \tau$, then $\Gamma \vdash e \sim e : \tau$.*

Proof We are to show that, if $\Gamma \vdash e : \tau$ and $\gamma \sim_\Gamma \gamma'$, then $\hat{\gamma}(e) \sim_\tau \widehat{\gamma'}(e)$. The proof proceeds by induction on typing derivations; we consider two representative cases.

Consider the case of rule (8.4a), in which $\tau = \tau_1 \to \tau_2$ and $e = \lambda(x : \tau_1) e_2$. We are to show that

$$\lambda(x : \tau_1) \hat{\gamma}(e_2) \sim_{\tau_1 \to \tau_2} \lambda(x : \tau_1) \widehat{\gamma'}(e_2).$$

Assume that $e_1 \sim_{\tau_1} e_1'$; by Lemma 46.11, it is enough to show that $[e_1/x]\hat{\gamma}(e_2) \sim_{\tau_2} [e_1'/x]\widehat{\gamma'}(e_2)$. Let $\gamma_2 = \gamma \otimes x \hookrightarrow e_1$ and $\gamma_2' = \gamma' \otimes x \hookrightarrow e_1'$, and observe that $\gamma_2 \sim_{\Gamma,x:\tau_1} \gamma_2'$. Therefore, by induction, we have $\hat{\gamma_2}(e_2) \sim_{\tau_2} \hat{\gamma_2'}(e_2)$, from which the result follows easily.

Now consider the case of rule (9.1d), for which we are to show that

$$\mathtt{rec}\{\hat{\gamma}(e_0); x.y.\hat{\gamma}(e_1)\}(\hat{\gamma}(e)) \sim_\tau \mathtt{rec}\{\widehat{\gamma'}(e_0); x.y.\widehat{\gamma'}(e_1)\}(\widehat{\gamma'}(e)).$$

By the induction hypothesis applied to the first premise of rule (9.1d), we have

$$\hat{\gamma}(e) \sim_{\mathtt{nat}} \widehat{\gamma'}(e).$$

We proceed by $\mathtt{nat}$-induction. It suffices to show that

$$\mathtt{rec}\{\hat{\gamma}(e_0); x.y.\hat{\gamma}(e_1)\}(\mathtt{z}) \sim_\tau \mathtt{rec}\{\widehat{\gamma'}(e_0); x.y.\widehat{\gamma'}(e_1)\}(\mathtt{z}), \tag{46.2}$$

and that

$$\mathtt{rec}\{\hat{\gamma}(e_0); x.y.\hat{\gamma}(e_1)\}(\mathtt{s}(\overline{n})) \sim_\tau \mathtt{rec}\{\widehat{\gamma'}(e_0); x.y.\widehat{\gamma'}(e_1)\}(\mathtt{s}(\overline{n})), \tag{46.3}$$

assuming

$$\mathtt{rec}\{\hat{\gamma}(e_0); x.y.\hat{\gamma}(e_1)\}(\overline{n}) \sim_\tau \mathtt{rec}\{\widehat{\gamma'}(e_0); x.y.\widehat{\gamma'}(e_1)\}(\overline{n}). \tag{46.4}$$

To show (46.2), by Lemma 46.11 it is enough to show that $\hat{\gamma}(e_0) \sim_\tau \widehat{\gamma'}(e_0)$. This condition is assured by the outer inductive hypothesis applied to the second premise of rule (9.1d).

To show (46.3), define

$$\delta = \gamma \otimes x \hookrightarrow \overline{n} \otimes y \hookrightarrow \mathtt{rec}\{\hat{\gamma}(e_0); x.y.\hat{\gamma}(e_1)\}(\overline{n})$$

and

$$\delta' = \gamma' \otimes x \hookrightarrow \overline{n} \otimes y \hookrightarrow \mathtt{rec}\{\widehat{\gamma'}(e_0); x.y.\widehat{\gamma'}(e_1)\}(\overline{n}).$$

By (46.4), we have $\delta \sim_{\Gamma,x:\mathtt{nat},y:\tau} \delta'$. Consequently, by the outer inductive hypothesis applied to the third premise of rule (9.1d), and Lemma 46.11, the required follows. $\square$

Corollary 46.14 (Equivalence). *Open logical equivalence is an equivalence relation.*

Corollary 46.15 (Termination). *If $e : \mathtt{nat}$, then $e \longmapsto^* e'$ for some e' val.*

Lemma 46.16 (Congruence). *If $\mathcal{C}_0 : (\Gamma \triangleright \tau) \rightsquigarrow (\Gamma_0 \triangleright \tau_0)$, and $\Gamma \vdash e \sim e' : \tau$, then $\Gamma_0 \vdash \mathcal{C}_0\{e\} \sim \mathcal{C}_0\{e'\} : \tau_0$.*

Proof By induction on the derivation of the typing of C_0. We consider a representative case in which $C_0 = \lambda(x:\tau_1)C_2$ so that $C_0 : (\Gamma \rhd \tau) \rightsquigarrow (\Gamma_0 \rhd \tau_1 \to \tau_2)$ and $C_2 : (\Gamma \rhd \tau) \rightsquigarrow (\Gamma_0, x : \tau_1 \rhd \tau_2)$. Assuming $\Gamma \vdash e \sim e' : \tau$, we are to show that

$$\Gamma_0 \vdash C_0\{e\} \sim C_0\{e'\} : \tau_1 \to \tau_2,$$

which is to say

$$\Gamma_0 \vdash \lambda(x:\tau_1)C_2\{e\} \sim \lambda(x:\tau_1)C_2\{e'\} : \tau_1 \to \tau_2.$$

We know, by induction, that

$$\Gamma_0, x : \tau_1 \vdash C_2\{e\} \sim C_2\{e'\} : \tau_2.$$

Suppose that $\gamma_0 \sim_{\Gamma_0} \gamma_0'$, and that $e_1 \sim_{\tau_1} e_1'$. Let $\gamma_1 = \gamma_0 \otimes x \hookrightarrow e_1$, $\gamma_1' = \gamma_0' \otimes x \hookrightarrow e_1'$, and observe that $\gamma_1 \sim_{\Gamma_0, x:\tau_1} \gamma_1'$. By Definition 46.8, it is enough to show that

$$\hat{\gamma_1}(C_2\{e\}) \sim_{\tau_2} \hat{\gamma_1'}(C_2\{e'\}),$$

which follows from the inductive hypothesis. $\square$

Theorem 46.17. *If $\Gamma \vdash e \sim e' : \tau$, then $\Gamma \vdash e \cong e' : \tau$.*

Proof By Lemmas 46.12 and 46.16, and Theorem 46.6. $\square$

Corollary 46.18. *If $e : nat$, then $e \cong_{nat} \overline{n}$, for some $n \geq 0$.*

Proof By Theorem 46.13, we have $e \sim_{nat} e$. Hence, for some $n \geq 0$, we have $e \sim_{nat} \overline{n}$, and so by Theorem 46.17, $e \cong_{nat} \overline{n}$. $\square$

Lemma 46.19. *For closed expressions $e : \tau$ and $e' : \tau$, if $e \cong_\tau e'$, then $e \sim_\tau e'$.*

Proof We proceed by induction on the structure of τ. If $\tau = nat$, consider the empty context to obtain $e \cong e'$, and hence $e \sim_{nat} e'$. If $\tau = \tau_1 \to \tau_2$, then we are to show that whenever $e_1 \sim_{\tau_1} e_1'$, we have $e(e_1) \sim_{\tau_2} e'(e_1')$. By Theorem 46.17 we have $e_1 \cong_{\tau_1} e_1'$, and, hence, by congruence of observational equivalence, it follows that $e(e_1) \cong_{\tau_2} e'(e_1')$, from which the result follows by induction. $\square$

Theorem 46.20. *If $\Gamma \vdash e \cong e' : \tau$, then $\Gamma \vdash e \sim e' : \tau$.*

Proof Assume that $\Gamma \vdash e \cong e' : \tau$, and that $\gamma \sim_\Gamma \gamma'$. By Theorem 46.17, we have $\gamma \cong_\Gamma \gamma'$, so by Lemma 46.7 $\hat{\gamma}(e) \cong_\tau \hat{\gamma'}(e')$. Therefore, by Lemma 46.19, $\hat{\gamma}(e) \sim_\tau \hat{\gamma}(e')$. $\square$

Corollary 46.21. $\Gamma \vdash e \cong e' : \tau$ *iff* $\Gamma \vdash e \sim e' : \tau$.

Definitional equality is sufficient for observational equivalence:

Theorem 46.22. *If* $\Gamma \vdash e \equiv e' : \tau$, *then* $\Gamma \vdash e \sim e' : \tau$, *and hence* $\Gamma \vdash e \cong e' : \tau$.

Proof By an argument similar to that used in the proof of Theorem 46.13 and Lemma 46.16, then appealing to Theorem 46.17.   □

Corollary 46.23. *If* $e \equiv e' : nat$, *then there exists* $n \geq 0$ *such that* $e \longmapsto^* \overline{n}$ *and* $e' \longmapsto^* \overline{n}$.

Proof By Theorem 46.22 we have $e \sim_{\text{nat}} e'$ and hence $e \simeq e'$.   □

46.4 Some Laws of Equality

In this section, we summarize some useful principles of observational equivalence for **T**. For the most part, these are laws of logical equivalence and then transferred to observational equivalence by appeal to Corollary 46.21. The laws are presented as inference rules with the meaning that if all of the premises are true judgments about observational equivalence, then so are the conclusions. In other words, each rule is admissible as a principle of observational equivalence.

46.4.1 General Laws

Logical equivalence is indeed an equivalence relation: it is reflexive, symmetric, and transitive.

$$\overline{\Gamma \vdash e \cong e : \tau} \tag{46.5a}$$

$$\frac{\Gamma \vdash e' \cong e : \tau}{\Gamma \vdash e \cong e' : \tau} \tag{46.5b}$$

$$\frac{\Gamma \vdash e \cong e' : \tau \quad \Gamma \vdash e' \cong e'' : \tau}{\Gamma \vdash e \cong e'' : \tau} \tag{46.5c}$$

Reflexivity is an instance of a more general principle, that all definitional equalities are observational equivalences.

$$\frac{\Gamma \vdash e \equiv e' : \tau}{\Gamma \vdash e \cong e' : \tau} \tag{46.6a}$$

Observational equivalence is a congruence: we may replace equals by equals anywhere in an expression.

$$\frac{\Gamma \vdash e \cong e' : \tau \quad \mathcal{C} : (\Gamma \rhd \tau) \rightsquigarrow (\Gamma' \rhd \tau')}{\Gamma' \vdash \mathcal{C}\{e\} \cong \mathcal{C}\{e'\} : \tau'} \tag{46.7a}$$

Equivalence is stable under substitution for free variables, and substituting equivalent expressions in an expression gives equivalent results.

$$\frac{\Gamma \vdash e : \tau \quad \Gamma, x : \tau \vdash e_2 \cong e_2' : \tau'}{\Gamma \vdash [e/x]e_2 \cong [e/x]e_2' : \tau'} \tag{46.8a}$$

$$\frac{\Gamma \vdash e_1 \cong e_1' : \tau \quad \Gamma, x : \tau \vdash e_2 \cong e_2' : \tau'}{\Gamma \vdash [e_1/x]e_2 \cong [e_1'/x]e_2' : \tau'} \tag{46.8b}$$

46.4.2 Equality Laws

Two functions are equal if they are equal on all arguments.

$$\frac{\Gamma, x : \tau_1 \vdash e(x) \cong e'(x) : \tau_2}{\Gamma \vdash e \cong e' : \tau_1 \rightarrow \tau_2} \tag{46.9}$$

Consequently, every expression of function type is equal to a λ-abstraction:

$$\frac{}{\Gamma \vdash e \cong \lambda\,(x : \tau_1)\,e(x) : \tau_1 \rightarrow \tau_2} \tag{46.10}$$

46.4.3 Induction Law

An equation involving a free variable x of type nat can be proved by induction on x.

$$\frac{\Gamma \vdash [\overline{n}/x]e \cong [\overline{n}/x]e' : \tau \text{ (for every } n \in \mathbb{N})}{\Gamma, x : \text{nat} \vdash e \cong e' : \tau} \tag{46.11a}$$

To apply the induction rule, we proceed by mathematical induction on $n \in \mathbb{N}$, which reduces to showing:

1. $\Gamma \vdash [\text{z}/x]e \cong [\text{z}/x]e' : \tau$, and
2. $\Gamma \vdash [\text{s}(\overline{n})/x]e \cong [\text{s}(\overline{n})/x]e' : \tau$, if $\Gamma \vdash [\overline{n}/x]e \cong [\overline{n}/x]e' : \tau$.

46.5 Notes

The method of *logical relations* interprets types as relations (here, equivalence relations) by associating with each type constructor a relational action that transforms the relation interpreting its arguments to the relation interpreting the constructed type. Logical relations (Statman, 1985) are a fundamental tool in proof theory and provide the foundation for the semantics of the NuPRL type theory (Constable, 1986; Allen, 1987; Harper, 1992). The use of logical relations to characterize observational equivalence is an adaptation of the NuPRL semantics to the simpler setting of Gödel's System **T**.

47   Equality for System PCF

In this chapter, we develop the theory of observational equivalence for **PCF**, with an eager interpretation of the type of natural numbers. The development proceeds along lines similar to those in Chapter 46 but is complicated by the presence of general recursion. The proof depends on the concept of an *admissible relation*, one that admits the principle of *proof by fixed point induction*.

47.1 Observational Equivalence

The definition of observational equivalence, along with the auxiliary notion of Kleene equivalence, are defined similarly to Chapter 46 but modified to account for the possibility of non-termination.

The collection of well-formed **PCF** contexts is inductively defined in a manner directly analogous to that in Chapter 46. Specifically, we define the judgment $\mathcal{C} : (\Gamma \rhd \tau) \rightsquigarrow (\Gamma' \rhd \tau')$ by rules similar to rules (46.1), modified for **PCF**. (We leave the precise definition as an exercise for the reader.) When Γ and Γ' are empty, we write just $\mathcal{C} : \tau \rightsquigarrow \tau'$.

A *complete program* is a closed expression of type nat.

Definition 47.1. *We say that two complete programs, e and e', are* Kleene equal, *written $e \simeq e'$, iff for every $n \geq 0$, $e \longmapsto^* \overline{n}$ iff $e' \longmapsto^* \overline{n}$.*

Kleene equality is clearly an equivalence relation and is closed under converse evaluation. Moreover, $\overline{0} \not\simeq \overline{1}$ and, if e and e' are both divergent, then $e \simeq e'$.

Observational equivalence is defined just as it is in Chapter 46.

Definition 47.2. *We say that $\Gamma \vdash e : \tau$ and $\Gamma \vdash e' : \tau$ are* observationally, *or* contextually, equivalent *iff for every program context $\mathcal{C} : (\Gamma \rhd \tau) \rightsquigarrow (\emptyset \rhd nat)$, $\mathcal{C}\{e\} \simeq \mathcal{C}\{e'\}$.*

Theorem 47.3. *Observational equivalence is the coarsest consistent congruence.*

Proof   See the proof of Theorem 46.6. $\square$

Lemma 47.4 (Substitution and Functionality). *If $\Gamma \vdash e \cong e' : \tau$ and $\gamma : \Gamma$, then $\hat{\gamma}(e) \cong_\tau \hat{\gamma}(e')$. Moreover, if $\gamma \cong_\Gamma \gamma'$, then $\hat{\gamma}(e) \cong_\tau \hat{\gamma}'(e)$ and $\hat{\gamma}(e') \cong_\tau \hat{\gamma}'(e')$.*

Proof   See Lemma 46.7.   □

47.2 Logical Equivalence

Definition 47.5. Logical equivalence, $e \sim_\tau e'$, between closed expressions of type τ is defined by induction on τ as follows:

$$e \sim_{nat} e' \quad \text{iff} \quad e \simeq e'$$

$$e \sim_{\tau_1 \to \tau_2} e' \quad \text{iff} \quad e_1 \sim_{\tau_1} e'_1 \text{ implies } e(e_1) \sim_{\tau_2} e'(e'_1)$$

Formally, logical equivalence is defined as in Chapter 46, except that the definition of Kleene equivalence is altered to account for non-termination. Logical equivalence is extended to open terms by substitution. Specifically, we define $\Gamma \vdash e \sim e' : \tau$ to mean that $\hat{\gamma}(e) \sim_\tau \widehat{\gamma'}(e')$ whenever $\gamma \sim_\Gamma \gamma'$.

By the same argument as given in the proof of Lemma 46.9, logical equivalence is symmetric and transitive, as is its open extension.

Lemma 47.6 (Strictness). *If $e : \tau$ and $e' : \tau$ are both divergent, then $e \sim_\tau e'$.*

Proof   By induction on the structure of τ. If $\tau = \texttt{nat}$, then the result follows immediately from the definition of Kleene equivalence. If $\tau = \tau_1 \rightharpoonup \tau_2$, then $e(e_1)$ and $e'(e'_1)$ diverge, so by induction $e(e_1) \sim_{\tau_2} e'(e'_1)$, as required.   □

Lemma 47.7 (Converse Evaluation). *Suppose that $e \sim_\tau e'$. If $d \longmapsto e$, then $d \sim_\tau e'$, and if $d' \longmapsto e'$, then $e \sim_\tau d'$.*

47.3 Logical and Observational Equivalence Coincide

The proof of coincidence of logical and observational equivalence relies on the concept of *bounded recursion*, which we define by induction on $m \geq 0$ as follows:

$$\texttt{fix}^0 \, x : \tau \text{ is } e \triangleq \texttt{fix} \, x : \tau \text{ is } x$$

$$\texttt{fix}^{m+1} \, x : \tau \text{ is } e \triangleq [\texttt{fix}^m \, x : \tau \text{ is } e/x]e$$

When $m = 0$, bounded recursion is defined to be a divergent expression of type τ. When $m > 0$, bounded recursion is defined by unrolling the recursion m times by iterated substitution. Intuitively, the bounded recursive expression $\texttt{fix}^m \, x : \tau \text{ is } e$ is as good as $\texttt{fix} \, x : \tau \text{ is } e$ for up to m unrollings, after which it is divergent.

It is easy to check that the follow rule is derivable for each $m \geq 0$:

$$\frac{\Gamma, x : \tau \vdash e : \tau}{\Gamma \vdash \mathtt{fix}^m\{\tau\}(x.e) : \tau} \, . \tag{47.1a}$$

The proof is by induction on $m \geq 0$, and amounts to an iteration of the substitution lemma for the statics of **PCF**.

The key property of bounded recursion is the principle of fixed point induction, which permits reasoning about a recursive computation by induction on the number of unrollings required to reach a value. The proof relies on *compactness*, which will be stated and proved in Section 47.4 below.

Theorem 47.8 (Fixed Point Induction). *Suppose that $x : \tau \vdash e : \tau$. If*

$$(\forall m \geq 0) \; fix^m \, x : \tau \; \mathrm{is} \; e \sim_\tau fix^m \, x : \tau \; \mathrm{is} \; e',$$

then $\mathrm{fix} \, x : \tau \; \mathrm{is} \; e \sim_\tau \mathrm{fix} \, x : \tau \; \mathrm{is} \; e'$.

Proof   Define an *applicative context* $\mathcal{A}$ to be either a hole, $\circ$, or an application of the form $\mathcal{A}(e)$, where $\mathcal{A}$ is an applicative context. The typing judgment for applicative contexts, $\mathcal{A} : \tau_0 \rightsquigarrow \tau$, is a special case of the general typing judgment for contexts. Define logical equivalence of applicative contexts, $\mathcal{A} \sim \mathcal{A}' : \tau_0 \rightsquigarrow \tau$, by induction on the structure of $\mathcal{A}$ as follows:

1. $\circ \sim \circ : \tau_0 \rightsquigarrow \tau_0$;
2. if $\mathcal{A} \sim \mathcal{A}' : \tau_0 \rightsquigarrow \tau_2 \rightharpoonup \tau$ and $e_2 \sim_{\tau_2} e_2'$, then $\mathcal{A}(e_2) \sim \mathcal{A}'(e_2') : \tau_0 \rightsquigarrow \tau$.

We prove by induction on the structure of τ, if $\mathcal{A} \sim \mathcal{A}' : \tau_0 \rightsquigarrow \tau$ and

$$\text{for every } m \geq 0, \; \mathcal{A}\{\mathtt{fix}^m \, x : \tau_0 \, \mathrm{is} \, e\} \sim_\tau \mathcal{A}'\{\mathtt{fix}^m \, x : \tau_0 \, \mathrm{is} \, e'\}, \tag{47.2}$$

then

$$\mathcal{A}\{\mathrm{fix} \, x : \tau_0 \, \mathrm{is} \, e\} \sim_\tau \mathcal{A}'\{\mathrm{fix} \, x : \tau_0 \, \mathrm{is} \, e'\}. \tag{47.3}$$

Choosing $\mathcal{A} = \mathcal{A}' = \circ$ with $\tau_0 = \tau$ completes the proof.

If $\tau = \mathtt{nat}$, then assume that $\mathcal{A} \sim \mathcal{A}' : \tau_0 \rightsquigarrow \mathtt{nat}$ and (47.2). By Definition 47.5, we are to show

$$\mathcal{A}\{\mathrm{fix} \, x : \tau_0 \, \mathrm{is} \, e\} \simeq \mathcal{A}'\{\mathrm{fix} \, x : \tau_0 \, \mathrm{is} \, e'\}.$$

By Corollary 47.17 there exists $m \geq 0$ such that

$$\mathcal{A}\{\mathrm{fix} \, x : \tau_0 \, \mathrm{is} \, e\} \simeq \mathcal{A}\{\mathtt{fix}^m \, x : \tau_0 \, \mathrm{is} \, e\}.$$

By (47.2) we have

$$\mathcal{A}\{\mathtt{fix}^m \, x : \tau_0 \, \mathrm{is} \, e\} \simeq \mathcal{A}'\{\mathtt{fix}^m \, x : \tau_0 \, \mathrm{is} \, e'\}.$$

By Corollary 47.17

$$\mathcal{A}'\{\mathtt{fix}^m\, x : \tau_0 \text{ is } e'\} \simeq \mathcal{A}'\{\mathtt{fix}\, x : \tau_0 \text{ is } e'\}.$$

The result follows by transitivity of Kleene equivalence.

If $\tau = \tau_1 \rightharpoonup \tau_2$, then by Definition 47.5, it is enough to show

$$\mathcal{A}\{\mathtt{fix}\, x : \tau_0 \text{ is } e\}(e_1) \sim_{\tau_2} \mathcal{A}'\{\mathtt{fix}\, x : \tau_0 \text{ is } e'\}(e_1')$$

whenever $e_1 \sim_{\tau_1} e_1'$. Let $\mathcal{A}_2 = \mathcal{A}(e_1)$ and $\mathcal{A}_2' = \mathcal{A}'(e_1')$. It follows from (47.2) that for every $m \ge 0$

$$\mathcal{A}_2\{\mathtt{fix}^m\, x : \tau_0 \text{ is } e\} \sim_{\tau_2} \mathcal{A}_2'\{\mathtt{fix}^m\, x : \tau_0 \text{ is } e'\}.$$

Noting that $\mathcal{A}_2 \sim \mathcal{A}_2' : \tau_0 \rightsquigarrow \tau_2$, we have by induction

$$\mathcal{A}_2\{\mathtt{fix}\, x : \tau_0 \text{ is } e\} \sim_{\tau_2} \mathcal{A}_2'\{\mathtt{fix}\, x : \tau_0 \text{ is } e'\},$$

as required.   □

Lemma 47.9 (Reflexivity). *If $\Gamma \vdash e : \tau$, then $\Gamma \vdash e \sim e : \tau$.*

Proof   The proof proceeds along the same lines as the proof of Theorem 46.13. The main difference is the treatment of general recursion, which is proved by fixed point induction. Consider rule (19.1g). Assuming $\gamma \sim_\Gamma \gamma'$, we are to show that

$$\mathtt{fix}\, x : \tau \text{ is } \hat{\gamma}(e) \sim_\tau \mathtt{fix}\, x : \tau \text{ is } \widehat{\gamma'}(e).$$

By Theorem 47.8, it is enough to show that, for every $m \ge 0$,

$$\mathtt{fix}^m\, x : \tau \text{ is } \hat{\gamma}(e) \sim_\tau \mathtt{fix}^m\, x : \tau \text{ is } \widehat{\gamma'}(e).$$

We proceed by an inner induction on m. When $m = 0$, the result is immediate, because both sides of the desired equivalence diverge. Assuming the result for m, and applying Lemma 47.7, it is enough to show that $\hat{\gamma}(e_1) \sim_\tau \widehat{\gamma'}(e_1)$, where

$$e_1 = [\mathtt{fix}^m\, x : \tau \text{ is } \hat{\gamma}(e)/x]\hat{\gamma}(e), \text{ and} \tag{47.4}$$

$$e_1' = [\mathtt{fix}^m\, x : \tau \text{ is } \widehat{\gamma'}(e)/x]\widehat{\gamma'}(e). \tag{47.5}$$

But this follows directly from the inner and outer inductive hypotheses. For by the outer inductive hypothesis, if

$$\mathtt{fix}^m\, x : \tau \text{ is } \hat{\gamma}(e) \sim_\tau \mathtt{fix}^m\, x : \tau \text{ is } \widehat{\gamma'}(e),$$

then

$$[\mathtt{fix}^m\, x : \tau \text{ is } \hat{\gamma}(e)/x]\hat{\gamma}(e) \sim_\tau [\mathtt{fix}^m\, x : \tau \text{ is } \widehat{\gamma'}(e)/x]\widehat{\gamma'}(e).$$

But the hypothesis holds by the inner inductive hypothesis, from which the result follows.

To handle the conditional $\mathtt{ifz}\, e\, \{\mathtt{z} \hookrightarrow e_0 \mid \mathtt{s}(x) \hookrightarrow e_1\}$, we proceed by cases on whether e diverges, in which case the conditional is divergent and therefore self-related by Lemma 47.6, or e converges, in which case we can proceed by an inner mathematical induction on its value, appealing to the inductive hypotheses governing the branches of the conditional to complete the argument.   □

Symmetry and transitivity of eager logical equivalence are easily established by induction on types, noting that Kleene equivalence is symmetric and transitive. Eager logical equivalence is therefore an equivalence relation.

Lemma 47.10 (Congruence). *If $\mathcal{C}_0 : (\Gamma \triangleright \tau) \rightsquigarrow (\Gamma_0 \triangleright \tau_0)$, and $\Gamma \vdash e \sim e' : \tau$, then $\Gamma_0 \vdash \mathcal{C}_0\{e\} \sim \mathcal{C}_0\{e'\} : \tau_0$.*

Proof By induction on the derivation of the typing of $\mathcal{C}_0$, following along similar lines to the proof of Lemma 47.9. ◻

Logical equivalence is consistent, by definition. Consequently, it is contained in observational equivalence.

Theorem 47.11. *If $\Gamma \vdash e \sim e' : \tau$, then $\Gamma \vdash e \cong e' : \tau$.*

Proof By consistency and congruence of logical equivalence. ◻

Lemma 47.12. *If $e \cong_\tau e'$, then $e \sim_\tau e'$.*

Proof By induction on the structure of τ. If $\tau = \mathtt{nat}$, then the result is immediate, because the empty expression context is a program context. If $\tau = \tau_1 \rightharpoonup \tau_2$, then suppose that $e_1 \sim_{\tau_1} e_1'$. We are to show that $e(e_1) \sim_{\tau_2} e'(e_1')$. By Theorem 47.11 $e_1 \cong_{\tau_1} e_1'$, and hence by Lemma 47.4 $e(e_1) \cong_{\tau_2} e'(e_1')$, from which the result follows by induction. ◻

Theorem 47.13. *If $\Gamma \vdash e \cong e' : \tau$, then $\Gamma \vdash e \sim e' : \tau$.*

Proof Assume that $\Gamma \vdash e \cong e' : \tau$. Suppose that $\gamma \sim_\Gamma \gamma'$. By Theorem 47.11, we have $\gamma \cong_\Gamma \gamma'$, and so by Lemma 47.4, we have

$$\hat{\gamma}(e) \cong_\tau \hat{\gamma}'(e').$$

Therefore, by Lemma 47.12, we have

$$\hat{\gamma}(e) \sim_\tau \hat{\gamma}'(e').$$ ◻

Corollary 47.14. *$\Gamma \vdash e \cong e' : \tau$ iff $\Gamma \vdash e \sim e' : \tau$.*

47.4 Compactness

The principle of fixed point induction is derived from a critical property of **PCF**, called *compactness*. This property states that only finitely many unwindings of a fixed point expression are needed in a complete evaluation of a program. Although intuitively obvious (one cannot complete infinitely many recursive calls in a finite computation), it is rather tricky to state and prove rigorously.

The proof of compactness (Theorem 47.16) makes use of the stack machine for **PCF** defined in Chapter 28, augmented with the following transitions for bounded recursive expressions:

$$\frac{}{k \rhd \mathtt{fix}^0\, x : \tau \mathtt{\ is\ } e \longmapsto k \rhd \mathtt{fix}^0\, x : \tau \mathtt{\ is\ } e} \qquad (47.6a)$$

$$\frac{}{k \rhd \mathtt{fix}^{m+1}\, x : \tau \mathtt{\ is\ } e \longmapsto k \rhd [\mathtt{fix}^m\, x : \tau \mathtt{\ is\ } e/x]e} \qquad (47.6b)$$

It is not difficult to extend the proof of Corollary 28.4 to account for bounded recursion.

To get a feel for what is involved in the compactness proof, consider first the factorial function f in **PCF**:

$$\mathtt{fix}\, f : \mathtt{nat} \rightharpoonup \mathtt{nat\ is\ } \lambda\, (x : \mathtt{nat})\, \mathtt{ifz}\, x\, \{\mathtt{z} \hookrightarrow \mathtt{s(z)} \mid \mathtt{s}(x') \hookrightarrow x * f(x')\}.$$

Obviously evaluation of $f(\overline{n})$ requires n recursive calls to the function itself. That is, for a given input n we may place a *bound* m on the recursion that is sufficient to ensure termination of the computation. This property can be expressed formally using the m-bounded form of general recursion,

$$\mathtt{fix}^m\, f : \mathtt{nat} \rightharpoonup \mathtt{nat\ is\ } \lambda\, (x : \mathtt{nat})\, \mathtt{ifz}\, x\, \{\mathtt{z} \hookrightarrow \mathtt{s(z)} \mid \mathtt{s}(x') \hookrightarrow x * f(x')\}.$$

Call this expression $f^{(m)}$. It follows from the definition of f that if $f(\overline{n}) \longmapsto^* \overline{p}$, then $f^{(m)}(\overline{n}) \longmapsto^* \overline{p}$ for some $m \geq 0$ (in fact, $m = n$ suffices).

When considering expressions of higher type, we cannot expect to get the *same* result from the bounded recursion as from the unbounded. For example, consider the addition function a of type $\tau = \mathtt{nat} \rightharpoonup (\mathtt{nat} \rightharpoonup \mathtt{nat})$, given by the expression

$$\mathtt{fix}\, p : \tau \mathtt{\ is\ } \lambda\, (x : \mathtt{nat})\, \mathtt{ifz}\, x\, \{\mathtt{z} \hookrightarrow id \mid \mathtt{s}(x') \hookrightarrow s \circ (p(x'))\},$$

where $id = \lambda\, (y : \mathtt{nat})\, y$ is the identity, $e' \circ e = \lambda\, (x : \tau)\, e'(e(x))$ is composition, and $s = \lambda\, (x : \mathtt{nat})\, \mathtt{s}(x)$ is the successor function. The application $a(\overline{n})$ terminates after three transitions, regardless of the value of n, resulting in a λ-abstraction. When n is positive, the result contains a *residual* copy of a itself, which is applied to $n - 1$ as a recursive call. The m-bounded version of a, written $a^{(m)}$, is also such that $a^{(m)}(\overline{n})$ terminates in three steps, provided that $m > 0$. But the result is not the same, because the residuals of a appear as $a^{(m-1)}$, rather than as a itself.

Turning now to the proof of compactness, it is helpful to introduce some notation. Suppose that $x : \tau \vdash e_x : \tau$ for some arbitrary abstractor $x.e_x$. Let $f^{(\omega)} = \mathtt{fix}\, x : \tau \mathtt{\ is\ } e_x$, and let $f^{(m)} = \mathtt{fix}^m\, x : \tau \mathtt{\ is\ } e_x$. Observe that $f^{(\omega)} : \tau$ and $f^{(m)} : \tau$ for any $m \geq 0$.

The following technical lemma governing the stack machine allows the bound on occurrences of a recursive expression to be raised without affecting the outcome of evaluation.

Lemma 47.15. *For every* $m \geq 0$, *if* $[f^{(m)}/y]k \rhd [f^{(m)}/y]e \longmapsto^* \epsilon \lhd \overline{n}$, *then* $[f^{(m+1)}/y]k \rhd [f^{(m+1)}/y]e \longmapsto^* \epsilon \lhd \overline{n}$.

Proof By induction on $m \geq 0$, and then induction on transition. $\qquad\qquad\square$

Theorem 47.16 (Compactness). *Suppose that $y : \tau \vdash e : \text{nat}$ where $y \notin f^{(\omega)}$. If $[f^{(\omega)}/y]e \longmapsto^* \overline{n}$, then there exists $m \geq 0$ such that $[f^{(m)}/y]e \longmapsto^* \overline{n}$.*

Proof We prove simultaneously the stronger statements that if

$$[f^{(\omega)}/y]k \triangleright [f^{(\omega)}/y]e \longmapsto^* \epsilon \triangleleft \overline{n},$$

then for some $m \geq 0$,

$$[f^{(m)}/y]k \triangleright [f^{(m)}/y]e \longmapsto^* \epsilon \triangleleft \overline{n},$$

and if

$$[f^{(\omega)}/y]k \triangleleft [f^{(\omega)}/y]e \longmapsto^* \epsilon \triangleleft \overline{n}$$

then for some $m \geq 0$,

$$[f^{(m)}/y]k \triangleleft [f^{(m)}/y]e \longmapsto^* \epsilon \triangleleft \overline{n}.$$

(Note that if $[f^{(\omega)}/y]e$ val, then $[f^{(m)}/y]e$ val for all $m \geq 0$.) The result then follows by the correctness of the stack machine (Corollary 28.4).

We proceed by induction on transition. Suppose that the initial state is

$$[f^{(\omega)}/y]k \triangleright f^{(\omega)},$$

which arises when $e = y$, and the transition sequence is as follows:

$$[f^{(\omega)}/y]k \triangleright f^{(\omega)} \longmapsto [f^{(\omega)}/y]k \triangleright [f^{(\omega)}/x]e_x \longmapsto^* \epsilon \triangleleft \overline{n}.$$

Noting that $[f^{(\omega)}/x]e_x = [f^{(\omega)}/y][y/x]e_x$, we have by induction that there exists $m \geq 0$ such that

$$[f^{(m)}/y]k \triangleright [f^{(m)}/x]e_x \longmapsto^* \epsilon \triangleleft \overline{n}.$$

By Lemma 47.15,

$$[f^{(m+1)}/y]k \triangleright [f^{(m)}/x]e_x \longmapsto^* \epsilon \triangleleft \overline{n}$$

and we need only recall that

$$[f^{(m+1)}/y]k \triangleright f^{(m+1)} = [f^{(m+1)}/y]k \triangleright [f^{(m)}/x]e_x$$

to complete the proof. If, on the other hand, the initial step is an unrolling, but $e \neq y$, then we have for some $z \notin f^{(\omega)}$ and $z \neq y$

$$[f^{(\omega)}/y]k \triangleright \text{fix}\, z : \tau \text{ is}\, d_\omega \longmapsto [f^{(\omega)}/y]k \triangleright [\text{fix}\, z : \tau \text{ is}\, d_\omega/z]d_\omega \longmapsto^* \epsilon \triangleleft \overline{n}.$$

where $d_\omega = [f^{(\omega)}/y]d$. By induction there exists $m \geq 0$ such that

$$[f^{(m)}/y]k \triangleright [\text{fix}\, z : \tau \text{ is}\, d_m/z]d_m \longmapsto^* \epsilon \triangleleft \overline{n},$$

where $d_m = [f^{(m)}/y]d$. But then by Lemma 47.15 we have

$$[f^{(m+1)}/y]k \triangleright [\text{fix}\, z : \tau \text{ is}\, d_{m+1}/z]d_{m+1} \longmapsto^* \epsilon \triangleleft \overline{n},$$

where $d_{m+1} = [f^{(m+1)}/y]d$, from which the result follows directly. $\square$

Corollary 47.17. *There exists $m \geq 0$ such that $[f^{(\omega)}/y]e \simeq [f^{(m)}/y]e$.*

Proof If $[f^{(\omega)}/y]e$ diverges, then it suffices to take m to be zero. Otherwise, apply Theorem 47.16 to obtain m, and note that the required Kleene equivalence follows.   □

47.5 Lazy Natural Numbers

Recall from Chapter 19 that, if the successor is evaluated lazily, then the type nat changes its meaning to that of the lazy natural numbers, which we shall write lnat for emphasis. This type contains an "infinite number" ω, which is essentially an endless stack of successors.

To account for the lazy successor, the definition of logical equivalence must be reformulated. Rather than being defined *inductively* as the strongest relation closed under specified conditions, it is now defined *coinductively* as the weakest relation consistent with two analogous conditions. We may then show that two expressions are related using the principle of *proof by coinduction*.

The definition of Kleene equivalence must be altered to account for the lazily evaluated successor operation. To account for ω, two computations are compared based solely on the outermost form of their values, if any. We define $e \simeq e'$ to hold iff (a) if $e \longmapsto^* z$, then $e' \longmapsto^* z$, and *vice versa*; and (b) if $e \longmapsto^* s(e_1)$, then $e' \longmapsto^* s(e_1')$, and *vice versa*.

Corollary 47.17 can be proved for the co-natural numbers by essentially the same argument as before.

The definition of logical equivalence at type lnat is defined to be the *weakest* equivalence relation $\mathcal{E}$ between closed terms of type lnat satisfying the following *consistency conditions*: if $e \, \mathcal{E} \, e'$: lnat, then

1. If $e \longmapsto^* z$, then $e' \longmapsto^* z$, and *vice versa*.
2. If $e \longmapsto^* s(e_1)$, then $e' \longmapsto^* s(e_1')$ with $e_1 \, \mathcal{E} \, e_1'$: lnat, and *vice versa*.

It is immediate that if $e \sim_{\text{lnat}} e'$, then $e \simeq e'$, and so logical equivalence is consistent. It is also strict in that if e and e' are both divergent expressions of type lnat, then $e \sim_{\text{lnat}} e'$.

The principle of *proof by coinduction* states that to show $e \sim_{\text{lnat}} e'$, it suffices to exhibit a relation, $\mathcal{E}$, such that

1. $e \, \mathcal{E} \, e'$: lnat, and
2. $\mathcal{E}$ satisfies the above consistency conditions.

If these requirements hold, then $\mathcal{E}$ is contained in logical equivalence at type lnat, and hence $e \sim_{\text{lnat}} e'$, as required.

As an application of coinduction, let us consider the proof of Theorem 47.8. The overall argument remains as before, but the proof for the type lnat must be altered as follows. Suppose that $\mathcal{A} \sim \mathcal{A}' : \tau_0 \rightsquigarrow \texttt{lnat}$, and let $a = \mathcal{A}\{\texttt{fix}\, x : \tau_0 \,\texttt{is}\, e\}$ and $a' = \mathcal{A}'\{\texttt{fix}\, x : \tau_0 \,\texttt{is}\, e'\}$. Writing $a^{(m)} = \mathcal{A}\{\texttt{fix}^m\, x : \tau_0 \,\texttt{is}\, e\}$ and $a'^{(m)} = \mathcal{A}'\{\texttt{fix}^m\, x : \tau_0 \,\texttt{is}\, e'\}$, assume that

$$\text{for every } m \geq 0, \ a^{(m)} \sim_{\texttt{lnat}} a'^{(m)}.$$

We are to show that

$$a \sim_{\texttt{lnat}} a'.$$

Define the functions p_n for $n \geq 0$ on closed terms of type $\texttt{lnat}$ by the following equations:

$$p_0(d) = d$$

$$p_{(n+1)}(d) = \begin{cases} d' & \text{if } p_n(d) \longmapsto^* \texttt{s}(d') \\ undefined & \text{otherwise} \end{cases}$$

For $n \geq 0$, let $a_n = p_n(a)$ and $a'_n = p_n(a')$. Correspondingly, let $a_n^{(m)} = p_n(a^{(m)})$ and $a'^{(m)}_n = p_n(a'^{(m)})$. Define $\mathcal{E}$ to be the strongest relation such that $a_n \mathrel{\mathcal{E}} a'_n : \texttt{lnat}$ for all $n \geq 0$. We will show that the relation $\mathcal{E}$ satisfies the consistency conditions, and so it is contained in logical equivalence. Because $a \mathrel{\mathcal{E}} a' : \texttt{lnat}$ (by construction), the result follows immediately.

To show that $\mathcal{E}$ is consistent, suppose that $a_n \mathrel{\mathcal{E}} a'_n : \texttt{lnat}$ for some $n \geq 0$. We have by Corollary 47.17 $a_n \simeq a_n^{(m)}$, for some $m \geq 0$, and hence, by the assumption, $a_n \simeq a'^{(m)}_n$, and so by Corollary 47.17 again, $a'^{(m)}_n \simeq a'_n$. Now if $a_n \longmapsto^* \texttt{s}(b_n)$, then $a_n^{(m)} \longmapsto^* \texttt{s}(b_n^{(m)})$ for some $b_n^{(m)}$, and hence there exists $b'^{(m)}_n$ such that $a'^{(m)}_n \longmapsto^* b'^{(m)}_n$, and so there exists b'_n such that $a'_n \longmapsto^* \texttt{s}(b'_n)$. But $b_n = p_{n+1}(a)$ and $b'_n = p_{n+1}(a')$, and we have $b_n \mathrel{\mathcal{E}} b'_n : \texttt{lnat}$ by construction, as required.

47.6 Notes

The use of logical relations to characterize observational equivalence for **PCF** is inspired by the treatment of partiality in type theory by Constable and Smith (1987) and by the studies of observational equivalence by Pitts (2000). Although the technical details differ, the proof of compactness here is inspired by Pitts's structurally inductive characterization of termination using an abstract machine. It is critical to restrict attention to transition systems whose states are complete programs (closed expressions of observable type). Structural operational semantics usually does not fulfill this requirement, thereby requiring a considerably more complex argument than given here.

48

Parametricity

The main motivation for polymorphism is to enable more programs to be written—those that are "generic" in one or more types, such as the composition function given in Chapter 16. If a program *does not* depend on the choice of types, we can code it using polymorphism. Moreover, if we wish to insist that a program *cannot* depend on a choice of types, we demand that it be polymorphic. Thus, polymorphism can be used both to expand the collection of programs we may write and to limit the collection of programs that are permissible in a given context.

The restrictions imposed by polymorphic typing give rise to the experience that in a polymorphic functional language, if the types are correct, then the program is correct. Roughly speaking, if a function has a polymorphic type, then the strictures of type genericity cut down the set of programs with that type. Thus, if you have written a program with this type, it is more likely to be the one you intended!

The technical foundation for these remarks is called *parametricity*. The goal of this chapter is to give an account of parametricity for **F** under a call-by-name interpretation.

48.1 Overview

We will begin with an informal discussion of parametricity based on a "seat of the pants" understanding of the set of well-formed programs of a type.

Suppose that a function value f has the type $\forall(t.t \to t)$. What function could it be? When instantiated at a type τ it should evaluate to a function g of type $\tau \to \tau$ that, when further applied to a value v of type τ returns a value v' of type τ. Because f is polymorphic, g cannot depend on v, so v' must be v. In other words, g must be the identity function at type τ, and f must therefore be the *polymorphic identity*.

Suppose that f is a function of type $\forall(t.t)$. What function could it be? A moment's thought reveals that it cannot exist at all. For it must, when instantiated at a type τ, return a value of that type. But not every type has a value (including this one), so this is an impossible assignment. The only conclusion is that $\forall(t.t)$ is an *empty* type.

Let N be the type of polymorphic Church numerals introduced in Chapter 16, namely $\forall(t.t \to (t \to t) \to t)$. What are the values of this type? Given any type τ, and values $z : \tau$ and $s : \tau \to \tau$, the expression

$$f[\tau](z)(s)$$

must yield a value of type τ. Moreover, it must behave uniformly with respect to the choice of τ. What values could it yield? The only way to build a value of type τ is by using the element z and the function s passed to it. A moment's thought reveals that the application must amount to the n-fold composition

$$s(s(\ldots s(z)\ldots)).$$

That is, the elements of N are in one-to-one correspondence with the natural numbers.

48.2 Observational Equivalence

The definition of observational equivalence given in Chapters 46 and 47 is based on identifying a type of *answers* that are observable outcomes of complete programs. Values of function type are not regarded as answers, but are treated as "black boxes" with no internal structure, only input-output behavior. In **F**, however, there are no (closed) base types. Every type is either a function type or a polymorphic type, and hence no types suitable to serve as observable answers.

One way to manage this difficulty is to augment **F** with a base type of answers to serve as the observable outcomes of a computation. The only requirement is that this type have two elements that can be immediately distinguished from each other by evaluation. We may achieve this by enriching **F** with a base type **2** containing two constants, **tt** and **ff**, that serve as possible answers for a complete computation. A complete program is a closed expression of type **2**.

Kleene equality is defined for complete programs by requiring that $e \simeq e'$ iff either (a) $e \longmapsto^{*}$ **tt** and $e' \longmapsto^{*}$ **tt**; or (b) $e \longmapsto^{*}$ **ff** and $e' \longmapsto^{*}$ **ff**. This relation is an equivalence, and it is immediate that **tt** $\not\simeq$ **ff**, because these are two distinct constants. As before, we say that a type-indexed family of equivalence relations between closed expressions of the same type is *consistent* if it implies Kleene equality at the answer type **2**.

To define observational equivalence, we must first define the concept of an expression context for **F** as an expression with a "hole" in it. More precisely, we may give an inductive definition of the judgment

$$\mathcal{C} : (\Delta; \Gamma \rhd \tau) \rightsquigarrow (\Delta'; \Gamma' \rhd \tau'),$$

which states that $\mathcal{C}$ is an expression context that, when filled with an expression $\Delta; \Gamma \vdash e : \tau$ yields an expression $\Delta'; \Gamma' \vdash \mathcal{C}\{e\} : \tau'$. (We leave the precise definition of this judgment, and the verification of its properties, as an exercise for the reader.)

Definition 48.1. *Two expressions of the same type are* observationally equivalent, *written* $\Delta; \Gamma \vdash e \cong e' : \tau$, *iff* $\mathcal{C}\{e\} \simeq \mathcal{C}\{e'\}$ *whenever* $\mathcal{C} : (\Delta; \Gamma \rhd \tau) \rightsquigarrow (\emptyset; \emptyset \rhd \mathbf{2})$.

Lemma 48.2. *Observational equivalence is the coarsest consistent congruence.*

Proof   Essentially the same as the the proof of Theorem 46.6.   □

Lemma 48.3.

1. *If* $\Delta, t; \Gamma \vdash e \cong e' : \tau$ *and* τ_0 *type, then* $\Delta; [\tau_0/t]\Gamma \vdash [\tau_0/t]e \cong [\tau_0/t]e' : [\tau_0/t]\tau$.

2. *If* $\emptyset; \Gamma, x : \tau_0 \vdash e \cong e' : \tau$ *and* $d : \tau_0$, *then* $\emptyset; \Gamma \vdash [d/x]e \cong [d/x]e' : \tau$. *Moreover, if* $d \cong_{\tau_0} d'$, *then* $\emptyset; \Gamma \vdash [d/x]e \cong [d'/x]e : \tau$ *and* $\emptyset; \Gamma \vdash [d/x]e' \cong [d'/x]e' : \tau$.

Proof   1. Let $\mathcal{C} : (\Delta; [\tau_0/t]\Gamma \rhd [\tau_0/t]\tau) \rightsquigarrow (\emptyset \rhd \mathbf{2})$ be a program context. We are to show that

$$\mathcal{C}\{[\tau_0/t]e\} \simeq \mathcal{C}\{[\tau_0/t]e'\}.$$

Because $\mathcal{C}$ is closed, this is equivalent to

$$[\tau_0/t]\mathcal{C}\{e\} \simeq [\tau_0/t]\mathcal{C}\{e'\}.$$

Let $\mathcal{C}'$ be the context $\Lambda(t)\mathcal{C}\{\circ\}[\tau_0]$, and observe that

$$\mathcal{C}' : (\Delta, t; \Gamma \rhd \tau) \rightsquigarrow (\emptyset \rhd \mathbf{2}).$$

Therefore, from the assumption,

$$\mathcal{C}'\{e\} \simeq \mathcal{C}'\{e'\}.$$

But $\mathcal{C}'\{e\} \simeq [\tau_0/t]\mathcal{C}\{e\}$, and $\mathcal{C}'\{e'\} \simeq [\tau_0/t]\mathcal{C}\{e'\}$, from which the result follows.

2. By an argument similar to that for Lemma 46.7.   □

48.3 Logical Equivalence

In this section, we introduce a form of logical equivalence that captures the informal concept of parametricity, and also provides a characterization of observational equivalence. This characterization will permit us to derive properties of observational equivalence of polymorphic programs of the kind suggested earlier.

The definition of logical equivalence for **F** is somewhat more complex than for **T**. The main idea is to define logical equivalence for a polymorphic type $\forall(t.\tau)$ to satisfy a very strong condition that captures the essence of parametricity. As a first approximation, we might say that two expressions e and e' of this type should be logically equivalent if they are logically equivalent for "all possible" interpretations of the type t. More precisely, we might require that $e[\rho]$ be related to $e'[\rho]$ at type $[\rho/t]\tau$, for any choice of type ρ. But this runs into two problems, one technical, the other conceptual. The same device will be used to solve both problems.

The technical problem stems from impredicativity. In Chapter 46, logical equivalence is defined by induction on the structure of types. But when polymorphism is impredicative, the type $[\rho/t]\tau$ might well be larger than $\forall(t.\tau)$. At the very least, we would have to justify the definition of logical equivalence on some other grounds, but no criterion appears to be available. The conceptual problem is that, even if we could make sense of the definition of logical equivalence, it would be too restrictive. For such a definition amounts to saying that the unknown type t is interpreted as logical equivalence at whatever type it is when instantiated. To obtain useful parametricity results, we shall ask for much more than this. What we shall do is to consider *separately* instances of e and e' by types ρ and ρ', and treat the type variable t as standing for *any relation* (of some form) between ρ and ρ'. We may suspect that this is asking too much: perhaps logical equivalence is the *empty* relation. Surprisingly, this is not the case, and indeed it is this very feature of the definition that we shall exploit to derive parametricity results about the language.

To manage both of these problems, we will consider a generalization of logical equivalence that is parameterized by a relational interpretation of the free type variables of its classifier. The parameters determine a separate binding for each free type variable in the classifier for each side of the equation, with the discrepancy being mediated by a specified relation between them. Thus, related expressions need not have the same type, with the differences between them mediated by the given relation.

We will restrict attention to a certain collection of "admissible" binary relations between closed expressions. The conditions are imposed to ensure that logical equivalence and observational equivalence coincide.

Definition 48.4 (Admissibility). *A relation R between expressions of types ρ and ρ' is admissible, written $R : \rho \leftrightarrow \rho'$, iff it satisfies two requirements:*

1. *Respect for observational equivalence: if $R(e, e')$ and $d \cong_\rho e$ and $d' \cong_{\rho'} e'$, then $R(d, d')$.*
2. *Closure under converse evaluation: if $R(e, e')$, then if $d \longmapsto e$, then $R(d, e')$ and if $d' \longmapsto e'$, then $R(e, d')$.*

Closure under converse evaluation is a consequence of respect for observational equivalence, but we are not yet in a position to establish this fact.

The judgment $\delta : \Delta$ states that δ is a *type substitution* that assigns a closed type to each type variable $t \in \Delta$. A type substitution δ induces a substitution function $\hat{\delta}$ on types given by the equation

$$\hat{\delta}(\tau) = [\delta(t_1), \ldots, \delta(t_n)/t_1, \ldots, t_n]\tau,$$

and similarly for expressions. Substitution is extended to contexts point-wise by defining $\hat{\delta}(\Gamma)(x) = \hat{\delta}(\Gamma(x))$ for each $x \in dom(\Gamma)$.

Let δ and δ' be two type substitutions of closed types to the type variables in Δ. An *admissible relation assignment* η between δ and δ' is an assignment of an admissible relation $\eta(t) : \delta(t) \leftrightarrow \delta'(t)$ to each $t \in \Delta$. The judgment $\eta : \delta \leftrightarrow \delta'$ states that η is an admissible relation assignment between δ and δ'.

Logical equivalence is defined in terms of its generalization, called *parametric logical equivalence*, written $e \sim_\tau e' [\eta : \delta \leftrightarrow \delta']$, defined as follows.

Definition 48.5 (Parametric Logical Equivalence). *The relation* $e \sim_\tau e'$ $[\eta : \delta \leftrightarrow \delta']$ *is defined by induction on the structure of τ by the following conditions:*

$$
\begin{aligned}
e \sim_t e' \, [\eta : \delta \leftrightarrow \delta'] \quad &iff \quad \eta(t)(e, e') \\
e \sim_2 e' \, [\eta : \delta \leftrightarrow \delta'] \quad &iff \quad e \simeq e' \\
e \sim_{\tau_1 \to \tau_2} e' \, [\eta : \delta \leftrightarrow \delta'] \quad &iff \quad e_1 \sim_{\tau_1} e_1' \, [\eta : \delta \leftrightarrow \delta'] \, implies \\
&\qquad e(e_1) \sim_{\tau_2} e'(e_1') \, [\eta : \delta \leftrightarrow \delta'] \\
e \sim_{\forall(t.\tau)} e' \, [\eta : \delta \leftrightarrow \delta'] \quad &iff \quad for \; every \; \rho, \; \rho', \; and \; every \; admissible \; R : \rho \leftrightarrow \rho', \\
&\qquad e[\rho] \sim_\tau e'[\rho'] \, [\eta \otimes t \hookrightarrow R : \delta \otimes t \hookrightarrow \rho \leftrightarrow \delta' \otimes t \hookrightarrow \rho']
\end{aligned}
$$

Logical equivalence is defined in terms of parametric logical equivalence by considering all possible interpretations of its free type- and expression variables. An *expression substitution* γ for a context Γ, written $\gamma : \Gamma$, is a substitution of a closed expression $\gamma(x) : \Gamma(x)$ to each variable $x \in dom(\Gamma)$. An expression substitution $\gamma : \Gamma$ induces a substitution function, $\hat{\gamma}$, defined by the equation

$$\hat{\gamma}(e) = [\gamma(x_1), \ldots, \gamma(x_n)/x_1, \ldots, x_n]e,$$

where the domain of Γ consists of the variables $x_1, \ldots, x_n$. The relation $\gamma \sim_\Gamma \gamma'$ $[\eta : \delta \leftrightarrow \delta']$ is defined to hold iff $dom(\gamma) = dom(\gamma') = dom(\Gamma)$, and $\gamma(x) \sim_{\Gamma(x)} \gamma'(x)$ $[\eta : \delta \leftrightarrow \delta']$ for every variable x in their common domain.

Definition 48.6 (Logical Equivalence). *The expressions $\Delta; \Gamma \vdash e : \tau$ and $\Delta; \Gamma \vdash e' : \tau$ are* logically equivalent, *written $\Delta; \Gamma \vdash e \sim e' : \tau$ iff, for every assignment δ and δ' of closed types to type variables in Δ, and every admissible relation assignment $\eta : \delta \leftrightarrow \delta'$, if $\gamma \sim_\Gamma \gamma'$ $[\eta : \delta \leftrightarrow \delta']$, then $\hat{\gamma}(\hat{\delta}(e)) \sim_\tau \widehat{\gamma'}(\widehat{\delta'}(e'))$ $[\eta : \delta \leftrightarrow \delta']$.*

When e, e', and τ are closed, this definition states that $e \sim_\tau e'$ iff $e \sim_\tau e'$ $[\emptyset : \emptyset \leftrightarrow \emptyset]$, so that logical equivalence is indeed a special case of its generalization.

Lemma 48.7 (Closure under Converse Evaluation). *Suppose that $e \sim_\tau e'$ $[\eta : \delta \leftrightarrow \delta']$. If $d \longmapsto e$, then $d \sim_\tau e'$, and if $d' \longmapsto e'$, then $e \sim_\tau d'$.*

Proof By induction on the structure of τ. When $\tau = t$, the result holds by the definition of admissibility. Otherwise, the result follows by induction, making use of the definition of the transition relation for applications and type applications. $\square$

Lemma 48.8 (Respect for Observational Equivalence). *Suppose that $e \sim_\tau e'$ $[\eta : \delta \leftrightarrow \delta']$. If $d \cong_{\hat{\delta}(\tau)} e$ and $d' \cong_{\widehat{\delta'}(\tau)} e'$, then $d \sim_\tau d'$ $[\eta : \delta \leftrightarrow \delta']$.*

Proof By induction on the structure of τ, relying on the definition of admissibility, and the congruence property of observational equivalence. For example, if $\tau = \forall(t.\tau_2)$, then we are to show that for every admissible $R : \rho \leftrightarrow \rho'$,

$$d[\rho] \sim_{\tau_2} d'[\rho'] \, [\eta \otimes t \hookrightarrow R : \delta \otimes t \hookrightarrow \rho \leftrightarrow \delta' \otimes t \hookrightarrow \rho'].$$

Because observational equivalence is a congruence, we have $d[\rho] \cong_{[\rho/t]\hat{\delta}(\tau_2)} e[\rho]$, and $d'[\rho'] \cong_{[\rho'/t]\widehat{\delta'}(\tau_2)} e'[\rho]$. It follows that

$$e[\rho] \sim_{\tau_2} e'[\rho'] \, [\eta \otimes t \hookrightarrow R : \delta \otimes t \hookrightarrow \rho \leftrightarrow \delta' \otimes t \hookrightarrow \rho'],$$

from which the result follows by induction. $\square$

Corollary 48.9. *The relation* $e \sim_\tau e' \, [\eta : \delta \leftrightarrow \delta']$ *is an admissible relation between closed types* $\hat{\delta}(\tau)$ *and* $\widehat{\delta'}(\tau)$.

Proof By Lemmas 48.7 and 48.8. $\square$

Corollary 48.10. *If* $\Delta; \Gamma \vdash e \sim e' : \tau$, *and* $\Delta; \Gamma \vdash d \cong e : \tau$ *and* $\Delta; \Gamma \vdash d' \cong e' : \tau$, *then* $\Delta; \Gamma \vdash d \sim d' : \tau$.

Proof By Lemma 48.3 and Corollary 48.9. $\square$

Lemma 48.11 (Compositionality). *Let* $R : \hat{\delta}(\rho) \leftrightarrow \widehat{\delta'}(\rho)$ *be the relational interpretation of some type* ρ, *which is to say* $R(d, d')$ *holds iff* $d \sim_\rho d' \, [\eta : \delta \leftrightarrow \delta']$. *Then* $e \sim_{[\rho/t]\tau} e' \, [\eta : \delta \leftrightarrow \delta']$ *if, and only if,*

$$e \sim_\tau e' \, [\eta \otimes t \hookrightarrow R : \delta \otimes t \hookrightarrow \hat{\delta}(\rho) \leftrightarrow \delta' \otimes t \hookrightarrow \widehat{\delta'}(\rho)].$$

Proof By induction on the structure of τ. When $\tau = t$, the result is immediate from the choice of the relation R. When $\tau = t' \neq t$, the result follows from Definition 48.5. When $\tau = \tau_1 \to \tau_2$, the result follows by induction, using Definition 48.5. Similarly, when or $\tau = \forall(u.\tau_1)$, the result follows by induction, noting that we may assume, without loss of generality, that $u \neq t$ and $u \notin \rho$. $\square$

Despite the strong conditions on polymorphic types, logical equivalence is not too restrictive—every expression satisfies its constraints. This result is often called the *parametricity theorem* or the *abstraction theorem*:

Theorem 48.12 (Parametricity). *If* $\Delta; \Gamma \vdash e : \tau$, *then* $\Delta; \Gamma \vdash e \sim e : \tau$.

Proof By rule induction on the statics of **F** given by rules (16.2).
We consider two representative cases here.

  Rule (16.2d) Suppose $\delta : \Delta$, $\delta' : \Delta$, $\eta : \delta \leftrightarrow \delta'$, and $\gamma \sim_\Gamma \gamma' \, [\eta : \delta \leftrightarrow \delta']$. By induction we have that for all ρ, ρ', and admissible $R : \rho \leftrightarrow \rho'$,

$$[\rho/t]\hat{\gamma}(\hat{\delta}(e)) \sim_\tau [\rho'/t]\widehat{\gamma'}(\widehat{\delta'}(e)) \, [\eta_* : \delta_* \leftrightarrow \delta'_*],$$

  where $\eta_* = \eta \otimes t \hookrightarrow R$, $\delta_* = \delta \otimes t \hookrightarrow \rho$, and $\delta'_* = \delta' \otimes t \hookrightarrow \rho'$. Because

$$\Lambda(t) \, \hat{\gamma}(\hat{\delta}(e))[\rho] \longmapsto^* [\rho/t]\hat{\gamma}(\hat{\delta}(e))$$

and

$$\Lambda(t)\,\widehat{\gamma'}(\widehat{\delta'}(e))[\rho'] \longmapsto^* [\rho'/t]\widehat{\gamma'}(\widehat{\delta'}(e)),$$

the result follows by Lemma 48.7.

Rule (16.2e) Suppose $\delta : \Delta$, $\delta' : \Delta$, $\eta : \delta \leftrightarrow \delta'$, and $\gamma \sim_\Gamma \gamma'\,[\eta : \delta \leftrightarrow \delta']$. By induction we have

$$\hat{\gamma}(\hat{\delta}(e)) \sim_{\forall(t.\tau)} \widehat{\gamma'}(\widehat{\delta'}(e))\,[\eta : \delta \leftrightarrow \delta']$$

Let $\hat{\rho} = \hat{\delta}(\rho)$ and $\hat{\rho}' = \widehat{\delta'}(\rho)$. Define the relation $R : \hat{\rho} \leftrightarrow \hat{\rho}'$ by $R(d, d')$ iff $d \sim_\rho d'\,[\eta : \delta \leftrightarrow \delta']$. By Corollary 48.9, this relation is admissible.

By the definition of logical equivalence at polymorphic types, we obtain

$$\hat{\gamma}(\hat{\delta}(e))[\hat{\rho}] \sim_\tau \widehat{\gamma'}(\widehat{\delta'}(e))[\hat{\rho}']\,[\eta \otimes t \hookrightarrow R : \delta \otimes t \hookrightarrow \hat{\rho} \leftrightarrow \delta' \otimes t \hookrightarrow \hat{\rho}'].$$

By Lemma 48.11

$$\hat{\gamma}(\hat{\delta}(e))[\hat{\rho}] \sim_{[\rho/t]\tau} \widehat{\gamma'}(\widehat{\delta'}(e))[\hat{\rho}']\,[\eta : \delta \leftrightarrow \delta']$$

But

$$\hat{\gamma}(\hat{\delta}(e))[\hat{\rho}] = \hat{\gamma}(\hat{\delta}(e))[\hat{\delta}(\rho)] \tag{48.1}$$
$$= \hat{\gamma}(\hat{\delta}(e[\rho])), \tag{48.2}$$

and similarly

$$\widehat{\gamma'}(\widehat{\delta'}(e))[\hat{\rho}'] = \widehat{\gamma'}(\widehat{\delta'}(e))[\widehat{\delta'}(\rho)] \tag{48.3}$$
$$= \widehat{\gamma'}(\widehat{\delta'}(e[\rho])), \tag{48.4}$$

from which the result follows. □

Corollary 48.13. *If $\Delta; \Gamma \vdash e \cong e' : \tau$, then $\Delta; \Gamma \vdash e \sim e' : \tau$.*

Proof By Theorem 48.12 $\Delta; \Gamma \vdash e \sim e : \tau$, and hence by Corollary 48.10, $\Delta; \Gamma \vdash e \sim e' : \tau$. □

Lemma 48.14 (Congruence). *If $\Delta; \Gamma \vdash e \sim e' : \tau$ and $\mathcal{C} : (\Delta; \Gamma \triangleright \tau) \rightsquigarrow (\Delta'; \Gamma' \triangleright \tau')$, then $\Delta'; \Gamma' \vdash \mathcal{C}\{e\} \sim \mathcal{C}\{e'\} : \tau'$.*

Proof By induction on the structure of $\mathcal{C}$, following along very similar lines to the proof of Theorem 48.12. □

Lemma 48.15 (Consistency). *Logical equivalence is consistent.*

Proof Follows from the definition of logical equivalence. □

Corollary 48.16. *If $\Delta; \Gamma \vdash e \sim e' : \tau$, then $\Delta; \Gamma \vdash e \cong e' : \tau$.*

Proof   By Lemma 48.15, logical equivalence is consistent, and by Lemma 48.14, it is a congruence, and hence is contained in observational equivalence.   □

Corollary 48.17. *Logical and observational equivalence coincide.*

Proof   By Corollaries 48.13 and 48.16.   □

If $d : \tau$ and $d \longmapsto e$, then $d \sim_\tau e$, and hence by Corollary 48.16, $d \cong_\tau e$. Therefore, if a relation respects observational equivalence, it must also be closed under converse evaluation. The second condition on admissibility is superfluous, now that we have established the coincidence of logical and observational equivalence.

Corollary 48.18 (Extensionality)**.**

1. $e \cong_{\tau_1 \to \tau_2} e'$ *iff for all* $e_1 : \tau_1$, $e(e_1) \cong_{\tau_2} e'(e_1)$.
2. $e \cong_{\forall(t.\tau)} e'$ *iff for all* ρ, $e[\rho] \cong_{[\rho/t]\tau} e'[\rho]$.

Proof   The forward direction is immediate in both cases, because observational equivalence is a congruence, by definition. The backward direction is proved similarly in both cases, by appeal to Theorem 48.12. In the first case, by Corollary 48.17 it suffices to show that $e \sim_{\tau_1 \to \tau_2} e'$. To this end, suppose that $e_1 \sim_{\tau_1} e_1'$. We are to show that $e(e_1) \sim_{\tau_2} e'(e_1')$. By the assumption, we have $e(e_1') \cong_{\tau_2} e'(e_1')$. By parametricity, we have $e \sim_{\tau_1 \to \tau_2} e$, and hence $e(e_1) \sim_{\tau_2} e(e_1')$. The result then follows by Lemma 48.8. In the second case, by Corollary 48.17 it is sufficient to show that $e \sim_{\forall(t.\tau)} e'$. Suppose that $R : \rho \leftrightarrow \rho'$ for some closed types ρ and ρ'. It suffices to show that $e[\rho] \sim_\tau e'[\rho'] [\eta : \delta \leftrightarrow \delta']$, where $\eta(t) = R$, $\delta(t) = \rho$, and $\delta'(t) = \rho'$. By the assumption, we have $e[\rho'] \cong_{[\rho'/t]\tau} e'[\rho']$. By parametricity $e \sim_{\forall(t.\tau)} e$, and hence $e[\rho] \sim_\tau e'[\rho'] [\eta : \delta \leftrightarrow \delta']$. The result then follows by Lemma 48.8.   □

Lemma 48.19 (Identity Extension)**.** *Let* $\eta : \delta \leftrightarrow \delta$ *be such that* $\eta(t)$ *is observational equivalence at type* $\delta(t)$ *for each* $t \in dom(\delta)$. *Then* $e \sim_\tau e' [\eta : \delta \leftrightarrow \delta]$ *iff* $e \cong_{\delta(\tau)} e'$.

Proof   The backward direction follows from Theorem 48.12 and respect for observational equivalence. The forward direction is proved by induction on the structure of τ, appealing to Corollary 48.18 to establish observational equivalence at function and polymorphic types.   □

48.4 Parametricity Properties

The parametricity theorem enables us to deduce properties of expressions of **F** that hold solely because of their type. The stringencies of parametricity ensure that a polymorphic type has very few inhabitants. For example, we may prove that *every* expression of type $\forall(t.t \to t)$ behaves like the identity function.

Theorem 48.20. *Let* $e : \forall(t.t \to t)$ *be arbitrary, and let id be* $\Lambda(t)\lambda(x:t)x$. *Then* $e \cong_{\forall(t.t \to t)} id$.

Proof By Corollary 48.17 it is sufficient to show that $e \sim_{\forall(t.t \to t)} id$. Let ρ and ρ' be arbitrary closed types, let $R : \rho \leftrightarrow \rho'$ be an admissible relation, and suppose that $e_0 \; R \; e_0'$. We are to show

$$e[\rho](e_0) \; R \; id[\rho](e_0'),$$

which, given the definition of *id* and closure under converse evaluation, is to say

$$e[\rho](e_0) \; R \; e_0'.$$

It suffices to show that $e[\rho](e_0) \cong_\rho e_0$, for then the result follows by the admissibility of R and the assumption $e_0 \; R \; e_0'$.

By Theorem 48.12, we have $e \sim_{\forall(t.t \to t)} e$. Let the relation $S : \rho \leftrightarrow \rho$ be defined by $d \; S \; d'$ iff $d \cong_\rho e_0$ and $d' \cong_\rho e_0$. This relation is clearly admissible, and we have $e_0 \; S \; e_0$. It follows that

$$e[\rho](e_0) \; S \; e[\rho](e_0),$$

and so, by the definition of the relation S, $e[\rho](e_0) \cong_\rho e_0$. $\square$

In Chapter 16, we showed that product, sum, and natural numbers types are all definable in **F**. The proof of definability in each case consisted of showing that the type and its associated introduction and elimination forms are encodable in **F**. The encodings are correct in the (weak) sense that the dynamics of these constructs as given in the earlier chapters is derivable from the dynamics of **F** via these definitions. By taking advantage of parametricity, we may extend these results to obtain a strong correspondence between these types and their encodings.

As a first example, let us consider the representation of the unit type, unit, in **F**, as defined in Chapter 16 by the following equations:

$$unit = \forall(r.r \to r)$$
$$\langle\rangle = \Lambda(r)\lambda(x:r)x$$

It is easy to see that $\langle\rangle$: unit according to these definitions. But this says that the type unit is inhabited (has an element). What we would like to know is that, up to observational equivalence, the expression $\langle\rangle$ is the *only* element of that type. But this is the content of Theorem 48.20. We say that the type unit is *strongly definable* within **F**.

Continuing in this vein, let us examine the definition of the binary product type in **F**, also given in Chapter 16:

$$\tau_1 \times \tau_2 = \forall(r.(\tau_1 \to \tau_2 \to r) \to r)$$

$$\langle e_1, e_2 \rangle = \Lambda(r)\, \lambda\,(x : \tau_1 \to \tau_2 \to r)\, x(e_1)(e_2)$$

$$e \cdot 1 = e[\tau_1](\lambda\,(x : \tau_1)\, \lambda\,(y : \tau_2)\, x)$$

$$e \cdot \mathbf{r} = e[\tau_2](\lambda\,(x : \tau_1)\, \lambda\,(y : \tau_2)\, y)$$

It is easy to check that $\langle e_1, e_2 \rangle \cdot 1 \cong_{\tau_1} e_1$ and $\langle e_1, e_2 \rangle \cdot \mathbf{r} \cong_{\tau_2} e_2$ by a direct calculation.

We wish to show that the ordered pair, as defined above, is the unique such expression, and hence that Cartesian products are strongly definable in **F**. We will make use of a lemma governing the behavior of the elements of the product type whose proof relies on Theorem 48.12.

Lemma 48.21. *If $e : \tau_1 \times \tau_2$, then $e \cong_{\tau_1 \times \tau_2} \langle e_1, e_2 \rangle$ for some $e_1 : \tau_1$ and $e_2 : \tau_2$.*

Proof Expanding the definitions of pairing and the product type, and applying Corollary 48.17, we let ρ and ρ' be arbitrary closed types, and let $R : \rho \leftrightarrow \rho'$ be an admissible relation between them. Suppose further that

$$h \sim_{\tau_1 \to \tau_2 \to t} h'\, [\eta : \delta \leftrightarrow \delta'],$$

where $\eta(t) = R$, $\delta(t) = \rho$, and $\delta'(t) = \rho'$ (and each is undefined on $t' \neq t$). We are to show that for some $e_1 : \tau_1$ and $e_2 : \tau_2$,

$$e[\rho](h) \sim_t h'(e_1)(e_2)\, [\eta : \delta \leftrightarrow \delta'],$$

which is to say

$$e[\rho](h)\ R\ h'(e_1)(e_2).$$

Now by Theorem 48.12 we have $e \sim_{\tau_1 \times \tau_2} e$. Define the relation $S : \rho \leftrightarrow \rho'$ by $d\ S\ d'$ iff the following conditions are satisfied:

1. $d \cong_\rho h(d_1)(d_2)$ for some $d_1 : \tau_1$ and $d_2 : \tau_2$;
2. $d' \cong_{\rho'} h'(d_1')(d_2')$ for some $d_1' : \tau_1$ and $d_2' : \tau_2$;
3. $d\ R\ d'$.

This relation is clearly admissible. Noting that

$$h \sim_{\tau_1 \to \tau_2 \to t} h'\, [\eta' : \delta \leftrightarrow \delta'],$$

where $\eta'(t) = S$ and $\eta'(t')$ is undefined for $t' \neq t$, we conclude that $e[\rho](h)\ S\ e[\rho'](h')$, and hence

$$e[\rho](h)\ R\ h'(d_1')(d_2'),$$

as required. $\square$

Now suppose that $e : \tau_1 \times \tau_2$ is such that $e \cdot 1 \cong_{\tau_1} e_1$ and $e \cdot r \cong_{\tau_2} e_2$. We wish to show that $e \cong_{\tau_1 \times \tau_2} \langle e_1, e_2 \rangle$. From Lemma 48.21 it follows that $e \cong_{\tau_1 \times \tau_2} \langle e \cdot 1, e \cdot r \rangle$ by congruence and direct calculation. Hence, by congruence we have $e \cong_{\tau_1 \times \tau_2} \langle e_1, e_2 \rangle$.

By a similar line of reasoning, we may show that the Church encoding of the natural numbers given in Chapter 16 strongly defines the natural numbers in that the following properties hold:

1. $\texttt{iter}\, \texttt{z}\, \{\texttt{z} \hookrightarrow e_0 \mid \texttt{s}(x) \hookrightarrow e_1\} \cong_\rho e_0$.
2. $\texttt{iter}\, \texttt{s}(e)\, \{\texttt{z} \hookrightarrow e_0 \mid \texttt{s}(x) \hookrightarrow e_1\} \cong_\rho [\texttt{iter}\, e\, \{\texttt{z} \hookrightarrow e_0 \mid \texttt{s}(x) \hookrightarrow e_1\}/x]e_1$.
3. Suppose that $x : \texttt{nat} \vdash r(x) : \rho$. If
   (a) $r(\texttt{z}) \cong_\rho e_0$, and
   (b) $r(\texttt{s}(e)) \cong_\rho [r(e)/x]e_1$,
   then for every $e : \texttt{nat}$, $r(e) \cong_\rho \texttt{iter}\, e\, \{\texttt{z} \hookrightarrow e_0 \mid \texttt{s}(x) \hookrightarrow e_1\}$.

The first two equations, which constitute weak definability, are easily established by calculation, using the definitions given in Chapter 16. The third property, the unicity of the iterator, is proved using parametricity by showing that every closed expression of type $\texttt{nat}$ is observationally equivalent to a numeral $\overline{n}$. We then argue for unicity of the iterator by mathematical induction on $n \geq 0$.

Lemma 48.22. *If $e : nat$, then either $e \cong_{nat} z$, or there exists $e' : nat$ such that $e \cong_{nat} s(e')$. Consequently, there exists $n \geq 0$ such that $e \cong_{nat} \overline{n}$.*

Proof By Theorem 48.12, we have $e \sim_{\texttt{nat}} e$. Define the relation $R : \texttt{nat} \leftrightarrow \texttt{nat}$ to be the strongest relation such that $d\, R\, d'$ iff either $d \cong_{\texttt{nat}} \texttt{z}$ and $d' \cong_{\texttt{nat}} \texttt{z}$, or $d \cong_{\texttt{nat}} \texttt{s}(d_1)$ and $d' \cong_{\texttt{nat}} \texttt{s}(d_1')$ and $d_1\, R\, d_1'$. It is easy to see that $\texttt{z}\, R\, \texttt{z}$, and if $e\, R\, e'$, then $\texttt{s}(e)\, R\, \texttt{s}(e')$. Letting $\texttt{zero} = \texttt{z}$ and $\texttt{succ} = \lambda\, (x : \texttt{nat})\, \texttt{s}(x)$, we have

$$e[\texttt{nat}](\texttt{zero})(\texttt{succ})\, R\, e[\texttt{nat}](\texttt{zero})(\texttt{succ}).$$

The result follows by the induction principle arising from the definition of R as the strongest relation satisfying its defining conditions. $\qquad\square$

48.5 Representation Independence, Revisited

In Section 17.4, we discussed the property of *representation independence* for abstract types. If two implementations of an abstract type are "similar," then the client behavior is not affected by replacing one for the other. The crux of the matter is the definition of similarity of two implementations. Informally, two implementations of an abstract type are similar if there is a relation R between their representation types that is *preserved* by the operations of the type. The relation R may be thought of as expressing the "equivalence" of the two representations; checking that each operation preserves R amounts to checking that the result of performing that operation on equivalent representations yields equivalent results.

As an example, we argued in Section 17.4 that two implementations of a queue abstraction are similar. The two representations of queues are related by a relation R such that $q\ R\ (b, f)$ iff q is b followed by the reversal of f. When then argued that the operations preserve this relationship, and then claimed, without proof, that the behavior of the client would not be disrupted by changing one implementation to the other.

The proof of this claim relies on parametricity, as may be seen by considering the definability of existential types in **F** given in Section 17.3. According to that definition, the client, e, of an abstract type $\exists(t.\tau)$ is a polymorphic function of type $\forall(t.\tau \to \tau_2)$, where τ_2, the result type of the computation, does not involve the type variable t. Being polymorphic, the client enjoys the parametricity property given by Theorem 48.12. Specifically, suppose that ρ_1 and ρ_2 are two closed representation types and that $R : \rho_1 \leftrightarrow \rho_2$ is an admissible relation between them. For example, in the case of the queue abstraction, ρ_1 is the type of lists of elements of the queue, ρ_2 is the type of a pair of lists of elements, and R is the relation given above. Suppose further that $e_1 : [\rho_1/t]\tau$ and $e_2 : [\rho_2/t]\tau$ are two implementations of the operations such that

$$e_1 \sim_\tau e_2\ [\eta : \delta_1 \leftrightarrow \delta_2], \tag{48.5}$$

where $\eta(t) = R$, $\delta_1(t) = \rho_1$, and $\delta_2(t) = \rho_2$. In the case of the queues example, the expression e_1 is the implementation of the queue operations in terms of lists, and the e_2 is the implementation in terms of pairs of lists described earlier. Condition (48.5) states that the two implementations are similar in that they preserve the relation R between the representation types. By Theorem 48.12, it follows that the client e satisfies

$$e \sim_{\tau_2} e\ [\eta : \delta_1 \leftrightarrow \delta_2].$$

But because τ_2 is a closed type (in particular, does not involve t), this is equivalent to

$$e \sim_{\tau_2} e\ [\emptyset : \emptyset \leftrightarrow \emptyset].$$

But then by Lemma 48.19 we have

$$e[\rho_1](e_1) \cong_{\tau_2} e[\rho_2](e_2).$$

That is, the client behavior is not affected by the change of representation.

48.6 Notes

The concept of parametricity is latent in the proof of normalization for System **F** (Girard, 1972). Reynolds (1983), though technically flawed due to its reliance on a (non-existent) set-theoretic model of polymorphism, emphasizes the centrality of logical equivalence for characterizing equality of polymorphic programs. The application of parametricity to representation independence was suggested by Reynolds and developed for existential types by Mitchell (1986) and Pitts (1998). The extension of System **F** with a "positive" (inductively defined) observable type appears to be needed to even define observational equivalence, but this point seems not to have been made elsewhere in the literature.

49

Process Equivalence

As the name implies, a process is an ongoing computation that may interact with other processes by sending and receiving messages. From this point of view, a concurrent computation has no definite "final outcome" but rather affords an opportunity for interaction that may well continue indefinitely. The notion of equivalence of processes must therefore be based on their potential for interaction, rather than on the "answer" that they may compute. Let P and Q be such that $\vdash_\Sigma P$ proc and $\vdash_\Sigma Q$ proc. We say that P and Q are *equivalent*, written $P \approx_\Sigma Q$, iff there is a bisimulation $\mathcal{R}$ such that $P\,\mathcal{R}_\Sigma\,Q$. A family of relations $\mathcal{R} = \{\mathcal{R}_\Sigma\}_\Sigma$ is a *bisimulation* iff whenever P may evolve to P' taking the action α, then Q may also evolve to some process Q' taking the same action such that $P'\,\mathcal{R}_\Sigma\,Q'$, and, conversely, if Q may evolve to Q' taking action α, then P may evolve to P' taking the same action, and $P'\,\mathcal{R}_\Sigma\,Q'$. This correspondence captures the idea that the two processes afford the same opportunities for interaction in that they each simulate each other's behavior with respect to their ability to interact with their environment.

49.1 Process Calculus

We will consider a process calculus that consolidates the main ideas explored in Chapters 39 and 40. We assume as given an ambient language of expressions that includes the type `clsfd` of classified values (see Chapter 33). Channels are treated as dynamically generated classes with which to build messages, as described in Chapter 40.

The syntax of the process calculus is given by the following grammar:

Proc	P	$::=$	stop	$\mathbf{1}$	inert
			$\mathrm{conc}(P_1; P_2)$	$P_1 \otimes P_2$	composition
			$\mathrm{await}(E)$	$\$\,E$	synchronize
			$\mathrm{new}[\tau](a.P)$	$\nu\,a \sim \tau.P$	allocation
			$\mathrm{emit}(e)$	$!\,e$	broadcast
Evt	E	$::=$	null	$\mathbf{0}$	null
			$\mathrm{or}(E_1; E_2)$	$E_1 + E_2$	choice
			$\mathrm{acc}(x.P)$	$?\,(x.P)$	acceptance

The statics is given by the judgments $\Gamma \vdash_\Sigma P$ proc and $\Gamma \vdash_\Sigma E$ event defined by the following rules. We assume as given a judgment $\Gamma \vdash_\Sigma e : \tau$ for τ a type including the type clsfd of classified values.

$$\frac{}{\Gamma \vdash_\Sigma \mathbf{1} \text{ proc}} \tag{49.1a}$$

$$\frac{\Gamma \vdash_\Sigma P_1 \text{ proc} \quad \Gamma \vdash_\Sigma P_2 \text{ proc}}{\Gamma \vdash_\Sigma P_1 \otimes P_2 \text{ proc}} \tag{49.1b}$$

$$\frac{\Gamma \vdash_\Sigma E \text{ event}}{\Gamma \vdash_\Sigma \$E \text{ proc}} \tag{49.1c}$$

$$\frac{\Gamma \vdash_{\Sigma,a\sim\tau} P \text{ proc}}{\Gamma \vdash_\Sigma \nu\, a \sim \tau.P \text{ proc}} \tag{49.1d}$$

$$\frac{\Gamma \vdash_\Sigma e : \text{clsfd}}{\Gamma \vdash_\Sigma \,!\, e \text{ proc}} \tag{49.1e}$$

$$\frac{}{\Gamma \vdash_\Sigma \mathbf{0} \text{ event}} \tag{49.1f}$$

$$\frac{\Gamma \vdash_\Sigma E_1 \text{ event} \quad \Gamma \vdash_\Sigma E_2 \text{ event}}{\Gamma \vdash_\Sigma E_1 + E_2 \text{ event}} \tag{49.1g}$$

$$\frac{\Gamma, x : \text{clsfd} \vdash_\Sigma P \text{ proc}}{\Gamma \vdash_\Sigma \,?\,(x.P) \text{ event}} \tag{49.1h}$$

The dynamics is given by the judgments $P \overset{\alpha}{\underset{\Sigma}{\mapsto}} P'$ and $E \overset{\alpha}{\underset{\Sigma}{\Rightarrow}} P$, defined as in Chapter 39. We assume as given the judgments $e \underset{\Sigma}{\mapsto} e'$ and $e \text{ val}_\Sigma$ for expressions. Processes and events are identified up to structural congruence, as described in Chapter 39.

$$\frac{P_1 \overset{\alpha}{\underset{\Sigma}{\mapsto}} P_1'}{P_1 \otimes P_2 \overset{\alpha}{\underset{\Sigma}{\mapsto}} P_1' \otimes P_2} \tag{49.2a}$$

$$\frac{P_1 \overset{\alpha}{\underset{\Sigma}{\mapsto}} P_1' \quad P_2 \overset{\overline{\alpha}}{\underset{\Sigma}{\mapsto}} P_2'}{P_1 \otimes P_2 \overset{\varepsilon}{\underset{\Sigma}{\mapsto}} P_1' \otimes P_2'} \tag{49.2b}$$

$$\frac{E \overset{\alpha}{\underset{\Sigma}{\Rightarrow}} P}{\$E \overset{\alpha}{\underset{\Sigma}{\mapsto}} P} \tag{49.2c}$$

$$\frac{P \xrightarrow[\Sigma,a\sim\tau]{\alpha} P' \quad \vdash_\Sigma \alpha \text{ action}}{\nu\, a \sim \tau.P \overset{\alpha}{\underset{\Sigma}{\mapsto}} \nu\, a \sim \tau.P'} \tag{49.2d}$$

$$\frac{e \text{ val}_\Sigma \quad \vdash_\Sigma e : \text{clsfd}}{!\, e \overset{e!}{\underset{\Sigma}{\mapsto}} \mathbf{1}} \tag{49.2e}$$

$$\frac{E_1 \overset{\alpha}{\underset{\Sigma}{\Rightarrow}} P}{E_1 + E_2 \overset{\alpha}{\underset{\Sigma}{\Rightarrow}} P} \tag{49.2f}$$

$$\frac{e \; \mathsf{val}_\Sigma}{?\,(x.P) \overset{e?}{\underset{\Sigma}{\Rightarrow}} [e/x]P} \tag{49.2g}$$

Assuming that substitution is valid for expressions, it is also valid for processes and events.

Lemma 49.1.

1. If $\Gamma, x : \tau \vdash_\Sigma P$ proc and $\Gamma \vdash_\Sigma e : \tau$, then $\Gamma \vdash_\Sigma [e/x]P$ proc.
2. If $\Gamma, x : \tau \vdash_\Sigma E$ event and $\Gamma \vdash_\Sigma e : \tau$, then $\Gamma \vdash_\Sigma [e/x]E$ event.

Transitions preserve well-formedness of processes and events.

Lemma 49.2.

1. If $\vdash_\Sigma P$ proc and $P \overset{\alpha}{\underset{\Sigma}{\mapsto}} P'$, then $\vdash_\Sigma P'$ proc.
2. If $\vdash_\Sigma E$ event and $E \overset{\alpha}{\underset{\Sigma}{\Rightarrow}} P$, then $\vdash_\Sigma P$ proc.

49.2 Strong Equivalence

Bisimilarity makes precise the informal idea that two processes are equivalent if they each can take the same actions and, in doing so, evolve into equivalent processes. A *process relation* $\mathcal{P}$ is a family $\{\mathcal{P}_\Sigma\}$ of binary relations between processes P and Q such that $\vdash_\Sigma P$ proc and $\vdash_\Sigma Q$ proc, and an *event relation* $\mathcal{E}$ is a family $\{\mathcal{E}_\Sigma\}$ of binary relations between events E and F such that $\vdash_\Sigma E$ event and $\vdash_\Sigma F$ event. A *(strong) bisimulation* is a pair $(\mathcal{P}, \mathcal{E})$ consisting of a process relation $\mathcal{P}$ and an event relation $\mathcal{E}$ satisfying the following conditions:

1. If $P \; \mathcal{P}_\Sigma \; Q$, then
   (a) if $P \overset{\alpha}{\underset{\Sigma}{\mapsto}} P'$, then there exists Q' such that $Q \overset{\alpha}{\underset{\Sigma}{\mapsto}} Q'$ with $P' \; \mathcal{P}_\Sigma \; Q'$, and
   (b) if $Q \overset{\alpha}{\underset{\Sigma}{\mapsto}} Q'$, then there exists P' such that $P \overset{\alpha}{\underset{\Sigma}{\mapsto}} P'$ with $P' \; \mathcal{P}_\Sigma \; Q'$.
2. If $E \; \mathcal{E}_\Sigma \; F$, then
   (a) if $E \overset{\alpha}{\underset{\Sigma}{\Rightarrow}} P$, then there exists Q such that $F \overset{\alpha}{\underset{\Sigma}{\Rightarrow}} Q$ with $P \; \mathcal{P}_\Sigma \; Q$, and
   (b) if $F \overset{\alpha}{\underset{\Sigma}{\Rightarrow}} Q$, then there exists P such that $E \overset{\alpha}{\underset{\Sigma}{\Rightarrow}} P$ with $P \; \mathcal{P}_\Sigma \; Q$.

The qualifier "strong" refers to the fact that the action α in the conditions on being a bisimulation include the silent action ε. (In Section 49.3, we discuss another notion of bisimulation in which the silent actions are treated specially.)

(Strong) equivalence is the pair $(\approx, \approx)$ of process and event relations such that $P \approx_\Sigma Q$ and $E \approx_\Sigma F$ iff there exists a strong bisimulation $(\mathcal{P}, \mathcal{E})$ such that $P \mathrel{\mathcal{P}_\Sigma} Q$, and $E \mathrel{\mathcal{E}_\Sigma} F$.

Lemma 49.3. *Strong equivalence is a strong bisimulation.*

Proof   Follows immediately from the definition.   □

The definition of strong equivalence gives rise to the principle of *proof by coinduction*. To show that $P \approx_\Sigma Q$, it is enough to give a bisimulation $(\mathcal{P}, \mathcal{E})$ such that $P \mathrel{\mathcal{P}_\Sigma} Q$ (and similarly for events). An instance of coinduction that arises fairly often is to choose $(\mathcal{P}, \mathcal{E})$ to be $(\approx \cup \mathcal{P}_0, \approx \cup \mathcal{E}_0)$ for some $\mathcal{P}_0$ and $\mathcal{E}_0$ such that $P \mathrel{\mathcal{P}_0} Q$, and show that this expansion is a bisimulation. Because strong equivalence is itself a bisimulation, this reduces to show that if $P' \mathrel{\mathcal{P}_0} Q'$ and $P' \overset{\alpha}{\underset{\Sigma}{\mapsto}} P''$, then $Q' \overset{\alpha}{\underset{\Sigma}{\mapsto}} Q''$ for some Q'' such that either $P'' \approx_\Sigma Q''$ or $P'' \mathrel{\mathcal{P}_0} Q''$ (and analogously for transitions from Q', and similarly for event transitions). This proof method amounts to *assuming what we are trying to prove* and showing that this assumption is tenable. The proof that the expanded relation is a bisimulation may make use of the assumptions $\mathcal{P}_0$ and $\mathcal{E}_0$; in this sense "circular reasoning" is a perfectly valid method of proof.

Lemma 49.4. *Strong equivalence is an equivalence relation.*

Proof   For reflexivity and symmetry, it suffices to note that the identity relation is a bisimulation, as is the converse of a bisimulation. For transitivity, we need that the composition of two bisimulations is again a bisimulation, which follows directly from the definition.   □

It remains to verify that strong equivalence is a congruence, which means that each of the process- and event-forming constructs respects strong equivalence. To show this we require the *open extension* of strong equivalence to processes and events with free variables. The relation $\Gamma \vdash_\Sigma P \approx Q$ is defined for processes P and Q such that $\Gamma \vdash_\Sigma P$ proc and $\Gamma \vdash_\Sigma Q$ proc to mean that $\hat{\gamma}(P) \approx_\Sigma \hat{\gamma}(Q)$ for every substitution, γ, of closed values of appropriate type for the variables Γ.

Lemma 49.5. *If $\Gamma, x : \mathtt{clsfd} \vdash_\Sigma P \approx Q$, then $\Gamma \vdash_\Sigma \mathop{?}(x.P) \approx \mathop{?}(x.Q)$.*

Proof   Fix a closing substitution γ for Γ, and let $\hat{P} = \hat{\gamma}(P)$ and $\hat{Q} = \hat{\gamma}(Q)$. By assumption, we have $x : \mathtt{clsfd} \vdash_\Sigma \hat{P} \approx \hat{Q}$. We are to show that $\mathop{?}(x.\hat{P}) \approx_\Sigma \mathop{?}(x.\hat{Q})$. The proof is by coinduction, taking $\mathcal{P} = \approx$ and $\mathcal{E} = \approx \cup \mathcal{E}_0$, where

$$\mathcal{E}_0 = \{ (\mathop{?}(x.P'), \mathop{?}(x.Q')) \mid x : \mathtt{clsfd} \vdash_\Sigma P' \approx Q' \}.$$

Clearly, $\mathop{?}(x.\hat{P}) \mathrel{\mathcal{E}_0} \mathop{?}(x.\hat{Q})$. Suppose that $\mathop{?}(x.P') \mathrel{\mathcal{E}_0} \mathop{?}(x.Q')$. By inspection of rules (49.2), if $\mathop{?}(x.P') \overset{\alpha}{\underset{\Sigma}{\Rightarrow}} P''$, then $\alpha = v\,?$ and $P'' = [v/x]P'$ for some v $\mathtt{val}_\Sigma$ such that $\vdash_\Sigma v : \mathtt{clsfd}$.

But $? (x . Q') \overset{v?}{\underset{\Sigma}{\Rightarrow}} [v/x] Q'$, and we have that $[v/x] P' \approx_\Sigma [v/x] Q'$ by the definition of $\mathcal{E}_0$, and hence $[v/x] P' \; \mathcal{E}_0 \; [v/x] Q'$, as required. The symmetric case follows symmetrically, completing the proof. $\qquad\square$

Lemma 49.6. *If* $\Gamma \vdash_{\Sigma, a \sim \tau} P \approx Q$, *then* $\Gamma \vdash_\Sigma \nu\, a \sim \tau . P \approx \nu\, a \sim \tau . Q$.

Proof Fix a closing value substitution γ for Γ, and let $\hat{P} = \hat{\gamma}(P)$ and $\hat{Q} = \hat{\gamma}(Q)$. Assuming that $\hat{P} \approx_{\Sigma, a \sim \tau} \hat{Q}$, we are to show that $\nu\, a \sim \tau . \hat{P} \approx_\Sigma \nu\, a \sim \tau . \hat{Q}$. The proof is by coinduction, taking $\mathcal{P} = {\approx} \cup \mathcal{P}_0$ and $\mathcal{E} = {\approx}$, where

$$\mathcal{P}_0 = \{ (\nu\, a \sim \tau . P', \nu\, a \sim \tau . Q') \mid P' \approx_{\Sigma, a \sim \tau} Q' \}.$$

Clearly, $\nu\, a \sim \tau . \hat{P} \; \mathcal{P}_0 \; \nu\, a \sim \tau . \hat{Q}$. Suppose that $\nu\, a \sim \tau . P' \; \mathcal{P}_0 \; \nu\, a \sim \tau . Q'$, and that $\nu\, a \sim \tau . P' \overset{\alpha}{\underset{\Sigma}{\mapsto}} P''$. By inspection of rules (49.2), we see that $\vdash_\Sigma \alpha$ action and that $P'' = \nu\, a \sim \tau . P'''$ for some P''' such that $P' \overset{\alpha}{\underset{\Sigma, a \sim \tau}{\longmapsto}} P'''$. But by definition of $\mathcal{P}_0$, we have $P' \approx_{\Sigma, a \sim \tau} Q'$, and hence $Q' \overset{\alpha}{\underset{\Sigma, a \sim \tau}{\longmapsto}} Q'''$ with $P''' \approx_{\Sigma, a \sim \tau} Q'''$. Letting $Q'' = \nu\, a \sim \tau . Q'$, we have that $\nu\, a \sim \tau . Q' \overset{\alpha}{\underset{\Sigma, a \sim \tau}{\longmapsto}} Q''$ and by definition of $\mathcal{P}_0$ we have $P'' \; \mathcal{P}_0 \; Q''$, as required. The symmetric case is proved symmetrically, completing the proof. $\qquad\square$

Lemmas 49.5 and 49.6 capture two different cases of binding, the former of variables, and the latter of classes. The hypothesis of Lemma 49.5 relates all substitutions for the variable x in the recipient processes, whereas the hypothesis of Lemma 49.6 relates the constituent processes schematically in the class name, a. This makes all the difference, for if we were to consider all substitution instances of a class name by another class name, then a class would no longer be "new" within its scope, because we could identify it with an "old" class by substitution. On the other hand, we *must* consider substitution instances for variables, because the meaning of a variable is given in such terms. This shows that classes and variables must be distinct concepts. (See Chapter 33 for an example of what goes wrong when the two concepts are confused.)

Lemma 49.7. *If* $\Gamma \vdash_\Sigma P_1 \approx Q_1$ *and* $\Gamma \vdash_\Sigma P_2 \approx Q_2$, *then* $\Gamma \vdash_\Sigma P_1 \otimes P_2 \approx Q_1 \otimes Q_2$.

Proof Let γ be a closing value substitution for Γ, and let $\hat{P}_i = \hat{\gamma}(P_i)$ and $\hat{Q}_i = \hat{\gamma}(Q_i)$ for $i = 1, 2$. The proof is by coinduction, considering the relation $\mathcal{P} = {\approx} \cup \mathcal{P}_0$ and $\mathcal{E} = {\approx}$, where

$$\mathcal{P}_0 = \{ (P_1' \otimes P_2', Q_1' \otimes Q_2') \mid P_1' \approx_\Sigma Q_1' \text{ and } P_2' \approx_\Sigma Q_2' \}.$$

Suppose that $P_1' \otimes P_2' \; \mathcal{P}_0 \; Q_1' \otimes Q_2'$, and that $P_1' \otimes P_2' \overset{\alpha}{\underset{\Sigma}{\mapsto}} P''$. There are two cases to consider, the interesting one being rule (49.2b). In this case, we have $P'' = P_1'' \otimes P_2''$ with $P_1' \overset{\alpha}{\underset{\Sigma}{\mapsto}} P_1''$ and $P_2' \overset{\bar{\alpha}}{\underset{\Sigma}{\mapsto}} P_2''$. By definition of $\mathcal{P}_0$, we have that $Q_1' \overset{\alpha}{\underset{\Sigma}{\mapsto}} Q_1''$ and $Q_2' \overset{\bar{\alpha}}{\underset{\Sigma}{\mapsto}} Q_2''$ with $P_1'' \approx_\Sigma Q_1''$ and $P_2'' \approx_\Sigma Q_2''$. Letting $Q'' = Q_1'' \otimes Q_2''$, we have that $P'' \; \mathcal{P}_0 \; Q''$, as required. The symmetric case is handled symmetrically, and rule (49.2a) is handled similarly. $\qquad\square$

Lemma 49.8. *If* $\Gamma \vdash_\Sigma E_1 \approx F_1$ *and* $\Gamma \vdash_\Sigma E_2 \approx F_2$, *then* $\Gamma \vdash_\Sigma E_1 + E_2 \approx F_1 + F_2$.

Proof Follows immediately from rules (49.2) and the definition of bisimulation. ☐

Lemma 49.9. *If* $\Gamma \vdash_\Sigma E \approx F$, *then* $\Gamma \vdash_\Sigma \$\, E \approx \$\, F$.

Proof Follows immediately from rules (49.2) and the definition of bisimulation. ☐

Lemma 49.10. *If* $\Gamma \vdash_\Sigma d \cong e : \mathtt{clsfd}$, *then* $\Gamma \vdash_\Sigma \,! d \approx \,! e$.

Proof The process calculus introduces no new observations on expressions, so that d and e remain indistinguishable as actions. ☐

Theorem 49.11. *Strong equivalence is a congruence.*

Proof Follows immediately from the preceding lemmas, which cover each case separately. ☐

49.3 Weak Equivalence

Strong equivalence expresses the idea that two processes are equivalent if they simulate each other step-by-step. Every action taken by one process is matched by a corresponding action taken by the other. This seems natural for the non-trivial actions $e\,!$ and $e\,?$ but is arguably overly restrictive for the silent action ε. Silent actions correspond to the actual steps of computation, whereas the send and receive actions express the potential to interact with another process. Silent steps are therefore of a very different flavor than the other forms of action, and therefore might usefully be treated differently from them. Weak equivalence seeks to do just that.

Silent actions arise within the process calculus itself (when two processes communicate), but they play an even more important role when the dynamics of expressions is considered explicitly (as in Chapter 40). For then each step $e \xmapsto{}_{\Sigma} e'$ of evaluation of an expression corresponds to a silent transition for any process in which it is embedded. In particular, $!e \xmapsto{\varepsilon}_{\Sigma} !e'$ whenever $e \mapsto_{\Sigma} e'$. We may also consider atomic processes of the form $\mathrm{run}(m)$ consisting of a command to be executed in accordance with the rules of some underlying dynamics. Here again we would expect that each step of command execution induces a silent transition from one atomic process to another.

From the point of view of equivalence, it therefore seems sensible to allow that a silent action by one process may be mimicked by one or more silent actions by another. For example, there is little to be gained by distinguishing, say, $\mathrm{run}(\mathtt{ret}\ 3{+}4)$ from $\mathrm{run}(\mathtt{ret}\ (1{+}2){+}(2{+}2))$ merely because the latter takes more steps to compute the same value than the former! The purpose of weak equivalence is precisely to disregard such trivial distinctions by allowing a transition to be matched by a matching transition, possibly preceded by any number of silent transitions.

A *weak bisimulation* is a pair $(\mathcal{P}, \mathcal{E})$ consisting of a process relation $\mathcal{P}$ and an event relation $\mathcal{E}$ satisfying the following conditions:

1. If $P \; \mathcal{P}_\Sigma \; Q$, then
   (a) if $P \overset{\alpha}{\underset{\Sigma}{\mapsto}} P'$, where $\alpha \neq \varepsilon$, then there exists Q'' and Q' such that $Q \overset{\varepsilon}{\underset{\Sigma}{\mapsto}}{}^* Q'' \overset{\alpha}{\underset{\Sigma}{\mapsto}} Q'$
   with $P' \; \mathcal{P}_\Sigma \; Q'$, and if $P \overset{\varepsilon}{\underset{\Sigma}{\mapsto}} P'$, then $Q \overset{\varepsilon}{\underset{\Sigma}{\mapsto}}{}^* Q'$ with $P' \; \mathcal{P}_\Sigma \; Q'$;
   (b) if $Q \overset{\alpha}{\underset{\Sigma}{\mapsto}} Q'$, where $\alpha \neq \varepsilon$, then there exists P'' and P' such that $P \overset{\varepsilon}{\underset{\Sigma}{\mapsto}}{}^* P'' \overset{\alpha}{\underset{\Sigma}{\mapsto}} P'$
   with $P' \; \mathcal{P}_\Sigma \; Q'$, and if $Q \overset{\varepsilon}{\underset{\Sigma}{\mapsto}} Q'$, then $P \overset{\varepsilon}{\underset{\Sigma}{\mapsto}}{}^* P'$ with $P' \; \mathcal{P}_\Sigma \; Q'$;
2. If $E \; \mathcal{E}_\Sigma \; F$, then
   (a) if $E \overset{\alpha}{\underset{\Sigma}{\Rightarrow}} P$, then there exists Q such that $F \overset{\alpha}{\underset{\Sigma}{\Rightarrow}} Q$ with $P \; \mathcal{P}_\Sigma \; Q$, and
   (b) if $F \overset{\alpha}{\underset{\Sigma}{\Rightarrow}} Q$, then there exists P such that $E \overset{\alpha}{\underset{\Sigma}{\Rightarrow}} P$ with $P \; \mathcal{P}_\Sigma \; Q$.

(The conditions on the event relation are the same as for strong bisimilarity because there are, in this calculus, no silent actions on events.)

Weak equivalence is the pair $(\sim, \sim)$ of process and event relations defined by $P \sim_\Sigma Q$ and $E \sim_\Sigma F$ iff there exists a weak bisimulation $(\mathcal{P}, \mathcal{E})$ such that $P \; \mathcal{P}_\Sigma \; Q$, and $E \; \mathcal{E}_\Sigma \; F$. The open extension of weak equivalence, written $\Gamma \vdash_\Sigma P \sim Q$ and $\Gamma \vdash_\Sigma E \sim F$, is defined exactly as is the open extension of strong equivalence.

Theorem 49.12. *Weak equivalence is an equivalence relation and a congruence.*

Proof   The proof proceeds along similar lines to that of Theorem 49.11.   □

49.4 Notes

The literature on process equivalence is extensive. Numerous variations have been considered for an equally numerous array of formalisms. Milner recounts the history and development of the concept of bisimilarity in his monograph on the π-calculus (Milner, 1999), crediting David Park with its original conception (Park, 1981). The development in this chapter is inspired by Milner, and by a proof of congruence of strong bisimilarity given by Bernardo Toninho for the process calculus considered in Chapter 39.

PART XIX

Appendices

A   Background on Finite Sets

We make frequent use of the concepts of a *finite set* of *discrete objects* and of *finite functions* between them. A set X is *discrete* iff equality of its elements is decidable: for every $x, y \in X$, either $x = y \in X$ or $x \neq y \in X$. This condition is to be understood constructively as stating that we may effectively determine whether any two elements of the set X are equal. Perhaps the most basic example of a discrete set is the set $\mathbb{N}$ of natural numbers. A set X is *countable* iff there is a bijection $f : X \cong \mathbb{N}$ between X and the set of natural numbers, and it is *finite* iff there is a bijection, $f : X \cong \{0, \ldots, n - 1\}$, where $n \in \mathbb{N}$, between it and some inital segment of the natural numbers. This condition is again to be understood constructively in terms of computable mappings, so that countable and finite sets are computably enumerable and, in the finite case, have a computable size.

Given countable sets, U and V, a *finite function* is a computable partial function $\phi : U \to V$ between them. The *domain $dom(\phi)$* of ϕ is the set $\{u \in U \mid \phi(u) \downarrow \}$, of objects $u \in U$ such that $\phi(u) = v$ for some $v \in V$. Two finite functions, ϕ and ψ, between U and V are *disjoint* iff $dom(\phi) \cap dom(\psi) = \emptyset$. The *empty* finite function, $\emptyset$, between U and V is the totally undefined partial function between them. If $u \in U$ and $v \in V$, then the finite function, $u \hookrightarrow v$, between U and V sends u to v, and is undefined otherwise; its domain is therefore the singleton set $\{u\}$. In some situations, we write $u \sim v$ for the finite function $u \hookrightarrow v$.

If ϕ and ψ are two disjoint finite functions from U to V, then $\phi \otimes \psi$ is the finite function from U to V defined by the equation

$$(\phi \otimes \psi)(u) = \begin{cases} \phi(u) & \text{if } u \in dom(\phi) \\ \psi(v) & \text{if } v \in dom(\psi) \\ \text{undefined} & \text{otherwise} \end{cases}$$

If $u_1, \ldots, u_n \in U$ are pairwise distinct, and $v_1, \ldots, v_n \in V$, then we sometimes write $u_1 \hookrightarrow v_1, \ldots, u_n \hookrightarrow v_n$, or $u_1 \sim v_1, \ldots, u_n \sim v_n$, for the finite function $u_1 \hookrightarrow v_1 \otimes \ldots \otimes u_n \hookrightarrow v_n$.

Bibliography

Martín Abadi and Luca Cardelli. *A Theory of Objects*. Springer-Verlag, 1996.

Peter Aczel. An introduction to inductive definitions. In Jon Barwise, editor, *Handbook of Mathematical Logic*, chapter C.7, pages 783–818. North-Holland, 1977.

John Allen. *Anatomy of LISP*. Computer Science Series. McGraw-Hill, 1978.

S. F. Allen, M. Bickford, R. L. Constable, R. Eaton, C. Kreitz, L. Lorigo, and E. Moran. Innovations in computational type theory using Nuprl. *Journal of Applied Logic*, 4(4):428–469, 2006. ISSN 1570-8683. doi: 10.1016/j.jal.2005.10.005.

Stuart Allen. A non-type-theoretic definition of Martin-Löf's types. In *LICS*, pages 215–221, 1987.

Zena M. Ariola and Matthias Felleisen. The call-by-need lambda calculus. *J. Funct. Program.*, 7(3):265–301, 1997.

Arvind, Rishiyur S. Nikhil, and Keshav Pingali. I-structures: Data structures for parallel computing. In Joseph H. Fasel and Robert M. Keller, editors, *Graph Reduction*, volume 279 of *Lecture Notes in Computer Science*, pages 336–369. Springer, 1986. ISBN 3-540-18420-1.

Arnon Avron. Simple consequence relations. *Information and Computation*, 92:105–139, 1991.

Henk Barendregt. *The Lambda Calculus, Its Syntax and Semantics*, volume 103 of *Studies in Logic and the Foundations of Mathematics*. North-Holland, 1984.

Henk Barendregt. Lambda calculi with types. In S. Abramsky, D. M. Gabbay, and T. S. E. Maibaum, editors, *Handbook of Logic in Computer Science*, volume 2, *Computational Structures*. Oxford University Press, 1992.

Yves Bertot, Gérard Huet, Jean-Jacques Lévy, and Gordon Plotkin, editors. *From Semantics to Computer Science: Essays in Honor of Gilles Kahn*. Cambridge University Press, 2009.

Guy E. Blelloch. *Vector Models for Data-Parallel Computing*. MIT Press, 1990. ISBN 0-262-02313-X.

Guy E. Blelloch and John Greiner. Parallelism in sequential functional languages. In *FPCA*, pages 226–237, 1995.

Guy E. Blelloch and John Greiner. A provable time and space efficient implementation of NESL. In *ICFP*, pages 213–225, 1996.

Manuel Blum. On the size of machines. *Information and Control*, 11(3):257–265, September 1967.

Stephen D. Brookes. The essence of parallel algol. *Inf. Comput.*, 179(1):118–149, 2002.

Samuel R. Buss, editor. *Handbook of Proof Theory*. Elsevier, 1998.

Luca Cardelli. Structural subtyping and the notion of power type. In *Proc. ACM Symposium on Principles of Programming Languages*, pages 70–79, 1988.

Luca Cardelli. Program fragments, linking, and modularization. In *Proc. ACM Symposium on Principles of Programming Languages*, pages 266–277, 1997.

Giuseppe Castagna and Benjamin C. Pierce. Decidable bounded quantification. In *Proc. ACM Symposium on Principles of Programming Languages*, pages 151–162, 1994.

Alonzo Church. *The Calculi of Lambda-Conversion*. Princeton University Press, 1941.

Robert L. Constable. *Implementing Mathematics with the Nuprl Proof Development System*. Prentice-Hall, 1986.

Robert L. Constable. Types in logic, mathematics, and programming. In Buss (1998), chapter X.

Robert L. Constable and Scott F. Smith. Partial objects in constructive type theory. In *LICS*, pages 183–193. IEEE Computer Society, 1987.

William R. Cook. On understanding data abstraction, revisited. In *OOPSLA*, pages 557–572, 2009.

Rowan Davies. *Practical Refinement-Type Checking*. PhD thesis, Carnegie Mellon University School of Computer Science, May 2005. Available as Technical Report CMU–CS–05–110.

Rowan Davies and Frank Pfenning. Intersection types and computational effects. In Martin Odersky and Philip Wadler, editors, *ICFP*, pages 198–208. ACM, 2000. ISBN 1-58113-202-6.

Ewen Denney. Refinement types for specification. In David Gries and Willem P. de Roever, editors, *PROCOMET*, volume 125 of *IFIP Conference Proceedings*, pages 148–166. Chapman & Hall, 1998. ISBN 0-412-83760-9.

Derek Dreyer. *Understanding and Evolving the ML Module System*. PhD thesis, Carnegie Mellon University, Pittsburgh, PA, May 2005.

Joshua Dunfield and Frank Pfenning. Type assignment for intersections and unions in call-by-value languages. In Andrew D. Gordon, editor, *FoSSaCS*, volume 2620 of *Lecture Notes in Computer Science*, pages 250–266. Springer, 2003. ISBN 3-540-00897-7.

Uffe Engberg and Mogens Nielsen. A calculus of communicating systems with label passing—ten years after. In Gordon D. Plotkin, Colin Stirling, and Mads Tofte, editors, *Proof, Language, and Interaction, Essays in Honour of Robin Milner*, pages 599–622. The MIT Press, 2000.

Matthias Felleisen and Robert Hieb. The revised report on the syntactic theories of sequential control and state. *TCS: Theoretical Computer Science*, 103, 1992.

Tim Freeman and Frank Pfenning. Refinement types for ml. In David S. Wise, editor, *PLDI*, pages 268–277. ACM, 1991. ISBN 0-89791-428-7.

Daniel Friedman and David Wise. The impact of applicative programming on multiprocessing. In *International Conference on Parallel Processing*, 1976.

David Gelernter. Generative communication in Linda. *ACM Trans. Program. Lang. Syst.*, 7(1):80–112, 1985.

Gerhard Gentzen. Investigations into logical deduction. In M. E. Szabo, editor, *The Collected Papers of Gerhard Gentzen*, pages 68–213. North-Holland, 1969.

J.-Y. Girard. *Interpretation fonctionelle et elimination des coupures de l'arithmetique d'ordre superieur*. These d'etat, Universite Paris VII, 1972.

Jean-Yves Girard. *Proofs and Types*. Cambridge University Press, 1989. Translated by Paul Taylor and Yves Lafont.

Kurt Gödel. On a hitherto unexploited extension of the finitary standpoint. *Journal of Philosophical Logic*, 9:133–142, 1980. Translated by Wilfrid Hodges and Bruce Watson.

Gödel Von Kurt. Über eine bisher noch nicht benützte erweiterung des finiten standpunktes. *dialectica*, 12(3-4):280–287, 1958.

Michael J. Gordon, Arthur J. Milner, and Christopher P. Wadsworth. *Edinburgh LCF*, volume 78 of *Lecture Notes in Computer Science*. Springer-Verlag, 1979.

John Greiner and Guy E. Blelloch. A provably time-efficient parallel implementation of full speculation. *ACM Trans. Program. Lang. Syst.*, 21(2):240–285, 1999.

Timothy Griffin. A formulae-as-types notion of control. In *Proc. ACM Symposium on Principles of Programming Languages*, pages 47–58, 1990.

Carl Gunter. *Semantics of Programming Languages*. Foundations of Computing Series. MIT Press, 1992.

Robert H. Halstead, Jr. Multilisp: A language for concurrent symbolic computation. *ACM Trans. Program. Lang. Syst.*, 7(4):501–538, 1985.

Robert Harper. Constructing type systems over an operational semantics. *J. Symb. Comput.*, 14(1):71–84, 1992.

Robert Harper. A simplified account of polymorphic references. *Inf. Process. Lett.*, 51(4): 201–206, 1994.

Robert Harper, Furio Honsell, and Gordon Plotkin. A framework for defining logics. *Journal of the Association for Computing Machinery*, 40:194–204, 1993.

Robert Harper and Mark Lillibridge. A type-theoretic approach to higher-order modules with sharing. In *Proc. ACM Symposium on Principles of Programming Languages*, pages 123–137, 1994.

Robert Harper, John C. Mitchell, and Eugenio Moggi. Higher-order modules and the phase distinction. In *Proc. ACM Symposium on Principles of Programming Languages*, pages 341–354, 1990.

Ralf Hinze and Johan Jeuring. Generic Haskell: Practice and theory. In Roland Carl Backhouse and Jeremy Gibbons, editors, *Generic Programming*, volume 2793 of *Lecture Notes in Computer Science*, pages 1–56. Springer, 2003. ISBN 3-540-20194-7.

C. A. R. Hoare. Communicating sequential processes. *Commun. ACM*, 21(8):666–677, 1978.

Tony Hoare. Null references: The billion dollar mistake. Presentation at QCon 2009, August 2009.

S. C. Kleene. *Introduction to Metamathematics*. Van Nostrand, 1952.

Imre Lakatos. *Proofs and Refutations: The Logic of Mathematical Discovery*. Cambridge University Press, 1976.

P. J. Landin. A correspondence between Algol 60 and Church's lambda notation. *CACM*, 8:89–101; 158–165, 1965.

Daniel K. Lee, Karl Crary, and Robert Harper. Towards a mechanized metatheory of standard ml. In *Proc. ACM Symposium on Principles of Programming Languages*, pages 173–184, 2007.

Xavier Leroy. Manifest types, modules, and separate compilation. In *Proc. ACM Symposium on Principles of Programming Languages*, pages 109–122, 1994.

Xavier Leroy. Applicative functors and fully transparent higher-order modules. In *Proc. ACM Symposium on Principles of Programming Languages*, pages 142–153, 1995.

Mark Lillibridge. *Translucent Sums: A Foundation for Higher-Order Module Systems*. PhD thesis, Carnegie Mellon University School of Computer Science, Pittsburgh, PA, May 1997.

Barbara Liskov and Jeannette M. Wing. A behavioral notion of subtyping. *ACM Trans. Program. Lang. Syst.*, 16(6):1811–1841, 1994.

Saunders MacLane. *Categories for the Working Mathematician*. Graduate Texts in Mathematics. Springer-Verlag, second edition, 1998.

David B. MacQueen. Using dependent types to express modular structure. In *Proc. ACM Symposium on Principles of Programming Langues*, pages 277–286, 1986.

David B. MacQueen. Kahn networks at the dawn of functional programming. In Bertot et al. (2009), chapter 5.

Yitzhak Mandelbaum, David Walker, and Robert Harper. An effective theory of type refinements. In Runciman and Shivers (2003), pages 213–225. ISBN 1-58113-756-7.

Per Martin-Löf. Constructive mathematics and computer programming. In *Logic, Methodology and Philosophy of Science IV*, pages 153–175. North-Holland, 1980.

Per Martin-Löf. On the meanings of the logical constants and the justifications of the logical laws. Unpublished Lecture Notes, 1983.

Per Martin-Löf. *Intuitionistic Type Theory*. Studies in Proof Theory. Bibliopolis, Naples, Italy, 1984.

Per Martin-Löf. Truth of a proposition, evidence of a judgement, validity of a proof. *Synthese*, 73(3):407–420, 1987.

John McCarthy. *LISP 1.5 Programmer's Manual*. MIT Press, 1965.

N. P. Mendler. Recursive types and type constraints in second-order lambda calculus. In *LICS*, pages 30–36, 1987.

Robin Milner. A theory of type polymorphism in programming. *JCSS*, 17:348–375, 1978.

Robin Milner. *Communicating and mobile systems—the Pi-calculus*. Cambridge University Press, 1999. ISBN 978-0-521-65869-0.

Robin Milner, Mads Tofte, Robert Harper, and David MacQueen. *The Definition of Standard ML (Revised)*. MIT Press, 1997.

John C. Mitchell. Coercion and type inference. In *Proc. ACM Symposium on Principles of Programming Languages*, pages 175–185, 1984.

John C. Mitchell. Representation independence and data abstraction. In *Proc. ACM Symposium on Principles of Programming Languages*, pages 263–276, 1986.

John C. Mitchell. *Foundations for Programming Languages*. MIT Press, 1996.

John C. Mitchell and Gordon D. Plotkin. Abstract types have existential type. *ACM Trans. Program. Lang. Syst.*, 10(3):470–502, 1988.

Eugenio Moggi. Computational lambda-calculus and monads. In *LICS*, pages 14–23. IEEE Computer Society, 1989. ISBN 0-8186-1954-6.

Tom Murphy VII, Karl Crary, Robert Harper, and Frank Pfenning. A symmetric modal lambda calculus for distributed computing. In *LICS*, pages 286–295, 2004.

Chetan R. Murthy. An evaluation semantics for classical proofs. In *LICS*, pages 96–107. IEEE Computer Society, 1991.

Aleksandar Nanevski. From dynamic binding to state via modal possibility. In *PPDP*, pages 207–218. ACM, 2003. ISBN 1-58113-705-2.

R. P. Nederpelt, J. H. Geuvers, and R. C. de Vrijer, editors. *Selected Papers on Automath*, volume 133 of *Studies in Logic and the Foundations of Mathematics*. North-Holland, 1994.

B. Nordstrom, K. Petersson, and J. M. Smith. *Programming in Martin-Löf's Type Theory*. Oxford University Press, 1990. URL http://www.cs.chalmers.se/Cs/Research/Logic/book.

OCaml. Ocaml, 2012. URL http://caml.inria.fr/ocaml/.

David Michael Ritchie Park. Concurrency and automata on infinite sequences. In Peter Deussen, editor, *Theoretical Computer Science*, volume 104 of *Lecture Notes in Computer Science*, pages 167–183. Springer, 1981. ISBN 3-540-10576-X.

Frank Pfenning and Rowan Davies. A judgmental reconstruction of modal logic. *Mathematical Structures in Computer Science*, 11(4):511–540, 2001.

Benjamin C. Pierce. *Types and Programming Languages*. MIT Press, 2002.

Benjamin C. Pierce. *Advanced Topics in Types and Programming Languages*. MIT Press, 2004.

Andrew M. Pitts. Existential types: Logical relations and operational equivalence. In Kim Guldstrand Larsen, Sven Skyum, and Glynn Winskel, editors, *ICALP*, volume 1443 of *Lecture Notes in Computer Science*, pages 309–326. Springer, 1998. ISBN 3-540-64781-3.

Andrew M. Pitts. Operational semantics and program equivalence. In Gilles Barthe, Peter Dybjer, Luis Pinto, and João Saraiva, editors, *APPSEM*, volume 2395 of *Lecture Notes in Computer Science*, pages 378–412. Springer, 2000. ISBN 3-540-44044-5.

Andrew M. Pitts and Ian D. B. Stark. Observable properties of higher order functions that dynamically create local names, or what's new? In Andrzej M. Borzyszkowski and Stefan Sokolowski, editors, *MFCS*, volume 711 of *Lecture Notes in Computer Science*, pages 122–141. Springer, 1993. ISBN 3-540-57182-5.

G. D. Plotkin. A structural approach to operational semantics. Technical Report DAIMI FN-19, Aarhus University Computer Science Department, 1981.

Gordon D. Plotkin. LCF considered as a programming language. *Theor. Comput. Sci.*, 5 (3):223–255, 1977.

Gordon D. Plotkin. The origins of structural operational semantics. *J. of Logic and Algebraic Programming*, 60:3–15, 2004.

John H. Reppy. *Concurrent Programming in ML*. Cambridge University Press, 1999.

J. C. Reynolds. Types, abstraction, and parametric polymorphism. In *Information Processing '83*, pages 513–523. North-Holland, 1983.

John C. Reynolds. Towards a theory of type structure. In Bernard Robinet, editor, *Symposium on Programming*, volume 19 of *Lecture Notes in Computer Science*, pages 408–423. Springer, 1974. ISBN 3-540-06859-7.

John C. Reynolds. Using category theory to design implicit conversions and generic operators. In Neil D. Jones, editor, *Semantics-Directed Compiler Generation*, volume 94 of *Lecture Notes in Computer Science*, pages 211–258. Springer, 1980. ISBN 3-540-10250-7.

John C. Reynolds. The essence of Algol. In *Proceedings of the 1981 International Symposium on Algorithmic Languages*, pages 345–372. North-Holland, 1981.

John C. Reynolds. The discoveries of continuations. *Lisp and Symbolic Computation*, 6 (3-4):233–248, 1993.

John C. Reynolds. *Theories of Programming Languages*. Cambridge University Press, 1998.

Andreas Rossberg, Claudio V. Russo, and Derek Dreyer. F-ing modules. In Andrew Kennedy and Nick Benton, editors, *TLDI*, pages 89–102. ACM, 2010. ISBN 978-1-60558-891-9.

Colin Runciman and Olin Shivers, editors. *Proceedings of the Eighth ACM SIGPLAN International Conference on Functional Programming, ICFP 2003, Uppsala, Sweden, August 25-29, 2003*, 2003. ACM. ISBN 1-58113-756-7.

Dana Scott. Lambda calculus: Some models, some philosophy. In J. Barwise, H. J. Keisler, and K. Kunen, editors, *The Kleene Symposium*, pages 223–265. North Holland, 1980a.

Dana S. Scott. Data types as lattices. *SIAM J. Comput.*, 5(3):522–587, 1976.

Dana S. Scott. Relating theories of the lambda calculus. *To HB Curry: Essays on combinatory logic, lambda calculus and formalism*, pages 403–450, 1980b.

Dana S. Scott. Domains for denotational semantics. In Mogens Nielsen and Erik Meineche Schmidt, editors, *ICALP*, volume 140 of *Lecture Notes in Computer Science*, pages 577–613. Springer, 1982. ISBN 3-540-11576-5.

Michael B. Smyth and Gordon D. Plotkin. The category-theoretic solution of recursive domain equations. *SIAM J. Comput.*, 11(4):761–783, 1982.

Richard Statman. Logical relations and the typed lambda-calculus. *Information and Control*, 65(2/3):85–97, 1985.

Guy L. Steele. *Common Lisp: The Language*. Digital Press, 2nd edition edition, 1990.

Christopher A. Stone and Robert Harper. Extensional equivalence and singleton types. *ACM Trans. Comput. Log.*, 7(4):676–722, 2006.

Paul Taylor. *Practical Foundations of Mathematics*. Cambridge Studies in Advanced Mathematics. Cambridge University Press, 1999.

P. W. Trinder, K. Hammond, H.-W. Loidl, and S. L. Peyton Jones. Algorithm + strategy = parallelism. *Journal of Functional Programming*, 8:23–60, 1998.

Jaap van Oosten. Realizability: A historical essay. *Mathematical Structures in Computer Science*, 12(3):239–263, 2002.

Philip Wadler. Theorems for free! In *FPCA*, pages 347–359, 1989.

Philip Wadler. Comprehending monads. *Mathematical Structures in Computer Science*, 2 (4):461–493, 1992.

Philip Wadler. Call-by-value is dual to call-by-name. In Runciman and Shivers (2003), pages 189–201. ISBN 1-58113-756-7.

Mitchell Wand. Fixed-point constructions in order-enriched categories. *Theor. Comput. Sci.*, 8:13–30, 1979.

Stephen A. Ward and Robert H. Halstead. *Computation structures*. MIT Electrical Engineering and Computer Science Series. MIT Press, 1990. ISBN 978-0-262-23139-8.

Kevin Watkins, Iliano Cervesato, Frank Pfenning, and David Walker. Specifying properties of concurrent computations in clf. *Electr. Notes Theor. Comput. Sci.*, 199:67–87, 2008.

Andrew K. Wright and Matthias Felleisen. A syntactic approach to type soundness. *Inf. Comput.*, 115(1):38–94, 1994.

Hongwei Xi and Frank Pfenning. Eliminating array bound checking through dependent types. In Jack W. Davidson, Keith D. Cooper, and A. Michael Berman, editors, *PLDI*, pages 249–257. ACM, 1998. ISBN 0-89791-987-4.

Index

Printed in the United States
By Bookmasters